W9-ARB-659

WITHDRAWN
from
NEWTON PUBLIC LIBRARY

NEWTON PUBLIC LIBRARY
NEWTON, KANSAS 67114

ROLLING
AWAY
THE
STONE

Religion in North America
Catherine L. Albanese and Stephen J. Stein, editors

289.509

MAY 1 1 2006

ROLLING AWAY
THE
STONE

*Mary Baker Eddy's
Challenge to Materialism*

Stephen Gottschalk

INDIANA
University Press
Bloomington & Indianapolis

NEWTON PUBLIC LIBRARY
NEWTON, KANSAS 67114

Much primary material for this work has been drawn from
The Mary Baker Eddy Collection and the Mary Baker Eddy Library
for the Betterment of Humanity. Any opinions expressed
in this book are solely those of the author and are not endorsed by
The Mary Baker Eddy Collection or The Mary Baker Eddy Library
for the Betterment of Humanity.

The author is grateful to the Rare Book and Manuscript Library
at Columbia University for permission to quote from their
collection of the New York World Papers.

This book is a publication of

Indiana University Press
601 North Morton Street
Bloomington, IN 47404-3797 USA

http://iupress.indiana.edu

Telephone orders 800-842-6796
Fax orders 812-855-7931
Orders by e-mail iuporder@indiana.edu

© 2006 by Stephen Gottschalk
All rights reserved

No part of this book may be reproduced or utilized in any
form or by any means, electronic or mechanical, including
photocopying and recording, or by any information storage
and retrieval system, without permission in writing from the
publisher. The Association of American University Presses'
Resolution on Permissions constitutes the only exception
to this prohibition.

The paper used in this publication meets the minimum
requirements of American National Standard for Information
Sciences—Permanence of Paper for Printed Library
Materials, ANSI Z39.48-1984.

Manufactured in the United States of America

Library of Congress Cataloging-in-Publication Data

Gottschalk, Stephen.
    Rolling away the stone : Mary Baker Eddy's challenge to materialism /
Stephen Gottschalk.
        p. cm. — (Religion in North America)
Includes bibliographical references and index.
    ISBN 0-253-34673-8 (hardcover : alk. paper)
    1. Eddy, Mary Baker, 1821–1910. 2. Materialism. I. Title. II. Series.
BX6995.G68 2005
289.5'092—dc22   2005014174

1 2 3 4 5 11 10 09 08 07 06

To Mary and Jennie

Glory be to God, and peace to the struggling hearts! Christ hath rolled away the stone from the door of human hope and faith, and through the revelation and demonstration of life in God, hath elevated them to possible at-one-ment with the spiritual idea of man and his divine Principle, Love.
       —Mary Baker Eddy, *Science and Health with Key to the Scriptures*

Contents

CONTENTS

Foreword

A certain sadness accompanies the appearance of this volume by Stephen Gottschalk, who struggled with illness and died while engaged in the last stages of revising his manuscript in preparation for its publication. During the difficult weeks of his illness prior to his death, he persisted in and completed the task, assisted by his wife, Mary. We regret that Stephen Gottschalk will not be present to engage the readers of his book and to receive the positive responses we anticipate for this volume.

Gottschalk, an intellectual historian par excellence, was uniquely positioned as a Christian Science insider to interpret the historical development of the religious tradition. In fact, not since the late Robert Peel, also a Christian Scientist, has any insider been better equipped to interpret the religious thought of Mary Baker Eddy. Moreover, the project of taking Eddy seriously as a theologian cannot be overrated. This volume cuts through and rolls away a number of barriers beyond the one to which its title alludes. It takes seriously the theological production of an individual outside the well-groomed tradition of professional Protestant theologizing, an individual with only a modicum of formal education, and a woman at that.

From the point of view of Christian Science theologizing itself, this book is decidedly revisionist. A few years ago the directors of the Mother Church countenanced the publication of a book that more or less deified Eddy. By doing so, the church obtained millions of dollars when the work appeared in print. In the context of that event and of the theological stance that it apparently represented for some in the church, Stephen Gottschalk's new book is a timely polemical intervention. It points to Christian Science's antimaterialist roots in the theology of its founder. In fact, according to Gottschalk, Mary Baker Eddy identified the primary error of the Christian tradition with belief in materialism and the corollary (false) judgment that God created a world in which mortality and materialism were essential elements. She declared that misunderstanding to be destroyed by the birth, healing ministry, and resurrection of Jesus. She thought that the medical, scientific, and ecclesiastical spheres of her day were dominated by that basic theological misunderstanding. For that reason the church she founded rested on her antimaterialist views.

With its years of research into Eddy's writings, her historical context, the persons who surrounded her and opposed her, and the scholarly literature that deals with her and Christian Science, Gottschalk's work provides a searching study of the last two decades of Eddy's life. He has focused his attention on the efforts she made during those years to ensure the centrality of her antimaterialist views in the church she founded. Although those years were a time of "retirement" for her, she felt forced to move from one controversy to another. In these circumstances she demonstrated the strength of her person and her ideas. In emphasizing these themes, Gottschalk initially focuses on the Next Friends suit in 1907, a planned effort by her critics to discredit her and take control of her substantial assets. Indeed and ironically, the effort even involved her only son, George—long separated and alienated—who joined in the attack. In this context, the Next Friends suit provides Gottschalk an occasion to insist on the theme of the "atheism of matter," which is a key theological reading in the volume. That episode also provides an excellent measure of the stature that Eddy had attained by the end of her life.

In the course of this book, Gottschalk casts instructive light on a number of major figures who intersected with Mary Baker Eddy. One such figure was Mark Twain, who is usually featured as the caustic critic of Eddy and Christian Science. Gottschalk's erudite and creative reading of Twain strikes a different note, pointing to shared qualities of mind that Eddy and Twain possessed. Other persons whose relationships with Eddy are discussed at length in their complexity include Adam Dickey and Foster Eddy, two men who were closer to her than her son, and Augusta Stetson and Josephine Woodbury, gifted female followers whose interactions with Eddy degenerated into open conflict.

With all of the complexities and conflicts that involved Eddy and her relationships with others, Gottschalk has still written an admiring—and instructive—study of the closing decades of her life. Richly informed and informing about Eddy and all of Christian Science, Gottschalk's production is exceedingly worth the reading not only for insiders but especially for outsiders to the tradition and its perplexities—and among them those who study the theological and interpersonal dynamics that shape religious traditions. We think this volume is a fitting conclusion to a significant career.

Catherine L. Albanese and
Stephen J. Stein, Series Editors

Acknowledgments

This book would not be what it is without the help of many wise and generous individuals who have contributed insights, questions, criticism, and support of all kinds. It is difficult to list all the ways in which so many have contributed, but I would like to make a general accounting in appreciation of their efforts.

In January of this year, it was good to meet Michael Lundell and Beth Marsh, two of the editors at Indiana University Press who were instrumental in handling the initial manuscript and its revision in the back and forth through readers and editors. Putting faces with names and e-mail addresses added warmth to the sometimes impersonal world of electronic editing, which had already been filled with efficiency, timely responses, and support. Also to be acknowledged for insightful criticism and encouragement are the editors of the series, *Religion in North America,* Cathy Albanese and Steve Stein.

My daughter, Jennie, collaborated with me for over a year doing research at the new Mary Baker Eddy Library in Boston. Kathleen Schwartz generously researched photographs for the book at the same library. Judy Huenneke and her staff at the research room of the Mary Baker Eddy Library were always knowledgeable and helpful to me and others working on this project. The rich resources they make available to scholars and researchers are invaluable. Jon Trotter did useful research at the Rare Book and Manuscript Library, Columbia University.

Steve Howard, curator of the Longyear Museum, offered valuable insights on portions of the manuscript. I am grateful to Ralph Byron Copper, who shared a wealth of resources for several chapters and took on fact-checking and editing for a large portion of the final manuscript. I also had expert help from Mike Davis and Keith McNeil.

Editorial assistance early in the process involved a friend and excellent editor, Barbara Wagstaff of Berkeley, California, and free-lance editor Vincent P. Bynack of Bronxville, New York. Other eyes on various revisions included the following: David Anable, David Andrews, Joan Andrews, Julian Baum, Ramona Cole, Jamae and Bart van Eck, Jennie and Mary Gottschalk, Todd Hollenberg, Alice Hummer, Mary Aileen Jamieson, Tom Johnsen, Diane Johnson, Margaret Millar, Darren Nelson, Allen and Lenore Parker, Skip Phinney, Scott Preller, Nancy Reinert, Kathleen Schwartz, Susan Stark, Lisa Rennie Sytsma, Patricia Tuttle, and Christopher Wagstaff.

I am especially grateful for grants for editorial assistance and research from individuals who prefer to remain anonymous and from the Marlène F. Johnson Memorial Fund for Scholarly Research on Christian Science, Inc. Barbara Martin, who designed books for Black Sparrow Press from its inception, offered suggestions and drawings for jacket designs. Other kinds of professional support came from Jim Halferty and Zick Rubin, among others.

The culminating editorial assistance came through Julian Baum. He brought the eye of a journalist and the diligence and dedication of a decades-long friend to the work. Of course, this book could not have been completed without the steadfastness of my wife, Mary.

Finally, I am grateful to the Christian Science Board of Directors for continuing to make the writings of Mary Baker Eddy available to the public and to the Mary Baker Eddy Collection for permission to include material from her unpublished writings.

Stephen Gottschalk
Wellesley, Massachusetts
January 2005

Note on Textual Usages

Gender questions have in recent years become important in public discourse and scholarly writing. In keeping with current practice, I have referred to Mary Baker Eddy—except in quoted material—as "Eddy" rather than "Mrs. Eddy," though the latter was customarily used by Christian Scientists, as well as other supporters and detractors. Prior to taking the name Eddy, she was known by her maiden name and her two previous married names. To avoid confusion, I have simply used the name Eddy in discussing her life before she took that name.

Eddy generally used the term "man" in a generic sense to refer to both men and women, whereas today "people," "humanity," and "individuals" have become the norm. In keeping with her usage, I have at points used the term "man" in this sense, but with no sexist implications. Another usage that may seem unusual to some readers is not capitalizing the pronouns "he," "him," and "his" when referring to God. Eddy's practice of capitalizing synonyms she used for God, such as Spirit, Mind, and Soul, however, has been maintained for the sake of historical accuracy.

In quotations from her letters and papers, many of which were written in haste, her original punctuation and spelling have been retained, except in instances where slight modification is needed to clarify her meaning. In her correspondence, Eddy typically underlined important words and phrases. In this book, following current practice, such phrases are reproduced in italics. Finally, Eddy and her followers frequently spoke of Christian Science as her "discovery." This book generally uses this term without quotation marks to avoid awkwardness, but with no suggestion as to the validity of her teaching one way or another.

ROLLING

AWAY

THE

STONE

Introduction

IN 1889, AT THE AGE OF SIXTY-EIGHT, MARY BAKER EDDY ABRUPTLY LEFT Boston, where she had lived and worked since 1882. Settling in Concord, New Hampshire, near her birthplace, she looked forward to what she believed would be a period of rest and retirement from the labors that had all but exhausted her over the past seven years. Instead, and perhaps to her own surprise, she entered into a period of just over twenty years of productive work in which the demands on her did not diminish but grew.

This book is a study of these last two consummatory decades of her life, during which she brought her work in Christian Science, begun in 1866, to completion. Other books have dealt with this period, most notably *Mary Baker Eddy: The Years of Authority*, the final volume of Robert Peel's biographical trilogy. This book, however, focuses on the dominant theme in her life during these two decades: her effort to protect and perpetuate a religious teaching that could provide an alternative to the materialism she saw as potentially engulfing traditional Christianity. In so doing, she acted not only as a Christian thinker confronting some of the most persistent issues of faith, but as a religious leader guiding a movement that in the two decades before her death in 1910 would grow to national and even international proportions.

Although she desired seclusion, Eddy felt that it was incumbent upon her during this period to take on the demands of leading the Christian Science movement, despite being a woman in a male-dominated society—and an elderly woman in her seventies and eighties at that. Beginning in the early 1890s, Eddy faced a continuing series of crises and problems linked, as she saw it, not only to the survival of the denomination she had founded, but to the future vitality of Christianity as a whole.

The phrase "rolling away the stone" in the title of this book is drawn from a metaphor she used at various points to suggest what Christian

Science, if conscientiously practiced, could mean to Christianity. It refers to the Gospel accounts of the rolling away of the stone from the place where the resurrected Jesus had been entombed. "What is it," Eddy asked at an Easter service in Boston two months before her departure for Concord, "that seems a stone between us and the resurrection morning?" That stone, she said, "is the belief of mind in matter." A sermon she had given earlier was based on the text from Mark, "Who shall roll us away the stone from the sepulchre?" Here she says that "this stone, in a spiritual sense, is the human view entertained of the power, resistance, and substance of matter as opposed to the might and supremacy of Spirit."[1]

To her, that stone was the obstacle that would hide from our view the power of the spirit of Christ to redeem the whole of human life. The advent of Christian Science, she insisted, marked a fresh new sense of the continuing presence of Christ, which had been embodied in the man Jesus but remained a healing presence for humanity. She saw the healing ministry of Christian Science as helping to rouse Christians to the great promise of restoring the power of the original Gospel.

What blocked the fuller realization of this promise, in her view, was what might be called the hidden metaphysics of traditional Christianity. Christian teaching in nearly all its forms held to the virtually axiomatic assumption that God was the creator of matter and finitude, and thereby the ultimate source of the suffering and death that human beings must endure. But the belief that man is physical, finite, and mortal, Eddy emphasized, is exactly what had been challenged and reversed by Jesus' resurrection, which she fully accepted as a literal historical fact. She taught, moreover, that just as the power of Christ had rolled away the stone from the tomb in which the crucified Jesus had been buried, so the continuing power of Christ as presented through Christian Science has rolled away the stone of the belief of life in matter from the sepulchre of mortality in which human hopes have been buried.

Christians, she maintained, without ever quite realizing it, held to the belief in the effective supremacy of matter over Spirit in daily life. If they not only held to but defended this belief, they could not, in her view, escape the iron logic of seeing God as the ultimate source of suffering and death. For Eddy, as for countless others, this problem of what is technically termed "theodicy" was not a problem of logic but a problem of life. It urged itself upon her as an issue that arose directly from the rigors of her own experience—from the pain and terror of the illnesses of her youth, the multiplying personal losses of the first three decades of her life, and the loneliness and near-invalidism she experienced as a result.

The problem of evil, declared theologian Hans Kung, has become in the age of Auschwitz "the rock of atheism." But atheism was no option for Eddy, who had been raised in the religious culture of latter-day

New England Puritanism, the major expression in the New World of the broader Calvinist tradition. Eddy strongly questioned the doctrine of predestination, which most Puritans, along with other Calvinists, affirmed. But it would never have occurred to her to question the reality of one sovereign God–hence the spiritual quest that dominated the first half of her life. As she put it later in her autobiographical work *Retrospection and Introspection*, "I was impelled, by a hunger and thirst after divine things,—a desire for something higher and better than matter, and apart from it,—to seek diligently for the knowledge of God as the one great and ever-present relief from human woe."[2]

In 1866, at almost the exact midpoint of her life, she experienced what she believed to be a major spiritual breakthrough as the result of being healed of the effects of a severe injury. This breakthrough she called her "discovery" of Christian Science. The metaphysics and theology of Christian Science were therefore far from being merely a statement of her personal religious views. But they were, for her, a making explicit of permanent spiritual truth that had been implicit in the Scriptures all along—a *re*discovery, as she saw it, of the continuing truth and undiminished power of biblical revelation that traditional Christianity had largely failed to discern and act upon.

Her healing in early 1866, she later said, "included a glimpse of the great fact that I have since tried to make plain to others, namely, Life in and of Spirit; this Life being the sole reality of existence." To Eddy, this breakthrough marked a revelatory understanding of God's true nature: that his being is infinite, an all-inclusive Spirit, and that his creation must be, like him, spiritual. For her, this was not merely a conclusion arrived at through abstract metaphysical speculation. It was an inescapable consequence of what the Bible, rightly understood, reveals.

Pursuing the logic of this conviction wherever it led, she concluded that the true understanding of biblical revelation ran counter to the assumption that God was the creator of matter and finitude. "The Scriptures," she wrote, "give the keynote of Christian Science from Genesis to Revelation, and this was the prolonged tone: 'For the Lord He is God, and there is *none beside Him.*' "[3]

Eddy believed that her teaching stood in stark contrast to and in active defiance of the worldview of materialism. In the broadest sense, she saw Christian Science as challenging this materialism, whether it took the form of the increasing domination of scientific materialism in Western thought, the pervasive assumptions of medical materialism, the ecclesiastical materialism that submerged spirituality in outward forms of ritual and creed, and especially the tacit materialism that nominally admitted the reality of God but denied that his power could have any direct effect in human experience.

The bedrock tenet of scientific materialism, asserted Stephen M. Barr in his book *Modern Physics and Ancient Faith*, is "that nothing exists except matter, and that everything in the world must therefore be the result of the strict mathematical laws of physics and blind chance."[4] Materialism in this basic sense inevitably has a shaping effect on human values, leading to the sometimes unspoken assumption that having material possessions, comforts, and power is the only valid measure of fulfillment and meaning in human life.

In an insightful summary of the modern materialist ethos, Richard Tarnas in his book *The Passion of the Western Mind* wrote that in contrast to earlier worldviews, materialism depicts the universe as "an impersonal phenomenon, governed by regular natural laws, and understandable in exclusively physical and mathematical terms." As this materialism took form, any sense of even a "residual divine reality . . . if unsupported by scientific investigation of the visible world, disappeared altogether." As a result,

> Science replaced religion as preeminent intellectual authority, as definer, judge, and guardian of the cultural world view. Human reason and empirical observation replaced theological doctrine and scriptural revelation as the principal means for comprehending the universe. The domains of religion and metaphysics became gradually compartmentalized, regarded as personal, subjective, speculative, and fundamentally distinct from public objective knowledge of the empirical world.[5]

For Eddy, materialism had deepened and become more intransigent—not because it was on the ascendancy, but because it was fighting for its life. As she put it on the first page of *Science and Health*, the "cold conventionality of materialism" was fading away. "The broadcast powers of evil so conspicuous to-day," she also wrote in that book, "show themselves in the materialism and sensualism of the age, struggling against the advancing spiritual era." As she saw it, the only form of spirituality worthy of the name must engage to some degree in this crucial struggle with the materialism that claims to define and limit our possibilities at every point. "The mortality of material man," she wrote, "proves that error has been ingrafted into the premises and conclusions of material and mortal humanity."[6]

Traditional Christianity, she believed, had not sufficiently broken with these premises and conclusions to realize the full saving power of the Gospel. Most forms of traditional Christianity teach that those who are saved are sinning, imperfect mortals now, but will become spiritual and immortal in a future life. For Eddy, this was a false point of departure in attaining the salvation that Christians seek, a spiritually crippling misunderstanding of the revelation that Jesus brought to humanity. "The divine nature," she wrote in *Science and Health*, "was best expressed in Christ Jesus, who threw upon mortals the truer reflection of God and lifted their lives higher than their poor thought-models would allow,—thoughts which presented man as fallen, sick, sinning, and dying. The Christlike understanding of scientific being and divine healing includes a perfect Principle and idea,—perfect God and perfect man,—as the basis of thought and demonstration."[7]

Beginning on this basis, Eddy insisted, provides a whole new understanding of what salvation actually means and requires. It certainly does not mean that men and women as we behold them now are perfect. Indeed, she sometimes outdoes Calvin in characterizing the sinfulness of the mortal picture of man. She spoke of "the total depravity of mortals" and characterized "the common conception of mortal man" as a "burlesque of God's man." But, she believed, God's man—the man Jesus exemplified and revealed—*is* spiritual, perfect, and immortal right now.[8]

The true path to salvation lay in recognizing what she held to be this supreme spiritual fact and bringing it to light in daily life. "The great spiritual fact," she wrote, "must be brought out that man *is*, not *shall be*, perfect and immortal . . . the evidence of man's immortality will become more apparent, as material beliefs are given up and the immortal facts of being are admitted." The struggle in which Christians must be engaged, therefore, is not the futile effort to make a poor sinning mortal into a perfect sinless immortal, for this can never be done. It is to give up the "material beliefs" that operate with hypnotic intensity in human experience, and to admit and adhere to the "immortal facts of being" despite the evidence of sensory testimony to the contrary.[9]

In her many descriptions of this struggle, Eddy characteristically employed military metaphors. She spoke of a "warfare with the flesh, in which we must conquer sin, sickness, death, either here or hereafter," of the need for Christians to "take up arms against error at home and abroad," of the fact that "Christian Science and the senses are at war," and that it is a "revolutionary struggle." Eddy held little hope for the future of Christianity if it was not fighting on the right side—if it was not found struggling on behalf of the "advancing spiritual era" by breaking thoroughly from the hold of materialism, whatever form it took.[10]

This conflict, she believed, was not theoretical but took place on the rough ground of everyday life through acts of spiritual healing. In her teaching, to understand that God's kingdom is, as Jesus said, "at hand" enlarges one's sense of God's presence. Individuals begin to give up the fears and false convictions that proceed inevitably from the belief that material conditions are the final arbiter of human life and well-being.

In proportion as this happens, what seem to be intractable physical conditions begin to change. Healing happens—not, in her view, through blind faith or miraculous divine intervention, but through understanding more of God's love and the supremacy of his power. This, said Eddy, was the basis of healing in New Testament times that she had rediscovered and made available in our own.

She believed that the God whom Christians claimed to worship must be a real God, having real effects in the world. If, however, humanity continued to be plagued by ineradicable woes from which Christianity offered no hope of surcease, she strongly doubted if Christianity had the staying power to survive the inroads of secular materialism. Since the last decades of the twentieth century, a new theological consensus has arisen among many influential theologians—so much so that it has been called a "new orthodoxy." Briefly, this viewpoint holds that the older conception of God as all powerful is impossible to sustain, that he is unable to prevent human suffering, but that he is nevertheless present to us, suffering with us in pain he cannot prevent.[11]

In Eddy's view, the true understanding of God's omnipotence acts powerfully to *ameliorate* suffering, bringing practical healing to humanity through the recognition of his presence. In this context, she saw Christianity as coming to a crossroads. Far from accepting for Christian Science a marginal place on the fringes of Christian experience, Eddy saw its challenge to materialism as potentially having a major bearing on the future of Christianity as a whole—but only if Christian Scientists practiced what she taught with sufficient dedication and effectiveness to give evidence of its truth.

During the two decades before her death, the Christian Science movement grew with surprising speed. Largely, it gathered adherents from the ranks of disaffected Protestants who, like Eddy in earlier years, had not only experienced suffering, but found in that suffering a strong challenge to their belief in a God who could be responsible for evil. Artlessly yet pointedly, the *Christian Science Journal* telescoped the whole issue by citing the story of a boy looking out of his window and telling his mother: "It's a funeral, mamma, God has been killing someone else."[12]

For many converts to Christian Science, Eddy's teaching validated the Christianity in which they desperately wanted to believe. As one Christian Scientist early in the century put it in a testimony reprinted in *Science and Health*, that teaching did not really dissent from orthodoxy but represented "an *ascent*, an expansion, a going onward and upward from the point where dogmatic teaching and theology leave off." To new adherents from Christian backgrounds, Eddy's teaching felt like

Christianity made alive again, released from the trammels of tradition but more fully free to realize the promise of the Gospel.[13]

Each of the chapters of this book revolves around a cluster of events and problems that Eddy faced during the last two decades of her life. In each instance, she confronted issues that proceeded from her effort to define and advance a new form of Christian spirituality that challenged materialism in its various forms. Since many of the problems she dealt with overlapped in time, the book is organized, after the Prelude, according to a broadly chronological, yet topical plan. (For readers who wish to track the specific sequence of events in Eddy's life, a chronology emphasizing the period covered in depth in this book is provided.)

The prelude, entitled "The World's 'leaden weight,'" focuses on a widely publicized lawsuit in 1907 challenging Eddy's mental competence and introduces issues explored in greater detail as the book progresses. The first chapter, " 'O God, *is it all!,*'" explores her struggle with the problem of evil, counterpoising the direction she took with Mark Twain's anguished confrontation with the same issue in the later part of his life. Chapter 2, "Becoming 'Mrs. Eddy,'" focuses on how, after leaving Boston abruptly for Concord in 1889, she sought and found renewal in her own spiritual life as a Christian, becoming over the next several years the "Mrs. Eddy" with whom history has become familiar. The basis of her growing authority within the movement in the early to mid-1890s is explored in the following two chapters, "By What Authority? On Christian Ground" and "By What Authority? Listening and Leading." The fact that she was a woman leading a burgeoning religious movement raises a number of issues about the nature of feminine spirituality brought into focus in Chapter 5, " 'Woman goes forth.'" The next two chapters, " 'This visible unity of spirit'" and " 'The preparation of the heart,'" revolve around Eddy's work on behalf of her church during the middle and late 1890s. Chapter 8, " 'Ayont hate's thrall,'" explores the implications of a major crisis in Eddy's life when she faced a lawsuit engendered by a former student, Josephine Curtis Woodbury. Partially as a result of this crisis, she formed a remarkable community of workers in her household, delineated in Chapter 9, "A Power, Not a Place."

In the first decade of the twentieth century, Eddy dealt with a series of issues revolving around what she saw as the opposition of materialism to Christian Science healing practice—or what she once characterized in terms adapted as the chapter's title, " 'The outflowing life of Christianity.'" Concurrently, her efforts to confront the evidences of materialism within the Christian Science movement itself are discussed in Chapter 11, "The Kingdoms of This World." The final chapter, "Elijah's Mantle," dwells on Eddy's more interior experience during her last several years, while the Coda, "The Prophetic Voice," points to her larger legacy as a Christian thinker.

In the process of measuring up to the unforeseeable day-to-day demands that devolved on her, Eddy found herself thrown back on the necessity of finding in Christian Science itself a basis for understanding the situations she faced, gaining the spiritual guidance she needed to meet them, and achieving the strength and staying power to go on leading the movement well into her eighties. The last two decades of her life, examined in this framework, offer a fresh perspective on the tough, persistent character of her own spirituality—as well as a persuasive gauge of the integrity involved in her rigorous commitment to living what she taught. In the words of religious historian Martin E. Marty,

> There's no doubt that in one sense she is doing what everyone from atheists like Sartre to intense believers like Pope John XXIII are doing; they are putting their banner up against forces of meaninglessness and saying, I defy them: I don't have to be merely passive. . . . Whether people can follow where her banner would lead is a very different question; but I think one has to say: Here's a steadfast, decades long attempt not thus to be overwhelmed.[14]

Prelude: The World's "Leaden Weight"

In Media Res

IN THE FIRST HALF OF 1907, MARY BAKER EDDY, THEN EIGHTY-FIVE YEARS OF age, suddenly became the most controversial and widely discussed woman in the United States. Disliking publicity and dubious of its value to the church she led, she had lived for fifteen years in the relative peace and seclusion of her Pleasant View home in Concord, New Hampshire. Yet within the space of several months, she became the central figure in one of the twentieth century's first major media events: a highly charged lawsuit in which her mental competence was challenged and her freedom to conduct her own affairs was seriously jeopardized.

The suit had been instigated by one of the world's most widely read English-language newspapers, Joseph Pulitzer's *New York World*, and prosecuted by one of the most powerful political figures in the country, former senator William Chandler of New Hampshire. Although Eddy was ultimately vindicated, the episode was at once the culminating crisis of her life, a pivotal moment in the history of the movement she led, and, in the words of her biographer Robert Peel, "one of the most bizarre cases in American legal history."[1]

Ostensibly, the suit had the just purpose of saving a dying and decrepit Eddy from a cabal in control of her person and her fortune, then turning control of both over to several relatives—in legal terms, her "next friends." This was the version of events proffered by the *World*. However great the *World*'s influence and circulation, it did not represent the broad range of editorial sentiment in the nation's press about what came to be called the "Next Friends Suit." Far more characteristic were the words of an editorial in the small town of Perry, New York: "It has been the experience of nearly every religious sect to suffer persecution to a greater or lesser extent, and the leader of any radical movement has had to bear his or her brunt of it."[2]

Eddy found the Next Friends Suit an ordeal. But she was not shocked by it. Seven years before the suit began, she had declared in her *Message to The Mother Church for 1900:* "Conflict and persecution are the truest signs that can be given of the greatness of a cause or of an individual, provided this warfare is honest and a world-imposed struggle. Such conflict never ends till unconquerable right is begun anew, and hath gained fresh energy and final victory."[3]

To her, Christian Science was the most vital of all causes. As she put it in the "Prospectus" for the first issue of the *Journal of Christian Science* in 1883, "To-day we behold but the first faint beams of a more spiritual Christianity that embraces a deeper and broader philosophy, and a more rational and divine healing." By the time the Next Friends Suit was launched almost a quarter of a century later, the "first faint beams of a more spiritual Christianity" had become very visible indeed, taking form in a distinct religious denomination fast gaining ground in the United States and in other lands. As Eddy saw it, Christian Science aroused predictable hostility and opposition, not so much because particular individuals opposed it, but because the broad currents of materialism always have been ranged against the advent of genuine spirituality in any form. "The earthly price of spirituality in religion and medicine in a material age," as she put it in a newspaper article published in 1901, "is persecution."[4]

The *New York World* editors, Chandler, and others responsible for the suit may have felt they were hard-boiled men of the world acting out of comprehensible motives of their own. But in Eddy's view, they were actually reenacting a scenario that had long been part of the spiritual history of humanity. Over many years she had written of the opposition undergone by Jesus, Paul, and later Christian figures such as Polycarp and Luther. Still, it would appear that at the age of eighty-five she would have been well past the point of having to endure such persecution herself. "Physical torture," Eddy said, "affords but a slight illustration of the pangs which come to one upon whom the world of sense falls with its leaden weight in the endeavor to crush out of a career its divine destiny."[5]

A half-century before the *World's* attack began, it would have been difficult to think of anyone in New England who had less promise of a significant career, let alone a "divine destiny." Eddy was born in 1821 into a vigorous New England family in Bow, New Hampshire, a short distance from Concord. A largely idyllic early girlhood, marred only by intermittent illness, was followed by a series of hammer blows that left her a virtual invalid by her mid-thirties: severe illness throughout her teens, the death of her favorite brother when she was twenty, of her first husband when she was twenty-two, and of her much-adored mother and her fiancé within three weeks of each other nearly six years later, a failed second marriage that eventually ended in divorce, and a conspiracy between her father and second husband to deprive her of any contact with her only son, who had been placed in foster care due to her physical inability to care for him. Plunged into virtual invalidism after the boy was taken out west with his foster parents in 1856, she endured months of near isolation in the remote, sometimes snowbound town of North Groton in the foothills of the White Mountains.

Eddy's life at this point appeared to be without prospects, but it was not without purpose. Her spiritual search reached its goal at almost the exact midpoint of her life of nearly ninety years. But it by no means followed a direct path. It led through her investigations of various medical theories into experiments with the medical system of homeopathy, through which she concluded that disease is rooted in the fears and anxieties of the human mind, to a pivotal association over nearly four years beginning in 1862 with the Maine healer Phineas Parkhurst Quimby, who influenced and stimulated her own spiritual search.

A severe injury from a fall in early 1866 might well have marked an acceleration of the downward spiral of her life. Instead, she saw it as leading to her discovery of how disease could be healed, humanity redeemed, and the power of original Christianity restored through the action of God, the divine Mind, on human minds and bodies. Turning, as she later recalled, to a Gospel account of healing, she experienced a spiritual illumination so intense that it brought about not only recovery from her injury, but a redirection of the course of her life.[6]

What Eddy called the "nine years of hard labor" that followed this experience began with scriptural study and healing work, continued with teaching a small group of students and the further clarification of her teaching, and climaxed with the publication in 1875 of her major work, *Science and Health* (later entitled *Science and Health with Key to the Scriptures*), the "textbook" of Christian Science, which she continued to revise for the rest of her life. "That work," she wrote in 1884, "is the outgrowth of my whole life. . . . It was learned of God, never from an author, or a person. It was learned through . . . *a life-long experience* that still *goes* on." As if to reassure herself of what she had learned from that "life-long experience," in the late spring of 1907 after the suit had been launched, Eddy for the first time read through *Science and Health* consecutively, as she put it in the preface to the book, "to elucidate her idealism."[7]

Her early efforts to establish and build up the Christian Science movement, although eventually successful, were marked by a series of apparent failures. Disaffection among her students left her early labors to build up the movement in Lynn, Massachusetts, during the 1870s in ruins. A promising move to Boston in 1882 began inauspiciously with the death later that year of her third husband, Asa Gilbert Eddy, on whose support she had relied since their marriage in 1877.

Yet it was during Eddy's years in Boston from 1882 to 1889 that Christian Science became a significant movement in American religious life. During those years, she labored intensely, teaching, preaching, writing, and gaining a growing following composed largely of disaffected mainstream Protestants. As a result, Christian Science became the focus of attacks from an increasingly perplexed clergy concerned with losing some of the most faithful members of their flock to what they saw as a dangerous heresy. In addition, the very survival of the movement sometimes appeared to be threatened by the rivalry of various "mind-cure" groups that, as Eddy saw it, appropriated her terminology, but sought healing through the powers of the very human mentality she saw as responsible for disease. In 1889, Eddy took the bold and, to many of her students, irrational step of abruptly leaving Boston. Exhausted, she "retired" to Concord, New Hampshire, settling three years later into her Pleasant View home with a small staff. Her relative seclusion, however, did not mean idleness. In a dictated memo probably written sometime in the 1890s, she retorted to those who would "whine" over that seclusion: "Mrs. Eddy is no recluse. She is in constant company. To care for 20,000 members of her Church, to peruse if not attend to 20 letters per day . . . demands seclusion when this much is done faithfully."[8]

During the decade after she left Boston, she gained in authority within the movement and public recognition outside of it. In 1892, she formally reorganized the Church of Christ, Scientist, founded in 1879, into the Mother Church and its worldwide "branches." In 1895, she published the *Manual of The Mother Church,* a slim body of bylaws codifying her plan for church government and providing guidance for members. At the same time, growing public recognition of her as a woman religious leader in a male-dominated society, together with the challenge posed by her teaching to conventional religion, had made her the subject of mounting controversy, which reached its climax in the Next Friends Suit of 1907.

THE INVASION

By the time the Next Friends Suit was instigated, Eddy was no stranger to litigation. In 1878, at the behest of an extremely litigious

289.509
Gottschalk

follower, Edward J. Arens, she had with little success sued several of her early students for recovery of unpaid tuition fees as well as royalties on their healing practices. Five years later, she sued Arens for infringement of her copyright on *Science and Health.* Though she won the case, the suit generated enormously bitter ill feeling that had severe repercussions on Eddy. For the remainder of her life, a period of almost three decades, she brought no legal action against anyone.

Her thoroughgoing distaste for litigation was compounded by a suit for libel brought against her by ex-student Josephine Curtis Woodbury in 1899. The suit, which stretched over nearly two years after it was first instituted, was extremely hard on Eddy's peace of mind and on her physical health as well. As a later chapter on Woodbury's animus against Eddy makes clear, the 1899 suit for libel had intricate connections with the Next Friends Suit itself.[9]

Although the Next Friends Suit was instituted and resolved in far less time than the Woodbury litigation, it was potentially more damaging to Eddy than any of the many crises that had marked her work in Christian Science. If the suit was an example of religious persecution, it was persecution in the distinctly twentieth-century form of a media event—indeed, a media-*orchestrated* event. Whatever its wider ramifications, it was instigated by the *New York World* to accomplish one of Joseph Pulitzer's major aims: selling newspapers.

Pulitzer's journalistic legacy and accomplishments were complex. He was in part motivated by a passionate desire to expose the abuse of the American political system at the hands of corrupt politicians controlled by monied interests. In this effort, he scored some notable triumphs, becoming one of the premier muckrakers in the field of journalism when there was a great deal of muck to rake. There was a difference, however, between muckraking—which, aside from Pulitzer's *World* and some other newspapers, was usually the province of periodicals such as *McClure's* magazine—and the outright sensationalism associated with "yellow journalism," the main exponent of which was Pulitzer's archrival, William Randolph Hearst. But the difference was not absolute. "Pulitzer's audacity and his historical accomplishment," writes historian Richard Norton Smith, "lay in trying to supply it all—high-minded editorials and socially conscious crusades alongside a gritty procession of headless corpses, adulterous clergy, and circulation-boosting stunts. He offered readers a journalistic supermarket, not a Holiday Inn."[10]

Pulitzer himself probably had no knowledge of the *World*'s investigation of Eddy until it was launched. By 1907, blind, ill, and in a state of chronic nervous collapse, he spent most of his time on a soundproof yacht moored in Maine and manned by a crew of sixty. But the paper

NEWTON PUBLIC LIBRARY
NEWTON, KANSAS 67114

still pursued the course he had set for it in the 1880s, when he found a journalistic formula that caused the *World*'s sales to surge dramatically. Giving free reign to what Smith calls his "instinct for lurid profitability," as well as his capacity for moral indignation, Pulitzer treated the public to a steady fare of sex, tragedy, and disaster. When news was not at hand to report, Pulitzer had no hesitancy in manufacturing it. In 1889, for example, he sent one Nellie Bly on a seventy-two-day trip around the world to best the record of Jules Verne's Phineas Fogg, thereby creating enormous public excitement to feed on the *World*'s coverage of a story it had itself created.

In effect, the newspaper created the Next Friends Suit the same way. In the summer of 1906, Bradford Merrill, its financial manager, dispatched two reporters to Concord to develop a story based on what turned out to be a baseless rumor that Eddy was decrepit, dying, or perhaps already dead. Knowing that a series of articles about her was soon slated for publication in its muckraking counterpart, *McClure*'s, the *World*'s editors were not about to be bested. Besides, growing public interest in Christian Science made Eddy not only good copy, but, for a portion of the press, fair game.

In June 1906, public attention had focused on Christian Science when widely reported dedication services were held in the vast extension of the more modest original Mother Church edifice built in 1894. By this time the Church of Christ, Scientist, had attained a membership of around forty thousand. The number was small for an American denomination, but not for such a new one. Six services were required to accommodate the thirty thousand who filled the impressive domed spaces of the new church with their prayers and song. In her message read at each of the services, Eddy reminded her followers, "The pride of place or power is the prince of this world that hath nothing in Christ." On many previous occasions she had cautioned them to avoid love of display in pridefully dedicating imposing church edifices—"I hope the church shows are now over," she had written in 1897.[11] Although she had supported the enterprise of building the extension, the dedication of it proved to be the biggest show of all, with the sheer numbers in attendance drawing unprecedented media attention to Christian Science and its founder.

Whatever advantage her church gained thereby, the results for Eddy were disastrous. After the glory of the hour faded, she was left in the spotlight of public attention. At the time of the dedication she had not made any public appearances for three years. It would have been extremely taxing for a woman in her mid-eighties to be the focus of attention at so crowded an occasion. In addition, she was intent on deflecting attention from herself personally. In April 1906, she had written to the directors of the Mother Church in the *Christian Science Sentinel*: "Now is the time to *throttle the lie* that students worship me, or that I claim their homage."[12]

Bookending this message was an article published in the *Sentinel* a month after the dedication. Entitled "Personal Contagion," it warned against the dangers of personal adulation of religious leaders, with specific but not exclusive reference to herself. Obviously, for her to occupy center stage at the dedication would have had exactly the opposite effect. "I left Boston in the height of prosperity to *retreat* from the *world*," Eddy stated, "and to seek the one divine Person, whereby and wherein to show others the footsteps from sense to Soul. To give me this opportunity is all that I ask of mankind."[13]

The request was the last thing mankind was prepared to grant, especially when newspapers across the land were running stories about the phenomenal growth of Christian Science. But Eddy's request was sincere. "O for the peace of a dog in my old age," she had written in a letter some years before.[14] To be sure, she found a measure of that peace in her Pleasant View home. Yet given the intensity of the life that she lived there, perhaps the only thing pleasant about Pleasant View *was* the view.

The balcony off Eddy's study commanded a sweeping view of the Merrimack Valley. To the south, as she was fond of pointing out to visitors, lay the hills of Bow, where she had been born. "Do you not find this a delightful view?" she asked a reporter just after the Next Friends Suit concluded. "I love to sit here or on the verandas and watch this quiet stretch of countryside. . . . But you know, I cannot always sit and dream. I have much work to do—a great correspondence to answer and I am always busy."[15]

Part abbey, part farmhouse, part fortress, Pleasant View was a highly unusual community, the quiet hub of a religious movement that was fast gaining momentum. It was this secluded and somewhat remote community that the news media invaded when two *World* reporters, Slaght and Lithchild, knocked on the door on October 14, 1906.

HAVING IT BOTH WAYS

Demanding an interview with Calvin Frye, Eddy's longtime major domo, the reporters said they would be satisfied only if they could determine for themselves that she was alive. Accordingly, they were presented to her briefly the next day in the presence of a somewhat hostile neighbor, who identified her as the veritable Eddy. Upon leaving, Lithchild said to Lewis Strang, one of Eddy's secretaries, with apparent conviction, "She is certainly a well preserved woman for her years." Strang said that Slaght, the senior of the two, "gave me to understand that he was thoroughly satisfied as to the soundness of Mrs. Eddy's physical and mental condition."[16] But the picture presented to the readers of the *New York World* gave a very different impression.

No, Eddy was not dead, the story admitted. But the headline splashed across the Sunday, October 28, paper read: "MRS. MARY BAKER G. EDDY DYING: FOOTMAN AND 'DUMMY' CONTROL HER—Founder of X Science Suffering from Cancer and Nearing Her End, Is Immured at Pleasant View, While Another Woman Impersonates Her in the Streets of Concord." Virtually nothing in this headline and the story that followed bore any resemblance to the truth, as a series of affidavits, interviews, and public statements from leading citizens of Concord who saw Eddy frequently made clear. "When any one tells Concord that Mrs. Eddy is not one of our busiest, most helpful, and most beloved and respected citizens, in full possession of her illustrious faculties of mind," declared the *Concord Evening Monitor,* "Concord has a prompt and impregnable answer:—'We all know better!' "[17] But the publication on October 28 of the *World*'s interview gave rise to what would today be described as a media feeding frenzy, as more reporters descended upon Concord demanding interviews with her.

To put the matter to rest, Eddy consented to a collective interview by a battery of eleven reporters just before her 1:00 P.M. daily drive on Tuesday, October 30. Some Christian Scientists viewed their leader as virtually impervious to human weakness, and just the day before she had shown unusual vigor. But even friendly accounts indicate that she displayed visible signs of weakness during the meeting, which lasted about a minute. Strang, who accompanied Eddy on the occasion, suggested that she "step right into the room and face the newspaper people there squarely," but "the mental blast seemed to beat her back momentarily when she reached the door." The impression she made, Strang conceded, "was not quite so positive as we could have wished."[18]

Some newspaper reports were mawkish to the point of absurdity— "she stood before them shaking with palsy, a physical wreck, tottering, pallid like a vision from beyond the grave."[19] Eddy's affirmations of good health in response to the several questions put to her seemed to be belied by her frail appearance on the occasion. The issue remained as to whether her physical appearance was representative of her general physical condition or a response to the occasion itself. Dr. Allan McLane Hamilton, grandson of Alexander Hamilton and perhaps the

William E. Chandler, n.d.
Courtesy of The Mary Baker
Eddy Collection.

country's leading alienist (a psychologist specializing in the legal aspects of mental competence), who examined Eddy at the time of the suit, observed: "One journalistic inquisitor is frequently enough to perturb an ordinarily sane person. What can you expect, therefore, when an army of them is suddenly let loose upon you?"[20] Yet the results of the interview more than gratified the *World*'s editors. Their problem at this point was how to keep the story alive. To this end they hit upon a brilliant scheme.

No public figure in New Hampshire was better known than former senator William E. Chandler, owner of one of Concord's two newspapers, friend of Theodore Roosevelt, former secretary of the navy, and chairman of the Spanish Treaty Claims Commission arising from the Spanish-American War. Feisty and resolute, the bespectacled ex-senator, known as the "Stormy Petrel of New Hampshire Politics," had developed a well-earned reputation for sarcastic invective in political debate and for the tenacious pursuit of any cause he embraced. Nine years before the Next Friends Suit, Eddy had commented, "Our Senator Chandler is a bristling man at best." In the words of Chandler's admiring biographer, he was "cocky, confident, never at loss for retort, always master of

himself and usually master of the situation, never in doubt of his ability to hold his own no matter who his opponent might be."[21]

As a resident of New Hampshire, Chandler could file a lawsuit in the
state where Eddy lived. If he could be enlisted to initiate a suit on behalf
of her heirs against those presumed to be presently controlling her, the
story could be both escalated and kept indefinitely alive. Chandler was
intrigued when the *World*'s editors contacted him in November with the
prospect of taking up a case that could also be seen as a cause.

The most curious aspect of his acceptance was how little time he
lost in convincing himself that the facts of the case were in line with
the picture the *World* had drawn, when so much testimony from
Concord's leading citizens, whom he knew, contradicted it—including
that of future senator George Moses, then editor of the *Concord Monitor*,
which Chandler owned. But in Robert Peel's apt explanation, "in some
degree the *World*, Chandler, and the so-called next friends were all victims of the myth which the newspaper itself had created."[22]

Next to Chandler, the most important of these victims was Eddy's
son by her first marriage, George Glover, then in his sixties and a longtime resident of South Dakota. Shortly after Chandler accepted the case,
the insistent Slaght was dispatched to convince Glover that his mother
was the prisoner of an unscrupulous clique and that for her sake and for
preservation of his own interests, a lawsuit was in order. After confer-
ring with Chandler in Washington, D.C., and making an unannounced
visit to Pleasant View with his daughter, Mary, Glover concluded that
the suit was justified. Nor did Slaght encounter much difficulty in persuading Eddy's adopted son, Ebenezer J. Foster Eddy, now estranged
from her, to join the suit, which he did ten days after it was filed.

On March 1, 1907, a bill of equity was filed in the Merrimack
County Superior Court in Eddy's name by her "next friends"—at that
point, consisting of George and Mary Glover and a nephew of Eddy's—
against a church cabal assumed to be in control of her person and fortune. By that date, Eddy had reason to believe that danger of some sort
was impending. A letter from George Glover's former attorney had
warned her of "breakers" ahead and urged her to retrieve from her son
potentially damaging letters she had sent to him, some embarrassingly
critical of members of her own household.[23] After making an unsuccessful effort to retrieve the letters by an offer of a $125,000 trust fund
for Glover and his family, she began in mid-February to plan for a
trust placing her property in the hands of three men of unimpeachable
reputation.

It was a step she well might have eventually taken anyway. As she
explained to Joseph Armstrong, one of the directors of the Mother

Church, "The demands upon my time, attention and labors are constantly increasing, whereas my advancing years seem to demand for me less work and more quietude."[24] But the prospect of some sort of legal action against her impelled Eddy to hasten the formation of the trust, which was formalized on March 6, 1907. On March 1, she showed her cousin, General Henry M. Baker, who had occasionally served as her legal counsel, a letter she had just received from George questioning her mental competence—a letter that, because of its very cogency, she knew could not have been written by her semiliterate son. What she did not know when they met was that the Next Friends Suit was being filed in the Concord court that very day.

In a letter to Judge Robert N. Chamberlin of the New Hampshire Superior Court dated May 16, Eddy said she had begun planning the trust well before the suit was formally filed.[25] She thus made it possible for her attorney, General Frank Streeter, to pursue what turned out to be an effective strategy. Streeter argued that the issue in the case must be confined to the single question of whether Eddy had been able to "manage her business affairs March 1, 1907." This, he said, would establish her "absolute competency to deal with her affairs . . . during the last two weeks of February, the last two weeks before this suit was brought."[26] Judge Chamberlin agreed. Thus, in appointing a three-person panel of masters to examine Eddy, he gave explicit instructions to Judge Edgar Aldrich as senior master that they confine themselves to the single question of her mental competence as of March 1, 1907.

On March 7, the day after the trust was signed, the *World*'s headlines announced, "Bill in Equity Filed at Concord . . . Alleges That the Enormous Income of Mary Baker Eddy Is Wrongfully Withheld from Proper Management—Plaintiffs Declare Her Helpless in the Hands of Calvin Frye, Alfred Farlow, and Other Leaders." The month before the suit was filed, however, the *World* severed all connection with the case. The *World*'s Bradford Merrill, who had instigated the Eddy exposé, left the newspaper, eventually defecting to the chain of William Randolph Hearst. His departure precipitated a review of the *World*'s relation to the lawsuit.

Having created a media event on which the paper could continue to feed, its managers, now captained by Pulitzer's son Ralph, saw no profit and potential risk in continuing to support the suit themselves. After a conference with Chandler and members of the newspaper's staff on February 3, Ralph Pulitzer informed Chandler that he was now strictly on his own. In reply, the dismayed Chandler, playing on his relation to Eddy's son and granddaughter, responded: "Shall we tell them to go back home, helpless, heart-broken and feeling that they have been betrayed?"[27]

Pulitzer then gave Chandler $5,000 for services rendered, but left no doubt that the *World* would cease to support the suit. Nor did an appeal by Chandler to Joseph Pulitzer to override this decision succeed. Yet Chandler convinced himself that it was his duty to plunge ahead to right a wrong being perpetrated against Eddy and her heirs. As he wrote to Joseph Pulitzer, "This thing begun must go through to the end—a full and public accounting by the conspirators."[28]

The *World*, in effect, had it both ways. By severing its connection with the suit, it absolved itself of all risks. But it also had its story in a high drama to be played out in a Concord courtroom—and as events proved, in a crucial examination of Eddy's mental competence in her own home.

EDDY IN CHARGE

One characteristic noted by those who left recollections of Eddy during her later years was her astonishing recuperative powers. At some points she would be afflicted with illness so severe that her household workers feared for her survival. Then, often to their surprise, she would rise up with new strength to accomplish immense amounts of work while they puttered about like zombies.

When the *World*'s attack hit home, quite literally, in the fall of 1906, Eddy was to some extent caught off guard in a way that gave the impression of frailty and diminishing strength. Actually, her health at that time was generally quite good. Just nine days before the damaging October 15 interview with the reporters, she had written to her cousin that symptoms of illnesses she had struggled with earlier "are *gone buried* and plucked up by the roots."[29] After the suit was initiated, however, she became thoroughly aroused to the need of the hour and was soon back in high gear, doing what needed to be done.

Despite the difficulty of the experience, Eddy never lost the edge of ironic wit that was part of her makeup. Even the excesses of the *World*'s sensational October 28 article announcing her imminent demise did not seem to faze her. The next day, Eddy stepped inside the door of her Pleasant View living room, where a carpenter was working, and quipped, "Good morning, Mr. Frost, I am so glad we are not all dead this morning." Her attorney, Frank S. Streeter, who accompanied the mayor of Concord on a visit to Eddy in her study, observed, "You have a cosy corner here, I see." "Yes," Eddy replied quickly, "and some people want to see me in an even closer corner." Not infrequently, her

Mary Baker Eddy, ca. 1907, the year of the Next Friends Suit.
Courtesy of The Mary Baker Eddy Collection.

irony verged on sarcasm, as when she commented to Leigh Mitchell Hodges of the *Philadelphia North American*, "My son, whom I took care of for many years, wants to take care of me because he is suddenly impressed with my incapacity for managing my business. It might not appear from his present condition that he himself has any surplus of ability in this line."[30]

Yet Eddy hardly sailed through the experience of the Next Friends Suit with equipoise and assurance. The situation was enormously threatening and there were points when she was plunged into the depths.

"Mrs. Eddy met this trial bravely," recalled her personal maid Adelaide Still, who was nearly always by her side, "and trusted that divine Love would deliver her, but there were times when there would creep in the fear that her enemies might take her from her home and friends." On one of these occasions, another household worker found Eddy looking depressed and speaking sadly as if to herself, saying, "I don't know, perhaps they will have their way." Her coachman, August Mann, recalled her saying as she alighted from her carriage during the suit, "It is very hard"—at which point he wept.[31]

In this situation, it was characteristic of Eddy to turn to the Bible for direction and support. "I live with the Bible," she said to Lida Fitzpatrick, a household member, in April 1907. One morning the same month, for example, as the suit was gathering steam, Eddy took comfort when she opened her Bible to the twenty-second chapter of II Samuel, a psalm of David thanking God for having "delivered him out of the hands of his enemies." The psalm includes the words, "He sent from above; he took me; he drew me out of many waters; . . . The Lord liveth and blessed be my rock, and exalted be the God of the rock of my salvation."[32]

Eddy also counseled her students and household workers to continually affirm God's presence and his dominion over all phases of human experience. As she put it to one of them during the suit, "We can, and do, trust in our God to deliver us from the persecutions of those who war against Truth and Love. But there is but *one* God, one infinite *mind,* there is *no law but the divine* and this law reigns and rules this hour. Let us *know this* and rejoice—know that the judge of the whole earth *will do right.*" Young Calvin Hill, who lived at Pleasant View during part of the suit, recalled saying to her, "I know the case is all right and we will win it." But this, Eddy replied, was not the way to approach the situation at all: God's government must be *demonstrated,* proven real through prayer and obedience to Him, not merely assumed. Hill noted that, according to her instructions for praying about the lawsuit, "I was not to outline what the verdict would be but to know that Truth would prevail and that divine Mind would direct the verdict—which it certainly did."[33]

Eddy herself gained greatly in assurance and command by the time the suit was launched in March 1907. For one thing, she insisted upon following every aspect of the case closely. During the early days of the trial, one of her secretaries tried to withhold from her a report in a Concord newspaper on the day's courtroom proceedings. She asked why the paper had not been brought to her as usual, insisted upon reading it, examined the article with care, then explained to the secretary the "importance of keeping her in close *touch* with the case so that she might give it all necessary attention." To make sure she was duly informed, she instructed one of her followers to "attend to the hearing of our case in Court each day and report to me daily how goes the battle," adding, "Oh for the spiritual understanding that knows it is all governed by God, infinite Truth, and Love."[34]

Eddy also conferred with her lawyers and took steps to counter the aggressive publicity in the pages of the *World* and in the ongoing series of muckraking attacks in *McClure's*. The first of these articles was so misleading that Eddy commented, "Of all the history of lies ever written I believe this article is the most in excess." Yet she trusted the long-term sanity and fairness of the *vox populi,* which "will redress wrongs and rectify injustice." This appeared to be palpably happening in other newspapers, even as the *World* continued its steady drumbeat of stories about the developing litigation. The *New York American,* long critical of the *World,* ran a trenchant editorial condemning "The *World's* Disgraceful Attack on Eddy" as "an attack upon a woman . . . upon old age . . . and upon religious belief. . . . And we trust that the *New York World,* as far as it is possible, will see fit to confine its attacks to MEN, and, if it must attack WOMEN, that it will at least exempt THOSE PAST FOURSCORE."[35] During the first part of 1907, as the case developed and press accounts multiplied, public fascination with Eddy mounted to unprecedented proportions. In May alone, eight national magazines ran stories highly favorable to her.

This sea change was in part Eddy's doing. To one office of her church, its Committee on Publication, she had assigned the duty of correcting misconceptions about her and Christian Science. Although the job was on the whole capably done by one of her most trusted lieutenants, Alfred Farlow, during the months of the Next Friends Suit, Eddy herself took over much of the work.

Long hesitant to give press interviews, she abruptly reversed course and during June through August of 1907 gave a half-dozen widely read interviews that strongly affected public perception of her. "There is no hysterical gush, no fanatic spirit of ecstasy, but a calm, self-possessed, well-poised mental equilibrium that is remarkable in a woman of her years," wrote playwright Charles Klein in the February 1907 issue of *Cosmopolitan.* As a recent convert to Christian Science, Klein was understandably sympathetic. No reporter had a greater reputation for tough-mindedness than Arthur Brisbane, editor of the *New York Evening Journal* and a former editor of the *World.* And no reporter appeared more impressed by his encounter with Eddy, who, as he recalled, "looked like a flaming spirit imprisoned in a body almost transparent." Eddy, he wrote after his interview with her on June 8, "has accumulated power in this world. She possesses it, she exercises it, and she knows it. But it is a gentle power, and it is possessed by a gentle, diffident, and modest woman." Summing up his impression, Brisbane said, "It is quite certain that nobody could see this beautiful and venerable woman and ever again speak of her except in terms of affectionate reverence and sympathy."[36]

For a reporter so hard-boiled as Brisbane to write this way about anyone was startling. Yet such characterizations of Eddy were increasingly commonplace in the national press, in which the Next Friends Suit intermittently held center stage during the spring and summer of 1907. Some of the coverage, particularly in Boston, was actively hostile. Between March and August 1907, the *Boston Herald* published over ninety articles unfavorable to Eddy, over half of them on the front page. In most instances, however, the manifest unfairness of the case against her, together with natural sympathy for a woman of her years, produced a backlash of favorable coverage. Article after article surrounded her image with a soft-focus grandmotherly haze. A comment from a heartland newspaper in Abilene, Kansas, is typical: "In strange contrast to the greed and malevolence of these 'next friends' is the sweet, pure, and holy life of this venerable woman."[37]

Such characterizations were one sided. Eddy could be motherly, domestic, and tender. But she could also be demanding, difficult, even imperious. She had not only "discovered" and defined Christian Science, but had founded and led the movement against formidable odds through its stormy early history, organizing and then reorganizing her church to provide channels for its growth. Some of the journalists who interviewed her caught her sharpness and quick wit. But neither they nor the editorial writers who commented on the case quite fathomed the toughness that had been required to build up and sustain the cause of Christian Science.

Hers was not so much a male toughness as a fierce motherly protectiveness, well characterized by Adam H. Dickey, who spent nearly three years as a member of Eddy's household and who was appointed by her to serve as a director of the Mother Church. Throughout the animal kingdom, Dickey observed, "the female of the species has always been defender of the offspring. . . . Hunters of wild animals much prefer to meet the father than to encounter a lioness or tigress who is protecting her young." Describing her efforts to preserve the movement against the inroads of rival "mind-cure" movements in the late 1880s, Eddy spoke of herself with little exaggeration as "a lioness deprived of her young."[38]

The situation she now faced was equally if not more threatening. In March 1907, she wrote to Calvin Hill, "This hour is going to test Christian Scientists and the fate of our Cause, and they must not be found wanting. . . . I see this clearly, that the prosperity of our Cause hangs in this balance." Others outside the movement shared her estimate of what was at stake. Christian Science has "no lack of open foes and of unbelievers ready to seize on any seeming weakness to attack it," commented an editorial in the *New Haven Register,* and if Chandler's claims as to the delusionary basis of her teaching were sustained in court, its foes "will accept that decision as the overthrow of the whole Christian Science faith."[39]

For Eddy, this was precisely the issue. She saw Christian Science as more than her own personal teaching and the Next Friends Suit as more than a threat to her person. "This movement of thought," she had written of Christian Science a decade before, "must push on the ages: it must start the wheels of reason aright, educate the affections to higher resources, and leave Christianity unbiased by the superstitions of a senior period."[40] By 1907, Christian Science was advancing so rapidly that it seemed to her to be fulfilling the destiny she had predicted for it. If an attack on her could discredit Christian Science as it was taking hold, her lifework would be reduced to ruins just as it was reaching fruition.

ADVERSARIES

This is exactly what Chandler aimed at accomplishing. He maintained that he was motivated by righteous outrage at the spectacle of an elderly woman and her heirs being victimized by money-hungry conspirators. But his repeated objections to Christian Science show that he looked upon Eddy as a fraud and her teaching as sheer humbuggery. As he wrote in a letter shortly after the suit came to trial, "the imposture of Eddyism grows bigger and more atrocious than I expected to find it."[41] In framing a strategy for the lawsuit, he went hammer and tongs after her fundamental claims as a religious thinker and leader.

As a professional man at the upper echelons of the WASP establishment, Chandler was naturally sympathetic with others who, for their own reasons, disliked Eddy as much as he did. She was, after all, a woman intruding into what they saw as exclusively male domains of leadership. Much of the invective directed against her reflected chauvinist hostility against this presumed intrusion. Repeatedly, such invective expressed the view that, while men could be taken seriously as writers and thinkers, women could not. Joseph Pulitzer, for example, once commented of Christian Science, "There is a strong leaning towards the view that the misguided religious people are hysterical women and weakminded men."[42]

It was only natural, after Ralph Pulitzer had thrust him out so abruptly on his own, for Chandler to go networking among other male professionals, both to obtain practical support for the litigation and to organize more far-reaching opposition to Christian Science. In March, he implored the president of the New York Medical Society to "originate a movement of physicians and surgeons . . . to expose and oppose" Christian Science healing, adding, "Please also consider whether there ought not to be a similar movement on the part of the ministers of the gospel of all denominations." There were enemies for Chandler to mobilize in both professions. Eddy had launched into American religious life a teaching that aroused the most serious questions for both theology and medicine. She cherished what she called "vital Christianity" wherever she found it. Yet if what she taught were true, some time-honored Christian doctrines were not. Just so, she paid genuine tribute to caring members of the medical profession, praising them as "grand men and women" over those who practiced Christian Science for anything less than Christian motives. But if her analysis of the mental basis of disease was correct, and if healing actually resulted from the practice of what she taught, conventional medicine could no longer claim preemptive supremacy either in explaining disease or in curing it.[43]

Since the mid-1880s, when Christian Science first attracted a substantial following in Boston, stemming the tide of the new movement had become a pressing subject for discussion at ministerial associations, and anti-Christian Science literature had become a virtual subgenre in Protestant church life. From their own theological standpoint, clergymen had reason to be alarmed at the inroads Christian Science was making as thousands left their old church homes to join a new and most dubious fold. Some clergymen struck a moderate and mournful note. A Universalist pastor, for example, introducing a Christian Science lecturer in 1900, observed, "One of the most serious objections I would find with Christian Science is that it has claimed as its own, too many of the most liberal and helpful members in my own church." Others, however, went to rhetorical extremes in blasting the new faith and its founder. In 1906, when the church extension was dedicated, the Reverend A. Lincoln Moore, pastor of the Riverside Baptist Church in New York, told his congregation that Christian Science is "unchristian, anti-Christian, anti-Biblical, Christless, Godless,—in brief, Pagan" and that "the attitude of the Christian Church must be one of uncompromising hostility" against it.[44]

The medical war against Christian Science was just as focused and determined. In 1899, the *Albany Morning Express* had reported that physicians in Philadelphia planned "to commence a national war against the Christian Scientists," with the goal of persuading the United States Congress to act against the group. The attack, while not centrally planned, was conducted by local medical societies in virtually every state. Christian Science periodicals reported a series of skirmishes in which efforts to ban the practice of Christian Science healing were carried on in state courts and legislatures. Such efforts met with little success. Christian Scientists mustered convincing accounts of healing to blunt the charge that their practice was ineffectual, while the strong tradition of First Amendment religious freedom made it difficult to impose legal restraints on a form of healing that was also an integral part of a religious practice. Even Mark Twain, who wrote scathingly of Eddy, observed that under the medical practice acts then being proposed, "if the second Advent should happen now," Jesus himself "could not heal the sick in the state of New York."[45]

Chandler, however, had little success in gaining allies for his anti-Eddy crusade. Some of those to whom he appealed may have realized, as Chandler apparently did not, that press coverage of the suit was creating a backlash of public opinion in her favor and that overt support for the suit would be an extraordinarily misguided tactic for those who most fervently wished Eddy ill. Like the *World*'s editors, Eddy's opponents left the ex-senator to press forward in a suit that, if won, would serve their interests, but that, if lost, would leave him alone, twisting impecuniously in the wind.

IN THE BALANCE

The Next Friends Suit came to trial in a Concord courtroom on August 13, 1907, five months after it was filed. As senior master, Judge Edgar Aldrich, an imposing, white-haired gentleman with a well-earned reputation for fair-mindedness, presided over the proceedings in a crowded courtroom. He, along with the two other masters, one an alienist and the other an attorney, were under instructions from Judge Chamberlin of the Supreme Court of New Hampshire to pursue one mission: to determine whether Eddy was legally competent when she executed the March 6, 1907, deed of trust.

Anticipating that he might not be able to prove his case against her mental competence, Chandler had decided upon a two-pronged legal strategy. During his long political career, he had proven himself an extremely adept tactician. His maneuvering as Republican national chairman following the disputed election of 1876 had been largely responsible for securing the presidency for Rutherford B. Hayes. Chandler's primary strategy in order to establish Eddy's incompetence to manage her own affairs was to seek a jury trial in which she would be forced to testify in open court. Judge Aldrich ruled against Chandler, insisting that in deference to her age, Eddy be examined not before a jury, but by the three masters in her own home.

This ruling forced Chandler to lay the groundwork for a second strategy: persuading the masters that her mind was controlled by religious delusions that made her unfit to make decisions relative to her property. To a physician with whom he corresponded about the case, Chandler confided his hope that "Mrs. Eddy will go to pieces mentally on view by the Masters, but if she does not and shows some intelligence in connection with business affairs, we wish immediately to press forward inquiry into and exposure of her delusions which unfit her for business acts."[46]

During his opening argument, after complaining at some length over the disadvantages under which he labored in preparing his case, Chandler enumerated delusions from which he claimed Eddy suffered—each of them, he insisted, open for all to see in her book *Science and Health*. Eddy's attorney did not engage Chandler on these points, which were obviously matters of religious belief outside the scope of the issues at trial. But he did agree with Judge Aldrich that the examination of her by the three masters should proceed as quickly as possible.

At two o'clock in the afternoon of August 14, the second day of the hearing, the three masters, along with Chandler, Eddy's attorney, and a court stenographer, met with her in her study. When the suit collapsed just a week later, well-wishers and followers rejoiced in a victory that seemed more inevitable than it actually was.

If Eddy had been as overcome on this occasion as when she faced the battery of reporters the previous October, Chandler may have been able to create sufficient doubts about her mental state to keep the case alive and perhaps even to win it. As events proved, she was more than equal to the occasion. Looking out of her tower window while awaiting the masters' arrival, she commented with quiet irony, "The 'Nexters' have fine weather for their trial." Recalling Eddy's demeanor just before the interview, Adelaide Still wrote that she showed "no sign of fear . . . and I was sure that the moment the opposing lawyer saw her sitting there, he knew he had not a chance of winning his case."[47]

Most of the initial questioning was carried on by Judge Aldrich in an atmosphere that, at the outset, was formal and strained. There were questions about her Pleasant View home, why she came to Concord, and her public-spirited efforts on the city's behalf. When the masters turned to financial questions—why and how she had established a trust, the kinds of investments she considered sound—her answers were deft, closing off any question as to her competence in business affairs. After a detour into a discussion of the development of Christian Science, tensions relaxed to the point that more personal and informal subjects were introduced. Eddy described her daily drive around Concord, work habits, and correspondence. Responding to a question as to whether she was fond of music, she insisted upon playing for the masters a gramophone she had recently come to enjoy. In the words of a biographer generally hostile to Eddy, "She greeted her visitors with the air of a gracious hostess, and, despite their efforts to maintain the frigid decorum of a court-room, she soon carried the interview into the easy atmosphere of an afternoon call."[48]

As the interview concluded, Judge Aldrich, who had begun the proceedings with nervous tentativeness, departed from the agenda with which he began. He volunteered that his own mother was still living and was eighty-seven years old, just a year older than Eddy. Seizing upon this opening, she commented, "God bless her. She is not a day older for her eighty-seven years if she is growing in grace." Eddy then spoke briefly of the mental basis of physical conditions, including the process of aging, then continued, "Now my thought is, that if we keep our mind fixed on Truth, God, Life and Love, He will advance us in our years to a higher understanding; He will change our hope into faith, our faith into spiritual understanding, our words into works, and our ultimate into the fruition of entering into the Kingdom."[49]

On the surface, Eddy's words sounded innocuous: an elderly lady sharing her religious faith about entering into the kingdom of God. Yet they afford a clue as to why her teaching aroused so much controversy that Judge Aldrich and the other two masters found themselves in her home on that August afternoon. In traditional Christian teaching, the kingdom of God is generally regarded as a supernatural realm into which those who are saved will enter in another life. In more liberal forms of Christianity, it has been portrayed more as the progressive amelioration of human affairs. Eddy taught neither of these conceptions.

For her, the kingdom of God is neither a far-off realm in the beyond nor an improved state of present human existence. Rather, it is a *present* spiritual reality to which conventional human thinking remains largely blind. As she put it in her short work *Unity of Good*, "Our Master said, 'The kingdom of heaven is at hand.' Then God and heaven, or Life, are present, and death is not the real stepping-stone to

Life and happiness. They are now and here; and a change in human consciousness, from sin to holiness, would reveal this wonder of being."[50] By putting off the sin-bound limits of the human mentality and admitting more fully the reality and presence of God, she taught, one begins to break through conventional limits of perception in a way that brings forth healing. The power that heals, she consistently emphasized, is not the human mind, which she saw as the cause and not the cure of disease, but the yielding of the human mind to what she called "Divine Mind," the Mind that is God. A key aspect of Eddy's interview with the masters at Pleasant View was her insistence that they understand this point.

During the interview, she had responded at some length to a question about "the development of your special religion." In response, she described one of her experiments in the 1850s with the medical system of homeopathy, through which she stumbled on the crucial point that, in her words, "mind governed the whole issue" of the patient's recovery— a conclusion that helped turn her thoughts to the "new channels" and led to the discovery of Christian Science. At that point, the interview took a detour into questions about other matters. But as the masters were leaving, Eddy recalled them, along with the attorneys and stenographer, so that she could complete what she was saying about the footsteps that led her to Christian Science.

"When I came to the point that it was mind that did the healing," she said, picking up where she had left off, "then I wanted to know what mind it was. Was it the Mind which was in Christ Jesus, or was it the human mind or human will?" She spoke of investigating spiritualism, mesmerism, and hypnotism, but failing "to find God there," then of finding through the Bible "that human will was the cause of disease rather than its cure. . . . All the power that Christian Scientists have," she concluded, "comes from on High. We haven't any other power and no faith in any other power."

By this point in the interview, Eddy's mental competence had been established beyond reasonable question. As an editorial in the *New York American* put it, the investigation into her mental condition "has revealed that the head of the Christian Science faith is quite the mental equal of the examiners; that she knows as much about her financial affairs as is necessary for her to know, and that at eighty-seven she is considerably more vigorous in mind and body than a number of United States Senators who are in their seventies."[51] Consequently, once Eddy had proven her ability to discuss business affairs and other matters rationally, Chandler had no option but to make the rationality of Christian Science itself the main issue in the case.

Delusions?

"The aged head of the movement," commented an editorial in the *Boston Journal*, "went through her examination with what may fairly be called flying colors."[52]

Chandler knew this as well as anyone. As the masters returned to the courtroom after the interview, he was heard to comment with no little disgust, "She's sharper than a steel trap." A year after the suit, Dr. George F. Jelly, a Boston alienist and one of the masters, was reported to have said that, having never met Eddy before, he had not been in the room with her for five minutes "when I realized I was in the presence of the most intelligent and spiritual woman I had ever met." Chandler obviously did not share this opinion, but he well knew by the end of the interview that his case had been dealt a crippling blow. Still, he tried to put the best face he could on the situation. To a confidant, he hypothesized that Eddy "is stimulated into a state of high exaltation when she is to have important interviews" and regretted that "we did not remain to see any collapse"—which never occurred. To Ralph Pulitzer, he conceded that she "showed mental activity on ordinary subjects"; but when it came to Christian Science, her "crazy notions" provided "symptoms of delusion abundantly vindicating my opening statement."[53]

The next four days of the hearing saw Chandler and his associates vainly trying to return to the ground he had staked out in that statement, in which he enumerated aspects of Eddy's teaching so "delusionary" as to render her unfit to conduct business acts. Chandler was frustrated from making his case by the strict rules of evidence imposed by Judge Chamberlin to the effect that the hearing was not an inquiry into Eddy's religious beliefs. Nevertheless, his way of defining these beliefs, even in his fiercest attack mode, caught some of the sharp contours and radical edges of her teaching that others, more sympathetic to her, easily passed over.

Thus he asserted that the first of the "delusions" propounded in *Science and Health* "is the delusion, a fundamental delusion, a widespread and deep rooted delusion, the delusion of non-existence and unreality of the physical universe, organic and inorganic. All her delusions are built upon this fundamental delusion."[54]

Eddy did hold that reality is, in truth, spiritual—that matter is not objectively substantial, but represents a finite, limited view of God's creation, which is spiritual and solidly present. Yet she made no blanket denial of the meaningfulness of human experience as a whole. Far from an assertion that all we experience is unreal—that there are no rocks, mountains, flowers, or trees, or that others whom we encounter and love do not exist—her view was akin to Paul's statement that "We see through a glass darkly." She acknowledged fully that within the limits of our present, distorted way of looking at things, matter, evil, and all forms of suffering *appear* thoroughly real, often more real than anything else. But she also wrote, "To take all earth's beauty into one gulp of vacuity and label beauty nothing, is ignorantly to caricature God's creation. . . . In our immature sense of spiritual things, let us say to the beauties of the sensuous universe: 'I love your promise; and shall know, some time, the spiritual reality and substance of form, light, and color, of what I now through you discern dimly.'"[55]

Chandler also overstated the case when he argued that her second "delusion" was "the supernatural character of the Science she calls her own and of the supernatural manner in which it was discovered by her." Eddy did see Christian Science as a spiritual breakthrough of major proportions. Yet she was far from viewing herself, in his words, as "miraculously and supernaturally selected by Almighty God to receive divine revelations directly from God." "My discovery of Science," she told a household worker in 1902, "was the result of experience and growth. It was not a case of instantaneous conversion in which, I could say, 'Now the past is nothing, begin entirely anew.'"[56] Indeed, when she called the masters back to share some of the steps she believed led to her discovery of Christian Science, she put particular stress on the role of homeopathy in her development.

To Chandler, Eddy's claim that the practice of her teaching produced healing results, thus helping to revivify Christian healing, constituted yet another delusion: "She has been possessed all these years of a delusion as to the cause of all the diseases of mankind; a delusion as to the cure of disease; a delusion as to the prevention of disease. And this insane systematized delusion of Eddy comprises and includes a complete system as to the mode by which alone disease is cured."

Chandler's phrase "complete system," while meant invidiously, was in one sense perceptive. Eddy did not merely offer a method by which disease as conventionally understood could be eliminated, or even a claim that disease has a fundamentally mental cause, although she certainly held this to be true. She saw disease in a biblical and theological context as a constituent part of the mortal condition from which humanity needs to be redeemed. The spiritual healing of disease, like the healing of sin, was for her a phase of a full salvation from fleshliness and mortality, proving that the true understanding of God dissolves rather than legitimizes physical suffering. Eddy stated that Christian Science had summoned the world to battle over these issues, writing that on the basis of "actual demonstration"—the healing works Christian Scientists accomplished—it would have a "fair fight."[57] In this way, she put the issue outside the realm of dialectical argument or opinion, hers or Chandler's.

Accounts of healing have been included in every issue of the *Christian Science Journal* and *Christian Science Sentinel* since they began publication in 1883 and 1898, respectively. Even if one excludes accounts that might involve questionable diagnoses or exaggeration, there still remains evidence of cures—in many cases medically diagnosed and confirmed—that Christian Scientists have emphasized cannot be medically explained. The question then as now is how these and other forms of nonmedical healing are to be evaluated, and this question remains extremely complex. Chandler's response, however, was simplistic. His bedrock contention was that such healings did not and could not in principle occur. On the third day of the hearing, one of his associates asserted categorically that "a practical condition" such as cancer cannot be healed through prayer: "With a cancer prayers come, the cancer remains; more prayers, the cancer remains, the patient dies."[58]

Cutting directly across this assertion were a series of healings in the Christian Science periodicals in 1907, the year of the Next Friends Suit, containing accounts of the healing, not only of cancer, but of numerous other definite and severe disorders, along with some accounts in which the condition being healed was more vaguely defined. An abstract list of illnesses reported as cured, however, gives little idea of the impact of these healing experiences, however they are evaluated, on individual lives.

One healing had far-reaching effects on the Next Friends Suit itself. In 1903, the son of newspaper publisher William Randolph Hearst was born with a condition called a closed pylorus. In Hearst's recollection, the baby was unable to take any nourishment or keep down "a teaspoonful of milk or even water." His condition grew desperate as he wasted away "to an actual skeleton." After medical resources had been exhausted, the Hearsts turned to a Christian Science practitioner. According to Hearst's account written years later, the child was healed overnight and his son "is now a little over six feet tall, and weighs 180 pounds, and runs a newspaper considerably better than his father can."[59] The way the elder Hearst ran his newspaper at the time of the Next Friends Suit was profoundly affected by this experience. Not only did he give direct orders that no Hearst newspaper should attack Eddy, but his newspapers showed uniform sympathy to her, and all of them printed the interview by Arthur Brisbane, editor of the *New York Journal*, a Hearst publication.

The question of the validity and meaning of such healings will not simply lie down as a remote quarrel in the early years of the twentieth century. In recent years, this question has not abated, but has become more complicated and intense. On the one hand, there is a substantial body of evidence of nonmedical cures, both in and out of Christian Science, which cannot reasonably be written off through recourse to such catch-all explanations as "spontaneous remission." This body of evidence points to the need for serious rethinking, not only of prevalent theories of medical causation, but of the presuppositions behind any form of scientific reductionism and materialism. On the other hand, important developments in molecular biology, genetic engineering, and related disciplines have been used to support the argument that the universe is so constituted that physical cause and effect reign supreme, and that matter is the absolute arbiter of the issues of life.[60]

Such were the issues that this "venerable" lady helped to project into the American environment. Though not a philosopher or professional theologian, Eddy articulated such long-range questions as starkly as anyone in her time and, what is more, founded a church committed to validating the answers she gave.

As far as the Concord court was concerned, on the basis of the First Amendment, the truth or falsity of her answers to these questions was not within the jurisdiction of any court to decide. Chandler made numerous efforts to present Christian Science as essentially a form of medicine, rather than a religious teaching that included spiritual healing as part of its practice. But the interview with Eddy left no doubt that Christian Science healing must be understood within a religious framework. And as the hearing progressed, it became apparent that Chandler's strategy was on a clear collision course with the First Amendment to the U.S. Constitution.

Judge Aldrich pointed out that Eddy was plainly not the only individual who believed in and advocated her religious teachings. If healing in Christian Science was in principle a delusion, then there were many others guilty of harboring it. In view of the fact that she had many thousands of followers, the conclusion followed that not only Eddy, but every believer in Christian Science was incapable of managing his or her business affairs—and, more broadly, that the holding of any religious belief contrary to popular convictions could be construed as evidence of insanity. As Judge Aldrich put it, *"The truth or falsity of a religious belief is beyond the scope of a judicial inquiry."*[61]

CHANDLER'S TRUMP CARD

In the four days that remained of the hearing after the masters' interview, Chandler was especially anxious to bring before the court what he saw as the most impressive *prima facie* evidence of Eddy's insanity: "the delusion as to the existence and nature of Malicious Animal Magnetism . . . that Malicious Animal Magnetism is capable of producing all manner of evil, is capable by mental suggestion, of poisoning mankind and producing death." In preparing for the case, Chandler and his associates expended enormous efforts in accumulating letters and testimony as to Eddy's views on this subject, and in his opening statement, he dwelt on it at greater length than any other aspect of her teaching. This was his trump card, and for Chandler, perhaps the most frustrating aspect of the trial was that he never got to play it.

The term "animal magnetism" as Eddy used it was not as mysterious as Chandler supposed. In her definition, "animal magnetism" was "the specific term for error or mortal mind"—that is, of all that opposed and denied God's reality and what to her was the basic fact of his inseparable relation to all his children. It was a term in general use, but was elastic enough to bear the freight of meaning she assigned to it, suggesting as it does the blind, primitive pull or mesmeric operation of error. She therefore characterized it by the use of gerunds: "so-called mortal mind controlling mortal mind; error, working out the designs of error; one belief preying upon another."[62]

The sense of the term as she employed it further conveys her conviction that, while error must ultimately be reduced to "its native nothingness," until that point is reached, error cannot be described as a mere blank. Rather, its operation carries with it the sense of denial, threat, meaninglessness, and mental darkness. For Eddy, it was crucial to see that this destructive mental influence has nothing substantive behind it—no reality before God, no existence as a personal Satan or actual power. Its apparent operation claims to have a temporary hold on people only through unchallenged mesmeric suggestion. As this is exposed and rejected, she maintained, the reality of God becomes so vivid that the magnetic pull of evil is broken, its grip on one's mentality is broken, and one is freer to understand that there can be no actual mind or power apart from God.

Eddy saw what she termed "mental malpractice" as a form of animal magnetism in which mesmeric influence was used to accomplish destructive ends. "Mental malpractice," she wrote, "is the injurious action of one mind controlling another from wrong motives, and is practiced either with a mistaken or a wicked purpose."[63] On the basis of what she said was long-term observation, Eddy concluded that the influence of mental malpractice, if undetected and unresisted, could have negative effects on the well-being of others, even though they remain utterly unaware of its operation. "The modes of mental malpractice," she wrote, can work "so subtly that we mistake its suggestions for the impulses of our own thought."[64]

In Chandler's opinion, the mere contention that mental influences could have such damaging effects was so inconceivable as to constitute evidence of paranoid delusion in itself. From her standpoint, exposing the effects of mental malice was far from an irrational obsession. On the contrary, it was bringing a much-needed light to an area of human experience of which conventional thinking remained largely unaware, but which could be negated and disarmed in the spirit of the Ninety-first Psalm, which she often quoted and had recourse to in her private devotions: "He that dwelleth in the secret place of the most High shall abide under the shadow of the Almighty. I will say of the Lord, He is my refuge and my fortress: my God; in him will I trust. . . . Thou shalt not be afraid for the terror by night; nor for the arrow that flieth by day."

One of Eddy's strongest assertions of this conviction is found in a brief editorial published in the *Christian Science Sentinel* and *Journal* of November 1907, just months after the conclusion of the Next Friends Suit. The editorial was occasioned by an article in the October issue of the *Arena,* written by Benjamin O. Flower, a longtime supporter. Flower's article gave full credence to the power of evil and hypnotism in a way Eddy believed needed correcting. She heavily revised the draft of an article by the editor of the Christian Science periodicals whom she had commissioned to write a rejoinder to the piece—so heavily that the editorial eventually published under his name was in substance her own.

Entitled "Evil Is Not Power," it acknowledged the effects of evil, including malicious mental attacks, when unopposed. But it asserted that one is never without a sure defense against these apparent effects: the understanding that evil can have no actual, self-constituted power in a universe governed by one omnipotent God. "That evil is real or has power," the editorial asserted, "is an unthinkable proposition unless we utterly and absolutely repudiate God. . . . The one thing from which mortals suffer is their belief in evil, that it is real and has power."[65] Minus this awakened understanding of the inherent powerlessness of evil, Eddy taught, mortals feel its effects, especially in the form of mentally projected malice, in ways they barely understand.

The question of the actual effects of the mentally projected "terror by night" and "arrow that flieth by day" remains controversial, although some recent studies suggest that the possibility of negative thought transference across distances should at least be taken seriously even by the skeptical.[66] What is not controversial is the intensity of the feeling directed against Eddy, especially in the context of the Next Friends Suit. "It is a curious fact, one worthy of study by psychologists," commented an Illinois newspaper, "that the Founder or Leader of such a peculiarly pacific faith as that of Eddy should be subjected to such bitter, unrelenting, hostility."[67]

Chandler's own conduct may be said to furnish an example. A man of singular powers of intellect, he became remarkably blind to facts bearing on Eddy's mental state obvious to almost everyone else. Even after the case was lost, he pursued the possibility of reopening it while she was alive and of contesting her will when she died with something more than the dogged tenacity for which he was known. When Eddy was rumored to be ill in 1909, he instituted a virtual death watch outside her home so as to spring into action if she died. He also planned to have a representative present should an autopsy be performed. Recuperating from a severe illness of his own at the time of her death in December 1910, Chandler traveled to Boston at the risk of his own health a year and a half later to take advantage of the possibility of contesting her will. After this challenge proved unsuccessful, he wrote to Eddy's son, George Glover, "You and I are old and feeble but we must keep fighting till the last gun is fired."[68]

The obsessiveness with which he pursued the litigation against Eddy was not, however, self-generated. The fire of his fury against her was persistently inflamed by his own junior counsel in the suit, Frederick W. Peabody. Peabody, in turn, was a virtual mouthpiece for one of Eddy's most determined enemies, Josephine Curtis Woodbury.[69] Peabody not only wrote and spoke against Christian Science, but also fed such information, or misinformation, as he had gathered to both Georgine Milmine and Willa Cather, who respectively originated and completed the muckraking series in *McClure's*, published in book form under Milmine's name in 1909.

As letters from Peabody to Mark Twain attest, Peabody also tried to stoke Twain's dislike of Eddy—a dislike so virulent that even Twain could hardly understand it. When the *World* began its attack on Eddy, its staff also turned to Peabody as a resource. As a Boston-based attorney, Peabody then became junior counsel to Chandler. Chandler for his part grew so weary of Peabody's lengthy and frequent letters that he once wrote to him, "Your basketful of communications is received." Two years later, he became so put off by Peabody's rancorous disposition that he castigated him for his "ungovernable temper," which had "made a *failure*" of his life.[70] Ironically, what Chandler could not see was that Peabody's obsessive hostility to Eddy had contributed to his own myopic failure of judgment in prosecuting the Next Friends Suit.

So emotionally intense was the whole situation, so irrational was the hostility it engendered, that it called forth a number of outraged responses. Some indication of the emotional temperature stirred up by the Next Friends Suit can be gleaned from the savage irony of a letter signed "A Sympathizer" received by George Glover in 1907:

> I want to congratulate you on the suit you have brought against your mother in Concord, N.H.. The spectacle of the old lady being dragged to the court will convulse the world with laughter. Such action on your part at her time of life will undoubtedly kill her by its indignity. . . . As one who sympathizes with you I hope that you will be in Concord to see your mother at the age of 86 dragged from her home, insulted by the rabble, and corkscrewed by your lawyer, Frederick W. Peabody.[71]

THE AFTERMATH

There could be little doubt after the masters' interview with Eddy that the suit would collapse, as it did just a week later, when Chandler, with no prospect of victory, asked to withdraw the petition with no finding from the court, pro or con, on the merits of the case. The request was granted, though over the objections of Eddy's counsel, Frank Streeter, who argued with some passion but no effectiveness that she should be fully vindicated by a conclusive finding as to her competence.

Yet the ordeal of the suit was not quite over for her when Chandler asked to withdraw the plaintiffs' petition. His so doing did not remove the possibility that another move on behalf of Eddy's "next friends" might be taken at some point in the future. In view of this brooding threat, her attorneys reached a compromise settlement with the plaintiffs, which among other provisions ensured that her every expenditure would be closely watched for the remainder of her life. Eddy also faced the possibility that the suit could be reopened, as well as the likelihood that her will would be challenged after her death, which it was.

Although Eddy won the suit, in the sense that the original complaint was withdrawn by the plaintiffs, it took a heavy toll on her personally. To her household, it became apparent that, despite intermittent periods of vitality, her old resilience was less evident than it had been before the suit, which had wounded her deeply. The very fact that both her son and her adopted son had been induced to join in the legal proceedings against her was more than hurtful. Since she had had no contact with Foster Eddy for nearly a decade after the suit began, his joining in the proceedings was probably no surprise. But the involvement of her natural son George was wounding. As she wrote to him in June 1906, "I love you, my only child. Why do you allow yourself to be used to bring this great grief and trouble on your own aged mother?"[72]

The effect of the suit on those close to her was destructive as well. Joseph Armstrong, a faithful and longtime director of the Mother Church, died at the end of 1907. Pamelia Leonard, a Christian Science teacher from Brooklyn who worked with Eddy at Pleasant View, had been caught up in the publicity surrounding the suit when the *World* maintained that to mislead the press, she had been impersonating Eddy on her daily drives. Probably as a result, an illness from which she had intermittently suffered intensified to the point that she went home and died in January 1908. A young Christian Scientist whom Eddy called to Pleasant View, Mary Tomlinson, became so agitated by the crisis that in April, she suddenly lost her reason and committed suicide, reportedly leaping from a window of the Parker House in Boston just above the room where Chandler, Peabody, and their associates were planning their strategy for the case.[73]

Eddy's most immediate challenge after the termination of the Next Friends Suit was to break through the miasma of malice and rancor that it had created. The clearest public recognition of her disposition to do this came in the form of an interview given by Clara Barton, founder of the American Red Cross, in the *New York American* early in 1908. "How beautifully," Barton wrote of Eddy, "she has managed her own unfortunate trials! Without malice, always with a kindness and charity that is almost beyond human comprehension, has this woman fought antagonism and that only with love."[74]

That Eddy did seek to meet antagonism with love was evident in some measure when she first heard that the suit was being withdrawn. According to the recollections of Calvin Hill, who brought her daily news of the court proceedings, she immediately wrote a letter "of over-flowing forgiveness" to one of those who had signed onto the suit.[75] The following November, she examined proofs of a book documenting the suit by Michael Meehan, the admiring young editor of the *Concord Patriot*. Without requiring him to do so, she asked Meehan to abandon the project, offering to pay his expenses several times over in order to prevent publication of a book that, although favorable to her, would have kept the memory of the suit alive. (The book eventually was published, although in truncated form.)[76]

The month after the suit was settled, Eddy even contemplated inviting Chandler to visit and talk with her, hoping that personal contact might bring a measure of healing forgiveness to a still-troubled situation. The idea was dropped only after Streeter, her attorney, advised her strongly against it, arguing that Chandler's "only purpose in going to your house would be to get some advantage over you" and that he "would not meet you with the same spirit with which you would receive him. I advise you not to invite him." In closing, Streeter commented: "Let me add that your policy of dignified silence with reference to these enemies of yourself has commended itself to the strong men who have talked with me and who have not the pleasure of knowing you personally."[77]

Eddy's long-run aim, however, was to wrest something of value from the ordeal, in the conviction, as she once put it, that "when these things cease to bless, they will cease to occur." Part of the blessing, as Christian Scientists and others sympathetic to Eddy read the situation, was the backlash in her favor represented by the general tenor of press opinion about the suit, as well as a wave of new interest in Christian Science that publicity about the suit occasioned. As Benjamin O. Flower, the editor of the *Arena*, put it in a letter to Eddy, "This persecution is wonderfully strengthening and promoting the Cause of Christian Science. It is arousing a feeling of deep resentment and holy indignation in the breasts of tens of thousands of people who love fair play and who . . . have never heretofore been interested in Christian Science."[78]

The major blessing Eddy wrought from the Next Friends Suit, however, took form in her decision in the early summer of 1908 to found a newspaper, the *Christian Science Monitor*. Far from a knee-jerk response to the *World*'s attack, the founding of the *Monitor* was a natural development from journalistic experiments she had already undertaken. Yet the specific impulse to begin a newspaper at that point was obviously influenced by the *World*'s example of journalism at its worst.

Though she did not know it at the time, the founding of the *Monitor* gave concrete content to her prophetic response to a reporter's question the month before the suit was tried. When asked, "What do you feel will be the result of the present controversy?" she replied during her interview with Leigh Mitchell Hodges of the *Philadelphia North American*:

> Why some good must come of it, of course. Hard as it is to bear, it cannot but cause the truth to stand out more clearly in the end. . . . You know, however, it is only through fermentation that the yeast fits the dough for the bread that will nourish. And this is only a fermentation under the waters which will bring the impurities to the surface and slough them off, leaving the residuum clearer and purer than before.[79]

The "fermentation" surrounding the Next Friends Suit can be appraised in several contexts: in a feminist context, as an example of male chauvinism; in a constitutional context, as an issue of religious liberty; in a journalistic context, as an early-twentieth-century media event. But Eddy's statement to the *North American* shows that she saw the Next Friends Suit primarily within a Christian context. As she put it in a letter written in late May 1907, "I can bear all things for Christ's sake and Truth, Christ, has come so near to this age that error is rampant to save itself from destruction! O that I may prove myself willing in the day of God's power to bear the cross and serve Him best whom I love most."[80]

To her, the ordeal reflected the pattern of sacrifice and triumph that must mark the experience of Christians throughout the ages, a pattern she explores most fully in the chapter "Atonement and Eucharist" in *Science and Health*. As she stated in a message to her church nearly five months before the suit came to trial, her life "is best explained by its fruits, and by the life of our Lord as depicted in 'Atonement and Eucharist.' " Intrigued by her statement that this chapter explained her life, Chandler wrote to a friend that he had reread it and considered it "insanity."[81]

As a rationalist Unitarian, Chandler could hardly have been sympathetic with Eddy's belief in the power of Christianity to radically transform human life. As she put it in a passage from "Atonement and Eucharist," "If all who ever partook of the sacrament had really commemorated the sufferings of Jesus and drunk of his cup, they would have revolutionized the world."[82] She believed that unless the limits of Christian experience were drastically expanded, Christianity might have no future at all. Her discovery of Christian Science in 1866, she was convinced, had "rolled away the stone" of the belief that God created and sustained mortality, undercutting the assumption that so drastically limited Christian faith and experience. Over the next thirty-five years, she worked assiduously so that her teaching could take root in the soil of people's lives.

This cost her much personally, as the Next Friends Suit clearly shows. Although the suit failed in its purpose, an understanding of just how the world's "leaden weight" came down on her so heavily during her last years takes us a considerable distance toward understanding why she was and remains so controversial. An editorial in the *St. Louis Post-Dispatch* put it well: "If Mrs. Eddy had not been an innovator in religion and in healing she would not have been troubled with this clumsy attempt to discover the processes of her mind." For a woman to take on such a role was in itself provocative—a point Eddy grasped when she commented, "If I had been a man they would not have treated me so."[83]

Any honest accounting of Eddy's life and character would reveal a woman with obvious frailties and weakness, but also a woman who grasped—or was grasped by—some of the most pressing and enduring issues of Christian faith. To date, an overall assessment of how she responded to these issues and what her response means within the broad framework of the Christian tradition has been largely obscured by the storm clouds of controversy she aroused in her own time, especially in the period of the Next Friends Suit. But now, in an era when the accomplishments of women are taken with new seriousness, it should be possible to arrive at a more even-handed assessment of her character and stature as a Christian thinker—an assessment free of stereotyping and polemicism, pro or con.

The best place to begin is with some understanding of the spiritual question that dominated the first half of her life—and, ironically enough, that became equally compelling for her best-known adversary, Mark Twain.

1

"O God, *is it all!*"

FROM GLORY UNTO GLORY

THE NEXT FRIENDS SUIT WAS THE CULMINATING ORDEAL OF MARY BAKER Eddy's life and in some ways the most threatening. She was ultimately vindicated and even rose in public esteem. Yet if the Next Friends had prevailed, the "insanity" imputed to her would inevitably have colored public perceptions of the religion she had founded. She would have lost control over her own person and property, and the movement she led would have suffered a severe and perhaps insurmountable setback.

Yet in Eddy's view there was a kind of glory to this experience—not the glory the world gives, but the glory that comes from enduring the malice that she saw as always threatening to extinguish spiritual light. This is the glory of the sacrificial love that Eddy felt made possible Jesus' triumph over hatred and death. In the chapter "Atonement and Eucharist" in *Science and Health,* she spoke of his "treading alone his loving pathway up to the throne of glory," of "the great glory of an everlasting victory" that overshadowed the Last Supper, of "his night of gloom and glory in the garden" of Gethsemane, and of his meeting with his disciples by the Sea of Galilee after the Resurrection, when "his gloom had passed into glory."[1] All Christians must share his suffering to some degree, she felt, in order to follow their Master and partake in some measure of that glory.

If the summer of 1907 proved to be Eddy's time of glory in this Christian sense, it was a summer of a different kind of glory for another notable American, Mark Twain. Accurately, if immodestly, he declared in a passage in his autobiography that for a generation he had been "as widely celebrated a literary person as America has ever produced."[2] He was both flattered and gratified when in early May he was invited to receive an honorary degree from Oxford University, to be bestowed the

Mark Twain in 1907.
Courtesy of The Mark Twain
Project, The Bancroft
Library.

next month. Until then, as he noted with some pique, he had received
no academic honors commensurate with his popularity and fame.

Yet it would have been hard even for Twain to imagine how an old
lion such as he could have been better lionized. When he disembarked
in London, stevedores stopped their labor to applaud him. Old friends,
photographers, and miscellaneous admirers queued up to greet him at
Brown's Hotel in London. He made the social rounds, marched about
London in his trademark white suit, spoke with King Edward VII at a
garden party at Windsor Castle, and was given special leave by the queen
to wear his hat in the royal presence. At the Oxford degree ceremony,
he received louder cheers than fellow honorees Rudyard Kipling, General
William Booth, Auguste Rodin, and Camille Saint-Saëns.

Twain was now at the apex of his public career, his long-standing
thirst for honors temporarily satiated. When he arrived back in the
United States in late July, New York newspapers ran headlines announcing that Mark Twain had come home.

By mid-August, the front pages of the same newspapers were crowded with news of the Next Friends Suit. Twain remained publicly silent on the controversy. In early May, he had made a passing reference to Eddy when he was misreported as having been lost at sea in a yachting accident off the coast of Virginia. As he told the *New York Times* with his usual aplomb, he was investigating the report of his demise himself, adding that he was definitely not absent from New York because he was "dodging Mrs. Eddy." Later, when he docked in London and reporters asked him about the Next Friends Suit, he told them that he had nothing further to say about Eddy, that he had "said it all" before.[3]

By that time, Twain had said quite a lot about Christian Science and its founder. His first public comment on the subject was an article in the October 1899 issue of *Cosmopolitan*, later reprinted in his book *Christian Science, with Notes Containing Corrections to Date*. The piece was a burlesque of Christian Science, written in 1898 while he was living in Vienna. It purported to be the memoirs of a traveler in the Swiss Alps who fell over "a cliff seventy-five feet high," bounced off and broke a series of boulders, was so badly injured that he looked "like a hat-rack," and was cured through the ministrations of a Christian Science practitioner summering in a nearby village.[4] His portrait of the frumpy and officious practitioner is wickedly effective, although neither here nor in his later writings did he deny that spiritual healing does occur.

Once Twain began writing about Christian Science, he could not let the subject rest. In the words of Twain scholar Hamlin Hill, "Twain was obsessed with Christian Science and Mary Baker Eddy." In 1901 and 1902 he vented his fears that the fast-growing movement was becoming hugely powerful in an unpublished fantasy called "The Secret History of Eddypus, the World-Empire." In the "Eddypus" manuscript, the voice of a chronicler in the future bewails the fact that Christian Science had grown to such mammoth proportions as to become, in combination with Roman Catholicism, the dominant force on the planet. In this vast new dark age to come, "the World-Empire of Holy Eddypus covers and governs all the globe" except China, and humanity regresses to a kind of supermedieval authoritarianism. The new religion of this empire is called "Eddymania"; the word *religion* itself has been replaced by "Eddygush," Christmas has given way to "Eddymas," religious rituals now consist of formulas from *Science and Health* called "Eddymush," the dollar becomes "Eddyplunk," and so on.[5]

Work on the manuscript lapsed, but in 1903 Twain was back writing about Christian Science, planning a book for Harper and Brothers to consist of the *Cosmopolitan* material along with additional chapters, including some of the "Eddypus" manuscript. Although the book was set in type, proofread, and advertised, Harper's abruptly withdrew it—according to Twain, because "the Xn Scientist cult . . . had scared the biggest publisher in the Union!" In February 1907, Harper's did publish the book, probably because the growing stir over Eddy made doing so irresistible. In the meantime, most of its contents had been published in four articles he wrote for the *North American Review* between December 1902 and April 1903. By this time, Twain's focus had shifted from Christian Science as a healing method to Eddy herself. The picture he drew of her in the *North American Review* articles and the "Eddypus" manuscript was at the very least overwrought. Measured in terms of her achievement, he wrote, "it is thirteen hundred years since the world has produced anyone who could reach up to Mrs. Eddy's waistbelt." She is "the most daring and masculine and masterful woman that has appeared in the earth in centuries."[6]

Yet there is nothing admiring in Twain's listing of the qualities that led to her rise to prominence, among which he included "extraordinary daring," "indestructible persistency," "devouring ambition," "limitless selfishness," and "a never-wavering confidence in herself"—traits usually associated with men. He depicts her as the ultimate control freak, whose entire motivation can be reduced to vanity, ambition, and the naked will to power. The bylaws in the *Church Manual* (Twain had borrowed a copy from Frederick Peabody) showed that "the master-passion in Mrs. Eddy's heart is a hunger for power and glory."[7]

Replying in the *New York Herald* in January 1903 to the first of Twain's *North American Review* articles, Eddy wrote that his "wit was not wasted in certain directions." For one thing, it afforded her an occasion to disavow the personal self-exaltation Twain had attributed to her, declaring that she regarded "self-deification as blasphemous." In response to the merry romp he had with the fact that her students often referred to her endearingly as "Mother," she maintained that this was not of her doing and she had asked them to stop. She specifically rejected the view that she was any kind of latter-day Virgin Mary, then set forth unequivocally and in the broadest terms the status she felt she had earned: "I stand in relation to this century as a Christian Discoverer, Founder, and Leader."[8]

Twain, like many other men of his time, would have preferred that women, including Eddy, remain on their domestic pedestals, as his own wife, Olivia ("Livy"), had done and so many other women were forced to do. Although Eddy was not primarily concerned with feminist issues, her life was a textbook case on how to live outside of conventional feminine roles. Her words in reply to Twain underscore the point: she not only discovered Christian Science, but insisted on implementing her discovery by founding a church, then leading it with decisive authority.

In her reply to Twain, she also affirmed that she was "less lauded, pampered, provided for, and cheered" than others. Years before, she had written to the editor of the *Christian Science Journal* that, rather than being some kind of pope, "I have always been for this cause, the household drudge, the servant of servants."[9] There was much work that needed attending to: finding better ways to communicate Christian Science to the public, honing the church structure, correcting and counseling the church's board of directors, encouraging and supporting students through private letters, sending messages to her followers, and putting *Science and Health* through its final major revisions.

Indeed, the final major revision of *Science and Health* appeared in 1907, the very year in which Twain proclaimed in his work *Christian Science* that Eddy was so lacking in cultivation and intelligence that she could not possibly have written the book, precisely because the book was so well written. By commenting positively on the literary merit of the work, he in effect retracted his earlier caustic comments on *Science and Health* in his 1899 article for the *Cosmopolitan* as the most "strange, and frantic, and incomprehensible, and uninterpretable" of books. Its language, he said, was at first unfamiliar to him, but upon further examination he no longer found it hard to grasp. He now spoke of *Science and Health* as "a compact, grammatical, dignified, and workman-like body of literature" and, of an extended passage he quoted from the opening chapter on "Prayer," as "wise and sane and elevated and lucid and compact"—no small tribute from a writer of Twain's stature.[10]

Here, as elsewhere, Twain finds a good deal to praise in Christian Science, although he continued to damn its founder. In her published response to Twain's criticisms, Eddy said simply, "What I am remains to be proved by the good I do," and Twain conceded that she had done much good. Eddy noted this herself, commenting to Alfred Farlow, her spokesperson, that she detected an "undertone" in the article "which is very complimentary to Christian Science." So did Frederick Peabody, Chandler's junior counsel in the Next Friends Suit, who wrote Twain candidly that he found Twain's first article in the *Review* "somewhat disappointing," while the *Philadelphia Medical Journal* said scathingly, "Mr. Clemens himself comes so near to being a follower of Mrs. Eddy that he has not critical insight enough left to see that her claim to be able to abolish disease is the gist of the whole humbug. . . . Clearly, Mark Twain is already four-fifths Eddyite, and of all the blatherskite he has ever written his latest is a little the most senile."[11]

While Twain's comments about Eddy were almost all negative and mocking, when he takes up the effects of her teaching in people's lives, he often speaks of Christian Science with warm eloquence and poetic feeling. In his book *Christian Science,* for example, he remarks on the distinctive spirituality that permeates her teaching:

> The Christian Scientist believes that the Spirit of God (life and love) pervades the universe like an atmosphere; that whoso will study *Science and Health* can get from it the secret of how to inhale that transforming air; that to breathe it is to be made new; that from the new man all sorrow, all care, all miseries of the mind vanish away . . . ; that it purifies the body from disease, which is a vicious creation of the gross human mind, and cannot continue to exist in the presence of the Immortal Mind, the renewing Spirit of God.[12]

A SHARED MORAL PASSION

What impelled the man who was then the best-loved writer in the English language to speak so warmly of a religious teaching, when almost all his other comments on Christianity are shot through with mocking negativity? Why should he have returned almost obsessively to the subject of Christian Science and its founder for nearly a decade? Why, after telling reporters in the summer of 1907 that he had "said it all" before about Eddy, could he not resist taking another whack at her the very next year in a satirical passage of several pages in the final version of *The Mysterious Stranger*?[13] How, having spoken repeatedly of Eddy as a hypocrite and a fraud, could he praise the spirituality he saw in Christian Science and its effects on people's lives?

As deeply as Twain distrusted Eddy, as vehemently as he railed against her, he agreed with her that Christianity must be an active healing presence that could heal the ills of the flesh as well as regenerate the sins of the soul. "Any Christian," he said in *Christian Science,* "who was in earnest and not a make-believe, not a policy-Christian, not a Christian for revenue only, had that healing power."[14] Despite their vast differences otherwise, Twain and Eddy were most alike in their shared passion for separating what they believed to be authentic from sham religion. Beneath his showmanship burned a genuine moral passion that took savage joy in winnowing truth from falsehood, authenticity from pretense.

The child of a rough-hewn religious culture in the mid-continental heartland of America, Twain had a brash, boyish impudence that prevented him from taking formal pieties too seriously. What he said in his autobiography about a friend during his youth, a giant of a fellow named Wales McCormick, applies equally to himself: "Among his shining characteristics was the most limitless and adorable irreverence."[15]

For the sake of his wife, Livy, whom he married in 1870 when he was thirty-four, Twain made spasmodic efforts to conform himself to the conventional Christianity in which she found comfort. Twain ended up not only abandoning such efforts, but helping to subvert Livy's faith as well. When he traveled through Illinois the year after his marriage, he wrote her about a church service he had attended with the evident intention of affording reassurance of his own regularity in religious matters. But his description was saturated with a faint sense of the absurd. He described "the stiff pews; the black velvet contribution-purses . . . ; the wheezy melodeon in the gallery-front; the old maid behind it in severe simplicity of dress." When he spoke of "the gallery, with ascending seats . . . ; six boys scattered through it, with secret spit-ball designs on the bald-headed man dozing below," he obviously identified with the boys.[16]

It has often been observed that Twain's personal acquaintance with tragedy and suffering, as well as his moral passion, gave a special edge to his humor. There was certainly a serious moral undertone to the often withering wit that came into play when Twain touched upon conventional religiosity. Professing Christians in both *Tom Sawyer* and *Huckleberry Finn* are portrayed as almost unrelievedly complacent and smug. But Huck and Jim express the native compassion and generosity of spirit that Twain saw as truly Christian. When these qualities were living and real—as they were to him, at least imaginatively, as embodied in these characters—there was no need for the language of Christianity to explain or justify them. They were simply and convincingly *there*. And when Twain was working at his height as an artist, he could render their presence naturally and movingly.

He was at least as adept in exposing the absence of natural and unaffected Christianity when he believed it should have been present. Twain felt with deeply committed moral passion that it was his vocation as an artist to expose the hypocrisies of a nominally Christian civilization. In 1866, he wrote to a friend entering the ministry: "I wanted to be a minister myself—it was the only genuine ambition I ever had—but somehow I never had any qualification for it but the ambition." The year before, discussing this ambition in a letter to his brother, he explained that he never felt the call to realize his ambition to become a preacher "*because* I could not supply myself with the necessary stock in trade—i.e. religion." His aspirations in that direction were, therefore, "the very ecstasy of presumption." But, he went on, he did feel the " 'call' to literature, of a low order—i.e. humorous. It is nothing to be proud of, but it is my strongest suit."[17]

These confessions were not casual: Twain was serious about the religious imperative he felt, not so much to preach Christianity directly, but to show the vast disparity between faith and practice in a culture that assumed itself to be Christian. In book after book, story after story, he used the lance of his wit to puncture the boil of his culture's self-esteem, the pretensions that masked a baseness he came to see more and more as lying at the very core of humanity. Among the most powerful instances of this wit is a short piece of fifteen pages called "The Stupendous Procession." Written early in 1901, it surveys the world of imperialism in which the United States, to his horror, was playing a leading role through the suppression of the Philippine insurrection. At the head of the stupendous procession that "moved across the world" was Christendom, "a majestic matron, in flowing robes drenched with blood. On her head, a golden crown of thorns; impaled on its spines, the bleeding heads of patriots who died for their countries."[18]

Twain saw imperialism as humanity at its most corrupt, using the rhetoric of Christianity to mask its crimes. In contrast, he spoke of Christian Science warmly during the very years in which he was denouncing imperialism because he saw it as doing what Christianity should be doing: "through loving mercifulness and compassion, to heal fleshly ills and pains and grief."[19] Little wonder that Twain found much to praise in the first chapter of *Science and Health*, entitled "Prayer," where Eddy repeatedly condemns, as he so frequently did, the self-satisfied solemnity of audible prayer that fails to correspond with the desires of the heart.

As a young person, she also had been capable of irreverence toward religiosity in its more externalized forms. In later years, she recalled how she expressed her annoyance at the interminable prayers her father uttered daily while his captive family was made to kneel. She crawled beneath his chair and inserted a pin into the area where it would do the most good, then quickly made her escape. As she matured, she grew into her own characterization of herself as "a heart wholly in protest." Quite early in her life, that protest took decisive form. When she was being questioned for church membership at the age of seventeen, she publicly rejected the Calvinist doctrine of predestination.[20]

The scene was archetypal. Much of the creative energy of New England's religious and literary life in this period grew out of the wholesale reaction of sensitive young people to a stark Calvinism they could no longer abide. Later, Eddy's challenge to the theological establishment took a more radical form, and there was little humor to soften the blow. Although Twain railed against conventional religion throughout most of his life, Eddy proved to be far more practically defiant of religious convention than he. Twain was popular and cherished his

popularity. Fearful of losing the affections of his vast and largely orthodox audience, he deliberately suppressed his strongest assaults on
Christianity during his lifetime.

Despite this, he would have agreed with Eddy's words, "Hypocrisy
is fatal to religion."[21] But she was not willing to see religion die. She
believed that in Christian Science she had discovered a working basis
for the renewal of Christianity that directly addressed the deepest sources
of Christians' defection from biblical faith. Among them, none was more
basic than the problem of how a good and all-powerful God could create or even coexist with a world so full of human suffering. This was the
problem that impelled her decades-long search that led finally to her
discovery of Christian Science. It was also the problem most responsible for Twain's angry, near-nihilistic rejection of Christian orthodoxy.

DESCENT INTO HELL

Among the reasons why Twain so detested conventional Christianity
was what he saw as the monstrous injustice of its scheme of salvation.
God made man subservient to various passions and appetites—"has so
contrived him that all his goings out and comings in are beset by traps
which he cannot possibly avoid, and which compel him to commit
what are called sins—and then God punishes him for doing these very
things which from the beginning of time he has always intended that he
should do." The same sentiment in substance is found in two statements
that Twain may well have read in *Science and Health:*

> In common justice, we must admit that God will not punish man for
> doing what He created man capable of doing, and knew from the outset
> that man would do. It would be contrary to our highest ideas of God to
> suppose Him capable of first arranging law and causation so as to bring
> about certain evil results, and then punishing the helpless victims of His
> volition for doing what they could not avoid doing.[22]

Whether or not Twain's words echoed his reading of *Science and
Health,* he and Eddy were in thorough agreement on this point. Neither
was temperamentally or intellectually disposed to accept one of the
major traditional Christian explanations for the presence of so much
suffering in the world: that it results from the sinful misuse human
beings make of the freedom God gives them to love him voluntarily. In
Eddy's theology, the meaning of sin did not lie so much in our personal
violation of this freedom, but rather in the larger *impersonal* belief or
mesmeric error that we are by nature separate from God and thus disposed to sin. "The real man," in her words, "cannot depart from holiness,

nor can God, by whom man is evolved, engender the capacity or freedom to sin."[23] They could not, therefore, abide a cosmic scheme whereby a supposedly sovereign and all-loving God subjects his creatures to impossible moral tests and then punishes them when they fail, inflicts them with devastating personal losses for their supposed moral betterment, or plunges them into the mortal condition through which they become susceptible to all the pains of the flesh and helpless victims of such natural calamities as he pleases to send their way.

Nor could either Twain or Eddy accept the evasions and compromises by which conventional Christianity sought to avoid or paper over what they both saw as this massive anomaly in Christian faith. In their response to this problem, they arrived at totally irreconcilable positions. But almost alone among their contemporaries, they insisted on facing it head on, without compromise or evasion, and they did so outside a professional theological context without easy escape routes into theological formulations that would have saved them from confronting the problem of pain in an intensely personal way.

To begin with, both felt instinctively that religious issues overshadow and determine the entire historical life of humanity. History was organized, as Twain put it in an essay in 1891, according to "changes in the Deity—or in men's conception of the Deity." Eight years before, Eddy had delivered a sermon in Boston, "The People's Idea of God, Its Effect on Health and Christianity," that argued essentially the same point: "The crudest ideals of speculative theology have made monsters of men. . . . The eternal roasting amidst noxious vapours,—the election of the minority to be saved and the majority to be eternally punished; the wrath of God to be appeased by the sacrifice and torture of his favorite Son; are some of the false beliefs that have produced sin, sickness and death."[24]

Twain detested these doctrines as passionately as did Eddy, but had nothing to put in their place. Intellectually, he gained his freedom from the constraints of Calvinist orthodoxy early in life. When he was eleven or twelve, he was exposed to sermons which, as the narrator of *Tom Sawyer* puts it, "dealt in limitless fire and brimstone and thinned the predestined elect down to a company so small as to be hardly worth the saving."[25] Twain may have felt mockingly impervious to such doctrines, but his continued exposure to them formed an emotional residue that would not go away. The revivalist camp meetings that flourished in and around Hannibal, Missouri, along with his fascination with the religion of African American slaves, developed in him a complex of sin, guilt, and fear that existed side by side with his comic sense, although it never completely overwhelmed it.

In his *Autobiography*, Twain registers vividly his feelings on that stormy night when he received the news of the death of Injun Joe, a mixed-blood inhabitant of his hometown who would reappear as a character in *Tom Sawyer:*

> By my teachings I perfectly well knew what all that wild rumpus was for—Satan had come to get Injun Joe from the underworld. . . . With every glare of lightning I shriveled and shrank together in mortal terror, and in the interval of black darkness that followed I poured out my lamentings over my lost condition, and my supplications for just one more chance, with an energy and feeling and sincerity quite foreign to my nature.[26]

The fear, terror, guilt, and the imagination of hell encapsulated in this passage took hold of Twain's religious sensibility early on. It was as if he were systematically drained of all religious convictions except for the emotional effects that a primitive and undeveloped religious experience had left on his highly suggestible imagination.

What seems to have impressed him more than anything was the reinforcement that his exposure to religion provided for the sense of danger and even terror in human experience. Life in Hannibal was rough, and Twain remembered the sight of hangings, drownings, murders, lynchings, and rapes. He recalled with horror how he had given matches to a drunken tramp who then accidentally burned himself to death in the town jail.[27] He lost a sister when he was three, a brother when he was six, and his father when he was eleven, after which he had the horrifying experience of peering through a keyhole as his father's body was opened for an autopsy.

Then as later, Twain reacted to the losses of family members and friends with a mixture of grief and guilt. So deeply had he internalized the sense of sin that he interpreted each disaster that befell a loved one as somehow his fault. When Twain was twenty-two, his brother Henry, whom he spoke of as "my darling, my pride, my glory, my *all*," died after being terribly burned when four boilers blew up on a steamboat near Memphis. Twain blamed himself for having arranged for his brother to be on the boat. Again, when his firstborn child, Langdon, died at the age of nineteen months in 1872, Twain recriminated himself for having kept the boy out too long in the cold, although the cause of death was diphtheria.[28]

Over the next fifteen years, however, Twain's fortunes prospered in every respect. His popularity exploded with the publication of *The Adventures of Tom Sawyer, The Prince and the Pauper, Life on the Mississippi,* and *The Adventures of Huckleberry Finn.* Samuel Langhorne Clemens had become Mark Twain, America's most beloved man of letters, the most striking and best-known literary hero the nation had produced, a living literary incarnation of the nineteenth-century ideal of success. Then the nightmare began.

Twain was a man of his time, for whom horizons had to be unlimited. However much he had, he always wanted more. Much of his income was expended in building and maintaining a large house in Hartford, where he flourished between 1874 and 1891, entertaining on a lavish scale. To meet escalating expenses and finally attain wealth and financial security, in 1886 he organized a company to manufacture and market an automatic typesetting machine, pouring all his resources into the gamble. It was not a bad machine, but a better one had been invented and tested. So Twain lost on a big scale. His creditors closing in on him, he embarked in 1891 on a trip abroad. Three years later, after a firm he had established to publish his own works failed, he declared bankruptcy. Filled with remorse and devastated by disappointment, he set out in the summer of 1895 on a year-long lecture tour around the world that taxed his strength, but did much to restore his spirits and material prosperity.

A year later, Twain was living in a town in Surrey, England, restored and in a relaxed mood. Then came the most shattering blow of his life: the news that his favorite daughter, Susy, had died of spinal meningitis in Hartford. Unlike the death of his infant son, who had been sickly during his life of nineteen months and whose demise was not unexpected, Susy's death at twenty-four was a total shock. Twain's grief was intensified by the conviction that the financial recklessness that had led to his sojourn abroad had made his daughter "a pauper and an exile." So great was his pain and loss, he wrote, that it "would bankrupt the vocabularies of all the languages to put it into words."[29] And so enormous was his guilt that he threw himself into his grief, rehashing every circumstance of his daughter's last days. Concurrently, Twain and his wife were forced to confront the painful fact that their daughter Jean, whose mood changes had perplexed them for some months, was suffering from epilepsy.

Railing against the hellishness of the world, raging against a God who permitted his creatures to suffer so much pain, Twain became an increasingly burdensome presence in the home circle of Livy and two surviving daughters. Livy grieved over Susy and anguished over Jean's attacks. But it was her husband's engulfing blackness and raging instability that most aggravated the nervous prostration and heart disease from which she had suffered since the early 1890s. She loathed the bitter Socratic dialogue *What Is Man?*, Twain's self-styled "Bible" expressing his despairing view of the human condition, and forbade its publication. As her health failed beginning in the summer of 1902, she took increasing refuge in the isolation of her sickroom. During that fall and winter, while Twain was completing his articles for the *North American Review,* Livy's physicians insisted on severely limiting his visits with her. Although they lived together in the same house in Riverdale, New York, Twain did not see her at all over a three-month period until late December, when he was permitted a five-minute visit. Late the following year, at her doctors' suggestion they went to Florence, Italy, where Livy died on June 5, 1904, at the age of fifty-nine.

Twain's *Autobiography,* the major work of his last decade, chronicles the deaths of his daughter and wife: "I lost Susy thirteen years ago; I lost her mother—her incomparable mother!—five and a half years ago."[30] There was more. The spring of 1909 saw the passing of his best friend, the businessman Henry H. Rogers, who had helped Twain negotiate his way out of bankruptcy. But the final blow was like a page from the last act of *King Lear.*

On Christmas Eve 1909, Twain's daughter Jean, with whom he lived on a hilltop home in Connecticut, apparently had an epileptic seizure in the bathtub and drowned. "And now I have lost Jean," Twain intoned in the last dictated entry for his *Autobiography:*

> How poor I am, who was once so rich! Seven months ago Mr. Rogers died—one of the best friends I ever had, and the nearest perfect, as man and gentleman. . . . Jean lies yonder, I sit here; . . . we kissed hands good-by at this door last night—and it was forever, we never suspecting it. She lies there, and I sit here—writing, busying myself, to keep my heart from breaking. How dazzlingly the sunshine is flooding the hills around! It is like a mockery.[31]

Twain spent the rest of his days, less than half a year, in the house where Jean died, the house he had built for them both to live in. And so he asked himself: "Why did I build this house, two years ago? To shelter this vast emptiness?" "I am full of malice, saturated with malignity," he declared during that last year, as he continued to rail against the God he held responsible for his pain and the pain of the whole world, as well.[32]

In *Letters from the Earth,* a short work written in 1909 about a half year before his death, Twain expressed in the most pointed language he could muster the reasons for his utter rejection of the God of Christian orthodoxy. The Christian, he wrote, begins with the "uncompromising proposition" that "God is all-knowing and all-powerful."

> Therefore nothing can happen without his "knowing before hand that it is going to happen," or without his permission and consent. Then, having

thus made the Creator responsible for all those pains and diseases and miseries above enumerated, and which he could have prevented, the Christian blandly calls him Our Father! . . . He equips the Creator with every trait that goes to the making of a fiend, and then arrives at the conclusion that a fiend and a father are the same thing![33]

This statement and others like it were not so much reasoned theological reflections as the cry of a wounded animal. What had wounded Twain, he believed, was not simple chance or brute physical force, but rather the God whom orthodox Christians claimed to love and worship.

Twain could have taken an entirely different course and embraced the atheistic denial that there is any God at all. But so thoroughly were his mind and heart immersed in the culture of evangelical orthodoxy that this route was effectively closed to him. Like one citizen quoted by Lord James Bryce in his *American Commonwealth*, Twain did not mind "going a good way along the plank," but he liked "to stop short of the jump-off."[34]

For Twain, God existed, but had become a kind of cosmic monster. "We call Him Father," he railed in an autobiographical dictation for June 19, 1906, "and not in derision, although we would detest and denounce any earthly father who should inflict upon his child a thousandth part of the pains and miseries and cruelties which our God deals out to his children every day."[35] This taste of Twain's rhetoric shows the merciless logic he pursued to its end. Given the massive disappointments of his life, his incredible ability to detect and express the immense gap between human ideals and practical realities, and above all his commitment to telling the flat-out, unvarnished truth, there is a power and honesty in his rhetoric, however immoderate, however extreme.

Others had endured misery and catastrophe without reviling God in this way, often treading the time-worn path of resignation to suffering as somehow the will of God. But Twain insisted upon pushing the question: If the God of the Bible is real, and if he is both sovereign and good, why are so many in pain, and can God do no more than hear their anguished wails? If the Bible, God's Word, gives comfort and cheer to the sick and dying, then why are they sick and dying in the first place? No one in America had asked this same question more insistently than Mary Baker Eddy.

"THE ORIGINAL BEAUTY OF HOLINESS"

After the first of Twain's *North American Review* articles was published, he was contacted by William D. McCrackan, who as the church's one-person Committee on Publication for New York had the responsibility of correcting public misconceptions of Christian Science. Converted to Christian Science in 1900, McCrackan moved with ease among literary circles, where he was well known as a political progressive and author. He visited and corresponded with Twain about his *North American Review* articles, in addition to furnishing a rejoinder to the *Review,* which Twain said he read with pleasure and profit.

Their first interview was tense and at points stormy. McCrackan recalled that Twain walked the room "shaking his shaggy head like a caged lion." But in subsequent visits, telephone conversations, and exchanges of letters, the atmosphere thawed, and the two men developed a cordial relationship. McCrackan recalled a particularly illuminating conversation that telescopes why Twain and Eddy, despite their huge differences, found themselves sharing common ground.

"They tell me that God is all powerful, He can do everything," Twain said. "Then I think of the miners down there in Pennsylvania working for a pittance in the dark. I think of the cruelties, oppressions, injustices everywhere and according to this, God is responsible for all of them. Why, I'd rather have Satan any day than that kind of a God." To which McCrackan replied, "So would I, for that God is not God at all."[36]

Behind this conversation lurks the huge dilemma of the problem of evil which so profoundly engaged both Twain and Eddy. It was not their personal dilemma so much as the basic spiritual problem that was beginning to erode religious belief in the nineteenth century and that continues to undermine it at the beginning of the twenty-first.

By the late nineteenth century, strict Calvinism was all but dead. Most seminaries taught, and most Protestants believed, that God is not an inscrutable judge and taskmaster, but a God of love, warmly solicitous of his children, anxious to save sinners, freely offering his grace to all. Thus was born the benign God of nineteenth-century Protestantism, which by the last decades of the century had all but vanquished the last remnants of Calvinist theology from America's seminaries and pulpits.

But this theological compromise left the basic problem of evil largely untouched. In fact, it made it worse. The more God was viewed as loving and good, the more perplexing became the question of why human life should contain so much misery and pain. One might disbelieve in a God who consigned the majority of his children to hell. One might discredit the belief that there could be a hell at all. But what about the sheer hellishness of human existence itself? If one could no longer worship the God of Calvinism, how could one worship a God who could prevent evil and yet chose not to? Would not such a God be morally worse than his worshipers?

Twain, as well as Eddy, faced this question directly—not because it was a theological conundrum, which neither had any interest in solving, but because it confronted them directly in the circumstances of life. The suffering Twain endured, however, came late in his life after he had reached the peak of success. With Eddy, it began in her childhood and early teens.

Sickness was endemic among the six children in the family of Mark and Abigail Baker, as it was in many other New England families. Remarkably, given the high rates of infant mortality in the period, none of them died in childhood. Yet it remained a question in the Baker household as to whether Mary, the youngest, would live to become an adult. In 1837, when she was seventeen, her older sister, Abigail, wrote: "Mary spent the last week with me and appears quite comfortable, but the poor girl can never enjoy life as most of us can should she live any time, and this is altogether uncertain." With considerable sensitivity, Robert David Thomas in his book *"With Bleeding Footsteps": Mary Baker Eddy's Path to Religious Leadership* wrote of the long-term effects of Mary Baker's childhood illnesses, which "contributed to Mary's bottomless empathy for children, which was virtually lifelong," and left her with an early and precocious "awareness of the unpredictability and fragility of life."[37]

This awareness was all the more difficult to bear because it so strongly conflicted with the life-affirming tendencies of her nature—her innate ebullience, high-spiritedness, and love of life. Years later, a cousin who knew her when she was fifteen recalled her as "a frail, fair young maiden with transparent skin & brilliant blue eyes, cheerful, hopeful, enthusiastic." Given these qualities of Eddy's mind and temperament, her youthful rebellion against the harsh God of her father's Calvinism becomes all the more understandable. Her struggle with the problems of suffering remained. But after a crucial experience in which she recovered quickly from a burning fever after her mother bade her to "lean on God's love," she wrote, "the 'horrible decree' of predestination—as John Calvin rightly called his own tenet—forever lost its power over me."[38]

Not so with Mark Twain. Until the very end of his days, Twain found himself still haunted by the specter of the Calvinist God. His spiritual journey took him full circle: he ended up embracing a secularized Calvinist deity just as vengeful, merciless, and arbitrary as the one he sought to reject. Instead of fearing a hell that lay in the future, he found himself descending into a living hell on earth.

While Eddy struggled with and rejected the harsh God of predestinarian Calvinism, she did so within a religious culture that gave her a place to go. Eddy's formative years coincided with a crucial transition in the religious life of New England. In Jacksonian America, the growth of transportation and commerce was accelerating, and the population was fanning out to the West, where Christianity took on the heated quality of the evangelical culture in which Twain was raised. Yet in New England enclaves such as Bow, Concord, and Sanbornton, where Mary Baker was raised, the embers of the original Puritan fire still glowed.

The character of this rich and resonant culture was beautifully caught by poetess Lucy Larcom, who was born in a small community in rural Massachusetts in 1824. "The religion of our fathers," she wrote, "overhung us children like the shadow of a mighty tree against the trunk of which we rested. . . . Some of the boughs were already decaying, so that perhaps we began to see a little more of the sky than our elders; but the tree was sound at its heart. There was life in it that can never be lost to the world."[39]

That "life . . . that can never be lost" was an expression of what historian Perry Miller called "the Augustinian strain of piety." By this term Miller meant, not simply Augustine's theology, but "his insatiable quest for satisfactions that nothing of this earth was ever able to supply him." As Augustine wrote about the period of his early theological questionings: "O Truth, Truth! how inwardly even then did the marrow of my soul pant after Thee, . . . I hungered and thirsted . . . after Thee Thyself, the Truth." Within the New England religious tradition, this piety was most fully reflected in the "Personal Narrative" of the towering figure in Eddy's spiritual background, the eighteenth-century theologian Jonathan Edwards. Edwards had preached perhaps the most famous of all hell-fire sermons, wherein he intoned to a thoroughly cowed congregation, "It is nothing but God's mere pleasure that keeps you from being this moment swallowed up in everlasting destruction"—a passage that Eddy referred to in her *Message to The Mother Church for 1901.* Far more characteristic of his piety and influence was the testimony in his "Personal Narrative" in which he declared, "I had vehement longings of soul after God and Christ, and after more holiness; wherewith my heart seemed to be full, and ready to break."[40]

Edwards's pastoral labors had been in part responsible for what was called the First Great Awakening in 1734. His strenuous efforts to rekindle the fires he had helped to stoke became so burdensome that his parishioners ousted him from his pulpit in Northampton, Massachusetts, in 1750. But his long-range influence was immense. He also developed and passed on to Eddy's religious mentors a rich theology of the "religious affections"—the new disposition of the heart awakened through the "spiritual sense" that only God's grace and love could effect. The renewal of religion, Edwards and his followers maintained, begins with a change in the inner life. But this change was seen as a new experience of something that is actually there. Once spiritual sense is touched and activated, he explained, men get new affections—a new sense of the excellency of God and his creation that results in a spiritual awakening not otherwise to be had. Religion for Edwards thus came to center less on creeds than on the changed sense of experience wrought by this new affection of the heart. "For although to true religion, there must indeed be something else besides affection; yet true religion consists so much in the affections, that there can be no true religion without them."[41]

Edwards became the fountainhead of what came to be known as the New Light tradition, or the New England Theology. Underlying everything Eddy felt and said about religion was the thoroughly Edwardsian conviction that true religion is a matter of the affections and must have a direct bearing on every phase of practical experience. This concept of the religious affections took root in her own affections, shaping both her spiritual quest and its final outcome in her mature teaching in a decisive way. Indeed, it was thoroughly natural to her, when writing of her own search for "the knowledge of God as the one great and ever-present relief from human woe," to do so in thoroughly Edwardsian terms, writing that from childhood she had been impelled by "a hunger and thirst after divine things."[42]

Just so, in later years she looked back with great fondness to those "grand old divines" who introduced her to the reality of religion during her youth. What they transmitted to her was the spirit of New England Puritanism at its considerable best—the godliness that reflected the more universal dimensions of Christianity, rather than the narrowly circumscribed doctrines of Calvinism in its terminal stages. Her tribute to them, written when she was seventy-nine, communicates better than any summary could how the reality of religion was woven into the fabric of her being. "Why I loved Christians of the old sort," she wrote, was because

> I could not help loving them. Full of charity and good works, busy about their Master's business, they had no time or desire to defame their fellow-men. God seemed to shield the whole world in their hearts, and they were willing to renounce all for Him. When infidels assailed them, however, the courage of their convictions was seen. They were heroes in the strife; they armed quickly, aimed deadly, and spared no denunciation. Their convictions were honest, and they lived them; and the sermons their lives preached caused me to love their doctrines. . . . With them Love was the governing impulse of every action; their piety was the all-important consideration of their being, the original beauty of holiness that to-day seems to be fading so sensibly from our sight.[43]

These words convey the element in New England Puritanism that became permanent in Eddy's own religious affections. Just so, throughout her life, she responded warmly to Christians she saw as exemplifying this spirit of godliness. But she never showed a very deep attachment to conventional forms of Christian theology and worship. It is true that she was the only one of the six Baker children to join her parents' Congregational church. But in the very act of doing so at the age of seventeen, as she later recalled, she protested vehemently against the doctrine of predestination. Her pleadings of disbelief in this doctrine so moved her minister and the congregation that "he received me into their communion, and my protest along with me."[44]

She had already fought a number of pitched battles over this issue with her rigidly Calvinist father. In *Retrospection and Introspection*, Eddy summarizes the aspect of Calvinism she came to loathe: "My father's relentless theology emphasized belief in a final judgment-day, in the danger of endless punishment, and in a Jehovah merciless towards unbelievers."[45] However conflicted their relationship, she also owed to him more than to any other her rock-solid conviction that religion is the single most important factor in human life. But again, the form that this conviction took in her own life differed sharply from the sentimental piety considered appropriate for young women in the early Victorian Age.

At times Mary Baker would try to accommodate herself to the mold of a more conventional piety that was natural to her. But one cannot imagine her writing, except in parody, in the pious tones of one Lydia Ann Holmes, sister of her best friend Augusta Holmes, in August 1838: "When shall I cease to be allured by the follies & vanities of life, & my disenthralled spirit soar above this polluted atmosphere?" Lydia Ann rejoices that her sister's friend, Mary Baker, is a "sympathising companion" to whom she can unbosom her whole heart. "Give my love to her . . . & say to her, . . . tho' you now walk *alone,* in the straight & narrow path, I hope the time is not *far* distant, that many through *your example,* will be led to seek the same heavenly inheritance."[46]

Lydia Ann would no doubt have been appalled if she had known where Mary Baker's path was heading. Mary did indeed partake of the Augustinian strain of piety: the religion that was all around her had found its own home within her—in her private devotions and Bible reading and in her total conviction that God is unquestionably real. But her piety was unsettled, troubled, questioning. The Reverend Enoch Corser, who examined her for church membership, already knew something of her highly independent spirit in religious matters because he had become her tutor after the Bakers moved to Sanbornton Bridge, New Hampshire, in 1836. He later commented to his son Bartlett that she was, even at this early age, "superior both intellectually and spiritually to any other woman" in the community—a view that Bartlett Corser echoed when he spoke of "her depth and independence of thought, and not least, spiritual-mindedness."[47]

"THIS CRUSHING OUT OF LIFE, OF HOPE, OR LOVE"

British historian H. A. L. Fisher was right when he observed, in a book largely critical of Eddy, "Prayer, meditation, eager and puzzled interrogation of the Bible, had claimed from childhood much of her energy." But her real spiritual questioning did not end at this point. In fact it had barely begun. During a sermon, Eddy's brother George Sullivan Baker dashed off a long note posing a question that was tormenting many of his contemporaries. Man, he wrote, "is doom'd to sustain the existence impos'd upon him by creation, by toil and fatigue, hardship and revolting exposure, physically, of every description! . . . But further, he is doom'd to endure the pangs of disease, and the sufferings of the decay of nature and even the pangs of death."[48]

George Sullivan was an artless fellow, not really disposed to enter very deeply into the long-term spiritual questions that his sister could not and would not avoid. Is existence actually so structured that pain and disease are simply inherent phases of the human condition, intractable and unavoidable? For her, this issue was no philosophical abstraction to be logically comprehended and parsed. It was a question that increasingly urged itself upon her through the mounting suffering and losses she endured as she moved into adulthood. With illusions about the stability of life shattered by the vicissitudes of her own precarious health, the larger problem of human vulnerability was driven home to her in the most immediate way.

In 1841, the Baker family circle was devastated by the premature death at age thirty-one of Mary's adored brother and mentor, Albert, just at the point when he was about to emerge on the national political stage. The decisive point in her own encounter with mortality and suffering came later, at the age of twenty-two, as she watched for over a week at the bedside of her first husband, a gregarious, handsome young man named George Glover. Glover had business interests in the South, and the two went to live in Charleston, South Carolina. The promise of her new life was increased when she and George discovered that she was expecting a child. Then everything fell apart. Glover, an enterprising businessman whose success was attained by leaping from one high-risk enterprise to another, had put most of his money into building supplies for the construction of a cathedral in Haiti. In June 1844, the supplies were entirely lost, leaving him nearly indigent. Then he contracted yellow fever, lingered about nine days, and died.

An account, very likely written by Eddy for an 1846 Odd Fellow publication, although tinged with sentimental rhetoric, sets forth with graphic starkness what she must have endured during the hours of Glover's death:

> Who that has watched beside the sick—the dying couch of a beloved being—does not remember the dreary, desolate blank that succeeds the moment of dissolution. To smooth the pillow—to watch over the unquiet slumber—to sweeten the bitter aught with affection's hand—to read the languid eye, and anticipate the broken wish: these and a thousand other kindly offices, fill up the weary hours, and twine the loved one in its helplessness closer and closer round the heart. But when the last scene has closed on the being we have so loved and tended—when the warm heart can no longer feel our care, nor the beaming eye smile its thanks—then it is that the weary frame and crushed spirit sink together in utter, hopeless, loneliness.[49]

Nothing in her life had quite prepared her for the cold horror and isolation of this naked confrontation with mortality. She now saw how sickness and death could utterly blast human life and hope, destroying in a moment every cherished plan for happiness and fulfillment. But she also came to realize that the sheer terror of mortality was not just her problem, her experience. She gained a compassion for the human condition which she had not fully felt before. Looking back, she could see the ordeal in this expanded perspective as breaking open the shell of her own self-concern, developing a new sympathy for human suffering. In a letter written in the last decade of her life, she spoke of Glover's death, asking if "that midnight shadow, falling upon the bridal wreath," had fulfilled "the merciful design of divine Love" that helped her to "evolve that larger sympathy for suffering humanity which is emancipating it with the morning beams and noonday glory of Christian Science?"[50]

Early widowhood deepened her compassion, but further difficult lessons were to follow. From the moment George Glover died in June 1844, her life slipped sharply downhill. The journey of fourteen hundred miles by steamer and railroad back to New Hampshire in the mid-summer heat was grueling, and the birth of her child in September was difficult. Her health, always precarious, broke down to the point that she was bedridden for several months. Her native resilience reasserted itself in various efforts to make something of a life that appeared to

Earliest known photograph of Mary Baker Eddy, ca. 1850–54. Courtesy of The Mary Baker Eddy Collection.

have poor prospects. She was living as a dependent in her father's household, intermittently ill, trying to care for an increasingly boisterous child, and with no way to provide either for herself or him.

The year 1849 brought another crisis that plunged her fortunes still lower. Her mother, described by contemporaries as a saintly woman, became worn down and finally worn out by a difficult husband and the need to care for a large family. When she died in November, Eddy, who had been especially close to her, wrote to a brother, "What is left of earth to *me*!"[51] At the time, however, one thing appeared to be left. She had become engaged to John Bartlett, a young, Harvard-trained lawyer whom she had known since their teens. When her mother died, Bartlett was in California seeking to establish himself amid the new opportunities offered by the Gold Rush. Soon she received word that he had survived the rugged journey to the coast, only to die in Sacramento on December 11, just three weeks after Abigail Baker's death.

Her mother's death and the loss of her marital prospects changed everything. Her father made plans to remarry, but had no intention of letting Mary's son remain in the house. As a result, Georgy was sent in 1851 to live with foster parents, who soon settled with him in North

Groton, New Hampshire, a village in the foothills of the White Mountains, some forty miles away. Immensely saddened, Eddy was in no position to protest, or come up with an alternative plan. Despair over the separation plunged her into months of invalidism. With the resilience that seemed so much a part of her nature, she again tried to put her life back together, only to meet with further and even more crushing defeats.

In June 1853, she married a bluff and handsome dentist named Daniel Patterson. The marriage, which at first gave every evidence of a lively affection, slowly unraveled. Patterson was something of a dandy, and after multiple infidelities, he deserted his wife in the summer of 1866, eloping with another woman. Seven years later, she sued for divorce. A harbinger of future trouble was Patterson's utter—and to some degree understandable—distaste for George. In 1855, Mary persuaded Patterson to move to North Groton, near George, now a rather obstreperous ten-year-old. The next year, without informing Mary beforehand, Patterson and Mark Baker worked out a plan for George's foster parents to take the boy with them to Minnesota. Mary had no idea of where her son had been taken, would have no contact with him for five years, and would not see him again for nearly a quarter of a century.

George was not dead, but she was separated from him by a distance of space and time that seemed to her as impassable as death itself. Her life by that time was so permeated by weakness and pain, both physical and emotional, that she seemed to live in some middle kingdom between life and death. During the winter months, she was surrounded by snow and silence. Her existence had contracted so drastically that her world became almost wholly an inner one, and there was precious little to fill it.

On a page of a scrapbook she kept during this period, she assembled a series of obituaries and poems bearing on the deaths of people she had loved: her brother Albert in 1841, her first husband in 1844, her mother and fiancé in 1849. Like a Chinese ideogram in which meaning emerges from the juxtaposition of elements, these items play off one another in an unselfconscious way as mute testimony to a life repeatedly punctuated by impotence, pain, and sorrow. The scrapbook also contained masses of "graveyard poetry" that, however naively, touched the aching chord of devastation she felt through repeated experiences of separation and death.[52] For her, the issue of mortality was personal, springing from the intensity of her own repeated encounters with the death of loved ones and the prospect that she, too, might not survive for long.

In March 1860, her life reached its nadir. Six months before, her sister Martha had been forced to foreclose on the mortgage she held on the Pattersons' small house in North Groton. As Eddy left town, a neighbor with whom Daniel Patterson had quarreled—most likely over a financial matter—tolled the church's bell in triumph. Myra Smith, a blind girl who often stayed with Eddy as a maid, walked along behind the carriage rather than hear her sobs. Never was Eddy to know a moment of greater humiliation and defeat. Beneath a copybook entry in which she recorded her sister's foreclosure of the mortgage on their house, she wrote a poem that distills what she experienced in that period:

> Father didst not thou the dark wave treading,
> Lift from despair the struggler with the sea?
> And seest Thou not the scalding tears I'm shedding,
> And knowest thou not my pain and agony?
> O! is this weight of anguish which they bind
> On life, this searing to the quick of mind,
> That but to God its own free path would crave,
> This crushing out of life, of hope, or love.
> Thy *will* O God?—Then stay me from above
> For my sick soul is darkened unto death,
> With stygian shadows from this world of woe;
> The strong foundations of my early faith
> Shrink from beneath me, whither shall I flee?
> Hide me O, rock of ages! hide in thee.[53]

Different as they were in so many ways, Twain and Eddy both experienced defining moments of absolute blackness and despair. In the snowbound isolation of her North Groton home, she knew something of that "vast emptiness" Twain had come to feel at the death of his wife, two daughters, and son. Given her multiplied personal losses, isolation, and invalidism, it would be difficult to think of anyone in New England who at that point would seem to have had less of a future. Yet, astonishingly, nearly a half-century later, Twain himself could write of her as "in several ways . . . the most interesting woman that ever lived, and the most extraordinary."[54] Just so, it would be hard to anticipate from the picture Twain presented in the 1880s—a period when he was at the height of his powers, living more than comfortably, adored by his wife and children—that he would pass through a financial debacle, suffer devastating personal losses, lose much of his creative edge, and descend into the bitterness and near nihilism of his later years.

To a large extent, these greatly differing trajectories in their lives depended on how each of them answered the question Eddy had framed for herself when she was twenty-two and in a state of emotional and physical exhaustion. She then copied and underlined words in a dirge-like poem by Barry Cornwall that ended:

> We toil through *pain* and *wrong*,
> We *fight* and *fly*,
> We love, and then ere long
> Stone dead we lie.
> Oh! life is all thy song
> *Endure, and die!*[55]

In the margins of the poem, she wrote "(O God) *is it all!*" In these five words she distilled the question that already overshadowed her life and that would dominate it until her work in Christian Science began.

Her language is terse, but loaded. She does not frame the problem of being abstractly, saying, as she might have said, "Is struggle and eventual death all there is to existence?" Nor does she question the reality of God. Rather she addresses him directly with the exclamatory question: "*Is it all!*" She underlines these words, just as in the poem she had underlined the words *pain, wrong, fight, fly, endure, die.* They are the "it"—the struggle, suffering, and eventual death that constitute the mortal condition—and she asks if this is all there is to being. Yet even while she feels the engulfing reality of that "it," God, too, remains real.

Which one, then, occupied the ground of being, God or that "it"? Mary Baker Eddy's whole life was built on the conviction that it could not be both.

NEW PATHS

"(O God) *is it all!*" Eddy eventually defined Christian Science as being in total and resolute opposition to the materialism that holds the "it" of physical existence as comprising the whole of life. In her words from *Science and Health*, "Belief in a material basis, from which may be deduced all rationality, is slowly yielding to the idea of a metaphysical basis, looking away from matter to Mind as the cause of every effect."[56] For her, the first step in breaking the hold of this materialism and defining an alternative to it came through her experiments in the early 1850s with the medical system known as homeopathy, one of the forms of medical treatment through which she sought relief from physical ills.

Homeopathy is based on the theory that cures can be attained by stimulating the system to range its vital forces against a disease and that this can be accomplished by administering doses of a substance that will produce in a healthy body symptoms of the disease to be cured. Most forms of homeopathic theory also stressed that the more minute the dose, the greater will be its diffusion throughout the body's system—a point that Abraham Lincoln mocked when he said that one of his opponent's positions was "as thin as the homeopathic soup that was made by boiling the shadow of a pigeon that had starved to death." During the 1850s, in one of the cases she treated in her small homeopathic practice, Eddy not only diluted drugs to a near vanishing point, but also administered unmedicated pellets to a patient, who continued to improve. Anticipating current theories about the placebo effect, she concluded that homeo-pathic cures are effected, not through any properties in the drugs, but from faith in the drugs on the part of both the patients and those who administered them.[57]

On the surface, it would seem difficult to understand how Eddy's homeopathic experiments could have anything to do with her spiritual search. It was, however, part of the process she described when she wrote: "St. Paul declared that the law was the schoolmaster, to bring him to Christ. Even so was I led into the mazes of divine metaphysics through the gospel of suffering, the providence of God, and the cross of Christ." Seen in this framework, Eddy's experiments with homeopathy were an initial phase of her exploration of "the mazes of divine metaphysics."[58]

By the late 1850s Eddy had become disenchanted with homeopa-thy as a remedial form of treatment. But what she had learned from it no doubt prepared her to pursue yet another new path in the journey that led to her work in Christian Science: her association with Phineas Parkhurst Quimby of Portland, Maine, from October 1862 until just before his death in January 1866.

The extent of Quimby's influence on Eddy's development has been the most controversial and divisive issue in the literature on Christian Science. Extremes have ranged from the contention that he was an ignorant mesmerist whose role in the gestation of her ideas was negli-gible, to the assertion that she virtually stole the substance of Christian Science from him. Some scholars, including Robert Peel, who was a Christian Scientist, and Gillian Gill, who is not, have sought to grapple with the complex evidence bearing on this issue. Others have taken extreme and largely indefensible positions on both sides of the ques-tion. Irving Tomlinson, for example, in speaking of her discovery in *Twelve Years with Mary Baker Eddy,* dismisses any serious influence Quimby may have had on her: "the assistance he gave her was one factor impelling her to search further for true spiritual healing." Others in the hostile biographical tradition, building largely on the extremely partisan Milmine series on Eddy's life for *McClure's,* have treated the

Phineas P. Quimby, n.d.
Courtesy of The Mary Baker
Eddy Collection.

assumption that Quimby was the true originator of Christian Science as axiomatic.[59]

As in other instances when unresolved controversies over intellectual influences are concerned, one suspects that a basic problem lies in the either-or model in which the conflicting claims have been framed. Here an alternative and potentially useful line of inquiry is suggested by a phrase used by the literary critic Harold Bloom in his seminal book, *The Anxiety of Influence: A Theory of Poetry*. Bloom uses the phrase "creative misreading" in explaining how younger poets grapple with issues raised by their feeling of dependence on precursors who have influenced them.[60] Applying this phrase, though not Bloom's theory as a whole, to Eddy's relation to Quimby, points to what may be a more balanced assessment that takes account of both his role as a stimulus to her development and the fact that she was pursuing a path that would diverge sharply from his own.

Eddy, it can be said, was involved in a "creative misreading" of Quimby's beliefs for about a decade after their first encounter in 1862. These encounters, which amounted to a total of about a year of intermittent visits, began in October 1862 when Eddy appeared in his

Portland, Maine, office seeking relief from her long-standing physical problems. Though she initially benefited from his ministrations, her health continued to fluctuate in the several years that followed. Of much greater importance, however, was the stimulus and direction she gained through her engagement with Quimby's ideas.

That she was misreading Quimby in terms of her own settled Christian convictions is illustrated by an article entitled "Experience of a Patient with Dr. Quimby" that found its way into the major collection of Quimby's writings, which actually consist of notes and articles he dictated to family and friends who served as copyists.[61] The patient spoken of in the article is identified as "Mrs. P." There can hardly be any doubt that this "Mrs. P." was Mrs. Daniel Patterson. She speaks of herself as suffering from a spinal ailment, clearly identifies herself as a deeply convinced Christian, and questions Quimby as to the charge that he was practicing spiritualism or animal magnetism. This was the very charge that Eddy raised and countered in the first of two effusive letters praising Quimby she wrote for publication in the *Portland Evening Courier* just a month after her first meeting him.

In the article, "Mrs. P." shows Quimby enlisting what he perceives as her strong religious convictions in her own behalf. He explains that the "Christ or God in us" that operated through Jesus is still present to "set you free from the evils of man's opinions that bind burdens upon you in the form of a disease." So successful is he in this enterprise that in the last paragraph, "Mrs. P.," now completely convinced of the truth of Quimby's words, declares, "I would rather part with everything on earth than part with the truth which is my shepherd that leadeth me through the dark valley of the shadow of death." Flushed with spiritual expectancy, she attributes to Quimby the Christian conviction that "we cannot be separated from our Heavenly Father"—a conviction that is wholly at odds with the tenor of his writings, but that clearly reflects her own strongly Christian religious upbringing and convictions.

Broadly characterizing Quimby's influence on Eddy, Karl Holl wrote in his article *Der Szientismus*, "it was her earnest Puritan faith in God that separated her from Quimby from the beginning." Though rejecting the harsh Calvinist deity of her father's "relentless theology," she never doubted the existence of the God enshrined in the Westminister Creed: "There is but one only living and true God, who is infinite in being and perfection, a most pure spirit, invisible, without body, parts or passions, immutable, immense, eternal, incomprehensible, almighty, most wise, most holy, most free, most absolute, working all things according to the counsel of his own immutable and most righteous will for his own glory." Far from questioning the reality of this God, Eddy came to believe that through her discovery of Christian Science, she had grasped the reality of his sovereignty in its fullness. "In this new departure of metaphysics," she wrote of her teaching, "God is regarded more as absolute, supreme; . . . God's fatherliness as Life, Truth, and Love, makes His sovereignty glorious."[62]

By no means was Quimby destitute of religious feeling. But his religious views were located at the opposite end of the theological spectrum from the theism Eddy absorbed as a child of the New England Puritan tradition. It is not enough to say that he saw God as immanent rather than transcendent, if this suggests a view of God as an immediate presence to whom our affections can be opened. He did speak of God as the "First Cause," a kind of supermagnetic force that calls man into being, and the "invisible Wisdom which fills all space, whose attributes are all light, all goodness and love, which is free from all selfishness and hypocrisy." But this Wisdom, which he also spoke of as Christ and Science, he saw more as potentiality *within* the human mentality than as a force or power exterior to it.[63]

Quimby studied and referred to the Bible frequently, often using accounts of Jesus as a reference point in speaking of his own methods of cure. Having begun his own healing work in the culture of American mesmerism, he was familiar with the stock-in-trade concept of mesmerist theoreticians that were replicating the healing works of Jesus. But for Quimby, this contention was no mere rhetorical gesture but an ardently held conviction. He saw Jesus as unique, not because he was humanity's Savior in any traditional sense, but because he exemplified and utilized Wisdom more fully than had any human individual before or since.

This Wisdom was a beneficent clairvoyant power to discern the mentality of the sick and liberate them from the errors that held them in bondage to their suffering. As such, it was the inner agency or force that Quimby sought to exercise in his own healing practice. "The homeopath," he wrote, "puts virtue into a powder which must be powerful. The Spiritualist puts intelligence into the dead. The Christian who is taught that prayer can cure believes the remedy to be in the prayer. All have something external to themselves in which to locate the curative power. I have not."[64]

Eddy's own spiritual quest was her passionate search for that "something." There can be little question that what she absorbed from Quimby was a powerful stimulus to her own spiritual quest. Expanding and developing some elements of his working concepts and vocabulary, she incorporated what she had learned from him into her own framework, which took shape over the course of several years following his death in January 1866. There is no evidence, to cite several examples, that previous to her encounter with Quimby, she had come to the conclusion that there was a discoverable science of healing underlying Jesus' cures, that because of this Christianity must be linked to science, that disease was an "error" of the human mind, that there is a fundamental polarity between "truth" and "error," and that physicians and the clergy were both guilty of fastening on humanity the errors that needlessly bound them to disease.

At the same time, the meaning that she ultimately attributed to the concepts and ideas she adapted from Quimby cannot be assimilated back into the orbit of his thought. The science she believed she had discovered was more than a method for replicating Jesus' healings. It was an all-embracing reconception of the nature of being. The healing works of Jesus she saw as more than enlightened acts that freed human beings from the slavery of false opinions that bound them to disease. They were, rather, evidences that "Jesus beheld in Science the perfect man, who appeared to him where sinning mortal man appears to mortals." They were confirmations of what she saw, in Robert Peel's words, as the "logical implications of the birth and Resurrection of Jesus, with their smashing of accepted physical law at each end of human life."[65]

Similarly, the conflict between "truth and error" of which Eddy so often spoke was not a war between misguided and enlightened views of the influence of opinions on human happiness and disease. It was an enormous, virtually cosmic struggle between the absolute reality of God, divine Truth, and the wholesale negation of that Truth by the error from which all materiality and suffering springs. Little wonder that George Quimby, a strong champion of his father's originality, wrote, "Don't confuse his method of healing with Mrs. Eddy's Christian Science, so far as her religious teachings go. . . . The *religion* which she teaches certainly *is hers,* for which I cannot be too thankful; for I should be loath to go down into my grave feeling that my father was in any way connected with 'Christian Science.' "[66]

As George Quimby's words suggest, Quimby and Eddy thought within fundamentally different frameworks. There were, so to speak, transcendental fringes at the edges of Quimby's beliefs. But the horizons of his thinking were more or less defined by his practical humanitarian efforts as a healer. From her teenage years, Eddy had been gripped by the largest possible questions, as epitomized in her near-despairing cry at the age of twenty-two, "O God, *is it all!*" When she used the term "Spirit," for example, it was in the biblical and deific sense of that which is distinct from "the flesh." With Quimby, the word "spirit" was generally used as part of the phrase "spiritual matter," meaning the mind as a "spiritual substance that can be changed," thus producing a corresponding change in the body.[67]

So great was her gratitude to Quimby, however, that Eddy remained largely unaware of the underlying disparity between them for about six years after her initial efforts to define and develop her own teaching began. In early 1872, she was embroiled in a newspaper controversy with a former student, Wallace W. Wright. He had argued publicly in a letter to the *Lynn Transcript* that, despite Eddy's protestations to the contrary, she taught mesmerism pure and simple, which he defined broadly as the influence of mind on mind. Grappling with this issue, she asserted in her rejoinder that Christianity and mesmerism "are separated by barriers that neither a geometrical figure nor a malicious falsehood would ever unite." She had stated in reply to an earlier letter from Wright that Quimby had started "from the stand-point of magnetism thence going forward and leaving that behind."[68] But she could no longer escape the conclusion that Quimby's thought remained within the orbit of mesmerism, in the broad sense in which Wright had defined it.

Wright used the term "mesmerism" in the same sense as had the widest-ranging and most influential early theoretician of mental healing, the former Methodist minister Warren Felt Evans. Though Evans was not a disciple of Quimby per se, Quimby had given his blessing to Evans's work. Evans's thinking had developed along somewhat parallel lines, except for the fact that he combined mesmeric theories with an ardently embraced commitment to the ideas of the Swedish scientist and theologian Emanuel Swedenborg.

In his book *The Mental Cure,* published in 1869, Evans spoke of "a variety of phenomena, passing under the names of Mesmerism, Psychology, Biology, Animal Magnetism, Pantheism, Hypnotism, and even Psychometry, that are reducible to one general principle,—the influence or action of mind upon mind." Defending her teaching in the exchange with Wright, Eddy made the distinction between it and mesmerism in this sense of the term categorical. In the first edition of *Science and Health,* which she began to write just the next month, Eddy stated that when she knew him, Quimby was "growing out of mesmerism." But she also concluded that Quimby "never studied this science, but reached his own high standpoint and grew to it through his own, and not another's progress."[69]

When she wrote these words, Eddy's love for and loyalty to Quimby remained undiminished. No evidence indicates that she had any vested interest in divorcing her teaching from his, but rather a strong personal desire to maintain whatever legitimate connection with him she could defend. Reluctantly and possibly painfully, she was

forced to relinquish the misreading of Quimby that had largely dominated her thinking up to that point. She therefore found herself forced
into accepting her own status as an independent thinker, along with
the weight of responsibility that went with it.

THE CARDINAL POINT

Eddy's contact with Quimby has received so much attention that it
has largely obscured what may in the final analysis be a larger and
more significant issue: how she assimilated into her own framework of
thought any term, argument, or concept that she found useful in conveying what she fundamentally—and uniquely—had to say. Even if
one combines all the conceptual and linguistic sources upon which
Eddy arguably drew, one could not derive from or find in them the
unique and defining teaching of Christian Science, which Eddy most
succinctly expressed as "the great fact of Life in and of Spirit; this Life
being the sole reality of existence."[70]

Eddy wrote frankly at many points of the difficulty she faced in
finding the appropriate language to communicate her ideas most effectively, and she was perfectly willing to appropriate any term into her
own framework to accomplish this end.[71] Hence the verbal echoes one
finds in her writings of various writers, including not only Quimby, but
Swedenborg and the highly influential "seer of Poughkeepsie," Andrew
Jackson Davis, whose combination of Swedenborgian and mesmeric
concepts probably influenced Quimby as well.

She may have developed some second-hand familiarity with the
ideas and language of these and other writers from conversations with
Quimby. She may also have been exposed to them through other
channels in ways now impossible to trace. It is apparent, however, that
her core convictions remained basically and, one might say, adamantly
Christian. Many of the most essential terms in her vocabulary—such as
"God," "Spirit," " Love," "sin," "evil," "the carnal mind," "salvation," "the
new birth," "regeneration," and "the Kingdom of God"—were specifically biblical and Christian. Yet she found the language of Christian
orthodoxy inadequate to convey the full dimension of the radically
new understanding of biblical Christianity as she understood it, hence
her adoption of terms from various sources to achieve this end.

The term "personal sense," for example, which is used extensively
in the first edition of *Science and Health* as the opposite of spiritual sense,
she largely dropped in working out the second edition, published in
1878. There she employed the term "mortal mind" in place of personal

sense and at the same time began to write of Mind with a capital "M" as a deific synonym wholly distinct from the mortal, human, or carnal mind. Again, while she used the term "metaphysics" hardly at all in the first edition, she employed it as the title of the new chapter "Metaphysics," which appeared for the first time in the second. Her use of this term at this point and in her later writings may be due to two congenial visits in early 1876 with one of Concord's luminaries, Emerson's seraphic friend and comrade Amos Bronson Alcott, for whom the word "metaphysics" was a virtual staple. After meeting with Eddy and her students in February, for example, he noted in his journal that they had passed the evening in "discussing metaphysical problems."[72]

Even the term "metaphysics," however, she employed in her own way that differs from its largely neo-Platonic use by Alcott and other exponents of various forms of philosophic idealism. For her, metaphysics became a means of expressing the implications of the new experience and enlarged understanding of God that she believed her teaching was opening to humanity. The metaphysics she taught, wrote Eddy, is "far from dry and abstract." It "treats of the existence of God, His essence, relations, and attributes."[73] If one experiences the reality and goodness of God as infinite Spirit and Love, then, Eddy believed, hatred, sin, and all material limitation must have a correspondingly diminished reality.

This, she taught, is what actually happened in biblical accounts of the overwhelming consciousness of God's presence characteristic of the patriarchs, the prophets, of Jesus, and of his apostles. "From Genesis to Revelation," she wrote, "the Scriptures teach an infinite God, and none beside Him; and on this basis Messiah and prophet saved the sinner and raised the dead,—uplifting the human understanding, buried in a false sense of being." For Eddy, one grasps and demonstrates the power of God's presence, in proportion as the reality of any other presence is seen to be illusory and denied. Hence her statement, which she knew to be thoroughly at odds with conventional human rationality: "Truth is immortal; error is mortal. Truth is limitless; error is limited. Truth is intelligent; error is non-intelligent. Moreover, Truth is real, and error is unreal. This last statement contains the point you will most reluctantly admit, although first and last it is the most important to understand."[74]

For her, this conclusion was not the result of philosophical speculation. It was based on the experience of God's reality that was open to all. One could come to no other conclusion, she insisted, if one is willing to accept without qualification what she saw as the core truth of scriptural revelation: that God is infinite Spirit, without an opposite and without limits. In the light of this truth, she maintained, matter and all forms of evil must be seen as having no ontological reality. Hence what she called "the cardinal point of the difference in my metaphysical system . . . that *by knowing the unreality of disease, sin, and death, you demonstrate the allness of God.*"[75]

It is hard to quarrel with the uniqueness of Christian Science as defined by Eddy in these terms. Minus her consistent and radical assertion of the demonstrability of the unreality of evil in the light of the absolute reality of God, Christian Science might well be accounted a derivative or variant of some other system of thought. The "cardinal point" in her metaphysical system, however, is not one that Quimby advanced, nor is it consistent with the underlying metaphysics of Christian orthodoxy, or coordinate with the substance and implications of Hindu cosmology.

Far from trying to obscure or downplay the unique and defining teaching of Christian Science, Eddy reiterated it at a number of points in her writings, giving it as precise and forthright expression as she could, as when she wrote of "the pith of the basal statement, the cardinal point in Christian Science, that matter and evil (including all inharmony, sin, disease, death) are *unreal.*" By "unreal," Eddy obviously did not mean that matter and evil are unreal to human beings, for whom they constitute vivid realities. She meant to convey that matter and evil had no ultimate or basic reality as aspects of being that God created and sustained. They are, in other words, without *ontological* reality. They seem totally vivid and real, but only within the limits of conventional human consciousness—the mortal-mindedness that by its very nature shut out the true sense of Spirit.[76]

Eddy also took pains at many points in her writings to affirm that we are not presently locked into some sphere of being in which everything we experience is wholly illusory and unreal. In her words, "The sweet, sacred sense and permanence of man's unity with his Maker, in Science, illumines our present existence with the ever-presence and power of God, good."[77]

This fact, she taught, was attested to by the revelation that Jesus's very life brought to humanity. Jesus, she believed, lived outside the limits of conventional human experience as much as was possible to one visible to humanity now. He did so because for him the overflowing goodness of God was the present reality of being—because he lived within the Kingdom of God even while he walked the earth. Thus Jesus' very life illustrated "the human and divine coincidence . . . as divinity embracing humanity in Life and its demonstration—reducing to human perception and understanding the Life which is God."[78]

"WITH SUCH A LIGHT AND SUCH A PRESENCE"

To begin to live this Life, she said, required the new birth, a spiritual awakening that sees beyond the limits imposed by sense-bound human consciousness, and this new birth or awakening must eventually be experienced by all. "Mortal mind," she wrote, "must waken to spiritual life before it cares to solve the problem of being, hence the author's experience; but when this awakening comes, existence will be on a new standpoint." That awakening, she believed, occurred in her life over the course of most of the year 1866, beginning with a transforming healing experience in February. The "new standpoint" of which she spoke meant a reappraisal of the nature of being from the perspective of an unqualified conviction that God is infinite, all-embracing Spirit. Looking back years later, she saw the gaining of this new standpoint as having been preceded by a collapse of "the illusion that this so-called life could be a real and abiding rest":

> Thus it was when the moment arrived of the heart's bridal to more spiritual existence. When the door opened, I was waiting and watching; and, lo, the bridegroom came! The character of the Christ was illuminated by the midnight torches of Spirit. My heart knew its Redeemer. He whom my affections had diligently sought was as the One "altogether lovely," as "the chiefest," the only, "among ten thousand." Soulless famine had fled. Agnosticism, pantheism, and theosophy were void. Being was beautiful, its substance, cause, and currents were God and His idea. I had touched the hem of Christian Science.[79]

In part, this collapse of the illusion that human life could be "a real and abiding rest" can be understood in terms of Eddy's changed circumstances. There is no evidence that the death of her father, Mark Baker, in October 1865 marked a crucial turning point for her, since the two had never been really close. But she felt the death of Quimby on January 16, 1866, and the continued unraveling of her marriage to Daniel Patterson as definite losses. Both of these developments were part of the downward spiral that Eddy saw as having prepared her for the spiritual breakthrough that began with her sudden recovery from the effects of a severe accident on February 1 of that year.

On her way to a meeting of the Good Templars with friends, she fell on icy pavement, striking her head and back. According to a contemporary newspaper account, the doctor who attended her found her injuries to be "internal, and of a very serious nature, inducing spasms and intense suffering." Eddy later recalled that, after being carried to a nearby house and attended by a physician, she remained unable to walk until, three days after the accident, she asked for a Bible, read an account of one of Jesus' healings, and experienced a moment so transforming that she was healed. She also recalled that she had a momentary relapse when her doctor expressed doubt that she had recovered without medicine, until "it all seemed to come to me again with such a light and such a presence" that she "rose right up again" with the feeling that she could never again be conquered.[80]

There has been much controversy over this incident in the literature on Christian Science, most of it centering on the issue of how serious her injuries were. But of far greater long-range importance is the fact that looking back, she saw the pivotal meaning of that experience, not so much in the physical healing itself, but in the transforming sense of God's presence that had brought it forth. In later years, she spoke to Alfred Farlow about what this new sense of God meant to her. In his words summarizing their conversation:

> At that time it was not clear to Mrs. Eddy by what process she had been instantaneously healed, but she knew that her thought had turned away from all else in contemplation of God, His omnipotence and everpresence, His infinite love and power. It eventually dawned upon her that this overwhelming consciousness of the divine presence had destroyed her fear and consciousness of disease exactly as the light dispels the darkness.[81]

The healing that she associated with this revelatory breakthrough was not, however, on the order of a dramatic "road to Damascus" experience or a turning point as clear-cut as Luther's decision, upon nearly being struck by lightning, to become a monk. In the grip of fear that she might suffer a relapse and again be reduced to invalidism, Eddy wrote eleven days after her recovery to Julius Dresser, a Quimby devotee whom she had come to know in Portland, asking if he might take up Quimby's mantle and help her, although he replied that he felt unworthy to do either.[82]

In the next months, her life appeared to be unraveling fast. Although able to walk, she was so near destitution after being temporarily deserted by Patterson in March that she petitioned the city of Lynn for damages because of the unsafe condition of the street where her accident had occurred. After being briefly reunited with Patterson, she was again deserted by him in August; and while he made at least one attempt to reunite with her, she concluded that the relationship had irretrievably broken down. Over the next few months, she stayed with one friend after another. Finally, in autumn she took refuge in the Swampscott home of the village schoolmaster and his mother, where her own search for a positive principle of spiritual healing was to begin in earnest.

Mary Baker Eddy around the time she was working on her notes on Genesis, ca. 1867–68. Courtesy of The Mary Baker Eddy Collection.

Quite possibly, several healings she effected during the latter part of 1866 made a crucial difference in impelling her to begin this search. According to one account, during the summer of 1866 Eddy encountered a mother whose seven-year-old son had never walked because of a severe condition of clubfoot. Leaving the boy on his pillow on the sand for a short time, the mother was surprised to find him taking his first feeble steps hand in hand with Eddy. This event, along with several other instances of healing, may have confirmed Eddy's conviction that what she had glimpsed at the point of her own healing in February 1866 pointed to a larger truth that needed sustained investigation. Thus she spoke in later years of that healing as the "falling apple" that led to her discovery. The discovery itself she identified with the conviction that came to her in the latter part of 1866, when, as she put it in *Retrospection and Introspection,* "I gained the scientific certainty that all causation was Mind, and every effect a mental phenomenon."[83]

It was at this point that she emerged from months of wavering and self-searching to become a woman with a spiritual mission. She devoted herself to developing the spiritual insight she had first glimpsed at the point of her healing and set forth—haltingly, and then with increasing assurance and conviction—on the road that led to the publication of *Science and Health* in 1875.

THE GENESIS OF CHRISTIAN SCIENCE AND THE GENESIS OF ORTHODOXY

"Our thoughts of the Bible utter our lives," Eddy wrote in 1902. This statement was discernibly true of Mark Twain, whose acceptance of the conventional view of the creator God of Genesis shaped his entire religious outlook.[84]

Twain had read the Bible by the time he was fifteen, but interpreted it through the lens of a flat-out biblical literalism. Beginning in the early 1870s, he became almost obsessed with writing a series of fantasies, farces, and satires on the creation stories in Genesis and its account of the story of Adam and Eve's fall and expulsion from the Garden of Eden. Where Twain continued to view assent to the literal word of the Bible as virtually synonymous with religious belief, Eddy broke utterly with biblical literalism. Indeed, she spoke of this literalism as "the reading of the carnal mind, which is enmity toward God, Spirit."[85] For Eddy, the early chapters of Genesis were full of revelatory power—but only if interpreted in terms of their underlying spiritual meaning.

That meaning for her revolved around a crucial distinction made in her mature teaching between the two accounts of creation stated respectively in the first and second chapters of Genesis. In the first, God created all things, including man in his "image" and "likeness" and pronounced all that he made "very good." Eddy wrote of this account of creation as a symbolic depiction of God's true creation, which is spiritual and complete. In the second account, the "Lord God" supposedly recreates man, Adam, out of the "dust of the ground," and woman from him. It was in the first account that Eddy located the true or divinely normative account of creation. The second account, Eddy noted, begins with the text: "But there went up a mist from the earth, and watered the whole face of the ground." For her, the mist symbolizes the obscuring of the reality of the Creator and his creation as presented in the first chapter of Genesis and the opening verses of the second. It is after the mist arose that the "God" of the first account becomes the "Lord God" of the second. This Lord God then infuses life into matter; whereas for Eddy, God is Life and cannot be infused into a finite form. It is not in Adam's fall, but in the root error of a material sense of creation that Eddy located the source of mortal iniquity and suffering.[86]

This clear-cut distinction emerged only as her teaching took distinct shape in the first edition of *Science and Health*. Eddy's own path toward the full articulation of Christian Science first spelled out in that book began with an intense study of the book of Genesis that occupied her from the autumn of 1866 into early 1869. Her intent was to develop the implications of her healing experience in February 1866 through a projected study of the spiritual meaning of the Bible as a whole. She intended a close investigation of the book of Genesis to be a first step in this process, but it turned out to be a huge leap.

In later years, she referred to the sprawling Genesis manuscript she wrote during this time as showing "her comparative ignorance of the stupendous Life-problem up to that time, and the degrees by which she came at length to its solution."[87] This document of several hundred pages shows the fundamental metaphysics of Christian Science in the process of emerging. Even amid the relative chaos of the notes on Genesis, Eddy established a basic premise, which she called her "principle unchanging": that existence, understood from the standpoint of God as its creative Principle, must be spiritual, that to regard it as material is to be in error, and that it is from this error alone that sickness and death arise. From this standpoint, our belief that we are shaped and determined by matter is actually brought about by our submergence in error, and not by an actual God-created condition. In this way, she challenged the consensus within traditional Christianity that God is the creator of mortality.

How had this assumption become so much a part of Christian teaching? This did not occur naturally, as if it were simply in the course of things to affirm that God created matter. Rather, it can be traced to a complex series of developments in the second and third centuries. Some major church fathers, believing it was imperative to stem the rising tide of what they saw as the gnostic heresy, came to two conclusions they regarded as definitive: that the creation account in the book Genesis affirms that God made his creation material, and that the sanctity of matter was confirmed through the incarnation of Jesus in the flesh. Their conclusions on this issue became a fixed part of Christian teaching. But the solution to one problem led to another: how could a loving God be ultimately responsible for the suffering of the mortal condition? This was the problem that Eddy faced. And in attempting to do so through her own work on Genesis, she reached without quite knowing it back across the centuries to an opposite conclusion about God and creation that almost all Christians regarded as obvious.[88]

At some point during her work on Genesis, Eddy appears to have been struck with the revolutionary character of what she believed she was discovering. There she suddenly wrote in prophetic, almost apocalyptic accents of the massive spiritual illegitimacy of the mortal condition that Christians conventionally assume to be the effect of God's creative will. Envisioning the vast transition for humanity when it sees the error of its belief in life in matter separate from God, she exclaimed:

> Such a time as this hath not been from the beginning nor ever again will be. The first perception of the woe, the sin and suffering produced by material belief, by placing our intelligence in matter, may so ferment the passions of that age that the violent reaction of credulity after looking its first look upon the vagaries it has pursued, upon the phantom it has called reality, may baptize this monster error in the blood of its own believing, and the sun of its center be forever darkened in that great and notable day which shall be the end of the world to opinion & belief and the new happiness and new understanding of science. That the approaching light of science may come through sweeter footprints than were these, is the desire of my soul, yet not my will but thine, O Principle, father, be done.[89]

In her work on Genesis, however, Eddy was not merely searching for an abstract understanding of spiritual truth. She was seeking to define a working basis for the practice of spiritual healing, which practice in turn would confirm the truth of her discovery. Thus, in a strong defense of her textbook and its teaching written in 1898, Eddy spoke of healings she had effected of consumption in its last stages, malignant diphtheria, carious bones, and of cancer. Referring at another point in her writings to the healing of cancer, Eddy further defined the spiritual state that she saw as having produced the healing effect: "When I have most clearly seen and most sensibly felt that the infinite recognizes no disease, this has not separated me from God, but has so bound me to Him as to enable me instantaneously to heal a cancer which had eaten its way to the jugular vein." Enlarging on this point, she wrote of her conviction "that an acknowledgment of the perfection of the infinite Unseen confers a power nothing else can."[90]

Eddy was intensively involved in the healing work that flowed from this conviction, especially during the several years after her notes on Genesis were completed. (Although completed as a manuscript, the notes were never published by Eddy.) At the same time, she continued honing her statement of the implications that flowed from the total acknowledgment of God's presence and perfection and of man's true spiritual oneness with Him. She brought further clarification to the structure of her emerging teaching through various versions of a manuscript of questions and answers designed for teaching. The language of this manuscript, called "The Science of Man," which she began to use in 1870, was skeletal and spare. In it, she expressed the inner logic of her discovery, which was fleshed out through the writing of *Science and Health* from early 1872 through the late summer of 1874.

WHICH IS THE DREAM?

The radical, essential fact Eddy believed she had set forth in *Science and Health* is that Love, the Love that is God, is the burning reality at the heart of all being, so great that it can have in reality no opposite; that the pains and evils of everyday human life, however frighteningly real they seem, are the "waking dream-shadows"[91] that the human mentality, in its alienation from God, mistakes for reality; and that these are dissolved in the degree that we draw closer to God and understand our full relation to him, revealed in the life of Christ.

As warmly as he wrote about the healing effects of Christian Science, Twain could not bring himself to believe in the reality of a God who is synonymous with Love itself. He reached the same conclusion that Eddy had arrived at: the moral impossibility of the coexistence of a loving and all-powerful God with human evil and pain. Each affirmed, too, that there could be no compromise on this matter, no middle ground that reconciled the existence of such a God with the stark realities of mortal existence. But beyond this point, they absolutely parted company.

Eddy believed she had experienced the reality of divine Love as palpable fact—so much so that even the suffering she endured could be seen in the light of that Love's purpose. In her words, "The very circumstance, which your suffering sense deems wrathful and afflictive, Love can make an angel entertained unawares." To Twain, the sheer fact of human pain was so glaring a reality that it became the measure of the meaning of existence, so that no other option existed but to deny the love, if not the reality, of God. The result was that his later writings are replete with passionate invective against a God whom he could conceive of only as indifferent or malign. Thus, in the summer of 1897, a year after the death of his daughter Susy, he wrote, "There you lie, poor abused slave, set free from the unspeakable insult of life, and by the same Hand that flung it in your face in the beginning." And of the God on whom he blamed her death: "He never does a kindness. . . . He gives you a wife and children whom you adore, only that through the spectacle of the wanton shames and miseries which He will inflict upon them He may tear the palpitating heart out of your breast and slap you in the face with it."[92]

It would have been psychologically impossible for Twain or anyone to remain trapped within the debilitating bitterness of such rage and grief. He needed escape from the burden of this misery; and as at other points in his life, work provided the means. Beginning in 1897 and across much of the next decade, his imagination reached out to a differing vision of human existence as a dream, a view that may, at its inception, have owed something to his reading and rereading of *Science and Health*.

In that book, Eddy repeatedly used the word "dream" as a kind of metaphorical shorthand for the whole sense we conventionally entertain of being so many egos encased in material bodies and living in a physical world, in which, despite its positive elements, conflict, fear, and suffering remain constant and threatening presences. Because of the allness of God, Spirit, Eddy maintained that this sense of existence can be nothing but dreamlike. In proportion as we awaken to the reality of Spirit, she asserted, the sense of the reality of the dream dissolves. But until that point, like the dreamer in sleep, we believe that our dream experiences are real. For her, however, this did not mean that we must now live entirely within the dream. All the goodness, love, beauty, genuine creative attainment—everything we rightly value as of supreme worth in present experience—Eddy saw as having its source in the divine.

This fact she saw as supremely demonstrated in the life of Jesus, whose compassion, communion with God, and obedience to him mark the penetration of reality through the "mists of materiality" into present experience. Jesus' lifework, she taught, reveals the possibility of living *outside* the dream sense, but in the midst of everyday human experience—but only to the extent that we give all for Christ by cherishing and following his example. "A dream calleth itself a dreamer," she wrote, "but when the dream has passed, man is seen wholly apart from the dream."[93]

Twain toyed with the idea of ordinary life as a kind of dreamscape in which both space and time are distorted, with apparently solid realities and events losing their objective fixedness. But for him, there was no solid spiritual reality outside the dream. For him, the belief that human experience is a dream, and that a "dream-self" is a potentially real state of awareness, opened up—at least imaginatively—the possibility of freedom from material limits and the suffering they imposed. He had felt the effect of those limits so severely that he could not accept as a final report the conclusion that this world is simply and irretrievably out there and that we are stuck with it.[94]

His ultimate exploration of this dream theme was the one sustained fictional work he managed to complete during the last decade of his life. *No. 44, The Mysterious Stranger,* set in late-medieval Austria, revolves around the appearance of an unearthly young man who identifies himself as "44" and gradually reveals his remarkable powers to the young friend who narrates the book. No. 44 identifies himself as an emissary from a "realm and orbit . . . outside the human solar system," therefore not entirely comprehensible to one with a "limited human mentality." All things that exist, he explains, "were made out of thought," rather than material substance, so that the "troublesome limitations" of the human race are just that—the limitations of humankind, not inherent and unalterable aspects of existence. Yet the last chapter of *The Mysterious Stranger* contains a sudden deflation of all that has gone before. No. 44 reveals to his young friend the awful final fact: "*Life itself is only a vision, a dream. . . . Nothing* exists; all is a dream. God—man—the world,— the sun, the moon, the wilderness of stars: a dream, all a dream, they have no existence. *Nothing exists save empty space—and you!*"[95]

In this way, the book suddenly tramples on whatever shards of hope Twain had that existence might be other than the time-trapped horror which for him it had become. On the basis of his own bitter experience, Twain came to view evil as the basic, monstrous, unalterable fact to which every concept of reality must adjust itself and to regard this reality as so unendurable that it must be accounted a meaningless nightmare or dream.

Eddy insisted that evil in all its forms must have an insubstantial, dreamlike existence. Yet whenever she spoke of the dreamlike nature of human experience, her words were intended to have an empirical edge. She meant, literally and specifically, that human existence does not transpire in a context of physical substance-matter, but is thoroughly mental—that what we call "matter" is simply a name for the images of limitation we ignorantly entertain within our own mentalities. This was, she knew, a radical proposition. But she also maintained that it was a concrete truth made credible by thousands of healing works through which severe, crippling, and in many cases terminal illnesses had been healed.

"THE BENEFACTOR OF THE AGE"

Twain gave every indication of believing that such healings actually occurred. The simple fact is that religion had too strong a hold on his mind and heart for him simply to relinquish all possibilities of faith. To him, Christian Science appears to have echoed as nearly as any religious teaching he knew the genuine spirituality, warmth, and power that he sensed true Christianity must include. Yet his view of Christian Science remained cautiously ambiguous. William McCrackan recalled seeing Twain sitting in a box at a Christian Science lecture in Carnegie Hall, observing that "he railed at the subject, but could not let go of it. He was too honest to discard it, yet could not understand it."[96]

During their last visit, Twain said that he would be very glad to have McCrackan treat his ailing wife, Livy, but that she was such a staunch Presbyterian that she would rather die first. If the account of his confidant Albert Bigelow Paine is accurate, Twain at one point had to concede considerable merit to Eddy herself. Paine had commented that he had received some help from Christian Science, to which Twain replied: "Of course you have been benefited. Christian Science is humanity's boon. Mother Eddy deserves a place in the Trinity as much as any member of it. She has organized and made available a healing principle that for two thousand years has never been employed, except as the merest kind of guesswork. She is the benefactor of the age."[97] It is possible to make too much of these words—as did Twain's daughter Clara in her 1956 book *Awake to a Perfect Day*. In one of history's supreme ironies that Twain himself might have found perversely amusing, Clara, after having explored Eastern religious teachings for some years, eventually became a Christian Scientist, although probably not a very serious and consistent one. As part of a long-term effort to take some of the rough edges off the public image of her father, she made him far more moderate in his opposition to Eddy than he in fact was. Indeed, around the time he expressed such positive sentiments about Eddy to Paine, Twain also commented in a letter to a correspondent in Scotland that his view of Christian Science had not changed. Conceding that it is valuable, he added that "it has just the same value now that it had when Mrs. Eddy stole it from Quimby; . . . Mrs. Eddy the fraud, the humbug, *organized* that force and is *entitled to high credit for that.*"[98]

The letter has the same rhetorical flourish of Twain's other well-rehearsed fulminations against Eddy. But he struck a different tone in the closing chapter of his book *Christian Science*, where he wrote that Eddy has delivered to Christian Scientists

> a religion which has revolutionized their lives, banished the glooms that shadowed them, and filled them and flooded them with sunshine and gladness and peace; a religion which has no hell; a religion whose heaven is not put off to another time, with a break and gulf between, but begins here and now and melts into eternity.
>
> They believe it is a Christianity that is in the New Testament; that it has always been there; that in the drift of ages it was lost through disuse and neglect, and that this benefactor has found it and given it back to men, turning the night of life into day, its terrors into myths, its lamentations into songs of emancipation and rejoicing.[99]

In his own wrestlings with Christian Science, Twain found himself inadvertently plunged into the mental maelstrom that the broader controversy over Eddy had aroused. Nothing that Twain ever said about Eddy would have credited the basic charge in the Next Friends Suit that she and her teaching were insane—especially in view of the fact that he had made so much of her presumed capacities for business, which Chandler pointedly denied.

To her, the Next Friends Suit represented the suffering she was forced to endure in the process of fulfilling her mission, and Twain's own public disparagement of her motives, although not of her teaching, was clearly a harbinger of the ordeal. Hence her concluding words in her open reply to his attacks: "We need much humility, wisdom, and love to perform the functions of foreshadowing and foretasting heaven within us. This glory is molten in the furnace of affliction." In a letter written just after the publication of the first of Twain's *North American Review* articles, Eddy said that she considered it "a burlesque on C.S. and its discoverer," referring in another letter to Twain's "effusion of folly and falsehoods." But she never accused him of deliberate malice, nor did McCrackan, who conversed with him at length.[100]

In fact, McCrackan once urged Twain to visit with some of the citizens of Concord who knew Eddy well so that he might realize on the basis of first-hand testimony the wild inaccuracy of the picture he had drawn of her.[101] But by 1902, Livy had become so ill that he was hesitant to leave her, even for a day. One thing that McCrackan did not propose, however, was a meeting between Twain and Eddy herself. Quite possibly the two would have had much to talk about and would have enjoyed each other immensely. The result was that Twain and Eddy, among the best-known Americans of their time, appeared to be in an adversarial relationship with one another, although they actually shared more ground than either of them ever knew.

2

Becoming "Mrs. Eddy"

"THAT SUPREMELY PERSUADED PERSON"

BY THE TIME OF THE NEXT FRIENDS SUIT AND TWAIN'S WIDELY PUBLICIZED attacks on her, Eddy was among the best known and most controversial women in America. In scholarly literature it has largely become the convention to refer to her by her last name alone, since, as feminists have reasonably maintained, it is implicitly chauvinistic to identify a woman by her marital status through the designations "Miss" and "Mrs.," whereas no such gender designations are affixed to the names of men. Yet in her lifetime, and among many of her followers and opponents since, Mary Baker Eddy was almost universally known as "Mrs. Eddy."

The very phrase "Mrs. Eddy" conjures up the image of a slim, white-haired figure, immaculately dressed, controversial to be sure, but almost grandmotherly in appearance, and firmly in command of the movement she led. But this "Mrs. Eddy" emerged during the decade following her abrupt departure from Boston in May 1889, and the figure known by this name was in many respects very different from the Mary Baker Eddy one would have encountered during earlier phases of her life after her work in Christian Science began in 1866.

While Eddy had undergone many transformations up to this point, the change that came about as a result of her exit from Boston had the most decisive consequences for her growth, her reputation and stature, and the future of Christian Science. One thing remained constant. In the words of former Mother Church archivist Lee Z. Johnson, she was "that supremely persuaded person, who has something to say and must say it at all costs."[1]

The personal costs involved in implementing her discovery had always been great. During the several years following her healing in 1866, she was the lonely originator of a new religious teaching, exploring

Asa Gilbert Eddy, pencil drawing from photograph. Courtesy of The Mary Baker Eddy Collection.

its dimensions and defining its metaphysics and theology in near isolation and under great hardship. In the decade of the 1870s she became teacher, author, and founder, the central figure in the life of a fledgling religious movement largely confined to Lynn, Massachusetts, a shoe-manufacturing town just north of Boston. It was in January 1877 that she became, literally, "Mrs. Eddy" through her marriage on the first day of that year to her student Asa Gilbert Eddy.

Gilbert Eddy, a native of Vermont, was the first person to publicly identify himself as a Christian Scientist. Kindly and gentle in manner, "Gilbert," as Eddy called him, was also capable of surprising strength and determination. As events proved, however, his strength—spiritual and physical—was not sufficient to cope with the contentious currents that surrounded the new movement during the five and a half years of their marriage, when storm clouds gathered and burst with almost frightening regularity.

The small circle of Eddy's followers, most of them workers in the Lynn shoe industry, organized on July 4, 1876, as the "Christian Scientist Association," the first formal organization in the movement's history. But harmony rarely prevailed among them. Within months of

Eddy's marriage to Gilbert Eddy, Daniel Spofford, previously one of her most supportive students, broke with her. The next year another follower, Edward J. Arens, a student of Gilbert Eddy and a close friend of the Eddys, influenced them—probably to their later regret—into suing two students for unpaid tuition, another for unpaid royalties on his healing practice, and still another for breach of contract. But the biggest storm of all burst in October 1878, when Gilbert Eddy and Arens were charged with conspiracy to murder Spofford, who eventually turned up alive. Exactly who arranged and stood to profit from the machinations that led to this bizarre case is still a matter of debate, although biographer Robert Peel maintains that it was most probably her former student Richard Kennedy. But the charges against Arens and Gilbert Eddy were eventually dismissed early in 1879 after Spofford resurfaced and it was proven that two key witnesses in the case had lied.[2]

The whole affair sounds to modern ears like something of a comic opera. To the Eddys, however, the episode was a nightmare. Not only did Gilbert Eddy face the very real possibility of a criminal conviction, but the publicity attendant on the case did the shaky reputation of the young movement no good. Still, its prospects appeared to be on the upswing when, on April 12, 1879, about fifteen members of the Christian Scientist Association present voted to organize a new church, formally named "The Church of Christ, (Scientist)," when its charter was granted by the Commonwealth of Massachusetts in August of that year. (The church had originally been named the "Church of Christ," the word "Scientist" being added to distinguish it from a denomination that already existed.) With twenty-six members, the new church seemed full of promise.

The promise was brightened by the Eddys' two extended stays in Boston from 1878 to 1880, where she taught several classes and preached at the Baptist Tabernacle, the Parker Memorial Building, and Hawthorne Hall. Eddy had planted her standard in Boston and Christian Science was beginning to attract a limited following there. In January 1881, the Massachusetts Metaphysical College, which was to seed the movement with hundreds of students over the remainder of the decade, was chartered by the Commonwealth. A further progressive step was the publication in August of the second major revision of *Science and Health*.

Again, however, the promise of the period was shattered after the Eddys returned to Lynn. For some months, tensions among her followers had been gathering momentum. Eddy and those loyal to her believed that disaffected students were actively influencing other members of the Association to turn on her. In October 1881, eight students in the Association resigned, accusing her of "frequent ebullitions of temper, love of money, and the appearance of hypocrisy," declaring themselves unwilling to submit to her leadership any longer. The lawsuits launched by her several years before against some former students probably led to the charges of avarice and hypocrisy.[3]

A loyal remnant of the Association reaffirmed their support for Eddy, ordaining her as pastor of the church in November. But she decided that the time had come to quit Lynn altogether and to commit her energies entirely to building up the movement in Boston. In April 1882 the Eddys made the decisive move to Boston, where through her teaching and preaching Christian Science was beginning to arouse considerable interest. But two months later came the most shattering blow of all: the death of Asa Gilbert Eddy on June 3, 1882, scarcely a month after she had opened the Massachusetts Metaphysical College in Boston.

Perplexed and worn down by the multiple controversies that surrounded his wife, Gilbert Eddy as publisher of the second edition of *Science and Health* had nevertheless spearheaded a successful suit to protect the copyright on the book, which Arens had infringed in a pamphlet. Moreover, in a foreword to the third edition he had denounced Arens roundly, though not by name, giving examples of his blatant plagiarism from *Science and Health* and stating: "It would require ages and God's mercy to make the ignorant hypocrite who published that pamphlet originate its contents."[4]

Eddy was convinced that Gilbert Eddy's death was the direct result of malicious hatred aimed at them both by Arens, against which, she believed, her husband in his innocence had failed to protect himself. Nor was she reticent about making this claim public. Distraught and temporarily disoriented, she summoned members of the press, telling them that her husband had been deliberately murdered by poison mentally administered. In the words of one of her former students from the Lynn years, "Dr. Eddy's death had given rise to a multitude of rumors which threatened to bring ruin upon the cause, and disgrace to Mrs. Eddy and her followers, most of whom were utterly dismayed and overwhelmed."[5]

Nothing could have been better calculated to destroy her own sense of mission and discredit her teaching before the world—and this at the precise time she began her teaching work in Boston. After a month's stay at the home of a student in Barton, Vermont, she broke through the pall of grief sufficiently to return to Boston in August 1882—and to the most intense period of activity in her life.

THE DANGER OF PINNACLES, THE NECESSITY OF DESERTS

Every phase of Eddy's life, especially after her work in Christian Science began, was intense in its way. But the seven years between the renewal of her efforts in Boston in August 1882 and her sudden departure from the city in late May 1889 had a whirlwind quality that sets it apart from any other period. As the central figure of a controversial and fast-burgeoning religious movement, Eddy found herself acting simultaneously on a number of fronts.

First, she was pastor of the Christian Science church in Boston. But in Boston as in Lynn, her church congregation had as yet no home, and would not have one until the original Mother Church opened its doors on the last Sunday of 1894. Though services in the 1880s were by necessity held in a succession of hired halls, Eddy's sermons became a primary and powerful factor in galvanizing interest in the new faith throughout the decade. A natural-born teacher, her work at the Massachusetts Metaphysical College, beginning in May 1882, had even greater long-range impact on the development of Christian Science.

Possibly for this reason, biographers have tended to give short shrift to the importance of her work as pastor and preacher. Although around a dozen of her sermons were written out with sufficient coherence to warrant inclusion in her published works, they were most often largely extemporaneous. The rough notes and transcripts that have survived indicate that they were far more colloquial and free-wheeling than her published writings, and, judging from their effectiveness, richly communicative. To take one example from a sermon probably delivered in the early 1880s:

> It is high time that we put off our swaddling garments and look around for work, not with uncomprehending wonder or with the stupid eye of an animal, but with glorified vision, there to behold ourself busy with God and allied to Deity that sprung over chaos an arch of "awful beauty" and lighted up its myriad suns. An ever active and glorious mind breaking out in every nook and phase, from the flowers underneath our feet to those secrets that retreat in shadow where man grows giddy with surprise and halts weary before the infinite Truth.
>
> Then shall we not ask what is required of us and why the example is furnished us to act in the living present and act not for one but for all, to move onward and launch into human life meet its mutations, its melancholy or its ecstatic realities, its shame and its glory, its broken resolutions and its undying hopes, its close clinging to the low and groveling things of earth and its gravitation to glory, and meet this with a thirst greater than sense can satisfy to master them all and be an actor on the stage of Life?

All earthly distinctions, all comparisons of power, vanish before the calm
and steadfast purpose to wheel into the line of God and fight it out on this.[6]

"When God called the author to proclaim His Gospel to this age,"
Eddy wrote in the preface to *Science and Health*, "there came also the
charge to plant and water His vineyard."[7] If the planting and watering
began most conspicuously with her preaching, it bore fruit through her
teaching at the Massachusetts Metaphysical College. The immediate effect
of Eddy's teaching bound many of the nine hundred or more students
she taught in an ongoing relation of loyalty to her leadership, while the
relatively small number of students she had come to trust were to play
consequential roles in the future of Christian Science.

Students who studied under Eddy often said they had gained a sense
of the reality of God exceeding anything they had known before, that this
magnified sense of God opened up the Bible to them and made them
healers. As Eddy put it at the conclusion of one class, "You are going out
to demonstrate a living faith, a true sense of the infinite good, a sense
that does not limit God but brings out God." "The first three days in the
classroom," recalled one student, "gave overwhelming proof of
Mrs. Eddy's understanding of God and her consistent acceptance of the
fact that there was none beside Him. . . . She seemed to have obliter-
ated everything I had deemed substantial and actual. The word 'God'—
'God'—'God' was repeated over and over in my consciousness to the
exclusion of all else." Referring to one of her classes that had gone
unusually well, Eddy wrote a recent student: "They tell me that one
day was a Pentecostal hour. . . . I felt the power of God lifting me up,
and you know the Scripture saith in the words of Jesus When I am
lifted up I will draw all men unto me."[8]

Eddy's teaching work had begun slowly, with about twenty students
in 1882. When she left Boston in May 1889, one hundred and sixty appli-
cations from those wishing to study with her lay on her desk. By that
time, the advance of Christian Science had become a definite problem
and a growing threat for Boston's clergymen. Clerical rumblings against
the new faith and its founder began by 1884 with a scattering of attacks
in ministerial associations. The next year, the storm broke at one of the
Reverend Joseph Cook's popular Monday Lectures. Cook read an open
letter from the Boston Baptist clergyman Adoniram J. Gordon attacking
what he saw as the multiple heresies of the "lady apostle" of Christian
Science. Eddy requested the right to reply. She was granted just ten
minutes on March 16, 1885, to defend Christian Science before more
than two thousand of the assembled orthodox in Tremont Temple, peppered with a scattering of her supporters.

Mary Baker Eddy in 1886.
Courtesy of Longyear
Museum.

The day before, she had delivered a ringing sermon in a crowded Hawthorne Hall just a few blocks from Tremont Temple on the text from Matthew, "Thou art Peter, and upon this rock I will build my church; and the gates of hell shall not prevail against it." After her appearance in Tremont Temple she might have thought that the portals of hell nearly *had* prevailed. When Cook met Eddy, he was, recalled Julia Bartlett who accompanied her, "abusive and insulting. . . . It was a hard ordeal for her, to encounter this hatred and antagonism against the Truth"—so hard that upon leaving Tremont Temple Eddy, feeling quite devastated, went directly home and spent the rest of the day alone in her room.[9]

Facing a largely hostile audience in this wood-beamed bastion of male authority was no triumph. It was, however, the most conspicuous of various efforts she made to defend the movement from the onslaughts of an increasingly aroused clergy, whose assaults on Christian Science she saw as a testimony to its growing strength. In a *Journal* article published the month after her appearance in Tremont Temple, she declared that attacks in the "materialistic portion" of the pulpit and press indicated "fear and weakness" and were actually giving Christian Science "new impetus and energy."[10]

The most pressing threat to the new movement, however, was the rising tide of the mental healing groups, often referred to as "mind-cure," led largely by individuals who had studied with Eddy but found her leadership too rigid and her Christian doctrines too confining. As one scholar put it, some of Eddy's students "were simply people who had their own point of view and were not ready for her 'my way or the highway' approach to the teaching of Christian Science. Eddy was absolutely convinced that she alone was best qualified to lead the movement, but she was not always successful in convincing her students of that point." In December 1883, for example, she instructed her student Clara Choate, who later broke with her, to visit Chicago to help establish Christian Science there. Eddy's tone in this instance as in others was not so much cajoling as demanding: "Before you ever heard of Christian Science I had been commissioned of God to lead his children out of the darkness of today. You can never do this until your life is changed as you well know. Those that talk truth in one thing must *live* it in all things to be fit for pioneers."[11]

Choate, along with some other students of Eddy, was not willing to fulfill such a demanding behest. Those who broke off from the Christian Science movement were, in fact, united as much as anything by an ideology of strong individualism. What historian J. Stillson Judah said of New Thought applies even more to the leaders of the mental healing movements that preceded it: "One finds in New Thought some appealing ideas of well-educated, intelligent speakers and writers mingled very often with bizarre theories and wild, extravagant claims of the ignorant and simple-minded." Names of early mind-cure leaders such as Mary Plunkett and Luther Marston have largely faded into obscurity. Yet one name stands out: that of Emma Curtis Hopkins, who served as editor of the *Christian Science Journal* in 1884 and 1885. After being dismissed from her post for reasons that remain obscure, Hopkins began a long career as a teacher of many major New Thought leaders, among them Charles and Myrtle Fillmore, founders of the Unity School of Christianity, H. Emilie Cady, author of the highly popular *Lessons in Truth*, and Ernest Holmes, organizer of the Church of Religious Science.[12]

Hopkins, more than any other figure, became the link between the mental healing movements of the 1880s and New Thought. New Thought, along with an attenuated form of theosophy, in turn fed into the later forms of alternative spirituality collectively known as the New Age that emerged in the last decades of the twentieth century. In almost all their forms, these movements emphasized the positive therapeutic effects of the beneficent power and energy of the human mind and its potential rapport with the divine. This emphasis differed sharply from Eddy's conviction that the human mind, far from being a potentially curative agent, was the cause of disease rather than its cure.

From Eddy's standpoint, this was no metaphysical nicety but a matter of preserving the very identity of Christian Science. In her estimation, mind-curers made wholesale use of her language, often called themselves Christian Scientists, but turned her teaching on its head. Both mind-cure and New Thought reiterated the fundamental concept that the human mind is in harmonious rapport with the divine. But they often did so in language largely adapted from Christian Science—with the notable and revealing exception of terms Eddy employed revolving around the Christian concept of sin. Specifically, they rejected her insistence that the human or mortal mind is not natively congruent with, but in fundamental opposition to, the Mind that is God. Defending the Christianity of Christian Science in Tremont Temple, Eddy averred that its healing practice "is not one mind acting upon another mind. . . . It is Christ come to destroy the power of the flesh. . . . It is not one mortal thought transmitted to another's thought, from the human mind that holds within itself all evil."[13]

This was in 1885. As the decade progressed, the confusion of Christian Science with mind-cure had intensified in the press and public mind. Christian Science was growing; but it sometimes seemed that the mind-cure flood might drown it out. Mind-curers held conventions, started magazines, and began teaching institutes modeled on the Massachusetts Metaphysical College. According to one contemporary estimate, among those who had left Christian Science, less than one in five recognized Eddy as the discoverer and founder of Christian Science or as the sole leader of the movement. "In order to be thought wise in this generation," wrote an exasperated Eddy in an 1887 memorandum, "it is not well to take advantage of the present ignorance in relation to Christian Science Mind-healing or to flood our land with contradictory theories and practice. . . . The unweaned suckling may whine and spit out the breast-milk which sustains him." Eddy's exasperation with the whole matter can be gauged from an incident two years later. Mary Plunkett, whom Eddy believed had successfully sought to control Emma Curtis Hopkins, tried to embrace Eddy after she concluded an address in New York. Eddy then turned to her and said, "You are so full of mesmerism that your eyes stick out like a boiled codfish."[14]

Eddy fought back against the inroads of mind-cure, against theological attacks on Christian Science, and against dissension and defection in the ranks of the movement itself. By the mid-1890s the advance of Christian Science seemed unstoppable. Clerical attacks escalated with the advance of Christian Science but did not halt it; and mind-cure and mental science groups became the New Thought movement. From Eddy's standpoint, the tribulations and battles of the 1880s were part of a past that seemed remote from the triumphs of the present. In the introduction to her book *Miscellaneous Writings 1883–1896*, which included most of the articles she had written for the *Christian Science Journal* in the 1880s, she could look back to that period and say, "With tender tread, thought sometimes walks in memory, through the dim corridors of years, on to old battle-grounds, there sadly to survey the fields of the slain and the enemy's losses."[15]

The writing of the articles collected in *Miscellaneous Writings*, along with several longer works she composed during her Boston years, constitute another aspect of her labors during the period of her work there. By founding the *Journal* (originally named *Journal of Christian Science*) in April 1883, Eddy established a means to feed growing public interest in Christian Science, as well as to provide a forum through which she could reach Christian Scientists in the field.

Not only did Eddy edit the *Journal* in its first few years and contribute frequently to it, she also wrote other shorter books in response to problems the movement was facing. Taking up Gordon's and Cook's attacks on her teaching, she wrote "Defence of Christian Science" for the *Journal*, which was then issued as a pamphlet before she expanded it into the booklet *Christian Science: No and Yes* in 1887. That year and the next saw the publication, respectively, of the pamphlets *Rudiments and Rules of Divine Science* and *Unity of Good and Unreality of Evil*, both intended to clarify metaphysical and theological points that were becoming the subject of confusion among her followers. Some indication of the pressure under which these and her many articles for the *Journal* were written is the fact that *Unity of Good*, her most important short work of the decade, was dictated to a shivering Calvin Frye in the early morning hours during the first months of 1888.

Perhaps the greatest pressure Eddy felt during this tumultuous period arose from the necessity of coping with dissension in the ranks of the movement itself. Her correspondence from the period indicates that it was the sheer effort of holding the movement together that most weighed her down. Simmering discontent among a vocal minority of her students came to a boil in the early summer of 1888 as a result of Eddy's hands-off policy in dealing with the case of a student named Abby Corner, who had been indicted for manslaughter after being the Christian Science practitioner when her daughter gave birth to a child. Both the daughter and the child were lost. Believing that Corner had acted unwisely, and convinced that she would be acquitted (as was the case), Eddy refused to put the resources and reputation of the movement behind her. An outraged cabal of students in the association of Eddy's pupils persuaded about a third of its members to abandon the movement. "Everything was torn up in Boston," she wrote upon her returning to the city after a brief trip to Chicago, "like as if a cyclone had swept over our city—in my absence."[16]

Eddy had gone to Chicago to attend a meeting of the National Christian Scientist Association. About eight hundred Association members, along with more than three thousand members of the public, most of them probably students of Christian Science, filled Chicago's vast Central Music Hall. Though she had not intended to speak except for a few concluding remarks, Eddy was listed on the program as the main speaker for the occasion.[17]

Laura Sargent, who accompanied her, recalls having said to Eddy just before going to the platform, "God is with you," to which Eddy retorted, "I know that better than you do." Eddy then proceeded to deliver a powerful impromptu address revolving around the themes of how Christian Science has "inaugurated the irrepressible conflict" between the material senses and the reality of Spirit; that it must sustain its claims through healing; and that those who claim to practice Christian Science must reflect the spirit of unity and love. "When the speaker concluded," read one newspaper account, "the audience arose en masse and made a rush for the platform. . . . They mounted the reporters' table and vaulted to the rostrum like acrobats,"[18] then hugged and kissed Eddy beyond endurance. The hysteria was not all; there were hundreds who responded with a quiet devotion and genuine love. But that evening at a reception in her honor at Palmer House, events spun out of control. Crowds filled the stairways and corridors. Flowers were crushed, sleeves torn, jewels trampled under foot. With the level of excitement rising, Eddy was whisked away to safety.

Returning to Boston, she was met with the reverse of the wild acclaim she had encountered in Chicago. It may well have become clear to her around this time that the basic issues behind the Chicago episode and the rebellion of 1888 would not go away so long as she occupied such an indisputably central place in the day-to-day life of the movement. Though the crisis following the Corner case had been surmounted, it, too, made apparent that her presence in Boston and involvement in the day-to-day decision making for the movement would continue to make her the focal point of any conflict, the lightning rod for all dissent.

Fearing that after the defection of so many of her Boston students she could never rebuild the movement there, Eddy seriously discussed leaving for the West, meaning cities west of Boston, where she still had loyal students. Then, characteristically, she recouped and reversed course, throwing herself into a sustained effort to take hold of the situation where she was. By late 1888 she could report to a student: "Our cause has had a great propulsion from my late large classes. Over fifty members have gone into our C.S. Association since the stampede out of it." Yet nearly seven years of exacting labor on several fronts were wearing her down—at points, almost wearing her out.[19]

By 1888 she was sixty-seven years old and the weight of the responsibilities that had devolved upon her was fast becoming unsupportable. "I do not *want* to teach, I am *tired tired,* of teaching and being the slave of so many minds," she wrote in a letter less than three months before she left Boston. In one sense, Eddy was just plain tired. In 1884 she had written to two students that her many duties "make me too perplexed too mind worn often to think—so I would give up writing at a late hour would crawl into bed to toss all night and half asleep give directions on business *cares* that concern the good cause." As the decade progressed she had reason to feel increasingly drained. In March 1889, in the midst of her last full class, she confided to her student Edward A. Kimball and his wife as she sat curled up on a chair in her home on Commonwealth Avenue that "she deeply wished sometimes that she could be a little old lady in a cap with nothing much to do."[20]

Yet she found that there was much to do on a daily basis. "I shall fulfil my mission, fight the good fight, and keep the faith," she wrote in an article for the *Journal* in July 1888. But God's plan of battle, as Eddy came to discern it, was to cease to do battle in the old way: that is, by redoubling her efforts on the Boston scene. Her Boston students, she came to feel, must learn to grow on their own. As she put it in a letter written in July 1889, she had not seen any instance in which her Boston students had "walked over the spell of Hypnotism" and taken "the line of God in opposition to it" without her help, adding, "I *write this in tears.* But this shall be done, and they shall be left to their own direction until it is done, since I am convinced that they will never learn out of this blindness but by suffering."[21]

"Many times," she also wrote to another student, "I wish I could go to some place where I was not known and find the peace that I long for. How sad life seems to me I mean human life. O how cold and unconscious of others is the human heart. If I had not heaven in view the former would kill me. But I must bear and bear on to the end."[22] The end of her ability to "bear on" came ten days after writing this letter.

After teaching a class for one day on May 21, Eddy suddenly departed without explanation for Barre, Vermont, leaving an assistant to complete the class. Over the following fall and winter she proceeded to take the equally drastic step of dismantling most of the existing organizational structure of the movement. The Christian Scientist Association of Eddy's students was the first to go, disbanding upon her recommendation in September 1889. Having ceased teaching herself, she dissolved the Massachusetts Metaphysical College on October 29, reopening it as an auxiliary to her church in 1898. In December the Church of Christ, Scientist, founded in 1879, was formally disorganized, although its members continued, as a voluntary association, to hold Sunday services and Friday evening meetings as before. In May of the following year, the National Christian Scientist Association, the only national organization in the movement, adjourned for three years at her request.

Eddy did not, however, terminate all Christian Science activities on the Boston scene. The *Christian Science Journal* continued publication. She also encouraged her followers to go on organizing churches and appealed to several of the most able to prepare themselves for the pulpit. As her dismantling of the broader organizational structure of the movement proceeded apace, she admonished another student not to "say one word against my students' organization, churches and associations. . . . Remember that I approve of organizations and desire students to continue this at present." And she continued to encourage a project she and her students embarked upon in 1885: building a church edifice in Boston. Yet what seemed primary to most Christian Scientists in Boston was Eddy's own departure from the Boston scene and her termination of the organizational apparatus of the movement.[23]

Just to be sure that there could be no mistaking her intention to withdraw totally from day-to-day decision making for the movement, she issued in the September 1890 *Journal* "Seven Fixed Rules." Each began with the same peremptory statement, "I shall not be consulted verbally, or through letters," and then went on to specify the various matters about which she refused to be consulted: advertisements or material to be published in the *Journal;* family matters, disaffections, and personal relations among students; choice of pastors for churches; membership issues in churches and associations; and questions about the healing practice. As she put it, "Like a policeman who speaks politely, then orders sternly, then keeps back the crowd with a baton so must I at last."[24]

The risks of leaving Boston may have seemed high; but as she gauged the situation, the risks to the future of Christian Science would have been much higher had she stayed. Announcing the closing of the Massachusetts Metaphysical College in the *Journal,* she wrote, "The first and only College of Christian Science Mind-healing, after accomplishing the greatest work of the ages and at the pinnacle of prosperity, is closed."[25] For her, it was not a time to be on a pinnacle but rather to go back to the desert—to be in a still place spiritually and mentally where the original spiritual impulse that lay behind her work in Christian Science could be renewed.

FINDING HOME

By settling down eventually in Concord, New Hampshire, Eddy was returning home to the environs in which she had been raised. But she was also returning home in a more profound sense as well. She was returning to a rhythm of life that made the often hectic activity of her Boston years something of an aberration.

For long stretches of her life Eddy had grown accustomed to a much more interior existence. Her bouts with prolonged illness as a teenager, the near-invalidism that kept her immobilized for months at a time during her North Groton years, her three-year period of spiritual research while working out the rudiments of her teaching in the mid-1860s, and the prolonged period of work on the first edition of *Science and Health* from 1872 to 1874—all these were in differing ways periods of stillness, inwardness, of spiritual questioning and exploration. And they suited her temperament and preferences far more than the incessant activity of her Boston years.

In a 1904 letter to her student Emma Shipman, Eddy spoke of this tendency, writing, "I always, as now, kept alone and out of society and the public notice all that I could. A strange inclination to be alone with my Bible . . . has attended all my years." Lex Hixon caught something of this interior dimension of her life in speaking of her time in North Groton:

> Her physical problems, the delicacy of her system, all the unhappy things that happened to her, seem to all be converging on her to purify her, to make her experience the kind of renunciation that traditional spiritual practitioners have done—whether they have gone to the desert or gone to the monastery. . . . She was in the wilderness eating locusts and wild honey with John the Baptist right there in the middle of New England. And not because of her own personal choice or some role she thought she was playing, but simply because life—the discipline of the divine call—imposed this on her.

The desire for this kind of renunciation, for being in the wilderness where the discipline of the divine call could be fulfilled, became part of Eddy's nature, something she deeply craved. She wanted and deeply needed time for spiritual communion and renewal that her work in Boston made impossible to attain on a continuing basis. "Beholding the infinite tasks of truth," she wrote in *Science and Health*, "we pause,—wait on God."[26]

For her, the waiting, in the largest sense of the term, was all. It required a turning inward, prolonged times of silence, a withdrawal from overt activity. It required reentry into the inwardness that has always been a part of the religious life. Eddy apparently felt an acute need to regain and strengthen the spiritual equilibrium and centeredness that alone could equip her to accomplish her work. The expression of this yearning had punctuated her correspondence throughout her later Boston years. "I want quiet and a Christian life alone with God," she wrote to her son George Glover in late 1887. Within months of leaving Boston she found a measure of the peace she wanted. This peace meant more to her than a mere surcease of the daily demands she had faced in Boston. It meant entering more deeply into what she saw as the truth of her own discovery. "I have learned more of Christian Science the last year than I shall ever be able to communicate," she told one student, explaining, too, that her seclusion would be kept up "for an indefinite time."[27]

Yet Eddy needed more than time. A *place* to live and work and pray became almost as important—a true home where the peace she craved was possible. Finding the home and the peace was difficult. The tranquility she sought in her brief stay in Barre was blasted by summer musicians performing on the green close to her house. Her next step was to rent a house on North State Street in Concord, although that did not bring her the sense of home she sought. She considered moving to England or the suburbs of Philadelphia, but was persuaded by her student Ira Knapp in the spring of 1891 to buy a house in Roslindale, a suburb of Boston.

Moving there in May, she confided to her student Laura Sargent, "I have no desire to live in the place of beauty that the Roslindale home is—a beauty *unavailing* in *Christian Science*," emphasizing, "There is no retirement, no solitude, no *quiet* in it." Within a month she was back on North State Street in "dear, quaint old Concord." To Knapp, who had purchased the house in Roslindale on her behalf, she wrote, "I want,— *stillness* and *nature* and *God*. Oh I get so near Him when I can be *alone* that I dread to be interrupted. But I am all the time, and of late have done my writing in the *night time;* but when you read my book [*Retrospection and Introspection*, published some two months later] you will think it was written in the light."[28]

Within a few months the right place appeared: a farmhouse just out of town that commanded a lovely view of the hills of her native Bow. She bought it quickly, began renovations, and moved there in June 1892. Eddy called her new home Pleasant View, and it proved to be a home in the full sense of the word, an almost ideal context for entering into the consciousness she craved. Eddy's domestic instincts had always been strong, and she had tried to make wherever she lived into as much of a home as circumstance would allow. The home she shared with Daniel Patterson at North Groton in the 1850s, though small, was maintained with pristine neatness. During most of the decade after her healing in 1866, she was virtually homeless, moving, according to her later estimate, at least a dozen times in nine years. Thereafter she made as much a home as she could of the houses she occupied in Lynn and Boston. But not until she moved into Pleasant View did her ideal of home become something of a reality.

When she first saw it, the farmhouse that became Eddy's Pleasant View home was virtually dilapidated. What attracted her attention was the land upon which it stood, which she spoke of in a letter as "a cow pasture with a captivating view."[29] The view was especially good from the farmhouse, since it stood on a knoll overlooking fields and meadows that led south for several miles to the hills of Bow. To take advantage of the view, Eddy added a tower room with five large bay windows and a balcony at the southeast corner, along with a wide veranda at the back of the house. Once having moved to Pleasant View in June, she made sure that the grounds were as pleasant as the prospect from the tower room into which her work area was nestled. She was, after all, a farm girl, and quickly made Pleasant View into a model working farm as well as a comfortable dwelling. She had boggy areas drained and planted with rye, wheat, vegetables, and fruits. Eddy took enormous delight in getting Pleasant View into just the right shape. In August, two months after moving in, she wrote to a student, "Oh! The singing birds and glorious view from my 'sweet home' is so lovely I cannot be sufficiently thankful for it. 'Peace be within thy walls.'"[30]

Pleasant View became many things. For the nearly sixteen years Eddy lived there, it was the center of operations for the Christian Science movement. It was a home for Eddy and her small staff, consisting of about a half dozen people by the end of the century. It was a farm where fruits and vegetables were raised. It was a large, landscaped garden with orchards, shrubs, vines, flowers, and a pond. More than anything else, Pleasant View became the refuge she sought where she could meditate and pray in the way her soul required. Without the protection of her own inner life, there was no way to cultivate the godliness that she required—not as a luxury, but as an increasing necessity. Nothing less, as she saw it, than an intense and consistent prayer-life was adequate to sustain her in fulfilling the exacting daily demands of guiding a movement that was growing faster than anyone, probably including her, had expected.

Rear view of the east side of Pleasant View, 1901.
Courtesy of The Mary Baker Eddy Collection.

Should Eddy, then, be understood within the framework of the great Christian contemplative tradition, in which the highest good is the direct experience of the presence of God? To some degree, she must be so understood. To the meeting of the association of the Massachusetts Metaphysical College, she wrote in 1891, around the time she moved to Pleasant View:

> The eternal and infinite, already brought to your earnest consideration, so grow upon my vision that I cannot feel justified in turning aside for

one hour from the contemplation of them and of the faith unfeigned. When the verities of being seem to you as to me,—as they must sometime,—you will understand the necessity for my seclusion and its fulfillment of divine order. "Wherefore come out from among them, and be separate, saith the Lord."

All our thoughts should be given to the absolute demonstration of Christian Science.[31]

The way Eddy arranged her daily schedule at Pleasant view shows that she was deeply committed to living the life these words imply. At the same time, the demands of the day pressed hard upon her, and like some other figures she struggled to balance times of contemplation with requirements for action. What a biographer of Bernard of Clairvaux said about him applies to some degree to her: "In the concrete situations instanced in his letters, he showed that what he taught elsewhere in theoretical manner was truly feasible." At the same time, prayer and obedience for her could not be wholly separated. On the contrary, while moments of communion with God were fulfilling in themselves, they were the only way in which effective leadership could be impelled and sustained. Thus her words in the chapter "Prayer" in *Science and Health:* "If spiritual sense always guided men, there would grow out of ecstatic moments a higher experience and a better life, with more devout self-abnegation."[32]

THE "MYSTERY OF GODLINESS"

When Eddy worked out the penultimate major revision of *Science and Health,* published in 1902, one of her major changes was moving the chapter "Prayer," which had been located in the middle of the book, to the beginning. She begins this chapter with the words "The prayer that reforms the sinner and heals the sick is an absolute faith that all things are possible to God,—a spiritual understanding of Him, an unselfed love. Regardless of what another may say or think on this subject, I speak from experience."[33]

To read the chapter in the light of these words is to realize that she is indeed speaking from experience—from her own immersion in the life of prayer. While Eddy often quoted the biblical phrase "the mystery of godliness," she did not characterize the life of prayer as mysterious nor speak positively of mysticism. The authors of a fair-minded and perceptive account of Christian Science in the Roman Catholic magazine *Sign* noted in 1980 that one point of contact between Christian Science and

Roman Catholicism is "the perspective on mysticism which Science provides us. The word itself too often connotes a nebulous subjectivity (and so Mrs. Eddy rejected the word lest it be misleading); but Christian Science offers a mysticism devoid of mistiness. Scientists build their spiritual life on a foundation of faith as the derivative of experience." When toward the end of the chapter "Prayer" in *Science and Health* Eddy writes, "Christians rejoice in secret beauty and bounty, hidden from the world, but known to God," one senses that her words were rooted in her life.[34]

Prayer as she described it in this chapter and practiced it in her own daily devotions includes elements of trust, longing, stillness, self-surrender, acknowledgment, gratitude, petition, and praise. It is more likely to be genuine, she believed, when it is silent rather than audible. She saw prayer as making real in present life the basic, unshakeable fact of each individual's spiritual unity with God. Prayer for her was the consciousness of this unity. Jesus' humble prayers, she wrote, "were deep and conscientious protests of Truth,—of man's likeness to God and of man's unity with Truth and Love." As she put it elsewhere, "Prayer is the utilization of the love wherewith He loves us."[35]

The view with which she quarreled was any concept of God that conformed to the pattern of human personality, dispensing love at one moment and pain the next, listening to some prayers and not others, a God changeable in his moods and arbitrary in his deeds—hence her use, from her earliest teaching manuscripts onward, of the synonym "divine Principle" for God. "We must learn," she wrote, "that God is infinitely more than a person, or finite form, can contain; that God is a divine *Whole,* and *All,* an all-pervading intelligence and Love, a divine, infinite Principle; and that Christianity is a divine Science."[36]

Here, as in dozens of other places in her writings, she linked Principle and Love, in effect precluding the misunderstanding she pointed to when she wrote, "When the term divine Principle is used to signify Deity it may seem distant or cold, until better apprehended." If Principle were rightly apprehended as inseparable from Love itself, then it is possible, in her words, to "open our affections to the Principle that moves all in harmony,—from the falling of a sparrow to the rolling of a world."[37]

As these words indicate, Eddy found it alien and incommensurate with her own experience to conceive of God as a blind, impersonal force. Nor would she accept any rigid, rational alternatives that defined God in exclusively personal or impersonal terms. Like others in the Christian tradition from Thomas Aquinas to Jonathan Edwards to Paul Tillich, she spoke of God ontologically as Being itself—as the divine Principle and ordering cause of all existence. To amplify the nature of God as she understood it, she also drew from the Bible the words "Spirit," "Truth," "Life," and "Love" as deific synonyms. She further used the term "Soul" for God to indicate that he is the source of all individuality, bestowing qualities of warmth, joy, beauty, and expressiveness. She used the term "Mind" to express the basic metaphysical point in Christian Science that God is the one absolute Ego, not only the source but the substance of all true consciousness and intelligence.

These synonyms, however, were not intended by Eddy to confine God within human definitions. Rather, they were the best terms she found to help break open humanity's understanding of God so as to express what she called his "nature, essence, and wholeness."

They have the further purpose of defining the reason why, in her teaching, it is impossible to separate the being of God from that of the men and women he creates. If God is literally the Life, Soul, and Mind of all his children, then there can be no actual separation between them and their divine source. In her words, "As a drop of water is one with the ocean, a ray of light one with the sun, even so God and man, Father and son, are one in being."[38]

At the same time, she strongly rejected any religious teaching that failed to make a clear distinction between God and his children. She insisted that in their true and authentic being, all the sons and daughters of God are inseparable from him, but that God remains God and man, in the generic sense, remains man. Hence the possibility—for her the absolute necessity—of communion with God, not in the sense of establishing a relationship between two disjunct entities, but in the sense of becoming conscious of the spiritual unity that constitutes the true relation between God and each of his daughters and sons.

For her, this communion must mean more than a merely inward state. The oneness with God that worshipers felt in exalted moments required practical obedience to God. In her words, "The scientific unity which exists between God and man must be wrought out in life-practice, and God's will must be universally done." And the practical doing of God's will, expressed in such qualities as "humanity, honesty, affection, compassion, hope, faith, meekness, temperance," embraced Eddy's concept of the moral dimension of human experience.[39]

Eddy saw the moral in this sense as deeply necessary to the development of the full spirituality that eventually marks the appearing of man in God's image and likeness. Although she used the term "morality" only three times in her published writings, she used the term "moral" nearly two hundred times. She spoke, for example, of moral victory, moral courage, moral freedom, moral idiocy, moral obligation, moral might, moral strength, and moral death.

As this suggests, the truly moral for her is far more inclusive than the conventional sense of morality associated, for example, with sexual behavior or the consumption of alcoholic beverages. Eddy assumed that rigorously moral behavior in the more conventional sense was incumbent on all serious students of Christian Science, spoke out strongly against marital infidelity, and saw the use of alcohol and tobacco as a resort to artificial stimuli inconsistent with the practice of her teaching. Yet she was inclined to be more lenient with those who temporarily indulged in the more ordinary sins of the flesh than with those who exhibited hypocrisy, deceit, and personal ambition—in other words, the self-seeking that represents the conscious dishonoring of God's will in daily life.

When God's will *is* done, the individual knows God directly; for he or she learns to have one Mind, the Mind that is God, and becomes literally the obedient servant of divine Principle. Individuals enter into the spirit of Christliness and have a measure of the experience that Jesus through his example opened up to all humanity. They begin to fulfill Paul's injunction, to which Eddy refers a half-dozen times in her writings, "Let this mind be in you, which was also in Christ Jesus." They begin to know God as the "infinite Person" to whom one must respond with awe and wonder and love. "That God is either inconceivable, or is manlike," as she put it in a message to her church in 1901, "is not my sense of Him. In divine Science He is 'altogether lovely,' and consistently conceivable as the personality of infinite Love, infinite Spirit, than whom there is none other."[40]

On many occasions, Eddy expressed concern that the genuine spiritual experience not be submerged in metaphysical abstractions. In the 1970s, some young Christian Scientists visited Lora C. Rathvon, the elderly widow of William Rathvon, who had been quite close to Eddy during her last years. Drawing on his recollections, she responded to the question of what struck her most about Eddy. It was, she said, that Spirit was so very *real* to her. Often people talked about Spirit, Lora Rathvon said, "but to Mrs. Eddy, Spirit was as real as this table." Then she put her hand down forcefully on the table next to her as she said this, "startling us all."[41]

The evidences of Eddy's own prayer life show her responsiveness to what she saw as the reality of Spirit, or what she called "the personality of infinite Love." In 1883 she wrote to a student:

> I have a far off echo that is sweeter than vintage bells to the villagers on the Rhine. It is the Love that never fails me, the sweet, strong glorious friendship with my own Soul, with my individual God that is so infinite in Truth and Love. I cannot tell what His personality is, but this I do

know, that when all that is human fails this divine friendship goes on, and I and He come nearer. To this heart of hearts every day I flee and rest my weary head on His tender bosom. Should I offend in one single point this dear rest would take wings; then I am jealous of my own love to see that it be loyal—spiritual, pure, divine.[42]

For Eddy, having this numinous spiritual consciousness required entering into what the Ninety-first Psalm, a text she loved and often quoted, called "the secret place of the most High." This, she once said, is "the inner sanctuary of divine Science, in which mortals do not enter without a struggle or sharp experience, and in which they put off the human for the divine." Her own sharp experiences had, she believed, made it imperative that she enter into this sanctuary on a daily basis, and so doing took spiritual discipline. As she put it later in a letter to two friends, "God speaks clearest to me when I am *alone*." To another correspondent she wrote in 1892 after settling down at Pleasant View, "The *closet* is my home, and God has now given me all of earth that I desire."[43]

The "closet," as she uses the term, was adapted from Jesus' words on prayer: "When thou prayest, enter into thy closet, and, when thou hast shut thy door, pray to thy Father which is in secret; and thy Father, which seeth in secret, shall reward thee openly." Quoting this saying in the opening chapter on "Prayer" in *Science and Health*, she added,

> The closet typifies the sanctuary of Spirit, the door of which shuts out sinful sense but lets in Truth, Life, and Love. Closed to error, it is open to Truth, and *vice versa*. The Father in secret is unseen to the physical senses, but He knows all things and rewards according to motives, not according to speech. To enter into the heart of prayer, the door of the erring senses must be closed. Lips must be mute and materialism silent, that man may have audience with Spirit, the divine Principle, Love, which destroys all error.[44]

Eddy's own prayer life, as well as many admonitions in her writings, tells us much about the priority she placed on making time for communion with God. Doing this, as she understood it, requires sustained periods of quietness in which the insistent voice of the world and its materialism is silenced and those who would commune with God wait for his voice to be heard. A household member at Pleasant View recalled that Eddy spent little time in studying, as such, "but very much time praying." "He advances most in divine Science," she wrote, "who meditates most on infinite spiritual substance and intelligence." She saw this kind of meditation and disciplined spiritual listening as a deep necessity for the genuine practice of Christian Science and would accept no excuse for her students' failure to make room for it in their lives. As she put it in a 1901 letter, "God has shown me that the students need spiritualizing more than they need Metaphysics."[45]

In an 1885 *Journal* article she commented on Jesus' parable of the foolish virgins who failed to provide oil for their lamps: "We learn of this parable, that neither the cares of this world, nor the so-called pleasures or pains of material sense, are adequate to plead for the neglect of spiritual light; that must be tended, to keep aglow the flame of devotion whereby to enter into the joy of divine Science in demonstration." In a private letter to a student four years later, she was still making the same point:

> Our Father is as never before coming nearer the human race in ways mysterious and requirements spiritual. Darling, put daily, oil in your lamp, put into your heart and understanding the power and spirit of what God has spoken to you in Science and Health, and what I, his poor servant have taught you. Be ready for the midnight call, for the hour of darkness in which He comes to us who are faithful with illumination and revelation.[46]

During most of her Pleasant View years from 1892 until just after the Next Friends Suit Eddy followed a routine that made possible the spiritual centeredness she required of herself and those in her household as well. Her daily schedule was usually marked by few or any variations, with Sundays no different from any other day. Rising early, she dressed herself, ate a small breakfast, then reserved the rest of the morning hours until nine for prayer and meditation. Often during this period she would call in members of the household to share with them the fruits of her study. The remainder of the morning was generally devoted to her correspondence or writing projects.

Her daily drive around the environs of Concord just after lunch, promptly served at noon, typically lasted for an hour, sometimes longer. That activity was usually a welcome recreational break, although it could also become a burden when, in her last years, Eddy felt obliged to take her ride just to prove that she was up to it. Probably more often it was a time for reflection and prayer. As she put it late in her life, "I have uttered some of my best prayers in a carriage." In 1893, Calvin Frye recorded in his diary that as Eddy was driving out in her carriage at a time when she apparently felt quite ill he heard her pray, "God, give me holiness." Instantly, Frye wrote, "a voice which seemed outside of herself said 'and holiness is health!' At that moment *all her pains ceased.*"[47]

Typically, upon returning from her drive, Eddy rested for a while, then continued her writing and met with church officials and other visitors. After a meal served sharply at six, there was often some interaction with household members, letter writing, or work on messages

Mary Baker Eddy returning to Pleasant View, 1895, Calvin Frye on the box.
Courtesy of The Mary Baker Eddy Collection.

and articles. Then regularly, whatever the weather, Eddy spent from one to two hours on the veranda outside her study in order, as she put it, to "talk with God." Once she sent a note to Gilbert Carpenter, then serving as her secretary, requesting that he not speak to her unless it was necessary during this time, explaining, "I want to be *apart* then. You know I love to see you always but the swing chair hours are mine to be alone with God. You dear one will understand me." During her last visit to Pleasant View, Eddy's student Henrietta Chanfrau came to understand something about her private devotions. Coming to the door of the porch, she found Eddy praying on her knees and saying aloud over and over, "Lord, dear Lord, keep my students straight!"[48]

In *Science and Health* she wrote, "The Soul-inspired patriarchs heard the voice of Truth, and talked with God as consciously as man talks with man." When a student in 1887 commented in a letter that the earliest biblical figures lacked an understanding of "the facts of Being," Eddy responded that this was so, but that "their *faith* was more lucid and stronger in God as a personal friend and savior than that of the 19th century." It did not seem mystical or inexplicable to her that this conscious communion with God should be a part of her own prayer life and that of others. "She walked and talked with God," wrote her student

Thomas W. Hatten, "as veritably as did the man Jesus and the Prophets of old, and she indicated the ability and great need of students of Christian Science learning to do likewise."[49]

Eddy often spoke in an unselfconscious way of her own communion with God. To two followers in New York she wrote in 1896, "Our God seems so near to me this morning and is critically and strictly defining the hour the Way and how to walk in it."[50] To all her students she commended making sufficient time, whatever the cost, to attain that same sense of nearness to God. Christian Science, she taught, shows the way for all to have this experience, so that it is not just as the province of a few saintly souls. Rather, it came naturally to those who accepted what she saw as the scientific fact that each man and woman, in his or her authentic being, was a child of God and therefore has a direct relation to him, a relation that must be entered into and lived.

She acknowledged that to the human mentality, conditioned by the patterns of ordinary daily living, doing this may seem at first a difficult discipline. "The harder it is to pray," she once said, "the harder we have to pray." But once the naturalness and necessity of disciplined prayer is grasped, it becomes a discipline one willingly accepted—until such point as it becomes something one grows to love. Thus when Judge Septimus J. Hanna, almost overcome by his workload as reader in the Mother Church and editor of the *Journal,* asked her for leave to take a vacation, she advised him to do what she did, which meant barring his doors to all visitors and taking definite time for communion with God. At the time, Hanna lived in a residence on Commonwealth Avenue in Boston that Eddy owned and had herself occupied, which contained a small observatory in an upper floor. She counseled him:

> Go into your secret "upper chamber" (observatory) shut out observation and the world since the kingdom of good cometh not thereby—and pray. No better possible place hath earth for prayer than that. But to reap the reward take up your cross overcome the fear of man that bringeth a snare. Tell your wife and her servants never to disturb you at those hours of prayer fix them at four hours each day for reading prayer and meditation *alone* with God. Let your rule for this have no more exception than if you were on an island in the sea. Be strong and *firm* on this basis till you are ready to feel "I have had my vacation I am ready for harder work."[51]

In Eddy's view, taking such "intervals" for study and prayer was more than a luxury. It was a necessity, especially for Christian Scientists in positions that exposed them to criticism and attack. Pamelia J. Leonard of Brooklyn, to take one example, had been cited in the *World*'s 1906 articles on Eddy as having taken her place on carriage rides so as to deceive the press into believing that Eddy, whom the articles assumed was desperately ill, was well enough for these excursions. Hermann Hering, who knew Leonard well, recounts that at one point, Eddy stopped by her room at Pleasant View to inquire how much time she spent in praying for herself. Leonard said that as a busy practitioner and teacher, she was too busy to do so. Eddy replied that the more work Leonard did for herself, the less work she would need to do for her patients, telling an astonished Leonard that she must devote three hours a day to this work. Leonard demurred, saying that she could not take the time for it. Shortly after the conclusion of the Next Friends Suit, Leonard, who had suffered from intermittent illness, returned home and died. Her son related to another worker that "something seemed to come over" her and that she made no resistance to the thought of death but seemed "determined to go."[52]

During his visits at Pleasant View, James F. Gilman, an itinerant artist who worked with Eddy in 1893 as illustrator of her poem *Christ and Christmas*, had plentiful opportunity to observe how assiduously Eddy guarded her own times for study and prayer. Leaving him to paint in an upstairs room that had been provided for his use, she told him he could knock on her door if he needed her up until 11 A.M., saying: "I will not be knocked at by anybody after that until lunch time." As Gilman rightly judged, this time was sacred to her. "I had a glorious season with God," she wrote to him of one of her prayer hours. She still dreaded to be interrupted, and the interruption could come in any form. As she once put it in a note to Gilman, "Cannot see you before next week, a dress maker keeps me from heaven this week." On one occasion when Gilman's own work became the source of the interruption, he found her heading to the boathouse by the pond at Pleasant View. "You have driven me away from my devotions," she said somewhat reproachfully, "and I must go where I can be alone." The next month on another visit, as he approached the boathouse to ask her a question, he heard her in an expressive soprano singing a familiar hymn.[53]

When Eddy retreated to the boathouse by the pond to escape Gilman, she was trying to enter into what she had called on a number of occasions "the mystery of godliness." It is the "ever-present Christ," she wrote, that acquaints "sensual mortals with the mystery of godliness,— unchanging, unquenchable Love." Godliness, she said in *Science and Health,* always presents a mystery to the ungodly, hence the belief that the direct experience of God's presence was mystical in the sense of being mysterious. But to her it was neither. It was, in fact, natural to one who accepts the primacy of goodness and who is convinced, as she was, that through spiritual sense we can feel and know God's presence

with absolute experiential certainty. "This is the mystery of godliness—
that God, good, is never absent, and there is none beside good."[54]

For Eddy, entering into the mystery of godliness marked the necessary deepening of her own spirituality—her assimilation of what she
had discovered. Thus in a note probably written in 1894 she said:

> I first gave to the world the Truth, Life, and Love, that was revealed to
> me. I now give to the world the Truth, Life, and Love, that I am experi-
> encing. I did not understand in the first instance, but could tell what was
> revealed. I do understand in the second instance, and can testify from
> experience. What I did in healing at first was a manifestation of Divine
> power not understood. What I now do in healing is the manifestation of
> grace and spiritual understanding.[55]

Amid the growing demands on her time from the early 1890s to
the end of her life, she continued to yearn for even more time for
prayer and solitude than circumstances made possible. "God is so
good," she wrote in a letter to her British student Marjorie Colles, that
"all eternity is none too long to learn His goodness. And time is given
only to prepare us for this final *allness* of good." In 1898, in another letter she again expressed her yearning "for a life *wholly His* wherein
nothing material troubles us and Love Divine feeds clothes and sustains us. Shall I . . . ever here perfect this life of my seeking?"[56]

Given the demands on her, the answer to this question was almost
certainly no. Yet the life Eddy made for herself at Pleasant View and
later at Chestnut Hill made it possible for her to have this life in sufficient measure to sustain her work on behalf of the movement she led.

In Her Authentic Voice

Eddy believed that everyone, not just a few mystics and saints, has
an unimaginably rich potential relation to God that can be entered into
amidst everyday life. In addition to committing herself to living by this
conviction, she felt the need to impart it to others.

In her short book *No and Yes,* Eddy spoke of both the Boston church
and the Massachusetts Metaphysical College as the "outgrowth" of her
own experience. Explaining the purpose behind both these institutions, she wrote of herself, "After a lifetime of orthodoxy on the platform of doctrines, rites, and ceremonies, it became a sacred duty for
her to impart to others this new-old knowledge of God."[57] But after
leaving Boston, she turned again to the primary and more permanent
means through which she sought to impart what had grown out of her
own religious experience.

In her final year in Boston, she had begun to give attention to a thorough, and as she then thought, definitive revision of *Science and Health*, which was eventually published in early 1891 as the fiftieth edition of the book and which proved to be the most pivotal of the seven major revisions she undertook. (The book passed through more than four hundred printings or editions—so many that in 1906 they were no longer numbered. But the major revisions involved such extensive changes and resettings as to require new copyrights.) Indeed, she indicated that the main reason she retired from the Boston scene was to devote "the next two years of her life" to completing work on this project.[58]

If, as she later put it, she spoke from experience in writing of her understanding of God, it was only natural that the book would reflect the deepening of this experience during the years that intervened between the last major revision of *Science and Health* published in 1886 and her departure from Boston in 1889. She had taught hundreds of students, defended Christian Science against the onslaught of the clergy, and devoted passionate energies to withstanding the erosion of the movement through defections to mind-cure. She had weathered the highs and lows of her appearance in Chicago and the 1888 schism, and had seen the movement develop beyond the point that it could be written off as a temporary "Boston craze." During this time she had also written extensively, producing not only a continuing stream of articles for the *Journal* but three short books, eventually titled *No and Yes, Rudimental Divine Science,* and *Unity of Good.*

It was, therefore, natural that she would want to pour what she had learned from meeting the demands of this intense and crucial period into a revision of her major work. As she put it in a letter to a grateful reader the year the new edition was published, "My own growth and experience gave me this assurance that I could transfer some of its hallowed influences by showing more *minutely* the way of Life and Love." But there was an additional impetus to her efforts to bring *Science and Health* into more definitive form. She felt the need to do so was urgent since, as she indicated in a series of letters, her time left on earth might be short. In 1889 Eddy was sixty-eight years old. During her work on the revision she confessed to one student, "I do desire to depart. At times I feel heavenly-homesick!" She gave several indications of believing that she was finishing her life's work. As she wrote to a student in August 1890, "I want to remain with you on earth long enough to see my revised edition of Science & Health published, I need say no more."[59]

She appeared to want every last thing about the book exactly right; and the effort, combined with other demands, had taken its toll on her physically. She lost a great deal of weight, over fifty pounds, and had difficulty sleeping. Since she ceased tinting her hair after leaving Boston, it had turned almost white. Clara Shannon, a British student who lived intermittently in Eddy's household, visited her as the revision was being completed and recalled being "much moved, as I could see by her face what deep waters she was passing through." Noting her reaction, Eddy said, "The cup is bitter, bitter! But the Father makes it sweet!"[60]

Part of the sweetness, no doubt, was the satisfaction of seeing the fiftieth edition of *Science and Health* through to publication. As she put it to a friend upon completing the work: "My *last words for you all in the Book* Science and Health, were written yesterday and sent off." Shortly after the book was published, she wrote to another correspondent of the two years of "hard work" she had put into it, adding that while the older editions "did their work and did it well," the new edition "takes into its office that of *Teacher* as well as healer. . . . I have done for this edition what the lapidary does,—brought out the gems and placed them well burnished, *in sight.*"[61]

The fiftieth edition, though a landmark, did not contain Eddy's last word for readers of *Science and Health,* since she lived to put the book through two further major revisions. But in this edition she brought the work very close to its final form. For long stretches, the book reads very much like her last major revision of the book published in 1907. Her relative satisfaction with what she had achieved in the fiftieth edition is shown in the fact that while no more than five years separated the previous four revisions—issued in 1878, 1881, 1883, and 1886— she would not put the book through another major revision until 1902, eleven years after the fiftieth edition.

For anyone familiar with today's authorized version of *Science and Health,* the fiftieth is the first edition of the work that has the familiar feel of Eddy in full stride. In some respects, the fiftieth follows the pattern of previous editions in diminishing personal references and opinions, with fewer "I's" and "we's." The language is more universal, with the focus on what Eddy believed to be permanently true. Yet what emerged as her most authentic and characteristic voice is more in evidence than ever before.

If the fiftieth edition had been completed as it was begun, this would not have been so. In 1888 when first giving thought to a major revision, she enlisted the help of Joshua Bailey, then editor of the *Journal,* to make the arrangement of material in *Science and Health* more orderly. She asked him to go through the book and bring scattered passages on particular topics together. Though he approached his task with great devotion, the resulting scissors-and-paste operation turned out to be a botch that undermined the individual quality of Eddy's writing style.

Her writing had always been more musical than linear-rational in its construction. The chapters of *Science and Health,* the blocks of material within them, even individual paragraphs, partake of an essential musical and thematic construction. At every level of the book, she repeats, develops, links, and amplifies basic motifs, so that the reader assimilates her meaning without the need for a point-by-point rational analysis. Particular statements remain memorable, although their ideas seldom lie down in a schematic way. This very fact, in the eyes of critics, made her writing appear disjointed, rambling, incoherent, and contradictory. Mark Twain, displaying his own vacillation about Eddy's prose, characterized it once as "incoherent beyond imagination," commenting acerbically that she "is not herself when she is not disconnected."[62]

In April 1890 she asked the Reverend James Henry Wiggin for his opinion of the rearrangement that Bailey had made of the text in *Science and Health,* just when the revision was nearly ready for the printers. Wiggin, a former Unitarian minister, was witty, erudite, somewhat pompous, highly intelligent, and often a perceptive literary critic. Although he could speak of Eddy in supercilious tones to others, including Mark Twain, he was uniformly courteous and straightforward in communicating with her. She had profited greatly from his editorial labors on the sixteenth edition of *Science and Health* published in 1886, and he served capably as editor of the *Journal* from 1886 to 1889. When she sought his counsel on Bailey's work, he replied frankly, "I should suppose a cyclone had struck the leaves, and knocked them into unwonted corners," saying that the book had actually deteriorated.[63]

Eddy, who may well have sensed the same thing herself, promptly agreed. As a result, the process of revision began all over again, with Wiggin assuming a crucial editorial role. His continued editing aided in straightening out her sometimes tortured syntax, smoothing out her sentences, and making the text more coherent. She had instructed him never to change her meaning but to use his own good judgment to give the book "consistency, *beauty, strength,* and *honesty*" by helping to shape her ideas "and greatly improve their manner of expressing them."[64] Thus admonished, Wiggin contributed significantly to the coherence of the new edition of *Science and Health.* But the voice of the book was definitely Eddy's own. The material she added, amounting to about forty pages of text, has a remarkable range of expressiveness, reflecting the intensity of her own spiritual life over the five years since the previous full-scale revision.

The six-page conclusion added to the chapter, "The Apocalypse," attains a visionary power unsurpassed in any of Eddy's other prose. The new material was apparently written at one sitting as Eddy, preparing to go out, became absorbed in her writing and stayed in her chair, oblivious to all else, for the better portion of the day. One passage conveys something of the strong cadences and biblical resonance of these pages. Interpreting the text from Revelation 21, wherein John saw "a new heaven and a new earth," she wrote:

> . . . St. John's corporeal sense of the heavens and earth had vanished, and in place of this false sense was the spiritual sense, the subjective state by which he could see the new heaven and new earth, which involve the spiritual idea and consciousness of reality. This is Scriptural authority for concluding that such a recognition of being is, and has been, possible to men in this present state of existence,—that we can become conscious, here and now, of a cessation of death, sorrow, and pain. This is indeed a foretaste of absolute Christian Science. Take heart, dear sufferer, for this reality of being will surely appear sometime and in some way. There will be no more pain, and all tears will be wiped away. When you read this, remember Jesus' words, "The kingdom of God is within you." This spiritual consciousness is therefore a present possibility.[65]

Purely as writing, nothing in *Science and Health* or in Eddy's other works sustains the pervasive poetic dimension of the chapter "Atonement and Eucharist," now enlarged from sixteen to nearly forty pages. Eddy told a student that she read this chapter, which at the time also included the shorter chapter on prayer that now precedes it, more frequently than any other in the book. More than any other chapter in *Science and Health*, it has a moving, devotional quality, and it remained largely unchanged through subsequent editions of the work. The following paragraphs are characteristic:

> The efficacy of Jesus' spiritual offering is infinitely greater than can be expressed by our sense of human blood. The material blood of Jesus was no more efficacious to cleanse from sin when it was shed upon "the accursed tree," than when it was flowing in his veins as he went daily about his Father's business. His true flesh and blood were his Life; and they truly eat his flesh and drink his blood, who partake of that divine Life.
>
> While we adore Jesus, and the heart overflows with gratitude for what he did for mortals,—treading alone his loving pathway up to the throne of glory, in speechless agony exploring the way for us,—yet Jesus spares us not one individual experience, if we follow his commands faithfully; and all have the cup of sorrowful effort to drink in proportion to their demonstration of his love, till all are redeemed through divine Love.[66]

These and other passages show Eddy feeding into the Christian Science textbook some of the hard-won spiritual growth she had gained since the previous revision five years before. Language as Eddy understood it, whether in teaching or writing, was intimately related to action. If it was authentic, it reflected the life behind it and could reach the heart. After beginning work on the fiftieth edition, she wrote to a student, "I have had little else this year but loss & cross according to the senses."[67] This sense of "loss & cross," of the diminishment of human expectations and ego, was reflected in her retelling of a story from Luke's Gospel in a six-page introduction to a newly titled chapter, "Christian Science Practice."

The story relates how Jesus, while dining at the home of Simon the Pharisee, was approached by a prostitute who bathed his feet with her tears and wiped them with her hair. Explaining his compassion toward the woman to the incredulous Pharisee, Jesus pointed out that it was the love within her heart that won her forgiveness. "Do Christian Scientists seek Truth as Simon sought the Saviour, through material conservatism and for personal homage?" she asked.

> If Christian Scientists are like Simon, then it must be said of them also that they *love* little. On the other hand, do they show their regard for Truth, or Christ, by their genuine repentance, by their broken hearts, expressed by meekness and human affection, as did this woman? If so, then it may be said of them, as Jesus said of the unwelcome visitor, that they indeed love much, because much is forgiven them.[68]

This love, born of brokenness and humility, she saw as the indispensable element in the work of healing.

The chapter on "Christian Science Practice" in the fiftieth edition was followed by a new chapter, "Teaching Christian Science." Though it incorporated some material from earlier editions, the fact that Eddy for the first time devoted a whole chapter exclusively to teaching reflected her distress over what seemed to her the checkered, and in some cases disastrous, state of teaching in the movement. Her concern about this had been a primary reason for making a definitive revision a priority. Before it was published, she wrote a brief notice for the *Journal* that said: "Too much, instead of too little, Christian Science teaching is being done at this period for the Spirit is *lacking*. The world must gradually grow up to this great fact of Being; and the study of Science and Health with personal experience and individual growth, is better adapted to this end."[69]

She saw the study of the new edition as having the potential to enhance this growth, becoming teacher as well as textbook to its readers and including, in the process, instruction to teachers about how to teach. If Eddy spoke, as she said, from her own experience in writing *Science and Health*, she expected that teachers would speak from their own experience in teaching from it.

The burden of the chapter "Teaching Christian Science" is that effective teaching must be the authentic outgrowth of the life of the teacher. The chapter emphasizes the need for ethics on the part of the teacher, but extends the term beyond the conventional sense of moral conduct. It connotes more the integrity that allows teachers to speak from their hearts and out of their lives, rather than simply to convey language they have assimilated. "Right is radical," she stated. "The teacher must know the truth himself. He must live it and love it, or he cannot impart it to others."[70]

VALEDICTION AND RENEWAL

As a kind of coda to the fiftieth edition, Eddy enlarged a brief history of Christian Science she had first published in 1885 into an account of her own life. The title of the book, *Retrospection and Introspection*, reflects the Puritan tradition of relentless self-scrutiny. But the book itself is more than autobiographical. As the title indicates, it looks backward as well as inward. Perhaps even more importantly, it looks *forward* to what she believed Christian Scientists must do to carry on her lifework.

The first sections of the book are a kind of obligatory recital of Eddy's family background and early religious life. While this background was more than respectable—she was the youngest daughter in a vigorous and remarkable New England household—it was not particularly distinguished. As the author of *Science and Health*, Eddy could write that "wealth, fame, and social organizations . . . weigh not one jot in the balance of God."[71] Yet she had a very human tendency to build up her past so as to make it seem more consonant with what one would expect of a major religious leader.

This tendency was responsible for Eddy's flirtation over several years beginning in 1895 with the possibility of tracing her own ancestry to that of King David. Absurd as this proposition sounds now, it was in accord with the then widely accepted "Anglo-Israel" theory propounded by a respectable Yale professor to the effect that the tribes that currently made up the population of Great Britain were descendants of the ten lost tribes of Israel. When her student Julia Field-King brought the matter to her teacher's attention, Eddy was intrigued, at least temporarily, by the possibility that she might be of Davidic descent. Despite intermittent misgivings about the project as basically irrelevant and contradictory to Christian Science, Eddy encouraged Field-King, whom she had sent on missionary work to London in 1896, to carefully ascertain the facts of the matter. Since there were no facts, Eddy and Field-King eventually abandoned the project, which had been a wild goose chase from the beginning. Eddy's motive had been to use the proposition that she was descended from King David to authenticate her discovery by legitimizing her. As she put it in a letter to Field-King, "My reason for asking you to undertake this historical proof was that the people would sooner be convinced perhaps by it of my legitimate mission."[72]

It was largely the same motive that underlay Eddy's efforts in *Retrospection and Introspection* to make more of her family background than was actually warranted, prompting a gleeful Twain to dub her ancestry "worthy small-fry." The language in which she reviewed her past, measured against her best writing, has a conventional, uninspired quality—especially when contrasted with the book's last sections, including the chapters "Admonition," "Exemplification," "Waymarks," and "The Human Concept," which are written with far greater conviction and assurance.[73]

These later sections of the book dwell partly on the subject of teaching, which she saw as basic to the future of Christian Science. But this issue is embraced by something larger: the need for the spirit of genuine humility among students of Christian Science. She touches on the barrenness of worldly policies, the need to reckon with specific sins that retard students' growth, the self-sacrifice necessary for spiritual progress, and the requirement for simplicity and humility in bringing Christian Science to the attention of the world. "I am persuaded," she wrote at the close of the book, "that only by the modesty and distinguishing affection illustrated in Jesus' career, can Christian Scientists aid the establishment of Christ's kingdom on the earth."[74]

Her concluding words indicate that in her eyes, her own mission and the work of the movement she led must be understood as a direct continuation of Jesus' healing and redemptive mission and the power of early Christianity. "In the first century of the Christian era Jesus' teachings bore much fruit, and the Father was glorified therein. In this period and the forthcoming centuries, watered by dews of divine Science, this 'tree of life' will blossom into greater freedom, and its leaves will be 'for the healing of the nations.'"[75]

When Eddy wrote these words, she possibly did not believe that she would be around much longer to assist in this process. Despite her exertions and exhaustion she lived a good deal longer. If she had exited from the earthly scene in the summer of 1891 as suddenly as she had left Boston two years before, the valedictory tone of *Retrospection* would have made its own kind of sense. But this did not happen. In the last pages of the book she admonished Christian Scientists that they owed to themselves and to the world a struggle to demonstrate the truth of

Mary Baker Eddy, 1891.
Courtesy of The Mary Baker
Eddy Collection.

what she taught.[76] And there was no telling where that struggle might lead—in her case just as surely as in theirs.

Eddy, in fact, lived until the end of 1910, emerging, without having in the least anticipated it, into nearly two more decades of authoritative leadership that proved decisive for the future of Christian Science. She reorganized the church in a way she had not previously contemplated, fashioned the *Manual* for its government, which again she had not expected to do, passed through the ordeal of the Next Friends Suit, and in her eighty-eighth year founded the *Christian Science Monitor*, in the process becoming an internationally known figure.

Perhaps most important, she had become the individual known to her contemporaries and later to history as the leader of one of the United States' few indigenous religious denominations. She had, in short, become "Mrs. Eddy."

3

By What Authority? On Christian Ground

The Question of Authority

Four years after leaving Boston, when Eddy was comfortably settled at Pleasant View, she told a visitor that there was one incident in the life of George Washington that impressed her greatly: his refusal to be made a king after the American Revolution.[1]

It was a familiar story. Patriotic Americans knew it well. In view of her own sudden departure from Boston four years before, Washington's act of renunciation had special meaning for Eddy. Like Washington, she genuinely wanted to retreat into private life, but she also felt enormous responsibility for a cause beyond herself. Eventually she, too, found herself in a position of renewed authority, having involuntarily gained a new stature by virtue of a voluntary retreat from the center of affairs. Not that Eddy sought new authority in her decision to leave Boston, although that came in full measure within several years. What she sought was more the authenticity out of which that authority eventually would spring.

During the years of her life that remained to her after her move to Pleasant View in June 1892, she possessed and exercised that authority in increasing measure. It was, therefore, entirely apt that Robert Peel titled the concluding volume of his biographical trilogy, *Mary Baker Eddy: The Years of Authority*. Yet that authority did not come easily or all at once; it was, in fact, hard won, tested, and fortified, especially during the four years after she took up residence in her Pleasant View home. And it was with a considerable sense of assurance and command that she was able to declare in her 1903 reply to Mark Twain in the *New York Herald*, "I stand in relation to this century, as a Christian discoverer, founder, and leader," adding, "What I am remains to be proved by the good I do."[2]

From these and other similar statements—for example, her words to her followers in 1901 and again in 1902, "Follow your Leader, only so far as she follows Christ,"[3] it is apparent that Eddy did not rest her authority on authoritarian grounds, but pointed to what she believed she had accomplished, which she left others to judge for themselves.

Certainly Eddy did not rest her claim to authority on any supernaturally conferred status. Ira Knapp, a long-bearded New Hampshire farmer of unimpeachable rectitude who had been converted to Christian Science in 1884, saw her personally and literally as the "Woman of the Apocalypse" portrayed in the book of Revelation—a contention that became a factor in the lawsuit for libel brought against Eddy in 1899 by Josephine Curtis Woodbury, and that became hugely controversial within the Christian Science movement decades later. Eddy valued Knapp's loyalty and unwavering obedience, making him a member of the church's first board of directors after she reorganized it in 1892—a position that he held until his death in office just the month before her own in 1910. Yet she rejected any personal identification of herself with the figure of the Woman of Revelation. Nor did she believe that a direct revelation from God had simply descended upon her in some supernatural and inexplicable way.[4]

Joseph Smith, the founder of Mormonism, asserted that he had been divinely led to find the golden plates that he translated and published as the *Book of Mormon*. Mormons further believe that direct revelations from God continue in the church through its president. Eddy, by contrast, maintained that the revelation that came to her did not simply devolve upon her, but had the character of a gradual process of unfolding in which she played an active part. As she described this process: "From 1866 to 1875, I myself was learning Christian Science step by step—gradually developing the wonderful germ I had discovered as an honest investigator. It was practical evolution. I was reaching by experience and demonstration the scientific proof, and scientific statement, of what I had already discovered. My later teachings and writings show the steady growth of my spiritual ideal during those pregnant years." These words reflect the fact that Eddy, in the words of Lee. Z. Johnson, for nearly thirty years archivist of the Mother Church, "viewed herself not only a genuine Christian, of course, but also as a discoverer, a scientist investigating the nature and application of spiritual power. Seeking the truth wherever it might lead, she found Christian Science."[5]

Her claim to spiritual authority rested, therefore, on entirely different grounds than is usually the case within the framework of religious discourse. In his book *The Melody of Theology: A Philosophical*

Dictionary, religious historian Jaroslav Pelikan points out that an unchallenged assertion of authority makes it possible to stop any argument in its tracks, "since it promises to resolve all other matters of theological inquiry by making them its corollaries." Once this battle is won, "all other doctrines become thereby unarguable." It was this very concept of religious authority that Eddy rejected and, in her own way, subverted. She did claim scriptural authority for the truth of her teaching, but she made no unchallengeable assertion of authority for herself. She believed, rather, that she had discovered truths independent of herself that had definite consequences for life-experience, and that others would and should accept or reject her authority as discover, founder, and leader on this basis alone. "You can prove to yourself, dear reader," she wrote in *Science and Health,* "the Science of healing, and so ascertain if the author has given you the correct interpretation of Scripture."[6]

"MY ONLY AUTHORITY"

What she had discovered, Eddy believed, was rooted in and continuous with the authority of scriptural revelation. Therein lay the basis of her claim to authority and leadership. "I have found nothing in ancient or in modern systems on which to found my own," she stated in *Science and Health,* "except the teachings and demonstrations of our great Master and the lives of prophets and apostles. The Bible has been my only authority. I have had no other guide in 'the straight and narrow way' of Truth."[7] Eddy did not believe that she was so much adding to scriptural truth as throwing a new light upon it, making explicit what was already in substance there. It would never have occurred to her to view her teaching as a personal religious philosophy of her own devising, independent of biblical truth and precedent.

In this sense, she was a true child of the Reformed Protestant tradition, which held the Bible to be the supreme source of revealed truth. While she denied that Christian Scientists subscribe to a "religious creed," she did set forth what she called the "important points," or "religious tenets," of Christian Science, the first of them being: "As adherents of Truth, we take the inspired Word of the Bible as our sufficient guide to eternal Life."[8] It was natural for her in working out her own metaphysics to begin, not with a theoretical explanation of what she had seen at the point of her healing in February 1866, but with the immense and uncompleted project entitled *The Bible in Its Spiritual Meaning,* the first volume of which was to be the notes on the book of Genesis she began writing in 1866.

It was also natural for Eddy to turn to the Bible for guidance and illumination. Almost every morning, she would open the Bible at random, fastening upon whatever scriptural text her eyes first fell upon, so as "to take from its sacred pages a thought that enables me to meet 'the cares that infest the day.' "[9] Not only in periods of crisis, but on a daily basis, she sought in this way to understand the forces she was encountering, to find the direction she must take, and to confirm that she was on the right course.

The book of Psalms was particularly meaningful to her. As she said in a note dictated in 1891, "It is so now that every morning when I open my Psalms the passage that I open to will always give me warning of the experience of the day." On June 17, 1892, for example, the last day she spent in her house on North State Street in Concord before moving to Pleasant View, Eddy opened her Bible to Psalm 107, which speaks of God's goodness and mercy in gathering his own from the "wilderness," leading them "forth by the right way, that they might go to a city of habitation" and bringing them "unto their desired haven." On another occasion, Eddy's eyes fell upon Luke 9:1, which reads, "Then he [Jesus] called his twelve disciples together, and gave them power and authority over all devils, and to cure diseases." Relating this passage to Christian Science practice, she observed, "Jesus spake as one having authority. The mild pleasant words to a patient will do when it is to quiet fear, but when there is to be a real clinch with evil to destroy it you must *command* as one having authority." And on the day when she received a copy of the masters' report in the Next Friends Suit, which vindicated her entirely, Eddy recalled that she opened her Bible to the first chapter of Proverbs, which includes the verse, "Surely in vain the net is spread in the sight of any bird."[10]

In seeking guidance and support from the Bible in this way, Eddy was not simply turning to scripture for moments of uplift and inspiration. In the Edwardsian tradition in which she was raised, biblical events had a meaning that transcended their specific circumstances. This pattern of interpretation was known formally as typology. It harkens back to the days of the early Christian church, when it was used as a way of interpreting passages of scripture. "Traditionally," explains Edwards scholar Wallace C. Anderson, "typology involved the exercise of matching biblical 'types'—prophetic figures, events, or circumstances—in the Old Testament with their 'antitypes' or fulfilling figures, events, or circumstances in the New."[11] Primarily, this meant that events in the Old Testament prefigured, or were "types" of, events revolving around the redemptive work of Christ. The destruction of Pharaoh's army by drowning in the Red Sea, for example, was seen as prefiguring Jesus' defeat of Satan's power in his Resurrection.

Jonathan Edwards expanded the significance of typology so as to see the universe itself as a means of "God's communication of himself—and thereby of his glory—to the understanding and will of his creatures." Edwards saw the phenomena and events of the natural world as forerunners or "types" of the unfolding process of redemptive history, including "the coming of the new heaven and the new earth," but also the future punishment of the unredeemed in hell. Thus the progressive state of the world, manifested in the growth of a plant or of a fetus in the womb, is analogous to and expresses the "unfolding of the work of redemption." Edwards's focus in his lengthy notes on typology is on how the physical world "shadows forth" spiritual things. But he also sees these spiritual things as including the living experience of humanity understood in the context of redemptive history.[12]

It was this understanding of typology that Eddy inherited from the Edwardsian tradition, then generalized and broadened in her own way. Like her Puritan forebears, she repeatedly spoke of biblical events as "types." But more than this, she believed that biblical figures, narratives, and teachings—although representing different levels of inspiration—point to enduring spiritual truths and patterns of experience made explicit in Christian Science. Indeed, the final chapter in *Science and Health* entitled "Glossary" consists of twenty pages of 125 mostly biblical terms, wherein Eddy indicates what she sees as the metaphysical or spiritual sense of their meaning. In so doing, she may well have reflected the broadly disseminated influence of Emanuel Swedenborg, whose *Dictionary of Correspondences* also explained what he believed to be the inner spiritual meaning of Scripture. At a more fundamental level, however, the "Glossary" reflects Eddy's immersion in the Puritan typological tradition. At six different points in the chapter, she speaks of these definitions in explicitly typological terms, writing, for example, of Japhet, Noah's son, as "a type of spiritual peace" and of Moses as "a type of moral law and the demonstration thereof."[13]

Just as she held that what Edwards had called spiritual sense—the capacity to apprehend the things of God directly—to be inherent in every individual, not just in the elect, so she believed that biblical events could be taken as foreshadowing what all practicing Christians could and would experience in whatever era they lived.

Typology, understood in this broadened sense, helps to explain what Eddy meant when she spoke of *Science and Health* as illumining the inner meaning of the scriptures as a whole. An editorial in the *Journal* for April 1895 expressed her intent by stating that the book "is not, as many suppose, a mere commentary upon or criticism of the Bible, but . . . is what it purports to be, a Key to its spiritual meaning as a whole." In her last years, she contemplated changing the title of the book from *Science and Health with Key to the Scriptures* to *Science and Health, Key to the Scriptures* but was dissuaded from doing so only because of copyright problems that would have ensued. With the conviction that the two books, the Bible and *Science and Health,* belonged together, Eddy in 1893 broached to her printer the idea of having her book printed on Bible paper. Despite the technical problems involved, she insisted that it could be done, explaining that it has "always been my desire and expectation that my book should encourage more and more people to read the Bible" and that having the two books more similar in appearance would be "an aid in using them together."[14]

"AS IN BLEST PALESTINA'S HOUR"

During the 1890s, Eddy's conviction as to the scriptural basis, authority, and resonance of Christian Science became stronger than in former years. She often spoke of Christ as uniquely present in the life of the historical Jesus, yet not confined to him. To her, Christ is "the real man and his relation to God." It is "the Spirit which Jesus implied in his own statements: 'I am the way, the truth, and the life'; 'I and my Father are one.' This Christ, or divinity of the man Jesus, was his divine nature, the godliness which animated him."

While Jesus, who embodied or incarnated Christ, was no longer present to humanity, the spirit of Christ, she believed, is still as much a living presence as when Jesus walked by the Sea of Galilee. Her specific message to Christians was that it is possible now for all to share in the life of Christ in a fuller, more untrammeled way than most Christians were prepared to admit. "It is the living Christ, the practical Truth," she wrote, "which makes Jesus 'the resurrection and the life' to all who follow him in deed."[15]

At the end of the chapter "Atonement and Eucharist" in the fiftieth edition of *Science and Health,* Eddy had written in prophetic accents, "Christ's immortal ideal will sweep down the centuries, gathering beneath its wings the sick and sinning." By the end of the 1890s, a period of sustained growth for the movement, she changed the words "will sweep down the centuries" to "is sweeping down the centuries."[16]

The change reflected the increasing conviction she shared with her followers that the remarkable progress of Christian Science marked the transition from prophecy to fulfillment. *Christ and Christmas,* an illustrated poem in book form which she worked on during most of the year 1893, shows Eddy giving imaginative shape to this conviction.

It turned out to be among the most unusual and misunderstood of any of her writings—and, in her view, among the most important. Not only is the poem less personal in tone than her other religious poetry, it is also longer and more formally developed. Its substructure is a series of biblical texts reprinted in the glossary at the conclusion of the poem. The fifteen stanzas expand on the contemporary meaning of these texts, while the accompanying illustrations, executed by the itinerant New England artist James F. Gilman, attempt to give visual form to that meaning.

Eddy's preoccupation with this poem-book included writing it, supervising the accompanying illustrations, and seeing it through to publication. She had become convinced, probably through her appreciation for Phillips Brooks's illustrated poem "O Little Town of Bethlehem," that Christian Science must have an art to correlate with its Science.[17] The fortuitous arrival of Gilman, who had been commissioned by Eddy's photographer to draw a series of sketches of Pleasant View, gave her the opportunity to put this conviction to the test.

Besides, she liked having Gilman around. He was a bit odd, but he was interesting, a welcome contrast temperamentally to the students with whom she normally associated. Enlisted by Eddy in March to illustrate her poem, Gilman boarded near Pleasant View for most of the rest of the year and, working under her close supervision, produced illustrations corresponding to the fifteen stanzas of the poem.

The supervision was very close. Gilman acknowledged that the designs of the important illustrations were mainly hers, and she was obdurate as to how even their details should be executed. As if to symbolize the point, once, when he was sketching her, it became necessary to move the chair in which she was sitting. Not wanting her to shift positions, Gilman tried to move her and the chair together. Although she was quite slight at the time, he confessed, "I could lift a hundred pounds of grain easy, but I found I could not lift or move Mrs. Eddy." She could become exasperated with him when he failed to heed her exacting instructions as to how the illustrations should be rendered. When he showed her one draft sketch, she "vigorously pointed to the different figures that must come out, saying in the voice of indignant command, *'Take that out! and that! and that!'* " At other times, she could respond with ironic humor, as when she commented that the result of his efforts to draw some angels looked more like tadpoles.[18]

Gilman tried. The pictures are earnest, sentimental, perhaps a bit kitschy. Eddy had little schooling in the visual arts, and Gilman, a landscape painter of some talent, was out of his element in executing visionary religious art. In her work with students whom she relied upon to help build the movement, Eddy often pushed them to greater exertions and better service than they were capable of otherwise. There could be no doubt of Gilman's exertions. But despite her enthusiasm, the drawings were at best barely adequate illustrations of the visionary dimensions of her poem.

The first two stanzas of "Christ and Christmas" establish the broad perspective of God's revelation of Christ to humanity:[19]

> Fast circling on, from zone to zone,—
> Bright, blest, afar,—
> O'er the grim night of chaos shone
> One lone, brave star.
>
> In tender mercy, Spirit sped
> A loyal ray
> To rouse the living, wake the dead,
> And point the Way.

The poem then emphasizes the continuity of that first appearing with the coming of Divine Science:

> What the Beloved knew and taught,
> Science repeats,
> Through understanding, dearly sought,
> With fierce heart-beats.

Here Eddy uses the term "Science" in its largest meaning. In many, perhaps most, instances, in her writing, the terms "science" and "scientific" indicate that Christian Science expresses divine law. At several points she conjoined the terms "Principle," "rule," and "demonstration" in explaining why her teaching should be regarded as scientific, as when she stated, "Divine Science is absolute, and permits no half-way position in learning its Principle and rule—establishing it by demonstration."[20] But there is another meaning to her use of the term Science as well. This is indicated by her frequent association of science with the idea of interpretation, whereby science becomes God's own interpretation of his being and the universe.

"Science," she wrote characteristically, "is an emanation of divine Mind, and is alone able to interpret God aright." Divine Science for Eddy is that aspect of God's being through which he reveals and communicates his nature. "This Science of God and man," she wrote, "is the Holy Ghost, which reveals and sustains the unbroken and eternal harmony of both God and the universe."[21]

In ordinary parlance, science is a cool word, while the Holy Ghost is a warm one. But Eddy felt bound by no such discriminations. The Science that richly communicates and sustains the harmony of God's universe, she saw as the very Spirit of Holiness expressed in the phrase Holy Ghost or Holy Spirit. It is Science in this larger sense that Eddy conveys in the very title of her textbook *Science and Health*. In view of Eddy's repeated conjunction of health with the terms holiness and harmony, the sense of the term becomes God's revelation or interpretation of his own being that supports the health, holiness, and harmony of his creation.

She believed, moreover, that the breakthrough of Divine Science to humanity had been prophesied in Jesus' words from the Gospel of John spoken to his disciples at the close of the Last Supper. There Jesus promised the appearing to humanity of the Comforter, which he said was the Holy Ghost—"the Spirit of truth," that would "teach you all things, and bring all things to your remembrance, whatsoever I have said to you." In concluding the chapter "Atonement and Eucharist," Eddy wrote, "In the words of St. John: 'He shall give you another Comforter, that he may abide with you *forever.*' This Comforter I understand to be Divine Science."[22]

For her, its advent marked the second coming of Christ—not on clouds of glory—but as the breakthrough or reappearing of the continuing presence of Christ to which humanity has been largely blind. With the advent of Divine Science, she affirmed, came the revelation of "the living Christ"—Christ's eternal reality and saving power.

Christ and Christmas celebrates what Eddy believed to be the "final revelation" of God to humanity in the form of Divine Science.[23] Divine Science is the form that Christ—the same godliness that was embodied in Jesus—was assuming in its contemporary appearing. Now there is no need to look back on the coming of Christ as a past event to be celebrated through religious ritual or commemorated through a conventional Christmas. Those who "make merriment on Christmas eves" fail to fulfill "Truth's demands" to celebrate the new appearing of "Christ, eternal and divine." The meaning of Christ thus becomes wholly contemporary again:

> As in blest Palestina's hour,
> So in our age,
> 'Tis the same hand unfolds His power,
> And writes the page.

Eddy's message was unmistakable: once one sees that biblical revelation points to a living truth in the present, the present can be as fully invested with spiritual meaning as the past. Both in its language and in its illustrations, the book *Christ and Christmas* blends the biblical with the contemporary. Thus, in the second illustration, which depicts Jesus

"The Way" from *Christ and Christmas*.
Courtesy of The Mary Baker Eddy Collection.

raising a girl from the dead, he is shown traditionally in the raiment of his times, but the two women in the picture wear nineteenth-century clothing.

After the book was published, one critic noted that in the last illustration, called "The Way," which depicts the illumination of Jesus' Ascension shining in the sky above a rich landscape, the scene appeared to be located in Concord. Conversing with Eddy, Gilman said this was no doubt true, since the trees were characteristic of New Hampshire. "But," he said, "I do not know as we need to go back to Jesus' day in Palestine to represent this thought." Eddy enthusiastically agreed, responding, "There is too much looking backward two thousand years. They will find that there is a *Way* here in Concord as well as in Palestine."[24]

The references to the present in the book, however, go well beyond suggestions of trees in the landscape around Concord. In four illustrations, womanhood is portrayed as linked with spiritual light, reaching out for it or offering it. These include "Seeking and Finding," showing a woman pouring over the Bible; "Christian Science Healing," depicting a woman in prayer standing at a sickbed; "Christian Unity," representing a woman holding a scroll inscribed with the words "Christian Science" and standing by the seated figure of Jesus, who takes her hand;

and "Truth *versus* Error," depicting the spirit of Truth knocking at the door of humanity.

The perception of the book, then and since, has largely revolved around a controversy over one of these illustrations: that of a woman (who vaguely resembled Eddy) holding the hand of the seated figure of Jesus. It was foreign to Eddy to claim anything like equality with Jesus. As she would later tell Calvin Frye, "When I hear people speak of me or any other mortal as an equal with Jesus it makes me shiver, for I realize more & more as I apprehend his true character & work his infinite distance above us." But as a child of the New England Puritan tradition, it was part of the furniture of her mind to think in typological terms. Thus, she explained that the illustrations that certain clergymen branded as blasphemous "refer not to my personality, but rather foretell the typical appearing of the womanhood, as well as the manhood of God, our divine Father and Mother."[25]

That either Eddy's Protestant critics or her more worshipful followers would see it in this way turned out to be a serious miscalculation. Nor did she anticipate that Christian Scientists' gushing over the book, particularly their response to depictions of Jesus and a figure vaguely resembling her, could reach dangerous proportions. The poem celebrated the active presence of Christ in human experience now. But some Christian Scientists, taking Gilman's representation of Jesus as authoritative because Eddy had sanctioned it, treated it as a virtual icon and even as an aid to healing. When Judge Hanna told her that he had memorized "Christ and Christmas" and was using it in treating himself, she responded, "Please tell no one how you utilize 'Christ and Christmas'; used thus it is a mental opiate by which the dreamy ecstasy of the repeater lulls fear, nothing else." Referring to the pictures in the book, she wrote to another follower, "Some students are making more reality of them than I made or intended. They are types not realities."[26]

Because of the outcry over the book and its misuse among some of her followers, Eddy withdrew it from publication in January 1894, waiting nearly four years to republish it. She explained in a *Journal* article that the book "mayhap taught me more than it has others." What it taught her, she said, was "that contemplating finite personality impedes spiritual growth, even as holding in mind the consciousness of disease prevents the recovery of the sick."[27]

The issue of personality deflected attention from the meaning of *Christ and Christmas* when it was first published and has largely continued to do so. Yet no other single document captures so well the sense that came over her and so many of her followers in the early 1890s that Christian Science had a destiny and mission of truly biblical proportions.

Eddy's audacity in the book did not lie in representing herself in any personal way as Jesus' equal, but rather in the intensity of her conviction that Christ was decisively breaking through to humanity through the advent of Divine Science, that this advent was in continuity with scriptural revelation, and that if her followers were disciplined and faithful, it could mark the beginning of a new spiritual day for humanity— a day in which the presence of Christ could be as tangibly felt in the historical present as in "blest Palestina's hour."

"VANITY FAIR"

If one thing more than any other infuriated Eddy's orthodox opponents of Christian Science, it was her insistence that her discovery was Christian to the core. The intended effect of the Reverend A. J. Gordon's open letter condemning her teaching read by the Reverend Joseph Cook in Tremont Temple, for example, had been to consign Christian Science to what orthodox clergymen generally saw as Boston's spiritual underground, a miscellaneous collection of theosophists, occultists, spiritualists, and "mind-curers" outside the pale of acceptable Christianity.

Eddy refused to let Christian Science be thus marginalized, insisting in her brief rejoinder at Tremont Temple that the movement she led stood squarely on Christian ground. She underscored the point when, in her 1903 reply to Mark Twain, she defined her own concept of her status, and thus of the authority she claimed, as that of a *"Christian* discoverer, founder, and leader" (italics added). "Christian Science may absorb the attention of sage and philosopher," she wrote characteristically in *Science and Health,* "but the Christian alone can fathom it."[28]

Her teaching engaged the attention of sages, philosophers, and a good many others as well when, in September 1893, Christian Scientists participated in the World's Parliament of Religions, held in conjunction with the six-month Columbian Exposition in Chicago commemorating the four-hundredth anniversary of Columbus's discovery of the New World. Christian Scientists were exultant over this opportunity. Most comments on the event in the *Journal* were little short of euphoric. From the outset, Eddy had been suspicious of the enormous enthusiasm that the parliament aroused in her students—especially those who were directly involved in planning for and participating in the event. Christian Scientists' presence at the parliament, Eddy eventually came to believe, marked a setback in the perception of Christian Science as a valid expression of Christian faith and of herself as the legitimate leader of a Christian denomination.

Edward A. Kimball, n.d.
Courtesy of The Mary Baker
Eddy Collection.

The invitation for Christian Scientists to participate in the parliament did not arise out of any generosity toward the new denomination on the part of its sponsors. The parliament was largely the brainchild of the Reverend John Henry Barrows, an advocate of worldwide ecumenicism. He and his associates built support for this broadly inclusive meeting through massive publicity efforts, including a mailing list sent to some ten thousand religious figures in thirty countries. But the Christian Scientists were not initially among those so eagerly solicited.

It was Augusta Stetson of New York who strongly lobbied Christian Scientists in Chicago to press for the inclusion of the new faith at the exposition. Stetson, one of Eddy's most prominent students, was a major figure in the early history of Christian Science. Eventually excommunicated from the Mother Church, she was an imposing and highly capable woman who dominated the movement in New York City. Galvanizing interest in a huge public presentation of Christian Science such as the parliament was thoroughly representative of her ambition and capacity to get things done.

Far more measured—and certainly more trusted by Eddy—was Edward A. Kimball of Chicago. Kimball was an able and eloquent student of Eddy who would become the movement's most widely known and

respected lecturer and teacher. He also had been a successful businessman and knew how to make things happen. Through Stetson's lobby-
ing and his untiring efforts, the way was opened for a large display of
Christian Science literature at a conspicuous place in the exhibition.
But these efforts led to something far more important: the opportunity
for the Christian Scientists to hold their own denominational congress
at the parliament on September 20 and to present their teachings before
a plenary session of the parliament.

Initially, Eddy wanted to keep her distance from the parliament,
physically and spiritually. When Christian Scientists in Chicago invited
her to share their hospitality and attend the event, she placed a notice
in the *Journal* for April, saying that she had "a world of Wisdom and
Love to contemplate that concerns me and you infinitely beyond all
earthly expositions or exhibitions." To a student she also wrote frankly,
"I have no desire to be identified at present with this 'Vanity Fair.' "
And when the World's Parliament of Religions began, she spoke of it as
"a political movement to consolidate and unify error."[29]

Yet the enthusiasm of her students drew her, at least temporarily,
in an opposite direction. Kimball paved the way for Christian Science
to be represented by a booth at the exhibition, which was attended by
millions of visitors. But this only served as a backdrop to the Christian
Scientists' participation in the events of the parliament itself.

After the first session of the parliament on September 11, an obviously bedazzled observer reported on the "picturesque and impressive
spectacle" presented by representatives of a dozen world faiths on the
first day. At the center of the platform sat Cardinal Gibbons, the senior
Roman Catholic prelate in the United States, garbed in scarlet robes.
"On either side of him were grouped the Oriental delegates, whose
many-colored raiment vied with his own in brilliancy." The eloquent
Indian Swami, Vivekananda, was "clad in gorgeous red apparel, his
bronzed face surmounted with a huge turban of yellow," while the
Chinese and Japanese delegates were "arrayed in costly silk vestments
of all the colors of the rainbow."[30]

Two days before the plenary session, at which Hanna read an address
by Eddy, the Christian Scientists held their own denominational congress. Presided over by her adopted son Foster Eddy, it consisted of a
dozen speeches by prominent church members on major aspects of
Christian Science, such as "Spirit and Matter," "the Resurrection," and
"Healing the Sick." Charles C. Bonney, the guiding spirit and president of
the World's Congress Auxiliary of the Columbian Exposition, introduced
the meeting in glowing terms: "When science becomes Christian, then the
world indeed advances toward the millennial dawn. . . . Christian

Session of the World's Parliament of Religions.
From *The World's Parliament of Religions,* edited by the Rev. Henry Barrows,
D.D. Chicago: The Parliament Publishing Company, 1893, frontispiece.

Scientists were . . . called to declare and emphasize the real harmony between religion and science."[31]

Such warm acknowledgment was balm to the souls of the approximately four thousand Christian Scientists in attendance. The words were generous, and in a piece for the *Journal* Eddy quoted them gratefully. Yet Bonney missed the point of what Eddy meant to convey when she spoke of Christian Science as *scientific.* He championed the inclusive view that Christian teaching and physical science could harmoniously *co-exist,* each operative in its own distinctive sphere—that there could and should be no real conflict between them. But this was far from Eddy's attitude.

She did hold that natural science and Christian Science were in accord in that both worked according to law. But to her, that law could not be a series of physical processes, which she saw as the outcome of human belief. To the extent that the physical sciences challenge the commonsense view of how the universe works, Eddy also saw an important link between science as ordinarily understood and her own teaching. In several passages she used astronomy to make the point that the evidence of the corporeal senses "afford[s] no indication of the grand facts of being, even as these so-called senses receive no intimation of the earth's motions or of the science of astronomy, but yield assent to astronomical propositions on the authority of natural science."[32]

But then she took a leap beyond conclusions that physical sciences in any form could sustain. She asserted that "the facts of divine Science should be admitted—although the evidence as to these facts is not supported by evil, by matter, or by material sense,—because the evidence that God and man coexist is fully sustained by spiritual sense."[33] While there were some genuine points of contact between Christian Science and the methodology of the natural sciences, she saw Christian Science as *confronting* the conclusions of natural science more than concurring with them.

Understandably, this crucial distinction remained largely overlooked by the Christian Scientists caught up in the euphoria of the occasion, which appeared to be the most triumphal moment in the history of their cause to date. Reporting on September 21, the day after the plenary session at which Christian Science was represented, the *Chicago Tribune* noted that "one of the best congresses yet held in connection with the Parliament of Religions, judged by numbers and interest, was that of the Christian Scientists which took place yesterday afternoon in Washington hall." Sharing the platform with Hanna were the great social gospel minister Washington Gladden, who also gave an address, and the Reverend Joseph Cook, who had greeted Eddy with such disdain when she appeared in Tremont Temple eight years before.

Eddy had expended great care in developing an address for Hanna to deliver at the parliament, constructing it out of linked passages from her published writings. Prior to the reading of the speech, she wrote to Kimball, "Through tears of joy I thank you and our God for the dawn of a new day. The night is far spent."[34] The day after the event, a banner was placed on the porch at Pleasant View in honor of the triumph of Christian Science in Chicago, where Eddy's address read by Hanna had been commended in the press as one of the most notable and well received of the Parliament. Kimball duly reported the triumph to Eddy, and she and the household rejoiced—for the moment.

THE DOWNSIDE OF A TRIUMPH

Two days after his reading of Eddy's address, Hanna reported to her that a mishap had occurred: he, Foster Eddy, and Kimball had been pressured by reporters to turn over the text of the address for publication in a newspaper account of the proceedings. Fearing that a garbled text would be published anyway, they consented on condition that a note be attached stating that Hanna's address was composed of texts by Eddy. But the press reports omitted the note.

Eddy was more than outraged. She had given strict instructions to Hanna that the address should not pass from his hands until he gave it to Kimball for inclusion in a book commemorating the parliament. Hanna, Kimball, and Foster Eddy had violated these instructions, and to her this was an act of disobedience. For one thing, there was no indication in the address that she was its author. From her standpoint, even more harm was done by putting such a concentrated dose of her teaching before an unready public. She had fashioned the address so that her words could get a fair hearing before an ecumenical audience or in a book where it could be thoughtfully perused. It was never intended to be served up to the public in the secular press. To the consternation of Hanna and Kimball, she went so far as to cancel plans for the inclusion of her address, properly attributed, in any forthcoming volume. In conveying this decision to Reverend Barrows, she said, "I was opposed to having my numerous students take part in this World's Fair but yielded to their views on this subject. I cannot see that it is a fit opportunity to test the heart of Christianity but I may be mistaken."[35]

The shock of this mistake had the effect of reactivating the concerns Eddy had suppressed. She concluded that her initial distrust of having Christian Science prominently represented at the parliament had not been mistaken. Nor would she be placated on what she perceived to be the lack of wisdom and disobedience involved in conveying her address to the press, despite the commonsense rationale that it was the best course to take under the circumstances. Still flushed with success, Hanna and Kimball were by turns angry, crestfallen, and uncomprehending of the point she made repeatedly with them and others: that Christian Scientists were simply not ready for this kind of exposure and that their apparent success at the parliament was a mirage that would in time be dispelled.

This was not a conclusion that most Christian Scientists were prepared to understand. After so many years "of continuous hatred, scorn, ridicule," as one of them put it, the fact that their religion had been placed "before the public upon the same level with other Christian bodies was one of the *great victories* of its history."[36] Despite this euphoria, which found frequent expression in the *Journal*, the "hatred, scorn, ridicule" that had so long been accorded the Christian Scientists was not lessened by the parliament, but intensified.

They had, in a sense, won too big. They exulted over the fact that alone among the groups represented at the parliament, they had been given the opportunity of having both their own denominational congress and a place on the platform at the plenary session. They also rejoiced over the enthusiastic reception accorded Hanna, although this was in some measure accounted for by the fact that the audience was packed with Christian Scientists bent on making a splash. They rejoiced further that the parliament heralded a marvelous new day in which Christian Scientists would be accepted warmly into the Christian fold.

But that day did not arrive. Because Christian Scientists became so visible, the parliament became a wake-up call for the clergy as to how much of a threat to orthodoxy this upstart denomination had become. At the same time, the parliament handed Christian Scientists' clerical opponents ideal weapons with which to attack them.

"A GREAT GULF"

To many of Eddy's followers, their presence at the gathering was a great occasion on which to step before the world. Yet they stepped forth in the company of such groups as Vedanta, a form of Hinduism, and theosophy, an eclectic form of esoteric spirituality represented by Annie Besant. This was precisely the linkage Eddy feared, since it tended to disassociate Christian Science from Christianity and to identify it with religious teachings with which she insisted it had nothing in common.

She was especially dismayed by any linkage between Christian Science and theosophy, a movement that she saw as thoroughly occult in character and as the source of dangerously malign mental influences. The originator of modern theosophy (the term is an old one meaning knowledge and wisdom about God and the world based on mystical insight) was the Russian immigrant Madame Helena Blavatsky, who had for many years practiced spiritualism and who believed that advanced masters from another plane of existence revealed to her secrets about humanity's progress toward a new "cosmic consciousness." In a message to the Theosophical Convention in America in 1885, Blavatsky said that Christian Science, along with other forms of mental healing, represented distorted appearances of the occult and psychic powers germinating in humanity. "Understand once and for all," she declared, "that there is nothing 'spiritual' or 'divine' in ANY of these manifestations." Blavatsky's writings also approvingly link theosophy with animal magnetism, as when she stated that "animal magnetism (now called Suggestion and Hypnotism) . . . will be found to contain possibilities, the nature of which has never been even dreamt of by the oldest and most learned professors of the orthodox physical science."[37]

Eddy agreed, but far from approvingly. Although the rise of theosophy in the United States paralleled that of Christian Science, she saw it in wholly adversarial terms, viewing theosophy as the most distilled and dangerous expression of the occult spirit in her time. A generally sympathetic article on Christian Science in the *Chicago Inter-Ocean* for December 31, 1894, concluded that theosophy along with spiritualism were allied with Christian Science as movements that were "manifestations of a higher spirituality seeking expression." This was not a view Eddy would accept. In the *Manual,* she wrote, "When it is necessary to show the great gulf between Christian Science and theosophy, hypnotism, or spiritualism, do it, but without hard words." But the gulf, she insisted throughout her writings, between Christian Science and any teaching that emphasized the untapped occult powers of the human mind, was definitely there. In 1887, for example, she wrote this curt note to the Occult Publishing Society: "Sirs: My objection to having my book in your Catalogue is that I have nothing in common with the 'isms and 'ologies of the works you publish and *refuse* to have my book Science & Health or any of my works advertised by you. I should not put my books in your hands."[38]

Beginning in the mid-1880s, she had also contended with the attempts of defectors from Christian Science to link her teaching with various forms—often garbled and popularized—of Eastern religious thought. The relation of Christian Science to Hinduism and Buddhism is an issue that has not as yet received the attention it deserves, and is so complex that it can only be touched on here. Eddy herself knew comparatively little about either, nor is there any evidence that she was acquainted with any of the major texts of these traditions. She did permit the urbane Wiggin to insert an epigraph from the Bhagavad Gita at the head of a chapter in the sixteenth edition of *Science and Health* in 1886, though she removed it in the next full revision of 1891. She also made a complimentary reference in an 1893 letter to Buddhism, writing that "the sense of taking no thought for what we shall eat or drink, is Christ-like . . . a native Christianity which presages science— a denial of personal life and sensation."[39]

Yet her overriding interest was to establish the Christian identity of Christian Science. She therefore made several statements distinguishing Christian Science from the tendencies of Eastern thought, at least as popularly conceived. With reference to Hinduism, for example, she wrote that her teaching, which maintains that the identity of each man and woman is unique and permanent, "absolutely refutes the amalgamation, transmigration, absorption, or annihilation of individuality." In an undated memorandum, she also stated that the hypotheses of the Hindu prophet demand "that we look inwardly for all enlightenment. But Christian Science . . . demands as did St. Paul's Christianity, that we look outwardly for divine power, and away from human conscious-ness. St. Paul argues against introspection whereby to work out the sal-vation of men." As she put it elsewhere: "Man is not an iceberg. He is the image and likeness of his Maker." Answering the contention that Christian Science tended toward "Buddhism or any other 'ism,'" she flatly declared, "*Per contra*, Christian Science destroys such tendency." Clearly, she had no sympathy with the broadly eclectic views of her erstwhile student Emma Curtis Hopkins, who wrote that "the remark-able analogies of the Christian Bible and Hindoo Sacred Books, Egyptian Ancient Teachings, Persian Bibles, Chinese Great Learning, Oriental Yohar, Saga, and many others, show that the whole world has had life teachings so wonderfully identical as to make them all subjects for respectful attention and investigation by the thoughtful of our age."[40]

Some of these teachings did indeed become the subject of "respect-ful attention" at the parliament, making it the occasion at which Eastern religious thought most conspicuously penetrated popular attention in the United States. Vivekananda himself had written back to India that the Christian Scientists, who were "spreading by leaps and bounds and causing heartburn to the orthodox," were obviously Vedantans. "I mean," he explained, "they have picked up a few doctrines of the Advaita and grafted them upon the Bible. And they cure diseases by proclaiming. . . . 'I am He. I am He.'—through strength of mind. They all admire me highly."[41]

Through the 1890s and beyond, clergy critical of Christian Science repeatedly hammered it as a form of pantheism that had more affini-ties with Hinduism than legitimate Christianity. "Mrs. Eddy," stated the Presbyterian minister William P. McCorkle in his book *Christian Science, or The False Christ of 1866*, "in every important particular, teaches pre-cisely what has been taught for ages by the Hindu philosophy. That sys-tem is pantheistic." Indeed, so common had this accusation become that in her message to the Mother Church for 1898, Eddy felt obliged to dwell on the topic "Not Pantheism, but Christian Science," which became a booklet entitled *Christian Science versus Pantheism*. Here, as in her other writings, she taught a strict theism in which God is one and infinite, but rejected the pantheistic conclusion that he in any sense inhabits matter. For her, the central fact of God's allness does not wipe out the crucial distinction between God and his universe, inclusive of men and women, but is intended to indicate that his being embraces and includes all true being.[42]

Personally, she apparently felt no hard and fast inclination to dog-matically separate Christian Science from other religious teachings that differed from it in some or even most important respects. Her own warm comments about Buddhism in the earlier-quoted letter, for example, might have been the result of generally positive discussions at the dinner table at Pleasant View of Sir Edwin Arnold's popular poem on the life of Buddha, *The Light of Asia,* in which Arnold, himself a Christian, sought to demonstrate a fundamental likeness between the teachings of the Buddha and those of Jesus. An admirer of Arnold, Eddy recalled having sent him a copy of the first edition of *Science and Health,* which had been published in 1875, four years before *The Light of Asia* appeared.[43]

Nevertheless, when it came to Christian Science itself, Eddy believed it was confusing and counterproductive for students to attempt the amalgamation of her teaching with Eastern religious beliefs. She found any effort to censor what Christian Scientists in general read repugnant. But to already committed Christian Scientists she made it plain that by mixing her teaching with other and differing faiths, they risked losing sight of the distinctiveness of Christian Science and the rigorous demands of practicing it as she taught. Hence her words to a student in an 1888 class: "If you break a bottle you will be cut by the fragments, never by the whole vessel. There is a little truth in all creeds, isms and ologies, but if you try to find the truth in a part of the vessel, you will get cut. Study the Bible and *Science and Health* and leave the fragments alone."[44]

The parliament, to use her metaphor, presented Christian Science itself as one of these fragments—a brightly shining one, to be sure, but only one amidst a myriad of other fragments, equally if not more colorful. But what Eddy longed to see accomplished at the parliament— the linkage of Christian Science with legitimate Christianity—was the precise opposite of what actually occurred.

"GORGEOUS BUT GODLESS"

Eddy's specific aim in fashioning the address read by Hanna was to help cement the bonds of Christian Science and other Christians of good will so that at the very least they would find a place for her teaching within the Christian fold. She therefore entitled the address "Unity and Christian Science."

The long-run effects of the parliament undermined the unity of Christian Science with other Christian faiths. It also disrupted that unity in a small but significant fracas that occurred when Hanna delivered Eddy's address with her old adversary, the Reverend Cook, on the platform. Several times during the address, Clara Shannon recalled, the perturbed Reverend Cook tried to interrupt the proceedings. At one point when Hanna held up a copy of *Science and Health* to demonstrate that this book alone contained Eddy's teaching, Cook rose from his seat dramatically, held up a Bible, and proclaimed that it would be his "dying pillow." In his own report to Eddy, Hanna struck anything but a pacific note, relishing what amounted to an ecclesiastic joust in which Cook had made a fool of himself and been vanquished. "He was beside himself with rage," wrote Hanna to Eddy, "because he had been compelled to listen to so much from you, when he had flattered himself that he had choked you off."[45]

To Charles Bonney, a guiding light of the parliament who had introduced Hanna, she wrote, "Christian Science inculcates spiritual love for all men but no worldliness. I fear the ambition of my students was touched." In this instance, she might have said "male students." Looking back at the parliament in a memorandum written in April 1894, she declared: "In pioneering Christian Science for about thirty years, I have not found that sharp percussion and the grumble of artillery will stop the onslaught of error, and why not? Because metaphysics is mightier than physics & the din of battle is mental not material and the Divine will, armed with its wonders of goodness, disciplines any noisy will into stillness and meek obedience."[46]

Like almost every other group at the parliament, the Christian Scientists had an agenda of their own that they pushed forward capably, and in the short term successfully. But this agenda was not Eddy's. Her initial instincts about Christian Scientists' participation in the exposition had been motivated by her concern to protect the movement from exposure she felt it was ill-prepared to withstand, and by the conviction that Christian Science was not forwarded by worldly methods of promotion.

"Acting as others act on the world's parade days," as she put it, "is ominous departure from our scriptural motto 'Quench not the smoking flax till He send forth judgment unto victory,' till the field is ripe for harvest and the sickle is thrust into the bending grain. There was never a time when material methods could substitute divine grace." Her students at the parliament had, in her final estimate, done exactly this. Despite the religious trappings of the occasion, the fair was, as she put it in another memorandum dictated to Frye, "a mart, a market, an exchange, whatever is brought into it is a commodity set up for exhibition for valuation for exultation or desecration." The whole affair was "gorgeous but godless."[47]

Impressive as the occasion of the parliament was, Eddy came to believe, it was not the setting in which the Christianity of Christian Science could be best attested and proven to the world. Christian Science would have to stand or fall on the ground of daily living. "It is the spiritualization of thought and Christianization of daily life," she wrote, "in contrast with the results of the ghastly farce of material existence; it is chastity and purity, in contrast with the downward tendencies and earthward gravitation of sensualism and impurity, which really attest the divine origin and operation of Christian Science. The triumphs of Christian Science are recorded in the destruction of error and evil, from which are propagated the dismal beliefs of sin, sickness, and death."[48]

In effect, Eddy's experience with the parliament of 1893 brought her back to a renewed commitment to this conviction.

4

By What Authority? Listening and Leading

"GOD HAS BIDDEN ME"

LOOKING BACK AT THE CHRISTIAN SCIENTISTS' ROLE AT THE WORLD'S
Parliament of Religions, Eddy wrote to a student: "I warned them not
to go to the World's Fair. Mrs. Stetson carried it over me in the minds
of my students, I yielded, they went and exposed the power and numbers we had."[1] If Eddy had, by her own estimate, been less than decisive in her exercise of leadership on this matter, it was not a mistake
she would be likely to repeat. Indeed, the net effect of the incident may
well have been pivotal in establishing her own trust in her capacities as
a leader and the need to follow through on her intuitions—regardless
of opposition from well-meaning associates who believed they knew
better.

To her, these intuitions were not merely personal responses to situations, but the result of spiritual listening, of moment-by-moment
waiting for God's guidance. This conviction was well-expressed in her
best-known poem, "Feed My Sheep." Published in 1887, the poem was
a prayer for guidance in the midst of a decade of turmoil, with a deluge
of demands pouring in on her from all sides. Its first stanza, in final
form, reads:

> Shepherd, show me how to go
> O'er the hillside steep,
> How to gather, how to sow,—
> How to feed Thy sheep;
> I will listen for Thy voice,
> Lest my footsteps stray;
> I will follow and rejoice
> All the rugged way.

The poem, which has been set to music as a hymn, became something of a classic. Even Mark Twain was moved to comment on the poem reproduced in his copy of *Retrospection and Introspection:* "As poetry goes, in hymns it is pretty nearly first-rate."[2]

The discipline of Christian Science, Eddy said many times and in many ways, lay in the effort, not just to look to God for guidance in times of special need, but to claim and accept the Mind that is God as one's only Mind, therefore as the source of all of one's thoughts and acts. She saw this as extraordinarily demanding yet progressively possible—but not because human beings themselves possess the capacity to be spiritually minded and obedient to God. "Infinite Mind," she wrote in *Science and Health,* "could not possibly create a remedy outside of itself, but erring, finite, human mind has an absolute need of something beyond itself for its redemption and healing." It was only by acknowledging the utter incapacity of what she called "mortal mind" to better itself or to find wisdom within itself that one could wholeheartedly yield to the supremacy of the one Mind. This for her was the discipline most essential to spiritual growth. As she confided to Calvin Hill, a young Christian Scientist whom she had come to trust, "The first thing I do in the morning when I awake is to declare I shall have no other mind before divine Mind, and become fully conscious of this, and adhere to it throughout the entire day; then the evil cannot touch me."[3]

Living this life of Christian obedience was a struggle. She could at times be hard on herself if she felt she had not met the demands the struggle involved. "I keep a strict account with God," she once wrote, "and if I do what is not clearly right suffer for it." Yet she also saw discipleship and obedience as a possible way of life. In a *Journal* article she wrote, "Man should be found, not claiming equality with Him, but growing into that altitude of Mind which was in Christ Jesus." The only identity or selfhood Jesus had, she taught, flowed from his consistent obedience to God. Eddy wrote that Jesus "found the eternal Ego, and proved that he and the Father were inseparable as God and His reflection or spiritual man."[4] For her, this true selfhood is the Christ, and those who would have the "Mind which was in Christ Jesus" and find their own identity in Christ, follow him in the measure of their own obedience to God. She taught that it is possible to have this Mind as one's only Mind, and that so doing is being what men and women in their God-given identities truly are: the reflection or expression of God.

She therefore made a distinction between acting, as she once put it in a letter to Knapp, out of "the highest false sense that means well,

and the 'still small voice' of Good"—between the best of human intentions and the actual government of one's acts by God. Until Knapp was
able to "hear His voice," she wrote, "God will lend me to you to distinguish for you what is the false and what the true direction." On many
occasions, she said that she had no idea why Mind was bidding her to
take some particular course of action, but that she became accustomed
to doing as she was directed by God without asking for a reason.
Dictating a letter she saw as crucial to Clara Shannon, Eddy declared,
"God *bids* me to do *so and so* but I don't see the reason why." After the
letter was finished and she saw why it had to be written as it was, she
added: "I want you always to remember that Mother had to obey God
before she knew the reason why." Shannon adds that when news of
the effect of the letter reached Eddy, she had the proof that "she had
acted rightly and God's directions were carried out." In a letter to a
highly capable young man from New York, Carol Norton, she reiterated that "obedience to God, even when I can not understand, is to me
the condition of my divine light and success. Hence I cannot question
but obey the 'still small voice.' "[5]

Eddy did not claim, however, that every step she took was
impelled by God. It was possible, she believed, to strive to claim and
accept no other but the one divine Mind, but at the same time to
acknowledge mistakes and the continued need for growth. "I am never
satisfied with my Christian growth," she confided in a letter to a New
Hampshire Unitarian minister in 1897. "I can see increase of knowledge yearly, but do not see the spiritual progress that I need more than
all else. But the dear God is *merciful*, and Life is eternal wherein to gain
the goal thereof—and to obey the Divine demand, 'Be ye perfect.' " But
until this is accomplished, she wrote earlier, "the Christian Scientist
must continue to strive with sickness, sin, and death,—though in lessening degrees,—in order to complete this regeneration."[6]

This regeneration for her marked the practical appearing of what
she called the real man. Eddy frequently used the term "man" in a
generic sense to apply to all men and women, but without any sexist
connotations. This man was not just a potentiality of human beings as
we see them now. It was, for her, the only concrete and scientific man
there is or ever was. Each individual, she taught, must eventually go
through the experience of spiritual rebirth, put off fallible human selfhood, and become identified wholly with man in God's likeness.

This process of rebirth did not, in her view, terminate at the point
of death, after which one was plunged into a purgatory, a heaven, or a
hell. For her, these were not actual states of being in an afterlife, so
much as terms that describe presently possible conditions of thought.

She conceived of an afterlife more as a continuation of present existence than as a radically altered kind of being. "Mortals waken from the dream of death," she wrote in *Science and Health*, "with bodies unseen by those who think that they bury the body." A number of informal comments made by Eddy in conversation about this subject indicate that, for her, death marked less of a rupture with what we know and experience now than is commonly conceived. "If we were to pass on right here now in this room," she told household worker Lida Fitzpatrick in 1904, "we would waken right here, and nothing would be changed any more than you see it now." Eddy taught that after death, individuals retain conscious identity; that they awaken at the same point of spiritual development as before the transition, able to recognize and communicate with those who have gone before; and that they face the need for continuing spiritual growth and purgation until the belief of being a mortal separate from God is thoroughly extinguished. In her words in *Science and Health*, "The sin and error which possess us at the instant of death do not cease at that moment, but endure until the death of these errors."[7]

Christian Science, she said, provides a new basis for the probation and growth through which all must pass, but does not absolve anyone from this process, nor does it make moral and spiritual progress automatic or easy. In the preface to the final edition of *Science and Health*, she speaks of herself as still "a willing disciple at the heavenly gate, waiting for the Mind of Christ."[8] Yet this "willing disciple" was faced with day-to-day responsibilities she believed she dare not shirk. She felt she had the responsibility to make the movement *move*—to push forward needed projects and shape policy on a variety of crucial issues. At the same time, there was no one whose judgment she felt she had more reason to trust than her own. She therefore felt the continuing pressure to make decisions on an almost daily basis about matters that had far-ranging effects on others. In many instances, particularly those for which no precedent existed, she felt compelled to make the best judgment she could, the only regular factor being the unpredictability of the crises that arose and of her own responses to them.

Eddy often fretted, especially as she became older, about the work load she carried in meeting the daily demands of leading the movement—the continued correspondence, visits from church officials, and putting out fires that gave her little respite or peace. As she put it in a message to her church in 1900, she had long desired "to step aside" and have another take her place as leader, but "no one else has seemed equal to 'bear the burden and heat of the day.' "[9] The statement might sound disingenuously self-effacing, were it not for her repeated and apparently sincere protestations of her relish for quietness and seclusion. She therefore accepted the fact that, as Harry Truman later said of the American presidency, "The buck stops here." But there was a definite downside to this situation.

Having assumed the burden of being the final decision maker in all things concerning the movement, Eddy came to the point of brooking no contradiction of her judgment in making decisions that she felt were impelled by God, or in matters affecting the teaching and practice of Christian Science. She was generally open to advice and discussion when it came to practical day-to-day issues about matters affecting the church. But she could be easily set off by any questioning of her judgment and authority when it came to issues of real spiritual moment. In some cases, household workers tested the waters of her tolerance out of a desire to be honest with her, or perhaps out of curiosity as to what her response might be.

After Eddy administered what seemed clearly an unmerited rebuke to Laura Sargent, for example, Adelaide Still, Eddy's personal maid, was bold enough to tell Eddy that she was being influenced by animal magnetism. Eddy's response was to sharply remind Still that she, Eddy, was in a better position than Still could possibly be to judge in such matters, and that Still should never forget that. Given Eddy's experience and powers of intuitive judgment about people and situations, she was probably right far more often than wrong. But this did not make things any easier on those around her when she was mistaken—especially since, as Robert Peel observed, Eddy "seldom apologized."[10]

When she made mistakes, reversed her position, or put people in office and then removed them, she felt this was a necessary form of learning and that God was giving her and them the experience they needed. There were occasions—probably not many—when Eddy was ready to acknowledge that she could make mistakes, especially when she acted under pressure and in haste.

One instance in which she promptly expressed regret for hastily written words occurred in the midst of the complex process of working out the revision for *Science and Health* in 1890. She had written a sharply phrased letter to the Reverend James Henry Wiggin, whom she had engaged to help edit the book, saying that his failure to fulfill his promises was "unbusinesslike unjust and unbearable." When he protested the unfairness of her letter, which apparently was based on misleading information, she wrote back, "I humbly, tearfully, read it, now . . . and wish it had not been written. . . . Pardon me this once and I never will give you another occasion of this kind to grant me such a favor. . . . I felt pushed to make somebody move."[11]

In most instances, however, Eddy would take a different position or change course on some important issue without explaining her motives or trying to justify a decision she had reversed. "Now I am always saying the unexpected, which is a cross for me and trying no doubt to others. But God's ways are not as ours," she wrote to two students in 1895. As she explained in another letter in 1902: "For the sake of our cause I ofttimes change orders and veer like a weather-vane. A direction that is right under existing circumstances may change the next hour for circumstances alter cases, then I countermand my order and it works well."[12]

Since Eddy put greater value on what she saw as obedience to God than on logical consistency, trying to keep up with a leader who led in this way could be at times exasperating. Adam Dickey, who served in her household during the last three years of her life, said that "the changing of her mind was a privilege that our Leader reserved for herself, and she exercised it without any regard whatever for what had gone before." Her approach in working out a problem, as she explained to him, was to take a step as nearly as she could in the right direction. Perhaps she might shortly find it had been wrong, but the step gave her a new point of view that she would not have had if she had not taken it. "I would not condemn myself, therefore, for what seemed to be a mistake," she told him, "but would include it as part of the working out of the problem."[13]

The increasing assurance of Eddy's leadership rested on her growing conviction, and that of her followers as well, that her exercise of authority was grounded in this discipline of spiritual listening. In many instances when they were tardy in taking some step she saw as wise, she asserted that, as she once put it, "My moves are not mine but His that moveth me." Beginning in the mid-1890s, her correspondence is studded with reminders to this effect—that her demands did not express her own personal wishes but divine requirements, and that obedience to these demands was therefore imperative. Issuing an instruction to her church's board of directors in early 1895, for example, she began in a way that almost seems to echo St. Paul's words, "I command, yet not I, but the Lord," writing: "God has bidden me speak out this morning and if I do not the stones will cry out."[14]

When two prominent attorneys in a major legal case in 1900 did not take her advice seriously, she showed no hesitation in reminding them, even though they were not Christian Scientists, of her own hard-won spiritual authority. Why "you give no credence to what I say," she wrote one of them, "is beyond my comprehension." Referring to the large number of her followers who "are following my guidance with unprecedented prosperity," she added that "whenever one of them ceases to do this he loses his prosperity. This is proverbial; here let me say, it is not I but a power infinitely above me that guides my perception."[15]

"A RELUCTANT CHARISMATIC"

One can only imagine the amazement with which the recipient of this letter read Eddy's claims as to the spiritual source and rightness of her guidance of others. At the same time, she had a principled and visceral repugnance for anything approaching the worship of her person among Christian Scientists. As biographer Robert David Thomas observed: "I think Eddy was a very unusual leader in terms of charisma. If I had to characterize her, I would call her a reluctant charismatic."[16]

She did have a conviction that her mission was unique, hers alone to fulfill. But her expression of this conviction was by no means uniform in tone. At times she could write in biblical language that came so naturally to her: "To-day it is a marvel to me that God chose me for this mission, and that my life-work was the theme of ancient prophecy and I the scribe of His infinite way of Salvation!" At other points, in the accents of the Apostle Peter, who proclaimed that "God is no respecter of persons," she could say to a student, "It is not because I have been specially chosen to reveal this Science, but it is as if there were those standing near a window, and because I was nearest the pane, the light fell upon me."[17]

Always, however, she disdained personal worship, which, she once noted, "is holding on to the window frame." Some of her sharpest rebukes were occasioned by the need to confront directly what she felt was the tendency among some of her students to hold on to that frame. For example, the highest aim of some Christian Scientists was to see Eddy in person. To this end, they would remain for hours outside her home, hoping to catch a glimpse of her. One woman lingered by her gate so long that Eddy stopped her carriage and addressed her peremptorily: "Have you no God? . . . Then never come here again to see me." In 1904 she introduced a new *Manual* bylaw, eventually titled "The Golden Rule," which stated that a member of the Mother Church shall not "haunt Mrs. Eddy's drive"—an injunction both symbolic and practical in its significance.[18]

At points, Eddy used humor to discourage unduly reverential attitudes toward her on the part of students and followers. Soon after the dedication of the Mother Church, she invited the so-called First Members (a group of about forty who, along with the directors, were in charge of the affairs of the church) to meet with her in Christian Science Hall in Concord. After speaking to them for a while, she said that she now wanted to hear them. But the response from the group was an awed silence. So Eddy told them a story about a devout Baptist girl who wanted to be sure that her beloved kitten would be saved. The girl drew a bath half full of water and attempted to immerse the kitten. The kitten, having strong objections, scratched her hand and jumped out of the water. This happened again and again until the girl looked at the kitten and said hopelessly, "Be a 'Piscopal kitten and go to hell if you want to." Whereupon Eddy said to the group, "Now, let's talk in a social way." Again, when speaking to William McKenzie about the need to be faithful and obedient, tears came into his eyes "when looking in her heavenly face." Eddy then rebuked his sensitivity, telling him in no uncertain terms: "*Stonify* yourself." He commented that he got the point, realizing that God was helping him to "rise above sensitiveness."[19]

Late in life, she replied to a letter by a student who had addressed her with idolatrous fervor, saying that she found the student's letter "astounding," as if it had been written "like a maniac, more than a Scientist! You an idolater making a *god* of *me!* . . . Beware . . . in turning to a *person* instead of divine Principle to help in time of need. O that you are blind to this sin seems to me incredible!" Three days after, she sent another message to the student, asking, "Has my *startling* last letter shocked you out of a mesmeric influence that is fatal to all who do not know what causes it? If such is the result I am paid for the great cross I took up when writing thus to *you*. You do know I love you deeply and so I try to help you in an hour of great need."[20]

At numerous points in both her published writings and private communications, Eddy returned to her basic point spelled out in her article (later renamed "Deification of Personality") published when *Christ and Christmas* was withdrawn for a time from circulation: "Whosoever looks to me personally for health or holiness mistakes. He that by reason of human love or hatred, or any other cause, clings to my material personality, greatly errs, stops his own progress, and loses the path to health, happiness, and heaven." Another article called "Personal Contagion" written toward the end of her life spoke of the tendency of "certain individuals" to "cling to the personality of its leader" as "sickly; it is a contagion—a mental malady, which must be met and overcome. Why? Because it would dethrone the First Commandment, 'Thou shalt have one God.' . . . There was never a religion or philosophy lost to the centuries except by sinking its divine Principle in personality." When this article was first published in the *Christian Science Sentinel*, editor Archibald McLellan affirmed, on Eddy's instruction, that "Personal Contagion" was "one of the most important statements of inspired truth that she has given to the world since the publication of the Christian Science text-book."[21]

In an analysis of the inner dynamic of this "personal contagion" in an undated memorandum, Eddy observed that it was not what it appeared to be—that the love and devotion it expressed rang false since it could so easily be reversed. Students, she wrote, would "set me up as Dagon and think they loved me, and the world would say 'they worship her.'" But this essentially pagan mode of personal worship took no account of the humanity of the one being worshiped—in Eddy's own case, of her personal needs to which some of her most ardent followers remained totally blind. Thus their love "can only be shown in a pagan manner . . . since their so called god has no human need." Then, pulling down their Dagon, they would turn upon the former object of their worship—as Eddy found was the case with several students who began by idolizing her and ended up by attacking her.[22]

In a kind of air-clearing exercise, she dictated in the early 1890s a brief, unpublished statement entitled "To All to Whom It May Concern," clarifying her own estimation of how she saw herself. Contrary to all attempts to define her in terms of some supernatural status, she began:

> In belief, I am a human being and should be treated as such, and spoken of as such, until I find my place outside this state of being. . . . In the flesh I am not what I desire to be; I am not what imagination would make me. I am not a heathen concept nor idol. . . . I am not the Door through which to enter, nor the Rock whereon to build, but what God has spoken to this age through me is the *way* and *sure foundation,* and no man entereth by any other way into Christian Science.[23]

"MERE PERSONAL ATTACHMENT"

Members of Eddy's household and church officers who worked with her regularly were on the whole less susceptible to what she called "personal contagion" than were followers who viewed her from afar. Those who served under her roof well knew that under the pressures of the moment she could sometimes lose her bearings, lash out, make demands that seemed arbitrary, and criticize in ways that seemed unfair. They knew, too, that she sometimes regretted such outbursts and sought to make amends. And there was something like a covenant of silence on the part of many of those who, in recounting their years of service to Eddy, gave only the barest hint of what they sometimes called her "human side."

Like any other religious leader, she faced the need of contending with her own demons, including her personal susceptibilities, the pitfalls that are endemic to the human condition. Eddy had made it a rule of her church that, in the words of one of its *Manual* bylaws, "neither animosity nor mere personal attachment should impel the motives or acts of the members of The Mother Church." When writing about the "coincidence of the divine with the human," she spoke of "pure humanity, friendship, home, the interchange of love" as examples of uniting "terrestrial and celestial joys."[24] But "mere personal attachment" meant something different. It meant satisfying the personal human ego—its emotional needs and dependencies, its pride and self-satisfaction, its fascination with or worship of the personality of others. This kind of attachment, she taught, could dwarf one's spiritual development more surely than anything else.

The term "personal" as Eddy used it here and in her other writings, published and unpublished, is a key word in the lexicon of Christian Science. In the first formulations of her teaching, up through and beyond the first edition of *Science and Health,* she used the term "personal sense" where, beginning with the second edition in 1878, she would later use the more broadly inclusive term "mortal mind." Eddy did speak of God as person, meaning that he is the "infinite Person" to whom we respond in wonder and love. But she strongly rejected the conventional view of him as a "man-projected" God with personal human qualities. Just as such a God represented for her a diminished sense of God, so personal traits in human beings represented a limited, diminished sense of their true identities, their God-given authentic being. "Remember," she told her students at the end of one of her last classes at the Massachusetts Metaphysical College, "it is personality, and the sense of personality in God or in man, that limits man," whereas, as she put it in *Retrospection and Introspection,* "silencing self, *alias* rising above corporeal personality, is what reforms the sinner and destroys sin."[25]

This rising, this regeneration from self, Eddy saw as incumbent on every individual—not excluding herself. Even in her early seventies, Eddy realized that she had more to learn along these lines. "Dear me," she wrote in a letter, "how frail is our fortitude to annihilate the claims of personality! What a poor demonstrator of this am I. To resolve and re-resolve and then go on the same."[26]

If Eddy was not free from all these claims, it is also clear that they were reaching her primarily through her adopted son, Ebenezer J. Foster, who took the name Foster Eddy, the recipient of this letter. No personal relationship over the forty-five years of her work in Christian Science—perhaps over her entire life—seems so anomalous or plunged her into such turmoil.

The relationship turned out so badly as to raise the question of how it could have ever begun. The answer lies largely in the depth of Eddy's personal need when she adopted Foster Eddy in 1888. She was sixty-seven and feeling the pressure of leading the movement as an increasing daily burden she longed to lay down. Worn down physically and mentally and troubled about the movement's future, she felt a need for closer, more continuing support than any of her other students could provide. Probably wondering at this point how long she might survive, she was also considering the need for a successor.

Foster Eddy, who had taken a class with her in November 1887, appeared to be an impressive fellow with good medical credentials and a measure of charm. He had served as a drummer boy in the Civil War, then studied at a prominent homeopathic medical college in Philadelphia. After further training in allopathic medicine and two years' experience at allopathic clinics there, he moved to Waterbury, Vermont, where he established a respectable homeopathic practice. Impressed by the healing of an old army friend of a serious long-standing illness through Christian Science, he investigated the new faith, became persuaded of its truth, and, after instruction at the Massachusetts Metaphysical College, entered into correspondence with Eddy.

Foster commended himself to Eddy as a thoughtful ex-physician, a conscientious convert to Christian Science, and a man old enough to put immaturity behind him, but young enough to have a promising future. He also professed the greatest devotion to her welfare in a way that at the time was probably sincere. In the summer of 1888, he became a member of her household, accompanying her to Chicago in June for the meeting of the National Christian Scientist Association. In November, she adopted him, stating to the court that he "is now associated with your petitioner in business, home life, and life work, and she needs such interested care and relationship."[27]

For several years, Foster Eddy seemed to have just the right qualifications to be a surrogate son and second-in-command. When she adopted him, he was forty-one, just two years younger than her son George, who had brought his family for a less than successful visit to Boston during a six-month period beginning in November 1887, when Foster Eddy was coming into favor. The contrast between the two men could not have been greater. George was bluff, hearty, and uncouth to the point that his exit from Boston was a great relief to his mother. Foster Eddy was genial and charming, but also able to acquit himself well

Ebeneezer J. Foster Eddy,
n.d. Courtesy of The Mary
Baker Eddy Collection.

as Eddy's representative, as a teacher of obstetrics at her college before she closed it, and as the first president of the reorganized Mother Church in 1892.

Foster Eddy's presence was galling to some members of Eddy's inner circle. But she clearly thrived on the relationship, sending "Benny," as she called him, on numerous missions representing her, while enjoying his solicitous support at home. He played the piano and sang to her, and while he spent weekdays in Boston after becoming publisher of her works in 1893, he usually commuted to Concord to spend weekends at Pleasant View. He also appears to have been serious and sincere in his study of Christian Science, at least for the first several years after Eddy adopted him. His diary for 1890, for example, reflects his attempt to assimilate her teaching. "Today we received instruction on impersonal treatment," he wrote characteristically on January 2, 1890; "we are to stand with our face outward watching constantly and praying without ceasing."[28]

Yet Foster Eddy was not constituted for the life of watching and praying. He was unwilling or unable to bear the weight of the demands that being the adopted son of Mary Baker Eddy and being groomed for heavy-duty service in the movement imposed on him. She loved him sincerely, but her mothering love in his case was primarily expressed in unremitting efforts to help him measure up to the role she expected him to fulfill. She was not about to accept him as he really was, a charming, able, and somewhat vain fellow who relished his daily comforts. Foster Eddy's weaknesses and basic unsuitability were apparent to many of Eddy's older associates, but what they saw was only intermittently clear to Eddy during the several years that followed her adoption of him. She first believed, then went on trying to believe, that "Benny" was everything she wanted him to be, and he continued to stoke the fires of her affection. Typical of the tone of his correspondence with her, even as the relationship deteriorated, is a sententious passage from a letter to her on May Day 1894:

> This is a beautiful morning and is May day. I awoke early this morning, and my thought went out, as of old, to the flowers of Spring, but it did not stay with them long for at once I thought of a flower more beautiful and lovely than all the flowers of this earth—my Mama!! . . . May she be fanned by the breath of tenderness, administered unto by deft fingers of love, fed by angels upon the nectar of heaven, protected by the Ever-Presence of Good that her blessed influence may continue in the world to purify and redeem it.[29]

Eddy was far from insensible to Foster Eddy's faults once they began to appear. As early as September 1890, she packed him off to board for a week with her reliable longtime student Ira Knapp in the hope that Knapp would "labor with him by counsel to rise above personal considerations" and to show him "that he is governed, upheld, and made joyful by *divine* Love only. . . ." This was a lesson that, as she came to believe, Foster Eddy was never able to learn. "We never can know who is in reality a C.S.," Eddy wrote to Calvin Hill in 1905, "until he is tested under fire; then what is left are dregs unfit for use till purged and purified or they are qualities that evil cannot destroy and are held by the power of God." As Eddy once put it to Foster Eddy, "You cannot be in the fire and not be burned. You are not a sufficient Christian, not purged and made pure, sufficiently for that."[30]

Foster Eddy was simply not the sort of individual who was committed to this kind of spiritual purgation. He does not appear to have been natively a bad or an unscrupulous man. In some respects, he was a very able individual. He acquitted himself well, for example, when he presided over the Christian Scientists' denominational congress at the World's Parliament of Religions in September 1893. A student of Eddy's who knew Foster Eddy observed that when he was "right" he was "a fine demonstrator of Christian Science, but under the influence of evil, he was a great trial to us all."[31]

From Eddy's standpoint, however, he was unable to defend himself against the malice and mental attack that threatened anyone and anything that could advance the cause of Christian Science. One thing Foster Eddy obviously lacked was the moral strength that being Eddy's adopted son required of him. He was especially susceptible to the flattery abundantly bestowed on him by many of Eddy's own followers. Among Christian Scientists in Boston, Eddy's adopted son was a crown prince—an alternative recipient of the adulation she discouraged for herself. Foster Eddy proved susceptible to glamour and flattery, especially on the part of those trying to get closer to Eddy by fawning on him.

For a few years, he did Eddy dutiful service. But signs of his power seeking within the movement grew with every passing month. In his attitude toward other Christian Scientists, he sometimes spoke in terms of moral admonishment, as when he wrote to Joshua Bailey, former editor of the *Journal*, "There is so much of this chronic *self* with all its past beliefs of error to be atoned for and wiped out, so much disobedience and rebellion towards God that it leads us into severe experiences at times." Ironically, Eddy often admonished her much loved but increasingly wayward adopted son in similar terms. In early 1893, for example, he was angling for the very visible position of pastor of the church at Boston. Aware of his ambitions, she wrote to him that he was "not ready to take the pulpit, and if you should take it with no higher, infinitely higher growth in the conception of what is required of you to preach the Truth, you would have to leave it just as others have had. Oh do not think of preaching till your life goes up to God in a fuller sense than at present."[32]

Much as she longed—and as much as he may at points have longed—for this to happen, Foster Eddy was not living the life that "goes up to God," but one of increasing evasiveness. The result was that Eddy was plunged into an excruciating alternation between efforts to reform him and despair that he was slipping beyond reclamation. By late 1893 she gave clear evidence of abandoning the hope that he could be reclaimed as a son and working Christian Scientist. To the new director Joseph Armstrong, whom Foster Eddy detested, she wrote in November, "He will *ruin you* unless you defend yourself mentally against his influence. . . . What shall I do to defend the cause against him? He knows no more than an *insane* man the nature of his actions and thinks it is all right till I struggle hours with him to get his eyes open and then he repents. . . . But in a few days does it right over again." Nonetheless, as she admitted to Foster Eddy in 1892, "No living mortal can give me so much *pain* or *pleasure* as you can, hence this present necessity of relieving my burdens if you cannot help bear them."[33]

Eddy eventually recognized the danger of focusing so much of her personal happiness on Foster Eddy. Early in their relationship, she had written to the Knapps, "He is to me *all* of *earth*, and instead of wanting him to be more in my thought and affections, I try to have him less, but do not succeed very much. I have feared that I thought of him more than I ought to think of any mortal or earthly object."[34] Yet by 1894, Foster Eddy's sloth became so noticeable, his behavior so deceitful, and his power seeking so obvious that almost no one could bear him, sometimes not even Eddy herself.

He became sometimes surly at Pleasant View, defensive of his eroding position in the household. Fearing that he might do her violent harm, Eddy once called for several old students, including Joseph Armstrong and his wife, to come to her. "I don't know how soon he will put his foot on my throat," she told them; "destruction is his aim." Then Foster Eddy, who had come into the room, went over to three of those she had called, whom he held responsible for doing him harm, saying chillingly, "These three I hated." Suddenly he got down on his knees by Eddy, cried, and pleaded with her to give him another chance—which she did, although he soon became worse than ever.[35]

The recollection of this event, made years later by one of the recipients of Foster Eddy's animus, may be supercharged, but Eddy's apprehension was undeniable. She had no clear idea of what her son was capable of doing when he was away from her, supposedly attending to his duties in Boston. As publisher of her writings, he made a handsome income, but repeatedly shirked doing the work the job required. William Dana Orcutt, employed by Eddy's printer, was dismayed when Foster Eddy arrived at the press in sartorial splendor, being conveyed there by a cab, when Eddy herself in times past had used a less luxurious horse car. He was, said Orcutt, agreeable to suggestions but repeatedly failed to get things done.[36]

The job of publisher was remunerative, but unglamorous. Losing his bid to become pastor of the Mother Church, Foster Eddy lobbied assiduously for the post of its first reader after personal preaching was dropped in early 1895. But in May of that year, his outright deception of Eddy brought matters to a head. Still publisher of her writings, he brought a married woman, Nellie Courtney, from a long distance to serve as his secretary. Although a student of Eddy, her practice of Christian Science was checkered at best. Eddy and others suspected that she was serving him in other ways—she was, Eddy wrote, "his private, *very* private secretary."[37]

Foster Eddy defended himself adamantly against the charge that any impropriety was involved, and Eddy eventually took him at his word. But the fact that she had been deceived about the very existence of a relationship that seemed so suspicious to others made the incident a turning point, especially after a noisy scene at Pleasant View. When

Foster Eddy read Calvin Frye's reference in a letter to Courtney as his "paramour," he rushed up to defend himself before his mother. She refused to see him, and her frustrated son pounded on her door, shoved Clara Shannon aside when she tried to prevent him from entering, then burst into Eddy's study with such force that she locked herself in an adjoining room for protection.[38]

"And Loss is Gain"

Over the next few years, Eddy counseled and cajoled Foster Eddy in a long series of letters that were in one sense the same letter written over and over again. In most of them, she expressed tender, continuing affection, but chastised him for continuing deceptions and abuses of her trust. There were times when he seemed repentant and hope for his improvement resurfaced. On October 15, 1895, for example, she spoke of a recent occasion when he knelt beside her and prayed for strength. "I did hope anew," she wrote, "that my faith could mount upward and that I should yet see of the travail of my motherhood, joy instead of sorrow, and its pangs cease forever." But the pangs continued to such an extent that Eddy wrote him less than four months later, "Now I have the painful task to tell you that you are growing dark fast. . . . It is enough to discourage the angels to see you decline so soon from where I got you after such awful experiences."[39]

One indication of Foster Eddy's "decline" was his behavior two weeks before this letter was written. When Eddy gave her second and last address in the Mother Church on January 5, 1896, Foster Eddy escorted her to the platform. Frye observed that, having taken Foster Eddy's arm before entering the church, she tried to withdraw her arm from his, but he clung to her, refusing to let her do so. Then, according to the hearing and memory of another witness, when Foster Eddy introduced her, he spoke of Eddy as "my mother and your mother," putting so much emphasis on "my" that Eddy, in an apparently involuntary gesture, suddenly clenched her fists.[40]

This angry and perhaps embarrassed reaction was understandable, considering the devolution of their relationship over the previous two years. Yet it took another year and a half before Eddy made a permanent break with her adopted son. In August 1896, she had packed him off to Philadelphia, where she instructed him to start a new branch church. Failing to accomplish this, he joined another branch church, where his jockeying for power thoroughly antagonized much of the membership. In August 1897, the Philadelphia church voted to expel him. At this point, Eddy forbade Foster Eddy to come to Pleasant View for three years until he showed definite signs of improvement, using the formal term "Dear *Doctor*" as a salutation and signing the letter, not "Mother" as usual, but "Yours only in Truth, Mary Baker Eddy."[41] Foster Eddy's rehabilitation never occurred, with the result that he and Eddy never saw one another again.

After a period of travel, Foster Eddy settled down to a quiet existence back in Waterbury Centre, Vermont. In formal terms, his relation to Eddy never changed: he remained by law her adopted son, thus making it possible for him to again become a factor in her life when he became a plaintiff in the Next Friends Suit a decade after their final break. Despite his initial professions of loyalty to Eddy when the *New York World*'s attack on her began, he became a party to the suit, claiming in a newspaper interview at the time that he had "only been awaiting an opportunity to strike a blow for the rescue of the kind-hearted woman who made me her son." Perhaps a more accurate gauge of his actual attitude was his disingenuous claim in the same interview that he had kept himself out of the public eye, living in his remote home location, because he feared assassination at the hands of the group controlling Eddy at Pleasant View. Just as revealing is the report that he was observed snickering in the courtroom when allegations detrimental to Eddy were made during the trial.[42]

By that point, she had long come to realize the toll that the relationship had taken on her, seeing in it the cause of some of the worst difficulties she had endured during the years since she adopted him in 1888. To a friend, Eddy wrote of her relationship with Foster Eddy as "seven almost eight long years I have had the indescribable, 'sharper than vinegar to the teeth.'" The anguish was still there, she said, "notwithstanding all that I have done for him, all my prayers and 'Mother's evening Hymn'"[43]—a poem she had written in 1893, a critical year during which she still retained a shred of the vanishing hope for Foster Eddy's reformation.

Like her other six poems eventually set to music as hymns, "Mother's Evening Hymn" (eventually titled "The Mother's Evening Prayer") was essentially a prayer—but a prayer that moves at two levels. At one level, it is a prayer on behalf of the son she loved, who can be identified with the child spoken of in its first stanza:

> O gentle presence, peace and joy and power;
> O Life divine, that owns each waiting hour,
> Thou Love that guards the nestling's faltering flight!
> Keep Thou my child on upward wing tonight.[44]

At another level, however, the poem was a prayer for the movement she mothered in an even larger sense. Read in this way, the poem makes just as much sense and is equally if not more moving. Echoing the Ninety-first Psalm, it reflects a sense of love and spiritual trust in divine protection so inclusive that the personal elements that initially gave rise to its writing seem beside the point. The ambiguity of the poem reflects the duality Eddy felt between the fulfillment of her personal needs on the one hand and her role as leader of her church on the other. Just how much suffering the frustration of her human yearning cost her can be felt in the third stanza, which poignantly expresses the tortuous character of the experience through which she was passing:

> O make me glad for every scalding tear,
> For hope deferred, ingratitude, disdain!
> Wait, and love more for every hate, and fear
> No ill,—since God is good, and loss is gain.

What had been lost, certainly, was a relationship that she treasured and poured her heart into. But in the process of losing so much, something had been gained. As she once observed in a letter to Augusta Stetson, "God always takes the one we love most in the flesh wherewith to rebuke our pride and chasten our lives in the flesh till we are above the flesh and all human designs and safe in the place of His abiding." In her relation with Foster Eddy, Eddy was forced to fulfill the demands involved in her words to Laura Sargent and Calvin Frye when, in early 1896, she told them that she was about to give them the whole of Christian Science in a nutshell: "Is God Love? Is Love infinite? Yes. Can you get outside the focal distance of infinity? I love. I do not formulate what I love but I love. If we personalize or have an object, love becomes finite instead of divine and infinite, and we lose the divine reflection. But if it is impersonal Love it opens up boundless resources whereby we can do good in every way."[45]

"ONE CAUSE AND EFFECT"

As her relation to Foster Eddy was winding down during the mid-1890s, Eddy—no doubt relieved from the psychological burden of trying to make it work—became better able, in her words, to "do good in every way." She became more fruitful and active in her work for the church, writing its *Manual,* pushing forward the construction of the Mother Church, and finding a variety of ways to galvanize her followers in the study and practice of Christian Science. In 1896, she also wrote perhaps the most authoritative and succinct statement of her teaching: a 2,700-word article for the *Granite Monthly*, a New Hampshire periodical, in October.

Ironically, the untitled article (which she later called "One Cause and Effect") was preceded by a biographical portrait of her by Hanna calibrated to the magazine's air of folksy respectability. Amid such regional fare as "Aunt Betsy's Thank-Offering," "New Hampshire Necrology," and "The Midnight Storm" came a lengthy and rather tame treatment of Eddy's life and accomplishments. In framing his portrait of her, Hanna seemed enamored with impressive statistics: the number of students she had taught, the sales of *Science and Health,* the current membership of the Mother Church, and the growing number of branch churches. He also spoke of her "pious parents"; made it seem as if she had been finely educated; referred to her "self-culture," modesty, and selflessness; described the relatively modest Pleasant View as her "beautiful home on the outskirts of Concord"; and referred to her "fine estate with ornamental grounds" at Roslindale, a rather extravagant description of the home where she had lived for a brief time after leaving Boston.[46]

With all of Hanna's praise of her, the picture he paints misses the element of authority that gives "One Cause and Effect" its own strong effect. Nor would one guess from the folksy context in which the article appeared how much controversy its author had caused or how deeply her teaching affronted the worlds of theology and medicine. Oddly enough, Eddy's article is not even listed in the contents, but tacked on to Hanna's descriptive piece, with a brief introduction by her stating, "At the request of the editor of this popular magazine, I have written for its columns this bit on the subject of my doctrine."

The "bit" she contributed to the pages of this regional magazine was adapted to a non–Christian Science readership in the sense that it took them along a line of logical progression into the heart of her teaching. In "One Cause and Effect," Eddy by no means sought to conceal the substance of Christian Science from first-time inquirers or to offer the public a watered-down version of its teaching. She stressed the biblical basis of Christian Science, even while bringing into sharp relief the great difference between her teaching and Christian orthodoxy.

"One Cause and Effect" begins with a short paragraph spanning the whole Bible before concluding with a terse statement of the crux of Christian Science:

> Christian Science begins with the First Commandment of the Hebrew Decalogue, "Thou shalt have no other gods before me." It goes on in perfect unity with Christ's Sermon on the Mount, and in that age culminates

in the Revelation of St. John, who, while on earth and in the flesh, like ourselves, beheld "a new heaven and a new earth,"—the spiritual universe, whereof Christian Science now bears testimony.

Asserting that her teaching departs from the trend of other denominations only through "increase of spirituality," Eddy defines the basis of that spirituality by quoting what she calls her "first plank in the platform of Christian Science," her "scientific statement of being" from the chapter, "Recapitulation," in *Science and Health:* "There is no life, truth, intelligence, nor substance in matter. All is infinite Mind and its infinite manifestation, for God is All-in-all. Spirit is immortal Truth; matter is mortal error. Spirit is the real and eternal; matter is the unreal and temporal. Spirit is God, and man is His image and likeness. Therefore man is not material; he is spiritual."[47]

In this short statement of some sixty words, Eddy used the word *is* no fewer than eleven times. By so doing, she telescoped her conviction that spiritual being is the only actual kind of existence, now or anytime, here or hereafter—that all is Mind and its manifestation, in which matter has no part.

If she were simply stating that mind or spirit is *ultimately* real and that all we perceive now is a form of illusion, her teaching might indeed have been classed within the framework of, say, Hindu cosmology. But for her, the denial of the reality of matter as a consequence of the primacy and infinitude of Spirit did not wipe out the reality of nature and the meaning of present experience. She used an ordinary object to ask an extraordinary question: "Is a stone spiritual?" "To erring material sense," she wrote, "No!" But to a more accurate spiritual perception, she continued, the only actual existence of a stone, as "a small manifestation of Mind," is spiritual. "Take away the mortal sense of substance, and the stone itself would disappear, only to reappear in the spiritual sense thereof." She then reached the bottom line of her metaphysics: "The only logical conclusion is that all is Mind and its manifestation, from the rolling of worlds, in the most subtle ether, to a potato-patch."[48]

That "potato-patch" does not fit into the conventional Christian cosmology that pictures two kinds of reality: the ultimate reality of God and his kingdom into which we will pass after death, as well as the immediate, tangible reality of the human condition in which we now dwell. God's universe, she said, is the only actual creation, and it is really here in all its multifarious expressions of life and varieties of form, color, and outline. She insisted that it is human limitation alone that mistakes the true spiritual nature of that universe by defining it as mortal and material.

Yet traditional Christian theology, as she saw it, perpetuated that limitation instead of challenging it. In "One Cause and Effect," Eddy asked if the power and reality of God could be combined with belief in the power and reality of matter. Is God "cause" and matter "effect"? Protestant, Catholic, and Judaic theology in almost all their forms say yes. The crux of Eddy's metaphysics lies in her insistence that truly biblical religion says no: "That there is but one God or Life, one cause and one effect, is the *multum in parvo* of Christian Science; and to my understanding it is the heart of Christianity, the religion that Jesus taught and demonstrated." From this standpoint, the oneness of God the creator with his creation is the only view consistent with a pure monotheism: "Was it Mind or matter that spake in creation, 'and it was done'? The answer is self-evident, and the command remains, 'Thou shalt have no other gods before me.' "

It would be difficult to overestimate how much the Old Testament command to have but one God entered into and shaped her theology. The impulse to acknowledge the reality of "the God of Abraham, Isaac, and Jacob," of the great "I AM" worshiped by Moses, of the one God of whom the psalmist sang, lay at the core of Eddy's sensibility. "If Mind was first chronologically, is first potentially, and must be first eternally," she wrote in *Science and Health*, "then give to Mind the glory, honor, dominion, and power everlastingly due its holy name."[49]

For Eddy, doing this—however great the violation of cherished human assumptions, however intense the opposition from entrenched material views—puts one on holy ground. It restores one to the world of the Bible. Fully acknowledging the sovereignty of God, Eddy insisted, rather than adapting our views of him down to the limits of conventional human beliefs, opens human thinking to grasp anew the reality of God.

If God has been acknowledged in his fullness as truly absolute, sovereign, supreme, then for his sake and in his name, she maintained, one must oppose the belief that there is intelligence, substance, and life apart from him. In the words of a verse in Deuteronomy that she quoted repeatedly in her writings, "The Lord he is God; there is none else beside him." Every element of suffering and evil in the world she identified as, at base, the result of the root error of belief in the reality of a power apart from God. This error of belief she saw as idolatry— "the shocking human idolatry that presupposes Life, substance, Soul, and intelligence in matter,—which is the antipode of God, and yet governs mankind."[50] In dozens of passages and in a variety of ways, Eddy inveighs against what she sees as this besetting sin and error, asserting in "One Cause and Effect" that Christian Science "translates matter into Mind, rejects all other theories of causation, restores the spiritual and original meaning of the Scriptures, and explains the teachings and life of our Lord."

These were strong claims, and Eddy appealed to Jesus' healing works to substantiate them: "The great Way-shower illustrated Life unconfined, uncontaminated, untrammelled, by matter. He proved the superiority of Mind over the flesh, opened the door to the captive, and enabled man to demonstrate the law of Life, which St. Paul declares 'hath made me free from the law of sin and death.' "

In concluding "One Cause and Effect," however, she again appealed to the readers' own experiences. If this understanding of Christianity seems mystical, she wrote, "the mist of materialism will vanish as we approach spirituality, the realm of reality; cleanse our lives in Christ's righteousness; bathe in the baptism of Spirit, and awake in His likeness."

5

Woman Goes Forth

A Different Kind of Thinker, a Different Kind of Thinking

After the publication of "One Cause and Effect," an editorial note by Hanna in the *Journal* commented that even to the longtime student of *Science and Health* "some of the statements of this article come with startling force . . . because of the forceful originality of their putting." He spoke of it as "one of the strongest and most comprehensive epitomes of the doctrine of Christian Science we have ever read."[1] It was a tightly reasoned and closely argued piece of metaphysics and theology, and it was, furthermore, the product of a woman's pen—a point of some importance, when one takes into account that during the period in which Eddy lived, the tradition of Christian theology had been to an overwhelming degree a male enterprise.

By the latter part of the twentieth century, women were to play an increasing role in the life of the church—in theology, liturgy, and expressions of spirituality. Historically, however, the makers of Christian doctrine from Augustine and Aquinas through Luther and Calvin to Schleiermacher and Barth were men. The intellectual bastions of Christianity have been monasteries and seminaries populated until recent decades almost wholly by men. Christian doctrine has reached the laity largely through preaching in pulpits by men. Within most Christian communions, the sacraments have been and are administered almost entirely by men. Mary Baker Eddy was in some respects the beneficiary of male thinkers such as Augustine, Calvin, Luther, and Edwards—especially Jonathan Edwards, the progenitor of the New Light Theology in which she was raised. But she did not aspire to be elevated to some theological Mount Rushmore, dialoging across the ages with the great male figures of the Christian tradition.

Eddy accounted herself both less and more than a Christian theologian: less, because she had neither the temperament nor the opportunity to enter into what was almost exclusively a male professional world; more, because she believed she was accomplishing something far closer to the bone of daily life than the development of new theological insights for their own sake. In the words of feminist historian Jean A. McDonald, Eddy was "not motivated as a theologian in an abstract way, just thinking 'well, how do the ideas fit together?' She was much more interested in what will make a difference in human life. What is true about God?—this was the main thing in her life. She was not getting answers, and she had to find answers that would make a difference in her own experience and in the experience of others."[2]

To Eddy, making this difference was crucial. Unlike many major figures in the fields of theology and philosophy, she had no interest in constructing an intellectual system as such. She used metaphysical and theological concepts to communicate the spiritual meaning she believed she had discovered in the Bible. Her intent in so doing was to make as intelligible as possible how individuals today could experience and demonstrate God's total sovereignty in daily life. Thus, in Eddy's view, she was not offering the world a new theory, but was articulating an empowering spiritual truth of major proportions.

One might also ask how Eddy should be regarded in the broad stream of Christian thought. Was she a theologian? Religious historian Martin E. Marty responds in the negative, "because in my definition a theologian has no words to use until there is a believing community. I don't think Paul was a theologian in the Christian tradition. He was an immediate, primary experiencer who just set it forth. So in that sense a philosopher of religion and progenitor of religious vision is what I would call her."[3] Other women within the Christian tradition, such as the mystics Julian of Norwich, Teresa of Avila, and Catherine of Sienna, have been primary experiencers, setting forth what they experienced in enduring classics of mystical literature. But Eddy believed that she had made a conclusive discovery about the nature of being that began with, but went well beyond, the borders of her own subjective spiritual life.

Acting on this conviction, Eddy wrote what she believed to be a textbook for Christian practice. Yet she would have been the first to object had her book gained merely intellectual status as yet another tome on library shelves to be analyzed and compared with other works. She did address briefly some of the differences between her thinking and the idealism of Kant and Berkeley.[4] Yet she was no more interested in debating philosophical points than in engaging in theological disputes that did not have a direct bearing on life as lived.

To Eddy, the most basic issue of all came down to a choice between two totally contrary positions. As she put it in *Science and Health:* "The theories I combat are these: (1) that all is matter; (2) that matter originates in Mind, and is as real as Mind, possessing intelligence and life. . . . One only of the following statements can be true: (1) that everything is matter; (2) that everything is Mind. Which one is it?"[5]

On the essential point that all must be "infinite Mind and its infinite manifestation," there could be no compromise, no equivocation. "Materialistic hypotheses challenge metaphysics to meet in final combat," she wrote in *Science and Health.* "In this revolutionary period, like the shepherd-boy with his sling, woman goes forth to battle with Goliath."[6] Just as the shepherd-boy with his sling lacked worldly weapons, so Eddy knew that she lacked the academic training and professional status to challenge materialistic hypotheses, as would be required of a male in the intellectual and religious worlds. Yet a purely conceptual challenge could not possibly go far enough. The only effectual challenge to the "Goliath" of materialism must come from the staying power and pure spirituality she saw as inseparably linked with womanhood in the fullest sense of the term.

This is not to deny that Eddy was a serious thinker, but to specify the kind of thinker she was. As a woman to whom the profession of the ministry was closed, she thought, as it were, with her life. She had no choice but to stick close to and learn from the texture and day-to-day involvements of that life: from her family relationships and her friendships, her search for health across several decades, her reading, research, and personal quest for truth. Was this a loss? Not according to some writers in the field of feminine spirituality who point out that women have a distinct advantage in pursuing their own path to spiritual insight and discovery. Eddy, like other New England women of her day, thought about and struggled over pressing issues such as predestination, grace, endless punishment, and atonement perhaps more than males, then or since, have been prone to acknowledge.

Male professionals in seminaries and pulpits dealt with these issues in sermons, books, and theological journals. But they did so within the protocols and limits that a highly structured theological tradition was bound to impose. From one standpoint, the very fact that women were confined to largely domestic roles or to professional tasks such as nursing and teaching was limiting. From another, the act of relating to others within a family context of mothering and other forms of nurturing could provide genuine sources of insight not as readily available within the framework of male professional life. In the words of Carol Ochs, a scholar in the field of feminine spirituality, "A woman can bring a unique perspective to spiritual questions based on experiences that are unique to her. What is required is a consciousness that will reflect on an experience and not let go until its value has been understood. Many experiences undergone only by women can be quite ordinary, yet nonetheless reveal the nature of reality and shed light upon the questions of meaning and value."[7]

In the spirit of these words, we cannot validly separate the spiritual problems that impelled Eddy's quest from the personal and familial context in which they arose. British historian H. A. L. Fisher wrote that "the great ideas of God, of immortality, of the soul, of a life penetrated by Christianity, were never far from her mind."[8] If it is true that these "great ideas" were never far from Eddy's mind in her early years, that mind was never far, at least for long, from the lively realities of daily existence within a close-knit family on a New England farm.

Family life was the horizon of her existence, and her rebellion as a young woman against predestinarian Calvinism was woven inextricably into the fabric of her family relationships. In later years, Eddy unselfconsciously couched her account of this rebellion in terms of the enormous disparity between her father's adherence to his "relentless theology" and her mother's much-treasured example of pure goodness and love. Again, when she publicly proclaimed her rejection of predestination during her examination for church membership, she did so more in familial than doctrinal terms: "I stoutly maintained that I was willing to trust God, and take my chance of spiritual safety with my brothers and sisters,—not one of whom had then made any profession of religion,—even if my creedal doubts left me outside the doors."[9]

Over the next two decades, it was her own bitter experiences and personal losses, rather than theological ratiocination as such, that impelled her search for a practical answer to the problem of human suffering. In this sense, there was no sharp separation between the spiritual search that led Eddy to the discovery of Christian Science and her ensuing efforts to found and lead a movement built on that discovery. The impulse that prompted her to pursue the answer to life's basic questions until a breakthrough occurred was the same impulse that impelled her to share the fruits of what she discovered with others.

Temperamentally she would have much preferred a quiet life of introspection and retirement to the demanding work that devolved upon her in founding and leading the movement. Yet she also felt strongly impelled to continue the work of mothering and nurturing the movement so that the practical truth she believed she had discovered would have a rooted and ongoing life of its own.

WOMANHOOD AND MOTHERHOOD

For Eddy, mothering was the most immediate practical expression of the strength and staying power of womanhood. "The affection of a human mind—however exalted—is not Divine," she wrote in a letter in 1896, "but nearer to that than any other expression of human love is a mother's love."[10]

In its largest sense, mothering was inextricably bound in both her teaching and practice with the hitherto unexplored dimensions of the motherhood of God. Eddy never claimed to have originated the idea of God's motherhood, as well as fatherhood. She was surely familiar with the fact that the American Shakers of New England had spoken of God as Mother as well as Father. The great preacher and theologian Theodore Parker, whom she much admired, had spoken of God in this way. For many years Parker included in his public prayers appeals to "Our Father and our Mother God," as Louisa May Alcott movingly recalled:

> The slow, soft folding of the hands, the reverent bowing of the good gray head, the tears that sometimes veiled the voice, the simplicity, frankness, and devout earnestness, made both words and manner wonderfully eloquent; and the phrase, "Our Father and our Mother God," was inexpressibly sweet and beautiful,—seeming to invoke both power and love to sustain and comfort the anxious, overburdened hearts of those who listened and went away to labor and to wait with fresh hope and faith.[11]

Something of the same note was sounded by Eddy during the last class she taught to a group of select students in 1898. Explaining her concept of God, she said: "It is like the Father protecting and caring for His child, it is like the Mother taking the little one in Her arms, and feeding it with the milk of the Word, it is like the tender Shepherd, caring for His flock, going out into the marshes after the lost lamb, calling, calling—listening for its little plaintive voice, taking it in His arms, carrying it home and doing it over and over again."[12]

For students of Christian Science, this view of God's motherhood as well as his fatherhood often struck a deeply responsive chord. As one Christian Scientist whose testimony appeared in the chapter "Fruitage" in *Science and Health* put it: "Through Christian Science, Mrs. Eddy had given me what I had longed for all my life,—a Mother, a perfect 'Father-Mother God.' . . . All the years of bitterness, hate, and fear melted away. I knew then, as I know now, that nothing satisfies but Love."

"'God is Love,'" wrote Eddy in the chapter "Prayer" in *Science and Health*. "More than this we cannot ask, higher we cannot look, farther we cannot go." This understanding of God as Mother was not primarily conceptual. It was a way of expressing the core truth that she felt Christian Science had brought to humanity: the understanding of God, not just as loving, but as Love itself, and of Love as the supremely powerful, sustaining, and healing reality in the midst of daily human experience.[13]

Eddy's followers often said that her own expression of Love's motherhood imparted a strong immediate sense of its reality and presence. One of them recounted the effect of a brief encounter she and her children had with Eddy on September 4, 1899, when Eddy had invited Christian Scientists for a brief visit on the grounds of Pleasant View. "I saw for the first time the real mother love," she later wrote,

> I looked down at the grass and the flowers and there was the same Love resting on them. It is difficult for me to put into words what I saw. This Love was everywhere, like the light, but it was divine not mere human affection.
> I looked at the people milling around on the lawn and I saw it poured out on them. I thought of the various discords in this field, the absolute unreality of everything but this infinite Love. It was not only everywhere present, like the light, but it was an intelligent presence that spoke to me, and I found myself weeping as I walked back and forth under the trees and saying out loud, "Why did I never know you before? Why have I not known you always?"[14]

Eddy spoke of her leadership of the Christian Science movement as reflecting the immense nurturing power of God's mothering love. Yet she also often spoke of her leadership more in military terms as a general commanding his troops—especially when there was an immediate need to galvanize her students into action. In the midst of one difficult situation in early 1896, she wrote to her student John F. Linscott, who had been a Union captain in the Civil War, "I am as a General looking over and giving orders for taking that stronghold. . . . Ask of me all that is needed by you as a faithful earnest soldier and Captain, to reinforce you and forward the march onward. . . . I am as ever your Teacher guide and mother."[15]

As her final words to Linscott suggest, the more male and military aspect of her role complemented, rather than conflicted with, its more feminine side as "Teacher guide and mother." Mothering the movement, at least as much as issuing orders, was what she did on a day-to-day basis. Doing this kept Eddy busy at her post in the larger field of Christian Science, guiding and encouraging students, attending to details, putting out fires, counseling and cajoling officers of the church.

Taken together, Eddy's correspondence on church matters forms an important ongoing aspect of her published and unpublished writings. This correspondence includes major messages to the Mother Church, frequent instructions to its board of directors, letters to branch churches, usually on the occasion of their dedication, and counsel to individual students involved in church issues. Judging from the amount of time she devoted to it, Eddy obviously considered this pastoral work on behalf of her church as a basic means through which her leadership was exercised. Some idea of the sheer volume of her correspondence can be gleaned from the fact that, to the ten individuals with whom she corresponded the most, she wrote a total of nearly 2,500 letters from the late 1880s until her death.[16]

Conscious that she would not be indefinitely present to offer such support, she instructed church members in a letter to be placed in the permanent records of the church to turn to the by-laws and the Bible—especially to the letters of Paul, which were largely directed to the infant churches he had established.

Indeed, Garry Wills, in an uneven essay in his book *Certain Trumpets: The Call of Leaders,* compares Eddy's leadership with that of Paul, who, preeminently "among the first great Christian leaders . . . roughed out doctrine, organized churches and evangelized." As Wills further notes, "Paul's Corinthian community was full of people suing and denouncing each other—for committing incest, for offering pagan sacrifices. Paul responded with tough assertions of his own authority—and so did Eddy." The departure of some of the students to whom she wrote may not have been as bizarre as in Paul's day, and Wills misses the pastoral nurturing in the efforts of both Paul and Eddy to protect and sustain the churches they had done so much to found. But he is right to point to this aspect of her work as a major element in her leadership.[17]

Almost no one, she frequently complained in her correspondence, understood the pressures and demands that relentlessly piled in upon her. To Laura Lathrop of New York she wrote late in 1891, "Your worst dilemma would be in my history quite a gala day." Similar sentiments are like a drumbeat in her correspondence. Four years later she wrote to the Hannas: "Pardon me for saying the Leader in our cause is shocked daily by burdens that to others would be insupportable. The detail of the cold world's harsh business of attention to housekeeping lawn farm etc. with a posse of sinners ever at your heels and the whole field of Christian Science calling on you—means somewhat to three score years and ten."[18]

In the largest sense, the Christian Science movement itself was and would remain her child. At points, it had appeared that the relationship with Foster Eddy threatened to distract her from this larger affection. But that affection, that mothering commitment, was strong—so strong that it eventually won out. In 1892, when a branch church in Denver was about to be dedicated, she wrote: "I as a corporeal person, am not in your midst. I as a dictator, arbiter or ruler, am not present; but I as a mother whose heart pulsates with every throb of theirs for the welfare of her children, am present and rejoice with them that rejoice."[19]

By that time, Christian Scientists had generally begun speaking of Eddy, and to her, as "Mother." During her years in Boston she had been known primarily as "Teacher." But in May 1889, the very month she left for New Hampshire, a *Journal* piece voiced what many students felt: "She has never claimed either the name or the substance of Christian Science as a property. But the Child is hers. She is its Mother, and she watches over it with more than an earthly mother's solicitude and love. Her labors and watching have planted Christian Science, and her tears have watered its growth in mortal consciousness."[20]

The affectionate title caught on—in her words, it "spread like wild-fire"—and in so doing became an easy mark for critics. In 1901 when Eddy complained to Alfred Farlow about the press's jeering references to her as "Mother Eddy," he frankly informed her that Christian Scientists were themselves to blame: they used it so much in the Wednesday evening meetings, "on the street cars and everywhere as to cause this vulgar use of it in the press." The next year, Mark Twain, in the first of his *North American Review* articles, made sport of Eddy's "army of disciples" who reverently called her "Our Mother"—predicting the inevitable day when "Mary the Matron" would be given precedence over "Mary the Virgin." Eddy palpably winced. In her rejoinder to Twain in the *New York Herald,* she said that she had at first begged her students not to call her "Mother" but that they continued to do so nonetheless. Shortly afterward, owing to "public misunderstanding," as she put it, Eddy changed a *Manual* bylaw that had reserved the appellation "Mother" for herself among Christian Scientists (except, of course, for its normal familial use). The change required Christian Scientists to drop the appellation and to refer to her as "Leader" instead.[21]

Although Eddy felt compelled to relinquish the name of "Mother" for public purposes, students close to her went on using it for the rest of her days. More important, she went on mothering her flock just as before. She had always shown solicitude for her students' progress, counseling them through letters and visits. But until she left for New Hampshire, meeting the demands of church work and the needs of students in the Boston area absorbed most of her attention. Once having left, she found herself thinking more in terms of the welfare of the movement as a whole.

Eddy had come to see dissension among her students, constant elbowing for power and place, and competition for a place in her affections as the primary dangers threatening the growing prosperity of the movement. Nothing caused her more concern for its future or more heartache on its behalf. As she put it in a letter written in March 1890 when speaking of a quarrel among factions in Chicago: "I love all my students and when I was asked what side I was on answered both sides. Can a mother choose between her children?" Upon leaving Boston she grew more acutely conscious of the need to foster greater unity and love among Christian Scientists. In the words of biographer Richard Nenneman, "she believed that unless Christian Science was to be signally identified as a religion of the truly reborn—that is, by self-lessness, humility, and love without expectation of reward—it would eventually lose the day."[22]

Like a mother seeking to promote harmony among warring children, one of Eddy's first initiatives upon leaving Boston was to write a series of letters to students throughout the United States, urging them to show more of the spirit of love and unity that she saw as lying at the very heart of Christian Science. "Love, love alone," she wrote to Laura Lathrop in New York, "will found, upbuild, and establish forever both the Christian Scientist and our Cause. But envy, jealousy, or rivalry, will kill the spirit of this Science in the person who possesses it and will thwart the establishment of it in this age." To a prominent Christian Scientist in Chicago who had broken relations with another worker there, she pleaded: "O do show me how great is your love for God by forgiving, yea more, by loving all mankind and for once I ask it show yourself the best Christian of the two by taking the *first* step towards reconciliation. Will you do this dear? My heart bleeds . . . that we are not *brethren*. I would humble myself in the dust to have this otherwise."[23]

Until the last few years of her life Eddy continued her letter-writing ministry to former students and other promising Christian Scientists, many of them far from Boston. Among the hundreds of such letters she wrote over the years was this counsel to Frank Walter Gale, a student from California, written in 1891:

> You are *growing*. The Father has sealed you, and the opening of these seals must not surprise you. The character of Christ is wrought out in our lives by just such processes. The tares and wheat appear to grow together until the harvest; then the tares are *first* gathered, that is, you have seasons of seeing your errors—and afterwards by reason of this very seeing, the tares are burned, the error is destroyed. Then you see Truth plainly and the wheat is "gathered into barns," it becomes permanent in the understanding.

Mary Baker Eddy working in her Pleasant View study, ca. 1903–06.
Courtesy of The Mary Baker Eddy Collection.

Eddy often felt it her duty to lay bare a chronic fault in a student that she saw as retarding needed spiritual progress. In an 1892 letter to Ira Knapp, written in the midst of a serious church crisis, she expressed appreciation for his deep Christianity, then pointed to one thing she urged Knapp to correct: "Rouse yourself from *morbid slowness*. . . . This slowness . . . arises from *fear* and not daring to act instantaneously lest you are not right. Now commit your way to God, *trust* Him, and act *quickly*."[24]

Eddy took no joy in administering what she saw as needed rebukes to her students. It was, as she put it in an 1893 address to the Christian Scientist Association, a duty she could not in conscience avoid: "However keenly the human affections yearn to forgive a mistake, and pass a friend over it, sympathy can neither atone for error, advance individual growth, nor change this immutable decree of Love,—'Be ye perfect.'" Once after a severe tongue-lashing to James Gilman, Eddy held his hand, then as he recalled, said yearningly like a mother: "It seems hard to bear, I know. You won't feel hard toward me, will you? I felt I must be severe because you needed it; but it was hard for me to be so. . . . Oh!" she said with great feeling, "You don't know what burdens I have borne through the necessity I have felt for rebuking students, but who could not receive my rebuke as coming from true love for them. This is the great test of the true student." The great test for Eddy herself was not only bearing the burden of administering needed rebuke to students, but to know when to let them learn from their own mistakes. "Know this," she wrote to one of them in 1891, "that a Mother's love encourages self dependence and trust in God. . . . It would not be love that would keep her child a lifelong suckling! All these things, like Mary of old, I 'ponder in my heart,' and try to do by my students as I would have them do by me."[25]

In her own relation with the board of directors, documented by hundreds of communications over the years, Eddy made an effort to awaken them to their own duties and capacity to perform them. She knew that she would not be personally present to guide them indefinitely and wanted to get out from under the burden of being constantly appealed to for instructions on the one hand, or needing to undo the messes they had made on the other. Her sometimes gentle, often caustic, and always very definite instructions typically sound at some points like a mother scolding truant children, at others like a general issuing orders.

Take, for example, the episode of the Westminster chimes. When the Mother Church was opened at the end of 1894, its bell tower featured chimes imported from Westminster, England. Eddy was informed by the directors in a casual communication that the chimes would ring every fifteen minutes, thus pleasantly reminding the citizens of Boston's Back Bay of the presence of Christian Science. What the incessant ringing did accomplish was to aggravate Back Bay residents to the point that a Boston newspaper reported they were being kept awake at night.

Eddy sought to pacify the waters by writing two graciously comic letters to the *Boston Herald*. Saying it would ease her conscience to confess her part in the blunder of the chimes, she told its readers that she had paid scant attention when she was informed of the project of installing them: "So the Directors purposing to show their generosity to the public, fell into the ignorant atrocity of calling the costly clock from across the waters to disturb the peace of Boston." The chimes, she promised, would be "let loose but *thrice* per day." When this proved an insufficient concession, she wrote yet another letter declaring that the chimes would be "heard no more in the Old Bay State. May it rest pacific on the shores of the Atlantic."[26]

Eddy then wrote to the directors calling their attention to the more serious implications of the episode: through their actions, they had reversed the press's mostly friendly response to the new church building, thus falling in with the aim of those who would injure Christian

Science. At the same time, she took herself to task for not seeing the danger beforehand: "Now, why did I consent? It was Mary that answered without waiting for God. Oh the pity! I *will watch*—that she does this not again, she did not even know what Westminster chimes were." In this as in other instances, Eddy concluded, "Mother has to go over the ground and patch up the fissures as best she can. 'These things ought not so to be.'"[27] But that is the way they largely were.

WOMAN'S HOUR, WOMAN'S POWER

Over the decade of the 1890s, Eddy grew enormously in the sureness of her leadership of the Christian Science movement. The power she exercised as a leader, while it had enormous authority behind it, was essentially a nurturing kind of power. "The true mother," she wrote with great feeling in *Retrospection and Introspection,*

> never willingly neglects her children in their early and sacred hours, consigning them to the care of nurse or stranger. Who can feel and comprehend the needs of her babe like the ardent mother? What other heart yearns with her solicitude, endures with her patience, waits with her hope, and labors with her love, to promote the welfare and happiness of her children? Thus must the Mother in Israel give all her hours to those first sacred tasks, till her children can walk steadfastly in wisdom's ways.[28]

Eddy came to discover that there was immense power in this kind of mothering—not so much power to coerce others as power to further their growth. Actually, the term "mother" as adopted by Eddy's followers and applied to her was less domestic than it may have sounded. It had been used a generation before as a term for women who operated outside that sphere: that is, to nurses during the Civil War, who were often affectionately called "mother" by the soldiers they tended. Motherhood in this sense is linked to the idea of ministering, nurturing love, and suggests the strength and staying power of a Florence Nightingale or Clara Barton. The term also has biblical roots in the scriptural designation of the Hebrew prophetess Deborah as "a mother in Israel." In *Retrospection and Introspection* Eddy applies that term to herself, showing that for her it was linked to the idea of God-impelled leadership, well beyond its more sentimental and affectionate usage.

Eddy incontestably exercised enormous power within her church. She caused bylaws to be added or altered to its *Manual,* guided the directors on important matters, and shaped church policy on a variety of important matters. But in her mind and the minds of her followers, she did so out of a fierce motherly love for the movement, and from a vantage point that had repeatedly detected and forewarned against a danger, or with prescience had initiated steps that proved to be progressive for Christian Science.

This was a form of leadership that Mark Twain, for one, was ill equipped to understand. He saw Eddy's exercise of power within the context of power as he understood it—that is, male power, with all its competitiveness, domination, and planning. The picture of her he drew corresponded to his view of the captains of industry: she was ambitious, selfish, self-confident. Twain saw Eddy in mannish terms as a supreme organizer and power wielder. What he could not stand was that this kind of power was being exercised by a woman, and what he could not understand was that power as she exercised it did not correspond to male power at all.

Throughout much of his life Twain revered, indeed, virtually idolized, one woman who wielded enormous power—Joan of Arc. In the midst of his dire financial crisis in the 1890s, he found relief through work on his book *Personal Recollections of Joan of Arc,* which he esteemed more than any of his other works. Joan's spirituality attracted him and her achievements stupefied him. Twain imagined contemporaries of Joan who gazed upon her—"the wonder of the time, and destined to be the wonder of all times!"—and said:

> Can it be true; is it believable, that it is this little creature, this girl, this child with the good face, the sweet face, the beautiful face, the dear and bonny face, that has carried fortresses by storm, charged at the head of victorious armies, blown the might of England out of her path with a breath, and fought a long campaign, solitary and alone, against the massed brains and learning of France—and had won it if the fight had been fair![29]

Twain's book about Joan has been widely regarded as among the least effective of his oeuvre, in part because of its one-dimensional portrayal of the heroine. George Bernard Shaw, author of his own work on the subject, referred to Twain's Joan as "an unimpeachable American school teacher in armor."[30] Though a leader of armies, in every other important respect she corresponded to the nineteenth-century image of femininity. Her instincts were safely domestic, she wanted nothing more than to leave the male realm of warfare and politics and return to her brothers and sisters in her village, and her military efforts were specifically at the service of a man—the French king. Twain's wife, whose sensibilities were safely at home in the cage of conventional femininity, agreed with him that the book was her husband's best. Alone among his books, Twain dedicated *Joan of Arc* to Livy.

As much as any woman in America, Eddy lived outside that cage. She dearly loved her home at Pleasant View, supervised its landscaping with meticulous care, and kept close watch on the daily running of the household. She also had a strongly feminine side in a more conventional sense of the term, expressed among other ways in her frustrated but genuine maternal instincts, her love of bonnets and other accoutrements, and in some of her more sentimental prose and poetry. Yet these tendencies never really defined her.

In this respect, Eddy differed markedly from her much adored mother, Abigail Baker. She revered her mother more than any other figure in her life. Their relation was exceptionally close—so much so that she could barely speak of her in *Retrospection and Introspection,* "for memory recalls qualities to which the pen can never do justice."[31] Abigail Baker's memory was so suffused with quietly sustaining love that her daughter came to see it as reflecting in a particularly pure way the very love of God. Yet Eddy was temperamentally incapable of imitating her mother's quiet submissiveness to an intractable husband, to doctrines that young Mary Baker could not accept in her heart, and to the restrictive role imposed on women in American society.

Eddy did support feminist reforms, including women's suffrage and expanded rights for women to hold property. But neither in principle nor in practice was she a feminist in the full sense of the term. Emma Curtis Hopkins, by contrast, was so energetically devoted to feminism among other social reforms that a biographer spoke of "the feminist eclecticism that placed her at odds with Eddy," observing as well that Eddy "clearly considered herself a revelatory prophet on a divine mission, functioning on a path parallel to the prevailing patriarchal religious system."[32] For her, the accomplishments of women in the social sphere were only the harbinger of what they should and could accomplish in the spiritual transformation of humanity.

Noting that women had played a crucial role in social reform movements, she observed in 1882 that if women working in Christian Science translated the same energies into spiritual pursuits, there was no limit to what they would accomplish:

It is glorious to see what the women *alone* are doing here for temperance. More than ever man has done. This is the period of *women, they* are to move and to carry all the great moral and Christian reforms, I know it. Now darling, let us work as the industrious Suffragists are at work who are getting a hearing all over the land. Let us work as they do in love 'preferring one another' . . . and then the puny kicks of mesmerism will give up the ghost before such *union.*[33]

"This is woman's hour in all the sweet amenities, charities, and reforms of to-day," Eddy wrote in a *Journal* article three years later. Yet she was thinking in terms of a much more decisive transformation in human life than either the equalizing of power among the sexes or the elevation of man through the virtue of woman could effect.

For her, the period in which Christian Science was beginning to thrive was "woman's hour" in a far larger sense. It was the hour in which the spirituality of womanhood was beginning to make an inestimable contribution to the spiritual awakening of humanity. Jesus, she wrote, needed no such awakening: he possessed innately a full understanding of his relation to God and demonstrated that relation completely. But "to one 'born of the flesh,'" wrote Eddy in her autobiography,

> divine Science must be a discovery. Woman must give it birth. It must be begotten of spirituality, since none but the pure in heart can see God,— the Principle of all things pure; and none but the "poor in spirit" could first state this Principle, could know yet more of the nothingness of matter and the allness of Spirit, could utilize Truth, and absolutely reduce the demonstration of being, in Science, to the apprehension of the age.[34]

EMPOWERMENT

This conception of womanhood transcended the sentimental Victorian piety that saw women as the repository of ineffectual religious feelings, with men making a real difference in the world. For Eddy, the spirituality of true womanhood had the power to make a radical difference, even though it was not the kind of power the world could easily understand.

After one class at the Massachusetts Metaphysical College in the mid-1880s, for instance, Eddy asked a student what she was going to do with the knowledge that had been imparted to her. The student answered, "I don't know what I am to do with it!" Eddy replied, "You are going to heal with it!" These were words of empowerment, and they were addressed to a woman. Within the framework of American religion, a sizable proportion of the active church membership were women. This was largely the case in other denominations as well. But the proportion of women to men was especially high in Christian Science. In 1900, of 2,564 practitioners, 79 percent were women; in 1910, of 4,350 practitioners, 89 percent were women.[35]

Historical and sociological explanations of why this was the case have tended to emphasize one factor: women gravitated to Christian Science because they saw it as a means for gaining status and power in a male-dominated society that otherwise consigned them to limiting and stifling domestic roles. In the scholarly literature on Christian Science, this view has, ironically enough, been sometimes voiced by feminist scholars. In her article "Protest in Piety: Christian Science Revisited," for example, Margery Fox writes that "Christian Science originally attracted women like Mrs. Eddy who came to be healed and found dominance roles within the sect that were denied them in the larger society." It was "an unconscious protest movement . . . directed specifically against women's social disabilities in the latter part of the 19th century." Eddy, she concluded, discovered "a new power role for herself that repudiated the traditional 19th century female stereotype." Seeing Eddy through this interpretive lens, Janice Klein in her article "Ann Lee and Mary Baker Eddy: The Parenting of New Religions" writes that for Eddy, Christian Science was "a means of rebellion, and a form of coping," without which she would have been "powerless and helpless," someone who "counted for nothing."[36]

As Jean A. McDonald explained in her path-breaking 1986 article, "Mary Baker Eddy and the Nineteenth-Century 'Public' Woman: A Feminist Reappraisal," the stereotype of Eddy and her women followers that results from such portrayals "matches in striking detail the traditional male portrait of 'public' women who have left their 'proper sphere,' thus potentially threatening men." McDonald goes on to document her contention abundantly, pointing out multiple examples in which Eddy was referred to in clerical, medical, and academic descriptions by such epithets as "a pope in petticoats," "the Lydia Pinkham of the Soul," a "Kaiser" greedy for money and power.

In a close analysis of a number of letters of testimony in Christian Science periodicals written by women converts, McDonald further observes that women were drawn to Eddy's teaching for much the same reason as men: "For these women and men the passion for certainty, their hunger for reality, had not been stemmed but deepened by the explosions set off by Darwinism and the undermining of religious faith by other secular influences." These documents, she concludes, "do not provide even hidden evidence for the motivations traditionally assigned to public women—the thirst for money and power; rather they testify to a great need to *know*." Raising the question as to why their theological hunger has been so long ignored, she writes that "one answer may lie in the stereotype that while men seek religion to satisfy their sense of reason and truth, women seek religion to satisfy their emotional needs."[37]

Some other feminist writers have also challenged this stereotype of Eddy. In her book *The Religious Imagination of American Women*, for example, Mary Farrell Bednarowski writes that "Mary Baker Eddy's creative medium was religious thought, and it is possible to see in her writings and in the healing movement she founded the play of religious ideas," adding accurately that "Eddy was not so interested in creating a systematic theology as she was in healing as a demonstration . . . of her understanding of God and reality. For Eddy there was a practical reciprocity between theology and healing: to know the true nature of God and reality was to be healed of both sin and suffering."[38]

Such appraisals have, however, been relatively rare in the feminist scholarship on Eddy. Despite its truth in some instances, the view that women in the early years of Christian Science were merely compensating for their lack of social and economic power verges on reductionism. As advocated by some recent feminist scholars, it suggests that Eddy herself cannot be taken seriously as a thinker. In terms of the movement as a whole, it obscures rather than explains motives of women who took prominent roles in the early history of Christian Science, giving wholly inadequate attention to their frequently remarkable achievements.

At the end of her article "Pond and Purpose," Eddy invited her readers to "drink with me the living waters of the spirit of my life-purpose,—to impress humanity with the genuine recognition of practical, operative Christian Science."[39] Many women did just this, finding thereby scope for the realization of talents and abilities beyond the confines of the home. Some, of course, may have been interested in financial gain. But there were many instances in which women pioneers of Christian Science threw themselves into the work of establishing the movement with the greatest possible earnestness.

The pivotal role of women in building up the new faith has been to some extent obscured by the fact that during Eddy's lifetime and for some decades afterward, men with few exceptions served the church in such visible roles as directors, editors, trustees, committees on publication, and lecturers. While Eddy had little patience with the kind of maleness that thought itself superior to womanhood, she pointed to the special strength of the male mentality as a vital support to her and the cause of Christian Science. In one of her last published notices to the field early in 1910, Eddy wrote: "Men are very important factors in our field of labor for Christian Science. The male element is a strong supporting arm to religion as well as to politics, and we need in our ranks of divine energy, the strong, the faithful, the untiring spiritual armament." Soon after the construction of the original Mother Church, for example, she wrote to the directors: "You are in a serious difficulty and men of business and capital can only, through God's dear help, see the way through this. Take the advice of these men whom you know are true as Christian Scientists and have experience in business."[40]

In part, Eddy appointed men to visible posts in the movement, not because she saw them as having superior capacities, but because they were more acceptable to society at the time than women would have been in the same roles. She specified, for example, that it was preferable for Committees on Publication, who dealt regularly with editors as well as legislators, to be men.[41] Similarly, her first appointments to the Christian Science Board of Lectureship were five men (although in a few months she added two women). In this instance, as in the case of Alfred Farlow, the first manager of the Committees on Publication, the men were very visible indeed. It was not unusual, for example, for Edward A. Kimball or other lecturers to speak to audiences numbering in the thousands. And some men entered vigorously into building up Christian Science in their local communities through healing and founding churches, often partnering with their wives in this work. But largely, the work of movement building across the whole field of Christian Science in the period of its earliest and most fertile growth was undertaken by women.

If Eddy looked to men as the public face of Christian Science, she largely looked to women to make things happen—that is, to build the movement from the ground up. This they did in considerable numbers, so that outside Eddy's own labors, the work of women was probably the single most important element in the spread of the Christian Science movement in the period before her death. Their labors as healers, teachers, and organizers of churches accounted in large measure for the development of Christian Science, for example, in Minneapolis, New York, Spokane, San Francisco, southern Los Angeles, Detroit, and also in such European cities as London, Hanover, and Berlin.

Julia Bartlett was the earliest of Eddy's students to remain loyal to her throughout. Her work in the town of Littleton, New Hampshire, gives some idea of how women in the movement felt that Christian Science had transformed their lives and what they were in consequence able to accomplish. A New Englander in her late thirties, Bartlett had endured seven years of invalidism and intense suffering when she saw a circular in 1880 of a new church designed "to perpetuate the teachings of Jesus, to reinstate primitive Christianity, and to restore its lost element of healing." Coming to Boston from her native Connecticut, she sought help from Asa Eddy and was soon healed. "I felt like one let out of prison," she wrote of her feeling at the time:

> The fetters of material beliefs and laws were giving way to the higher law of Spirit and the sufferings were correspondingly disappearing. I never could describe the sense of freedom that came with a glimpse of this glorious truth. The world was another world to me. All things were seen from a different viewpoint and there was a halo of beauty over all.

Julia Bartlett, n.d.
Courtesy of Longyear
Museum.

After studying with Eddy, she joined the Church of Christ, Scientist, and began her own healing practice. One of her patients was a young woman from New Hampshire whose healing impelled her former physician to request Bartlett to visit the town. After giving two talks on Christian Science, she found herself overwhelmed with patients. "I was seeing and treating seventy patients a day," she recalled, ". . . and although I could give each one but a few minutes of my time, most of them were healed quickly." Her healing work made Christian Science "the one topic of conversation in town and on the outbound trains, and much antagonism was expressed by certain clergymen and M.D.s when their people and patients rejoiced in the proof of the great healing power of Truth and trusted in it for their help."

Despite this opposition, when the young woman whom she had healed visited another town in Vermont, Bartlett was called there with similar results, including the healing of a case of double curvature of the spine and of acute heart disease. To her, these experiences proved that "God is ever present with us and that however difficult the situation His great love is right here sufficient to fill the need if we put our whole trust in Him, and a greater work is done than mortals are capable of doing."[42]

Other students who may have seemed equally unprepossessing undertook enormous tasks at Eddy's bidding, in many instances accomplishing them. In 1886, for example, Eddy instructed Sue Ella Bradshaw from San Jose, California, who had just studied with her, to establish Christian Science in the San Francisco area. Bradshaw then proceeded to open the first Christian Science institute, to become the first advertised practitioner, and to organize the first Christian Science church in the area. The difficulty of this missionary work was compounded because of the inroads of the mind-cure movement, which at first attracted many more newcomers than were drawn by Bradshaw's efforts. "The contest appears to be a very uneven one, so few against a multitude," she wrote to Eddy. "Trumpet-blowing calls together large classes, who desire Truth, but are misled by the bait of cheapness." But she ended on a resolute note: "I have no compromise to make, nor will I turn hypocrite, even if I can not succeed honestly."[43]

In 1897, with the moral and financial support of Mary Beecher Longyear, a prominent wealthy Christian Scientist, Laura Lathrop sent yet another young woman to help found Christian Science in Germany. Raised in a strongly religious home, Frances Thurber Seal had watched her mother die after years of intense suffering. After the further loss of one loved one after another, she felt an irresistible longing for a deeper understanding of the Bible and a more believable God.

Attending a Christian Science testimony meeting for the first time, she heard a new message "that man suffers not because of the will of God, but through ignorance of God." Quickly healed of long-standing physical difficulties, she began an intensive study of Christian Science, taking a class with Lathrop. Still feeling like a novice in Christian Science, she was prevailed upon by her teacher to answer a long-standing request from some German Christian Scientists for a worker to be sent to Dresden to establish the movement there. By her account, the healing of two cases that had come to her—one of rheumatism and the other of cancer—convinced her that she could undertake the work, and so she sailed to Germany in 1897.

The voyage was rough, but she found her thought "lifted above the storm into the peace of God," so that her calmness and strength attracted others to hear about Christian Science. The healings that followed her arrival in Germany, though at first she could speak no German, included by her testimony cures of Bright's disease, an advanced case of cancer of the uterus, ulcers, and tuberculosis of the hip. After returning to America and taking further instruction in Christian Science, Seal settled in Berlin, where her healing and teaching work grew. Later, after she had thoroughly proven her healing abilities and fulfilled her mission admirably, Seal returned briefly to the United States. Upon visiting Concord, she was told that Eddy was not receiving visitors that summer. Nevertheless, Eddy took the unusual step of calling on Seal at her hotel to thank her "for being brave and true, for facing error courageously and standing with Truth."[44]

Other women, too, acted with sometimes astonishing success as movement builders in diverse locales, mainly in the United States. In 1888, for example, the *Journal* published a letter to Eddy from a student of Julia Bartlett who had gone to a town in Indiana to establish Christian Science. Soon after her arrival, she was immersed in the healing work. Among the healings she recounted was that of a ten-year-old child with medically incurable cancer of the hip, several cases of spinal curvature, a healing of brain fever, and another of mental derangement. "Dear Mrs. Eddy," the letter continued,

> I am satisfied that it is not words but works that you want, as a reward for your teachings. This city is the hardest place I ever tried to establish Christian Science in; but now it is done, and the harvest is great. . . . I have not seen but one Christian Scientist since I was in Boston, but I do not feel lonely or weary, for I had such a longing desire to conquer this city with Truth, that I would not mind if I were in a desert.

Two years later another pioneer arrived at a small town in Wisconsin "without patients, money, or any other call than the desire to proclaim Truth to these people by works of healing." Building on healing work that had already gone on, she worked hard for over two years. "The struggles, loneliness, privations, disappointments, joys, and victories," she said, "were of priceless value to me, and resulted in awakening a few to the understanding of Truth."[45]

In some cases, women in the movement who were engaged in the work of healing faced not only hardship and loneliness, but serious danger. One of them was Phoebe Haines of Minnesota, to whom Eddy wrote several warm and encouraging letters. Haines recalled that in the winter of 1893 at five in the afternoon she was telegraphed to see a seriously ill little boy in a neighboring town. Riding seven hours in thirty-below weather over roads almost drifted full with snow, she arrived around midnight and immediately began to pray. By the next morning the child had made a strong recovery. At the noon meal the boy's grandfather burst in carrying a gun, determined, if the boy had died, to shoot "that old woman on sight."[46]

THE MALE AND FEMALE OF GOD'S CREATING

What Eddy most desired in Christian Scientists and sought herself to exemplify was a kind of spiritual completeness based on the conjoining of male and female qualities. Both men and women, she held, needed to be freed from human gender weaknesses that crippled their spiritual capacities. In her words from her unpublished 1900 essay "Man and Woman": "The feminine weakness that talks when it has nothing to say, that gossips, slanders, unwittingly or unconsciously, that envies or scorns when it should only pity, is out of line with being in Science, and in line with the masculine element that robs innocence of purity, and peoples of liberty and life, in the name of the rights of might."[47]

In her various contacts with men who played a part in the movement—including former lawyers, judges, businessmen, and military officers—Eddy repeatedly found it necessary to hold her ground in the face of would-be male competence that threatened to be overbearing, even with her. In some cases, their latent, and not so latent, chauvinism made them bridle at the very idea of working under the direction of a woman. This was especially the case with men of proven executive ability who relied on business methods, rational planning, or sheer male aggressiveness. To the male mentality that conceived of the progress of Christian Science as a series of bold, well-planned initiatives, Eddy's womanly and intuitive pattern of leadership was often difficult to understand, much less to submit to.

During the Next Friends Suit, to take a conspicuous example, Eddy employed a battery of excellent attorneys, among them General Frank S. Streeter, a leader of the New Hampshire bar, and noted Boston attorney Samuel J. Elder. Though she profited from their services, she, not they, directed strategy in the case. In later years, Elder was fond of recalling Eddy's discussion of strategy with her lawyers on a crucial issue in the pending litigation. During a "tense hour of controversy," the lawyers presented her "in language respectful, but emphatic" with reasons for following a particular course on the point at issue. They were forbearing because of her age and sex: "Her person commanded deference," Elder's daughter recorded him as saying, "but clearly her legal opinion was valueless." Leaving for her daily drive, Eddy stopped by Streeter's office, to which the lawyers had adjourned, called Elder down to her carriage, and putting her hand on his arm told him that he was wrong and should ask the others to reconsider the matter. "The result was that they reversed their decision, followed the lines insisted upon by Mrs. Eddy, and during the trial it became indubitably clear that she had been right."[48]

Others were not nearly so compliant or understanding. Some of her followers who held tenaciously to an essentially sexist view devised a rationale that went something like this: Eddy had discovered and fully stated the Science of Christianity, and for that we are everlastingly in her debt. But as a woman, she cannot be expected to devise the most effective means through which her discovery should be implemented and brought to the attention of humanity. It would be better if, in such matters, she stepped aside and allowed men with far greater worldly experience to settle such questions.

This was the position taken by several students when Eddy abruptly closed her college and left Boston for Concord in 1889. As another student put it, "They said as far as spiritual things were concerned there was no question as to our teacher's judgment and ability, but in matters of business it was not expected she would understand." These men of the world requested a visit with Eddy to share their concerns. She received them cordially, then had a few minutes conversation with them that "opened their eyes and their understanding." When she asked each in turn what they wanted to see her about, none had anything to say. Later when they related what had happened, they said that "they would have been glad if the floor had opened and let them down out of sight."[49]

One student who began to play an important part in the movement at this time did not give up so easily. William G. Nixon was a hard-nosed businessman from South Dakota whom Eddy would describe as "a Western sharper." After he and his wife took a class from Eddy in 1889, she appointed him her publisher. But she soon found that his considerable business skills were obviated by his almost complete lack of spiritual intuition and his strong advocacy of conventional views about marketing and promotion. In Robert Peel's words, for Nixon, "business was business. Advertising, promotion, publicity were the obvious tools of selling. When some of his carefully thought-out campaigns along this line failed to produce results, the reason seemed to him clear: it was Eddy's feminine instability, her arbitrary orders and sudden changes of direction."[50]

Her basic view of the matter was clearly spelled out in a letter to Nixon written after one of his campaigns to increase sales of *Science and Health* had backfired: "If you believe that my writings are inspired, you certainly can read them and thus learn that you are instigating means and measures contrary to the divine directions. This must stop, or you will force me to take the side of God . . . which is opposed to your worldly material means and maintain it against you." Otherwise the only alternative would be to "let Mr. Nixon rule my students and have in business the same material motives that the world acts from."[51]

Nixon eventually did leave the movement, returning to it as a semi-invalid shortly before his death. But his essential approach did not lack for advocates, among them a Judge Joseph Clarkson of Omaha.

Eddy recognized Clarkson's ability, and although he was a relative new-comer to Christian Science, she included him in her last class in 1898. One of his comments during the class seemed so personally adulatory of her that she commented, "I trust that no personal sense of me will ever stand between you and Christian Science."[52] As in other instances, Clarkson's adulation of Eddy was subject to being turned on its head. His strongly personal worship of her remained just as personal, even as it was flipped-flopped into a superior and dismissive attitude.

At first, he appeared to be an impressive advocate for Christian Science. Appointed to the Board of Lectureship in 1899, he lectured to large audiences in Tremont Temple, then in a number of midwestern and eastern states. Returning to New England after a lecture tour in 1900, he consulted with some of the church officials involved in pending litigation initiated by Josephine Woodbury. Finding himself in disagreement with their approach and with Eddy's, he was emboldened to assert the superiority of male reasoning to hers in broader matters concerning the growth of Christian Science. A two-hour interview with Eddy was followed by an invitation to dine with her a few days later, since there were evidently some unsettled points to discuss. Calvin Frye noted in his diary: "Judge Clarkson dined with Mrs. Eddy today & after dinner tried to convince her again that she was mistaken & the cause was going to ruin & the men were essential to take the lead of the cause of C.S. & to assert their rights without her dictation."[53] Failing to do so, he left the movement soon thereafter, severed entirely his connection with Christian Science, and lent support to the plaintiffs in the Next Friends Suit.

From Eddy's standpoint, the problem with both Clarkson and Nixon was that they were relying on a kind of rational maleness entirely disconnected from the humility and love that the practice of Christian Science required. However effective Eddy's organizational abilities, they sprang from a different source than the self-confident planning so often advocated by some of her male students and associates. Hers was a form of leadership inclined not to human strategizing, competition, and combat, but to less obvious and less aggressive methods. If necessary, it would give the appearance of yielding in order to survive.

Eddy once recalled that someone had observed, "No one but a fool or a woman would have written Science and Health." Then she went on to say:

He was right. Either a fool who did not know the consequences of writing that book or a woman who would have humility enough to go down like the grass under the persecution. A man might have been more apt to resist and to resist these persecutions would have been fatal. I had to learn the lesson of the grass. When the wind blew I bowed before it and when mortal mind put its heel upon me I went down and down in humility and waited on God. . . . Waited until it took its foot off and then I rose up.[54]

Such humility was often a hard lesson for the male mind to absorb and practice, so deeply ingrained are cultural and perhaps instinctual habits that give rise to competition, quarrelsomeness, and the habit of responding to aggression with more aggression. But the lesson of Eddy's life and of the work of women who shared the purpose of that life was that in this womanhood there was great and sustaining strength.

She did not see that womanhood and that strength as the exclusive property of women. Even if women exemplified it more often than men, she believed, the qualities of womanhood and of manhood belonged generically to all God's children. Christian Science may have been the ultimate expression for Eddy of the fact that her time was "woman's hour." But it was not the triumph of woman so much as the completeness of each of God's daughters and sons that she sought to establish and vindicate. As she put it in a note dictated to Calvin Frye in 1895, "There is no superiority of the sexes but there is equality in man and woman and the new woman will be seen in the new man & the new man in the new woman." *Science and Health* summarizes this point in the brief but trenchant exclamation: "Let the 'male and female' of God's creating appear." "Both sexes," she wrote in that book, "should be loving, pure, tender, and strong."[55]

Annie Knott, for example, was a doughty student of Eddy who was appointed to the Board of Lectureship in 1898. When she received at first few invitations, her friends told her that this was to be expected. But Eddy advised her otherwise, saying that she "must rise to the altitude of true womanhood, and then the whole world will want you as it wants Mother." Knott went on to become not only a widely heard lecturer but also the first woman director of the Mother Church. Conversely, Eddy wrote to Irving Tomlinson, a former Universalist clergyman who had converted to Christian Science and was appointed as a lecturer, to "have a cell less in the brain and a fibre more in the heart in yourself and it will do much for your lectures and in healing the sick."[56]

The last thing she wanted was a kind of role reversal that made for dominating, power-seeking women and pusillanimous, weak-minded men. In *Science and Health* she urged, "Give up the belief that mind is, even temporarily, compressed within the skull, and you will quickly become more manly or womanly." Possibly with a sidelong reference to Foster Eddy, she wrote in "Pond and Purpose" that "scientific growth manifests no weakness, no emasculation, no illusive vision, no dreamy absentness, no insubordination to the laws that be, no loss nor lack of what constitutes true manhood." She was not advocating female domination over males any more than male domination over females. She was advocating the end of domination by either sex.[57]

She also recognized that there was a cultural bias to be redressed. "The equality of man and woman is established in the premises of this Science," she stated in her unpublished essay "Man and Woman," written and copyrighted within days of her last visit with Judge Clarkson. "The masculine element has had precedence in history." But this element "must not murmur if at some period . . . the verdict should take a turn in behalf of woman, and say,—Her time has come, and the reflection of God's feminine nature is permitted consideration, has come to the front, and will be heard and understood." This, however, did not mean that "God has at any period bestowed a superabundance of His image and likeness on man more than on woman, or vice versa," since he was not a "respecter of persons," only that the long-suppressed spirituality of womanhood was at last coming into its own. Since masculine and feminine elements were *both* aspects of all individuals understood in their completeness, there can be "no suggestion of preeminence, or disseverance of the masculine and feminine elements of God's creating—no question of whom shall be the greatest."[58]

In the spirit of these words, Eddy sought to establish equality in her church, with women included as lecturers and editors, and not excluded from service on the board of directors. Men, Eddy knew, were needed to carry on the work of Christian Science, especially in a world in which most structures of power in government, law, the economy, and society were under male control. But what animated the movement fundamentally, she believed, was the spirituality, strength, and staying power that flowed from an understanding of God's Motherhood, no less than God's Fatherhood, as the true source of power.

6

"The Visible Unity of Spirit"

HAVING CHURCH

WHEN EDDY LEFT BOSTON AND WITHDREW FROM ACTIVE INVOLVEMENT IN THE day-to-day affairs of the movement, it was not because she did not care about the future of Christian Science but because she needed to care for herself. She may have resigned herself temporarily to the possibility of not remaining on earth for long. But so strong were her motherly instincts that she could not resign herself to seeing the movement founder and perhaps eventually fail. Her whole history since 1866 showed that the inner dynamic of her sense of mission demanded something more.

Exhausted as she was after her intense labors in Boston, she was not about to see Christian Science perish and that mission go unfulfilled. It was to forestall this eventuality that she threw herself into a major revision of *Science and Health* in the conviction that this was the most she could do to ensure the continuity of Christian Science. But as events proved, there was a great deal more that needed to be done. And perhaps to her own surprise, she survived to do it.

Had Eddy not survived into the 1890s and beyond, she may have been known as the discoverer of Christian Science. But so uncertain were the prospects of the movement that she would most likely not have been known as its founder. Every step she took in the 1890s shows how fully she remained committed, not just to stating Christian Science compellingly in written form, but to making sure that the vision contained in *Science and Health* took shape as a visible religious movement and church.

The appearance of some of Eddy's best-known students at the Christian Science Congress of the World's Parliament of Religions had made the movement very visible indeed. For Eddy, reared in the Congregational Church tradition of New England, there was every difference between a rooted, vital church life on the one hand, and the fleeting clamor and acclaim of the parliament on the other. She once spoke of herself as "a child of the Church, an eager lover and student of vital Christianity."[1] It was inconceivable to this "child of the Church" that Christian Science should be known mainly as an upstart movement making a public splash in the religious world, or that it was anything other than a community of Christians dedicated to making vital Christianity the center of their lives.

For Eddy, this community could take plural forms. It could be expressed in branch churches, societies, and informal groups; at the Mother Church itself; in associations of students of Christian Science teachers; in informal relations among Christian Scientists in a given area; and in her household at Pleasant View and later at Chestnut Hill. Whatever form it took, the community of love she sought to inculcate in the movement was not primarily organizational.

Eddy, in fact, was deeply suspicious of the spirit of ecclesiastical organization. For her, organization was secondary to community. To William B. Johnson, one of the directors, she wrote, "Let there first be a Church of Christ in *reality*—and in the hearts of men before one is organized." That reality, for her, lay at the heart of the church organization that was to be formed a month later in September 1892, a month after the letter was written. The branch churches, she once observed in a conversation with Irving Tomlinson, were "over-organized."[2] But organization as such was not, she finally concluded, an evil in itself. It was obstructive when it became the vehicle for conflict and rivalry, or when it assumed such importance as to be spiritually deadening. When organization was alive with the spirit of warmth and tenderness, when it expressed mutual love and support of those working for a common purpose, Eddy saw it as a necessary good.

She therefore rejected the belief of some Christian Scientists that they could function autonomously, separate from any church community whatever. To Eddy this was little less than inconceivable. When Julia Bartlett, whose healing work was unusually effective, said to Eddy, "You know I do not act with the church but alone," a short time later she received a letter with this quiet rebuke: "Now Julia dear this thought is impressed on you by mental malpractice. Rise above it. You have done and are doing *good* and how can you separate that work from His church? You cannot, and do not. *Realize* this and feel and take your place with the church as you used to."[3]

Spiritual conversion and renewal, Eddy taught, began with individuals yielding to the power of Christ. But it inevitability led to the forming of bonds of unity with others. Eddy spoke in *Science and Health* of Jesus' mission as "both individual and collective," saying that he "did life's work aright not only in justice to himself, but in mercy to mortals,—to show them how to do theirs, but not to do it for them nor to relieve them of a single responsibility."[4] Just so, when she specified what she expected of individual Christian Scientists, she spoke of the need for the transformation that began in their own hearts, but then flowed outward to bless and include others in practical ways.

This outflowing process is evident in the progression of the prayer that Eddy in the *Church Manual* enjoins on every member of the Mother Church to pray each day: "'Thy kingdom come;' let the reign of divine Truth, Life, and Love be established in me, and rule out of me all sin; and may Thy Word enrich the affections of all mankind, and govern them!" Prayer as Eddy understood it is always an expression of the heart's right desire. By beginning the "Daily Prayer" with the words "Thy kingdom come," drawn from the prayer that Jesus taught his disciples, she established at the outset that the motivation of prayer in Christian Science is linked with and proceeds from what she called the "one bond of unity, one nucleus or point of convergence" that all Christian churches have in common: the Lord's Prayer. The following two sequences of the Daily Prayer expand on the meaning of this petition. First comes the willingness for God's kingdom, or reign, to be "in me"—in the individual's own heart. But this prayer, if genuine and felt, has the immediate effect of expanding the affections, for it leads naturally beyond the individual into prayer for the divine Word to enrich and govern the affections of "all mankind."[5]

For Eddy, valid spiritual endeavor can never be rightly seen as the isolated activity of single individuals separated from the needs of the world or the community of church. "Our watchwords are Truth and Love," she wrote in 1888, "and if we abide in these, they will abound in us, and we shall be one in heart, one in motive, purpose, pursuit. Abiding in these, not one of you can be separated from me, and the sweet sense of journeying on. 'Doing unto others as ye would they should do unto you,' conquers all opposition, surmounts all obstacles, and secures success."[6]

This "sweet sense of journeying on" and the power that came from such united action became for Eddy the true gauge of whether the spirit of church was or was not present among her followers. Having church in this sense was never for her merely a concession to necessity. It was itself the primary necessity for which she struggled during most of the 1890s when Christian Science emerged as a recognized denomination on the American religious scene.

A MISSION TO BUILD

The same month in 1889 when Eddy dissolved the church organization in Boston, she also executed a deed of trust creating a board of directors authorized to hold services as a voluntary association and to organize a church at an appropriate time. The same deed of trust also created a board of trustees authorized to hold the lot of land and collect funds to build a church edifice on the property. Yet even as Eddy did this, she remained uncertain, even mistrustful, of a fully functioning organization for the Church of Christ, Scientist.

For several years after she dismantled the Boston church organization, Eddy made a number of statements, many of them quite strong, questioning the utility of church organization. In a major letter to the church when she disorganized it, she observed that the Boston church had been her "patient seven years." When she thought the church was "well nigh healed a relapse came and a large portion of her flock would forsake the better portion." God, she wrote, had "bidden her to disorganize saying 'I will try her and prove her on the pure basis of spiritual bonds, loving the brethren, keeping peace and pursuing it.' . . . And if she is saved as a Church, it will be on this basis alone." She therefore admonished its members "after ten years of sad experience in material bonds to cast them off and cast their net on the spiritual side of Christianity. To drop all material rules whereby to regulate Christ, Christianity, and adopt alone the golden rule for unification, progress, and a better example as the Mother Church."[7]

A few months later a *Journal* editorial underscored her intent by explaining, "The dissolution of the visible organization of the Church is the sequence and complement of that of the College Corporation and Association. The College disappeared, 'that the spirit of Christ might have freer course among its students and all who come into the understanding of Divine Science'; the bonds of organization of the Church were thrown away, so that its members might assemble themselves together and 'provoke one another to good works' in the bond only of Love."[8]

The question was: Would this work? Could the church advance and fulfill its purpose on this basis? The eventual answer was no. There was no way for Eddy to determine this, however, without giving the experiment time to work and without feeling her own way forward in the process, awaiting what she sometimes called "the logic of events" and seeking divine guidance at every step. Never once, however, did she ask the members of the church in Boston or elsewhere to cease working and worshiping together as a congregation.

As Eddy's representatives stood before the eyes of the world at the World's Parliament of Religions in September 1893, only one of the approximately one hundred congregations of Christian Scientists (in Oconto, Wisconsin) was worshiping in its own church building. And the long-planned construction of a Mother Church edifice in Boston had not even yet begun. In particular, she always supported the project of constructing a church edifice on the lot in Boston's Back Bay that had been purchased in 1886. At that point and for nearly nine years thereafter, Boston Christian Scientists held church services mostly in rented halls. What Eddy and most of her followers longed for was a church home of their own. Through all the vicissitudes that preceded the completion of the Mother Church in late 1894, she remained determined that it must be built as a focus for the loyalties of Christian Scientists everywhere—a visible sign of the unity she tried so hard to inculcate in the movement, as well as evidence that Christian Science was and would remain a presence on the religious scene.

The struggle to build the original Mother Church was one of the most complex odysseys in the early history of Christian Science. If that church was to symbolize the unity of spirit that prevailed among Eddy's followers, that unity took nearly nine years to achieve. And for a good portion of that time, it appeared that rivalry, fractiousness, and sheer confusion would continue to hold the upper hand. Eddy wanted to see the new church built, to protect the title to the land upon which it was to be constructed, and to do so in a way that would unify Christian Scientists rather than providing occasion for further divisions in their ranks.

In realizing these ends, she refused to be prodded into actions she intuitively felt were wrong. Her instinct at all points was to keep her options open, to decline to shut any doors until there seemed to be a definite and, as she believed, divinely impelled rightness to moving in a new direction. Then, once this became apparent, she would act with speed and do what had to be done. After The Church of Christ, Scientist, had been reorganized, the original Mother Church edifice built, and its first *Manual* published, it became easier to lose sight of this pattern of Eddy's decision making, and thus of the struggles that attended each of these efforts, the outcome of which did not seem obvious at the time.

In the lore of the Christian Science church, there has been a long-standing myth that Eddy retreated from Boston in order to contemplate in long-range abstract fashion the best form of government for her church. Yet it was uncharacteristic of her to define a desirable objective, then fashion a thoroughly worked-out plan whereby to attain it. Proceeding in this way would have made her more of a man than a woman, an ecclesiastical version of a captain of industry building up a great organization through a series of rationally calculated plans. Mark Twain developed his portrayal of Eddy's authority on that very premise, crediting her with a genius for organization but absolutely missing the genius she actually had, which had far more to do with an intuitive response to the needs of the moment than any kind of business acumen.

There was, in fact, an element of sheer unpredictability in the process whereby Eddy arrived at a workable plan for the governance of her church and provided for the construction of the original Mother Church. Robert Peel sometimes likened the steps she took in this direction to how Eliza in *Uncle Tom's Cabin* escaped from her pursuers by stepping from one ice floe to another until she eventually reached the other side of the river.[9] Eddy's followers had increasingly come to trust that her steps in this, as in other matters, were intuitively right and that there was reason to believe that eventually she and they would get across that river. These steps *resulted* in the development of a new overall structure of church government when, in September 1892, Eddy reorganized the church she had founded in 1879 into what would eventually become its present form as the Mother Church and its branches. The other side of the river was reached in public, visible terms when the Mother Church edifice was dedicated on January 6, 1895. But these steps began, not with any intent to arrive at a new overall plan of church government, but with her efforts to make possible the building of the church edifice in Boston.

The saga began in June 1886 when a committee acting for the church found a site in Boston's Back Bay on which to build. The lot was purchased with a three-year mortgage due in July 1889. How to pay off the mortgage became the immediate problem for which church members, most of whom were former members of evangelical churches, had a familiar solution. Accustomed to fund-raising through holding church socials, suppers, and bazaars, they proposed holding a fair that would raise a large portion of the $5,800 mortgage due. Eddy objected to the plan on grounds that it marked a throwback to older methods of fund-raising.

In a sermon she delivered a few months before the fair, she recounted the Gospel story of how the disciples had been called by Jesus to become fishers of men, but after the crucifixion "relapsed, turned back to their nets, and were ensnared in them again." They "toiled all night but caught nothing" until Jesus appeared and directed them to "cast their nets on the right side of the ship." This, said Eddy, is "the important thing to understand, Which is the right side? Is it the material or the spiritual side of life and its pursuits?" Only after learning their mistake through their own "bitter experience" had the disciples at last yielded to Christ's command and cast their nets on the other side and "gathered an abundance of fish."[10]

The sermon could not have been more pointed. Yet when it came to setting up the fair, the church members insisted on carrying out their plan, and Eddy, convinced that they needed to learn from their own experience, not only conceded to it but made an appearance at the fair held from December 19 to 21, 1887. It was an elaborate occasion with eleven different committees providing flowers, decorations, and refreshments, along with various commodities for sale. At first, the fair seemed eminently successful as well, raising nearly all the money needed to pay off the mortgage. Then, three months after the general rejoicing, the church's treasurer absconded with all the funds—including proceeds from the fair as well as hard-earned contributions from single individuals such as Julia Bartlett—leaving the church back where it was before the plans for the fair began.

To Eddy and some of the now chagrined church members, the lesson was painfully obvious. She even went so far as to say that the treasurer was by nature an honest man if "free from the evil influence that opposes the building of a church which is being established on a spiritual foundation." The long-range problem for the church was acute: lacking sufficient funds, the church would lose the lot when the final payment became due the next year. To prevent that from happening, Eddy intervened in late 1888 and, through a complex series of transactions, obtained legal control of the church lot, arranged for title to the property to be transferred to Ira Knapp, then to three trustees charged with raising sufficient funds so as to begin building a church edifice.[11] It was at this point that the truly serious problems that impeded the completion of the building project began.

WORDS—AND THE POWER OF THE WORD

The first difficulty was the advancement of what to Eddy was a misconceived plan promoted by some of her more ardent followers in 1890 to make the new church a memorial to her. Once the plan, which quickly became popular among her followers, became known to Eddy, she made plain in the *Journal* that the land she gave to the church was for the purpose of "building thereon a house for the worship of God, and a home for Christian Scientists." She therefore objected to "such a departure from the Principle of Christian Science, as it would be, to be memorialized in a manner which should cause personal motives" for building the new church.[12]

It did not take long for another and even more troubling approach to the building of the church to gain traction and almost derail the project completely. The struggle this time involved nothing less than the future of Christian Science as a church, and in waging it Eddy faced a most capable and determined adversary, William Nixon, whom she would later chide in his capacity as publisher of *Science and Health* for his over-reliance on business methods. During an interview with him at the conclusion of the March 1889 class, Eddy said, "If you should ever turn from Christian Science you would become one of the strongest enemies it ever had."[13] The words turned out to be grimly prophetic. With capable people in short supply, she tried as best she could to harness Nixon's considerable business capabilities to advantage. She appointed him as manager of the Publishing Society in June 1889, then a few months later as one of three trustees responsible for the property on which the new church edifice was to be built, and in October 1891 as publisher of her writings.

In this capacity, Nixon made strong efforts to redirect the building program into channels defined by his business-oriented sensibility. He developed what a contemporary called an "obsession that the publication of literature was first in importance in the work of disseminating Christian Science."[14] In his capacity as trustee, Nixon lobbied hard for the view that the new church building should be designed primarily for the publication of Christian Science literature. Eddy herself had given him a relatively free hand to lobby for his agenda, since her deed of trust of 1889 included the requirement that the trustees not consult her on the building project. Nixon argued his point of view most persuasively, drawing the other trustees, two of the five directors, and Foster Eddy to his side.

Writing for the *Journal* in June 1891, Foster Eddy enthusiastically seconded the view that the building of a Christian Science publishing house was "a great work to be done for the cause, and for the whole world." The demand is "not upon any particular section of the country, but it is general, it comes to all Christian Scientists everywhere, because it is for the general good of humanity." Here was the crux of the argument: that a building geared mainly to publishing was preferable to a church dedicated to worship because people everywhere could benefit from reading church publications, while only those in Boston could benefit from attending the house of worship. But this was wholly contrary to Eddy's view. As early as April 1889, she had spoken of church membership in universal terms. Using the term the "mother church" for the first time publicly, she extended through the *Journal* an invitation "to my students everywhere, whether they have attended my classes or have received instruction through reading my books" to become "members of the 'mother church' here in Boston, and be received into its communion by writing without their personal presence. If you are united with us in thought and affection, you know in Science that you are not absent from us. I carry you all in my affection."[15]

Nixon and Foster Eddy, however, continued to urge what appeared to be the more practical viewpoint that Christian Scientists outside of Boston would have little reason to contribute to a building fund for a church to be used by worshipers in the Boston area. As an article in the *Journal* for May 1891 put it, "The movement is no longer confined to one of local or sectional interest merely, but is become one of national concern." On this plausible basis, Nixon gathered widespread support in Boston and beyond for the view that only a building primarily geared to publishing could enlist necessary support throughout the field. In Eddy's absence, and with these arguments enthusiastically propounded by most of her Boston followers, the "cry for a publishing house," in the words of William Lyman Johnson, son of one of the directors, "became an epidemic." Johnson recalled that his father and some of Eddy's other students "tried hard to stem the tide." The land Eddy had deeded, they argued, was for a church building and not a publishing operation— "this was all that she had in thought, all that she had given advice upon or consent to."[16]

This was true as far as it went, but the real issue ran deeper. The written word played a large role in the life of the movement, and Eddy went on to establish the Christian Science Publishing Society by a deed of trust in 1898—but only as a constituent element of a larger church entity, and as one way of carrying forward its primary mission of restoring "primitive Christianity and its lost element of healing." Minus the experience of the power of the divine Word in the act of healing, merely reiterating the words of Christian Science became in her view a vain parody, and an exclusive focus on publishing them an intoxicating substitute for the hard discipline that the actual practice of Christian Science required. In her words, "The demonstration of what I have taught them [her students] heals the Sick. It absolutely disgusts me to hear them babble the letter and after that fail in proving what they say! It is high time that they stop talking science or do prove their words true."[17]

Some years before, Eddy had begun a poem with the questions "Saw ye my Saviour? Heard ye the glad sound? Felt ye the power of the Word?"[18] Converts throughout the United States were increasingly answering yes to these questions. Congregations were being formed on the basis of the shared conviction that the power of the Word was being felt in the lives of thousands of Christians through acts of spiritual healing. On this basis, the movement in 1891 was gathering momentum in a way that astonished most Christian Scientists, probably including Eddy herself. And that momentum was taking shape in the form of worshiping congregations—visible bodies of Christians working together in unity of spirit.

Eddy saw such communities as vital to the advancement of the cause of Christian Science. "The spiritually minded," she wrote in her newly published book *Retrospection and Introspection* at the end of the year,

> meet on the stairs which lead up to spiritual Love. This affection, so far from being personal worship, fulfils the law of Love which Paul enjoined upon the Galatians. This is the Mind "which was also in Christ Jesus," and knows no material limitations. It is the unity of Good and bond of perfectness. This just affection serves to constitute the Mind-healer a wonder-worker,—as of old, on the Pentecost Day, when the disciples were of one accord.[19]

For Eddy, the advancement of Christian Science took natural form in this "just affection" and the "unity of Good and bond of perfectness" among her followers. By contrast, the strong emphasis on promoting the progress of the movement mainly through publication of written texts put spiritual community of any sort in a distinctly secondary place, if it did not leave it out of the picture altogether.

The ultimate question raised by Nixon's determined efforts to derail the church building project was, therefore, of fundamental importance: would Christian Science be essentially a Christian religious movement animated by the warmth of spiritual community, or a publication enterprise appealing primarily to single and separate individuals? The question hung in the balance until midsummer of 1892. During the summer of 1891 a strong current of opinion among Christian Scientists was being swayed by Nixon's view. As a letter in the July *Journal* expressed it, a church building in Boston was of lesser interest than a "business for the issue of true literature, which, as seed, can be scattered broadcast, to help in bringing the world to the *true Light*."[20] By early 1892, it appeared that the effort to make a publishing house the representative structure of Christian Science was sweeping all before it.

The March *Journal* presented its readers with a photogravure representation of the proposed edifice, together with a detailed description of exterior and interior design. As William Lyman Johnson commented later, no doubt echoing the thought of his father, the director William B. Johnson, it "would have been a most unchurchly looking edifice"—a square and severe building that contained a place for worship but looked more like a library or a courthouse than a church. So dominant, said Johnson, was the thought that the new building was primarily for the purpose of publishing that "outward semblances of a building for religious services were forgotten."[21]

But not by Eddy. She objected strongly to the plan published in the March *Journal*. In April she wrote to a student, "All my dear students are giving their money with this expectation [that a church would be built on what was once her lot] and speak so tenderly of *Mother's Church* and the Mother Church it seems awful for this *fraud*, as I deem it, to go on." Yet she let "this *fraud*" go on for almost another four months, as Nixon embarked on a tour of Christian Scientists in the West, persuading many to join with the faction he now led in Boston. William B. Johnson circulated a letter to students known to be loyal to Eddy explaining the whole situation and adding as a postscript: "I have just returned from Concord, and have talked with our beloved Teacher. She sees it all, and the stupidity of us students." But seeing it all, she refused for the time to be personally drawn into the conflict, believing at this point that it was better to leave the church to learn from its own mistakes. If the church "again sells her prosperity for a mess of pottage," she told Johnson in May, "it is not my fault."[22]

The trustees, however, had one trump card to play. Through their attorneys, they discovered that there were several technical defects in the December 1889 deed of trust through which the property had been conveyed to the trustees. On this basis, they appeared ready to obtain further funds sufficient to buy a lot and build a publishing edifice of their own wholly free from any restrictions that Eddy and the deed of trust imposed on them. This would have been tantamount, not just to rebellion against Eddy's leadership, but to usurpation of control over the church. Rather than dispute the technical issues on their merits, Eddy expressed in an article for the July *Journal* the hope that "with the spirit of Christ actuating all the parties concerned about this legal quibble, that it would be easily corrected to the satisfaction of all." She then went on to plead, "Do not, I implore you, stain the early history of Christian Science by the impulses of human will and pride; but let the divine will and the nobility of human meekness, rule this business transaction in obedience to the law of God, and the laws of our land."[23]

Through mid-August her instincts told her to wait, which for her meant waiting before taking a precipitate step that might make things worse. As she put it in a letter to Ira Knapp in mid-June, a victory could be won through "a material hard fought battle." But she chose to take "the other side so clearly revealed, namely, 'Be still and know that I am God'—I choose to take this side, and so do you. Now remain in watching and prayer, but take no legal steps toward breaking the deed . . . and let the Trustees meet the fearful sins that they alone commit."[24] Nixon had, in effect, chosen to take on Eddy. But she refused to take him on in a direct contest that would only exacerbate divisions. Rather, she waited until it became unmistakably clear that advertising for funds to build a publishing house as well as a church constituted a violation of her deed of trust. She then summoned Nixon and the other two trustees, along with Ira Knapp, who had deeded the property to them, to a meeting with her and her attorney (and Foster Eddy) at Pleasant View on July 16, 1892—which, coincidentally, happened to be her birthday.

Acting on a legal technicality, but motivated by the betrayal of her original intent that the property be used specifically for a church, Eddy terminated the trust. The step was decisive, for at this point she had become determined that the building of the church must proceed, but that this required a new church organization that would make faction-alization and conflict less likely, if not impossible. Still, her attitude toward Nixon, the fountainhead of so much of the recent conflict that had plagued the building project, remained one of forbearance. Seeing the need to reorganize the church, on August 9 she wrote to Alfred Lang, a trustee and treasurer of the building trust fund, with obvious reference to Nixon, "Let us prepare our hearts (if they are not already prepared) to receive God's dear benediction, else, we can not have it. This preparation, at this time, consists in cherishing no feeling towards a single actor *known* or *unknown* in this business transaction that we would not have God look upon, and ourselves could say of it,—'it was also the mind which was in Christ Jesus.' "[25]

There remained, however, one legal hurdle to surmount: Nixon and those allied to him argued that the church must reincorporate legally for the building project to proceed at all. In Eddy's estimation, so doing would only have prolonged the struggle over "who owned God's temple." Acting on her instructions, in August Eddy's attorneys found a Massachusetts statute that made it possible for officers of a church to be "deemed corporate bodies which could receive grants and donations and hold property."[26]

With this issue resolved, Eddy proceeded quickly. On August 19 she regained title to the property on which the new church was to be built and took measures to reorganize the church. Three days later she explained her motives:

All that I have done or advised doing in the direction of organizing a church at this time, has been at the beck of lawyers and infants in Christian Science. Now I shall deed my land *today*, and to certain persons

that I know to be seeking and finding Christ's Church in their hearts, and
let them use it for the benefit of Christian Science, for building thereon a
Church edifice in which to preach Christ, Truth, and to *demonstrate love
one for another.*

She drafted a new deed of trust that gave title of the land to four grantees,
who became thereby the directors of what would be the reorganized
Church of Christ, Scientist, now officially titled in the deed, "The First
Church of Christ, Scientist," but more informally spoken of since as "The
Mother Church." The directors were commissioned to build a church
edifice that would, according to the later rules of the church, belong to
Christian Scientists everywhere.[27]

"My task the past summer," Eddy wrote to a student in October
1892, "to breast the storm of *blind guides,* and deliver the people and
establish Christ's Church in Boston, has been beyond description. But
I was enabled to accomplish it. This new form of Church government
is a light set upon a hill." In a message to the field in the *Journal* the same
month, she made clear that the building fund was being reopened for
one exclusive purpose: to "build a church edifice in the interest of
Christian Science." Speaking obliquely but derisively of the scheme to
put primary emphasis on publication, she wrote, "I am confident that
all loyal Christian Scientists will gladly consecrate our church to a more
dignified end, than an exchange, or a place for business bickerings, bag
and baggage!—a church to be erected on a lot given, and regiven to
them under such difficult circumstances, by the author of *Science and
Health.*"[28]

Oneness of Heart

Within a year of the writing of these words, Christian Scientists
had contributed sufficient funds so that the long-delayed construction
of the Mother Church could begin. By May 1894, the initial work had
advanced to the point that the cornerstone could be laid. On the last
Sunday of the year, the first service was held in the completed church,
which was formally dedicated on January 6, 1895.

That church became the visible sign of the unity that had been
achieved among the ranks of Christian Scientists. For Eddy, building
that unity was in its way as demanding as the physical labor that others
put into the building of the church. It was the disunity among her followers—their contentiousness, elbowing for place and power, and tendency toward merciless judgment of one another—that frequently

brought her to the point of despair. "I must have love and *peace* prevail in the Mother Church," she wrote to Edward and Caroline Bates; "God cannot be, is not, where these are not. But God is everywhere. . . . Dear students let *us* keep ourselves aloof from all contention, all bitterness, all that is *unlike Christ*." When the directors tried to involve her in a conflict which had sprung up, she remonstrated, "You will bring my white hairs into remembrance in years to come when you remember the unchristian acts that keep me in perpetual broils."[29]

The conflict over whether the new church should be primarily a publishing society or a place for worship was the culmination of the factionalism that had plagued the movement since Eddy left Lynn in early 1882. Though she built up a solid core of loyal followers in Boston, dissension prevailed in many forms. Four of the early editors of the *Journal* she appointed for varying reasons turned against her. Former students such as Mary Plunkett, Emma Curtis Hopkins, and Ursula N. Gestefeld formed rival groups of their own. The rebellion against Eddy's leadership in 1888 in the wake of the Corner case disastrously disrupted the fragile unity of the movement. She had left Boston and dissolved most of the institutions of the movement partly to check the vitiating effect of this divisiveness—to begin again on what she called "a purely spiritual Christ-like basis" in which the quarrelsomeness that affected all human organizations would be minimized.[30]

Again emphasizing the need for love and unity among Christian Scientists, she wrote in the article "Love your Enemies" for the *Journal* in April 1890: "I want to take by the hand all who love me not, and say to them: '*I* love *you*, and would sooner pluck out my heart than to harm you. *Because* I feel thus, I say to you: hate no one; for hatred is a plague spot that kills at last, and will bring suffering upon suffering to you throughout time—and beyond the grave.'" Yet the currents of contention and disunity continued to seethe, especially in the wake of Nixon's effort to wrest from Eddy control over the direction of the movement on the question of the church building project. As she wrote to a student late in 1891 when the crisis he provoked was gathering momentum, "A tornado of inward pride and envy is tearing out the heart of Christian Science in many directions today. But God reigns, and I have noble, brave, selfsacrificing students that are firm as the sea girt rock. And on this 'Rock' Christ's Church must be built."[31]

After having dissolved the trust of December 1889 and regained title to the land in mid-August, Eddy proceeded to reorganize the church—but not by direct personal fiat that left her followers without any consent in the matter. Instead, she selected twelve students whom she knew to be thoroughly loyal to her, instructing them to meet together on

August 29, 1892. On that day they were told of Eddy's plan to create, under a deed of trust, a four-person board of directors that should constitute "a perpetual body or corporation" for the purpose of building and maintaining a church. The twelve gave their ready assent to the plan, and on September 1 the deed creating the "Christian Science Board of Directors" was formally executed.

The church itself was not officially reorganized until September 23, when these same handpicked students met again and voted into membership both themselves and twenty of Eddy's other students as "First Members." They also adopted the tenets and rules of the church as prepared by Eddy and elected a president, clerk, and treasurer.[32] The most crucial post, however, was filled in a uniquely different way. Not by formal vote, but by the new members' implicit acceptance of Eddy's September 1 deed of trust, the four trustees (or "directors") named in the deed became, in effect, the directors of the church. Underlying what appeared on the surface to be a risky surrender of political sovereignty by the First Members was a tested conviction on their part of Eddy's spiritual leadership.

In such a spirit of Christian fellowship and trust, far more than through any political protocol of governance, Eddy's church was reborn. Two months before in a *Journal* piece Eddy had described the complex transactions of conveying the land on which her church would be built as "a type morally and spiritually inalienable, but materially questionable—even after the manner that all spiritual good comes to Christian Scientists to the end of taxing their faith in God, and their adherence to the superiority of the claims of Spirit over matter or merely legal titles." Now, a month after the September reorganization, in reflecting on what had been accomplished, she expressed a similar thought to some students in Chicago: "God has given me the travail of my soul (sense) in the form of this church government. It is unity in bonds of love divine not human law."[33]

In future months, she sought to strengthen these bonds of love still further within the newly organized church. When the Reverend D. A. Easton, a former Congregational minister, became pastor of the church in March 1893, she wrote him:

> I feel it is my duty to state to you the special need of my old church in that City. It is in short a *revival*. An outpouring of love, of the *Spirit* that beareth witness. I found it essential, when the pastor of this church, to lead them by my own state of love and spirituality. By fervor in speaking the Word, by tenderness in searching into their needs—and specially by *feeling myself*—and uttering the *spirit* of Christian Science—together with the letter.

Oh! may the God of all grace and peace and joy and love give you wisdom to feed this dear flock. And He *will* if you *trust* Him and *obey* Him—these are *His* only conditions.[34]

The Reverend Easton did not live long enough to occupy the pastorate of the Mother Church and to continue shepherding its members in the way Eddy had pointed out. He died after just one year's work with his congregation. Yet possibly due in part to his efforts, the revival of community and love Eddy desired was beginning to occur by the time the cornerstone for the Mother Church was laid on May 21, 1894.

"I dedicated The Mother Church to God and humanity, spiritually, when the Corner-stone was laid—did it alone in my sweet, quiet communion with Him," she wrote to a student after the event. The inward act had its outward manifestation in a quiet ceremony, with only the directors of the Mother Church present. The cornerstone contained the Bible, copies of Eddy's writings, and the names of around fifty students who had each contributed one thousand dollars at her request to the building fund, along with the names of the directors, in Eddy's handwriting. Once the cornerstone was placed on rollers and pushed into place by hand, the workmen withdrew, the directors alone remaining. They uncovered their heads, each laid a hand on the stone, then prayed silently and repeated the Lord's Prayer together. That afternoon, Septimus Hanna's wife, Camilla, assistant editor for the *Journal,* took the train to Concord with the proof sheets for a *Journal* article Eddy had written for the occasion. "Mother, the Corner Stone was laid today," Camilla Hanna said upon seeing Eddy. "Yes," Eddy replied, "I laid it."[35]

In one sense this was understandable. But for her continued urgings, the laying of the cornerstone could have been delayed even further. Although exhausted by her efforts, Eddy, as was often the case, by that evening recovered her strength and energy rapidly, staying up most of the night to revise the message so that it would be ready for the directors the next morning. But the grinding weariness Eddy felt had been caused by more than the directors' slowness in bringing the project to the point that the cornerstone could be laid. In a larger sense, it was the effect of the struggle she had undergone in bringing her followers to the point where such united action became possible. Hence the mixed sense of relief and fulfillment in the first verse of the poem she wrote for the laying of the cornerstone of the Mother Church:

> Laus Deo, it is done.
> Rolled away from loving heart
> Is a stone,
> Lifted higher we depart
> Having one.[36]

This emphasis on Christian Scientists having one heart—one motive and affection—was carried even further in Eddy's words for the *Journal* written for the same occasion. Affirming the need for the church institution as a necessary "form of godliness," she prophesied that "the time cometh when the religious element, or Church of Christ, shall exist alone in the affections, and need no organization to express it." Rebuking the possible vanity of those whose names were listed within the cornerstone, she asked, "Does a single bosom burn for fame and power? . . . Then is he less than man to whom God gave 'dominion over all the earth,'—and the meek who 'inherit the earth.' . . . In our rock-bound friendship, delicate as dear, our names may melt into one, and common dust, and their modest sign be nothingness. Be this as it may, the visible unity of spirit remains." Concluding, Eddy yearned for the time when "the *hearts* of Christian Scientists are woven together as are some of their names in this web of history."[37]

The building of the Mother Church, which she called "our prayer in stone,"[38] marked a major step in this direction—the "our" being as important as the "prayer," the "prayer" being more important than the "stone."

Obedience

As biographer Gillian Gill writes, "The projected Mother Church as envisaged by Mrs. Eddy would serve and belong to the whole membership of Christian Science," while the newly organized church institution "was not merely accepted but welcomed by the membership at large. She had given the movement a new task, to build a Mother Church as soon as possible, and members set about their work with a zeal that aroused the admiration and envy of contemporaries and that still merits the descriptor *extraordinary*."[39]

Perhaps the most extraordinary thing about this whole process was that once the long-delayed building project had begun, it was completed in so short a time. On the last Sunday in December 1894, little more than seven months after the cornerstone was laid, the first service was held in the Mother Church. What animated the process was not the wisdom and ability of the woefully inexperienced directors, who were responsible for managing the project, nor even the determination of those Eddy entrusted with executing it. Rather, it was the spirit of obedience that Eddy had worked hard to cultivate—not, as she saw it, obedience to her personal demands, but to God's demands as she saw them, demands that she did not hesitate to communicate in the strongest possible terms.

Only by using her full authority to exact this obedience could she build the unity of action that would make it possible for the church to be built. The point is best illustrated by an address she wrote to be read in February 1893 at the meeting of the Christian Scientist Association, which was composed of Eddy's own pupils, many of whom were Christian Science teachers with pupils of their own. Nixon, now embittered, was still very much on the scene. Though he had recently resigned as publisher of both the *Journal* and Eddy's writings, his influence was felt among a faction of his supporters in Boston and elsewhere. His wife, Helen, who remained close to Eddy, recalled his "white face and expression"[40] when she spoke to a group of fellow Christian Scientists in strong support of the new church organization and signed the rolls as a member. But there were other potential sources of disaffection within the movement, especially within the Association.

The devotion of its members to Eddy was unquestionable. But their obedience to her direction was not automatic, especially when it came to the role and influence of the Association itself. This body, not the church, had been the seat of collective power in Boston during the 1880s. Although officially disbanded in 1889, the Association continued to meet as an informal group and remained an important factor. But with the new church government in place, the power it exercised passed to a group called the First Members, who had been appointed, on Eddy's recommendation, by the original twelve students she had selected to form the church. While the First Members were drawn from the ranks of the Association, the other members of the Association had to swallow the fact that their power was now largely a thing of the past.

In her address to the Association printed in the *Journal*, Eddy dealt with this and other potential sources of resentment and disunity in an impersonal way. She referred neither to Nixon nor to the grievances of some within the Association, but rather emphasized the need for all Christian Scientists to join together in the spirit of obedience to the God who is divine Love. In a pivotal passage, she related obedience to Love, and Love to the unity that so desperately needed to be built among Christian Scientists: "Obedience is the offspring of Love, and Love is the Principle of unity, the basis of all right thinking and acting. Love fulfils the law. We see eye to eye, know as we are known, reciprocate kindness and work wisely, in proportion as we love." She also voiced this warning:

> Until the student of Christian Science separates the tares from the wheat, discerns between the thought, motive and act superinduced by evil minds, and the true God-given intent and volition,—and arrests the

former, and obeys the latter, he is not on the safe side of practice. . . . God is the fountain of light, and He illumines our way in obedience. The disobedient make their moves before God makes His, or too late to follow Him. We should wait for God to direct our footsteps, then, hasten to obey under every circumstance.[41]

As subsequent events showed, she meant what she said. Frequently and unabashedly, she sought to galvanize the obedience required to impel forward the construction of the new church. The enemies, as she saw it, were confusion, sloth, delay, inaction, and lack of commitment and purpose. The remedy was an unremitting demand for concerted, purposeful action in obedience to what Eddy saw as God's mandate to her and all involved to get the work done. She further insisted that the new church be completed by the end of the year—probably not because of any objective reason for this target date, but to establish a definite deadline to spur the efforts of all concerned. As she wrote to one of the directors, "Be *obedient* that is all that is required, our Father Mother God will do the rest and blesses only His *obedient* children." Repeatedly she urged the board to action. Just as repeatedly they dallied, prompting this complaint to Foster Eddy: "As it is, I have to do most of the thinking, remembering, and all the guiding, and then speak to blanks almost, or have to listen to a long jabber of why they did forget. . . . Oh for Grace and Love infinite to meet this finite woe."[42]

Her words to the directors during the course of the actual building express better than any summary the sometimes cajoling but more often jolting effect of her efforts to ensure that the work was getting done:

- In September 1893, after a delay in laying the foundation, she wrote to them, "Why in the name of *common sense* do you not lay the foundation of our Church *as God bids you, at once?*"
- Twelve days later, after yet another delay: "Do not delay one other day to lay the foundation of our Church, the season will shut in upon you perhaps, and the *frost* hinder the work. God is with you, thrust in the spade, Oct. *1st* 1893."
- On July 19, 1894, giving direction on practical matters: "Make your contracts in writing, stipulate the time allowed for the fulfilment of contract,—the quality of the iron, and work to be done on it, and whatever else is requisite."
- In the same month after another slowdown: "To the *sleepers* in Boston, The C.S. Board of Directors . . . *Work* is *wanted, have it done. Now is the time.* . . . One *month gone,* your *best month,* and

nothing done is shocking! . . . May God open your eyes and *keep them open* or our cause in Boston is lost."

- In October after plastering the church was needlessly delayed: "I *regret* that you had not employed the highest priced *plasterer,* or have let me decide that question. Take no *risks now.* It is easier to supply money than time."
- In late November: "Finish the church on Saturday night or Sunday morning and hold services in it the last Sunday in this year. . . . Get the roof and the tower done if possible and I know it can be by putting enough men at work on the roof. . . . Let me know *at once* when your outside work is done & I implore you to keep the commandments in this letter."
- Then in December the definitive command: "Hold your services in the Mother Church Dec. 30, 1894, and dedicate this Church Jan. 6th."[43]

At points, Eddy's exasperation with the directors boiled over into scolding letters as severe as any she ever wrote. In October 1894, after the architect had said that the church could not be finished till the following April, she wrote to them: "The church could have been finished this year as easily as in twenty years, if you had done your duty and what God commanded. . . . God requires restitution, cross-bearing, obedience. Begin now, today, hear his voice and be as willing to follow his command in taking up your cross and carrying it till the Church is built, as to lay it down and sleep when he bids you watch with me in this evil hour."[44]

A COMMUNITY OF PURPOSE

Despite what Eddy saw as the intermittent sloth of the directors, the services were held and the church dedicated as planned. In July 1892, well before construction began, she wrote to the members of the church: "Built on the rock, our Church would stand the storm. . . . Our Church of Christ, our prayer in brick, should be a prophecy and monument of Christian Science. . . . This building begun, would have gone up and no one could suffer from it, for no one could resist the power that was behind it, and against this Church and temple 'the gates of hell could not prevail.' "[45]

As these words suggest, while Eddy demanded obedience, she could also inspire it. After one of her more rousing missives to the directors, Ira Knapp wrote to her that her letter "is the word of God and it seems

as though it would raise the dead and I think it has, myself included."[46]
For Eddy this was precisely the issue. The massed power of mortal
mind, the general weight of human resistance to God's demand, she
was convinced, always exerted a deadening effect on the fulfillment of
any divine purpose. The great need, therefore, was not to push the
recalcitrant along by the sheer force of human will so much as to rouse
the deadened thought to a new perception of God's requirements and
the ability of her followers to fulfill them. This meant specifically to
break the grip of torpor and inaction which she saw as predictably
resisting the completion of so great a project as the building of the
Mother Church.

What animated those who at Eddy's behest carried through the
building project was the force of her constant injunction that what
seemed impossible was, in fact, possible. From this standpoint, the work
was done essentially because of their common refusal to credit the
belief that it could *not* be done. Joseph Armstrong, the director whom
Eddy put in charge of the overall project, recalled that he visited her
hoping for "some way of escape" from the requirement "to complete
the church within the appointed year." But after a brief conversation
with her, "his doubts vanished forever. Like Elisha's servant when his
eyes were opened, he saw that 'they that be with us are more than
they that be with them,' and from this hour he knew as an absolute
certainty that, whatever the seeming, *the work would be done!*" Later,
Edward P. Bates, a businessman from Syracuse who oversaw the daily
construction of the building in its final critical stages, wrote about what
appeared to others to be a hopeless situation: "I could have been no
possible use in building the Church if I had doubted for a moment that
the work would be finished. When I went into that building I saw it
finished as it is today."[47] Both Bates and Armstrong noted that once
workmen and others involved in the project admitted that the building
could be completed by the end of the year, cooperation increased and
the work moved ahead.

For Bates, obedience to Eddy's orders, no matter how exacting, and
the unity of purpose built by this obedience guaranteed success. He was
convinced that Eddy, through her prayers in Concord, was empowering
the day-to-day work in Boston. Therefore, he said, "our whole duty
was to obey; when we did obey the work progressed rapidly,—so rapidly that it seemed as though, when we commenced a piece of work, it
was done." On December 8, for example, Eddy sent a peremptory note
requiring the ceiling to be lathed and the interior of the building plastered
immediately. When this was conveyed to the contractor for the interior
of the church, he said flatly that the church could not be finished that

The original Mother Church under construction, 1893.
Courtesy of The Mary Baker Eddy Collection.

year and that he would still be plastering ten or even twelve weeks from that day. This was not a proposition Bates was prepared to accept. Through a series of developments that appeared wholly remarkable, the plaster was delivered and applied by five o'clock the next morning. The contractor, reported Bates, "said he had never seen anything like it in his life. I am sure I never did, and all the plasterers said the same." What made all the difference, Bates continued, was Eddy's clear vision that the work could be done. "There was no time when it was safe to retreat a single inch: no matter what obstacle seemed to be in the way,—what resistance we met, we must press forward and carry out her demonstration."[48]

As the work proceeded, it appeared that the obstacles became not only monumental, but multiple. Prices rose during the course of the building, vital deliveries were repeatedly delayed, labor disputes and contractual complications threatened to disrupt the work, and the weather turned against them. Bates recalled that the snowfall that began in October "had been the worst that Boston ever knew. It was worse than the winter when the Pilgrims landed."[49] As problem after problem was surmounted, those involved in the work became convinced

Christian Science Board of Directors, 1895: Ira O. Knapp, William B.
Johnson, Joseph Armstrong, Stephen A. Chase.
Courtesy of The Mary Baker Eddy Collection.

that the church could be ready for services at the end of December as
Eddy required. Their obedience to her in turn helped to build a spirit of
community that Eddy captured in an impromptu poem she sent the
directors on November 23 as the final phase of the building process went
into high gear:

> When the *mists* have risen above us,
> As our Father knows his own,
> Face to face with those who love us,
> We shall know as we are known;
> Love beyond the orient meadows
> Floats the golden fringe of day,
> Heart to heart, we bide the shadows,
> Till the *mists* have cleared away.[50]

As vision was translated into fact, Christian Scientists involved in
the building process were forced into a community of purpose in
which rank and dignity of position counted for little. With less than two
weeks to go before the first service, painters labored all night to finish
work on the ceiling. Johnson, though a director and the clerk of the
church, snatched a scant two hours' sleep in a pile of gunny sacks and
painters' cloths in a corner of the vestry, so as to be on hand to deal with
problems that could arise in paying for extra help and overtime.

Finally, on Saturday, December 29, hours away from the opening Sunday service, the last of the pews were installed. Now just one thing more needed to be done to make the auditorium ready: a thorough cleaning. Respected teachers and practitioners worked in shirt sleeves and aprons amid the dust and dirt to remove the debris and clean up the mosaic floors. Johnson's son recalled that "brooms, dusters, buckets and mops were brought forth and there ensued such a loving, and joyous competition in work as has perhaps never been equaled. Intermingled with it was a holy happiness, a fresh urgence to preach the far-reaching truth of this great teaching."[51]

Not "in Commemoration but in Recognition of His Presence"

Purely as architecture, the Mother Church was impressive. A Romanesque structure of pink and gray granite from Eddy's home state of New Hampshire, it combined elements of the traditional with the modern in a way that was intended to please a younger generation who wanted something more contemporary than the plain Puritan style of church building.

The auditorium, which seated twelve hundred, was brilliantly lit by electric lights. On fair days, light poured through stained-glass windows depicting biblical images, while 144 electric lamps illuminated a sunburst of art glass in the ceiling with a seven-pointed star at its center. The finely carved seats on the readers' platform integrated with the curved lines of the interior design. Pews of strong-grained and mellow curly birch, upholstered in old rose plush that blended with the russet color of the walls, gave richness and warmth to the interior.

Eddy was less concerned with how the Mother Church looked than with what it meant, especially its broader effect on the Christian Science field. Had the Mother Church not been dedicated on time, she told Bates, it would have been a monument to error. But now that the church has been built, she said, "it will be easy for branch churches to build their structures as we have cleared the way." Over the next several years this proved to be the case. By 1897, Christian Science churches had been constructed or were underway in Missouri, Iowa, Oklahoma, Rhode Island, and Illinois. By the end of 1898, over thirty-two church buildings had been dedicated across the United States. As Eddy noted in 1895, "The *times* are *changed*—C.S. is taking the place that I knew it would when our church was built, hence my labor and efforts in that direction."[52]

As this veritable building boom of Christian Science churches proceeded, Eddy wrote letters of support to congregations in many cities where new edifices were being built and dedicated. These letters include sometimes sharp warnings against falling back into the spirit of complacency and self-satisfaction, instead of moving forward to realize the true purpose of having a church. The church as an institution, she had said in *Science and Health*, must give "proof of its utility." It was a means, not an end—a means of "rousing the dormant understanding from material beliefs to the apprehension of spiritual ideas and the demonstration of divine Science, thereby casting out devils, or error, and healing the sick."[53]

But the creeping materialism displayed by some Christian Scientists who virtually worshiped church edifices moved in the opposite direction. Hence Eddy's recommendation to the readers of a branch church in Troy, New York, that all churches "give no special publicity and particularly no public pictures of their churches. It is too commercial, too cheap looking, too little like things that come in course and to stay; and too like a surprise that one can have a church edifice!" As Eddy tersely put it in a message in 1904 on the occasion of the dedication of the Christian Science church in Concord, New Hampshire, which she largely financed: "Our proper reason for church edifices is, that Christians may therein worship God; not that Christians may worship church edifices!"[54]

Even during the building of the Mother Church, Eddy saw the need to check signs of pride, complacency, and incipient materialism in the directors. She wrote in November urging them to hasten the completion of the Mother Church: "Finish this church in 1894, even if you have to give up some of your gods such as mosaic floor in the auditorium or other decorations." In another letter to a group of students later the same month she wrote:

> I am sorely disappointed in the animus of Christian Scientists, that I cannot scarcely see a dividing line between the Ecclesiastes "soft-palm upturned to a lordly salary" and towers tremulous with beauty that turns the poor from the gate,—and the Mother Church in Boston! I would rather see 5000 hearers in a plain wooden Tabernacle listening to the Scriptures and Science & Health than pride contracted walls hemming in 1200 hungry hearers.[55]

There seems to have been little of the spirit of pride and coldness in the first service held in the Mother Church. On the contrary, according to William Lyman Johnson, the day was filled with a special illumination: "With the sunlight streaming into the clean, sweet auditorium, [it] seemed to veteran workers like a resurrection morning." It was

Communion Sunday. Judge Hanna, who had succeeded the Reverend Easton as pastor, read from Mark's account of the Last Supper followed by a passage from *Science and Health* portraying the risen Jesus' morning meal with his disciples by the Sea of Galilee, as depicted in the Gospel of John. "This spiritual meeting with our Lord, in the dawn of a new light," Eddy wrote in *Science and Health* at the time, "is the morning meal which Christian Scientists commemorate. They bow before Christ, Truth, to receive more of his reappearing, and silently to commune with the divine Principle thereof."[56]

Eventually Eddy abolished the Communion season at the Mother Church (although she retained it in branch churches), thereby countering any suggestion that the true meaning of the sacrament lay in an outward observance at any special location. Just as the Eucharist for her meant a continuously renewed spiritual experience of communion with God, so in her writings she speaks of the true significance of baptism as the purification of thought and daily life. She defines baptism as "purification by Spirit; submergence in Spirit." "We should strive to reach the Horeb height where God is revealed," she further states; "and the corner-stone of all spiritual building is purity. The baptism of Spirit, washing the body of all the impurities of flesh, signifies that the pure in heart see God and are approaching spiritual Life and its demonstration." As this happens, "Christ's baptism of fire, his purification through suffering, consumes whatever is of sin," and our genuine being as God's child becomes more apparent. Thus Christian Science, in Eddy's words, "lights the fires of the Holy Ghost, and floods the world with the baptism of Jesus"—the point at which he heard the Father's voice declaring, "This is my beloved Son, in whom I am well pleased."[57]

Those who have experienced baptism in this sense of the term, she believed, find themselves linked together in the spiritual unity of the newly born, and in this unity they find together the true spirit of church. Thus, speaking of church in the broadest sense, Eddy wrote in *Science and Health:*

> Our church is built on the divine Principle, Love. We can unite with this church only as we are new-born of Spirit, as we reach the Life which is Truth and the Truth which is Life by bringing forth the fruits of Love,— casting out error and healing the sick. Our Eucharist is spiritual communion with the one God. Our bread, "which cometh down from heaven," is Truth. Our cup is the cross. Our wine the inspiration of Love, the draught our Master drank and commended to his followers.

In other words, she was asking why observe a material ritual if one can incorporate in the fabric of one's daily life the spiritual realities it symbolizes? "Your feast days," she wrote to the branch church in Atlanta, Georgia, on its dedication in 1899, "will not be in commemoration but in recognition of His presence."[58]

"A SCIENTIFIC, POSITIVE SENSE OF UNITY WITH YOUR DIVINE SOURCE"

The last thing Eddy wanted was for her church to slip back in any way into the spirit of an ecclesiastical formalism she saw as deadening the life of Christianity. Certainly there was a sense of newness and moving forward—of what young Johnson had called a "fresh urgence"—at the first service held at the Mother Church. Even the weather was bright. By contrast, the day of the dedication a week later was gloomy, and the service—actually five consecutive services—had far more the feeling of an exterior public occasion. While it had been announced beforehand that Eddy would not be present at the dedication, her absence was conspicuous.

She was then seventy-three years of age. For her to participate personally in the opening festivities would have been strenuous. In any event, it was not something she was inclined to do. She had long since come to distrust the tendency of her students to heap personal adulation upon her. "When I go into the public assemblies," she wrote to Augusta Stetson a few weeks before the dedication, "there is such a desire to do me honor it spoils all my joy."[59]

If Eddy was not present in person, she was very much present in spirit. The characteristic quality of her leadership, especially her penchant for the unexpected, was distinctly present in the text of her sermon read at each of the dedication services by a capable, if not very inspired, elocutionist who was not a Christian Scientist. Eddy's sermon began by celebrating the spirit of the occasion and paying tribute to the beauty of the new church. "Both without and within," she said of the church she had not yet seen, "the spirit of beauty dominates The Mother Church, from its mosaic flooring to the soft shimmer of its starlit dome." Such beauty, she went on, must be taken as prefiguring something larger, "the 'house not made with hands, eternal in the heavens.'" It was natural, even expected, to make the transition from the symbol of holiness to its permanent essence, from the human to the divine. But her next words shifted into an entirely different mode.

Abruptly, she asked her listeners to imagine themselves in a situation directly opposite from the light and joy and harmony of their present surroundings: "With the mind's eye glance at the direful scenes of the war between China and Japan. Imagine yourselves in a poorly barricaded fort, fiercely besieged by the enemy." Why this sudden jarring of her hearers' sanguine joy? As the younger Johnson observed, the Christian Scientists at that point were "gathered together in the tender hush of a gladdening realization that the struggle was past, and that they were to dwell in the glorious sunshine of hope fulfilled."[60] But to her, the struggle in the largest sense was not past. In fact, it had barely begun.

Once she had written to Foster Eddy, "You will always think you are fully *aroused* to the present need when the glamour is deepest. You are always most safe when you realize you are in need of more conscious truth relative to the lie, and *its action*."[61] At that point, the glamour was deep, the sense of triumph palpable. But Eddy had a strong conviction as to what this triumph, gratifying as it was, actually meant: that it was temporary at best, that the very success of the Christian Scientists would inevitably bring forth a reaction, especially from the orthodox churches, which felt threatened by increasing conversions to the now very visible new faith.

How were her followers to face the situation they confronted? The heart of her dedicatory sermon lay in her answer to this question. She told her followers, in effect, that rather than being lulled by the satisfaction of the occasion, they must be awake to the resistance that would meet their every advancing step; that the only way to meet it was by entering more fully into the very heart of the truth she had discovered and by having the deep Christian experience it had opened up to them. They were to understand that "the real house in which 'we live, and move, and have our being,' is Spirit, God, the eternal harmony of infinite Soul. The enemy we confront would overthrow this sublime fortress, and it behooves us to defend our heritage."[62] The enemy, as she saw it, was never an outside force. It was the regressive mental tendency that denied our present capacity to have the consciousness of man's spiritual oneness with God.

Citing Jesus' words "The kingdom of God is within you," Eddy went on to say: "Know, then, that you possess sovereign power to think and act rightly, and that nothing can dispossess you of this heritage and trespass on Love." If one doubts one's ability to attain this spiritualized consciousness, the answer lies in the conscientious practice of fundamental truth she was certain she had discovered: "You have simply to preserve a scientific, positive sense of unity with your divine source, and daily demonstrate this. Then you will find that one is as important a factor as duodecillions in being and doing right, and thus demonstrating deific Principle."[63]

However beautiful the new church structure, however much comfort and assurance it gave to Christian Scientists, it had only one purpose: to be the visible symbol and sign of the unity of spirit that prevailed among those who share the conviction that conscious unity with God is an attainable basis for being a Christian in the contemporary world. In her view, on this basis, and no other, could the spiritual unity that she so yearned to see prevail among Christian Scientists be established. As this happened, she was convinced, a renewed resurrection to spiritual life, love, and power would occur, and her church would be able to withstand the opposition ranged against it. In her words to the six branch churches in Chicago in 1904:

> A great sanity, a mighty something buried in the depths of the unseen, has wrought a resurrection in your midst, and leaped into living love. What is this something, this phoenix fire, this pillar by day kindling, guiding, and guarding your way? It is *unity*, the bond of perfectness, the thousandfold expansion that will engirdle the world,—unity, that unfolds the thought most within us into the greater and better, the sum of all reality and good. This unity is reserved wisdom and strength; it builds upon the Rock 'gainst which envy, enmity, or malice beat in vain.[64]

7

"The Preparation of the Heart"

RELIGION OF THE HEART

It was not until nearly three months after the dedication service that Eddy first saw the Mother Church. On April 1, 1895, accompanied only by Calvin Frye and Clara Shannon, she took a train from Concord to Boston and went directly there. Instead of a procession and chimes, which, as she wrote in a letter, her Boston students had planned in case she should visit, she went " 'without shot of gun' . . . and God was manifest to me in more ways than I have time to tell."[1]

Shannon recalled how Eddy entered the auditorium immediately upon her arrival in mid-afternoon, walked slowly around, then knelt on the lowest step leading to the readers' platform in silent prayer. Nearly eight years later, in her public reply to Mark Twain, she spoke of what she felt at that moment. When kneeling on the steps, she said, "the foresplendor of the beginnings of truth fell mysteriously upon my spirit."[2]

Later in the evening, after having met with a few of her students, she returned to the church auditorium, now brilliantly lit, and stood behind the First Reader's desk and repeated aloud the words of the Ninety-first Psalm. Then, moving to the Second Reader's desk, she spoke the words of the hymn "Guide me, O Thou great Jehovah," which she had sung frequently during her girlhood. After Eddy finished no one spoke for a few minutes. Then she went over to talk with an old worker she had not seen since the 1880s. Now custodian for the new church, he was so overcome with joy mingled with memories of the past that he sat weeping with his head leaning on the pew in front of him. Sitting beside him, Eddy touched his shoulder and said, "Why, brother, don't you remember in the days gone by when we went to the hall to have our services there, how you and I had to pick up pieces of paper and bits of orange peel in order to make the room clean?" After brief exchanges with others in the auditorium, she returned to "Mother's Room," the apartment built for her in the church's tower, where she spent the night before returning to Concord the next morning.[3]

When Eddy entered the church for the first time, knelt in prayer, repeated the Ninety-first Psalm, recited a familiar hymn, and comforted a long-time worker in the cause, she was not making a series of gestures. She was simply being who she was: a Christian for whom praying, hymn singing, the reading of Scripture, and Christian community were natural. Shannon also recalled Eddy's encounter a few years after with a Methodist clergyman, the Reverend Richard S. Rust, with whom she had been friends in the 1840s. He was passing through Concord and had asked to see her. She found his visit most welcome. "Each knew, or expected," wrote Shannon,

> that it would be the last visit on this side that they would have together. I can still hear his words, "Sister, shall we sing a hymn together?" And her reply, with such a sound of joy, "Yes, let us sing 'The Sweet By and By.'" In the back parlor . . . I listened to those two voices praising God. I never forgot that song, sung by those two saints. Then they sang, "He Leadeth Me" and "Tell the Old, Old Story." It made me weep to hear and to see that communion; it was a communion of Saints.

Shannon recounted, too, as did others who worked closely with Eddy, how she urged her students to open their hearts to God in prayer. Quoting God's word in the Bible, "I will take away the stony heart . . . and I will give you an heart of flesh," Eddy described a stony heart as a heart hardened by materialism and lack of sympathy. Shannon recalled Eddy's instructions were that "we must look to God for deliverance and pray that He take away that heart and give us a heart of flesh, . . . a heart of love, seeing one another's need and supplying it with love which is divine."[4]

The word "heart" in the metaphorical sense associated with warmth and love is one of the most frequently used in Eddy's vocabulary, appearing several hundred times in her published writings. She counsels that "we should examine ourselves and learn what is the affection and purpose of the heart, for in this way only can we learn what we honestly are." In speaking of healing she states, "The poor suffering heart needs its rightful nutriment, such as peace, patience in tribulation, and a priceless sense of the dear Father's lovingkindness." And in her first address in the Mother Church she stated: "As we rise above the seeming mists of sense, we behold more clearly that all the heart's homage belongs to God."[5] In putting such strong emphasis on the preparation of the heart, Eddy was drawing on a biblical concept rooted in both the Old Testament and the New that played a key part in the Puritan tradition in which she was reared. In the words of historian Norman Pettit, "Seventeenth-century New Englanders examined their hearts with an intensity now quite alien to the American mind." When Eddy urged cultivation of the heart, she used language that came naturally to an heir of this tradition. As Pettit explains, "The heart could be 'proud' or 'humble,' 'stony' or 'fleshy,' the source of perpetual corruption, a jealous and indifferent barrier to grace, or the final realm of understanding, the ultimate dwelling place of God. When they touched their hearts, they touched their deepest faith. . . . Piety in New England demanded that the heart be put in order for the coming of the Spirit."[6]

Eddy, too, emphasized the need for the heart to be "put in order" so as to receive spiritual blessings. In her words to Sue Ella Bradshaw, "All things are prepared for us by the Father. Our part is to prepare ourselves to receive them." She commended such preparation to her followers on the occasion of the annual meeting of the Mother Church in 1896:

> One thing I have greatly desired, and again earnestly request, namely: that Christian Scientists here, and elsewhere, pray daily for themselves. Not verbally, nor on bended knee, but mentally, meekly, and importunately. When a hungry heart petitions the divine Father-Mother God for bread, it is not given a stone,—but more grace, obedience, and love. If this heart, humble and trustful, faithfully asks divine Love to feed it with the Bread of Heaven, health, holiness, it will be conformed to a fitness to receive the answer to its desire; then will flow into it the "river of His pleasure," the tributary of divine Love, and great growth in Christian Science will follow,—even that joy which finds one's own in another's good.[7]

"A SERMON FROM HIS PERSONAL GOD!"

"May God enable my students to take up the cross as I have done, and meet the pressing need of a proper preparation of heart to practise, teach, and live Christian Science!"[8] These words, taken from Eddy's address before the alumni of the Massachusetts Metaphysical College in 1895, express Eddy's underlying intent in taking a number of major steps during the several years after the Mother Church was dedicated.

In her dedicatory message read at that event, she rejoiced with her followers that Christian Scientists in Boston had a church of their own. Yet Eddy appears to have sensed a double edge in the apparent prosperity and progress of her church. What apparently concerned her the most was the prospect that the church would devolve into yet another ecclesiastical organization, "barren," to use her words in *Science and Health*, "of the vitality of spiritual power, by which material sense is made the servant of Science and religion becomes Christlike." "It is their *materiality* that clogs the student's progress," she wrote in a letter to students in 1893, while "spirituality is the basis of all true volition."[9] Eddy's work on behalf of her church, especially in the middle to late 1890s, included a series of determined efforts to foster a tough, disciplined spirituality in her followers so as to counter the materialism that threatened to "clog" their progress.

This materialism could, she believed, take on ecclesiastical form. It did so when Christian Scientists, conditioned by their earlier adherence to orthodoxy, failed to break with outworn tradition, ritual, and other merely exterior forms of worship. "Long prayers, ecclesiasticism, and creeds," she stated, "have clipped the divine pinions of Love, and clad religion in human robes. They materialize worship, hinder the Spirit, and keep man from demonstrating his power over error."[10]

By the time the Mother Church was dedicated, Eddy had come to believe that personal preaching in Christian Science worship services was among those pitfalls that tended to "clad religion in human robes." Some Christian Scientists in the field had already experimented with reading passages from the Bible and *Science and Health* in place of the sermon. Eddy decided that the time had come to adopt this practice in Boston. Less than two weeks before the first Mother Church service, she wrote to the Hannas, "I received last night a certain sound on the direction. . . . That no sermons are to be preached by mortals in the Mother Church as pastors appointed or placed over this Church. That the Bible and Science & Health are to be the preachers."[11]

The next day in the same letter in which she had instructed the directors to begin holding services in the Mother Church, she explained that "personal preaching has more or less of human views grafted into it. Whereas the pure Word contains only the living, health-giving Truth." Based on sermons she had read, these "human views" at points expressed teachings totally at variance with Christian Science.[12] So it was at the first Sunday service held at the Mother Church, when Hanna read passages on the Last Supper from the Bible and on Jesus' morning meal with his disciples from *Science and Health*. The congregation found to their surprise that the reading of these texts had replaced the sermon, which until that service had been the central element in all Christian Science Sunday worship.

As in other matters, Eddy took this step in an experimental spirit, with the intention that a precedent would be set for the branch

Judge Septimus B. Hanna, n.d. Courtesy of The Mary Baker Eddy Collection.

churches to follow if it worked out well. It did, and by June, Eddy was able to write to Ellen Linscott in Chicago, "The Pastor of our churches is getting popular." In the April *Journal* she had announced to the whole field, "Humbly, and as I believe, Divinely directed—I hereby ordain, that the Bible, and Science and Health with Key to the Scriptures, shall hereafter be the only pastor of the Church of Christ, Scientist, through-out our land, and in other lands."[13] Services would henceforth be con-ducted by two "readers," one reading from the Bible and the other from *Science and Health* in pre-selected texts which comprise the Bible lesson-sermon.

In one stroke Eddy had abolished all personal preaching in Christian Science churches. By so doing, she eliminated the role of a clergy in the denomination, making the Church of Christ, Scientist, into a lay church—a fact that proved to be as significant as the change effected by her abolition of personal preaching.

Eddy's institution of the impersonal pastor did not meet with her followers' universal acclaim—at least initially. Many church members normally loyal to her were dismayed by it. Older communicants had been so accustomed to hearing sermons preached in their former churches that the sudden loss of pastors often left them feeling bereft. Even sharper feelings were to be found among some of the pastors themselves. Hanna accepted his changed status from pastor to First Reader gracefully, saying, "I gladly lay down my charge at the foot of a higher and better ministry,—the unadulterated Word of God."[14] But as for other pastors in some of the 240 places where Christian Science services were being held at that time, many resented being so abruptly deprived of a post that had given them considerable prestige and control.

For Eddy and the majority of Christian Scientists who eventually came around to her point of view, this was the virtue of what an anonymous article in the *Journal* for July 1895 called "The New Order." This article, which had much influence among church members, argued that the step Eddy had taken was preventing the "evils of ecclesiasticism" such as "pride, self-congratulation, love of power, desire for distinction" from infecting the new movement: "Listening to sermons as of old, men felt gratified, or displeased with the speaker; hearing the Truth as it comes now with power in Christian Science services, people are healed of their sickness and sin." A branch church in Buffalo, New York, commented to the *Journal* that it had obeyed the order to institute the impersonal pastor with regret, and that for a time the congregation lessened considerably; but over several months it had increased to the point that it was larger than ever before, so that not "one of us would willingly return to the old order of service."[15]

While the institution of the impersonal pastor was an innovation within the Christian Science church, it followed the pattern of Eddy's departure from traditional ecclesiastical forms in other respects. "We have the least possible ceremony in our Church and its functions," she wrote to a student a few years later. Where traditional churches observed the rites of the Eucharist and baptism, it was Eddy's belief that sacraments would mean more, not less, to the extent that worshipers made the effort to incorporate into their lives the reality they symbolized. Her aim was to remove the humanly imposed filters that intervened between individuals and direct spiritual experience. In her words from an undated fragment, "The design of [Christian Science] is to open the human heart to the direct influence of the divine nature."[16]

To the extent that personal preaching interposed a filtering element between students of Christian Science and the core texts that contained the substance of their faith—the Bible and *Science and Health*—it, too, was a mediating element. Putting texts from the Bible and *Science and Health* at the center of both church worship and private devotional study was more consistent with the overall intent and pattern of worship as understood in Eddy's teaching. In this way, the daily work and study of

"Pioneer Days in Christian Science . . ." in Orange, Massachusetts. James E. Gilman.
Courtesy of The Mary Baker Eddy Collection.

church members, as well as their life together, brought them into continuous contact with the sources of spiritual growth and renewal. As Eddy stated in an explanatory note introduced in 1897, which today is read in its revised form by the First Reader in all Sunday services preceding the lesson-sermon: "The canonical writings, together with the word of our textbook, corroborating and explaining the Bible texts in their spiritual import and application to all ages, past, present, and future, constitute a sermon undivorced from truth, uncontaminated and unfettered by human hypotheses, and divinely authorized."[17]

In 1898 she made yet another consequential change. Since 1890, the Bible lessons studied by Christian Scientists had been composed of biblical passages and references from *Science and Health* that amplified their meaning, along with expository notes from reference works. But the topics themselves were adapted from a series of International Sunday-School Lessons in general use among Protestant churches. In 1898, Eddy outlined twenty-six topics, rotating twice yearly, that covered comprehensively major topics in Christian Science. Irving Tomlinson pointed out that in so doing, she united the movement in "one method of Bible study, one basis of teaching in the Sunday School, and one form of preaching in all Christian Science churches throughout the world."

Tomlinson also observed that, once having decided on a definite course of action, Eddy brooked no opposition. A few years later, as a member of the committee charged with assembling the texts for the Bible lessons, he expressed to Eddy the committee's view that there should be one topic for every Sunday, proposing a list of twenty-six further topics to augment the topics she had already chosen. Calling him to sit beside her when he visited some weeks later, Eddy turned to him and said, "so energetically that I almost jumped from the sofa, 'That will never do—that will never do!'" The additional topics, she explained, could all be used under the present list. "Tell the committee the original subjects were given of God—they are sufficient, and they will remain forever."[18]

Six years after the impersonal pastor was instituted, assessing the issue in a message to her church, Eddy wrote, "Whosoever saith there is no sermon without personal preaching, forgets what Christian Scientists do not, namely, that God is a Person, and that he should be willing to hear a sermon from his personal God!" Hence she spoke in the *Manual* of the Bible Lesson as "a lesson on which the prosperity of Christian Science largely depends."[19]

For Eddy to have instituted the "new order" so abruptly at the very point that her students were rejoicing in having a church like other churches might seem anomalous. Yet she was hardly worried about taking an unconventional step when so doing seemed to her God-directed. There was now a visible symbol in Boston of the church's hard-won identity. But she was not about to sacrifice that identity, especially at such a moment of triumph. On the contrary, by abolishing personal preaching she created an occasion to confirm its uniqueness.

A Resource and a Refuge

Far from believing that Christian Science was reserved for those who were already church members, it was Eddy's conviction that Christian Science was to be lived in the office and on Main Street, and be fully available to communities in which it had established a presence. Acting on this conviction, in 1899, she initiated a new bylaw requiring each Christian Science branch church to maintain a reading room. As amended and published the next year in the *Manual*, the bylaw stipulated also that churches in close proximity could have the same reading room, provided that these rooms were "centrally located." She emphasized the point in a letter to the board of directors in May 1900, when she wrote in peremptory tones: "Once more God thunders in your ears—*Get a reading room* in *Boston* and locate it in that part of the city where people will be most apt to go into it."[20]

As one facet of the church that she founded, reading rooms did not involve people of a given community coming to a Christian Science church so much as the church extending itself into the community. Reading rooms, as they took finished form, were the final stage in a development that Eddy and her students initiated in the late 1880s to fulfill the missionary function, in her words, of helping "those unable to pay for healing, and prevented by their circumstances from hearing the Glad Tidings unless taken to them by messengers of the Truth." Earlier missionary activity took form in what were known as "dispensaries," in which practitioners provided treatment free of charge or at reduced rates and made Christian Science literature available, sometimes in rough slum districts of major cities.[21]

The dispensary work in Boston served as an experimental prototype for dispensaries in other cities. This "mission work," Eddy said at a church service in April 1889, "will draw the world's attention more distinctly to the humane character of Science than any degree of generosity and self-sacrifice in the routine of a private practice could do." No sooner had Eddy said these words than the June *Journal* listed five dispensaries in four cities. By the end of the year, the number had grown to nineteen dispensaries in eighteen cities, including Boston, Chicago, Cleveland, and Montreal. *Journal* articles told of healings that occurred through the work of practitioners who served in them. Yet the work had its drawbacks. The demand was particularly great on missionaries who went from door to door to acquaint members of the community with the new service available to them. In Boston, as one observer noted, "the courage of many a volunteer going into the rougher districts fled between the time she rang or knocked upon the door and the answer."[22]

Parallel to the dispensary work during these years was the work of reading rooms, one of the earliest of which was located in the Hotel Boylston in Boston. It was described in the September 1888 *Journal* as "A New Home," meaning a new place that would serve as a publication room where the *Journal* could be read, as well as a salesroom for other Christian Science publications. The announcement went on to say that "it will also be a reading-room and social place for our friends,—a sort of clubroom."[23]

But maintaining both a dispensary and a reading room in Boston proved to be more complex and costly than the relatively small movement at this point could sustain. This became particularly apparent to Eddy in 1894, when her time and energy, along with that of her most faithful followers, became focused on the construction of the Mother Church edifice. Given this shifting of priorities, Eddy put a stop to the dispensary work and reading room in Boston, although these activities continued independently elsewhere.

In 1900, upon revisiting the whole issue, Eddy put into the *Manual* a bylaw establishing reading rooms on a uniform basis for the entire Christian Science field. After she did so, the character of reading rooms bore little relation to what had gone before. Under Eddy's new direction, reading rooms, as a constituent part of the church life of the denomination, shed the social, club-like feature of the late 1880s. They became instead congenial places, much like an extended library or living room, that combined the functions of making Christian Science literature accessible and providing a quiet space for meditation and prayer. They were, therefore, a kind of refuge or sanctuary in the midst of urban communities (and smaller towns as well) aimed at meeting the needs of the general public even more than of committed Christian Scientists.

The typical quietness of a place reserved for study and prayer has made reading rooms the easy butt of many a comedian's jest. But accounts in the church's periodicals have often told of inquirers finding Christian Science by being drawn to the quiet refuge of a reading room for comfort or healing. One testifier in 1909 from New Haven, Connecticut, for example, told how she injured herself on a city street, sharply aggravating already existing medical conditions considered to be incurable. Just as she cried out in extreme pain, "O God, help me!" her eyes fell on a sign pointing to a reading room where the "lady who met me (may God bless her abundantly) gently said, 'You know that all things are possible with God.'" Upon reading some Christian Science literature provided by this attendant, the testifier experienced immediate relief from pain and was drawn into the further study of Christian Science, gaining in the process more healings.[24]

Supported as a public service by all branch churches, reading rooms over the years have been the principal way in which *Science and Health* and other Christian Science literature were made accessible to the public. As Annie Knott put it in a 1910 *Sentinel* editorial, the reading room was a guarantee that "the growing demand for genuine Christian Science literature should be met in an adequate way."[25]

But the reading room as a refuge was just as important as the reading room as a resource. At the 1900 Annual Meeting of the Mother Church in June, the clerk's report noted that 212 reading rooms had already been established. They were "harbors of rest,—in the midst of the rush of the business districts"—where "the merchant and the shop-hand can escape from the whirl of daily life and find a resting-place where on a work-day they can think about God, and return to their tasks with sweeter thoughts, strengthened courage, and regenerated hopes."[26] The missionary function of reading rooms could therefore be thought of in dual terms. They were places where the heart could be prepared both to engage more fully with genuine Christian Science and to find welcome surcease from the pressures of modern life.

"IF THE LIVES OF CHRISTIAN SCIENTISTS . . ."

The institutions and church practices that Eddy developed during the 1890s served a more educational than ecclesiastical function. At the same time, she had no desire to distance Christian Science from fellowship with other Christian denominations. The day was long past when the *Journal* regularly printed jokes about clergymen and when Eddy had responded in sometimes severe language to her clerical critics. Particularly after the World's Parliament of Religions, she urged upon her followers the need to dwell in unity with other churches insofar as this was possible—even if she had no illusions about their preponderantly negative opinions of Christian Science.

Eddy, however, shared more with her Christian critics than they generally understood. The reverence in which she held the pastors of her youth, her lifelong immersion in the Bible and the hundreds of times she quoted it in her writings, her horror of mesmerism and other expressions of what she held to be the occult tradition, her love of the hymns she had learned as a girl, her insistence that Christian Science find expression in a church and not just a publishing organization, the hours she spent in private devotions and prayer—all these and more were evidences that her life was, in H. A. L. Fisher's words, "penetrated by Christianity."[27]

Although Eddy's denial of the deity of Jesus remained a sticking point for her orthodox critics, she was in spirit far closer to them than it might appear. As in other matters, Eddy's approach to the issue of the deity of Jesus has more to do with demonstration than with doctrine. For her, the question of how to think about Jesus was not a matter of staking out and defending a doctrinal position, but of exploring the practical implications of what Jesus means for how Christians must live their lives.

In her theology, to think of Jesus as God would leave an unbridgeable gap between Christians of today and Jesus, since it would therefore be idolatrous to even attempt to follow his example—in effect, becoming equal to God. At the same time, Eddy did not think of Jesus as just another human being. At many points she spoke of the unique divinity evident in his life, as when she wrote that "it required the divinity of our Master to perceive the real man, and to cast out the unreal or the counterfeit" and spoke of him as "our human and divine Master."[28] For her, the divine was not just a component of the human Jesus. It was the permeating identity of Jesus, as evidenced throughout his earthly life, from the virgin birth to his resurrection and ascension. Only Jesus, unique in all of human history, she taught, had so thoroughly manifested this divinity, or Christ, that he must be regarded as the Messiah. Thus Eddy insisted on maintaining an important distinction between Jesus and God, while also teaching Jesus' inseparability from the divine.

Her discovery of Jesus' mission and its consequences, Eddy believed, empowered Christian experience as no other form of Christian theology had. Through his life and sacrifice, she held, Jesus empowered his followers in all ages to partake of the sonship he showed was possible. He was, therefore, the unique "Wayshower" to humanity. Following in his way, Christians could expect to live a measure of the divine Sonship that Jesus lived, and thereby experience a proportionate measure of the salvation he made possible from sin, sickness, and eventually death itself.

"The life of Christ," she wrote, "is the predicate and postulate of all that I teach." Interestingly, it was a Jewish critic of Christian Science who most clearly grasped this point. At the Central Conference of American Rabbis at Baltimore in April 1912, Rabbi Maurice Lefkovitz refuted the argument of some Jewish converts to Christian Science that it was possible for a Jew to be a Christian Scientist and a believing Jew at the same time. Christian Science "does not believe in the deity of Jesus," he said. But by accepting the Virgin Birth, it "assigns to Jesus a position in human thought and belief that is absolutely unique and distinct. . . . The man who subscribes to the creed of Christian Science affirms his belief in this unique unmatched, and unmatchable position of Christ Jesus."[29]

A similar point was made four years later in Karl Holl's essay "Der Szientismus." By the time he wrote, Christian Science had gained enough adherents in Germany to arouse lively curiosity as to what it taught. Holl's essay contained some minor inaccuracies and he disagreed with the theology of Christian Science in some important respects. But he grasped the essential Christianity of Eddy's teaching as much, if not more than, any other non–Christian Science scholar before or since. He recognized that Eddy treated the revelation that came through Jesus as unique and absolutely necessary to human salvation, because through his "word and deed he brought to light the truth about God and reality. . . . His miracles, his resurrection and ascension" evidenced "the unity of man with the Father."[30]

As both Lefkovitz and Holl recognized, Eddy saw Jesus as the unique savior of humanity no less than did her orthodox Christian critics. The defining difference between her and other Christians lay not in the absolute centrality of that life to Christian faith and experience, but in her understanding of what his life meant and required of all Christians. Some of Eddy's clerical critics might well have been surprised by the fervor of her words about the blood of Christ in her short book *No and Yes:*

> The spilling of human blood was inadequate to represent the blood of Christ, the outpouring love that sustains man's at-one-ment with God; though shedding human blood brought to light the efficacy of divine Life and Love and its power over death. Jesus' sacrifice stands preeminently amidst physical suffering and human woe. . . . The real atonement—so infinitely beyond the heathen conception that God requires human blood to propitiate His justice and bring His mercy—needs to be understood. . . . Love bruised and bleeding, yet mounting to the throne of glory in purity and peace, over the steps of uplifted humanity,—this is the deep significance of the blood of Christ. Nameless woe, everlasting victories, are the blood, the vital currents of Christ Jesus' life, purchasing the freedom of mortals from sin and death. This blood of Jesus is everything to human hope and faith.[31]

Eddy's short book *Pulpit and Press,* published a few months after the dedication of the Mother Church, included a three-page note explaining her carefully balanced view of what today would be called the ecumenical question, along with two dozen press clippings covering the event. "To perpetuate a cold distance between our denomination and other sects," she wrote, "and close the door on church or individuals— however much this is done to us—is not Christian Science." It must be the spirit of Christ, rather than popularity and self-aggrandizement— "aught that can darken in any degree our spirituality"—that calls Christian Scientists into fellowship with other denominations. For Eddy, it was the practical spirituality of Christian Scientists—the healing work they accomplished, the living Christianity shown forth in their lives—that would be the decisive factor in the relation of Christian Scientists to other denominations. "If the lives of Christian Scientists attest their fidelity to Truth," she wrote, "I predict that in the twentieth century every Christian church in our land, and a few in far-off lands, will approximate the understanding of Christian Science sufficiently to heal the sick in his name."[32]

Historically, Christian Science was a significant, but not a sole, influence in stimulating a renewed commitment to spiritual healing across many denominations. Yet Eddy's "if" was and remains a very *big* if—especially given the distinction she consistently made between merely verbal adherence to Truth, and Truth actually lived. "Truth talked, but not demonstrated," she wrote in an 1889 article, "rolls on the human heart a stone, consigns sensibility to the charnel house of sensuality, ease, self-love, and self-justification, there to moulder and putrefy into nothingness."[33] The chapter on "Prayer" in *Science and Health* inveighs at many points against this dispiriting conventionalism: against pleading with God for undeserved benefits, remorse without real regeneration, audible prayers that do not correspond with actual convictions, and public displays of religiosity. A large portion of Eddy's energies during 1895 and 1896 particularly was devoted to trying to close the gap between word and deed among her followers.

So it was that her first address at a Mother Church service on May 26, 1895, partook not at all of the spirit of self-congratulation. Rather, it was a sharply worded wake-up call to a more vigorous and steely Christianity. The doors to a demanding, involving Christianity had been opened to Christian Scientists. But were they entering through those doors in sufficient numbers by the only means possible—the Christianization of their lives? The requirement that they do so underlay everything Eddy said when, to the great surprise of most of the congregation, she entered the church auditorium midway through the reading of the lesson-sermon.

The audience stood as she entered and, after bowing to them, she walked to the platform, sat down, and rested her head in silent prayer. A musical solo allowed the congregation to regain its composure. Then Eddy stepped to the desk and began speaking. Although she spoke distinctly and in a simple way, what she said was direct and at points severe. In her talk, which lasted fifteen or twenty minutes, Eddy spoke of the redemptive power of Christianity "seen in sore trials, self-denials, and crucifixions of the flesh," which come to the rescue of mortals and plant their feet "steadfastly in Christ"; of the need for self-forgetful, forgiving love; and, for most of the address, of the requirement on her followers to deal honestly with sin in themselves "before poor humanity is regenerated and Christian Science is demonstrated."[34]

With Foster Eddy's descent into what she saw as moral bankruptcy darkening her own personal life, she declared in perhaps the most uncompromising language she had ever used in speaking publicly on this subject: "The lack of seeing one's deformed mentality, and of *repentance* therefore, deep, never to be repented of, is retarding, and in certain morbid instances stopping, the growth of Christian Scientists. Without a knowledge of his sins, and repentance so severe that it destroys them, no person is or can be a Christian Scientist."

By sin, Eddy meant far more than the transgression of moral laws or even personal rebellion against God and his demands. Sin as she used the term connotes something far less personal and even more intransigent than sin in the more conventional sense. Eddy spoke of sin as an impersonal false belief: "the lying supposition that life, substance, and intelligence are both material and spiritual, and yet are separate from God." The great need for the individual who would be saved from sin, therefore, was not simply to choose to cease sinning, in the sense of committing sinful acts. This, Eddy taught, was sorely needed. But it can only be accomplished to the degree that one broke the hold of the hypnotic error of being a personal selfhood, a corporeal personality, torn between material and spiritual tendencies and separated by nature from God. While affirming the ultimately delusional character of sin, its unreality before God, she urged the congregation to serious and constant self-examination, so that they could maintain the childlikeness that Jesus loved, knowing that their "example, more than words, makes morals for mankind!"[35]

In Eddy's other communications with her followers over the next year and a half, she pursued almost relentlessly the same purpose: urging them to a more serious and disciplined Christianity by means of which alone they could incorporate the truth they professed into the fabric of their lives. The month after her first address in the Mother Church, she invited the alumni of the Massachusetts Metaphysical College to Pleasant View, telling them, "When you see sin in others, know that you have it in yourself and become repentant," upbraiding them for their failure to confront evil, and concluding with words drawn from Jeremiah: "Would that my head were a fountain of waters and my eyes rivers of tears that I might weep because of the apathy of my students and the little they have accomplished."[36]

There are clear evidences that in this period especially, she was deeply troubled by signs that the apathy and lack of spirituality among her students was not being remedied. In January 1896, she wrote to William and Daisette McKenzie, "I feel more and more that unless Christian Scientists grow rapidly more *spiritual* our cause will not be established. I feel a famine in the atmosphere of many oldest church members." To Caroline D. Noyes later in the same month she reiterated that "spirituality is so much needed in our ranks that sometimes it is disheartening to go among the oldest students and see its lack."[37]

It was on the occasion of her second and last appearance at a service at the Mother Church on Communion Sunday, January 5, 1896, that Eddy most forcefully summarized the tenor of her messages and instructions to its members following its dedication. She did not call them to account for their deficiencies but sought to rouse them to new spiritual efforts in a different way: by dwelling on what she saw as the Christian heart of her teaching. Again, she used the metaphor of rolling away a stone: "Divine Science has rolled away the stone from the sepulchre of our Lord; and there has risen to the awakened thought the majestic atonement of divine Love." The thrust of her message was what Jesus' atonement as understood in her teaching could, must, mean to her hearers. It must mean that "sinners suffer for their own sins, repent, forsake sin, love God, and keep His commandments, thence to receive the reward of righteousness: salvation from sin, not through the *death* of a man, but through a divine *Life*, which is our Redeemer." It must mean that they fulfill the meaning of "the last act of the tragedy on Calvary" that "rent the veil of matter, and unveiled Love's great legacy to mortals: *Love forgiving its enemies*." It must mean that in proportion to their spiritual progress, Christians today will "indeed drink of our Master's cup, and be baptized with his baptism! be purified as by fire," and thus have part in "Love's atonement." Only then could they "rest, in the understanding of divine Love that passeth all understanding."[38]

In thus dwelling on the need for repentance, more love, and willingness to pass through redemptive fire before rest and peace are attained, Eddy was trying to bring home to the congregation that they were pioneers in a new dispensation, a new spiritual era for humanity, and had better act like it. But how willing, she asked in effect, were they to break free of conventionalism and dedicate themselves to the demonstration of what she taught? Again, she expressed disappointment over what she perceived to be their state of thought. Shortly after returning to Pleasant View from her second public appearance at the Mother Church, she wrote to the Hannas: "I find the general atmosphere of my church as cold and still as the marble floors. God help you dear ones to not be paralyzed with the others." Later, writing to the Armstrongs, she explained further: "My students are doing a great, good work and the meeting and the way it was conducted rejoiced my heart. But O I did feel a coldness a lack of *inspiration* all through the dear hearts (not for me, Oh no, they are loyal to the highest degree) but it was a stillness a lack of spiritual energy and zeal that I felt."[39]

These observations help explain Eddy's efforts, especially during the second half of the 1890s, to kindle her followers' practice of her teaching into new life. Ironically, one of the most consequential of these efforts was one that she initially had no enthusiasm for undertaking.

"To Form the Budding Thought"

After the reorganization of September 1892, Eddy drafted and the First Members approved in an ad hoc fashion a number of rules regulating church meetings, admission of new members, and other procedures. As the rules multiplied and questions about them abounded, the need for a more orderly approach became evident—although not initially to her.

Yielding at last to the pressure of necessity, she appointed a committee to organize the rules she had drafted to that point into what became the *Church Manual*, which, after being further refined by her, was published in the late summer of 1895. When several more editions of the *Manual* followed in quick succession, she was again less than enthusiastic. Indeed, the first four editions did not even carry Eddy's name as author. Giving instructions the next year for yet another edition to be printed as soon as she wrote the last bylaw, she added: "O, I pray God it shall be the last I ever am called on to write." Within two or three years her negative view of having to put the *Manual* into place had changed. By late 1898 she had concluded, as she put it in a letter, "Our dear Father Mother God gives us the right rules for action and I have reason to believe that He has governed the writing of our Church Rules and By-laws."[40]

After a major revision of the *Manual* was published in 1903, Eddy wrote: "Heaps upon heaps of praise confront me, and for what? That of which I said in my heart, it will never be needed; namely, laws of limitation for a Christian Scientist. 'Thy ways are not as ours.' Thou knowest best what we need most, hence my disappointed hope and grateful joy." These words reflect in part Eddy's aversion to church rules, laws, and organization, but also her reluctant conviction of their necessity. Indeed, once she saw the practical need for a manual, she pushed the project forward with dispatch. A letter to a director urging more decisive action is a prime example of the peremptory style of one of her missives when she felt that an important project was being botched or delayed: "I direct you to get the *Manual* published *soon*. I mean just as soon as it can be. It must be *hurried*. . . . Now do not neglect this work for any other but push it as I say."[41]

The *Manual* was in one of its aspects a guidebook for the discipline and conduct of Mother Church members. But it was also a kind of constitution that spelled out the overall pattern of governance for the church. Eddy had no desire to establish an over-arching organization for its own sake. Long-term experience, however, had convinced her that without a coherent structure in which church life could proceed, it would be impossible for the Christian Science movement to withstand the disintegrative forces that assailed it from within and without. In this way, she came back to a position she had taken in responding to an ex-student who had decried church organization in 1887: "After over ten years of experience and success far beyond yours, I learned that nothing but organization would save this cause for mankind and protect it from the devouring disorganizers."[42]

By 1895, Eddy had learned through sometimes bitter lessons that her teaching could be mistaught and students of her book thus misled, that promising Christian Scientists could fall by the wayside through lack of spiritual discipline, and that factions and internal rivalries could severely undermine the stability of the church. She saw these and other problems as preventable if church members voluntarily obeyed basic rules for spiritual self-discipline, teaching and learning Christian Science, conducting church services, admitting new members and disciplining erring ones, and for working together within a clearly defined structure of church government. In this respect, she felt it was appropriate to refer to the *Manual* as "the Deuteronomy of Christian Science."[43]

In the *Manual,* Eddy recognized and provided for the disciplining of wayward church members, including church officers who failed to fulfill their duties. Yet she remained suspicious of the expectable tendency of some church officials to wield personal power through application of the *Manual*'s provisions for discipline beyond what was absolutely necessary. In a number of instances, she proved far more patient and charitable than her more zealous students. In 1902, she wrote to the board of directors, "If I were to have the students that break faith all excommunicated without sufficient effort on my part and on yours to save them how many members think you would be left in it?"[44]

As this statement illustrates, for Eddy, rules, regulations, and procedures—all the etceteras of organization—were never primary, never the truly essential factor in the life of the church at any level. If the branch churches, as Eddy later put it to Tomlinson, were "over-organized," she had no desire to over-organize the Mother Church itself. Eddy once wrote the Hannas that it had been her "life-long task to *experiment*," and her attempt to arrive at a practical basis for this government of her church showed that spirit at work. The *Manual* that she wrote for the church retained the open, experimental character of her leadership of the movement through the years. Its rules and bylaws, she explained at the time the first edition was published, were "written at different dates, and, as the occasion required; they sprang from necessity, the logic of events, from the immediate demand for them, a need that must be met for the honor and defense of our cause." In 1903, she further wrote to the directors that each of the bylaws

has met and mastered, or forestalled some contingency, some imminent peril, and will continue to do so. Its By-laws have preserved the sweet unity of this large church. . . . Many times a single By-law has cost me long nights of prayer and struggle, but it has won the victory over some sin and saved the walls of Zion from being torn down by disloyal students. We have proven that "in unity there is strength."

She therefore counseled them: "Never abandon the By-laws nor the denominational government of the Mother Church."[45]

For nine years after the church was reorganized—from 1892 to 1901—the First Members shared the primary responsibility for the running of the Mother Church with the four directors (who were also First Members). In its early years this body comprised about forty members (and, later, up to 100 members), all residing within five hundred miles of Boston. They met as necessary to vote on the adding of new church members, enact new *Manual* bylaws—all of them proposed or approved by Eddy—deal with cases of discipline, and transact other business of the church. The First Members were akin to lay bishops, though without jurisdictions of their own; and while Eddy's approval became a requirement for election of a new First Member, as a body they were answerable under the *Manual* to no one but themselves.

Eventually the system of trying to govern a far-flung and growing church through such a large body became unworkable. Tomlinson, who became a First Member in 1898, said that he had supposed that the First Members were "the flywheel of the church," praying about and harmoniously resolving church problems as they arose. Instead, he found that "they were not the flywheel, but were more like flies doing their best to stick to the wheel as it revolved." At one point, Eddy explained to a reporter, the First Members had five churches under discipline until she intervened. "Dissensions are dangerous in an infant church. I wrote to each church in tenderness, in exhortation, and in rebuke, and so brought all back to union and love again. If that is to be Pope," she added, "then you can judge for yourself."[46]

She did more than intervene to settle such disputes. These and other similar incidents convinced her that conducting the affairs of the church required a more coherent form of church government. So Eddy again made a fundamental change, requesting in 1901 that the First Members turn over the powers they had exercised to the board of directors. Yet she had no desire to exalt the board into a position of quasi-papal authority. While the board no longer had to share the responsibility of transacting the business of the church, its members operated under a number of constraints. Like all other church members, each director was under the discipline of the *Manual* bylaws. Each director was further required by deeds of trust incorporated into the *Manual* to be a "firm and consistent believer" in Christian Science as taught by her.[47] The Mother Church, the business of which the directors transacted, was forbidden from interfering in the affairs of branch churches and had no role in conducting the associations of pupils of recognized Christian Science teachers, living or deceased.

The directors were also obligated by thirty-two bylaws to obtain Eddy's consent for such required actions as important appointments, for major steps that only she could initiate, and for optional actions taken by the board.[48] Common law gave the board power to act as next in authority under these "consent clauses" after Eddy's decease. But her "consent" did not pass to the directors at that point, but was simply no longer necessary or even possible.

A small minority of disaffected church members after 1910 argued that by virtue of these "consent clauses," Eddy signified an intent that the *Manual*'s authority should cease at her death. Perhaps anticipating that this issue would arise, she wrote to the directors, "If I am not personally with you, the Word of God, and my instructions in the By-Laws, have led you hitherto and will remain to guide you safely on, and the teachings of St. Paul are as useful to-day as when they were first written."[49]

Just to make sure that this would be the case, in a major revision of the *Manual* published in 1903, she locked in the *Manual* as the indisputable constitution and governing law of her church in perpetuity. She did so by making a crucial change in a bylaw that had previously allowed the directors, with Eddy's consent or direction, to amend most bylaws by unanimous vote. The *Manual* revision, deleting any mention of the directors, gave to Eddy, and to no one else, the sole right to change church law and church doctrine: "No new Tenet or By-Law shall be adopted, nor any Tenet or By-Law amended or annulled, without the written consent of Mary Baker G. Eddy, the author of our textbook, Science and Health."[50]

But Eddy did not stop there. She added another deed of trust, executed in 1903, to the appendix of the *Manual* as a legal companion to the original 1892 deed of trust that had created the "Christian Science Board of Directors" as "a perpetual body." The new deed conveyed to the directors property on which an extension of the Mother Church edifice would soon be built. Incorporated into the new trust deed was wording similar to the revised bylaw that required Eddy's written consent in order for a "Tenet or By-Law" to be adopted or changed.[51]

By putting a second court document into a church manual, Eddy created an iron barrier against the possibility that in her absence the directors could make or revise the bylaws. This also gave legal underpinning to her intent that the *Manual of The Mother Church* would retain its essentially constitutional character. The book became the framework for a form of church government in which the directors, along with other church officers, remained accountable, not only in a moral and spiritual sense, but in a legal sense as well, defining their responsibilities and limiting their powers. As Boston attorney Walter A. Dane noted in 1919 during a major court case involving his clients, the Mother Church directors: "This Manual is the source and the measure, the limitation, of the responsibilities and the powers of the Board of Directors, and they are governed and controlled by its provisions; and in that respect they are the administrative unit of a highly developed form of constitutional church government." A month before the court ruled in favor of the directors' upholding of the *Manual* in this case, Adam Dickey, one of the five board members, gave a talk that was later printed in the *Journal*. In it he rejected the argument that Eddy had put the government of her church in the hands of five persons. "What she did," he insisted, "was to put the government of The Mother Church into the *By-laws*." He added, "The safety of the Christian Science church does not rest in the Board of Directors; it lies in the integrity of each individual member, and in the determination of the members to obey the By-laws."[52]

Even considering the far-reaching responsibilities of the directors, Eddy spoke of the church as a whole as "the mouthpiece of Christian Science." In words that apply to the Mother Church as well as to its branches, she identified the church with "equal rights and privileges, equality of the sexes, rotation in office." She made this statement in 1904 in a short article concerning the church's board of education. With the Mother Church very much in mind, she declared that "the Magna Charta of Christian Science" is "essentially democratic," since "its government is administered by the common consent of the governed, wherein and whereby man governed by his Creator is self-governed." When it came to the branch churches, she was even more emphatic, referring to their government as "distinctly democratic."[53]

The *Manual*, however, is not essentially a set of rules for how authority is to be distributed within the Church of Christ, Scientist. It is, rather, more a book about relationships within that church as a whole. It concerns the relation of Eddy to her church and its members, the Mother Church to the branch churches, teachers to students, practitioners to patients, church members to other church members, readers in churches to their congregations, Committees on Publication and members of the Board of Lectureship to the needs of the field they served.

One of the most able writers for the early church periodicals, Blanche Hersey Hogue of Portland, Oregon, explored this point in an article for the September 10, 1910, *Sentinel*. In an unusual gesture, Eddy commended it to the field as "practical and scientific," recommending its "careful study to all Christian Scientists." Hogue did not write of the *Manual* in legalistic terms, as so many of her fellow church members have done in her time and since. She spoke of the effect of the Bible and of *Science and Health* as correcting the individual thought and aiding the student to live in Christian discipleship. The *Manual,* she wrote, "bears definite relation to the other two books in that it shows us how to take the steps that will bring their teaching into our lives in all necessary relations with our fellow-men." Work within its organizational frame-work provides the Christian Scientist with "multiplied opportunities for surrendering his own will, his own opinion, and his own comfort to the good of the whole,—opportunities unafforded even by the home or by any outside life in the world." In this sense, Hogue concluded, no student should be indifferent to organization or feel that he or she has "outgrown" the need for it.[54]

In shaping the church organization spelled out in the *Manual,* Eddy confronted a long-term problem: how to provide a workable structure for her church without losing its heart and soul by sinking it in the pit of institutionalism. It was the spirit in which the *Manual* bylaws were to be administered that Eddy emphasized in a 1901 interview printed in the *Baltimore Sun,* when she stated, "I have made rigid by-laws for the gov-ernment of the church, and every one has been necessary, but they need to be administered in gentleness and forbearance, as well as in firmness with the erring."[55] The spirit she sought to inculcate in the church is reflected in the only bylaw to have remained virtually unchanged in the *Manual* from its first through its final edition. Entitled "A Rule for Motives and Acts," it reads:

> Neither animosity nor mere personal attachment should impel the motives or acts of the members of The Mother Church. In Science, divine Love alone governs man; and a Christian Scientist reflects the sweet amenities of Love, in rebuking sin, in true brotherliness, charitableness, and forgiveness. The members of this Church should daily watch and pray to be delivered from all evil, from prophesying, judging, condemn-ing, counseling, influencing or being influenced erroneously.[56]

"A Rule for Motives and Acts," with its strong emphasis on love and community, may be taken as sounding the keynote of the *Manual* as a whole and the motive that lay behind all its provisions. In the same letter in which she counseled the directors never to abandon the *Manual* bylaws, she said that the bylaws "have preserved the sweet unity" of the church. There could be no guarantee that the spirit of love and community Eddy hoped would prevail in her church would be forthcoming. But insofar as this was possible, she undertook in the *Manual* to nurture the qualities necessary to make the system of church government that it outlined work. "Of this I am sure," she wrote, "that each Rule and By-law in this Manual will increase the spirituality of him who obeys it, invigorate his capacity to heal the sick, to comfort such as mourn, and to awaken the sinner." The *Manual* "stands alone, uniquely adapted to form the budding thought and hedge it about with divine Love."[57]

"The Hitherto Unexplored Fields of Science"

Christian Science, Eddy insisted, was not a theory to be debated but a truth to be lived. Students bought and studied *Science and Health;* but how were they to grasp and practice what it contained? Eddy looked to the growing number of teachers in the movement to help accomplish this purpose. She well knew how difficult the task of teaching was, saying that "it requires a higher understanding to teach this subject properly and correctly than it does to heal the most difficult case."[58]

The dearth of good teaching was especially painful to her when Christian Science was making converts rapidly and new students needed to understand how to assimilate and practice what they were reading in *Science and Health.* It was to help accomplish this end that Eddy spent the latter part of 1896 assembling earlier occasional writings into a volume published in February 1897 with the title *Miscellaneous Writings— 1883–1896.* After the publication of an earlier book, she wrote, "The way is always blockaded in proportion to the weight of good that is to be carried over it." If this was true, then *Miscellaneous Writings* was destined to carry a very heavy "weight of good."[59]

To aid her in the editing process, Eddy hired a young Scottish Christian Scientist named Jessie Gorham. Gorham, working under Eddy's supervision, was energetic and made corrections of grammar and punctuation with dispatch. Eddy welcomed such improvements, encouraging her young helper to be critical and writing, "I can never prepare my manuscript on Christian Science for print, when I am composing it." But when Gorham assumed the prerogative of changing Eddy's language and her meaning, she needed to be reminded, as had Wiggin before her, that the meaning of the text was to be rendered clearer, not changed: "None but the author sees certain needs in the copy, and the less written by any other person the better." Gorham was not only sensitive but mercurial and subject to bouts of extreme depression and confusion over her tasks. Eddy's attempts to correct her were expressed in affectionate, sometimes humorous terms, as when she addressed her in a letter as "my loved literary Lassie." Eventually Gorham's services proved counterproductive and she was relieved of her duties. But the problems

with the manuscript continued. Calvin Frye, much to Eddy's consternation, wrestled for days with the apparently simple task of typing a
table of contents correctly. Then there was always the looming problem,
as Eddy put it, of the need "to fight the printing battle—breaking of
machinery and almost skulls."[60]

The book was finally published early in 1897. A month afterward,
Eddy announced to Christian Scientists the startling requirement that
teachers of Christian Science were to cease instructing students for one
year. The study of the new book, wrote Eddy in the *Journal,* "is calculated
to prepare the minds of all true thinkers to understand the Christian
Science Text-book more correctly than a student can."[61] The contents
of *Miscellaneous Writings* were partly shaped by the character of what
Eddy had written since the founding of the *Journal* in 1883. Its title was
surely justified, since she had written in a wide variety of genres: articles,
addresses, messages to the Mother Church, questions and answers,
letters, sermons, and poems. Given this range, the book has an open,
informal quality that reflects the relatively unstructured character of
the movement before it became a church with a more uniform pattern
of worship and teaching by the late 1890s.

The editing process winnowed out some articles in which Eddy
had allowed herself to write in surprisingly strong personal terms. She
had indirectly referred, for example, to one mind-curer as "an ass whose
ears stick out." As late as 1891 she had commented sharply on an article
in the Concord press that restated an English slight on American women
who became Christian Scientists: "The public cannot wisely swallow
reports of American affairs gathered from beer-bulged and surly sensu-
alists, or perchance from an aristocrat's lofty scorn of a community he
has never visited."[62]

While the writing in the new book was edited and smoothed out
for publication in more permanent form, it still had the immediacy
that came from grappling with urgent spiritual issues at the very point
when they had become urgent. In compiling and reworking her earlier
articles and other pieces for *Miscellaneous Writings,* Eddy adapted the accumulated lessons of the past to serve the immediate needs of the present.
In articles, letters, and messages since 1883, she had dealt with virtually
every problem, temptation, and obstacle that her students encountered
in trying to incorporate Christian Science into the fabric of their daily
lives. She had answered questions about its teaching, touched on a
variety of problems in the healing practice, helped students face and
understand clerical attack, encouraged and supported their efforts to
form church congregations, warned them against the dangers of internal
dissension; dealt with the persistent issue of the glorification of personality

(especially her own), and had spoken of the ways in which her teaching could be diluted and compromised.

In the largest sense, *Miscellaneous Writings* is a record of the struggle that Eddy faced in helping to ensure that the movement would survive. In the introduction to the book she wrote that, in compiling it, she had tried to "remove the pioneer signs and ensigns of war, and to retain at this date the privileged armaments of peace" and "with strong wing to lift my readers above the smoke of conflict into light and liberty."[63] Yet what Eddy put into her book was less the memories of the struggles she had made than the lessons learned from the battles she had waged. The book as a whole said, in effect: this is what you must undergo if you would incorporate the truths of Christian Science into your lives and demonstrate the spiritual power it opens to humanity. It addressed in various ways how to make good on this commitment—how to measure up to the demands of practicing Christian Science in a world that only grudgingly made room for it.

"May this volume," wrote Eddy in the preface, "be to the reader a graphic guide-book, pointing the path, dating the unseen, and enabling him to walk the untrodden in the hitherto unexplored fields of Science."[64] The new paths to traverse, though, were less in the public arena of building churches and holding services than in the chambers of the human heart. Many of the most memorable passages in the book explored what might be called the inner psychology of the Christian life as lived in the light of Christian Science.

An example is Eddy's treatment of the familiar Christian theme of baptism in the article "Pond and Purpose," which she set apart from other articles by making it a chapter all its own. The article began by thanking students who contributed to placing a pond on the grounds of Pleasant View. But Eddy went on to expand on the larger meaning of baptism that the waters of the pond symbolically implied.

She spoke of the baptism of repentance as "a stricken state of human consciousness . . . which rends the veil that hides mental deformity." So far Eddy was on familiar Christian ground. But then she moved on to what she saw as a second stage of baptism, the baptism of the Holy Ghost, in which mortals gained "new motives, new purposes, new affections." This stage marked the appearing of a consistent spirituality in human life: "Through the accession of spirituality, God, the divine Principle of Christian Science, literally governs the aims, ambition, and acts of the Scientist. The divine ruling gives prudence and energy; it banishes forever all envy, rivalry, evil thinking, evil speaking and acting; and mortal mind, thus purged, obtains peace and power outside of itself." Eddy went on to write that the complete achievement of a spiritualized condition—the "final immersion of human consciousness in the infinite ocean of Love"—came only with the baptism of Spirit, wherein all sin and mortality must ultimately vanish. But she insisted that no one had to wait for this ultimate spiritual state to begin living in what Eddy called elsewhere "the coincidence of the human and the divine." This was the new territory, the new latitude of consciousness, "the hitherto unexplored fields of Science," that she intended *Miscellaneous Writings* to help its readers explore.[65]

The intent behind *Miscellaneous Writings* had been to prepare its readers to understand better *Science and Health* and to discipline their lives so as to absorb the teaching it contained. Eddy also included at the end of her new book seventy-one pages of testimonies showing the healing effects of reading the textbook on first-time inquirers into Christian Science. Five years later in the 1902 revision of *Science and Health*, she did the same thing on a larger scale, incorporating a new chapter called "Fruitage," composed of one hundred pages of testimonies written by those healed by reading the book. Testifiers repeatedly related the startling, abrupt physical changes that had come about once they began to feel the power of the book, sometimes speaking of how they had endured years of invalidism and suffering up to that point. Others tell how their whole being was transformed through the truth that reading *Science and Health* had brought into their lives.

There was another aspect to her new book and its effect that William Lyman Johnson, then a young man, commented on in recalling the period. In contrast to *Science and Health* and most of Eddy's other published works, *Miscellaneous Writings* contained much that was personal. Articles such as "Voices of Spring," "Thanksgiving Dinner," and the poetry included as part of the book, reflected Eddy's own tastes, experiences, and observations on a variety of subjects outside of Christian Science. This dimension of the book, Johnson observed, acted as a "leaven" among Christian Scientists, some of whom had become so austere and serious that they looked upon "simple pleasures" almost as sins and would converse "almost always upon matters of Christian Science." What they found upon reading *Miscellaneous Writings* were a number of passages that illustrated a point Eddy had made in an address included in the book: "Pure humanity, friendship, home, the interchange of love, bring to earth a foretaste of heaven. They unite terrestrial and celestial joys, and crown them with blessings infinite."[66]

Eddy committed the pages of *Science and Health* to "honest seekers for Truth." *Miscellaneous Writings*, however, was dedicated "To Loyal Christian Scientists" who already believed that the convictions embodied in that textbook were true. It seems to have made a striking impression on those it was intended to reach, which included a large proportion of practicing Christian Scientists. Most of the articles comprising the book had been written for the *Journal* in the 1880s when the movement was much smaller than it had become by the time the book was published. As a result, the material in the book was completely new to a great many of its readers. Many of them expressed warm appreciation for the new book in letters to Eddy, some of them published in the *Journal*. Less fulsome but more perceptive than most were the words of Edward A. Kimball, one of those who had urged Eddy to compile the book. He spoke of "its rules for solving hard problems and dissolving hard hearts."[67] This for Eddy was perhaps the most difficult, but the most necessary, step of all.

"I Will Lift You into the Understanding"

Speaking of the early stages of her work in Christian Science, Eddy said that she had to "impart, while teaching its grand facts, the hue of spiritual ideas from her own spiritual condition."[68] After the one-year moratorium on teaching following the publication of *Miscellaneous Writings* had expired, Eddy still found the spiritual condition of teachers generally lacking in that divine hue.

In mid-November 1898 she sent identical telegrams to seventy students asking them to be at Christian Science Hall in Concord at 4 P.M. the following Sunday. When they all arrived (with two or three exceptions), Kimball read a letter from Eddy saying that they had been called to receive one or more lessons on Christian Science and that "this opportunity is designed to impart a fresh impulse to our spiritual attainments, the great need whereof I daily discern. And I have waited for the right hour, and to be called of God to contribute my part towards this result."[69]

The background of many of those present was impressive: they included ministers, judges, physicians, businessmen, and editors. Although the composition of the movement as a whole was predominantly female, the class included almost an equal number of men and women. Some had come from great distances: from Canada, England, Scotland, and the far West. But the distinguishing feature of the class was the inclusion of a number of promising young people such as John Lathrop, Ira Knapp's daughter Daphne, James Neal, and Augusta Stetson's protégé Carol Norton.

Eddy's precise instructions for the seating arrangement of the class reflected the importance she attached to their presence. The older and more experienced students were placed on the third bench, with their students in the second row, the first being reserved for newer and younger students who had learned only from *Science and Health*. When asked why she included so many young people in the class, she answered, "Because I want my teaching carried on."[70]

How did she intend to do this? Not merely through formal instruction on the main points in Christian Science. All present, with the exception of a couple of observers, had been well grounded in Christian Science, many of them having studied previously with her. There was some instruction on basic points in Christian Science, such as a statement on the Trinity that Eddy later had copied and sent to each member. On the face of it, however, much of the class was a prolonged examination in which she tested the spiritual fitness of her students. Looking directly at each of them in turn, she asked questions about what God meant to them and what they felt was most important in healing. She listened intently to their answers, sometimes correcting them or providing an answer of her own.

In part, Eddy was testing her students with an eye to assessing their fitness for future service. But given the kinds of questions she asked, the answers she provided to them beyond what her students had said, her other comments in the class, and the reaction of her students to the occasion, it is apparent that much more was going on. Speaking of the younger members of the class whom she desired to encourage, she said, "I will lift you into the understanding." Students' recollections of the class suggest that her underlying aim was to touch their hearts and enlarge their vision—to lift them into a larger understanding of God than more formal instruction could convey. The purpose of the gathering, she later commented to Irving Tomlinson, was "to spiritualize the Field," saying also that "her work with that class changed the character of the entire Field."[71]

As an experienced teacher, Eddy tried to do so without solemnity or even giving the appearance that this was her aim. Her questions were phrased almost pleadingly, as if the students were doing her a favor by sharing their responses. The class was informally structured, with considerable give and take. It included moments of humor, with Eddy relating an amusing story or two from her childhood to make a point. But from the interchange as recorded by students in the class, one can see the consistency of her underlying intent.

While the class did not include a systematic review of doctrinal points of Christian Science, Eddy did grill its members at one point on their understanding of the trinity. Finding less than satisfactory responses to her question, several weeks after the class was over she sent each one a note on the trinity, which she defined in these words:

> Father, is man's divine Principle, Love.
> Son, is God's man—His image, or spiritual idea.
> Holy Ghost, is Divine Science, the Messiah or Comforter.

Here as elsewhere she strongly affirmed the reality of one triune God, always with the underlying thought that the trinity does not consist in three distinct persons but, as she once put it, is "the same in essence, though multiform in office."[72]

When Eddy speaks of father, son, and holy spirit, she generally refers to the offices of God as revealed to humanity. But she was less interested in doctrinal formulations than in what it means to experience God's presence in daily life. Hence the frequent references to God as Life, Truth, and Love: Life corresponding to God as Father and Mother; Truth to Christ, God's son and full expression; and Love as God's sustaining presence, the Comforter or Holy Ghost. "The ego," as she summarized the issue, "is revealed as Father, Son, and Holy Ghost, but the full Truth is found only in Divine Science where we see God as Life, Truth, and Love." To raise her students to the fuller apprehension of this triune God, and so to impart a new impetus for spiritual growth to the field, was the essential purpose of the 1898 class.[73]

The home of a Christian Scientist, she said, "is in the understanding of God, his affections and interests are there, and his abiding place is there." Eddy's evident desire was to lift the vision of her students into a more immediate grasp of this positive truth of Christian Science. For this reason, she deliberately avoided any discussion of the nature of evil and mental malpractice. As she explained afterward in a letter to Hanna, that subject should already have been familiar, since it was covered in primary class instruction. But she also made it clear that, without an understanding of this issue, a student "cannot separate the tares from the wheat and destroy the tares—he cannot divide between an impartation from the immortal or divine Mind, and temptation, or the evil suggestion of human thought and argument."[74]

In this class the main effort was not to make that separation, but to focus wholly on the effort to lift her students into a more intense spiritual light. Repeatedly Eddy tried to take the thought of the class as a whole as far as they could go in this direction. At points, students later recalled, she went well beyond their understanding. Indeed, she explained in a letter that she had closed the class on the second day because she saw that the students "had gotten all they could digest" and because she did not want to "lose the strong impression (to some extent) already made on their minds." After Eddy had spoken on the dangers of worshiping her personality, recalled Daisette Stocking, "her voice became illumined, and she went on speaking with deep earnestness, her voice thrilling with love and power. . . . I tried earnestly to follow her words, but became aware that I was not understanding her at all. A feeling of great regret and loss passed over me. . . . She continued to speak for several minutes, and then paused a few moments and quietly took up her former line of instruction."[75]

During the class, Eddy showed particular interest in several students who had visionary experiences of the sort not usually encountered in Christian Science literature. One woman spoke of having been healed of several serious diseases, including a tumor and heart trouble. She had been healed, she said, by reading the Revelation of St. John, and a short time afterward experienced "a vision of being led to the light of Truth." Another young man rose to speak but was so moved that he had to sit down for a while before regaining his composure. He then told how Christian Science had brought him three times into "a vision of wonderful, intense light, in which he was simply bathed, a light beyond the brightness of the sun or any light that is known." Relating this, Sue Harper Mims, a student from Atlanta, said that she had never seen anything like the wonderful look on Eddy's face as he spoke.[76]

Mim's recollections of the class, like those of other students, contain some rather fulsome passages, as when she wrote of her first view of Eddy as she entered the hall: "She is the very picture of refined elegance, and were I to try to describe her to you exactly, the difficulty would be to find words to express how fine she is, how delicate, how sensitive, how exquisite."[77] Probably most students were affected far more viscerally than they had the ability to express. One account by Edward Norwood of Tennessee, who later helped to update the chapter "Fruitage" for the 1907 revision of *Science and Health*, is worth quoting at greater length for what it reveals, if stammeringly, about the experience:

> Suddenly it did seem a veil was lifted or a window opened, and I could see, in one of those supreme moments . . . the reality of things—the majestic oneness of the spiritual universe—its vast quietness—the infinite Mind—the eternal stillness. . . . And as I looked, the symbols around me, the personalities, the class, all externals, seemed to fade, and a wondrous sense of Reality appeared. . . . I got such a glimpse of the Way . . . and my heart yearned to go on! But anon the veil dropped down, and I was back again.[78]

Norwood's statement, however visionary, caught something essential about the spirit of Christian Science that was vitally important to Eddy, though less so to some of her more prosaic followers: that there is a different consciousness to be had now, the consciousness of a different reality from what is apprehended by sense-bound limits. But this consciousness, as Eddy had so often said, was not a consciousness of another sphere of being, as in some forms of Christian mysticism. It was, rather, a new apprehension of present being. While preparing for the class, Eddy had called Joseph Armstrong, one of the directors, to Pleasant View on another matter. When she shared with him what she hoped the class would accomplish, he said that for a few moments he saw what she saw, and that he had "never dreamed of such a Heaven on earth."[79]

1898

In December 1898 Eddy wrote to Carol Norton in New York, who had been a member of the class: "I have wrought day and night this year to make way for our church and a systematic order of action in the departments of CS." The year 1898 was, in fact, a prolific time of substantive achievement in Eddy's work on behalf of the future of her church. "I am at work continually for the good of all. The field is large the laborers are few," Eddy wrote in another letter of 1898.[80] That year she was giving those laborers a good deal to do. Almost every month brought forth some new development:

- In January, Eddy founded the church's Board of Lectureship, initially consisting of five lecturers but later expanded so as to respond to the enormous and growing public curiosity about Christian Science.
- Later in the same month, she executed a deed of trust organizing The Christian Science Publishing Society.
- In February, she took the first step in forming the Board of Education to resume the work of the Massachusetts Metaphysical College, the charter of which she had never surrendered, so as to provide for the teaching of teachers. (The first class was taught by Edward Kimball in January 1899.)
- In April, she defined twenty-six Bible lesson topics covering major aspects of the teaching of Christian Science. From July on, each topic would be repeated with a different set of texts twice every year.

- In May, Eddy shifted testimony meetings in all Christian
  Science churches from Friday to Wednesday, to take effect
  in June.

- In September came the first issue of a new periodical originally
  named the *Christian Science Weekly,* renamed the next year
  Christian Science Sentinel.

- In December and January, she laid the groundwork for the
  church's Committee on Publication, entrusting it with the
  mission of correcting misconceptions about Christian Science
  and injustices done to Eddy and church members.

Some of these changes—especially those that concerned services
and teaching—directly affected the internal life of the movement. But
the balance had shifted in an important way. To a large extent, the initiatives Eddy instituted in 1898 found their focus outside the Christian
Science movement itself. The new work of the Board of Lectureship,
Committee on Publication, and Christian Science Publishing Society
was geared primarily to reaching the general public, rather than exclusively to meeting the needs of Christian Scientists themselves.

As always, the dynamic of the growth of Christian Science lay in
individual conversions, healing experiences, and the forming of local
congregations. The purpose of the Board of Lectureship was to feed the
growing public interest that Christian Science healing practice had
aroused. The ideal lecture, said Eddy, *"persuades* and convinces by the
logic and the tenderness of Christian Science." In an era when lectures
were highly popular modes of communication, attendance at Christian
Science lectures in the United States and England was often huge.
Overflow crowds often jammed such large venues as Queen's Hall in
London and New York's Metropolitan Opera House and Carnegie Hall,
where, to cite but one instance, Carol Norton delivered a lecture to
about three thousand in December 1898.[81]

The heightened public interest in Christian Science naturally stimulated enormous public controversy, sometimes generated by the
clergy and medical fraternity. The great need, as Eddy saw it, was to
bring some balance and calm to the heated atmosphere created by a
growing literature of highly polemical newspaper articles, pamphlets,
sermons, and tracts. She therefore entrusted the Committee on
Publication with correcting "in a Christian manner" stereotypes and
misinformation that would otherwise shut out honest public reckoning
with what Christian Science actually stood for.

That office, she wrote to a state committee, requires "more than
the wisdom of Solomon to fill it for it calls for the meekness love and

Alfred Farlow speaking
to Mary Baker Eddy, ca.
1903–06. Courtesy of
The Mary Baker Eddy
Collection.

divine strength of our Master, Jesus, to wisely rebuke reform and regenerate this generation. Its vital best work must reach the Press whence the people draw their supplies." Eventually she assigned this work to one-person Committees on Publication in each state and later in foreign countries, all working under the direction of a manager in Boston. Beginning in 1900, that manager was Alfred Fallow, whose corrections in the press were so widely printed that he became the best-known Christian Scientist other than Eddy herself.[82]

The *Christian Science Weekly,* like the reading room work, had a dual function, since it was directed both to the inner life of the denomination and to the public. On the one hand, it was a means through which Eddy could communicate more readily with her followers than was possible through the monthly *Journal.* On the other, it reached the public not only with timely articles on Christian Science, but with coverage of current national and world news in every issue, making it thereby a forerunner of the *Christian Science Monitor,* established a decade later.

The establishment of the Christian Science Publishing Society under an 1898 deed of trust was, as Eddy stated in the deed itself, "for the purpose of more effectually promoting and extending the religion of Christian Science as taught by me." Here the words "by me" were crucial. Judge Hanna later recalled that in a conversation with Eddy a few days before she signed the trust deed, she said that she wished especially "to protect and preserve the literature of the movement in its purity and from aggressive attempts by enemies of the movement to adulterate the literature by injecting into it thoughts and teachings which would tend to becloud or destroy her teachings of Christian Science and thereby create chaos and confusion in the Christian Science ranks as well as to misrepresent her teachings to the outside world."[83]

Identifying these newly systematized activities of the church initiated in 1898, however, gives but a scant idea of the palpable sense of freshness and forward movement of which they were an essential part. At the beginning of this landmark year Eddy had asked in a Communion message to the Mother Church: "Beloved brethren, another Christmas has come and gone. Has it enabled us to know more of the healing Christ that saves from sickness and sin?"[84] By the end of the year she had effectively answered yes to the same question, in a poem called "Christmas Hymn" published in the *Journal* for December.

Unlike most of her other religious poetry, this poem, revised as "Christmas Morn," did not reflect a deep need of the movement as Eddy felt it. Rather, it celebrated, as its first stanza illustrates, the newness and spiritual light that had been breaking through in various ways during the course of the year:

> Blest Christmas morn, though murky clouds
> Pursue thy way,
> Thy light was born where storm enshrouds
> Nor dawn nor day![85]

By the end of 1898, however, storm clouds were definitely gathering again. In May 1899, Josephine Curtis Woodbury, who had been excommunicated from the Mother Church three years before and had come to attack Eddy with passionate intensity, wrote a damning article in the widely read magazine the *Arena*. Later that summer, in response to a controversial portion of Eddy's June message to the Mother Church, Woodbury instigated a lawsuit that made the next two years among the most torturous of Eddy's life.

8

"Ayont Hate's Thrall"

"Our Salvation is Through Love"

The conduct of Josephine Curtis Woodbury had constituted a severe and growing problem for the church in Boston since the mid-1880s. But the fact that she launched her lawsuit against Eddy in 1899, just after a period of sustained progress for the church, had its own kind of logic within the framework of Christian Science. To Eddy, it was predictable that any momentum in the progress of the movement would be met by the resistance of what she called the carnal or mortal mind. This was not so much a matter of the will of persons—even so troublesome a person to her as Woodbury—as an expression of the dynamics involved in the conflict between spirituality and materialism.

Eddy in no way credited the existence of a personal Satan. Nevertheless, she did believe that sin and evil oppose good at every turn until the true understanding of God's supreme power vanquishes all belief in a power opposed to him. Again, her perspective was biblical: "Whosoever lives most the life of Jesus in this age and declares best the power of Christian Science, will drink of his Master's cup. Resistance to Truth will haunt his steps, and he will incur the hatred of sinners, till 'wisdom is justified of her children.' " To Eddy, these words were not rhetoric but a precise statement of how Christian experience *happens*, from the crucifixion of Jesus to the resistance that she saw as attending each step in the growth of Christian Science. In her words from *Science and Health*, "the higher Truth lifts her voice, the louder error will scream, until its inarticulate sound is forever silenced in oblivion."[1]

Eddy's fundamental teaching, however, did not primarily concern the nature of evil and error, but rather the naturalness and reality of good.

Her theology may be said to turn on her insistence that God is not just the author or giver of good, but is—literally and substantively—goodness itself, pure, universal Love, infinite in quality and extent. To acknowledge this fact, she held, meant more than merely assenting to it: it meant acting as the reflection or expression of Love in daily human experience. As she put it in an article published in the *Journal* for May 1885 and included in *Miscellaneous Writings*:

> I shall never admit that love is something to be laid on a shelf, and taken down upon rare occasions with sugar-tongs and laid on a rose leaf. I make great demands upon it, call for active witnesses of it, and noble sacrifices and grand achievements from it; and unless these appear I cast aside the word as a counterfeit having not the ring of the true coin. It cannot be a mere abstraction, or goodness without power and presence.[2]

The issue of the nature, demands, and effects of what Eddy called "divine Love" had, in one way or another, always been central for her. It impelled her search for the understanding of God as both all-powerful and all-loving, gave rise to the discipline she imposed upon herself for sustained periods of what she saw as communion with Love, in her affirmation of God's Motherhood as the fullest expression of Love, in her efforts to foster love and unity in the movement and in her household, and in the emphasis she placed on the central role of Love in the healing practice of Christian Science. But in no instance did Eddy feel that stronger demands had been made on her own capacity to love in the face of extreme personal attack than in the period of crisis for the movement precipitated by Woodbury.

In a sense, the crisis continued all the way through the Next Friends Suit of 1907, since Woodbury's influence continued to be felt well beyond the lawsuit for libel she launched against Eddy in July 1899. This suit was settled in Eddy's favor in June 1901. But Woodbury's strong animus against Eddy found continued expression, especially in the pivotal role played by her attorney, Frederick W. Peabody. Peabody not only helped to fuel the attack on Eddy in both *McClure's* and the *New York World*. He also served as junior counsel to Senator Chandler in the Next Friends Suit, and continued his fulmination against Eddy in lectures and writings intermittently for a quarter of a century.

Through Peabody, and possibly through a series of contacts with the press as well, Woodbury helped indirectly to shape the contents and the tone of the slashing portrayal of Eddy in the negative biographical tradition represented by the Milmine and Cather series for *McClure's* and by the biography based upon it that was published in 1909. The immediate problem for Eddy stemming from the suit lay in facing what would have been dire consequences had Woodbury prevailed. In an even larger sense, however, Eddy—who turned eighty the year the suit was settled—faced the challenge of simply surviving in the atmosphere of threat and hostility that the suit had engendered. Doing so necessitated her bearing witness in her own life to the conviction she expressed in a memorandum she dictated to Calvin Frye in April 1890:

> Our salvation is through Love. Call God Love always and bend all your efforts towards achieving perfect love in thought word and deed. That is the way. All is won through it. Its presence gives me all. Its absence takes all away from me therefore "Love is the fulfilling of the law." Love is heaven, and hate is hell. Our only way to heaven is through Love. Our sure way to hell is through hate.[3]

Repeatedly, Eddy had counseled her students to express more of the spirit of this Love so that Christian Science could be validated as a Christian movement before the world. In 1890, the year in which she sent out a flood of letters urging her followers to reflect more of the spirit of forgiveness and love, she wrote to Foster Eddy: "You and all other students somewhat contend like the lower animals, and God is not in these battles."[4]

Eddy herself had been accused by those who turned against her of seeking ruthlessly to vanquish potential rivals to power in the Christian Science movement, a judgment often repeated in the negative biographical tradition. In fact, however, some of her closest students, including officers and First Members of the Mother Church, were sometimes critical of her for not taking more decisive action with her most recalcitrant and difficult students—and none seemed to her more recalcitrant and difficult than Josephine Woodbury.

THE PATH PERILOUS

In a book strongly critical of Eddy and Christian Science, Caroline Fraser speaks of Woodbury as "one of the most outrageous figures in a movement peopled by colorful characters," characterizing her also as "loopy." Other students of Eddy who caused her vexatious problems—for example, Emma Curtis Hopkins and Augusta E. Stetson—have their own merits and their own stories to tell; but a review of Woodbury's career and character make Fraser's judgment hard to refute, even though it might be tempered by the recognition of just how conflicted a woman she was.[5]

Woodbury's career in Christian Science spanned just over twenty years. The wife of E. Frank Woodbury, an original trustee of the

Josephine Curtis Woodbury,
n.d. Courtesy of The Mary
Baker Eddy Collection.

Massachusetts Metaphysical College and a distinguished civil engineer,
Woodbury was attracted to Christian Science in 1879, studied with Eddy
in 1884 and 1885, and the next year established her own Massachusetts
Academy of Christian Science. Over the years she passed from being one
of Eddy's most ardent disciples to her most stinging adversary. By 1896,
Eddy said with perfect realism that she had "no greater *enemy* on earth
than she is."[6] Yet she admitted this with sad resignation, having worked
assiduously to save her brilliant but errant student from the moral and
spiritual abyss into which she seemed intent upon plunging.

One reason for Eddy's great desire to reclaim Woodbury lay in the fact
that she was a vastly capable woman: an impressive speaker, writer, and
organizer. During the take-off years of the movement in the mid-1880s,
Eddy sorely needed and lacked qualified students as practitioners, teachers, and workers for the *Journal*. Moreover, Woodbury professed the most
ardent loyalty to Eddy until her excommunication from the Mother
Church in 1896. Unlike some other apostates from Christian Science,

Woodbury made not the slightest move throughout the 1880s to set up shop on her own outside the Christian Science movement.

Further, she remained pointedly Christian in almost everything she wrote—though not in everything she did. The most poignant fact about her was that she seemed at times to long deeply to measure up to the demanding Christian idealism she could articulate with greater facility than almost any of Eddy's other students. As a young woman, she had received religious instruction at a boarding school by the renowned evangelist Theodore Dwight Weld. In articles for the *Journal,* of which she was editor in 1885 and 1886, and in other venues as well, Woodbury spoke repeatedly, and sometimes movingly, of Jesus' ministry and the human need for salvation. In particular, she emphasized the need to follow Jesus' example through self-renunciation and cross bearing, so as to uproot

every poisonous weed of evil sown in the garden of self. Pride in birth or attainments; envy of others' prosperity; jealousy of the success gained by those more deserving than ourselves; ambition to be known of men; hatred, from its slightest degree, up to its most malicious one; yea, more than all, self-will and self-justification,—these all must be ploughed up, rooted up, and left to perish in the white light of Love.[7]

When Woodbury made such statements about the need to overcome pride, envy, jealousy, and ambition—and she made them often—she was speaking as one who knew how powerful these motivations could be. Alongside her idealization of Christian selflessness ran an intense desire for domination of others, that, if one credits the sincerity of her occasional expressions of remorse, she probably felt at times powerless to resist. By the end of the 1880s what apparently gnawed at Woodbury, possibly to her own dismay, was the desire to usurp Eddy's place within the movement and take its leadership from her. After her final break with Eddy, Woodbury's brother said that her motive was "to rule or ruin," quoting his sister as saying, "I will have Eddy's place or pull the whole thing down upon their heads."[8]

At her Academy of Christian Science on Boston's Dartmouth Street, Woodbury taught classes, preached, and met informally with a growing coterie of acolytes and sympathizers attracted less by her spirituality or healing power than by her glamour and dramatic flair. Woodbury's closest disciples, unlike the rank and file of the Christian Science movement, were imaginative and sentimental, with pronounced leanings toward the occult. They included musicians, artists, and would-be intellectuals. According to the Milmine and Cather account, "Woodbury and her students lived in a kind of miracle play of their own; had inspirations and revelations and premonitions; kept mental trysts; saw portents and mystic meanings in everything; and spoke of God as coming and going, agreeing and disagreeing with them." They interlaced discussions of Christian Science with bits of French, adorned their rooms with pictures of the Madonna, and in general acted more like a pre-Raphaelite cell than a group of committed Christians.[9]

Still, there was nothing whatever to bring Woodbury's loyalty to Eddy into question—at least not on the surface. On the contrary, she allied herself with her teacher against mind-cure factions as well as the members of the Christian Scientist Association involved in the schism of June 1888. She was also in the audience that greeted Eddy rapturously at the Chicago meeting of the National Christian Scientist Association in June just after the rebellion had broken out.

By Woodbury's own testimony, the occasion was a transforming experience in which "there dawned upon me revelations of a New Heaven and New Earth." Her words were published in a fulsome article for a Boston newspaper and reprinted in the *Journal*. In rapturous accents, they expressed awe at the very tide of emotional adulation that so repulsed Eddy:

> A mother, who failed to get near her, held high her babe, to look on their helper. Others touched the dress of their benefactor, not so much as asking for more.
>
> An aged woman, trembling with palsy, lifted her shaking hands at Mrs. Eddy's feet, crying, "Help, help!" and the cry was answered. Many such people were known to go away healed. Strong men turned aside to hide their tears, as the people thronged about Mrs. Eddy with blessings and thanks. . . .
>
> What wonder if the thoughts of those present went back to eighteen-hundred years ago, when through Jesus was manifested the healing power?[10]

Returning to Boston, Woodbury made an unsuccessful bid for power by attempting to parlay herself into the position of temporary pastor of the Boston church. Around the same time, she began a liaison with Henry L. Putnam, a student of hers who had studied with Eddy as well. Their relationship was passionately physical. Putnam, Woodbury told a friend, gave her "exquisite pleasure," with the result that she lost "every particle" of love for her husband.[11] Learning of the affair, Eddy sent Putnam back to Montreal, where he had a wife and family. This was a separation that Woodbury, who had two children of her own, refused to endure. Beginning in the fall of 1889 she paid lengthy visits to Montreal, ostensibly to further the growth of Christian Science there, but probably to continue the liaison with Putnam.

Coming back to Boston in early winter, Woodbury proceeded to close her academy and resign with her husband from the Boston church and from the Christian Scientist Association. The reason she gave was that Eddy, by leaving Boston, had moved beyond organization and she only wished to follow suit. But Eddy had neither required teachers to stop teaching nor asked church congregations to stop meeting. The real reason lay most likely in the fact that she was now visibly pregnant. It would have been difficult for her to face her followers, since she not only preached sexual abstinence, but had long since let it be known that she had ceased having marital relations with her husband.

When Woodbury's child was born in June 1890, her explanation of how this occurred was, in Gillian Gill's words, "a fascinating mixture of bold-faced lies and cynical manipulation." The child, whom Woodbury called the "Prince of Peace," had been conceived of the Holy Ghost through the spirit of Eddy, she said. According to Woodbury, she was only enacting what Eddy had taught: that a woman might conceive spiritually if she had become mentally pure through overcoming sensuality and sin. She further explained that until her child's "sharp birth-cry saluted my ears," she had not even been aware that she was pregnant, attributing her abdominal swelling to "some fungoid formation." Assembling a dozen or so followers on bluffs overlooking Ocean Point, Maine, Woodbury bathed the child, then commended the dirty bathwater to her obliging students to drink, which some of them did. She then baptized the child by three lengthy immersions in a rocky pool, named by her "the Pool of Bethesda" for the occasion. At that point, recalled Woodbury, the crowd of onlookers "joined in a spontaneously appropriate hymn of praise."[12]

Just before Woodbury's excommunication from the Mother Church, Eddy wrote to her, "How dare you, how dare you in the sight of God and with your character behind the curtain, and your own students ready to lift it on you—pursue the path perilous?" Woodbury had not only pursued this path through the 1890s but seemed to enjoy it. In late March 1895, she had a confidential interview with Julia Bartlett in which she showed herself not only fully capable of admitting her sins, but also relishing the shock value of the admission. According to Bartlett's testimony, Woodbury confessed to her that no one yet knew the "terrible sins she had committed," that sometimes it seemed "as if she were nothing but evil," and that "when she realized the enormity of her sins her agony was almost unbearable but fortunately these times did not last long." The last words of this confession are revealing. Woodbury was a classic example of the state of mind Eddy spoke of when she wrote, "We never need to despair of an honest heart; but there is little hope for those who come only spasmodically face to face with their wickedness and then seek to hide it." Although the words were written well before the problems with Woodbury began, they might have been spoken directly about her.[13]

Woodbury's disingenuous explanation for the birth of the little "Prince" made her a pariah among Christian Scientists. Far from publicly retracting her account of the Prince's miraculous birth, she continued to embroider on it so as to extract money from those remaining disciples whose gullibility apparently knew no bounds. They were cajoled into contributing funds for a home for the little Prince (strategically located within eyeshot of Eddy's Boston residence) and for lavish gifts whereby to do him homage. Even while placed on probationary membership in the Mother Church, Woodbury made conspicuous and unwelcome appearances with her entourage at Christian Science services, sometimes launching into long harangues at the evening testimony meetings, then held on Fridays.

Woodbury's hold on her followers can be partially explained by the fact that she was a strongly charismatic, almost overtly sexual figure. A photograph of her taken around the time of her excommunication shows a finely dressed woman with a somewhat coy and distant "come and get me" look on a very handsome face. There is no doubt that she used seductiveness as a means of getting her way. She once bragged that when a publisher hesitated to use an item she had written, she simply allowed him to smooth the sleeve of her dress admiringly. Then, said Woodbury, "I got my publishing done." More characteristic were her words to another shocked follower, "O Carrie, if you'll let a man roll over you once there's nothing he won't do for you." In another instance, while speaking to two prim disciples in Maine, she launched for no apparent reason into a graphic explanation of sodomy and "a crime called buggery."[14]

While Woodbury could be crude and enjoyed shocking her more maidenlike lady minions, she could also be artful. Charming and well educated, she kept up connections with intellectuals, particularly writers and editors. In particular, she used her charm and sophistication to ingratiate herself with the Reverend James Henry Wiggin, whose friendship with Eddy she may well have helped to undermine. She gained such influence over the normally urbane Wiggin that even after her well-publicized antics over the birth of the "Prince of Peace," he wrote in an enthusiastic endorsement of a book of her poetry that "her adherence to unusual ideas" had brought upon her "misrepresentation and what often seems like absolute persecution." He then went on to pay tribute to her "brain power," poetic temperament, capacity for sarcasm, and "lambiant wit," along with her "frankness in the discussion of mundane facts."[15]

Woodbury, however, had means other than beauty, charm, and intellectual sophistication for dominating others. She had a long-standing fascination with hypnotism before coming into Christian Science. In her articles for the *Journal* and in other writings, she returned frequently to the subject of hypnotic control, denouncing it as the most pernicious evil of the age. In an article originally published in the *Boston Transcript* for October 31, 1887, for example, she declared that if what Christian Scientists believe about "the grave problem of thought transference" is true, "then we stand face to face with a slavery heretofore unknown." She went on to speak of "innocent and malicious mental malpractice" as an evil of "swelling proportions." Despite her professed opposition to hypnotic control, the close and continuing attention she paid to the subject showed a strong fascination with what she called the "death-dealing" capacity of perverted mental power. Even in a short statement of a "Credo" published in several places in her writings, Woodbury, after speaking of the way of salvation through Jesus and extolling *Science and Health*, wrote that "heavenliness is oft hindered by cunning thought-transference" that would "deceive the unwary, by charging its own malice upon the heart-purity of others."[16]

Woodbury's excommunication from the Mother Church in April 1896 was largely prompted by what the First Members saw as convincing evidence that she practiced this "cunning thought-transference" herself. In her interview with Julia Bartlett, she had admitted attempts to do so, saying that Bartlett "had no idea of the number of people she had been the means of putting out of the cause of Christian Science" and that "it was through mental means that this was done." William B. Johnson, a director of the Mother Church, had also gathered from eight of Woodbury's former associates testimony as to her manipulativeness and attempts at mental control—testimony that was later amplified in the preparation for Eddy's defense in the lawsuit Woodbury initiated in 1899.

The picture presented by this evidence was chilling. In Montreal, outside the purview of Boston Christian Scientists, Johnson reported how Woodbury terrorized followers into submission by threatening to use her mental powers to bring physical suffering and financial ruin on them and their families. Mary Landry told him that Woodbury "used to say that Eddy was God and she was Mary," that her child was "conceived by Eddy" and was of "immortal conception," and that unless Landry saw this she would die. "A Mr. Seton," she also said, "left her and he dropped dead without a moment's warning." Another woman, Martha Burns, who had opposed Woodbury, said that she was told by her that "terrible calamities" would come to her and her family if she persisted in this opposition, and that "invariably I returned to her allegiance because of terror." Later, in testimony before the First Members of the Mother Church, Charles E. Nash of Augusta, Maine, who was not a Christian Scientist, told of how Woodbury assumed complete control of his young daughter, kept her a virtual prisoner in Boston during a protracted illness, and permitted her family to take her home only a few days before she died. According to the written opinions of two Maine physicians who attended the girl before her death, she had been the victim of systematic hypnosis.[17]

While hypnotism by the late nineteenth century was widely regarded as a therapeutic agent, Eddy made no distinction between mesmerism and hypnotism, which she saw as essentially similar forms of occult mental control. They were, therefore, closely linked phenomena—a point suggested by one of the longer titles of the twenty-six lesson sermon topics she put into place in 1898: "Ancient and Modern Necromancy, Alias Mesmerism and Hypnotism, Denounced." As Nathaniel Hawthorne himself commented on mesmeric healing, the "transmission of one spirit into another" in mesmeric healing violated "the sacredness of an individual" and thus intruded "into the holy of holies." In Eddy's view, projected mental control had such far-reaching and potentially lethal effects that she wrote with indirect yet unmistakable reference to Woodbury, "The crimes committed under this new-old *regime* of necromancy or diabolism are not easily reckoned. At present its mystery protects it, but its hidden modus and flagrance will finally be known, and the laws of our land will handle its thefts, adulteries, and murders, and will pass sentence on the darkest and deepest of human crimes."[18]

The discovery of this potentially lethal influence she saw as the downside, so to speak, of her discovery. Projected malice, she believed, was an aspect of human experience that on the basis of bitter experience she felt compelled, against her own inclination, to investigate. Speaking of her investigation into this subject in July and August 1880, some two decades before the Woodbury lawsuit, Eddy wrote:

> I shall not forget the cost of investigating, for this age the methods and power of error. The ways, means, and potency of Truth flowed into my consciousness as the morning light breaketh and the shadows flee; but the metaphysical mystery of error—its hidden paths, purpose, and fruits—at first defied me. I was saying all the time, "Come not thou into the secret!" I yielded at length to what I understood was God's command, and continued the research, which will, must, crush the serpent's head, even while it is biting at her heel.[19]

During the course of this investigation she experienced both shock and horror at what she took to be the sheer evil of the dangers she was uncovering. She was, she believed, exposing evils that she had first encountered during the early 1870s, when she formed a partnership in the healing practice in Lynn with a young man named Richard Kennedy. Kennedy, she believed, although superficially affable, had begun to practice mental manipulation consciously out of a fascinated preoccupation with the destructive power of thought. She saw her own health and the welfare of the movement as having been undermined by despotic mental control practiced by Kennedy, a form of mental control she saw as the diametrical opposite of Christian Science and its legitimate practice. The third edition of *Science and Health*, published in 1881, included a long chapter titled "Demonology" detailing in highly personal terms what she took to be the mental machinations of Kennedy and others.[20]

The climax of this phase of her preoccupation with the subject came with the death of her husband, Asa Gilbert Eddy, in June 1882 through what Eddy saw as deliberately projected mental malice by Edward J. Arens. This horrific episode marked the climax of one phase of Eddy's engagement with the issue of what she called mental malpractice. By the end of the 1880s, she came to see this phenomenon in far less personal terms and with a distinctly different emphasis. Addressing the subject in a class, she said she was going to "talk something up to talk it down." She took special pains to make sure that her students did not develop a morbid fascination with the subject—a fascination that in itself could verge on the occult. In the August 1890 *Journal* she wrote, "The discussion of malicious animal magnetism had better be dropped until Scientists understand clearly how to handle error." In their frantic zeal, some Christian Scientists, she maintained, were in "danger of dwarfing their growth in love." Only "patient, unceasing love for all mankind,—love that cannot mistake Love's aid,—can determine this question on the Principle of Christian Science."[21]

From that point on, Eddy's emphasis in dealing with the issue of projected mental malice lay on the protection attainable through the recognition of the presence and power of divine Love. "Clad in the panoply of Love, human hatred cannot reach you," she wrote in *Science and Health*. "Hatred and its effects on the body," she also stated, "are removed by Love." This emphasis found expression in a letter following the death of President William McKinley on September 14, 1901. McKinley had been expected to recover from the wound he received at the hands of an assassin, but died unexpectedly of complications from the injury, despite widespread prayers on his behalf. In answer to the question as to why he had not survived when so many Christians were praying for his recovery, Eddy wrote in a public letter a little over four months after the conclusion of the Woodbury suit: "Had prayer so fervently offered possessed no opposing element, and President McKinley's recovery been regarded as wholly contingent on the power of God,—on the power of divine Love to overrule the purposes of hate and the law of Spirit to control matter,—the result would have been scientific, and the patient would have recovered."[22]

"I Make Strong Demands on Love"

"The power of divine Love to overrule the purposes of hate" expresses a theme that had become central to Eddy's work over the previous decade. In 1895, for example, she wrote to the Linscotts, who were involved in factional quarrels in the Christian Science field in Chicago, "Argument, intellect, reason, never will accomplish the victory over self-mesmerism and m.a.m. [her abbreviation for malicious animal magnetism], *never*. There is but one thing at which you can beat the latter viz. *Love*. They can beat you every time in hate. Now pray constantly for Divine love to give you meekness, patience, and forgiveness towards your enemies."[23]

Eddy made a consistent effort to follow this advice herself. In this respect, she was far less rigid and doctrinaire than the general run of her students in positions of responsibility in the Mother Church, who sometimes saw her as being lenient to the point of weakness. This was especially the case in her dealings with Woodbury, who began to show signs of quarrelsomeness by the mid-1880s. In 1886, Eddy admonished her, "There is always a difficulty and misunderstanding in whatever you participate. When things are smooth you disturb them and when rough you make them harder to handle. I have again and again rebuked you to this and you have confessed, and I well know that it all lies in your habit of telling or implying that which is untrue." In answer to another rebuke, Woodbury replied with the fleeting remorse that characterized most of her responses to such admonitions: "I am sure now that animal magnetism claims the power to make me do and say things the exact opposite of my desires and intentions. . . . Now I am calmer again, and I will battle with the enemy on this question of sin."[24]

If her words were sincere, this was a battle she was ultimately to lose. So was formed the pattern that prevailed in Woodbury's relation to Eddy for more than a decade to come: Woodbury's transgressions, her teacher's rebukes, temporary seasons of confession and remorse on Woodbury's part, succeeded by renewed misconduct. Indeed, Woodbury became, if anything, more brazen as time went on. As the situation continued to devolve, Eddy at times grew thoroughly exasperated. Despite Woodbury's seasons of remorse, Robert Peel's comment remains valid: Woodbury was gifted with "complete freedom from a New England conscience."[25]

In this respect as in others, there was an immense disparity between the flamboyant Woodbury and most of Eddy's sober and upright Christian followers—including Ira Knapp, among the most sober and upright of them all. In July 1887 Eddy asked Knapp to arrange for Woodbury to give a talk in the town hall of his home town of Lisbon, New Hampshire. While Eddy had rebuked Woodbury for her quarrelsomeness, she seems to have regarded her at that point as a capable if mercurial student with a gift for public speaking.

It was natural for Knapp to welcome Woodbury into his home for a visit, especially since they had studied in the same class under Eddy. Knapp found the encounter shocking. While not accusing Woodbury of any effort to seduce him, he wrote Eddy frankly to the effect that Woodbury was more reminiscent of the Babylonish woman of Revelation than of a Christian Scientist. Eddy called Knapp to Boston for particulars, then summoned Woodbury for yet another sharp rebuke. Shortly thereafter, Eddy sent to the *Journal* for publication another letter Knapp had sent her after his meeting with Woodbury. Without referring to her by name, he couched the effect she made on him in biblical and apocalyptic terms, speaking of the "Scarlet Woman" of Revelation as "the mother of harlots" in whom "is found the blood of prophets and of saints." He prophesied the doom of the "beast of lust and sensualism, on which this woman rides."[26]

The "lust and sensualism" of which Knapp spoke became more evident in the sequence of events surrounding the birth of the "Prince of Peace" in June 1890. When it came to ordinary human derelictions, Eddy was not particularly given to shock or prudery, and it was not Woodbury's moral lapse in giving birth to a child out of wedlock that apparently troubled her most. The key issue was Woodbury's utter dishonesty in explaining the birth as the result of a spiritual conception and in attributing the whole idea of a birth without a sexual union to Eddy's teaching. Nevertheless, Eddy even at this juncture refused to abandon Woodbury once and for all. Putnam was the most likely father of the child, and before his liaison with Woodbury began Eddy had written to him, "Dear Mrs. W is not alone in the struggles of nature and grace. She is unfortunate in some things that hinder her progress. I rebuke and I encourage. I am stern and gentle by turns with her, but only to do her good—for I am not naturally mean in my mental states."[27]

Woodbury's pregnancy, along with her bizarre explanation of how it occurred, had outraged other Christian Scientists on the Boston scene. Eddy appeared ready to forgive her now disgraced student, apparently believing that if the error that gripped her was self-seen in sufficient measure, she could yet be rescued through the power of grace. Again, Woodbury appeared to be genuinely contrite—at least for a time. Visiting Eddy in 1895, she admitted that she well knew her child had not been immaculately conceived but had been "incarnated with the devil." In response to Eddy's question as to why she had resigned from the church in 1889, Woodbury admitted with evident shame, "What else could I do?" Speaking of these admissions in a letter written the next year, Eddy recalled: "During that visit you seemed deeply penitent and I pitied you sincerely. You referred to your past conduct and said, 'If it will save others from doing as I did it is all that I can ask now.' I forgave you then and there and told you I would try to have you admitted to our church if you so desired."[28]

Eddy had already made a strong effort to have Woodbury restore her standing in the church. In an 1894 letter, still referring to Woodbury as "My dear student," Eddy promised, "If you really desire me to, I will ask the church if it will receive you if you confess to the First Members as you did to me that you see your error in supposing your child incarnate and acknowledge it. Then I think it would love you again even as I do." Despite almost solid opposition from the First Members to admitting Woodbury, Eddy prevailed upon them to admit her to probationary membership in April 1895. But this concession did not prevent Woodbury from continuing much as before. Eddy wrote to her that she had pleaded with the directors on her behalf for two hours, but that her arguments were undermined by continuing evidence of Woodbury's dishonesty.[29] Once more she urged Woodbury to reform, saying that if she were to do so for one year, she would be readmitted to the church. But again this hope proved to be futile. A month later the First Members dropped Woodbury from membership in the Mother Church.

Still, Eddy refused to give up the effort to reclaim her, thereby reflecting the attitude she expressed in a sermon she had preached years earlier: "The wickedest man is but a temporary eclipse, not quite total, and in the great forever he must rotate towards Truth and Life. One ray, one speck of the emanation of the divine is eternal, and it finally lifts the gloom and lets in all light." In March 1896, Eddy wrote to the First Members requesting them to reconsider their excommunication. "This Christian forgiveness can do you no harm," she said, "and if it will help her spiritually this effort will be worthy of your Christian endeavors and of my sincere hope and inexhaustible charity." It was the church's duty, she wrote in a follow-up letter, to reinstate Woodbury on probation "and give her an opportunity to hear the Word of God from the pulpit—a little longer. This Church must be above censure. And more than all others *just* and *merciful*."[30]

Eddy was bringing the full weight of her authority to bear on the situation. As a result, Woodbury was reinstated to probationary membership, only to be excommunicated forever less than two weeks later. Once this occurred, a *Manual* bylaw went into effect making a second excommunication of a member irrevocable. But this, Eddy wrote to Judge Hanna, "by no means hinders the salvation of that sinner, for C. S. does not make the church responsible for his salvation as Catholicism does." As to her own motives, Eddy wrote to the directors that if called upon to explain Woodbury's excommunication to the press, they should say that it had occurred "for more than sufficient reasons" and that she would never have been readmitted to the church "had it not been for Mrs. Eddy's unprecedented mercy that holds on so long as a hope lasts for anybody and for everybody,—calling us to try to save her."[31]

It was Eddy's determined exercise of charity and forgiveness that animated her efforts on Woodbury's behalf, not any special feeling for Woodbury herself. Shortly after the lawsuit began, Eddy commented in a letter that, while she had done all she could to reform Woodbury, "she never was one I could love, but I helped her all the same." It may have been Eddy's own forbearance more than any other factor that intensified Woodbury's self-loathing to the point that it became unbearable. One construction that could be put on the behavior of this profoundly conflicted woman is that, unable to face her own demons, Woodbury's self-hate finally spilled over into overt hatred of her former teacher and friend. Her internal pain is observable in a letter to Eddy in 1893, where, referring to her already admitted sins, she wrote: "And you never speak of it; you never seem to remind me of it or remember it but always bless me so. I think I never suffered as I suffer now when I am beginning to understand you. Every time I see you it is harder to bear—this great chasm between your life and mine."[32]

An indication of how far Eddy was prepared to go to reclaim Woodbury is seen in Clara Shannon's account of an incident that probably occurred sometime in 1899. To Shannon's great surprise, Eddy wrote a letter to Woodbury inviting her to visit Pleasant View on one of two days of Woodbury's choosing. "Why did you write to her," asked Shannon, "when you know she is doing all she can to harm you, and not hiding it, but talking about it?" Eddy replied, "You must learn to love that woman." Shannon asked, "Do you love her?" "Yes, and I am trying to bless her! If you and I do not love her, who can or will?" Although there was no reply to the invitation, Eddy took her carriage ride early on the second day in case Woodbury should arrive. She then waited in the drawing room for most of the afternoon, while Frye at her instruction met several successive trains from Boston. "The last time it was late and too dark for her to have come, and our Leader sat in the parlor waiting till then; after which, she rose to return to her sitting room, and said, 'Oh, what a benediction of love she would have received! It would have saved and comforted her!' "[33]

IN THE *ARENA*

Woodbury was not ready for the benediction. In 1899 she began a campaign against Eddy by planting a series of letters, poems, and news items in newspapers from Maine to Colorado. These, however, proved to be merely a prelude to a major salvo in the form of the article "Christian Science and Its Prophetess," published in the May 1899 issue of the *Arena*, a mildly radical Boston magazine circulated mainly among intellectuals.

The *Arena* under its usual editor, Benjamin O. Flower, had been friendly to Christian Science. But it fell temporarily into the hands of an ardent advocate of occultism and psychic research who had little use for Eddy or her doctrines. The May issue included the article "Christian Science and its Prophetess" in two parts: Part I, "The Facts of the Case," was written by Horatio Dresser, son of Julius Dresser, who had been close to Phineas Quimby in Portland, during the years that Eddy was associated with him. In his article, Horatio Dresser championed his father's long-standing argument that Eddy had virtually stolen Christian Science from Quimby.

Part II, "The Book and the Woman," was a diatribe in which Woodbury at last poured forth vindictiveness toward Eddy that apparently had been building up for years, lashing out at her with a stinging ferocity unequaled, up to that point, in the literature on Christian Science. As a hostile biographer of Eddy put it, "Woodbury had launched an attack far exceeding in violence all that her combined opponents had said before." Woodbury began with a ploy adopted as a convention by later critics—listing Eddy's maiden and married names as a kind of put-down (although she got one of them wrong): "Mrs. Mary Mason [it was actually Morse] Baker Glover Patterson Eddy." The tone of the article is sustained along the lines of the following paragraph: "From Concord she issues her edicts and manifestos. Multitudes go thither to worship at her shrine; and are satisfied if they do not even touch the hem of her garment, but only see her from afar, as a beatific vision, while she speaks a few commonplace words, or repeats the Ninety-first Psalm." The article is further laced with such invective as Woodbury's assertion of "the utter lack of divine inspiration in Christian Science," her reference to the "incongruous paragraphs and jumble of antagonistic ideas" in *Science and Health,* and her concluding peroration: "What she has really 'discovered' are ways and means of perverting and prostituting the science of healing to her own ecclesiastical aggrandizement, and to the moral and physical depravity of her dupes. . . . What she has 'founded' is a commercial system, monumental in its proportions, but already tottering to its fall."[34]

Much of the article is built on Dresser's effort to attribute all that is worthy in Christian Science to Quimby. Woodbury's purpose in adopting this strategy went far beyond trying to establish that Eddy dishonestly claimed to be the originator of ideas that were not her own. The ultimate purport of Woodbury's article in conjunction with Dresser's struck far deeper.

By arguing at length that Eddy had stolen her leading ideas from Quimby, she was, in effect, maintaining that Christian Science, even if clothed in Christian language, belonged to the orbit of mesmerism rather than Christianity—not the specific practices of the magnetic doctors of the mid-nineteenth century, but the broader tradition of the control of one human mind by others. The issue raised by the *Arena* articles, therefore, was not so much who owed what to whom, but what Christian Science in substance was. Its most pronounced trait, she maintained, was what she called "the Christian Science disease" of "Demonophobia—the fear of demons, the fear of witchcraft. . . . Its advocates are crazy with the fear of a Satan of their own making; and this fear is stimulated by Eddy's constant allusions to the subject."

Yet Woodbury's own writings inadvertently betray her own deep personal involvement in the very practice she seemed to deplore. In her book *War in Heaven*, she gave a highly selective and self-serving account of her years in Christian Science up through her excommunication. With a measure of the honesty that occasionally brought her face to face with her own demons, she confessed: "In my own 'chambers of imagery' also there was mental bewilderment. At one moment all seemed surely good; yet the next hour the feeling supervened that wrong was the great ruler, and that mankind might exclaim with Milton's Satan, 'Evil, be thou my Good.'" She also advocated for the necessity of the spiritual darkness she claimed to expose: "As light both has and implies its correlative darkness, so spiritual life has its antagonistic corruption, acting through subtly malicious hypnotism, the more dangerous because unseen to the mortal eye." The "aspersion of hypnotism" attached to her name, Woodbury said, was a stigma she had to bear for "trying to unmask mental malpractice, never by conniving therewith and indulging therein." The imputation of evil to her was only an example of how "serpents poison the crushing heel" of those who would expose the ultimate sin and unseen error of mentally projected hate.[35]

A little more than a year later in the *Arena* article, Woodbury, having abandoned all hope of reclaiming her status in Christian Science, apparently dropped all faith in its teaching and condemned both it and Eddy with all the vehemence she could muster. Eddy was convinced that Woodbury's *Arena* attack must not stand unanswered. The newly instituted Committee on Publication under its first manager, Alfred Farlow, responded to the factual misrepresentations that arose out of the Woodbury suit—in Eddy's view inadequately. But she felt keenly the need to assess what Woodbury represented in broader terms. It was not Eddy's impulse—indeed, it was wholly contrary to her convictions—to attack Woodbury personally and by name, even if she found it no longer possible to influence the woman that Woodbury had become. Far more congenial to Eddy's mentality was to depict the biblical and typological pattern that she saw Woodbury as fulfilling.

Specifically, she came to see the spiritual warfare she was waging in the framework of the twelfth chapter of Revelation. In doing so, Eddy made use of the image of the "Babylonish woman" who stands in the seventeenth chapter of Revelation as a countertype to the "woman clothed with the sun" in the twelfth—the woman of whom Knapp had spoken when referring indirectly to Woodbury in his letter published in the *Journal* nearly a decade before. In her Communion message to the Mother Church for June 1899, the month after the *Arena* article was published, Eddy dropped into sundry remarks on the general progress of her church several paragraphs of striking intensity describing the Babylonish woman and her doom:

> This woman, "drunken with the blood of the saints, and with the blood of the martyrs of Jesus," "drunk with the wine of her fornication," would enter even the church,—the body of Christ, Truth; and, retaining the heart of the harlot and the purpose of the destroying angel, would pour wormwood into the waters—the disturbed human mind—to drown the strong swimmer struggling for the shore,—aiming for Truth,—and if possible, to poison such as drink of the living water. . . . That which the Revelator saw in spiritual vision will be accomplished. The Babylonish woman is fallen, and who should mourn over the widowhood of lust, of her that "is become the habitation of devils, and the hold of every foul spirit, and a cage of every unclean bird?"[36]

A little less than two months later, Woodbury filed for libel against Eddy as well as officers of the church involved in the publication of the message containing this passage.

Claiming that Eddy's words were "false, scandalous, malicious, and defamatory," Woodbury asked for damages of $150,000 for the four readings of the message in the Mother Church, its publication in the *Christian Science Journal* and *Sentinel*, and a Boston newspaper. She also asked for damages amounting to an additional $250,000 from church officers, including the board of directors and the trustees of the Publishing Society, whom she held accountable for the publication and dissemination of Eddy's message.[37] The original complaint, which ran to fifteen thousand words, contained other accusations disparaging Christian Science, Eddy's presumed claims for it, and the government of its church.

These were dismissed by the judge as irrelevant matters of belief that could not be tried in court. The one issue in dispute was whether Eddy had deliberately and personally libeled Woodbury by referring to her in a thinly disguised way as the Babylonish woman of Revelation. A corollary issue, important though unsuitable for resolution in court, was whether Eddy and her students viewed Eddy herself personally as the woman clothed with the sun. Did they believe that, in the wording of Woodbury's legal complaint, "in her own person and life, she is the fulfillment, or realization of this prophecy?"

By a strange irony in the literature of Christian Science, Eddy's name was first linked publicly with the figure of the Woman of Revelation by Woodbury herself. In an article for the July 1886 *Journal*, she wrote with clear reference to Eddy, "This woman, 'clothed with the sun' (the understanding of Good) with the 'moon under her feet' (matter and mortality denied and overcome) is indeed a voyager into a far country. The Key to happiness is in her hands." Yet this kind of personal identification of biblical symbols was entirely uncharacteristic of Eddy and the religious culture out of which she sprang. Thinking again in terms of typology, Eddy spoke of the dragon in the book of Revelation as the type of the "malicious animal instinct" that "incites mortals to kill morally and physically even their fellow-mortals, and worse still, to charge the innocent with the crime."

When she wrote in *Science and Health* that the twelfth chapter of the book of Revelation has a "special suggestiveness in relation to the nineteenth century," she was speaking within this typological mode of thought. What it suggested was the fulfillment of a type or pattern of spiritual experience portrayed in the appearing of "the Woman clothed with the sun," which Eddy says "symbolizes generic man, the spiritual idea of God." In Robert Peel's explanation, in Eddy's usage "the words 'woman' and 'womanhood' frequently refer not to a particular woman or to women as a sex but to woman as idea, or more specifically as that revelatory state of mind in which man is conceived to be the child of God."[38]

In a press interview, Edward Kimball, speaking for Eddy, answered the question as to whether she considered herself literally to be the woman clothed with the sun: "She does not. She does not teach or want anyone to teach that. On the contrary, we do not believe that the word 'woman' means any particular woman, but rather refers to conditions of thought, or the revelations of truth." During the trial, Ira Knapp was asked by Peabody whether he knew "it to be a part of Eddy's teaching . . . that she is what the Book of Revelation calls 'the woman clothed with the sun.' " While Knapp believed that she was personally "the woman" (a position his son Bliss later stoutly defended), he testified that he could not honestly say that this was part of her teaching or that her followers generally believed it. So he responded somewhat evasively with the simple statement, "I do not know."[39]

Partisans of the viewpoint that Eddy was specifically and personally "the woman" have argued that Kimball and Knapp were speaking for public consumption only and dissimulated in order to protect her. There is no evidence that she was particularly concerned with or anguished over the issue of her personal place in biblical prophecy, although she spoke often of her belief that the discovery of Christian Science fulfilled Jesus' prophecy of the coming of the Comforter. The day-to-day demands that confronted Eddy absorbed her time and attention almost completely, and she was not given to the contemplation of issues that seemed abstruse and remote from the immediate needs of the moment. During the period of the Woodbury trial, however, she was confronted with "the woman" question in a way that could hardly be avoided. What she wrote, in several private memos not intended for publication and in a brief book she eventually did not publish, confirmed the truth of the testimony Knapp and Kimball had given.

In one fragment she stated: "The woman whereof St. John prophesied in the Apocalypse and depicted is the type of a fair fresh promise crowned with stars, a beacon form of hope . . . of faith's fruition of the living light in all ages. . . . I never taught or thought that I was the Woman referred to in the dim distance of St. John's period. . . ." In a short book initially intended for publication she rejected any literal identification of herself with the woman, saying she could

> apply St. John's far-reaching thoughts only as type and shadow. . . . What St. John saw in prophetic vision and depicted as "a woman clothed with the sun and the moon under her feet" prefigured no speciality or individuality. His vision foretold a type, and this type applied to man as well as to woman. Another application or identification of his vision of the woman spoken of in the 12th chapter of Revelation is chimerical, it has no more validity than to fancy a statue of Liberty represented by a woman resembling some individual form or face, then name it that individual.[40]

Frederick W. Peabody, n.d.
Courtesy of The Mary Baker
Eddy Collection.

Regarding the figure of the Babylonish woman, she wrote similarly to her attorneys in the Woodbury suit, "I meant Mrs. Josephine C. Woodbury no more than I meant any other person *who is like her.* I meant what I think the Revelator means namely that the Babylonish woman is only a symbol *of lust,* but Woodbury has applied this symbol to herself."[41] There was, however, a hint that Eddy meant something more than this. Her message included the line, "And who shall mourn the widowhood of lust," which could be taken as a reference to the sudden decease of Woodbury's husband shortly after the *Arena* article was published. Fortunately for Eddy and the church officials also implicated in the suit, Peabody failed to make much of the point in court, and it did not affect the outcome of the suit.

"ONLY A WOMAN"

Woodbury's suit for libel against Eddy was filed on July 31, 1899, and dragged on through a number of preliminary hearings for nearly two years until it was lost by the plaintiff after a week's trial on June 5, 1901. The coverage of the four-day trial in both the *Boston Globe* and the *Boston Post* over the week beginning on May 29, 1901, was extensive, with ten out of a total of fifteen major stories featured on the newspapers' first pages. The tenor of the stories indicates that the atmosphere in the crowded courtroom was highly charged. Peabody, having devoted some two years to the preparation of the case, was extremely focused and intense in his questioning of Hanna, Ira Knapp, William B. Johnson, Edward Kimball, and other church officials. Besides Woodbury herself, both Clara Choate—a disaffected student of Eddy's from the early 1880s— and William Nixon both testified on behalf of the plaintiff. Woodbury made an impressive appearance. The *Boston Post* pictured her as "dark as a Spanish woman, and with big burning dark eyes, her curling grey hair showing under a . . . modish hat. She was cool, calm, collected."[42]

Eddy's victory, if not a vindication, seemed complete when on June 4 the judge ordered the jury to render a verdict for the defendant on grounds that Woodbury had not made a case. The *Boston Globe* in a front page story on June 6 reported that the Christian Scientists in the courtroom were "overjoyed at the outcome." While Eddy herself—along with the church officials named in the suit—was much relieved, she was far from overjoyed. The publicity generated by the suit was obviously damaging to Christian Science, and the wait for an outcome that could have been adverse to her was both prolonged and taxing.

At points during the nearly two years between the inception and conclusion of the suit, Eddy had spoken with her usual assurance about "the persecutions which I meet. *They* cannot *move* me. The winds and waves beat in vain against the foundations of my faith—they are built on the Rock whose shadow hath long been my shelter in the wilderness of human opinions." She also spoke at times with great hopefulness about the outcome of the suit, as when she wrote to Ira Knapp in November 1899, "The lust of Babylon will fall and the bright and morning star will arise with new splendor and the glory of our God will shine from the North to the South and from the east to the west."[43]

Mainly, however, her comments on the suit struck a darker note. For Eddy and her lieutenants involved, the case was a difficult ordeal. First, it was by no means certain that Woodbury would lose, and the negative and embarrassing effects that a loss in such a widely publicized case might bring to Eddy and Christian Science appeared to be incalculable. Were this to happen, the church officials named in the lawsuit had serious cause to be concerned, since they would have probably been required to pay damages out of their own pockets. Regardless of the outcome of the suit, the atmosphere of fear and malice that hung over the whole period was almost intolerable for Eddy and those closest to her. One of Eddy's most revealing comments is helpful in understanding her complex reaction to the ordeal. To a student she once said of herself, "As

Mary Baker Eddy, I am the weakest of mortals, but as the Discoverer and Founder of Christian Science, I am the bone and sinew of the world."[44]

On any given day it was hard for those around her to anticipate whether she would be responding to the demands of the hour as the personal and vulnerable Mary Baker Eddy or as the discoverer and founder of Christian Science. As the latter, Eddy acted very much as she did during any crisis affecting the church, relying on Christian Science itself to meet the need at hand. During the Woodbury suit, as well as the Next Friends Suit of 1907, where at times the outlook also seemed bleak, Eddy's primary recourse was to summon workers to pray about the case. In January 1901, she asked six students to come temporarily to Pleasant View for this purpose. With an eye to what Christian Scientists needed to learn from this ordeal, she also caused to be published in the twelfth edition of the *Manual* in 1899 the bylaw "Alertness to Duty." In its final form, this bylaw read: "It shall be the duty of every member of this church to defend himself daily against aggressive mental suggestion, and not to be made to forget nor to neglect his duty to God, to his Leader, and to mankind."[45]

That they were not doing so seemed clear to Eddy in a number of ways. For one thing, Judge Hanna's judgment, she came to believe, had become so clouded that he gave her what turned out to be disastrous legal advice, wrote several editorials that were so adulatory of her as to be inadvertently damaging to her legal position, and sided against her in a crucial meeting with her attorneys. Around the same time, young John Lathrop took the embarrassing step of writing on his own initiative to the judge on Eddy's behalf, urging a speedy dismissal of the case. Such mistakes, she explained in a letter to the First Members, required their immediate action on the bylaw. "Alertness to Duty," she believed, had become imperative, since "instead of vacations and good times and pleasure hunting this church needs most of all things to settle this question in the life of every member: am I obedient to this By-law?"[46]

Eddy believed that the key duty of any Christian Scientist was always prayer and that prayer would make a genuine difference. She therefore made an effort in her *Message to The Mother Church for 1901* to inspire her followers to pray more actively about the underlying issues at stake in the suit. She did not address the crisis directly, touching rather on a number of themes basic to Christian Science. But she inserted a number of points into the message that the more alert of her followers could not have missed if they were at all sensitive to what was occurring at the time. "The most deplorable sight," she wrote, "is to contemplate the infinite blessings that divine Love bestows on mortals, and their ingratitude and hate, filling up the measure of wickedness against all light. I can conceive of little short of the old orthodox hell to waken such a one from his deluded sense." The "unseen evil" of mental malpractice, she further wrote, "is the sin of sins; it is never forgiven. Even the agony and death that it must sooner or later cause the perpetrator, cannot blot out its effects on himself till he suffers up to its extinction and stops practicing it. The crimes committed under this new-old regime of necromancy or diabolism *are not easily reckoned.*"[47]

In these instances Eddy was acting as the discoverer and founder of Christian Science. But as Mary Baker Eddy, if not the "weakest of mortals," she still showed great vulnerability to fear, strain, and in one matter particularly, a defensiveness not otherwise characteristic of her. Two months after the Woodbury trial was lost by the plaintiffs, Frederick Peabody delivered a lecture in Boston's Tremont Temple entitled "Complete Exposure of Eddyism or Christian Science, and the Plain Truth Regarding Mary Baker G. Eddy, Founder of Christian Science." The lecture, which was published in pamphlet form, was a compendium of invective so disturbing to Eddy that she felt compelled to respond. Her insistence on doing so herself was impelled by Alfred Farlow's overly cautious response to what she called Peabody's "dirty pamphlet." "It was your duty," she wrote Farlow in a strongly worded letter, "to write historically correctly or to write nothing when a whipped lawyer exploded lies in Tremont Temple."[48]

Her own response to Peabody's pamphlet took the form of a highly defensive short book of about seventy pages entitled *Footprints Fadeless* in which she attempted to refute his main charges through a variety of letters, documents, and aggrieved personal statements. One passage illustrates something of the tone of the book as a whole. On the concluding page of *Retrospection and Introspection,* written a decade earlier, Eddy had said characteristically, "I am persuaded that only by the modesty and distinguishing affection illustrated in Jesus' career can Christian Scientists aid in the establishment of Christ's kingdom on earth." By contrast, the page entitled "Closing Words" of *Footprints Fadeless* includes the less than modest assertion, "Dear reader, I could introduce you to my witness across the sea, to Earl and Countess, Marquis and Marchioness, Lord and Lady; and to my native land to the best people in it, distinguished professors, poets, and authors, and Doctors of Medicine, and in my native state to New Hampshire's noblest sons and daughters."[49]

Eventually Eddy dropped the project and never took it up again. According to Adelaide Still, she had not intended for it to be published until a year after her death, but said no more about the project after Sibyl Wilbur's biography of 1908 defended her against many of Peabody's charges. Certainly nothing Eddy ever wrote for publication shows her to less advantage. Although *Footprints Fadeless* contains a few historically helpful passages, it was mainly a way of letting off some of the steam that had accumulated from the stress of the Woodbury trial. Suffering intermittent but severe bouts of illness during this period, along with many sleepless and trouble-filled nights, she along with members of her household sometimes wondered how long she could survive. Occasionally she roused herself into making defiant and even ironic statements, as when she wrote to Kimball in February 1901, "The hounds on my track may bark [but] they cannot bite me," or when she commented to her attorney Samuel J. Elder just after the suit concluded, "Have not two years closed one of the dirtiest dastardly libel suits that ever stained the clean records of the United States Courts?"[50]

More characteristically, her letters during the suit and for some months thereafter were punctuated with expressions of suffering and distress. "Error says I am failing, that I suffer, and fatal symptoms are appearing," she wrote in September 1899. The following July she confided in Kimball, "My prayer is now for *rest*. The persecution and prosecution of this year, the onslaught of M. A. M. and the prospect of being unclad unhelped and killed has discouraged me. My endurance and struggle has been more than you can know." In October 1900, she wrote to Alfred E. Baker, "I can not take another single finger's weight on my shoulders." Six weeks before the case came to trial, Calvin Frye wrote to Edward Kimball, who had been brought to Boston to take charge of the case, that Eddy "is literally living in agony from day to day waiting to have this case called up and disposed of and W. is pouring in her hot shot declaring she cannot live through the ordeal."[51]

In view of the tension and uncertainty that gripped her, Eddy was sometimes strained to the utmost in her dealings with her household staff, church officials, and the attorneys she had employed to defend her. Since Woodbury had filed her suits in both New Hampshire and Massachusetts, two attorneys—General Frank Streeter in New Hampshire and Samuel Elder in Massachusetts—were required to handle the defense. Coordinating strategies required a conference at Pleasant View attended by the attorneys, along with Hanna, Joseph Armstrong, and William B. Johnson. As in other matters connected with the case, Eddy's experience and intuition impelled her to argue for a course directly opposite to what her attorneys recommended. When she did so on an issue about which she was eventually proven right, Hanna and Armstrong remained silent, tacitly supporting her attorney's position rather than hers. Deeply wounded, she wrote to her Chicago student Judge Ewing the next day, "I felt so alone. Judge H. Mr. A. and Mr. J. sat with the lawyers in my room for hours—the latter cutting my heart out, the former speechless.

I felt as if I were in the presence of headsmen waiting to take me to the scaffold."[52]

Two days later, William McKenzie wrote of Eddy's missives to his fiancé, "It seems like a state of siege just now, & we scarcely get the debris from one shellburst cleared up before there comes another explosion. One thing we shall have to cease forever, & that is the superstitious worship of a personal leader." Eddy, he went on, was "in wild tumult raging with Elizabethan frankness against those who are serving her with their lives." McKenzie was deeply devoted to Eddy. But he was also a sensitive, poetic soul who had been a Presbyterian minister turned English professor. His term "Elizabethan frankness" was a euphemism for displays of temper that violated his image of Eddy. And his shock at what he called in another letter to his fiancé her "detonations and Sinaitic flashings" and "the extreme of unreasoning personal queenship" alienated him from her for some months. Far from being "the Woman of Revelation," he wrote that she was "in general exhibiting the characteristics of 'only a woman.' "[53]

"NOTHING IS LEFT TO CONSCIOUSNESS BUT LOVE"

If Eddy sometimes was "only a woman," and at times a difficult and unpredictable one at that, there were other occasions when her fundamental spiritual convictions suddenly surfaced. At these points she reasserted that the only thing that can ultimately triumph over radical evil and hate is an equally radical understanding of God as Love. She had ended the first version of her chapter on the Apocalypse in the sixteenth edition of *Science and Health* in 1886 with the following words, which remained unchanged through the final edition: "Love fulfils the law of Christian Science, and nothing short of this divine Principle, understood and demonstrated, can ever furnish the vision of the Apocalypse, open the seven seals of error with Truth, or uncover the myriad illusions of sin, sickness, and death."[54]

For Eddy, the malice and sheer destructiveness which Woodbury projected into the mental environment marked the appearing of a far more malign force than she as one finite personality was capable of generating. In this sense, as Eddy's use of language from the book of Revelation indicated, the whole struggle with Woodbury moved onto an apocalyptic plane, for it involved basic elements of the spiritual warfare that, in Eddy's view, the coming of Christian Science had inaugurated. And in waging this battle, only alignment with Love in the largest sense could make a real difference.

Mary Baker Eddy around
the time of the Woodbury
lawsuit, ca. 1900.
Courtesy of The Mary
Baker Eddy Collection.

For Love to mean anything, she believed, it must be woven into the texture of daily life and practice. "As Christian Scientists," she wrote in her *Message to The Mother Church for 1901*, "you seek to define God to your own consciousness by feeling and applying the nature and practical possibilities of divine Love." This is what Eddy herself found it necessary to do in her invitation to Woodbury but in more private moments as well. During one particularly disturbed night in the midst of the Woodbury suit, at 3 A.M. she reached out for help by asking Calvin Frye "what Love is." Neither he nor Laura Sargent, who also came to her assistance, could answer to her satisfaction. Another student was called whose response was more helpful. Then Sargent was called back again and "answered her heart's yearning that 'Love is selflessness forgetting self and laboring for the good of others.'" This answer "relieved her severe belief of constriction of air passages"; but it did so by defining God in a way that restored to her the sense of his presence.[55]

In this as on other occasions, the real challenge Eddy faced spiritually was to rise above the dense malice in the mental atmosphere so as to regain her own spiritual equilibrium. The clearest evidence of her doing so is the poem "Satisfied" that she wrote in January 1900:

> It matters not what be thy lot,
>   So Love doth guide;
> For storm or shine, pure peace is thine,
>   What e'er betide.
> And of these stones, or tyrants' thrones,
>   God able is
> To raise up seed—in thought and deed—
>   To faithful His.
> Aye, darkling sense, arise, go hence!
>   Our God is good.
> False fears are foes—truth tatters those,
>   When understood.
> Love looseth thee, and lifteth me,
>   Ayont hate's thrall:
> There Life is light, and wisdom might,
>   And God is All.
> The centuries break, the earth-bound wake,
>   God's glorified!
> Who doth His will—His likeness still—
>   Is satisfied.[56]

As with the previous six poems she wrote between 1867 and 1900 that were eventually set to music as hymns, "Satisfied" is in essence a prayer showing a traceable relation to the needs and struggles Eddy faced in founding Christian Science. "Feed My Sheep," for example, was a prayer for guidance written in 1887 in the midst of the multiple demands of one of Eddy's most tumultuous years in Boston. "Mother's Evening Hymn," written six years later, was a prayer on behalf of her adopted son, but also reflected her mothering instincts in relation to the movement as a whole. "Christmas Morn" was clearly expressive of the sense of a spiritual breakthrough associated with the year 1898, toward the end of which it was written.

A strong characteristic of Eddy's poem-prayers lay in the fact that they show her throwing herself in dependence upon God and speaking not just *about* God but directly *to* him—as, for example, in the words through which she spoke to God in another of these poems: "Thou the Truth in thought and deed," "Shepherd, show me how to go," "O Life divine," "Thou Love," "Thou to whose power our hope we give." In no instance is her sense of abandonment to God more pronounced than in "Satisfied." But unlike her other poems which address God directly, "Satisfied" builds on the sense of his immediate presence, but directly addresses the evil that seems so threatening in the first line of the fourth stanza: "Aye, darkling sense, arise, go hence!" The next stanza conveys in the line "Ayont hate's thrall" the specific nature of that "darkling sense."

The real point of the poem, however, is not the magnification of human hatred. Rather, it is the capacity of Love to offset and defeat such hatred—the recognition that "Love looseth thee, and lifteth me, ayont hate's thrall." The power of Love, even in the midst of the worst manifestations of human hate, became the theme of several of her most eloquent letters during this period. As she wrote in one of them,

> Your need will be supplied when you are so emboldened by the fire of the Holy Spirit as to be receptive of the one garment seamless having no rents or separate parts to be united but all one pure eternal sense of Love. Wait dear one, and some Christmas dawn will clothe you with this love . . . and the dear human love that was akin to the Divine will have on the wedding garment and be fully prepared for its bridal—unity with God.[57]

Shortly after the lawsuit concluded, a painter with whom Eddy had been in touch offered to paint for her a picture entitled *Gethsemane*. At her instruction, Calvin Frye responded by saying: "She thanks you heartily for the kind offer but says her life is so full of the Gethsemane experiences she must decline your offer to portray the scene." What she meant by "Gethsemane experiences" included more than a time of trial and testing. To her, it touched the profoundest depths of love. As she defined it in the glossary of biblical terms toward the end of *Science and Health*, Gethsemane meant "Patient woe; the human yielding to the divine; love meeting no response, but still remaining love." In "Atonement and Eucharist" she develops what this means by writing that Jesus' words "Not my will, but Thine, be done!" mark "the new understanding of spiritual Love. It gives all for Christ, or Truth. It blesses its enemies, heals the sick, casts out error, raises the dead from trespasses and sins, and preaches the gospel to the poor, the meek in heart."[58]

To love in this way, practically and without limit or reservation, became a persistent theme in Eddy's writing and correspondence in the aftermath of the Woodbury suit. "One uniform rule is mine," she wrote in 1902 to an overzealous would-be champion: " 'Overcome evil with good.' I take the sword of spirit, Love, to conquer my enemies and none other."[59]

In the context of the Woodbury suit which had concluded just the year before, Eddy's *Message to The Mother Church for 1902* distills what she had learned from the whole experience, though she does not refer to it directly at all. In her *Message for 1899* she had spoken of the type or mental quality represented by Woodbury in the accents of the book of

Revelation, identifying it in one of the passages just quoted, with "lust, hatred, and revenge." What she eventually distilled from her encounter with these elements, once the lesson had sunk in and she regained her health and spiritual balance, was a more focused sense of the power of Love and its necessity in forwarding the cause of Christian Science.

In communicating her new understanding of these demands and their centrality to her followers, she begins by invoking the First Commandment, always for her the most central of Scriptural texts: "Thou shalt have no other gods before me." Reiterating John's declaration "God is Love," she then portrays the living of love in human experience as the only way to obey the First Commandment. This, she writes, was what Jesus required of his disciples when he said at the Last Supper, "A new commandment I give unto you, That ye love one another; as I have loved you." In an earlier article entitled "The New Commandment," she said that in uttering these words, Jesus had seen that "Love had a new commandment even for him."[60]

In a sense, the commandment to render Love central became a "new commandment" for her as well. The power of Jesus' love, she had said in *Science and Health,* was the vital factor in making his Resurrection possible. "The efficacy of the crucifixion," she wrote in "Atonement and Eucharist," "lay in the practical affection and goodness it demonstrated for mankind."[61] Just so, a measure of this same affection and goodness she saw as crucial in meeting the onslaught of the crucifying hatred that she believed animated the Woodbury suit. In Eddy's words toward the close of her message, "The great Master triumphed in furnace fires. Then, Christian Scientists, trust, and trusting, you will find divine Science glorifies the cross and crowns the association with our Saviour in his life of love. There is no redundant drop in the cup that our Father permits us."

Her words in the *Message for 1902* distill what she had come to learn from the furnace fire of the Woodbury suit. "The Latin omni, which signifies all, used as an English prefix to the words potence, presence, science, signifies all-power, all-presence, all-science. Use these words to define God, and nothing is left to consciousness but Love, without beginning and without end, even the forever I Am and All than which there is naught else."[62]

9

A Power, Not a Place

LONELINESS, FAMILY, AND COMMUNITY

ON JULY 1, 1893, EDDY WAS CONVERSING WITH JAMES GILMAN IN THE LIBRARY at Pleasant View. The day was warm and she placed him by an open window where he could be cooled by the fragrant summer breeze. She directed his attention to a single flower on a single stalk growing on the lawn. "It looks beautifully sweet and courageous in its loneliness I think," Gilman commented. "Doesn't it?" replied Eddy feelingly; "that is the way it is in spiritual living—in Christian Science, often." She continued, "Oh, how often I have found myself standing entirely alone with God, standing for the right—for His word—with everyone striving to pull me back, offering every inducement to go some other way. How much I would have given sometimes if I only could have had some one to talk with, some one who knew more than I did."[1]

Not only did Eddy make major decisions affecting the welfare of her church largely on her own. She also had personal issues to work out: her emotional needs for home, domesticity and companionship, temperamental flare-ups often exacerbated by the stress of her responsibilities, and intermittent but sometimes severe health problems related to both stress and age. The stakes, as she saw them, were high, the pressure and demands on her enormous. If she was to meet these demands, Eddy knew she needed practical help and support. Far from concealing or downplaying her needs, she became more forthright about them during the first years of the new century, after she had turned eighty. During her remaining years, she built a community of household workers, including groundskeepers, cooks, housekeepers, personal maids, companions, corresponding secretaries, and metaphysical workers charged with praying under her direction for her and for issues affecting the cause of Christian Science. In the process of training her staff to live up to their responsibilities, she gradually brought into being a spiritual community that became, in effect, her family.

Like so much else in her life, the community that took form as her household was not consciously constructed, but emerged in an experimental, unselfconscious way. She was not seeking the realization of a communitarian ideal that had animated, say, the Oneida Community in New York or a religious order of the Roman Catholic Church. It was simply that there was work to do, and she surrounded herself with those whom she felt could be trained to do it. As in any religious order presided over by an indisputably central figure, there were rivalries among those who sought status by being close to Eddy and attaining her favor. In her last few years there were also divisions between old-timers and newcomers in the household, which grew from about a dozen by the turn of the century to nearly double that during her last years. But there was unity, too, a shared spirit of mutual support impelled by the demands of living and working in a home that was the nerve center of a far-flung and controversial religious movement.

"Home," Eddy wrote, "is the dearest spot on earth, and it should be the centre, though not the boundary, of the affections." Given the range of her concern for the movement as a whole, the boundary of her affections was large. But when she moved into Pleasant View in June 1892, that spot rapidly became the center of her affections and remained so even after her move in 1908 to Chestnut Hill. Yet she largely lacked "the sweet interchange of confidence and love" that would have made her home complete. Soon after moving to Pleasant View, her household consisted of herself, a cook, a housekeeper, and a caretaker, as well as Calvin Frye and either Laura Sargent or Clara Shannon, who took turns as her companion. With none of these individuals, however, did she have the biological kinship she tried to approximate by adopting Ebenezer J. Foster Eddy, or "Benny," as she called him. Any fulfillment Eddy could have conceivably found within the framework of biological family relations had ended decades earlier. In 1903, she wrote in a letter, "How oft I sigh for a relative to love me and care for me. I, the last of the large family, am alone on earth notwithstanding the thousands who love me, yet I feel alone with the world on my back; a human atlas burdened with materiality. Some darling students come to my side tenderly—but none can bear my burden."[2]

Aside from a few distant relatives, Eddy's remaining bloodline included only her son George and his five children (one of whom, daughter Evelyn, died in August 1903). However much she loved her son, reintegrating him into her life after a separation of more than twenty-three years proved impossible, although the fault lay neither with him nor with his mother. Rough-hewn, uncouth, and almost illiterate, George was a prospector in the Dakota territory when they finally arranged to meet in 1879, after having corresponded for some years. His visit to her in Lynn only served to prove how little they had in common. The gulf between them deepened after Glover refused to come when she appealed to him following the death of Asa Gilbert Eddy in 1882. A visit to Boston from Glover with his family in tow five years later lurched from the embarrassing to the disastrous. Although she was generous to Glover and his family, he was eventually manipulated into becoming the chief plaintiff against her in the Next Friends Suit of 1907.

By the time Glover was reunited with his mother in 1879, there was almost nothing left of the family affections that Eddy prized so highly. Her adored brother Albert and her mother were long since dead; her father, with whom she had never been close, died in 1865. In earlier years she had enjoyed a somewhat chummy relation with her brother George Sullivan Baker; but they had drifted apart and in 1867, blind and embittered, he too died. In the mid-1880s Eddy tried to revive her once close friendship with George's widow, Martha Rand Baker, but the overture was rejected. Her sisters, Martha and Abigail, embarrassed and put off by Eddy's work in Christian Science, had cooled to her nearly twenty years before their deaths in 1884 and 1886, respectively. The one relative to whom Eddy was able to maintain affectionate ties was, curiously, the widow of her eldest brother, Samuel, who had been the first of the Baker children to leave home and whom she knew least well of all.

Deprived of any conventional family life, but valuing it above all human goods, Eddy made a series of efforts over several decades to find a substitute for it in surrogate family relationships. She took intermittent satisfaction in being in the midst of families with whom she found temporary refuge in her years of wandering in the late 1860s, adopted a motherly relation with some of her male students in the late 1860s and early 1870s, and made several efforts to bring students' families within her own home. She also reached out through correspondence to form friendships, some of them temporary, some more enduring, with a variety of individuals—not all of them Christian Scientists. Among her own students, there was Hannah Larminie in the late 1880s, Augusta Stetson, and Edward Kimball. In some cases she found refreshing contacts with others who sympathized with, but were not adherents of, Christian Science. Among them were the poets James Terry White and Edward A. Jenks, a Unitarian minister, the Reverend Frank Lowe Phalen of Concord, and her printer, William Dana Orcutt.

Her longing for contacts with her own family remained largely unfulfilled. Mournfully, she wrote to a friend in 1897 about her son George and his family, "What would all the earth be to me compared with the joy of having him and my lovely grand Children *with me* and interested in what I am. Had I *time* of my own and was able to do all I am doing and teach them, I would be in *heaven right here.*" Even in the midst of the Woodbury lawsuit, she gave substantial attention to finding a way to improve the education of her grandchildren. When it became apparent that circumstances beyond her control made this impossible, she wrote to Kimball, "I have lost the education of my grand-children and my most cherished earthly plans for them."[3]

Adopting Foster Eddy in 1888 was Eddy's last and most desperate effort to build a close family relationship that would at least approxi-mate the warmth and intimacy of her home life in her early years. In so doing, she was still to some degree seeking fulfillment in family-defined terms. The period following her permanent break with Foster Eddy in mid-1897 appears to have been unusually lonely for her. "Oh life here is so lone so thorny," she confided to a friend later that year. "This world has never afforded aught but struggle care ingratitude to me. No helping hand here no friend in need. . . . God, dear God, alone helps me to live for others and *adore* Him." The next year, 1898, she spoke of her feelings to her son George in a letter that she may have regretted writing when it turned up in Georgine Milmine's slashing series in *McClure's* ten years later. "I am *alone* in the world," she wrote, "more lone than a solitary star. . . . My home is simply a house and a beautiful landscape. There is not one in it that I love only as I love everybody. I have no congeniality with my help inside of my house, they are no companions and scarcely fit to be *my* help."[4]

When she wrote these uncharacteristically sharp words, Eddy may have been still smarting from the realization that any possible support and satisfaction from biological kinship was irretrievably lost to her. Her apparent ingratitude toward her relatively small staff was a way of driving home to George how grievously she felt that he—and Foster Eddy as well—had failed her. Even as she wrote, however, a very dif-ferent, more satisfying kind of community was in process of forming.

"Who Shall be Called to Pleasant View?"

About one hundred Christian Scientists worked as household mem-bers over the period Eddy lived at Pleasant View and Chestnut Hill, some for a few days or weeks, others for months, still others for one or more years. Eddy made her need for support known in a startlingly public way in her *Message to The Mother Church for 1901*, less than three weeks after the termination of the Woodbury suit. Writing with oblique but obvious reference to her own "increasing years and needs," she asked if Christian Scientists had "looked after or even known of" what she called the "sore necessities" of the "aged reformer." In her words, "mortals in the advancing stages of their careers need the watchful and tender care of those who want to help them." In June of the next year she wrote more bluntly to Archibald McLellan, who later that month would succeed Hanna as editor: "Cowardice, deceit, will without wisdom, have imposed on me tasks incredible. It is wise to protect as far as possible a Leader, instead of putting her to the front in every battle, laying her on the altar and saving themselves. I have now no relatives to defend me and my age requires some consideration after thirty-six years of constant conflict."[5]

Here as elsewhere, she was frank in acknowledging that she could go on carrying the burdens of leadership only with practical help which at that point she did not have in sufficient measure. Calvin Frye, of course, remained a faithful fixture in her life, although he could buckle under the continuing pressure of being available to help Eddy anytime day or night and enduring her rebukes. On at least one such occasion, Frye simply walked out of the house until Eddy, noticing his absence, sent Joseph Mann to chase after him and talk him into coming back. Explaining Frye's duties at the time as well as his character, she wrote in 1894, "He is an *odd individual*, but a very *honest*-man."[6]

By 1902, he had been with her for twenty years, and while she could in exasperation call him "the prince of blunderers," she also recognized and told him on several occasions that no one had done more for her or been kinder to her than he. Six years later, probably after administering a strong rebuke to him, she sent a note to Frye saying, "Calvin dear. Because I love you most of persons on earth I try most to have you see the lies of m.a.m. [malicious animal magnetism]." Frye himself, with the wry humor that was characteristic of him, observed how little adequate support she had when in 1902 he noted in his diary: "Mrs. Eddy opened the Bible this morning to the passage 'Fear not O daughter of Zion for behold your king cometh sitting upon an ass & upon the colt of an ass.' (fools) Yes, I remarked that is about all you ride on."[7]

The situation that confronted Eddy was unusual. She had begun her work in Christian Science when she was almost forty-five, built up the movement in her fifties and sixties, "retired" as she approached her seventies, only to find herself within several years more deeply enmeshed as the hands-on leader of a growing movement than ever before. Eddy turned eighty in 1901, but the movement was becoming international in scope, giving her enlarged responsibilities even while she was in the last decade of a very long life. She knew she needed help, did not hesitate to ask for it and, when that help was not sufficiently forthcoming, to demand it. What those around Eddy least understood, Adam Dickey once observed, was the depth of her need. Most of her followers assumed that "she stood erect physically and mentally at all times and simply spoke the word to error and it would entirely disappear." At points, Dickey said, she did rise to this level. But at other times she would bend beneath the load she bore. "She seemed to feel that she was more or less alone in her sphere of work and that those by whom she was surrounded did not really understand her or sympathize with her in the way in which she truly wished."[8]

That Eddy was not a tower of spiritual strength at every moment was difficult for many of her followers to grasp, both during her lifetime and in future decades. Sensitive to some of her students' incomprehension of this point, she was quoted by William Rathvon, a member of the household at Chestnut Hill, as comparing herself to someone "buffeting the waves far out" from the shore, while being judged by another who is standing safely "in water knee deep," adding that she was going through things that may never come to others and that they could not understand.[9]

Eddy found it particularly painful when students did not give her the loving support she needed, especially in times of crisis. After a sudden onset of illness in May 1903, she wrote to the directors, "Some of the students went away from me in my sorest hour of need, and I regret to say it, apparently *heartless* in regard to my dire necessity. This has at times grieved me almost to death." This comment was made in explanation of a strongly worded *Manual* bylaw she had drafted shortly before entitled "Opportunity for Serving the Leader," which required any church member whom she had selected to go to her side within ten days and remain with her for twelve consecutive months on pain of excommunication from the Mother Church. In 1906 the bylaw was amended to require the time of service to be from one to three years at Eddy's request. She explained later to the directors that experience had taught her that "one year at Pleasant View is only a test and preparation for the next year's experience." In 1909 the term of service became a fixed three years.[10]

Eddy knew how controversial this bylaw would become, writing in 1903 that it would be "the hobby of my foes." Yet as she saw it, getting the help she required to carry on her work was a matter of necessity.

The Civil War was a living memory for Eddy's generation, and military metaphors came naturally to her pen. She wrote to the directors that the "principal *fort*" of the cause of Christian Science "needs fortification" and she was calling upon "soldiers to supply this need," just as a nation drafts more soldiers when it needs them. "My only sigh," Eddy concluded, "is that these soldiers of the cross have not been *volunteers*." One of these "soldiers of the cross" was Minnie Weygandt, Eddy's cook for nearly nine years. As Weygandt defined it, her work was not confined to kitchen labor. Drawing a parallel between the role of Eddy's household and that of the biblical figures Aaron and Hur, who supported Moses' hands while he upheld the rod of God during one of the Israelites' battles, Weygandt explained, "Our work was to patiently uphold her hands as his had been upheld."[11]

Eddy was conscious of the sacrifice she was calling for by asking students to leave their homes, drop their work in their own fields, and come to her aid. To her Brooklyn student Pamelia J. Leonard, she wrote in 1902: "I need you. . . . But whoever is here comes not for any cause but the cross and Christ. Are you the victor enough to come where people go thus from the cross to the crown, relinquish the world and its pastimes—give up all for Christ?" Leonard responded affirmatively, and she served off and on at Pleasant View for the next five years. Often the sacrifice required of those who were called to serve their leader was matched by the sacrifice of their loved ones left behind. When her husband first started working at Chestnut Hill, a forlorn Ella Rathvon in Colorado said that the separation was "the supreme test of my life." But "the burden vanished" when she read her husband's letter conveying Eddy's message to her: that what she and her husband were doing was "not sacrifice, but offering." "The joy that came to me," Ella said in her reply to Eddy, "is indescribable." In an unusual twist, within eight months Ella Rathvon joined William Rathvon as a member of Eddy's household.[12]

To find other workers, Eddy commissioned her student Calvin Hill to interview prospective candidates for service. She also tested the waters through a series of letters to older students probing their willingness and ability to come to her if needed. Over the next years Hill and others formed a committee whose members made trips into the Christian Science field to examine prospective members of Eddy's household before they were called to be interviewed by her and, if they passed muster, to begin service.

In a 1903 statement in the church's religious periodicals, Eddy answered the rhetorical question "Who shall be called to Pleasant View?" by reiterating that Christian Scientists' motives should be "to help their helper, and thus lose all selfishness, as she has lost it, and thereby help themselves and the whole world, as she has done."[13] In some cases, it soon became apparent that a promising new arrival was simply not up to the work and he or she was soon sent packing. Others, including corresponding secretaries and metaphysical workers, stayed for a year or more and left with her gratitude.

John Salchow, whom one biographer describes as a "simple, uneducated, tireless, and great-hearted man," came to Concord in January 1901 and remained with Eddy throughout her lifetime as a groundsman, handyman, and at times a serviceable bodyguard. None of those who served at Pleasant View came more willingly or more expeditiously or won more of Eddy's trust and love. Recommended for the job by his friend and teacher Joseph Mann, already serving at Pleasant View, Salchow had worked on his family's farm in Kansas. At ten o'clock in the morning he received the letter inviting him to come to Pleasant View and by noon he was on his way, having taken no time to settle his personal affairs.[14]

Salchow quickly proved himself not only extremely hardworking, but ready to undertake any task. Besides his assigned work as groundskeeper, he took on other jobs as the occasion required. Knowing nothing about plumbing, he learned enough to accomplish what a professional plumber had said could not be done. He also studied enough about electric wiring to rewire a part of the house, fashioned a wrought iron step for Eddy's carriage out of a stray piece of iron, and tested the safety of the balcony at Pleasant View by rigging a pulley-and-weight system to determine how much weight it could bear. When the need for a night watchman became evident, he took on that job as well for a period of three months, going without sleep much of the time. His work load was so great and the demands so manifold that he wrote to a relative in Kansas a few months after his arrival, "Now I work, not according to time but, *Eternity.*" Salchow did his work in a spirit of loving supportiveness that Eddy came to acknowledge and appreciate. In his words, "Somehow I could always see the depressing, discouraging burden of human thought which was constantly being piled upon Mrs. Eddy and I wanted with all my heart to do anything I could to help ease that burden."[15]

Something of Salchow's uncomplicated loyalty to Eddy and her affection for him was captured in an incident related by Henrietta Chanfrau. Just after the *New York World's* sensationalist articles on Eddy began, Salchow along with other men in the house was meeting with Eddy in her study. Suddenly Salchow, roused by the attacks, raised his fist in the air and declared that he would " 'go to New York and find that reporter and give him the beating he deserves!' There was silence for a moment, then Eddy, who had been looking down at the carpet, suddenly looked up at him with a slight twinkle in her eyes, 'And I really believe you could do it, John . . . I really do!' "[16]

Even though Eddy had not met Salchow before he came to Pleasant View, few of those she interviewed beforehand did her greater service. While many potential workers were called to Pleasant View, by no means were all of them chosen. The first question when someone was called to serve in Eddy's household was whether they would make the cut—that is, survive their first interview with her. Salchow, who often picked up prospective household workers at the Concord railway station, developed a keen intuition as to who would be invited to stay. If he concluded that they would be invited, he unhitched the carriage and went about his business. Otherwise, he left the carriage intact so as to be ready to drive a rejected candidate back to the station—and in his reminiscence he recalls that he was seldom wrong.[17]

One man who was invited to stay was George Kinter of Buffalo, among the first to serve under the conditions of the new bylaw. Kinter recalled that Eddy received him cordially, then peppered him with dozens of questions. Was he as well and strong as he looked? Could he come and stay a whole year? Did he love the cause of Christian Science more than anything else in the whole world? Kinter served at Pleasant View for a year with distinction and was called back for shorter stints when help was needed. In other cases, however, Eddy would interview a new recruit and detect an unfitness that those responsible for his or her selection had not discerned. Sometimes a new household member might last for a matter of days or weeks and then leave, voluntarily or at Eddy's request—some with much grace, others with none at all. According to Hermann Hering, himself a frequent visitor to Pleasant View though not a member of the household, one practitioner called to Pleasant View had good credentials, but was "so very queer that Mrs. Eddy could not have her around." Asked to serve as Eddy's maid, she lasted but two days. When Eddy rang for her to come, this individual "would open the door and stand there with folded hands and roll her eyes. Mrs. Eddy said, 'She acts as though she were in the presence of the Holy Ghost.' "[18]

There were the workers who began their service with enthusiasm but found they could not bear the demands of serving in Eddy's home. "I want to tell you that being with our leader is not all sunshine," recalled Mary Armstrong, who came as a temporary replacement to cook at Pleasant View. "I found all sorts of arguments of error to hinder me from staying with Mrs. Eddy. I was tried on all sides to give up and go home. The error would argue discouragement and tell me what a

Mary Baker Eddy speaking with John Lathrop, Pamelia Leonard,
and Lida Fitzpatrick, ca. 1903–06. Courtesy of
The Mary Baker Eddy Collection.

hard master Mrs. Eddy was, and to leave, and tell me I would not stand
to stay with her." But she could also write, "It was no trouble for me to
please Mother, for I thought of her, and loved her as my *own Mother*.
I saw her as very human, and she needed human care."[19]

The hardest thing for some workers was the realization that what
they were asked to do was considerably less exalted than what they
thought befitted their abilities. One practitioner called to Pleasant View
from the Midwest came believing that she had been summoned to do
mental work. Eddy informed her that she would like her to stay as her
housekeeper. The practitioner replied, "Why, Mother, I thought I had
gotten through with all *menial* work long ago!" In recalling the incident, she said Eddy "looked at her, it seemed to her for a long time, and
just as though she could see right through her, and then said very gently,
'Why, my dear, I did not know that there was any.'" This individual
repented of her less than humble attitude and stayed. But this was not
always the case. James Neal, who had done some outstanding healing
work and eventually became a director, almost saw his career in the

movement cut short by a serious misstep that Eddy found unsupportable. At the time, she was looking for a temporary substitute coachman
for Calvin Frye. Neal was recommended to her; so she called him to
Pleasant View and after a few days asked him to take on the job. Believing
it was beneath his dignity and abilities as a practitioner, Neal declined
on grounds that he suffered from catarrh, which was untrue. Eddy said
nothing at the time but apparently boiled over in the face of Neal's unwill-
ingness to serve and, more importantly, his willingness to prevaricate.
Calling Calvin Frye, she instructed him to put Neal out of the house
forthwith and send him on his way back to Boston. Neal, who eventually redeemed himself in her eyes, was obliged to take a taxi and wait
in zero degree weather before boarding the next train at 2 A.M.[20]

HAVING GOD

Probably few of the Christian Scientists who were plunged suddenly into life in Eddy's household were in the least prepared for the
intensity of the atmosphere and of the demands they encountered. The
idea of dwelling in their leader's home took on a sacrosanct aura in
the movement, so that serving there was thought by those who were
called to be more of a plum than a burden—that is, until they actually
arrived. Salchow wrote to family members that Christian Scientists
sometimes said to him "how lovely it must be" to work for Mrs. Eddy,
"what a good time you must have." But if they had "a real try at it, for
five minutes, how much would be left of them, for in spite of all the
blessing, those that come here, (many of them) will squirm as if you
were throwing hot water on their backs."[21]
   Few new recruits arriving at Pleasant View were at all prepared to
encounter Eddy as she really was. For one thing, she was extraordinarily sensitive to the mental atmosphere of those around her. Salchow
wrote to relatives in the same letter that "if you came into her presence
with discordant thoughts, either you would have to rid yourself of
your thoughts, or, your thoughts and all would go out of there a *flying*."
Household workers often found her manner of speaking tender and
helpful, but she could also be surprisingly direct. John Lathrop, who
served on different occasions at both Pleasant View and Chestnut Hill,
recorded a number of instances in which she spoke with a frankness
that would have dismayed many of her followers; for example, her
statement to him that "the letter"—that is, the letter without the spirit—
"has killed some of my old students deader than dead." The same year
he noted her sharp words: "*Heal Heal Heal* No more blabbing." Referring

to her students' failure to rebuke one another's sins, she also said, "You didn't talk *squarely* enough as I do."[22]

The intensity of life at Pleasant View often made it anything but pleasant. Eddy had exacting work to accomplish on behalf of the movement, and the primary focus of the household was on maintaining her ability to accomplish it. In measuring up to the demands this work imposed, her only recourse lay in the practice of her own teaching. In 1902, responding to a letter from a board member who had asked somewhat rhetorically, "When shall we learn the way?" she wrote:

> I reply, when you have *all faith* in *Truth,* no faith in error. Gain this point, overcome evil with the good by knowing that good is *supreme*—is the master of so-called evil. Work mentally with this consciousness and you will overcome evil just as I have done so many years, and carried on a cause in the midst of all opposition, to such heights of success.
>
> True, I am battle stained; but still I live and give orders that are blessed and foil the enemy.

Those who obeyed these orders shared with Eddy the conviction that the prosperity of Christian Science depended in great measure on her being mentally and spiritually in the place her own discovery had opened. For her, this required the discipline of maintaining as a kind of grid, or working basis for thought and action, what one worker called her "absolute reliance on God's allness as the basis of her revelation." It meant the discipline, not only of believing in this as a concept, but feeling its truth through what Eddy termed "spiritual sense," defined in *Science and Health* as "a conscious, constant capacity to understand God." Grateful as she was for the practical help of those who had been called to serve at Pleasant View, supporting her in the effort to maintain her own spiritual sense was, in her eyes, the greatest necessity of all.[23]

Those who worked with her often recalled that she was fearless in the face of illness. What did disturb Eddy greatly was the temporary eclipse of her spiritual sense, when so much depended on maintaining it. Having God, in the sense of having a conventional belief about God, was not enough to provide spiritual light. "Mortals try to believe without understanding Truth; yet God *is* Truth," she wrote in *Science and Health*. That passage came to Eddy's aid, according to an account by Calvin Frye, during an episode that occurred in the midst of the Woodbury trial. She had awakened at 3 A.M. in severe pain. After Frye and other workers had tried to help her for about an hour, one of them opened *Science and Health* to the page on which those words were written. Hearing this passage read aloud gave her help and courage. Frye then

Mary Baker Eddy in her
study at Pleasant View, ca.
1903–06. Courtesy of The
Mary Baker Eddy Collection.

called her attention to the last chapter of Second Thessalonians, which
opens with the verse "Finally, brethren, pray for us, that the word of
the Lord may have free course, and be glorified, even as it is with you"
and includes the assurance that "the Lord is faithful, who shall stablish
you, and keep you from evil" and the injunction to "be not weary in
well doing." Reading this chapter, Eddy "immediately exclaimed 'I have
got back my God' & was comforted & relieved & had a restful sleep."[24]

In the summer of 1910, she instructed members of the household
how to deal with times when they could not pray. Explaining the passage in the book of John where Jesus said, "The night cometh, when
no man can work," she said, "A temptation comes to all that we cannot
do our work. If we yield, we are in the night. This is what is meant by
'the night cometh, when no man can work.'" Eddy's worst moments
occurred when she felt this sense of being "in the night." Gilbert Carpenter,
who worked as a secretary in 1905 and 1906, later said that when she
was fearful, the fear did not arise "from the presence of suffering, old age,
or persecution. It entirely concerned the possibility of losing her spiritual sense." When she was in need, Carpenter observed, she was "like
a great airplane when the propellers stop." But as soon as she began to

get real help—as "that spiritual inflow," in his words, started again—
"everything was reversed; for, instead of being a receiver from, she
became a giver to, her students."[25]

Eddy considered the most important characteristic of true prayer as
this quality of unreserved openness to God. Above all else, she valued
the evidence of this openness in those who worked in her home. Salchow
treasured a note she wrote to him saying, "I find you live so near to
God that you see to do the things I need before I ask you to do them."
When her student Clara Shannon asked Eddy how to resolve a difficult
dilemma, saying, "It is getting serious, Mother," she replied: "But you
can meet it, dear. Let your heart cry out to divine Love, as a child cries
out to his mother, for more light, more truth, more love. Ask Love for
what you need and for what Love has to give and then take it and
demand of yourself to rise up and live it."[26]

When Eddy felt that household workers were not measuring up to
this demand, individually or collectively, she did not hesitate to bring
them up short. Sometimes she urged them to greater spiritual effort
with wry humor. Once at Chestnut Hill she called the workers to her
study, telling them they must work harder and accomplish more. One
of them recalled that the twitching of her lips showed how amused she
was at their protestations that they would do so. She told them of a
lazy worker on her father's farm who was about to be fired but promised to work hard for his week's board. Mark Baker told him that he
didn't earn his board in a week. "Well, sir," the worker said, "if I can't
earn it in one week, I'll do it in two." Eddy then commented that this
is what her own workers' promises sounded like to her: "You are not
doing your work as you should, and you protest that if you haven't
done it heretofore, you will hereafter." Joseph Mann also recalled that
"With her characteristic aliveness Mrs. Eddy once thunderingly rebuked
her household with the query: 'Have you no God?'—arousing us out of
a self-mesmeric barrenness resulting from a very liberal use of the letter quite devoid of the quickening spirit: that is, devoid of the grace of
God-with-us."[27]

THE COINCIDENCE OF THE DIVINE WITH THE HUMAN

In one sense, life in Eddy's home was so demanding that it might have
seemed to have had a monastic aspect. Yet the spirituality demanded of
members of the household had little in common with the mystical spirituality of the Roman Catholic tradition. Sibyl Wilbur, a well-known
feminist journalist who wrote a magazine series on Eddy countering

the articles in *McClure's*, linked her to the broad tradition of feminine mysticism, writing that when Eddy was "lifted out of herself," the "physical discomforts of her existence were swept away by an inrush of God's truth. . . . The ego slipped away from her in some supreme moment and she made the plunge of the true religious, the mystic who cries: 'My soul swims in the Being of God.' "[28]

Wilbur's own Catholicism made her responsive to the dimension of Eddy's sensibility that links it with the broad stream of feminine spirituality. But as the biography she wrote about Eddy shows, she missed the really defining aspect of Eddy's sensibility: her continual struggle, not to escape into mystic rapture, but to challenge illness, age, mortality, and spiritual darkness so as to live the things of Spirit in the midst of daily life. In speaking of what she called "the coincidence of the divine with the human," Eddy had written: "Pure humanity, friendship, home, the interchange of love, bring to earth a foretaste of heaven. They unite terrestrial and celestial joys, and crown them with blessings infinite."[29]

In various ways, Eddy tried to find at least a foretaste of heaven at Pleasant View. She jealously guarded her times to be alone with God for seasons of spiritual renewal. But she also craved contact with the warmth of everyday life. Joseph Mann observed that "to Mrs. Eddy the ideal was not transcendental. Her life did not elevate God above the world; but she made appreciable the Revelator's vision that God dwells with men and so shall be their God and they His people." He spoke, for example, "of her joy at haying time. The grass in the rich valley south of Pleasant View had been cut in the early morning, and in the evening before the dew fell the hay had all been raked . . . in the clean and careful manner which seemed to bespeak for Mrs. Eddy, as she viewed the hundred of restful little mounds all over the large field, a tender goodnight."[30]

There was also a vein of pure earthiness in Eddy's appeal to the board, saying that "a cook-book cook is not what I need. . . . What I need is a cook that knows how to boil, *broil,* bake, and fry meat. How to make good flour bread and *common* good puddings and pies. I am not fond of sweetmeats and fancy food, but relish the plain substantial cooking and food." In the same earthy vein she once shared with Mary Armstrong, serving temporarily as her cook, in great detail her recipe for making Boston baked beans, writing as well to Laura Sargent, who was away at the time, "We are having the *best corn* cucumbers peas and raspberries you ever tasted. I always think of you at the table."[31]

In later life she learned about a variety of subjects that elicited her interest—as her friend and printer William Dana Orcutt realized when in 1897 he showed her a copy of the *Kelmscott Chaucer,* designed and printed by William Morris, which had just made its appearance in the United

States. Some years before, she had said to Orcutt when discussing the art of bookmaking, "If a man has beauty in himself he can put beauty into anything." Believing that Morris's volume illustrated her point, he was surprised at her trenchant critique of Morris's efforts. Acknowledging that he indeed had "beauty in himself," she commented that he used a "strange method of expressing it. . . . Everything he has done shows the same overloading and overelaboration, even his efforts to reorganize society." This, she said, has kept him "shifting from one frustration to another." Orcutt had to acknowledge the correctness of her point, which he found expressed by only one other eminent individual, his former Harvard professor Charles Eliot Norton, ironically enough a bitter critic of Eddy.[32]

Eddy also had a playful side with a sense of humor that ran toward irony. Her cook Minnie Weygandt recalled that once in the effort to get tender lamb chops to serve Eddy, she obtained fresh meat from some young sheep, not realizing that meat needed time to age before it was fit to be cooked. Thinking they would be tender when they were actually quite tough, she served them to Eddy, who commented: "Lamb chops? They are tougher than old sheep. They are older than I am." Salchow recalled that after two distinguished-looking directors came to Pleasant View for an appointment with Eddy, upon leaving they were laughing over her comment that they "would make good pictures to hang on the wall." Salchow also recollected an incident at Chestnut Hill when Eddy was walking upstairs with her hand on his arm, humming some hymns. Suddenly she broke into the words of one hymn and paraphrased the last two lines of the first verse, "And step by step, since time began, / We see the steady gain of man," as follows: "And step by step as time moves on / Upwards the march of Mary and John."[33]

Eddy relished frequent contacts with townspeople in Concord, from local merchants to editors and children whom she stopped to greet on her daily carriage rides, which became a familiar aspect of town life. She had no objection to the building of a state fairgrounds bordering her property. To great applause, she appeared there on one occasion to witness with obvious glee a spectacular high dive act. In the springtime, the citizens of Concord were welcomed to view the tulip display on the Pleasant View grounds, and during apple season they were invited to pick whatever remained of the harvest after the household had gathered as much as was needed for winter storage.

There was, in short, no real distinction between the sacred and the secular to be observed at Pleasant View, no sense of holy distance from the doings of everyday life. But there was the persistent demand on every member of the household of being up to the necessity of doing daily whatever needed to be done.

Pauline Mann in the Pleasant View study waiting for Eddy to return from her drive. Courtesy of The Mary Baker Eddy Collection.

SURVIVING

"Healing physical sickness," Eddy wrote, "is the smallest part of Christian Science. It is only the bugle-call to thought and action, in the higher range of infinite goodness."[34] She saw the work of the household as being in that "higher range of infinite goodness." It concerned mainly the healing of sin in its larger forms: that is, the antagonism directed at her, along with the laxity and indiscipline among Christian Scientists themselves.

Within the household, therefore, the healing of physical problems had a secondary place. Eddy did not want coping with physical ailments among household members to become their central preoccupation. She therefore required that prospective workers be free from physical illness and from a history of significant illness when they arrived, believing that the atmosphere of mental hostility they would encounter there could activate a latent problem. In one instance, which workers sometimes cited as an example, a coachman who concealed a long-standing heart condition in order to work at Chestnut Hill was found dead in his bed after just a week or two of service. As a result, Eddy devoted intensive attention to a brief addition published in a forthcoming edition of *Science and Health*. In one of the relatively few statements in the book directly addressed to her followers, she counseled them, "Christian Scientists, be a law to yourselves that mental malpractice cannot harm you either when asleep or when awake"—an admonition she considered so important that she later instructed Christian Scientists to give it daily attention.[35]

Eddy did not believe in papering over or ignoring physical problems that needed attention, either in her own case or that of her staff. When a new worker named Ella Sweet came to serve at Pleasant View in 1904, she suffered a fall that severely injured a leg and was confined to her room. Eddy noticed her absence and asked what was wrong. Household workers who had not healed the case said reassuringly that she was all right. Eddy replied, "She is not all right." She then visited Sweet and asked what was wrong. Sweet replied, "It is being met," to which Eddy responded, "It is not being met." The injury, Eddy explained, was merely a means through which Sweet was being prevented from working effectively in the household. Sweet indicated that with this realization came the needed healing.[36]

In this as in other instances, Eddy was definite about facing physical problems directly and fearlessly. One example often cited in the literature on Christian Science was her vigorous rousing of Calvin Frye from a death-like stupor during a winter night in 1905. After having rung for him several times with no results, she called Kinter, who found Frye slumped in his armchair showing no signs of movement or life. Kinter concluded that Frye was dead. Although to all appearances this was the case, he may have been in a kind of self-induced catatonic state, resulting from sheer weariness and the desire to escape the rigors of daily life in a household where so much responsibility fell on his shoulders.

Despite the freezing cold, Eddy came to Frye's room clad only in her nightdress and began audibly to call him back to consciousness. Kinter supported her in his arms, urging her to return to bed, though she remained oblivious to his pleas. Laura Sargent wrapped her in a double blanket and put slippers on her feet, with Eddy paying not the slightest attention. She continued making strong declarations, Kinter recalled, "with such vehemence and eloquence, for a full hour, as I never have heard on any other occasion, even in that house." Still supported by Kinter in a half-stooping position, she made statements such as the following: "Calvin, wake up and be the man God made. . . . Calvin, all is Life! Life! Undying Life! Say 'God is my Life.' Say it after me; say it so I shall know you realize it. . . . Mother loves you for all your years of faithful service, but our dear God loves you infinitely better."

During this time Eddy chafed Frye's hands, slapped his face, and shook him briskly. After an hour he moved slightly, then said, "Don't call me back. Let me go, I am so tired," to which Eddy responded, "Oh yes, we shall persist in calling you back, for you have not been away. . . . You love life Calvin, and its activities, too well to fall asleep. . . . You know that divine Love is the liberator, and you are freed from the thraldom of hypnotism, alive unto God, your Saviour." In another half-hour Frye was restored to his normal condition. Afterward Eddy was half carried back to her bed, bidding her helpers good night by telling them "to go to our beds now and go to sleep, because we would have a busy day tomorrow."[37]

In all probability the day was busy. Until her last few years, Eddy held to a rigorously demanding work schedule. In 1905, when she wrote to her young friend Calvin Hill of her resolve each morning to have only the Mind that is God, she added, "I have done it but am a poor specimen of preservation. But the greatest miracle of the age is that I am alive."[38] That conversation occurred five years before her death in her ninetieth year. Eddy's longevity appears all the more impressive given the fact that there was no family history of great longevity except that of her maternal grandmother, who died at the age of ninety-one. When Eddy died, she was nine years older than her father had been at his death, twenty-four years older than her mother, thirty-four and nineteen years older than her sisters, and from about three to seven decades older than her brothers when they died. Dr. Allan McLane Hamilton, the alienist who examined her just before the Next Friends Suit was tried, declared that for a woman of her age—at that time eighty-six—she was "physically and mentally phenomenal."[39]

Eddy had endured serious and sometimes incapacitating illness during her lifetime. Her brother Albert died of kidney disease. Surviving family letters bearing on her own health suggest, though not conclusively, that she suffered from some combination of bladder and kidney difficulties. In 1903, and again in 1909 and 1910, there were several episodes when she endured painful kidney attacks, although her death was listed by the coroner as caused by pneumonia. Frye's diaries and other comments by household workers indicate that she suffered periodically from other difficulties, including breathing problems, rheumatism, loss of a sense of smell, and intermittent deafness, although her eyesight improved in later years.

When Eddy had a physical difficulty she was specific and up-front about her need. "I am always frank, or mean to be," she wrote in a letter in 1903, "and [do] not hide the worst side of a subject." A common phenomenon observed by those in the household was that she suffered, sometimes greatly, when working out a serious problem in the church, such as the formulation of a new bylaw for the *Manual*. At such times, according to Adam Dickey, "the physical effects of the discord she wished to overcome seemed to manifest themselves in her body and often she was prostrated with suffering." Adelaide Still recalled, for example, that at the time of the Communion service of the Mother Church in June 1908, Eddy in acute physical distress called for help, explaining that she had "always suffered for what was not right with my church." She then dictated a *Manual* bylaw abolishing the Communion service in the Mother Church, which had in her view become too much a vast and crowded public occasion, although the *Manual* retained the semi-annual observances in branch churches. When she told Frye to send the bylaw to the directors, he remonstrated, "Oh, Mother, I wouldn't do that, if I were you," to which she replied, "Calvin, *you do as I tell you*." Frye did so, but not without grumbling to Laura Sargent and Still, "She'll ruin her church."[40]

Most often when Eddy had a siege of physical illness she would call a mental worker to her room, explain her need in unvarnished terms, and require that the needed help be given, usually in the form of audible treatment—which she often listened to attentively, correcting mistakes when necessary. If she did not feel markedly better within twenty minutes or so, she would dismiss that worker and call another. New members of the household especially were sometimes taken aback when called upon to give treatment to Eddy. In one instance where Eddy experienced relief after asking Lida Fitzpatrick for help, Fitzpatrick asked her how she could have healed her "when I felt so helpless to do for some one who was so far above me?" Eddy replied that it was "through that helplessness you let the Truth in, and it was Christian Science that healed the case, not your own exertion."[41]

There could be no question that, by the time of her death, Eddy had lived long enough to fulfill what she saw as her mission and complete her lifework. Given the multiple ordeals of her life, she was not vastly exaggerating when she told Calvin Hill that her very survival and accomplishment of this work was the "miracle of the age."

GETTING IT RIGHT

"Orthodox Christians consider Sunday as a day of rest from secular employment, and special religious worship," wrote one household worker in retrospect. "Mrs. Eddy did not accept this view. Days were just days and every day was Sunday. Pleasant View was one place on earth where the presence of God was definitely felt. Serving Him was more important than doing anything else in the world. It was the place where demonstration was demanded." In this respect, Eddy made no particular distinction between, say, how well a meal was prepared, if her pin cushion was kept in an orderly manner, or if a mental worker completed an assignment effectively. What mattered to her was her estimation of whether the activity, no matter how apparently significant or insignificant, was done or not done under divine guidance through the consciousness that God is the only Mind, and thus done rightly—if it reflected, as one worker put it, "the exactness and divine order of God."[42]

Eddy had been temperamentally disposed to maintain extreme neatness in her surroundings since girlhood. Her rigorous demand for order in every phase of the life of the household might well be interpreted as an extension of this temperamental tendency, intensified by age. Adelaide Still, who loved and admired Eddy greatly, saw such demands in this light, writing that "just as with the rest of the human race, many of the traits, opinions, likes and dislikes which she manifested were the results of early environment, education and experience."[43] To Eddy herself, however, maintaining a household in which this sense of order became the norm assumed a much larger dimension. She saw learning to do what appeared to be little things in a right and orderly way as an important preparatory step in doing effective spiritual work involving larger matters.

The one thing Eddy most abhorred and rebuked was self-justification, which she saw as a mental state of acute resistance to genuine spiritual progress. In singling out the problem of self-justification in potentially disrupting the community she was trying to establish, Eddy touched upon what German theologian Dietrich Bonhoeffer later spoke of as a major impediment to a functioning Christian community. In his book *Life Together,* Bonhoeffer spoke of "the struggle of natural human beings for self-justification." This tendency, said Bonhoeffer, was part of "the natural drive to self-assertion," which disrupts or even destroys the capacity of a budding community to fulfill its possibilities. In the words of Hermann Hering, when workers failed to accomplish something they had been asked to do and had to report to Eddy, she would "not permit them to make any excuses," to justify themselves or even apologize; "she never stopped questioning them or talking with them until they admitted that error had made them do this or fail to do it. She said that unless you made this admission that error made you do it, you can't be healed of it."[44]

Her position is evident in the case of Caroline Foss, a New York practitioner whom Eddy called to Pleasant View to serve as her personal maid. Foss later wrote of her initial feeling of humility at the possibility of being with Eddy, but found that she was frequently rebuked for her resistance to correction. Eddy, she wrote in her reminiscences, "reproved me for something, and seeing me look quite distressed, she said, 'Remember, Caroline, the Bible says, No chastening for the present seemeth to be joyous, but grievous.' " Though it reflected ill on her, Foss reproduced in her reminiscence a letter sent to her by Eddy after she had returned to New York saying: "I have begged of you to quit telling me why you did a thing wrongly, but you have not obeyed me. I have told you it is like the sick excusing sickness—tell *why they are sick*, and you do know that this would tend to make it real and to *justify sickness*."[45]

A countervailing instance can be found in the reminiscence of John Lathrop, a young practitioner from New York of whom Eddy was quite fond. He was called to her study at Pleasant View and asked if he was doing his mental work. He replied that he was trying to do it. Eddy repeated the question and he replied as before. His account continues:

> She said, "Stop, stop!" and gave me one of her penetrating looks which went right through one. "I asked you if you were doing what I gave you to do. You replied, 'I am trying to do it.' Now you are either doing a thing or you are not doing it. Were you doing it?" "No, Mother, I was not doing it," I replied. She said quickly, "When are you going to do it?" "Now," I replied. "Let me see you do it now," she said sternly. I returned to my room. I knew that if I did not do the required mental work now, I would soon be taking a train to my home.[46]

Lathrop quickly gained the needed spiritual realization—and just as quickly Eddy called him back and gave him more work to do.

KEEPING THE WATCH

The work young Lathrop had been called upon to do was called in the household "watching." During the morning watch, which lasted from nine to ten, a worker in her home later recalled, "each student returned to his or her room to do the mental work to destroy fear, and to recognize the presence and power of God as supreme in the home as well as in the whole universe." Another hour for watching and prayer was observed from three to four, then again from eight to nine.[47]

Basically, all the activities of the household arranged themselves around these periods of watching. Eddy did not believe in prayer on the run. She saw the specific acts of prayer and metaphysical treatment as definite activities which must be carried on in a committed and focused way. In the midst of unpredictable and multiple demands, the greatest need of all, she believed, was for her and the household to maintain a schedule in which this work was central, thus to sustain the *progress* of Christian Science through the *practice* of Christian Science. Her teaching rested on the conviction that evil, having no entity or power in itself, could operate only in this one way: through suggestion and deception.

A large part of the mental work that went on in Eddy's household consisted in the effort to ensure that such suggestion, in whatever form, did not prevail. This involved the effort to put down any argument or condition that denied God's control of events, whether this concerned Eddy's health, a prevailing sense of darkness and gloom, a church crisis, a severe attack on her in the press, or even dangerous or threatening weather conditions. The great daily need in the household, therefore, was to maintain spiritual light and assurance against the inroads of anything that could threaten it.

What undermined this light and assurance, Eddy believed, was almost always the effect of the malice that, if unchecked, would blast her peace and health so as to undermine the progress and well-being of the Christian Science movement. In Salchow's words, "There were times when the attacks from outside were so malicious that everyone needed to be more alert than ever. It was the work of the household to shield and guard their Leader from these attacks."[48] Some of this hostility was obvious and overt. As Christian Science took hold in various communities, sermons, pamphlets, and books denouncing Eddy as a heretic circulated widely in the evangelical world. Twain's articles were stinging, and attacks in the media, especially the Milmine/Cather series in *McClure's* and the articles in the *New York World*, were savage.

Sometimes the malice Eddy saw as needing the watchers' attention could be identified in general terms as the resistance of the carnal mind to the advance of Christian Science. In other instances such malice had, as she believed, a more specific and identifiable source. She especially believed this to be the case in the animosity directed toward her by disaffected Christian Scientists who had learned of the possible misuse of mental power. Josephine Woodbury furnishes a case in point, since her antagonism toward Eddy was undisguised. About that antagonism there could be no doubt. What has been controversial is Eddy's belief that an atmosphere of enmity, including the intentional projection of mental malice, could have a destructive effect. Robert Peel's biography records one instance, just months after Woodbury's excommunication from the Mother Church in April 1896, when Eddy experienced a night of intense physical agony. In the morning came a telegram to Pleasant View signed "Greetings Woodbury."[49] From one standpoint, relating Eddy's suffering to Woodbury's mental influence amounts to sheer imagination playing on coincidence. From Eddy's standpoint, given Woodbury's history of mental control and her repeated avowals of hostility, making this link was simply a matter of connecting the dots.

Eddy stressed, however, that there was nothing inevitable in the suffering that projected malice could effect, since it was thoroughly possible to place oneself in an atmosphere of God's protection and love. Doing just this was what "watching" at Pleasant View and Chestnut Hill was all about. Since mental malpractice is mental, Eddy explained to one new worker in her Chestnut Hill home, "the only place I could meet it was within what seemed to be my own mentality and the only way that I could meet it was to give up the belief in a power and presence other than God or Truth."[50]

At any given time, several of the workers in Eddy's household were designated as watchers. Each watcher had a watch in which he or she worked alone, especially at night if Eddy had an acute physical problem or felt a loss of spiritual light. Usually she would give Frye hand-written slips of paper or dictate instructions for the lines of work to be taken up and amplified by each worker. Frye would then convey these instructions to the watchers, who would do the required work in their rooms, where they would also be on call in case Eddy wanted to instruct them further or ask them to work along different lines.

To Eddy, these watches—however esoteric they might seem from an outside perspective—had clear scriptural precedent. They involved acting on Jesus' words that Eddy quoted at the beginning of an article called "Watching versus Watching Out": "Our Lord and Master left to us the following sayings as living lights in our darkness: 'What I say unto you, I say unto all, Watch;' and 'If the goodman of the house had known what hour the thief would come, he would have watched, and not have suffered his house to be broken through.' "[51]

The article from which these words were taken was a correction on an editorial under the same title "Watching vs. Watching Out" that had appeared in the *Sentinel* for September 16, 1905, by John B. Willis. Probably Willis was prompted by his wife, who had recently served at Pleasant View for a year, and who interpreted Eddy's demand for dealing with evil through the practice of "watching" as excessive. Willis's editorial was built around the distinction between the two types of watching named in the title: "watching," which Willis characterized as calm, quiet, and confident, and that "minimizes the manifestations of evil," and "watching out," which is troubled and perturbed because it makes too much of evil. "The one knows the lions are chained, and goes forward with freedom and inward rejoicing; the other peoples the air with dragons and indulges in a strained and elaborate caution."[52]

Willis's editorial was a brief on behalf of a version of Christian Science in which adherents are depicted as perpetually calm, buoyant, undisturbed in the face of evil. But this approach to Christian Science flies in the face of Eddy's actual teaching and its demands. In a tightly worded comment published the week after Willis's editorial, Eddy undertook to correct his soft-grained version of Christian Science. In doing so she again advocated the point stressed throughout her writings: that the true practice of Christian Science involves directly naming and facing whatever errors seem threatening and need to be overcome. If self-examination or any other form of watching becomes frightening and discouraging, then one deals with and puts out whatever is frightening and disturbing. One does not put out one's watch. "One should watch to know what his errors are," she wrote; "and if this watching destroys his peace in error, should one watch against such a result? He should not."

Then what is the right kind of watching? In answering this question, Eddy once told John Lathrop a story about a Confederate soldier during the Civil War who crept through the underbrush approaching the breastworks of the enemy. Seeing a Union soldier marching up and down, he took aim. Just as he was about to fire, he heard the Union soldier singing a hymn. He then lowered his rifle and retreated. Years later after the war, the Confederate soldier heard what seemed a strangely familiar voice singing a hymn during an ocean crossing. After the service he asked the man if they had met. After comparing notes with him, he realized that the voice that sounded so familiar was that of the Union soldier he had almost shot and killed. The Union soldier told him that he had sung the hymn "because I was conscious of danger which I could not see or hear." The hymn was "Jesus, Lover of my Soul." When he finished singing the hymn, he said, he felt the danger was gone. "That man," said Eddy, "was watching. He was not afraid, but he was conscious of his danger. Now, Christian Scientists read their literature, go to church, to lectures, and to church meetings, but that is not *watching;* they are merely marching up and down the breastworks."[53]

Eddy saw herself as having a specially developed ability to be a "sentinel" for the cause of Christian Science—to feel a danger to her or the movement before it could have a damaging effect. "My students think they do well when they discover the burglar after he has broken in, and then succeed in throwing or driving him out"; she once declared, "but Mother watches and sees his intent before he gets in."[54]

Some of the dangers she instructed the watchers to deal with involved obvious and specific problems such as ill health, church crises, or legal entanglements. More often she stated the need in broader terms, identifying the line of thought that would deal with what she saw as some impending threat, rather than naming and describing the threat itself. The bottom line in most of the watches was attaining a greater sense of God's presence. One watch included the instruction, "Try to realize the omnipotence of Love and Life, the in-breathing of His presence. Arouse yourself to a true sense of God's power, the eternal and ever-conscious Mind that knows only Life." Other watches dealt with particular needs, for example one that related to problems on the board of directors: "You are to take up for the Directors daily: Mind is All. God is here. There is no darkness, no mental depression, no failure in God's Cause. *Do not name them by name.*" Sometimes, too, Eddy instructed the watchers to work so as to lift their own state of thought: "Now take up again for yourself every day, Love is All. Truth reigns. There is no lie and nothing to make a lie. No m.a.m. to darken thought. Love reigns and rules this and every hour. Truth declared *heals*. No reversal. God is All. 'Commit thy ways unto Him and He shall bring it to pass.' "[55]

These and other watches were not meant to be repeated by rote or as formulas. They were intended to set a direction for the worker's own treatment, which should then develop through inspiration in a way that would meet the need at hand. Whether it did so or not was the simple test of whether a watch was truly effective. Passing the test kept the watchers watching.

"My Family"

When household workers kept their watch, that work was done in quiet and solitude by the individual watcher in his or her room and fulfilled an individual trust. Yet the effort to "watch and pray," thus to sustain Eddy's ability to carry on her work, was a community effort that bound the watchers together, despite the solitariness of the watching itself. That community life was affirmed and carried forth in other more visible ways. There were, of course, meals together, usually well-prepared from foods raised at Pleasant View. There were quiet conversations and interchanges of support, and sometimes commiseration in the face of the exacting demands they all tried to fulfill. And there were convivial occasions when the household was called into Eddy's study for social conversation and sometimes for singing, in which she often happily joined.

But the times that meant the most, and that most deeply connected the members of the household to her and to each other, were the frequent occasions when they were called to her study in the morning. "I live with the Bible," Eddy told a member of her household in 1907.

Mary Baker Eddy sitting at her desk talking with Laura Sargent. Courtesy of The Mary Baker Eddy Collection.

At another time she said, "God talks to me through this book as a person talks to another, and has for forty years." When Eddy opened the Bible at random each morning, almost invariably finding a passage that she felt gave the needed light and direction for that day, she would then often summon some or all members of the household to share what she had found. Calling them together after she had read from the Gospel of John one morning, for example, she said that the words of the Bible were "as plain as though the person, John, were present." She then spoke with some feeling of what it meant to love one's neighbor in the light of Jesus' words in John about the oneness of God's children with him: "The neighbor is one with the Father; so are we; all one in Spirit. The 'I' is one, infinite. The one who sees this and abides in it, becomes unselfed and is then ready to do for his neighbor—is a Christian Scientist."[56]

Some of the household did indeed bear each other's burdens, consoling one another when Eddy's rebukes seemed unduly harsh, helping each other through periods of exhaustion or illness, supporting each other as well as Eddy during crises. There were times at Pleasant View and Chestnut Hill when the spirit of unity Eddy sought to maintain did prevail. But given the incessant demands, from the menial to the metaphysical, that household workers had to meet, the cooperative spirit she sought to establish was fragile. Eddy's own demands sometimes exacerbated the problem.

In part because of the illnesses she faced during much of her life, she had become accustomed, somewhat like a Southern belle, to having others wait upon her. Even during her years of relative poverty in North Groton and Rumney, she often had help, such as the blind girl, Myra Smith. This tendency continued, although for a largely differing reason, after 1866, when she was on the whole healthier than in earlier years. From that point on, she became increasingly fired with a sense of mission, which led her to expect that it was fitting for others to perform practical tasks, so as to make it possible for her to give attention to larger matters. Living with various families in the early years after her discovery, she put her own spiritual research and writing above all other considerations, contributing little if anything to the running of the household; understandably she was viewed at points as a difficult guest. Later, some of her early male students at Lynn such as George Barry and James Howard became part-time errand boys for Eddy.

There was no question that the members of Eddy's household were there to give her needed help and support at every level. Though she showed them much gratitude, she could also give the impression of taking the work of others on her behalf for granted, resulting in hurt feelings among those who served her. In addition, as Adelaide Still frankly recalled, Eddy could be quite stingy, at points cutting wages that, if anything, deserved to be raised and providing scantily for food she expected to be purchased for household meals. Still interpreted this tendency, along with a penchant for maintaining extreme orderliness, as an extension of older patterns. "Mrs. Eddy never got away," she wrote, "from the penuriousness of her days when she had nothing."[57]

Still touched on this issue in correspondence with Gilbert Carpenter, who after his service in Eddy's home wrote prolifically on his time there, giving sometimes exaggerated metaphysical meaning to almost everything Eddy did and said. With far greater realism, Still insisted that Eddy, especially with advancing age, manifested some very human tendencies that could be largely explained in common sense terms that did not discredit the enormity of her accomplishment and sincerity in the practice of her own teaching. In one such exchange with Carpenter, Still wrote that his defense of his views on these matters showed that he was "hopeless." Referring to Eddy's own unvarnished realism about human affairs, she continued, "As Mrs. Eddy once said, 'Some students would spiritualize anything; they would spiritualize a beefsteak.' She turned up her nose when she said it, and she could turn up her nose more effectually than anyone I have ever seen."[58]

While Eddy could be both parsimonious and extremely demanding of her household workers, she could also be generous and warmly

Mary Baker Eddy, ca. 1903–06. Courtesy of The Mary Baker Eddy Collection.

solicitous for their welfare. After calling Gilbert Carpenter's wife to Pleasant View for a year's service, Eddy asked Carpenter himself to come in her stead upon realizing that his wife had a two-year-old child to care for. She wrote to the Carpenters:

> You have healed that wound in my heart that was bleeding for just such an offering and now I will do my duty in the case. Yesterday I said, forgive me Father Mother Love, for my *selfishness* and provide some one for me that has not a babe to cry for her mother. . . . You are not yet quite situated so as to do this,—the baby I cannot have cry, I seem more weak on this point than you are now, but after being here sufficient time to have tied me to your dear heart and help, then you would have to leave one baby for your other! God bless you for what you have done and He will. Unpack your trunks, and accept my Soul's benediction for your love.[59]

Eddy's supportiveness for her staff was probably more the norm than her occasional outbursts and excessive demands. But there were times when relationships in the household simply broke down. Calvin Frye recorded in his diary for January 11, 1906, one instance in which his normally supportive and harmonious relation with Eddy was temporarily disrupted:

> Mrs. Eddy says I was under the spell of m.a.m. all day today and she could not by mild methods waken me. So at about 8.30 P.M. as I had not

gone to the swing to enquire after her she called me there; and when I came she said, *"What are you here for."* I said you were quiet & so I did not disturb you. How are you getting on? But she would not give me any satisfactory answer, and so I felt she was unjust and I got mad. This frightened her & made matters worse for us both. When she tried to go to her bedroom she could hardly walk and I had to hold onto her to keep her from falling. After retiring she called me to help her mentally, but I was so overcome by error & confused I said I could do nothing which scared her thoroughly to see me so & she called Carpenter & Mrs. Sargent & set them at work mentally after which I was able to recover myself & to quiet her fears so that about 10 P.M. we had both overcome the attack.[60]

Then, too, the fallibilities of human nature were factors to be contended with in Eddy's home. Probably the most disruptive and difficult of any of the household workers was Lewis Strang, a sophisticated Boston drama critic and author. Strang was the most intellectually capable of Eddy's secretaries. According to the recollection of others, he could also be self-willed and apparently carried on a serious affair with Grace Greene, a married woman who also worked in the household. Strang's liaison with her, however, became known to Salchow, among other workers at Pleasant View, one of whom saw Greene slipping into Strang's bedroom night after night. Once the situation came to Eddy's attention, she told Greene to return to her home. Instead, she remained at a hotel in Concord, where Strang continued to visit her. When Eddy confronted Strang on the matter, he was apparently repentant and broke off relations with Greene. Little wonder that shortly after this episode, Eddy wrote to Calvin Hill, who headed the committee charged with finding appropriate household help for her, that she was looking for someone "50 years old and as plain looking as possible."[61]

More problematic in the long run were the animosities that sprang up at Chestnut Hill during Eddy's last few years. Competition among some of the male members of the household sometimes reached serious proportions, particularly when several of them resolved to break what they perceived as Frye's domination of the household and undue influence on Eddy. She saw this sort of competition as the besetting sin that she strove to keep out of her church and her home. "Competition in commerce, deceit in councils, dishonor in nations, dishonesty in trusts," she wrote in 1902, "begin with 'Who shall be greatest?'"[62]

Life in the household, however, was a great leveler. Several of the women called to work there had been teachers with prominent positions within their own fields but with no special status among the other workers who served in the home. The household workers were very different types of people. They ranged all the way from Anna Machacek, a sweet-natured Czech immigrant who worked as laundress, then housekeeper from 1905 to 1908, to Mary Armstrong, the wife of a director of the Mother Church, who was asked to come to Pleasant View as an interim cook for a month in 1898. What knit them together and submerged rivalries and differences more than anything else was the urgency that brought them there—the sense that they were sorely needed to support Eddy and that her continued work was indispensable for the welfare of the church as a whole.

Eventually, and perhaps imperceptibly, Eddy found a measure of the sense of spiritual family and community in her household that was deeply satisfying to her. Despite one happy visit from her two grandsons in 1910, there was never a realistic possibility of establishing any kind of biological connectedness, especially with her son, George, after he became the chief plaintiff in the Next Friends Suit. During the suit when she was clearly saddened by the thought of how he had been used against her, she gained some comfort through the words of one of her household: "Cheer up, Mother, for this is the last channel of flesh-relationship through which evil could presume to reach you."[63]

Yet if fulfillment through the biological sense of family was denied her, she could act in the spirit of her own words: "We must resign with good grace what we are denied, and press on with what we are, for we cannot do more than we are, nor understand what is not ripening in us."[64] In her case, pressing on meant realizing more of the essence of spiritual family and community. This is what she did, perhaps not consciously, but nevertheless to surprising effect.

By her last decade, Eddy developed more feeling for a number of her household community than she may have thought possible in earlier years. Reminiscences by many household workers confirm her solicitude for their welfare, as reflected in notes of heartfelt appreciation for their service, unexpected small gifts, and sensitiveness to their personal needs.

When John Salchow became enamored of a local Concord girl, he hesitated to propose to her, not wanting his personal wishes to interfere with his service to Eddy. Learning of his feelings, she called him to her study, expressed deep appreciation for his consideration of her, and asked if he truly loved the girl. When he replied that he did, "she said at once, 'I wish you would get married just as soon as you can arrange to do so' "—which they happily proceeded to do.[65]

Acknowledging Eddy's liberal donations to the betterment of Concord, her cook Minnie Weygandt commented that it was "the smaller examples of loving interest to those within her immediate circle that counted most with me." One touching indication of this point was

John G. and Mary McNeil Salchow, 1906.
Courtesy of The Mary Baker Eddy Collection.

Eddy's response to news of the death in 1904 of Minnie Weygandt's sister Mary, of whom Eddy had grown very fond. After several years at Pleasant View, Mary had what appeared to be a nervous breakdown and went back home to recuperate. In a despondent state, she sought no help for her condition, refused to eat, weakened, and soon died. Eddy eagerly looked forward to her return, asking earnestly, "When *will* I get my Mary back?" When Minnie broke the news of Mary's death to Eddy, she "looked up at me, her hands groping before her, and cried out in a trembling voice, 'Minnie, Minnie, Minnie!' Two big tears rolled down her cheeks and splashed over her dress. She had loved my sister and could not bear to think of her loss at that moment."[66]

There were also moments of lightness, as when the household gathered together on New Year's Day of Eddy's last year, when she read from the Gospel of John and then *Science and Health,* after which her hymn "Mother's Evening Prayer" and several others were sung. Then Eddy gave them all her blessing, calling them back shortly to read an impromptu poem she had just written for the occasion. The next month she gathered them together and said, "Home is not a place, it is a power. Going home is doing right. If you cannot make a home here you cannot anywhere. I am glad all of you . . . are going with me homeward, and we will all meet there."

Now, when a member of the household had to leave for a time, she sometimes cried and welcomed him or her back with tender solicitude. In her own way, she was feeling the impact of Jesus' words which she had twice quoted in her published writings, "whosoever shall do the will of my Father which is in heaven, the same is my brother, and sister, and mother."[67]

While Eddy could always be demanding of household workers, more characteristically in her later years she became touchingly grateful to them. Shortly before she died she called one of the workers into her study just before her evening meal to express her gratitude for her home and those who were caring for it, saying how much it meant to her to have such a place in which to carry on her work. The month before her death she said to one of them, "I do not want any of you to leave me. When I get attached to a person I stick like a nit." On another occasion she said, "There is a great gulf between old age and middle age,—a second childhood. When a member of my family is absent now I watch and am anxious for his return the same as I did when I was a child."[68]

Speaking of her own age with that degree of objectivity was remarkable. But even more so was the naturalness with which she used a term for the members of her household that a decade before probably would not have occurred to her at all: "my family."

10

"The Outflowing Life of Christianity"

GLORIFYING GOD

IN A SERMON DELIVERED IN BOSTON IN THE EARLY 1880S, LATER REVISED FOR publication in *Miscellaneous Writings*, Eddy declared: "The so-called miracles contained in Holy Writ are neither supernatural nor preternatural; for God is good, and goodness is more natural than evil. The marvelous healing-power of goodness is the outflowing life of Christianity, and it characterized and dated the Christian era."[1]

In some testimonies shared by Christian Scientists, the point of healings was couched mainly in therapeutic terms—that is, in terms of their benefit to the testifier, who gives gratitude for the blessings conferred by the healing of illness in some form. Eddy's focus was different. Writing in a *Manual* bylaw of the purpose of testimonies, both in church periodicals and those given spontaneously in Wednesday evening church meetings, she gave priority to testimonies, not as a "mere rehearsal of blessings," but as a way of glorifying God and scaling "the pinnacle of praise."[2]

Eddy saw healing as less a therapy than an act of worship. In her writings, the metaphysics and theology that empower Christian Science healing proceed from the biblical impulse to worship, magnify, and glorify the one God. This spirit is emphasized throughout her works. As Eddy expressed it in *Science and Health*: "Mind is the grand creator, and there can be no power except that which is derived from Mind. If Mind was first chronologically, is first potentially, and must be first eternally, then give to Mind the glory, honor, dominion, and power everlastingly due its holy name."[3]

An example of a healing in which the emphasis distinctly falls on glorifying God is an account of an incident at Pleasant View in 1905. The reminiscence of George Kinter, Eddy's secretary at the time, tells of a severe illness that affected her, involving acute pain throughout her body from the waist up, along with fever, chills, nausea, and vomiting. She requested her staff one by one to treat her, but the condition grew worse over a thirty-six hour period. She then appealed to Kinter, asking if, after forty years of work for the cause, she must endure "such indescribable suffering." Could she not be healed? "Yes," Kinter answered, "and by God's good grace, you shall be." Sitting near her in a chair, he began a treatment he knew "*must* prove effective":

> I recall even now, quite vividly, my mental process. It came to me that there need be no fear, because God was a fact, a present reality, and that inasmuch as God dwells in heaven, then wherever God is, is heaven or harmony, and that as in heaven there is no sin, sickness, nor death, so there is none here. All *is* harmony, and the false claim of distressful suffering for Mrs. Eddy is a lie. God, omnipresent Love, is the fact, and divine Love is the liberator. She is free and she knows it.

Eddy's response, Kinter related, was immediate. She declared that she was free and well, then said, " 'Thank God! Oh thank the dear loving Father, *I am* healed! . . . Isn't it glorious. O, give thanks unto the Lord, for He is good.' Then she recited Psalm after Psalm, and rapturously reiterated her gratitude." Calling in the staff to share the good news, she walked easily to her usual evening seat on a swing where "she spent the entire evening, praising God for His goodness to her" and saying, " 'God *is* here! This *is* heaven, and we all know it now, don't we dear ones! Don't let us ever forget it again.' "[4]

Kinter's treatment was succinctly stated. But it included the key elements that go into healing prayer as Eddy described it. It began with a real God described as present fact. It challenged fear on the basis of his presence, and the presence of his heavenly kingdom, not just in a far-off realm, but here and now. On this basis it also challenged the appearance of evil and suffering as a reality "out there," a necessity to which one must submit. It recognized the appearance of "suffering," but identified this suffering as a temporary, false impression that has no staying power or authority. Kinter affirmed that Love's presence has an immediate, liberating, and healing effect. He therefore expected a change in what appeared to be a severe condition of suffering—in other words, a healing—and in this account, the healing occurred.

"I'M ASKING YOU, THE READER, TO TAKE PART"

The purpose of the church that Eddy and her students founded in 1879 was to restore "the marvelous healing-power of goodness" to contemporary Christianity. To revive the warmth and power of early Christianity was the motive of other American religious denominations as well—the way in which many Protestant groups defined their animating purpose. To the founders of the Disciples of Christ, this meant restoring the patterns of worship in the early church. To Baptists, it meant a return to the unchallenged authority of the Bible and the baptism of believers. To Methodists, it meant a fresh emphasis on the role of love in Christian life, the recovery of "living powers of refreshment" of apostolic Christianity. To Pentecostals at the beginning of the twentieth century, it meant the fresh outpouring of the Holy Spirit, including speaking in tongues, that marked the Day of Pentecost and the revival of apostolic healing as well. Yet none of these denominations took the healing work of the early church as their benchmark indication of the primitive Christianity that needed to be restored. To Eddy, however, her church was the only one that accepted the Gospel in its completeness. In her words from an undated memorandum: "Christ's seamless garment is rent in twain & one church accepts a portion of this garment & rejects another portion thereof. . . . Shall the church be accounted Christless or unchristian who accepts the entire teachings of Christ, demonstrates them in part & demands their entire proof in demonstration?"[5]

It seemed virtually axiomatic to Eddy that the power of Christ must be present for Christians to experience today. Nowhere was this belief more eloquently expressed by another than in the words of her adversary Mark Twain on Christian Science:

> The thing back of it is wholly gracious and beautiful: the power, through loving mercifulness and compassion, to heal fleshly ills and pains and griefs—*all*—with a word, with a touch of the hand! This power was given by the Saviour to the Disciples, and to *all* the converted. All—every one. It was *exercised* for generations afterwards. . . . These things are true, or they are not. If they were true seventeen and eighteen and nineteen centuries ago it would be difficult to satisfactorily explain why or how or by what argument that power should be non-existent in Christians now.[6]

Twain's words echo a point Eddy herself made repeatedly, as when she wrote in *Science and Health:* "Christians are under as direct orders now, as they were then, to be Christlike, to possess the Christ-spirit, to follow the Christ-example, and to heal the sick as well as the sinning." In that book—especially in the chapter "Atonement and Eucharist"— Eddy maintained that only by obedience to Jesus' orders can contemporary Christians participate in the meaning of his sacrifice on humanity's behalf. "It is the living Christ, the practical Truth," she wrote, "which makes Jesus 'the resurrection and the life' to all who follow him in deed."[7]

Eddy gave special emphasis to this obedience in the very way she structured the penultimate revision of *Science and Health*, published in 1902. The change in the character of *Science and Health* in this revision was one of the most far-reaching that had gone into any of the five major revisions of the book up to that point. Changes in the landmark fiftieth edition of 1891 had been substantial. But they were largely textual, clarifying Eddy's meaning, adding a significant amount of new material, and smoothing out her syntax. The major change in the 1902 revision was structural, involving an important rearrangement of the chapters at the beginning of the book and the addition of a new chapter at the end.

The last edition before the 1902 revision had begun, like those preceding it for eleven years, with the chapter "Science, Theology, Medicine." The new arrangement of 1902 brought forward to the beginning of the book the chapters on "Prayer" and "Atonement and Eucharist" that had formerly been in the last half of the book. The 1902 revision concluded with a hundred-page chapter called "Fruitage," establishing through multiple examples how spiritual reformation and healing have now become part of present Christian experience by "the perusal or study of this book."[8] (The same chapter appears in the 1907 revision, though with a different selection of testimonies.)

This permanent change in the structure of *Science and Health* has a crucial role in shaping the overall character of the book and its effect upon readers. By beginning the book with the chapters "Prayer" and "Atonement and Eucharist," Eddy establishes at the outset the Christian character and purpose of Christian Science. These chapters become the gateway through which one must pass to understand her teaching as a whole. "Prayer" and "Atonement and Eucharist" immediately focus the reader's attention on the spiritual transformation the book was intended to inspire—on the godliness gained from genuine prayer and on what it means to abide in the spirit of the living Christ.

Healing becomes the fruit of this godliness, rather than the reason for seeking to attain it. When Eddy named the last chapter "Fruitage," she was employing one of those biblically resonant words which, along with direct scriptural quotations and references, occur on virtually every page of her writings. The term "Fruitage" harkens back to Jesus' words to his disciples at the Last Supper in the Gospel of John: "He that abideth in me, and I in him, the same bringeth forth much fruit: for without me ye can do nothing. . . . Herein is my Father glorified, that ye bear much fruit; so shall ye be my disciples."[9]

The Christian, salvific purpose of healing in Christian Science was clearly grasped by the German historian Karl Holl. Rejecting the view that healing in Christian Science is only a therapy, Holl sees it as simple obedience to Jesus' "explicit command" that his followers "should imitate his great works." Eddy, he wrote, "feels called to rouse dormant Christendom and to restore the original, the whole Gospel." Healing is effected, not through human will, but through "practical godliness." Only through true prayer, "a silent yielding of self to God, an ever closer relationship to God, until His omnipresence and love are felt effectively by man," will evil collapse for man "into its own nothingness" and the fear that gives rise to disease be cast out by divine Love.[10]

As Holl recognized, physical healing is not the be-all and end-all of Christian Science, even if it remains its most conspicuous and publicly identifiable practical outcome. In most cases, those who became Eddy's followers came to Christian Science initially for physical healing. This was entirely in accord with her expectation and intent. Yet some Christian Scientists channeled Eddy's teaching into a narrow utilitarianism, a practical problem solver tailored to human use. In this way, the injunction "use your Christian Science" became something of a shibboleth in the movement, as if metaphysical concepts were to be applied for the sole purpose of solving physical problems and other human ills.[11]

While Eddy spoke of "the marvelous healing-power of goodness" as "the outflowing life of Christianity," she never confined healing to the cure of physical ailments. "The emphatic purpose of Christian Science," she wrote, "is the healing of sin; and this task, sometimes, may be harder than the cure of disease; because, while mortals love to sin, they do not love to be sick." Nor were healings so much miracles in the conventional sense of the term as the natural and inevitable results of a Christianity that is truly *alive*. "The life of Christ Jesus," stated Eddy, "was not miraculous, but it was indigenous to his spirituality,—the good soil wherein the seed of Truth springs up and bears much fruit."[12]

Her primary focus in *Science and Health* lay in developing the meaning of that spirituality—its opposition to materialism in every form, its great cost and demands, and the promise that meeting these demands holds for the renewal of Christianity. The arrangement of the chapters of *Science and Health* in the 1902 revision demonstrated through its very structure that, for its author, the book was far from a merely theoretical work to be examined and put back on the shelf. In the words of playwright Horton Foote about *Science and Health*, "It is not an indulgent work at all. It's not a work of ego. It's a very practical work. It's a work that says, 'Here it is. I'm asking you, the reader, to take part.'"[13]

"A STRUGGLE FOR ITS DEMONSTRATION"

It may appear that Eddy placed the chapters "Prayer" and "Atonement and Eucharist" at the beginning of the book for tactical reasons, since they dwelt on issues already familiar to its Christian readers. But if these chapters had the potential for moving such readers the most, they also moved her the most, because they were closer to the quick of what she was all about as a Christian thinker. The Reverend Richard Rust recalled that when he met with her at Pleasant View in 1902, he suggested that she make plain to others that she was still clinging to the old-time religion of the Bible. "Why, that," replied Eddy in the kindliest of tones, "is exactly what I am doing!"[14]

This point becomes especially apparent in the chapter "Christian Science Practice" that contains extensive instructions on mental treatment—the *do's* and *don'ts* that Eddy sees as helpful in praying for the sick, along with useful approaches to be taken in various kinds of cases. In the major fiftieth edition of *Science and Health* published in 1891, Eddy opened the chapter on "Christian Science Practice," not with technical advice on healing, but with a six-page meditation on the story from the gospel of Luke about the repentant sinner who washed Jesus' feet with her tears. Eddy thus addresses at the outset of the chapter the great need for the spiritual transformation of the practitioner—his or her growth in the Christliness, humility, and love that she saw as the most essential factor in the healing practice.[15]

Eddy's student Annie Dodge caught the point completely in an article for the *Journal* in 1908 entitled "Lowliness of Heart," for which Eddy warmly commended her. Speaking of Jesus' "boundless love and compassion for sinners," she wrote: "As an expression of his matchless love for humanity, his self-sacrifice, he became the servant of all, working for and saving all mankind. He made nothing of self, and all of God, serving Him unceasingly."

Then, speaking of the woman who won Jesus' forgiveness after bathing his feet with her tears, Dodge wrote, "It requires great Christian grace and lowliness of heart to acknowledge, or confess, one's sins, for by so doing one acknowledges the nothingness of the self that claims it can sin, and the allness of God, good, divine Love, in whom is no sin! All true lowliness of heart means the exaltation of the divine Principle, Love! Thus self disappears and unselfish love takes its place!"[16]

This, for Eddy, is the spiritual quickening that makes the work of the practitioner possible and effective. "If you fail to succeed in any case," she wrote elsewhere in *Science and Health*, "it is because you have not demonstrated the life of Christ, Truth, more in your own life,—because you have not obeyed the rule and proved the Principle of divine Science."[17] Only after this does she go on to define the method and rules for Christian Science practice. "Suffer no claim of sin or of sickness to grow upon the thought," she counseled. "When the body is supposed to say, 'I am sick,' never plead guilty." "Rise in the strength of Spirit to resist all that is unlike good." "Maintain the facts of Christian Science,— that Spirit is God, and therefore cannot be sick; that what is termed matter cannot be sick; that all causation is Mind, acting through spiritual law. Then hold your ground with the unshaken understanding of Truth and Love, and you will win."[18]

To maintain these facts often requires what Eddy calls "argument," that is, holding to the facts of being, God's goodness and allness, and the patient's perfection in his sight, and denying the validity and necessity of every evidence to the contrary. This process of argument, she asserted, does not in itself heal. In speaking to students about her own early healing work, she often said that she did not employ argument but turned to God with such a complete conviction of his presence and allness that the patient was healed. When William Rathvon read to Eddy an experience from the *Sentinel* of a Christian Scientist who was healed by declaring his divine sonship, she said, "No such experiences ever came to me. I reached the result without the intermediate steps." But her followers, she found, could not yet heal in this way, and thus needed the process of arguments as "reminders"—a useful discipline to prevent fear from dominating the human mind and to align thought with the power of divine Mind, which is the healing factor in all cases. In her words, "Remember that the letter and mental argument are only human auxiliaries to aid in bringing thought into accord with the spirit of Truth and Love, which heals the sick and the sinner."[19]

Gaining and maintaining this spirit she saw as the primary factor that breathes life into the rules for healing. However important it is to be well-versed in the rules that must govern Christian Science practice— and Eddy held this to be very important indeed—obedience must be conjoined with the spirit of love and Christliness in the healer. If this spiritual affection is absent, the practitioner lacks "that recognition of infinite Love which alone confers the healing power."[20] Only through this recognition, she maintained, can the fear that is the primary causal factor of disease be dissolved.

Eddy did not take the view that disease arises from fear alone, adding that it can also be occasioned by ignorance or sin. Nor did she maintain that one must entertain a specific fear of a specific disease in order to feel the effects of fear. If not alert, she said, we can be influenced by the concern of others for our welfare—for example, the fear of a mother for her child, by the general sense of anxiety occasioned by the belief that we are mortal and therefore always at risk of danger from accidents, infection, or other adverse environmental influences. In many instances, however, individuals do either consciously or unconsciously harbor specific fears of some sort, whether of hereditary disease, the recurrence of an illness, or coming down with an illness that has attracted popular attention. "A new name for an ailment," she wrote ironically but with a serious point, "affects people like a Parisian name for a novel garment. Every one hastens to get it."[21]

The answer to the problem posed by fear, she held, does not lie in repressing it but in uprooting it through the power of Love. In a number of places in her writings, she quoted from I John the passage "There is no fear in love; but perfect love casteth out fear," adding at one point, "Here is a definite and inspired proclamation of Christian Science." The Love that motivates the healer, she said, dispels fear by helping to dissolve the root belief that supports all fear: that we are mortals separate from God and his care, and therefore subject to conditions that can destroy our health and well-being. She instructed those who would heal through Christian Science to always begin their treatment "by allaying the fear of patients. Silently reassure them as to their exemption from disease and danger." The real work of the healer is to "leave self, the sense material, for the sense spiritual," and thus "become imbued with divine Love that casts out all fear."[22]

Underlying all of Eddy's instructions for Christian Science practice is her bedrock contention that because Mind and Spirit are all, "there is no life, intelligence or substance in matter." This is the element in her teaching that both Christian Scientists and non-Christian Scientists often find most difficult to reckon with. But Eddy regarded it as fundamental. As she once put it in counseling a student, "Do you find any difficulty in healing? If so strike for the higher sense of the *nothingness of matter.*" Why did Eddy consider this point of such basic importance? In "Christian Science Practice" she explained, "Admit the existence of matter, and you admit that mortality [and therefore disease] has a foundation in fact. Deny the existence of matter, and you can destroy the belief in material conditions."[23]

An article from a recent church periodical usefully enlarges on the meaning of Eddy's understanding of the nature of matter and its relation to Christian Science treatment:

Christian Science treatment could not possibly heal as it does if everything were as solidly material as it appears. But since it isn't, and what we see and experience so vividly and sometimes painfully is a subjective

mental impression, this fear and false impression about God and His man
can be changed by the omnipotence of divine Mind.

Numerous instances of healing, in which so-called material disease
does not follow its supposedly natural course after Christian Science
treatment has been introduced to the case, help to make this more apparent. Malaria, typhoid fever, cancer, pulmonary tuberculosis, for example,
have been arrested and healed in this way. Such experiences along with
others, the author concludes, lead "thought to become more willing to
explore the possibility that the impression of matter ruling and deter-
mining all is not accurate."[24]

For Eddy, the healer is never dealing with matter as such because
there *is* no matter as such. The question that one giving Christian Science
treatment needs to ask, therefore, is not primarily about the physical
condition of the patient, but rather about the nature, source, and effects
of the beliefs about body the patient is entertaining. Eddy instructed
the healer to deal with these beliefs, to establish the truth that the
apparent material condition appears to hide, and to treat the patient's
mind "to be Christly." The bodily condition, she insisted, will inevitably
correspond to change in thought that the healer's work has effected—
not through the healer's mentality, but through the operation of Truth
to which it bears witness. In the preface to *Science and Health,* she wrote
that physical healing in Christian Science is not "a phase of the action
of the human mind" but "results now, as in Jesus' time, from the operation of divine Principle, before which sin and disease lose their reality
in human consciousness and disappear as naturally and as necessarily
as darkness gives place to light and sin to reformation."[25]

Christian Science, Eddy also wrote, "excludes the human mind as
a spiritual factor in the healing work." Healing prayer, in her understanding, does not occur through the ability of one mind to impress
itself upon another, through the projection of will, or through metaphysical expertise. It occurs when the healer becomes transparent to
the power of Truth and Love, which alone heals. Healing in this sense
flows from the grace of God, which Eddy once defined as "the effect of
God understood." The true spiritual healer is always appealing and
yielding to divine resources outside of himself or herself. Hence Eddy's
counsel, "Hold perpetually this thought—that it is the spiritual idea,
the Holy Ghost and Christ, which enables you to demonstrate, with
scientific certainty, the rule of healing, based upon its divine Principle,
Love, underlying, overlying, and encompassing all true being."[26]

Spiritual healing, Eddy believed, had continued for several centuries after Jesus in the early Christian era—not because Christians

understood how healing was accomplished—but because the continuing power of Christ's living presence was so vivid that it brought forth the faith through which the healing was done. The purpose of Christian Science was to make explicit how the same healing power that so vitalized early Christianity was available to Christians in the present. For Eddy, this required that healings happen, but it also required that the basis of these healings be understood in a way that made the healing effect rational and repeatable. Describing the three years that followed her discovery of Christian Science in 1866, she wrote: "I knew the Principle of all harmonious Mind-action to be God, and that cures were produced in primitive Christian healing by holy, uplifting faith; but I must know the Science of this healing, and I won my way to absolute conclusions through divine revelation, reason, and demonstration."[27]

Lee Z. Johnson, archivist of the Mother Church for nearly thirty years, observed that other churches spoke of revelation and reason as the basis of their theology and church life. But, he said, "invariably, they will add tradition. She didn't. She put demonstration in, meaning that the works that her students did were to carry the day. . . . It was a demand to challenge the basic materialism that she saw as the plague of our times." This was a demand that Eddy made on herself especially during the several years immediately following what she saw as the revelatory breakthrough that came to her in early 1866. Eddy struggled for this demonstration throughout the remaining forty-five years of her life. But she did so in a particularly concentrated way in the first few years after the initial discovery. She saw her healing work as a phase of the spiritual breakthrough that had occurred in her life—the essential act that confirmed its truth. In a defense of her teaching published in 1898 when the healing practice of Christian Science was under sharp public attack, Eddy enumerated the kinds of cases she had healed during these early years, including consumption in its last stages, diphtheria, cancer, blindness, and pneumonia, as well as "hopeless organic diseases of almost every kind."[28]

These healings did not, of course, occur in a context that yielded hard medical evidence according to present-day standards. The healing experience for which one piece of significant historical evidence does exist, however, was the earliest and most consequential of them all—her recovery from the effects of a severe accident in early February 1866. No fully competent medical diagnosis of such internal injuries as she may have sustained was probably even available then, and it is certainly impossible to determine the question with any exactitude now. Some forty years after the event, the attending physician, Dr. Alvin M. Cushing, said in an affidavit published in the Milmine/Cather series in *McClure's*, then in the biography drawn from it, that he never believed her injuries were critical. But the *Lynn Weekly Reporter* for Saturday, February 3, 1866, told a different story. It stated that Dr. Cushing "found her injuries to be internal, and of a very serious nature," and that she "was removed to her home in Swampscott yesterday afternoon, though in a very critical condition."[29]

Another healing during this period for which there is some contemporary testimony is that of Eddy's twenty-three-year-old niece, Ellen Pilsbury. When her aunt was summoned back to Sanbornton Bridge, New Hampshire, in 1867, she found Ellen bedridden, in great pain from enteritis, and given up medically. Another of Ellen's aunts, Martha Rand Baker, later described that Eddy, then Mrs. Patterson, entered the room, prayed silently for a few moments, then asked the young woman to rise. Ellen did so, walking across the floor without suffering. The following day she was dressed and ate with her family. On the fourth day she went on a journey of about one hundred miles. "Such a change," recalled Martha Rand Baker, "came over the household. We all felt . . . 'the angel of the Lord appeared and glory shone round.' "[30]

Some other accounts of Eddy's healing work have a vaguely apocryphal air.[31] At the same time, such evidence as does exist cannot easily be dismissed. In its own historical context, it more than satisfied a growing number of people that spiritual healing as Eddy taught and practiced it was effective. She found, however, that to invest her major efforts in the work of healing was not the most appropriate way for her to advance the interests of Christian Science. To do the latter meant teaching others how to heal, which in turn required her to refine the statement of her teaching—its theology, metaphysics, and rules for practice. While she turned most cases over to students beginning around the time that *Science and Health* was first published, she was never wholly removed from the healing work either and continued throughout her life, in Robert Peel's words, "to reach out in impulsive help in emergency situations."[32]

Accounts by those who knew her from her decade in Lynn through her last years at Chestnut Hill speak of healings she accomplished on an intermittent basis, simply in the process of daily living. Laura Lathrop recounted a healing she had in 1886 when visiting Eddy in her home. Lathrop had long suffered from a serious hereditary heart condition that limited her ability to move freely. When Lathrop saw Eddy, then in her mid-sixties, run up a flight of stairs, she made the effort to do the same, although she had not made such an exertion for twenty-four years. Reaching the top of the stairs, she was seized with such a strong attack that it "seemed as though an iron hand gripped my heart and was squeezing the very life out of it." Eddy, she recalled, gave her one glance, then "spoke aloud to the error. We are told that when Jesus healed the sick, he spake as one having authority. On this occasion Mrs. Eddy also spoke as one having authority." Subsequently Lathrop was seized with one other attack which lasted but a moment, then found herself entirely free from the heart condition from which she had suffered so long—so free that she ran up stairs numerous times in the years that followed with no ill effects whatever.[33]

As Testimony

Eddy was far from believing that the healing practice was reserved for a few saintly and super-religious types, or that a genuine student of Christian Science needed to be an intellectual. If individuals were rightly motivated—if they earnestly sought to live morally, to love God and follow Jesus, to study and practice what her writings contained—then they had every reason to expect that they could both heal and be healed.

There were among the ranks of Christian Scientists a number of individuals so moved and shaken by their involvement in the new faith that they were willing to put everything on the line to hasten its advancement. Many such early workers hardly appeared to be very prepossessing or even unusually "religious" people in the conventional sense of the term. There were some distinguished individuals in the early ranks of the movement: judges, lawyers, scholars, military men, former ministers, and medical doctors. But far more typical—to take several examples from those who worked in Eddy's household—were people like Anna Machacek, George Kinter, John Salchow, and Minnie Weygandt, none of whom would have been particularly noteworthy for their accomplishments outside of their labors in Christian Science. What united them was the fact that they were among those to whom Eddy committed the pages of *Science and Health*—"honest seekers for Truth." When they believed they found the Truth they sought, they also found their spiritual capacities aroused to such an extent that they were unexpectedly plunged into a whole new life.

In Eddy's language, they became caught up in "the outflowing life of Christianity." And it was the lives of these early Christian Scientists—their healing work, and the effect of their testimonies of healing—that was largely responsible for the enormous growth of the movement beginning in the last decade of the nineteenth century. In a variety of contexts—from testimony meetings to the denomination's religious periodicals and hearings before state legislatures—Christian Scientists reported healings that, unless the facts involved were made out of whole cloth, could not reasonably be dismissed.

As Thomas Johnsen notes in his 1986 article, "Christian Scientists and the Medical Profession: A Historical Perspective": "Few critics charged that testimonies published in the church's periodicals were dishonest, but from a medical perspective, they were hardly written with laboratory exactitude. By their nature they involved life situations rather than clinical case studies." Traditional medical practitioners were, therefore, inclined to attribute reported healings to a variety of factors, among them "time, suggestion, *vis medicatrix naturae,* the placebo effect, misdiagnosis, the power of will." In spite of a widespread medical effort to debunk Christian Science healing, the evidence that it actually occurred was sufficiently strong and compelling that it would simply not go away. In many instances, the cases that fell to Christian Science were those that medicine had failed to cure. When a practitioner was brought in as a last resort, the disease had often reached a critical or sometimes terminal stage. Without exaggeration, Alfred Farlow wrote in 1902 that the majority of Christian Scientists "are recruits from the gravyards."[34]

On abstract theoretical grounds, the case against spiritual healing could sound convincing. But when specific instances of healing were presented in detail and in a credible way, the phenomenon of spiritual healing was not so easily dismissed. One comprehensive testimony published in the *Journal* for September 1901 attests to the healing work accomplished during the period in which the growth of the movement was rapidly accelerating. It was submitted by a practitioner from Fitchburg, Massachusetts, John W. Keyes, D. M. D. With twenty years' experience in dental surgery and a previously "fixed belief in the power of material medication," Dr. Keyes wrote knowledgeably of the cases he had witnessed in his subsequent healing practice in Christian Science:

> Memory furnishes the following classes of diseases . . . which . . . in my own ten years of exclusively Christian Science practice, I have seen yield to the power of Truth as taught in that marvelous book, "Science and Health with Key to the Scriptures:" Asthma, appendicitis, Bright's disease, catarrh, cataract, constipation, cancer, diarrhoea, dyspepsia, diabetes, erysipelas, eczema, epulis, fear, fever (typhoid and malarial), gravel, hemorrhoids, heart disease, inguinal hernia, insanity, liquor, opium, and tobacco habit, the grip, neuralgia, nervous prostration, obstetrics, polypus,

nasi, prolapsus uteri, pneumonia, pulmonary consumption, rupture of perineum, rheumatism, sciatica, shortened and withered limb, tumors, (cystic and fibroid), tonsilitis, and venereal diseases.[35]

"In many instances," Keyes continued, "the patients were considered by both the previous medical attendant and friends as past remedy." One such instance was recounted in the *Sentinel* for 1908 by Dr. Edmund F. Burton, who had for many years been a respected physician and surgeon. In 1902 he discovered that he had tuberculosis of the lungs, abandoned his medical practice in Chicago, and moved to Arizona, though the prognosis was that he could live for only several months. He had become heavily reliant upon opium and alcohol to control the symptoms of the disease and experimented with hypnotism. After this, Burton's account continues,

> . . . my physical and mental condition grew rapidly worse, until within a few weeks there was no reason left. After a period of entire irresponsibility, lasting about a week and followed by unconsciousness for something more than forty-eight hours, a number of physicians who had known me for several months, in consultation pronounced me incurable, and told my friends that I had from a few days to a few weeks to live.
>
> During the evening following this verdict a lady suggested with much trepidation the advisability of calling a Christian Science practitioner, and my wife consented that this be done, not with a feeling that anything could be accomplished, but in the same spirit of desperation in which any other harmless although probably useless thing would have been allowed. A practitioner came and remained with me three hours. At the end of the first hour I was sleeping quietly, and when I woke about eight o'clock in the morning it was with a clear mind and the absolute conviction, which has not changed since, that I was free and well. . . . So far as I know there is no instance in medical literature of the recovery of any one taking the amount of these drugs which I was taking up to the time referred to. And to one who knows the state of the nervous system and of the digestive organs which exists in such cases, it is stating it mildly to say that the most remarkable feature of the cure was that there was no period of convalescence. From the time of my waking on the morning following the treatment there was no nervousness or twitching, sleep was natural and quiet, appetite healthy, digestive functions all in good working order, and mind clear and composed.[36]

Taking up the study of *Science and Health*, Burton said he struggled for a time to reconcile his medical perspective with what he was learning from Christian Science. "I was forced by my own healing," he wrote, "to the conclusion that there was a power in Christian Science of which I had never taken account." Further experiences confirmed his conclusion:

> I myself have seen a broken bone and dislocated joint restored to normal condition and function within a few hours, and that without manipulation, splint, or bandage of any kind. I have seen a child of five years freed instantly from a congenital deformity without touch of hand or instrument. I have seen a woman, who, according to the verdict of the best medical talent, was within a few hours of death from cancer, restored to good health and spirits within a few days.
>
> Christian Science takes away from us nothing but ignorance and dependence upon falsities. It shows us that we have been making ourselves the slaves of the things for which we have been spending our lives, that we have belonged to them and not they to us. It is a thing to be lived. It is the way to live, the scientific way to live, the only way to live right and the way in which all men sooner or later must come to live, for it is the Christ-way, and at the name of Jesus every knee shall bow, and every tongue confess that Jesus Christ is Lord. It is the Science of being, the Science of Life. It is the truth that makes men free.[37]

Accounts of healing in the early literature of Christian Science went well beyond physical healing *per se*. A number of them spoke of instances where Christian Scientists were saved from the effects of accidents and natural disasters, including earthquakes, fires, and floods. In 1900, for example, the *Sentinel* carried the account of a woman relating how her family had survived the ravages of the hurricane which flooded Galveston, Texas, and nearly wiped out the entire city in one of the worst natural disasters in American history.

"The house, "she said," was rocking like a cradle, and it seemed almost beyond human belief that it could withstand such a terrific wind for even a single moment." Then the house came off its foundations, and the family huddled within it was in total darkness, with water at waist level. When the water reached chin level and all the furniture was floating, the account continues, for "just one brief moment fear tried to take possession of me, but its sway was brief, for almost with the next breath the thought came to me: 'Underneath are the Father's everlasting arms.' " The family found it possible to stand on the kitchen stove, which they did while continuing their prayers. They held to biblical promises such as the words of Isaiah: "Fear thou not; for I am with thee; be not dismayed; for I am thy God." They also "silently tried to realize God's Allness and to know that 'He holds the wind in His fist.' " The testifier wrote that the whole experience lasted from five in the afternoon until half past two the next morning. Once the waters subsided, the family saw that the houses around theirs "were piled up in mountains of wreckage," while their home, though torn from its foundations, remained intact. The account ends by saying that they had survived because they "had placed our safety in our Father's hands."[38]

Such accounts were by no means rarities, yet the practice of Christian Science healing could not be said to have been viewed by the public as a parade of unquestioned triumphs. In its earlier years as in more recent times, widely reported failures were often given extensive attention in the press by opponents of Christian Science and tended to hold the spotlight more than the myriad examples of effective healing that largely accounted for the movement's rapid early growth. Where successes caused a ripple, failures often caused a wave.

Failures in Christian Science practice, particularly in children's cases, sometimes drove communities to a pitch of fury. In 1889 a Christian Scientist in Pierre, South Dakota, described an extreme situation of this sort. The eleven-month-old child of a close friend died after both women had tried to help him through Christian Science treatment. The next morning, wrote the friend, a Methodist minister gathered a crowd on the street and denounced this "pernicious" doctrine, "till the people were infuriated and threatened mob law" against the practitioners. After a town meeting at which the same sentiment prevailed, the two women were informed by a committee that the community wished them to leave town. But the worst suffering that a Christian Scientist in such a case had to endure was not the hostility of the populace but grief and the sense of having failed. Like Twain, the woman whose friend's child had died asked in anguish, "Why this termination?" Unlike Twain, however, the Christian Scientist did not blame God for the failure, but condemned herself. Faith in God was not the question.[39]

Eddy addressed the issue of failures in the practice of Christian Science with frankness. Acknowledging the need for "so-called material pains and material pleasures to pass away, for both are unreal" and for mortals to gain "the true idea and divine Principle of all that really exists," she wrote, "This thought is apprehended slowly, and the interval before its attainment is attended with doubts and defeats as well as triumphs." She herself had too direct an experience of the grim side of human existence to dismiss its vicissitudes out of hand. Yet she did maintain that Christian Science healing practice was defensible, and that its practical worth had been so fully attested that denying its effectiveness outright must be the result of prejudice or ignorance of the facts. "By thousands of well-authenticated cases of healing," she stated in the preface to *Science and Health*, "she and her students have proved the worth of her teachings. These cases for the most part have been abandoned as hopeless by regular medical attendants."[40]

Taken together, the testimonies from the 1902 and 1907 revisions of *Science and Health* alone contain an impressive array of illnesses that were reported as healed through the study of that work. In most instances, the cases had been treated unsuccessfully through standard medical care. As in Keyes's account, another dimension of these testimonies speaks of the moral and spiritual transformation wrought in the lives of testifiers, including freedom from alcoholism, addiction to tobacco, and infidelity, as well as from mental darkness, atheism, and despair over life. Repeatedly in these accounts, healings are portrayed not just as physical cures but in much larger terms as essentially redemptive acts.

"To my darkened thought," said one of them about his mentality before embracing Christian Science, "man lived and died in matter, and then nothing—darkness—void. . . . My thought is now being satisfied in the contemplation of infinite Good." Many others spoke of the changed view of the Bible they gained through the study of *Science and Health*. Before coming to Christian Science, said one writer, he was "very cynical and disbelieving in regard to . . . God and religion. . . . I have found a God whom I can love and worship with my whole heart, and I now read my Bible with interest and understanding." "The Bible, which I regarded with suspicion," another testifier wrote, "has become my guide, and Christianity has become a sweet reality, because the Christian Science textbook has indeed been a 'Key to the Scriptures' and has breathed through the Gospel pages a sweet sense of harmony."[41]

One testimony in particular has become something of a classic in the literature of Christian Science. It tells of a moment of spiritual transformation that proved decisive in the life of a Massachusetts woman. Entitled "Born Again," the testimony relates how by the time she was twenty the testifier came to believe that though God "probably existed in some remote place," it was "impossible to connect Him with my present living." Then came many years of sorrow and the breakdown of her health, until reading *Science and Health*, given to her by a friend, wrought a complete transformation. But she still found herself looking back to be assured that the suffering that had plagued her had really gone. Seeking an answer, "I opened Science and Health and these words were before me, 'If God were understood, instead of being merely believed, this understanding would establish health.'" She continues:

> I saw that I must get the right understanding of God! I closed the book and with head bowed in prayer I waited with longing intensity for some

answer. How long I waited I do not know, but suddenly, like a wonder-ful burst of sunlight after a storm, came clearly this thought, "Be still, and know that I am God." I held my breath—deep into my hungering thought sank the infinite meaning of that "I." All self-conceit, egotism, selfishness, everything that constitutes the mortal "I," sank abashed out of sight. I trod, as it were, on holy ground. Words are inadequate to con-vey the fulness of that spiritual uplifting, but others who have had simi-lar experiences will understand.

From that hour I have had an intelligent consciousness of the ever-presence of an infinite God who is only good.[42]

HARBINGERS?

If the "healing-power of goodness is the outflowing life of Christi-anity," as Eddy once wrote, then it was not surprising that its reappear-ance would meet the same resistance that was accorded early Christianity. "Of old the cross was truth's central sign, and it is to-day," she wrote. "The modern lash is less material than the Roman scourge, but it is equally as cutting. Cold disdain, stubborn resistance, opposition from church, state laws, and the press, are still the harbingers of truth's full-orbed appearing."[43] A harbinger is a forerunner of someone or something announcing the approach of that which is to come. In this sense, Eddy took the very resistance aroused by Christian Science as a sign of its strength and efficacy.

In her analysis, opposition to Christian Science healing practice was especially intense because of a de facto alliance between the two "systems" of religion and medicine. There were those in the Protestant world who looked at Christian Science as a welcome sign of a revolt against materialism or saw in it a valuable reminder of the larger part spiritual healing needed to play in modern Christian life. A Baptist cler-gyman in Brooklyn, for example, wrote in 1897, "They tell me that the same Master who commanded us to baptize, also commanded us to heal. I do not know how to answer them." Similarly, a Presbyterian minister in Denver told his congregation in 1907, "The atonement covers the whole nature of man, and the failure of the church to see it has been a very serious mistake."[44] But these were minority reports. The predomi-nant form of American Protestantism in the early twentieth century was evangelical, and the predominant view of Christian Science in the evangelical world was overwhelmingly hostile and sometimes strident in its expression of this hostility.

Theological strictures against Christian Science multiplied as it became a more vital force in the religious world. The bottom-line as far as many clergymen were concerned revolved around Eddy's denial that God was in any sense the cause of finitude and mortality. Where Eddy declared, "Man is not matter; he is not made up of brain, blood, bones, and other material elements," the Reverend I. M. Haldeman in his book *Christian Science in the Light of Holy Scripture* wrote, "This body of flesh and bones is the most perfect piece of architecture in which life ever dwelt, the most perfect piece of machinery which ever responded to the human will." Where she argues that the verse in Genesis, "The Lord God formed man of the dust of the ground," expresses a false view of creation, the Reverend Henry Varley commented, "Man is declared, so far as his body is concerned, to be formed of matter; he indwells a material house, a body."[45]

Roman Catholic critics of Christian Science had reason to find Eddy's denial of the objective reality of matter and the validity of sense testimony even more grating than did her Protestant opponents. Although the tone of their comments was generally cooler and more rational, their opposition was no less uncompromising. The theology of St. Thomas Aquinas, which is basic to Catholic doctrine, holds that human reason based upon sense testimony can accurately inform us of earthly realities, but must leave to supernatural revelation the disclosure of ultimate matters of faith. In this light one can better understand the opposition of Catholics to the metaphysics of Christian Science. The Reverend Louis Lambert, defining common sense testimony as the united report of two or more of the five senses, wrote: "We conclude, then, that the common sense of mankind has not erred, and that it is one of the best authorities, in its own field, that the individual man can rest his convictions on; it is next to divine positive revelation and the divinely commissioned teacher of it."[46]

To Eddy, such assertions represented a subtle form of materialism unwittingly embraced by exponents of the Gospel. It was just at this point, she argued, that conventional medicine and orthodox theology joined hands. In making this linkage, Eddy echoed a point made frequently by Quimby, who saw physicians and clergymen as fostering needless and negative opinions that held the sick in bondage to disease. Eddy, if anything, saw this alliance in even broader terms: "Both anatomy and theology define man as both physical and mental, and place mind at the mercy of matter for every function, formation, and manifestation."[47]

For Eddy, it was this unholy alliance of anatomy and theology that explained why spiritual healing had largely disappeared from Christianity. "The theology of Christian Science includes healing the sick," she wrote. Why, she asked, has Christian healing been lost to Christianity, when "our Master's first article of faith propounded to his students was healing," and when healing was so much a part of early Christianity? "Because our systems of religion are governed more or less by our systems of medicine. . . . Such systems are barren of the vitality of spiritual power, by which material sense is made the servant of Science and religion becomes Christlike."[48] In this way, she believed, orthodox Christianity had unwittingly become to some degree the captive of a materialism it nominally opposed.

An Unlikely Ally

The year 1910 saw the deaths of three of the most notable figures in the United States. On April 21, Mark Twain, crushed by grief, died in his Connecticut home. A few months later, on August 26, the great American philosopher William James succumbed to a heart ailment. Mary Baker Eddy, who was twenty years older than James and fourteen years older than Twain, survived them both, dying in her ninetieth year on December 3.

While Eddy never met either Twain or James, the two men thought well of each other, were companions in the anti-imperialist cause, and maintained a cordial relationship, their paths crossing on several occasions. More important, the common concerns of all three intersected in an uncommon way. Eddy directly challenged the materialism that defined human existence in brute physical terms. Twain was nearly engulfed by materialist currents that he could neither embrace nor find a way to fully resist. James not only rejected materialistic theories conceptually, but made good on his opposition to medical materialism by publicly opposing efforts in Massachusetts to legally stamp out Christian Science healing.

In 1894, the Massachusetts medical profession sponsored a bill requiring that only those with a medical license could practice healing for either mind or body. The bill, which would have affected all non-regular healers, was specifically targeted at Christian Scientists, whose increasing presence in Boston made them conspicuous. Writing to the *Boston Transcript* with specific reference to mind-cure and Christian Science, James declared: "I assuredly hold no brief for any of these healers. . . . But their *facts* are patent and startling; and anything that interferes with the multiplication of such facts, and with our freest opportunity of observing and studying them, will, I believe, be a public calamity."[49]

The bill was tabled—but only temporarily. Four years later, the possible "calamity" against which James had warned took concrete

(1907)

William James, 1907. By
permission of Houghton
Library, Harvard University.

form when the legislature reconsidered the bill and asked James to testify
before the committee considering it. Appearing in a crowded chamber
during the second session of the committee meeting, James declared
that he had "no axes to grind, except the axe of truth, that 'Truth' for
which Harvard University, of which I am an officer, professes to exist."
As a doctor of medicine himself, James well knew the cost to his reputation among others in the medical profession, some of whom he
counted as close friends. "But I cannot look on passively, and I must urge
my point. That point is this: that the Commonwealth of Massachusetts
is not a medical body, has no right to a medical opinion, and should not
dare to take sides in a medical controversy."[50]

James did not underestimate the hostility his testimony aroused.
One of his biographers maintains that he had thus earned the enmity
of the Massachusetts medical profession for the rest of his life. In testifying, James wrote to a friend, "I never did anything that required as
much moral effort in my life. . . . But if Zola and Col. Picquart can face
the whole French army [referring to their roles in the Dreyfus Affair],
can't I face their disapproval?—much more easily than that of my own
conscience!"[51]

James's conscience was in part a matter of fidelity to the views he had developed in his own philosophy and conception of religious experience. His pragmatic theory of truth included the insistence that our concepts and ideas are useful in formulating the meaning of our experiences, but should never limit the experiences that are open to us. In his essay "The Will to Believe," James expressed a conviction that he considered vital enough to italicize: *"a rule of thinking which would absolutely prevent me from acknowledging certain kinds of truth if those kinds of truth were really there, would be an irrational rule."* He was specifically interested in the truths about religion and the cosmos that can be opened through paying serious attention to individual human experiences. Various forms of philosophic idealism championed the reality of a transcendent and ideal Absolute. But James believed that a merely philosophical idealism, however much it affirmed the spiritual dimension of experience, remained so conceptual that it lacks practical consequences. Far more, he believed, could be gained by expanding an empirical approach to experience into what he called "radical empiricism." "Let empiricism once become associated with religion," he wrote, "as hitherto, through some strange misunderstanding, it has been associated with irreligion, and I believe that a new era of religion as well as of philosophy will be ready to begin."[52]

On these grounds, James opposed any form of materialism that on principle excluded religious and mystical experiences as unscientific because they were not measurable in conventional empirical terms. In his seminal book *The Varieties of Religious Experience*, published in 1902, James uses illustrative material drawn of a highly mystical character. But he interprets the meaning of the experiences he draws upon as evidences of the fact *"that the conscious person is continuous with a wider self through which saving experiences come,"* of our actually living in a wider sphere of being than that embraced by our everyday consciousness. As he put it in an essay in *A Pluralistic Universe*, a collection of essays published in 1909, "the believer is continuous, to his own consciousness, at any rate, with a wider self from which saving experiences flow in. . . . We may be in the universe as dogs and cats are in our libraries, seeing the books and hearing the conversation, but having no inkling of the meaning of it all."[53]

Those religious innovators who are most likely to be open to participation in the wider sphere of being, James insists, are usually "twice-born," since they have endured extreme experiences that have resulted in the creation of a new inner person. They are "sick souls" for whom "pity, pain, and fear, and the sentiment of human helplessness" open them up to a new understanding of the meaning of being. The once-born, by contrast, believe that, through exploration of the self as it exists, they can tap into a subconscious self without the transformation that goes with the new or second birth. They become exponents of a "sky-blue" optimistic gospel, or what James also calls the "religion of healthy-mindedness" natural to those temperaments "organically weighted on the side of cheer and fatally forbidden to linger . . . over the darker aspects of the universe."[54]

Making no distinction between Christian Science and mind-cure, James saw Eddy as a purveyor of the gospel of optimism, writing that from the standpoint of her teaching, duty forbids us to pay evil "the compliment even of explicit attention." James was insufficiently acquainted with Eddy's life history to know that she was, if anything, a prime example of what it means to be "twice-born" in precisely his sense of the term. Indeed, in 1859, at one of the low points of her life when the mortgage on her home in North Groton was foreclosed, after asking if "this crushing out of life, of hope, or love [be] Thy *will* O God?" she declared, "Then stay me from above / For my sick soul is darkened unto death."[55]

A further factor is that James's attitude toward mind-cure and Christian Science was probably shaped by Horatio Dresser, at one time his graduate student and an assistant in the philosophy department at Harvard for eight years. The son of Julius Dresser, who had been part of Quimby's inner circle, Horatio Dresser teamed with Woodbury in writing on Christian Science in the *Arena*. He made little if any distinction between Christian Science and mind-cure, or mind-cure and Quimby's thought. By the time Mark Twain published his book *Christian Science* in 1907, however, that distinction had become sufficiently clear to him that he could write: "It is apparent . . . that in Christian Science it is not one man's mind acting upon another man's mind that heals; . . . that the healer's mind performs no office but to convey that force to the patient. . . . Therefore, if these things be true, mental-healing and Science-healing are separate and distinct processes, and no kinship exists between them."[56]

In his 1894 letter to the *Boston Transcript*, James professed to have little comprehension of the theoretical aspects of Christian Science and other methods of nonmedical cure. Nevertheless, his strongly voiced opposition to strictures on spiritual healing based on an *a priori* form of medical materialism reflected the open-mindedness for which he is justly known. In fact, James in 1909 was sufficiently open-minded to seek treatment for his own heart ailment and the depression that accompanied it from Lewis Strang—not, perhaps, the happiest of choices, considering Strang's misbehavior at Pleasant View several years before. James found Strang's twenty-one treatments ineffective. But he attributed this fact to his own failure as one of those who "can't back out of their system of finite prejudices and intellectual scruples, even though in *words* they may admit that there are other ways of living, and more successful ones."[57]

James, however, had already gone beyond mere verbal arguments by putting so much of his personal reputation on the line in defense of irregular forms of healing practice. Few other voices outside the ranks of Christian Scientists, and certainly none so prominent, were raised in public forums as the debate over the practice of Christian Science began to heat up in the legislatures of almost every state in America.

"THE BABE WE ARE TO CHERISH"

In an article from *Miscellaneous Writings*, "The Cry of Christmas-Tide," Eddy wrote: "In different ages the divine idea assumes different forms, according to humanity's needs. In this age it assumes, more intelligently than ever before, the form of Christian healing. This is the babe we are to cherish."[58] Here again, she is using the language of motherhood. The multiple attacks on Christian Science emanating from the world of professional medicine and seconded in the world of theology enlisted her strongest mothering instincts. Indeed, they did so more forcefully than at any time since she confronted clerical opposition and the inroads of mind-cure in the 1880s.

Historian Rennie B. Schoepflin, in his book *Christian Science on Trial: Religious Healing in America*, has graphed articles in medical journals about Christian Science from 1885 to 1925. Between 1890 and 1900, such articles, most of them wholly negative, increased from around twenty per year to an astounding one hundred and seventy, before declining to about forty annually by 1910 and the ensuing decades. It is not clear, he wrote, whether physicians were misinformed in overestimating the influence of Christian Science or "intentionally inflated the figures to exaggerate the Christian Science threat." What is clear is that physicians in the Progressive Era "worked to control the terms of the debate so that Scientists would appear marginal and foolish. Physicians defined Christian Science as a blatant example of the many past and present popular systems of religious and mental healing, quackery, and deceit, each posing a menace to the health and morals of an unwitting public." Noting, too, that physicians depicted the Christian Scientists as "a threat to their own status and income," Schoepflin concluded that physicians "unwittingly displayed both disdain for the public's judgment and anxiety about their own authority."[59]

Protective as she could be when the "babe" of Christian healing was threatened, Eddy's general demeanor toward the medical profession was far from adversarial. She was realistic, saying to a student that the time would come when "materia medica would threaten us with fines, imprisonment, and in every possible way interpose between and hinder Christian Science healing." Nevertheless, she wrote in *Science and Health* that "great respect is due the motives and philanthropy of the higher class of physicians." As the medical assault was getting under way, she wrote to a student that "envy and rivalry [among Christian Scientists] are causing the true Scientists more trouble and retarding our Cause much more than the medical men can."[60]

Eddy also well knew that Christian Scientists sometimes lost cases, that tragedies did occur, and that losses under Christian Science treatment were likely in some instances to come under the glare of public scrutiny. She had experienced one such major loss when her husband, Asa Gilbert Eddy, died in 1882. But she had no doubt that many Christian Scientists were achieving remarkable healing results, often inexplicable according to medical theories of causation. And she counted on the basic fair-mindedness of the public to acknowledge this point. In some cases such acknowledgments were forthcoming. For example, an editorial from the *Haverhill Evening Gazette* for November 11, 1898, observed, "If Christian Scientists are to be condemned for their failure to effect cures in individual instances they must in fairness be given credit for all they accomplish."[61]

The editorial was one among many at the time commenting on the most widely publicized death involving Christian Science treatment up to that point: that of the American novelist and journalist Harold Frederic, who had died in London in October. Frederic was both a distinguished author—his novel *The Damnation of Theron Ware* was something of a minor classic—and a correspondent for the *New York Times*. A sporadic Christian Scientist at best, he remained under the care of physicians during the course of a sudden illness. When informed that his case was hopeless, he asked for treatment from a friend who was a Christian Science practitioner. At the inquest following his death, she and the woman with whom Frederic lived at the time—a Christian Scientist, though not his wife—were indicted for manslaughter by a coroner's jury. When the case came to trial in December, both women were exonerated for lack of any evidence against them, but not before the whole matter had caused a major firestorm in the press in Britain, Canada, and the United States.

While some American newspapers came to the defense of the beleaguered Christian Scientists, Eddy evidently felt a more authoritative response was needed. She therefore wrote a strong defense of her teaching and its practice entitled "To the Christian World," published in the *New York Sun* on December 16 and in the *Concord Evening Monitor* on December 17, and then revised her response for publication in the Christian Science periodicals. Referring specifically to "the cruel attempt to criminate two innocent women and Christian Scientists," she spoke of the case as an instance of outright religious persecution, declaring that "a person's ignorance of Christian Science is a sufficient reason for his silence on the subject; but what can atone for the vulgar denunciation of what a man knows absolutely nothing?" She went on to enumerate the kinds of cases she had healed during the early years of her work in Christian Science and spoke of the "folly" of declaring that Christian Science healing was "limited to imaginary diseases" when "it has healed cases that I assert it were impossible for the surgeon, or *materia medica*, to cure." In concluding, she declared that "ignorance, slang and malice touch not the hem of the garment of Christian Scientists," and that the words in the New York press, "Mrs. Eddy not shaken," were valid.[62]

That she was neither shaken nor intimidated was fully borne out in her response to the next major controversy over the practice of Christian Science. The press coverage of the Frederic case turned out to be a kind of wake-up call to the medical community to move into high gear in its campaign to restrain the practice of Christian Science by law. Three years later a great deal more controversy, if not quite as much damage, was generated by what came to be known as the Brush Will case in New York in 1901. The case began when the sisters and brother of one Helen C. Brush, who died of consumption in July 1900, contested her will on grounds of testamentary incapacity due to the influence of Christian Scientists.

The will left the siblings a token amount, with the major portion of the estate, about $90,000, left to the First Church of Christ, Scientist, of New York City, dominated by Augusta Stetson. In contesting this will, her siblings maintained that she was laboring under insane delusions, one of which was that they were persecuting her because of her religious convictions. The other delusion, they claimed, was the belief in spiritual healing, which they held was *prima facie* evidence of insanity. The court did not agree, maintaining that it was "beyond the scope of a judicial inquiry" to pass upon the truth or falsity of a religious belief or to say that people who hold these religious convictions, however contrary to the beliefs of others, are mentally unsound—a judgment that was cited as precedent six years later by Eddy's lawyer in the Next Friends Suit.[63]

Before the decision was rendered in the Brush Will case, Eddy wrote for the *New York Sunday Journal* a substantial two-thousand word article published on February 21, 1901, under the title "Christian Science Healing Explained and Defended."[64] The piece began with Eddy writing in her most uncompromising mode: "To say that it is sin to ride to church on an electric car would not be more preposterous than to believe that man's Maker is not equal to the destruction of disease germs." After establishing that Christian Scientists scrupulously obey the laws of the land, she couched the underlying issue in the controversy over the Brush Will case in terms of the conflict between spirituality and materialism: "The earthly price of spirituality in religion and medicine at a material age—persecution—and the moral distance between Christianity and materialism precluded his [Jesus'] doctrine, then as now, from finding favor with certain purely human views."

Challenging the claim that reliance on spiritual means for healing is dangerous, she asserted that modes of healing *other* than spiritual means break the First Commandment, "Thou shall have no other gods before me." "Our Master conformed to this law," she wrote, "and instructed his followers, saying, 'He that believeth on me, the works that I do shall he do also.' This is enough." Then, after referring to Jesus' stricture on the lack of faith even in his disciples, she concluded: "Beyond the frail premises of human hypotheses, above the loosening grasp of creeds, the demonstrations of Christian Science stand revealed as practical science. Divine metaphysics is Christ Jesus' revelation of Truth and Love, for which he labored and suffered, then left a legacy to mankind, and which remains the divine standard for the understanding and practice of every man."

Since the mid-1880s, the *Journal* had reported sporadic efforts to criminalize the practice of Christian Science, both through state laws and the prosecution of its adherents. But the Harold Frederic and Brush Will cases, which generated enormous adverse publicity, galvanized a nationwide effort to restrain the practice of Christian Science by law. In state legislatures across the country, Christian Scientists offered an impressive array of evidence that their form of healing, however contrary to medical assumptions, actually accomplished much in benefiting the patient. Such testimony was especially effective when those who had been healed themselves were called upon to testify or were local residents of the state or community where the legal rights of Christian Scientists were in dispute.

Given the convincing nature of such accounts and the less than impressive record of conventional medical practice, plus the hesitancy of legislators to challenge constitutional freedoms of religious practice, attempts to restrict Christian Science healing by law ultimately failed. But in states where medical licensing laws were temporarily on the books, they were sometimes enforced in ways that Christian Scientists saw as brutally harsh. In Dayton, Ohio, in 1895, for example, Mr. and Mrs. Thomas Hatten, both practitioners, were arrested, brought before police authorities eight or nine times, twice in the night, taken from their homes three times in a patrol wagon for interrogation, and widely pilloried in the local press before being exonerated by the court. In another case, after a young woman agreed to pray for a man pretending to be sick, she was dragged to a police station, disrobed and searched, prompting a local newspaper to ask, "What did the police expect to find on Miss R—dangerous Bible texts?"[65]

"FROM EXTREMES TO INTERMEDIATE"

When Eddy as the preeminent spokesperson for Christian Science met public attacks on her teaching and its practice head on, she often did so in a strong and decisive way. In counseling Christian Scientists about state encroachment on their healing practice, however, she urged modesty and moderation. For one thing, Eddy had great faith in the American judicial system, specifically in the protection that would ultimately be afforded the practice of Christian Science under the First Amendment of the Constitution. That faith was justified by a landmark case, decided by the Supreme Court of Rhode Island in 1898, which held that prayer in Christian Science could not reasonably be mistaken for medical treatment in any normal sense of the term.[66]

Eddy's published statements and interviews likewise ran consistently to a defense of Christian Science practice on the constitutional grounds of religious freedom. As she put it in a message to the Mother Church in 1899: "A coroner's inquest, a Board of Health, or class legislation is less than the Constitution of the United States; and infinitely less than God's benign government, which is no respecter of persons. Truth crushed to earth springs spontaneously upward, and whispers in the breeze man's inalienable birthright—*Liberty*." "The Constitution of the United States," she wrote in her article for the *New York Sunday Journal*, "does not provide that *materia medica* shall make laws to regulate man's religion; rather does it imply that religion shall permeate our laws."[67]

Eddy, while concerned about the potential injustice done Christian Scientists by state legislatures, was equally concerned about unwise political maneuvering on the part of Christian Scientists themselves. Along with a number of statements expressing confidence in the working of the American constitutional system, she cautioned her followers to comport themselves with dignity and restraint in the face of legal challenges to their healing practice. What particularly troubled her was the use of political pressure tactics to maintain freedoms that she believed the Constitution would in the long run preserve anyway. To Augusta Stetson, who characteristically sought to defeat a threatening bill by organizing Christian Scientists to put pressure on state legislators, Eddy wrote in 1894 that such an action "dishonors the dignified grounds on which I have founded Christian Science. . . . I have no fears whatever of the passage of any law that can injure Christian Science and only fear the dishonor that comes from unwise measures taken by students."[68]

Rather than combatively asserting their rights and interests, Christian Scientists, Eddy counseled, needed most to win the support of society for their reasonableness and respect for the rights of others, along with the effectiveness of their healing work. In 1902, she advised her followers to submit to the process of vaccination and to report cases of infectious disease to the proper authorities when the law so required. She urged them to use careful judgment when considering whether to take a case of malignant disease, writing that "they should consider well as to their ability to cope with the case—and not overlook the fact that there are those lying in wait to catch them in their sayings; neither should they forget that, in their practice, whether successful or not, *they are not specially protected by law.*" When Christian Scientists in one state decided, in response to a restrictive ruling by that state's supreme court, to practice without fees, Eddy congratulated them "tenderly" on their decision and stated she would "thoroughly recommend it under the circumstances."[69]

Her fundamental approach was the opposite of fanaticism, whether reflected in her followers' sometimes militant efforts to oppose enactment of laws limiting spiritual healing practice or in the judgmental stance they sometimes assumed toward one another. Whereas some Christian Scientists could become bitterly critical of church members who opted for medical care, their judgment ran counter to Eddy's own. She did insist in *Science and Health* that "only through radical reliance on Truth can scientific healing power be realized."[70] But this statement meant simply that if one wishes to attain a healing effect through the practice of Christian Science, he or she must rely wholeheartedly on God to attain that aim. Taking the metaphysical system of Christian Science seriously, she did not feel it was either beneficial or possible for patients to be treated through two contrary methods—through both spiritual and material means—at the same time. Yet as her writings make clear, she always advocated for the right of each individual to choose his or her own way in the quest for healing.

She especially emphasized this point in *Science and Health*—not, as might be expected, in the chapter "Christian Science Practice"—but in the following chapter, "Teaching Christian Science." That chapter has as much to do with learning from one's own experience as it does with being taught in a class. Eddy begins "Teaching Christian Science" by pointing out that "systematic medical study" detracts "from entire confidence in omnipotent Mind as really possessing all power." But she also said that while certain Christian Scientists "severely condemned" such study, she felt "that all are privileged to work out their own salvation according to their light" without the personal judgment of others. In all cases, she advised students "to be charitable and kind, not only towards differing forms of religion and medicine, but to those who hold these differing opinions." She urged her followers to faithfully point out the Christ-way, to judge righteously, and never to condemn rashly. But what if some patients do not experience the healing power of Science and choose medical treatment instead? Her position was the same: "the Mind-physician should give up such cases, and leave invalids free to resort to whatever other systems they fancy will afford relief. Thus such invalids may learn the value of the apostolic precept: 'Reprove, rebuke, exhort with all longsuffering and doctrine.' "[71]

In this as in other matters, Eddy was taking realistic account of the fact that Christian Science was being practiced by people of widely different mentalities and backgrounds, and that it was therefore necessary to strike a balance between maintaining the doctrine and ethics of what Christian Science teaches on the one hand, and being compassionate and long-suffering on the other, to those practicing the teachings of Science, however imperfectly, in their daily lives.

In this regard, Eddy, too, had to learn from her own life experience. While she herself never sought medical treatment for healing after her work in Christian Science began, she found it necessary on a limited number of occasions to use morphine for the relief of extreme pain. One such instance occurred on May 3, 1903, when she endured a night of acute suffering. With no relief through the work of her helpers, Eddy consented to calling in a physician, not for medical treatment, but for the purpose of a diagnosis. A doctor came to her side at 2 A.M. and, after calling in another doctor for consultation, diagnosed the difficulty as renal calculi, or kidney stones. Later the next day when her suffering returned and became unbearable, she had a hypodermic injection of morphine to relieve the pain. Over the next few years Eddy had similar attacks involving such severe pain that she called again for relief by hypodermic injection, although in several other instances she refused such ministrations or was sufficiently helped by the mental workers that they were not needed.[72]

Morphine was not a cure for kidney stones, and in no instance after 1866 did Eddy ask for or consent to any form of medical treatment as a means of curing this or any other illness. But her own sense of integrity, true to her life experience, demanded that reasonable account be taken of the concession she made on those occasions. Thus, two years after the initial incident when morphine was administered she sent to the directors a statement to be inserted in the next printing of *Science and Health*. The statement in its final form reads:

> If from an injury or from any cause, a Christian Scientist were seized with pain so violent that he could not treat himself mentally,—and the Scientists had failed to relieve him,—the sufferer could call a surgeon, who would give him a hypodermic injection, then, when the belief of pain was lulled, he could handle his own case mentally. Thus it is that we "prove all things; [and] hold fast that which is good."[73]

The timing of this addition may have been prompted by her knowledge that a much-valued follower had just died in extreme pain, which if it had been alleviated, she believed, might have allowed him to deal more effectively with his own case. But she was obviously think- ing of her own experience as well. Lydia B. Hall, a household worker at Pleasant View, recalled Eddy saying something to the effect that she felt compelled to put the paragraph in *Science and Health* because doing it "was to be honest to God and the Cause."[74] Further, the context in which the statement was placed in *Science and Health* is revealing in itself. It comes at the end of the chapter "Teaching Christian Science." The preceding paragraph touched on her own seclusion and on the "time and toil" she expended on behalf of Christian Science, so that for the attentive reader there was a personal context for the paragraph that followed. The possible autobiographical application of her words about a hypodermic injection becomes even clearer in the sentence that fol- lows: "In founding a pathological system of Christianity, the author has labored to expound divine Principle, and not to exalt personality."

Some Christian Scientists in her day would have been hard pressed to understand how their leader could have made such a concession, and although the board of directors confirmed the facts of the matter as long ago as 1929, the issue has raised clouds of controversy among Christian Scientists for decades.[75] From one standpoint, it could be said that Eddy was rationalizing what could only be interpreted as a compromise; from another, she was anticipating through her own difficult personal expe- rience a dilemma that others might face in future years and helping them to resolve it without evasion or guilt.

In this as in other matters, Eddy proved more liberal than many of her more hard-line followers. Her advice to them on a broad range of issues was to go "from extremes to intermediate"—to attain a moderation that she saw as deeply Christian but difficult for most human beings to attain. In an 1890 letter she wrote:

> I have never known a student of Christian Science who has not inclined to extremes and it will take a long time as it now appears before Christian Scientists will see and then take the intermediate course that I take, recommend to others, and have taught in the class room. Jesus taught and I teach that there is in mortal mind a perpetual force impelling wrongly. . . . Now no one can take the temperate line of conclusion and action which is the only right one till they do see this and then bring forth the fruits of the Spirit which Paul said is "meekness, temperance."[76]

PRECEPT UPON PRECEPT

Eddy's attitude toward the protection of Christian Scientists' legal right to practice their faith was encapsulated in her statement, "It is of less importance that we receive from mankind justice, than that we deserve it." Impelled by this conviction, she remained concerned that the claims for the healing efficacy of Christian Science be substantiated by the healing works her followers performed. She gave special weight to the need for healing by placing in the *Manual* a bylaw entitled "Healing Better than Teaching," in which she recommends "that each member of this Church shall strive to demonstrate by his or her practice, that Christian Science heals the sick quickly and wholly, thus proving this Science to be all that we claim for it."[77]

One expression of how serious she was in insisting on this point was the close eye she kept on the publication of testimonies in the Christian Science periodicals. Again, her approach can be understood as seeking an intermediate position between extremes—in this instance, publishing an insufficient number of testimonies or too many. In 1903, when testimonies in the religious periodicals seemed to her too sparse, she wrote to the editor: "I started this great work and *woke the people* by demonstration, not words but works. Our periodicals must have more Testimonials in them. The Sentinel is of late a Shakespeare without a Hamlet. . . . Healing is the best sermon, healing is the best lecture, and the entire demonstration of *C.S.*" On the other hand, a few years before when testimonies seemed too numerous, she wrote to the Hannas that so many testimonies "lower the standard of Principle by appeals to person and mortal mind. They are in Metaphysics much like narcotics in medicine and fiction in literature."[78]

Yet as biographer Robert Peel commented, the healing work itself, rather than testimonies as such, was of first importance to her, and "there could not be too many *healings*." "I am sorely disappointed in the demonstration of C.S.," Eddy wrote to Kimball in 1903. "And it must improve or our cause will float into theory and we will not 'show our faith by our works.' A chatterer of C.S. is never a healer." Some five years later William Rathvon quoted her as saying, "I have no use for the smiling kind who say with their lips 'God is all' and sit with folded hands doing nothing in the way of proof. It is a lie to say that which implies proving, if we prove it not."[79]

A key aspect of Eddy's ongoing nurturing ministry to the Christian Science field was her efforts at different levels to encourage, upgrade, and inspire the healing work of her followers. In 1899, for example, she felt that an important question had been inadequately dealt with in the *Sentinel* and decided that she had to provide a corrective answer. The question was, "If all matter is unreal, why do we deny the existence of disease in the material body and not the body itself?" In answering it, Eddy gave special weight to the fact that Christian Science, though it rests on the basis of absolute Truth, must be demonstrated by degrees, and that the mere assertion of abstract truths without concrete proof is harmful to this demonstration. Thus she wrote, "We deny first the existence of disease, because we can meet this negation more readily than we can negative all that the body affirms." Jesus, she said, "restored the diseased body to its normal action, functions, and organization," and after the Resurrection "presented his *material* body absolved from death and the grave." "The *spiritual* body came," she explained, "with the *ascension*." She ended with the reminder that "the introduction of pure abstractions in Christian Science without their correlatives leaves its divine Principle unexplained" and "tends to confuse the mind of the reader."[80]

This and other episodes clarified and reaffirmed what Eddy saw as the scientific basis of spiritual healing practice. A large part of her continuing effort to support the work of healing took a more personal and pastoral form. Besides published admonitions to her followers, she continued until her last years to write frequent letters and notes for the support of students who were working out healings for themselves or treating others. Nothing she said in this counsel contradicted or added in substance to what her published writings contain. They were meant, rather, to respond to immediate situations and particular needs, or in some instances to correct points in Christian Science that she felt her students were ignoring or getting wrong. Her counsel in these matters to various students ran along the following lines:

> The body and you are not one. You are not in the body talking for it and it cannot talk for itself. . . . You are spiritual not material. You are my good faithful follower of Christ—the image of God; indeed, you are this idea

and have no strife with the flesh; you reflect God and are His image and like unto Spirit not matter. The flesh has no connection with you. Realize this and you are master of the situation.

The healing will grow more easy and be more immediate as you realize that God, Good, *is all* and Good is *Love*. You must gain Love, and lose the false sense called love. You must feel the Love that *never faileth,*—that perfect sense of divine power that makes healing no longer power but *grace*.

The healing of my students changes its stages as they learn from experience. It starts a marvel of power and then becomes a marvel of *grace*. The latter is gained by the spiritualization of practice. . . . More of the spirit than letter is required to reach this Christ-stage of healing sickness and sin.

In treating patients, do not repeat words over and over as it has the effect of morphine, soothing syrup or mesmerism. Christian Science treatment is prayer, but we do not plead with God to do what He has already done, but we know His work is finished, and man is His perfect idea, and "you shall know the Truth and the Truth shall make you free."

Put down this temptation that you cannot heal the sick, preach the gospel, and raise your dead faith to the life-giving realities and possibilities that enable you to meet the command of Christ to his students today the same as in the first century. Rise above this temptation . . . and "the Truth will make you free" and angels, right thoughts, will come to you.

God's way is the only true way. He bids us, "Flee as a bird to your mountain." The little bird does not hop his way to the mountain, he flies, straight and swift as the arrow. So in our healing, let us go straight and swift to the divine Father Mother Love. Let us go to God knowing that the work is His.[81]

Eddy's most widely quoted letter on the healing practice was written to James Neal, a likeable young man who showed remarkable adaptability for the work of spiritual healing before coming to Boston. He was one of those individuals in the early days of the movement who simply took hold of Christian Science with both hands—or rather, let it take hold of him.

Neal gave little evidence of having been a particularly unusual young man when in 1886 he developed a sudden, strong interest in Christian Science and began its practice. A cashier in Joseph Armstrong's bank in Irving, Kansas, he was so struck by the healing of Armstrong's wife that he spoke at length with the practitioner who had been on the case, began studying Christian Science literature, and healed the first of many cases before he had even read through *Science and Health*. From his own account, Christian Science became to him the discovery of a huge present reality that was simply there to be recognized and affirmed and that put everything else in daily life in a new light— especially the apparently intractable realities of sickness and pain.

To him, it seemed utterly natural to heal, which he proceeded to do professionally, moving from town to town in Kansas, healing along the way cases of cancer, deafness, blindness, and insanity.[82] Eddy had defined a miracle as "that which is divinely natural, but must be learned humanly."[83] To Neal, the basis of healing seemed to be just that: a divinely natural witnessing to the reality of an entirely good God and of his kingdom as an actual presence, an order of scientific fact. Coming to Boston as Armstrong's assistant, Neal longed to be back in the practice in Kansas. Eddy asked him to remain in Boston, which he did. In January 1897 she wrote him a letter expressing her satisfaction that she had "at least one student in Boston that promises to be a Healer such as I have long waited and hoped to see."

> Oh may the Love that looks on you and all guide your every thought and act up to the impersonal, spiritual model that is the only ideal—and constitutes the only scientific Healer.
>
> To this glorious end I ask you to still press on, and have no other ambition or aim. A real scientific *Healer* is the highest position attainable in this sphere of being. Its altitude is far above a Teacher or preacher; it includes all that is divinely high and holy. Darling James, leave behind all else and strive for this great achievement. . . . Your aid to reach this goal is *spiritualization*. To achieve this you must have *one God,* one affection, one way, one Mind. Society, flattery, popularity are temptations in your pursuit of growth spiritual. Avoid them as much as in you lies. Pray daily, never miss praying, no matter how often: "Lead me not into temptation,"—scientifically rendered,—Leave me not to lose sight of strict purity, clean pure thoughts; let all my thoughts and aims be high, unselfish, charitable, meek,—*spiritually minded.* With this altitude of thought your mind is losing materiality and gaining spirituality and this is the state of mind that *heals* the sick. . . . I welcome you into the *sanctum* of my fold. God bless you.[84]

11

"The Kingdoms of this World"

"OUR MAGNIFICENT TEMPLE"

"DIFFICULTY, ABNEGATION, CONSTANT BATTLE AGAINST THE WORLD, THE FLESH, and evil, tell my long-kept secret—evidence a heart wholly in protest, and unutterable in love."[1]

Eddy wrote these words in 1903 when she was almost eighty-two years old, yet her "battle against the world" had hardly ended. Indeed, as Christian Science gained ground, the world was becoming more aware of her than ever before. Reports of healings, conversions, and church building, public controversies over Christian Science healing practice, publicity generated by the Woodbury trial and Mark Twain's early articles, a barrage of attacks on the new faith from the pulpit—these and other factors made it impossible for most Americans not to have some awareness of, and an opinion about, Christian Science and its leader. In the coming years, this awareness would only increase, especially given the publicity surrounding the dedication of the massive extension of the Mother Church in 1906 and the Next Friends Suit that followed in its wake.

In the 1890s, Eddy and those closest to her were primarily involved with reorganizing the church, constructing the Mother Church edifice, and strengthening the movement. The following decade saw their focus shift outward to meet the reaction of the world to the growth of that church and the spread of the movement into virtually every state. In Eddy's usage, "the world" was largely a pejorative term for the worldliness and materialism from which humanity needs to be redeemed. It was worldliness in this sense that had crucified Jesus. In her words, "The real cross, which Jesus bore up the hill of grief, was the world's hatred of Truth and Love." Jesus, she also wrote, "met and conquered the resistance of the world." To be of help in redeeming this world, her followers needed to be free of its influence. As Eddy put it in her first address in the Mother Church in May 1895, "Beloved children, the world has need of you,—and more as children than as men and women: it needs your innocence, unselfishness, faithful affection, uncontaminated lives."[2]

If Christian Scientists had to do battle against the worldliness of the world, there was an even greater need to do battle against worldliness among themselves. In this respect, apparent triumphs could be more dangerous than outright defeats. Certainly the summer of 1906 appeared to be one of unparalleled triumph for the cause of Christian Science. The extension of the Mother Church, toward which Christian Scientists had pledged $2 million in 1902, was dedicated with great fanfare on June 10. Some thirty thousand proud followers of Eddy streamed into Boston for the great event, which received massive press coverage. "Nothing in the history of the Christian Science movement, it may be ventured," wrote one of Eddy's biographers, "served to awaken public attention all over the world to the fact and the growth of Christian Science more than the building of The Mother Church extension."[3]

Yet it was in that same summer that Eddy wrote to her young friend John Lathrop, who in 1902 had served for several months as a member of her Pleasant View household: "I mourn over the ease of Christian Scientists. They are not at ease in the pains of sense, but are at ease in its pleasures. Which drives out quickest the tenant you wish to get out of your house, the pleasant hours he enjoys in it or its unpleasantness?"[4] This is not to say that Eddy had reservations about the building of the extension. To her, as to most of her followers, the need for a larger church was not a luxury but a necessity. The original Mother Church, dedicated at the beginning of 1895, had soon proved inadequate to accommodate those who wished to worship there. Its twelve hundred seats filled quickly before services, forcing many to find what places they could at the back of the auditorium, along its sides, and around the doors. By April 1896, two services were being held each Sunday and by October 1905, three. Even with new congregations forming in Cambridge, Chelsea, Roxbury, and other Boston suburbs, the space problem remained acute. The influx into Boston of thousands of church members for annual meetings and communion season required larger quarters such as Tremont Temple, Symphony Hall, and Mechanics Hall to take care of the overflow.

Not wanting the church to go into debt, Eddy asked the directors to look for an existing building that would accommodate five thousand church members. By 1902 she agreed with those who held that the best alternative would be to construct a larger church. Accordingly, Edward Kimball moved at the church's annual meeting, attended by ten thousand church members, that an auditorium seating four or five thousand people be constructed and that Christian Scientists pledge themselves to contribute up to $2 million for this purpose. The motion was adopted unanimously without discussion, although the church had on hand less than $34,000 at the time.[5]

By April 1903, all the parcels constituting a triangular plot of land for the building of an extension to the original Mother Church had been purchased. The work of clearing the land was begun in October, the cornerstone laid in July 1904, and on Sunday, June 10, 1906, the extension was dedicated. Newspaper reports of the event made much of the fact that by this date the entire sum of $2 million had been collected, so that the new church building was dedicated free of debt. Eddy was far less involved in pushing forward the building of the extension than she had been in the construction of the original Mother Church in 1894. But she was deeply involved in the choice of the distinguished Chicago architect Solon S. Beman, a Christian Scientist whose work was later commended by one of America's greatest architects, Louis Sullivan. Beman was a strong champion of the classical idiom in architecture, which he suggested would best befit the Mother Church extension. Impressed with his recommendation, Eddy responded that his letter was "quite sufficient to determine the style of The Mother Church building. . . . We all bow to your skill in this matter."[6]

Beyond this, she selected and adapted an extensive series of quotations from the Bible and her writings to be carved into the walls of the new church. She also suggested eliminating from the extension stained glass windows that were so conspicuous a feature of the original Mother Church. But otherwise she counseled the board to defer to Beman's advice. She also counseled them as the building process began to beware of the materializing tendency that threatened to engulf the whole project:

> May our God who is Spirit be worshipped by you in Spirit, and the house you are about to erect be built on the Rock of ages; while you, my dearest ones, are rearing in your own consciousness a temple not "built with hands"—and consecrate alone to the One-and-All—apart from all material considerations. Be careful not to drop into the usages of other churches in thought or act only so far as you can unite on the one spiritual basis and not the material.[7]

By Communion Sunday in 1906, the church was completed successfully—in some respects, some might have said, too successfully. When the extension was dedicated on that day, understandable satisfaction at the completion of a needful task had largely given way to pride in the

Dedication Day of The Mother Church Extension, 1906.
Courtesy of The Mary Baker Eddy Collection.

magnitude of what had been accomplished. It is difficult to tell who was more impressed with what the Christian Scientists had achieved: the press or Christian Scientists themselves. In support of the motion to build the extension, Kimball had made his case in practical terms, saying, "We need to keep pace with our own growth and progress." But a different note was struck when the motion was seconded by Judge William

G. Ewing of Chicago: "As we have the best church in the world, and as we have the best expression of the religion of Jesus Christ, let us have the best material symbol of both of these, and in the best city in the world." At the annual meeting on June 12, 1906, two days after the extension was dedicated, the incoming president of the Mother Church echoed the same tone: "The world looks with wonder upon this grand achievement,—the completion and dedication of our magnificent temple."[8]

The pride may have been unseemly, but the words were accurate. The world's wonder was widely expressed in a spate of articles in the Boston press that were echoed throughout the United States and beyond. The *Boston Post* spoke of the "spacious and elegant edifice," saying that "in its simple grandeur" it would "surpass any church edifice erected in this city." The *New York Herald* commented, "This temple is one of the largest in the world. . . . Beside it the dome of the Massachusetts State House, which is the leading landmark of Boston, pales into insignificance." With some exaggeration, another *Post* article reported that "the gates of Boston are open wide in welcome to nobility. . . . Members of the titled aristocracy of the old world . . . are streaming into town . . . to attend the dedication." The *Boston Herald* was further impressed with the magnitude of the collections taken at the six services, in which the plates were "heaped high with bills, with silver, and with gold."[9]

Architectural opinion was less effusive. Constructing a church on so confining a location limited the architects' options from the start. Some commentators were severely critical of the building for its lack of a coherent style. Since its style had no kinship with the architecture of Italy or France, said one prominent critic, its structure "should have been essentially American and essentially Modern. As a matter of fact, it is neither." That may well have been true. But while the extension may have lacked conventional ornamentation and architectural reference points, other commentators found much to praise in its "evenly diffused light," and in what one called its "atmosphere of quiet, simplicity, restfulness."[10]

The extension did have a distinct quality of simplicity that contrasted not only with most traditional churches, but with some of the more elaborate Christian Science churches built over the next two decades. One would have scarcely concluded that this was the case from the abundant newspaper reports of the immense satisfaction Christian Scientists displayed in the dedication of their new temple. To some degree, they gave the impression of being so wholly caught up in the glamour and glory of the occasion as to forget what their religion was about. One report, however, penetrated the rhetoric and caught something of the life behind the devotion of Eddy's followers that resulted in the extension being funded so generously. An article in the *Boston Herald* observed that "quietly, without a trace of fanaticism, making their remarkable statements with a simplicity which sprang from the conviction that they would be believed, scores of Christian Scientists told of cures . . . of blindness, of consumption in its advanced stages, of heart disease, of cancer; . . . that when wasted unto death they had been made whole."[11]

Eddy's response to the occasion was complex. Biographer Gillian Gill writes that "as the leader of a growing movement, she was gladdened by the size and splendor of the new building, by the evidence it offered of success, and by the glowing reports it had elicited from the press and general public. As a spiritual guide, however, Mrs. Eddy worried, I think, that prosperity might prove more dangerous for her movement than adversity."[12] On the one hand, Eddy collected a wide sampling of press reports, some of which were breathless if not hyperbolic, for inclusion in a book to be published after her death with the title, *The First Church of Christ, Scientist, and Miscellany.* On the other, the dedicatory message she wrote for the occasion was anything but celebratory.

Entitled "Choose Ye," it shows Eddy speaking in her sternest mode. Toward the beginning of her message she stated almost peremptorily: "A Christian Scientist verifies his calling. *Choose ye!*" She continued with a series of warnings buttressed with Bible texts: "Lust, dishonesty, sin, disables the student; they preclude the practice or efficient teaching of Christian Science, the truth of man's being. The Scripture reads: 'He that taketh not his cross, and followeth after me, is not worthy of me.' On this basis, how many are following the Way-shower?" In words that could be taken as rebuking her followers' exultant pride in their new temple, she said: "The pride of place or power is the prince of this world that hath nothing in Christ. Our great Master said: 'Except ye become as a little child, ye cannot enter the kingdom of heaven.'" Toward the close of her message she declared: "We cannot serve two masters. Do we love God supremely? Are we honest, just, faithful? Are we true to ourselves? 'God is not mocked, Whatsoever a man soweth, that shall he also reap.'"[13]

Eddy's apparent intent in these unexpectedly strong words was similar to her message to the congregation when the original Mother Church was dedicated: to puncture the glamour of the occasion with a demanding spiritual realism intended to awaken, rather than merely to congratulate, her followers, at a point when they would be most asleep to imminent danger. As events turned out, the danger stemming from the massive publicity surrounding the dedication lay in its long-range consequences for Eddy herself. The *Boston Post* commented, with some hyperbole but with real point, on the change that had occurred in the public's view of her: "One does not need to accept the doctrines of Mrs. Eddy to recognize the fact that this wonderful woman is a world power. This is conclusive; it is conspicuously manifest." As a later biographer observed, "In these weeks of June, 1906, Mrs. Eddy was doubtless the most discussed woman in the world."[14]

One of the conspicuous features of the dedication was the absence from the scene of this "most discussed woman in the world." In view of the fact that she would be eighty-five the next month, had made but few public appearances in years, and was on record as disdaining personal adulation, her absence from what would have been a taxing and very public occasion was understandable. Yet so extensively reported was the dedication ceremony that the mere fact of her absence became a major story, leading to widespread rumors about the state of her health. Such rumors generated further press interest in the well-being of the secluded founder of Christian Science, helping to precipitate the chain of events that led to the Next Friends Suit and Eddy's departure from Concord to the Boston suburbs in January 1908.

"OH, SPLENDID MISERY"

"Choose Ye" was a relatively short message of about fourteen-hundred words. Although it was read at the dedication ceremony, it was only in the last two paragraphs that Eddy mentioned the extension specifically: "You have dexterously and wisely provided for The Mother Church of Christ, Scientist, a magnificent temple wherein to enter and pray. Greatly impressed and encouraged thereby, deeply do I thank you for this proof of your progress, unity, and love."

However positive her remarks about the extension, the smaller original Mother Church, which Eddy visited on three occasions, had a more prominent place in her affections. Just so, her Pleasant View home seemed more of a home to her than the mansion at Chestnut Hill into which she moved on January 26, 1908. The need for her relocation to the Boston area seemed as pressing and sensible as the commitment to build the extension had been six years earlier. Although Eddy had no desire to leave New Hampshire, its court system had failed to protect her from the Next Friends Suit, which she feared could be revived at some future time.

Her move back to Boston was not, however, occasioned by this one factor alone. Even before the suit ended, she had confided to John Salchow that it would soon be necessary to leave Pleasant View. Much as she loved her home, it was proving far too small for her growing

Mary Baker Eddy's residence at Chestnut Hill, Brookline, Massachusetts.
Photograph by David Brooks Andrews.

staff. When directors or Boston visitors needed to stay overnight, they
had to sleep on cots set up in the living room. So close was the house
at Pleasant View to the street that it was difficult to keep reporters and
other possible intruders away from the doorstep. By mid-July 1907,
Alfred Farlow and Archibald McLellan, then a director, were at Eddy's
very secret request looking for a new home for her in the Newton or
Brookline area near Boston.

The twenty-five-room stone mansion located on twelve acres of
grounds that McLellan purchased for her in Chestnut Hill in October
needed some renovations in order to accommodate her needs. Its most
useful feature may have been its proximity to the Brookline reservoir,
an apt and pleasant route for Eddy's daily carriage rides. But its enormity was incompatible with the simplicity of her taste. With notable
incomprehension of her mentality, at least in this respect, John Lathrop
wrote in a letter, "There is much about this location which seems particularly appropriate for our Leader's higher work. . . ." This was a view
that Eddy did not share, particularly on January 26, 1908, when the
household traveled on a special train from Concord to Chestnut Hill.
The departure of Concord's most distinguished citizen had been kept
secret from the press, the Concord townspeople, and, until the latest
possible moment, most of the Pleasant View staff.[15]

At 2:00, Eddy began her afternoon drive as usual but was taken to
the train rather than back to Pleasant View. When she arrived at the
station, McLellan and Tomlinson stepped up to assist her. According to

John Salchow, who was holding the horses' reins while she alighted the carriage, she "held out her little hand and said, 'I don't want you. I want my John.'" The train was underway by 2:45 and, after an uneventful journey, was switched onto a track leading directly into the Chestnut Hill station. By the time the party arrived at Eddy's new home, the press had ferreted out the news of her move and a corps of reporters and photographers were waiting for her. As the press began to crowd in upon her, she again appealed to Salchow, "Can you get me out of this, John?"—which he proceeded to do by scooping her up in his arms, taking her upstairs, and depositing her in a chair.[16]

She then began to take the measure of what she called the "great barn of a place" that was to be her new home. The house was overlit and overheated on that first cold January night. She had agreed that the study and bedroom be slightly larger than their equivalents at Pleasant View. But they turned to be twice again as large. Dark, rich wallpaper, which she disliked, and a rose-figured carpet created an atmosphere totally different from the lightness of her study at Pleasant View, while the windows were too high for her to gaze out as she sat in her chair. And, as she complained wryly to Adelaide Still, her new study was so large that she could not wait while a student walked across a great expanse of carpet from the door to where she sat. The whole house smacked of Gilded Age fustian—far removed from the rural New England atmosphere in which she felt at home, occasioning her outburst as she sat at her desk the next morning, "Oh, splendid misery, splendid misery."[17]

Over the next few months she directed renovations aimed at restoring her adjoining study and bedroom to the dimensions of her quarters at Pleasant View. Gradually she adjusted to her new residence, so that at some point it took on the aspect of a home to her—but never completely. To Salchow she confided that Pleasant View would always be her home, and to Archibald McLellan she explained: "The house that I now occupy was purchased for me before I saw it or had any correct idea of its dimensions and expense. When I . . . looked on the house I now own I was shocked, and went to my room and wept. . . . I have always declared against the display of material things and said the less we have of them the better." As she wrote to Alfred Farlow after rejecting the idea of purchasing a particular estate, "I dislike *arrogant* wealth, a great show of it, and especially for one who *works* as well as preaches for and of the nothingness of matter."[18]

On one occasion only did Eddy even make the effort to view the Mother Church extension closely. Boston newspapers reported that on February 6, 1908, less than two weeks after her move to Chestnut Hill, Eddy saw the exterior of the church fleetingly from her carriage window on one of her daily drives. Associating the extension with her Chestnut Hill home, Eddy is reported to have said "that the Extension was too extravagant, and that she did not like the elegance of Chestnut Hill. 'Too much matter.'"[19]

"THE PAGANIZATION OF CHRISTIAN SCIENCE"

Eddy had a visceral disdain for materiality, and when she found herself plunged into the midst of it in what was supposed to be her home, her misery was real. Some of her students, however, were thriving on a form of the very materiality she loathed.

In 1897, a Christian Scientist wrote of a relative, "He wants Christian Science only to heal the ills of the flesh. He wants to enjoy the pleasures of the world and has no idea of nor hunger for the great spiritual uplifting that would come with Science." As one Christian Scientist put it, "A demonstration of the allness of God in business does not always result in the attainment of some particular aim or object." Other Eddy followers were likewise aware of the tendency to materialize and secularize her teaching, thereby taking it out of the sphere of redemptive religion and placing it in the context of what scholar Sydney Ahlstrom has usefully called "harmonial religion." Ahlstrom writes of harmonialism as a diffuse tendency in which "spiritual composure, physical health, and even economic well-being are understood to flow from a person's rapport with the cosmos."[20] That many of her followers practiced an essentially harmonial form of Christian Science in order to maintain a comfortable, placid human existence is undeniable, underscoring the truth of Ahlstrom's observation in one respect.

Eddy's ideal of the Christian life, however, could not be more sharply at variance with the purpose of furthering these harmonial human aims. She placed a far higher value on spiritual striving than on spiritual composure, telling one class that "if we are struggling all the time, fasting . . . and praying, and are unsatisfied, it is a very hopeful condition." She most often spoke of harmony positively as the stability and peacefulness of God's universe, writing, for example, of heaven as "the harmony of being." But she also spoke of harmony as a false and misleading human ideal, writing that "the mistaken way, of hiding sin in order to maintain harmony, has licensed evil, allowing it first to smoulder, and then break out in devouring flames." Nor was physical healing for her an end in itself. Indeed, she said that "dis-ease in sin is better than ease in sin," and that "sickness is the schoolmaster, leading you to Christ."[21]

When students spoke to her of using Christian Science to "demonstrate" material objects and comfortable surroundings, she was appalled. She saw material comfort and the achievement of wealth as of no value whatever. "Break up cliques, level wealth with honesty, let worth be judged according to wisdom," she wrote, "and we get better views of humanity." Blanche Hersey Hogue, whose article on the *Manual* Eddy so appreciated, commented in an article for the *Sentinel*, "to find out whether we want health and success for the sake of it or in order that God may be glorified, is to determine the genuineness of our profession as Christian Scientists."[22]

A classic critique of a more secularized, harmonial version of Christian Science adapted to serve the ends of business success was written for the *American Businessman* by Alfred Farlow in 1908: "It seems to us," wrote Farlow, "that a Christian Scientist can judge better as to his real advancement by noting how many of his pet sins he is escaping, rather than by counting the amount of money he is gaining." Commending his article as *"grand,"* Eddy wrote to him, "You have shown the way and the ultimate of all success in Science."[23] In the light of her teaching, his argument was irrefutable. Yet among Eddy's followers generally and in the first decade of the twentieth century especially, the form of ultra-harmonial materialism he implicitly condemned became a distinctly traceable tendency.

For one prominent Christian Scientist, this tendency became a virtual ideology. Augusta Stetson, who by the turn of the century dominated the Christian Science scene in New York City, defended material acquisitiveness in words that transmuted the metaphysics of Christian Science into a rationale for opulence:

> We need health and strength and peace, and for these we look to God. But let us not forget that we also need *things*, things which are but the type and shadow of the real objects of God's creating, but which we can use and enjoy until we wake to see the real. We surely need clothes. Then why not manifest a beautiful concept? Clothes should, indeed, be as nearly perfect as possible, in texture, line and color. . . . It is certain, too, that we need homes. Then why not have beautiful homes? Our homes should express the highest sense of harmony and happiness. . . . We have a right to everything that is convenient, most comfortable, most harmonious.

These words were a major part of Stetson's message, and New York in the late years of the Gilded Age was the perfect locale in which to preach it. With some exaggeration, but with no little insight, a critical biographer of Eddy who had known Stetson wrote, "The paganization of Christian Science . . . had been going on for years, but Gussie Stetson was the

Augusta E. Stetson, 1924.
Courtesy of The Mary
Baker Eddy Collection.

first to avow it openly. And New York, the most pagan of American cities, was delighted with her teachings."[24]

Eddy first met Stetson in 1884 when the younger woman was forty. It was immediately apparent that Stetson had unusual ability along with striking force of character. She was well educated, a good musician, widely traveled, and a trained elocutionist. After taking several classes with Eddy, Stetson also proved herself to be an effective healer as well. In short, she was a potential asset to an infant religious movement woefully lacking in people of real capacity. Several capable women in the movement—including Clara Choate, Emma Hopkins, and even Josephine Woodbury—had shown great promise, but each of them for differing reasons eventually broke with Eddy. Not so with Stetson—at least not on the surface. In one sense, she took the very opposite road of loyalty to Eddy so effusively that it practically amounted to deifying her. Well before this tendency became apparent, Stetson had proven herself among the most obedient of Eddy's followers. When in 1886 Eddy requested Stetson to go to New York to help build up Christian Science,

Stetson complied, although all of her friends lived in Boston and she knew but two people in New York City. At least in the early stages of their relationship, Eddy was grateful for her loyalty and obedience. "On no one," wrote Robert Peel, "did Eddy lavish more care and affection than on this brilliant, wilful, ambitious woman whom, she explained, she loved for the incalculable good of which she was capable."[25]

Stetson's early years in New York appeared to fulfill Eddy's highest expectations. Her efforts began inauspiciously as she assembled a group of seventeen who met in a hired room above a drugstore in a poor district on Sixth Avenue. Over the ensuing years, the indefatigable Stetson marched steadily northward, with swelling congregations outgrowing one locale after another, until in 1899 a cornerstone was laid for a huge and expensive church at 96th Street and Central Park West. First Church of Christ, Scientist, New York City, opened its doors in 1901 to widespread acclaim. Its floor, columns, walls, and spiral stairway were of marble. Three great aisles in the central auditorium, each with border panels of red Italian marble and red carpets, led to the rostrum. A luxuriously appointed reading room on the third floor led into a large space containing cubicles for twenty-five practitioners, who were permitted to decorate the space where they met with and treated patients. Stetson at first occupied spacious quarters within the church itself, but a year after its dedication moved into a home that had been built adjoining the church at a cost of $100,000.

With specific reference to Stetson's grandiose church building, Eddy asked in an editorial written by her but signed by McLellan, "Are you striving, in Christian Science, to be the best Christian on earth, or are you striving to have the most costly edifice on earth? . . . The more modest and less imposing material superstructures indicate a spiritual state of thought; and vice versa." Eddy's congratulatory message read at the dedication of First Church, New York, also included this admonition: "Remember that a temple but foreshadows the idea of God—the 'house not made with hands, eternal in the heavens,' while a silent grand man or woman healing sickness and destroying sin builds a heaven-reacher. Only that group of men and women gain greatness who gain themselves, in a complete subordination of self."[26]

"A complete subordination of self" was not a phrase that aptly described Stetson's priorities or those who found her church congenial. First Church was located in the midst of a virtual colony of well-heeled converts who constituted something of a cross between a working congregation and a fan club for their unquestioned local leader. To help maintain the atmosphere of affluence that Stetson sought to establish in her church, a special room was provided just outside the auditorium containing expensive hand-me-downs of hats, furs, coats, and shoes donated by members of the congregation. These were then made available to poorer members so that they could attend services looking wealthier than they actually were.[27]

Stetson also sought to extend her influence beyond the precincts of her own church. She was extremely good copy, and New York newspapers reported her announcements and pronouncements frequently. In November 1908, one city newspaper announced that she had opened a subscription for the building of a new church on Riverside Drive. The new church would not only rival the recently dedicated Mother Church extension in size and magnificence, but would itself be a "branch" of Stetson's church, which would thereby become the "Mother Church" for other branches in New York City. Eddy lost no time in making sure that this scheme did not come to fruition. She largely wrote and had McLellan sign an editorial entitled "One Mother Church in Christian Science" for the *Sentinel*. The editorial explained why Stetson's plan violated the institutional framework established by Eddy for the structure of her church.[28]

On the date the article was published, Eddy summoned Stetson for a carriage ride around the reservoir. It would be the last time the two would meet, and ostensibly all was sweetness and light between them. In the course of their conversation, Stetson, according to her own version of the interchange, protested that the only reason for planning a new church was to take care of the overflow from services at First Church. Eddy then told her that those who wished to form a new church should do so on their own and that the funds collected for the new church must be returned. Stetson did as she was bidden, all the while denying that there ever was a plan for making her First Church into a New York version of the Mother Church.[29]

An Ambivalent Relationship

On one level, Eddy and Stetson were close and had great affection for one another. Eddy sent "Gussie," as she called her, hundreds of letters over the years, many of them quite affectionate and confiding. Stetson remained, at least ostensibly, intensely loyal to Eddy, giving her unstinting support in times of crisis, including the Woodbury and Next Friends Suits. She also gladly supplied her with a steady procession of bonnets and clothing that Eddy enjoyed and paid for, but had neither the time nor inclination to select for herself.

Augusta E. Stetson leaving
Pleasant View, n.d.
Courtesy of The Mary
Baker Eddy Collection.

Another side of the relationship, however, reveals a very different picture. Robert David Thomas, one of Eddy's biographers, appraised the relationship from a psychoanalytical standpoint. Catching something of the complexity of Stetson's attitude toward Eddy, he wrote that from the late nineties until her dismissal from the church in 1909, Stetson "wanted to cling to Mrs. Eddy's hand; she wanted to feel her arms around her; she wanted to share in her Mother's power and to reflect it. But another part of Stetson wished to throw aside the hand, to unwrap the arms, to usurp the mother's power." For her part, Eddy, in Robert Peel's words, "enjoyed and even admired Stetson's dash and sweep and she appreciated the flood of affection which her 'darling Augusta' poured on her. But she apparently recognized that such adulation could be a subtle form of self-exaltation."[30]

The ambivalence of their relationship was caught in a moment recorded by Henrietta Chanfrau, who served at Pleasant View irregularly over the years. At one point when Stetson was visiting she told those assembled at the dinner table, including Eddy, "many stories of her successes, the wealthy patients and students who were members of her church, the lavish gifts they had made her, and so on." Eddy listened quietly, giving no hint of approval or disapproval. Chanfrau spoke of the contrast between Stetson, as a "woman of position in the metropolitan world, dressed in the height of fashion, with flashing wit and brilliant conversation . . . the centre of attention," and Eddy, "a little woman, dressed conservatively, radiating simplicity in every movement, sitting quietly as though she were the humblest worker among us." When Stetson expressed pleasure in the many gifts showered upon her by her students, Eddy observed, "Yes, dear, *God* gives us many gifts, but it is His *correcting rod* we need most of all!"[31]

In 1893 Eddy apparently tried to give Stetson a much-needed lesson in humility. Stetson, who had pushed hard for the inclusion of Christian Science at the World's Parliament of Religions, was scheduled to give the last talk at the Christian Science Congress on September 20. Eddy, however, asked her to withdraw the paper on the Trinity she had already prepared and to substitute for it a piece by Eddy herself that had already been twice published in the *Journal* and was scheduled for republication in the issue following the parliament.

Entitled "An Allegory," it pictured the dangerous descent from a sacred celestial city of a "Stranger" through a valley into a city of sinners. One inhabitant of a mansion in which stupefied sinners dwell looks out at the Stranger through the clear pane of the need in his own heart. The Stranger seeks to awaken other sinners to follow him through the valley and up to the mountain summit, but to no avail. Eventually he meets the penitent one, who now hopes to follow him. "And the Stranger said unto him, 'Wilt thou ascend the Mountain, and take nothing of thine own with thee?' He answered, 'I will.' Then said the Stranger, 'Thou hast chosen the good part, follow me.'" Summarizing the meaning of this allegory, Eddy again brought home the lesson of the humility that opened one to the presence of Christ: "Dear reader, dost thou suspect that the valley is humility, and the mountain is heaven-crowned Christianity; and the Stranger, the ever-present Christ, who from the summit of bliss surveys the vale of the flesh to burst the bubbles of earth with a breath of Heaven; and acquaint sensual mortals with the mystery of godliness, unchanging unquenchable Love?"[32]

Flushed with pride in her triumph in helping to arrange for Christian Science representation at the parliament, Stetson was hardly prepared to take in the meaning of these words. Well aware of this tendency, Eddy's correspondence over the years was punctuated with cautions to others both to be patient with Stetson's foibles and to be watchful of her misdeeds. In 1894 she wrote to the Hannas, "You must make strong efforts to save poor Stetson or M.A.M. [malicious animal magnetism] will put out her light." The light appeared to be going out fast when

Eddy wrote in late 1897 to young Carol Norton, a protégé of Stetson's whom Stetson tried to dominate, of Stetson's ambitious schemes to unify New York churches under her rule: "All this propagating *unity* of churches is a subtle move to put my students to work in the interest of one individual. . . . Carol, dear, it is an old policy of some folks to make others catch the fish and they bag them! Have you not done just this for certain persons not knowing why?"[33]

Over the years Eddy, although frequently expressing affection for Stetson, continued to rebuke her sharply. In October 1897, Eddy wrote to her bluntly, "You have always been the most troublesome student that I call loyal." Two years later came another affirmation of Eddy's love along with yet another warning: "Dear child *watch* that you enter not into the ways of the world from which our Wayshower teaches us to separate." "Your material Church is another danger in your path," wrote Eddy to her in a letter in 1903. "It occupies too much of your attention. It savors of the goddess of the Ephesians, the great Diana. O turn ye to the *one God*."[34]

SUCCESSORSHIP

On July 1, 1904, Stetson made another of a number of public dis-avowals in the New York press of the widespread assumption that she sought to become Eddy's successor. "Mrs. Eddy," she declared, "is, and ever will be, the only Leader of the Christian Science movement." That Stetson sought and desired to become Eddy's successor was widely assumed as obvious, both within the Christian Science movement and in the press. Eddy herself alluded to it as if it were not even a question when she commented in the midst of a crisis involving Stetson that God had told her to "leave the successor question alone" for the time.[35] Stetson always denied that she had any such aspirations. But she had a large following and thus an unparalleled power base in the largest field in the movement outside Boston, and her appetite for power was well known.

Moreover, Stetson held a quasi-mystical view of Eddy as the feminine representative of God and claimed a special relationship with her that would continue even after Eddy's death. "Christ Jesus," wrote Stetson, was "the masculine representative of the fatherhood of God. In this age Mary Baker Eddy is the feminine representative of the motherhood of God." In this age she is "God's highest representative," "the ideal woman" who is "continuing to destroy all mortal mentality." As such, she expected that Eddy would *continue* to guide her from the next plane of existence: "If I thought you would ever cease to lead me, I would be utterly hopeless," she wrote Eddy. "If I thought there would come an hour when I could not hear you, mentally, or see you through the veil of the flesh, as spiritual substance idea, I could not press forward." Horrified, Eddy told her to drop "the spiritualistic illusion that I am your guiding spirit here or hereafter, for I am not; and you will sink the Principle of Christian Science in personality and ruin your scientific progress. . . . I am not your guardian spirit here, and I shall not be hereafter." This belief that Eddy would continue to guide her from the next plane of existence was woven into her private utterances imparted to her inner circle of practitioners who met with her at noon every weekday. According to evidence at her trial before the church's board of directors in Boston, Stetson believed that Eddy had appointed her to become the sole teacher of Christian Science and to bring salvation to the world after Eddy had been "translated" into pure spirit.[36]

In late July 1909, the issue of Stetson's role in New York and in the movement as a whole abruptly came to a head. Her coterie of practitioners gave her a gift of gold pieces, along with a letter filled with such sentiments as "May a purified life attest the endless gratitude I feel for the manifestation of the Christ you have given us, while, with Mary of old I cry, Rabboni—Teacher." In a flush of enthusiasm Stetson sent the gold and the letter along to Eddy saying, "I feel they belong to you, dearest, and are your fruit. . . . Precious Leader, my love for you is inexpressible." At this point, Eddy felt that Stetson had crossed the line between loyalty and respect for her leader into virtual deification of Eddy and herself. Forwarding the composite letter and Stetson's letter to her to the board of directors, she instructed them to "act, and act quickly. Handle the letters according to *Science and Health* and The Mother Church *Manual*."[37]

To Stetson she wrote tersely, "I thank you for acknowledging me as your Leader and I know that every true follower of Christian Science abides by the definite rules which demonstrate the true following of their Leader; therefore if you are sincere in your protestations and are doing as you say you are, you will be blessed in your obedience." The letter was published in the next issue of the *Sentinel*. When Stetson was shown it during a noon meeting with her practitioners, she became nearly hysterical. Several days later, Eddy sent Stetson yet another letter, the mildest of several drafts she had worked on, urging her to "awake, and arise from this temptation produced by animal magnetism upon yourself, allowing your students to deify you and me. Treat yourself for it and get your students to help you rise out of it. It will be your destruction if you do not do this. Answer this letter immediately."[38]

Called to Boston in early August, Stetson acquitted herself well and was easily able to put at rest charges of the one accuser. The matter seemed closed—for the moment. In September, the board began a round of questioning of Stetson's students as to her beliefs and practices. Based on what was disclosed in these interrogations, the board stripped Stetson of her status as an authorized practitioner and teacher of Christian Science. Then Eddy temporarily backtracked, possibly to head off legal action and a hostile mental backlash from Stetson and her supporters, also saying that it would be more appropriate for Stetson's own church to discipline her. But after fresh revelations of Stetson's continued derelictions from normative Christian Science, the problem was obviously a matter of Mother Church discipline beyond the purview of Stetson's branch. After three lengthy examinations before the board, from November 15 through November 17, Stetson was excommunicated from the Mother Church. Stetson's church predictably exploded in contention until a letter arrived from Eddy advising them "with all my soul to support the Directors of The Mother Church."[39]

THE POWER—AND POWERLESSNESS—OF "LIBERATED THOUGHT"

The original charges against Stetson included her claim that her branch church was the only legitimate one in New York City, that she attempted to dominate her students, and that her total condemnation of sexuality conflicted with Christian Science teaching. But the heart of the charges revolved around her intentional practice of what Eddy called malicious mental practice, the conscious use of destructive mental power to do others harm. Testimony as to her animosity toward those she saw as rivals and opponents was so plentiful that it was not difficult for the board of directors to sustain these charges.

Depending on one's general framework of beliefs, there are three attitudes that can be taken in regard to the issue of whether projected hatred can have a harmful effect. First, there is the position, conscientiously held by many, that this cannot and does not occur. For William E. Chandler, Eddy's belief that projected malice must be detected and countered constituted *prima facie* evidence that she and her teaching were insane. Edwin Franden Dakin, in his debunking biography, speaks of Eddy's "fearful belief in M.A.M. as an ever-active devil"—a "neurosis" constituted of "unreasoning fears that made her own life a torture." Far more moderate in tone, Robert David Thomas, in his generally sympathetic biography, speaks of the "paranoid features" of her "fears of malicious animal magnetism," stating that her "beliefs and fears about mesmerism emerged from an intricate web of relationships and experiences, thoughts, and feelings that stretched from childhood to Quimby and back again."[40]

Others maintain that Eddy's insistence upon recognizing and dealing with the effects of mentally projected hate was a valid response to a neglected aspect of human experience. From this standpoint, she was describing and defining how human life actually works—the mental mechanism that operates beneath its surface. It takes no close reading between the lines to see Robert Peel's discussion of this issue, especially in his depiction of the Woodbury and Stetson episodes, as an expression of this approach. Christian Scientists in the World War II era and since have often said that the grip that Hitler gained on Germany and its monstrous consequences are clear evidences of mesmerism on a mass scale. One article in the *Journal*, for example, asked: What "made a nation-apparently cultured, civilized—lawful, allow the attempted extermination of entire groups of people, including tiny children, when a fraudulent, unbalanced demagogue pointed the way? Mesmeric influence is the explanation that seems to get closest to the heart of the matter."[41]

In addition, there is substantial literature outside of writings about Christian Science that takes the phenomenon of projected mental influence seriously. Larry Dossey's book *Be Careful What you Pray for . . . You Just Might Get it,* though a popularized general treatment of the subject, points to a widespread literature, including one major database of experimental evidence documenting the effects of "distant intentionality." Dossey concludes on the basis of this and other studies that data exist suggesting "that, in principle, negative intent does have distant effects, whether we call these intentions prayers, curses, hexes, or spells."[42]

There is also an *intermediate* approach between the polar views of those who credit or discredit the possibility of projected hatred. This approach holds that both those who practice and those who believe they suffered from such malice are caught up in a climate of fear that itself produces destructive results. From this standpoint, entertaining the suggestion of the possible harm of malicious animal magnetism becomes a kind of self-fulfilling prophecy. The biography of Eddy by Ernest Sutherland Bates and John V. Dittemore, a member of the church board that excommunicated Stetson, argues that her efforts to practice "witchcraft" in New York may seem laughable from a later perspective. Yet these efforts "were far from laughable at the time to those who believed in their efficacy. And when her victims were of a suggestible disposition and were informed of the measures taken against them . . . there can be no doubt that serious mental injury often resulted."[43]

Whatever construction one places upon the evidence, the facts in Stetson's case are well attested: she believed in and practiced what Eddy called "despotic mental control," and many of those who became the object of her hostility apparently suffered and died as a result of what Stetson and those in her circle took to be the results of her baleful mental influence. In examining some of Stetson's students individually in September 1909, the board of directors nailed down the facts about Stetson's "treatments" of her enemies. Insisting upon direct "yes" and "no" answers to avoid evasiveness on the part of those being examined, their interrogation included questions such as: "Did you ever hear Mrs. Stetson in the course of one of those treatments say of any person that he or she was ripe for destruction?" "Did you ever hear her say in one of those treatments, 'Go to your place. If it be in God, then go there, but if not, then go to the other place?'" "Did you hear her make this declaration, after mentioning the name of some person: 'If the error in you is so great that you cannot save your body then let it die, it is nothing anyway?'" The answer to these questions in each case was "Yes."[44]

In framing their questions, the directors drew on the diary of Virgil Strickler, an able and genial lawyer from Omaha who had been healed by Christian Science, moved to New York in 1906, and became First Reader of Stetson's church and privy to her daily meetings with her circle of practitioners. Most of them, he wrote in his diary, "are in abject fear of her. . . . It is the sort of fear exhibited by a subject towards the hypnotist in whose control the subject is when the hypnotist is angry." Strickler became increasingly appalled at Stetson's intense hatred of the other five branch churches in New York City and their members. On February 25, 1909, he wrote that Stetson "is working for the destruction" of these churches "as well as the people who compose them." "I strike to kill," he recorded her saying on July 4, 1909. Several days later he noted her conviction that those who refused to recognize that Eddy is God and she, Stetson, is Christ "shall die and go out with suffering untold and die on the next plane of consciousness and the next and so on forever until they recognize her as Mrs. Eddy's first born and until they atone for the sin of having doubted or opposed her."[45]

Stetson sought to explain away Strickler's allegations by stating to the press that he misconstrued her intent, failing to discriminate between mental malpractice and "indispensable defence or self-protection." From this "fortress of defence," she declared, she would name the person she believed was attacking her mentally, "and then speak to the error which might be operating through the human mind for which he has been the avenue." But even this position was at odds with Eddy's teaching. Reflecting the lesson she had learned in dealing with the Woodbury suit, she had written to Stetson in 1905 that the only effective defense against aggressive mental assault lay in acting according to "the rule of our blessed Lord viz. Love your enemies; and return good for evil."[46]

After Stetson's excommunication, evidence began to surface of the harm done to her enemies by either the treatments she administered to them—or, alternatively, by their belief that these mental ministrations of hatred had power. The *Boston Herald* for April 27, 1910, noted that after her excommunication, a dozen of Stetson's followers had died, three of them by suicide. In each instance "it is said, the victims of self-destruction have been obsessed with the belief that some powerful mental influence urged them to end their lives." The article also refers to the earlier death of Carol Norton, Stetson's erstwhile protégé who broke with her after his marriage in 1901, contrary to her insistence that her students remain chaste. Eddy had an especially high opinion of the talented young New Yorker, made him a member of her last class in 1898, and carried on a correspondence with him, probably unknown to Stetson.

His death as a result of a freak accident in Chicago not long after alienating Stetson was a blow to Eddy, who cried copiously when she heard of it. Stetson's reaction, according to one of her ex-followers, was different: "She turned as white as a sheet and cried: 'God grant that Carol does not haunt me for that.'"[47] Whether or not Carol Norton haunted Stetson, her own conscience apparently did not. Strickler reported that her curses on those she saw as rivals and opponents grew increasingly malevolent over the months in which he kept his diary. But Strickler himself, who more than anyone was responsible for apprising the board of facts that led to Stetson's downfall, appears to have remained unaffected by her hostility. "I think that I am perhaps the only one who has never been mesmerized by her," he wrote on June 26. He recorded one instance during the following month which he interpreted as an unsuccessful effort on her part to hypnotize him. Just after he returned from being interrogated by the directors in Boston, she came to his office in the church. Behaving strangely, she positioned herself four feet from Strickler with her eyes fixed steadily on him. She began repeating in a "sing-song way 'God is all. God is love. I come to you in love.' 'There is nothing but love. God is love' etc. etc. all the while following my eyes with hers."

It dawned on Strickler that Stetson was trying to hypnotize him so that he would accept her version of what had transpired in Boston before she unfolded her plan of operations at the practitioners' meeting at noon. He began to declare to himself, as he put it, "that I could not be touched by her thought." Within a few minutes he felt completely freed from its influence.

Strickler's response on this occasion had far-reaching implications as an example of Eddy's approach to the issue of projected malice. She held unapologetically that what she called "the power of liberated thought . . . to accomplish an evil purpose" is an operative factor on the human scene. But she maintained that this power could be rendered powerless—seen as insubstantial suggestion and thus nullified. "Evil thoughts, lusts, and malicious purposes," she wrote in *Science and Health,* "cannot go forth, like wandering pollen, from one human mind to another, finding unsuspected lodgment, if virtue and truth build a strong defense." This defense was constituted on the recognition that through Christian discipleship, one can actually have, in words she quoted from Paul, "the mind that was in Christ Jesus." Therein, she believed, lay the source of the kind of freedom that Strickler achieved in countering what he saw as Stetson's attempted hypnotic control.[48]

STETSON AND THE LIVERY OF HEAVEN

Eddy's letter urging the members of First Church, New York, to support the directors following Stetson's excommunication did much to pacify the troubled waters of the congregation. With Stetson no longer in the church's midst, Strickler became its de facto guiding star. But it was to be some time before the church itself felt less impact from Stetson's thought, since she continued to exercise a controlling influence on many of her partisans who stayed within the church.

Stetson herself was put into an extremely awkward position of having to come up with some rationale for her apparent desertion by the leader she so revered. Eddy's action, Stetson maintained, was a covert means of relieving her from all burdens of material organization and thus another special sign of Eddy's continuing love. Far from turning against Eddy, Stetson developed an even more exalted view of her. Shortly after Eddy died, Stetson publicly proclaimed that Eddy would at some point reappear in the semblance of a human form and that Stetson herself "shall see Mrs. Eddy" and "walk by her side"—prompting evangelist Billy Sunday to exclaim, "If old Mother Eddy rises from the dead I'll eat polecat for breakfast and wash it down with booze!"[49]

The prediction was desperate. But the fact that it was unrealized seemed not to have troubled Stetson at all. Far from shrinking from the limelight, she channeled her abundant energies into new paths, becoming almost as ardent an apostle of right-wing Americanism as she had been of her own version of Christian Science. A trained musician, she founded a large patriotic chorus, sponsoring concerts at such venues as

Carnegie Hall and the stage of the Metropolitan Opera. She also devoted substantial energies to supporting a magazine called the *American Standard* that preached Nordic supremacy, racial purity, restricted immigration, and "Gentile Economic Emancipation," along with "100% Americanism." For several years in the mid-1920s, she held forth on religion and other matters on a popular radio station bankrolled by one of her students. Energetic to the last and looking far younger than her years, she averred that she would not die. When she finally did so after a brief illness, she was eighty-seven and had been vigorously active almost until the last.[50]

While Stetson's bid for successorship failed, it probably never had much chance of succeeding. Stetson was thoroughly unlike Josephine Curtis Woodbury, who did Eddy far more personal harm but whose bizarre behavior was extremely off-putting to the vast majority of Christian Scientists. Yet successorship had more than one face. Stetson was in one respect a unique phenomenon in the history of Christian Science. But she was also an extreme embodiment of tendencies that had other expressions.

Stetson's penchant for outsized and opulent architecture was not hers alone. Eddy's own preference was for simpler church architecture—for "churchy" churches with "something pointed upward" along traditional Protestant lines. While architectural styles in branch churches in smaller American communities were heterogeneous, some of them, like Bernard Maybeck's handsome and eclectic First Church in Berkeley, California, constructed in 1913, were truly notable. But the architecture of branch churches in many larger cities, among them Providence, Chicago, Kansas City, Minneapolis, Oakland, and Los Angeles, were mostly classical in conception—constructed in what has been called "the triumphal style," and conveying the message "Look, we have arrived!" Conspicuously positioned in downtown districts, often in affluent areas, they may look disconcertingly more like banks than places of worship.[51]

In her architectural tastes as well as other areas, Stetson overtly championed a version of materialism that associated the practice of Christian Science with "abundance" and an upper-class mentality and lifestyle. Yet her voluminous writings on Christian Science are filled with a wholly different kind of religious rhetoric, as when she wrote that "as humble followers of the meek and Holy One, but mighty in reflection of Spirit, Life, and Love, Christian Scientists must follow Christ and continually unfold in spiritual understanding and demonstration."[52]

This, however, was only one kind of illustration of a gap in Stetson's sensibility between rhetoric and reality that had another more serious dimension. Christian Scientists sometimes made use of the terms "absolute" and "relative" as a way of differentiating ultimate spiritual reality from the present human scene, although Eddy herself never paired the terms in this way. For her, it was inconceivable that one could claim purity of motive and action spiritually without making good on that claim in daily experience. "To assume that there are no claims of evil and yet to indulge them," wrote Eddy in *Science and Health*, "is a moral offence."[53]

Prior to her trial before the board of directors, however, Stetson had instructed her practitioners to testify "in the absolute" when answering the board's questions about the doses of mental malpractice she attempted to administer to her enemies. When reminded by Strickler that she had spoken words along these lines, Stetson flatly denied that she had ever said them. It was, she said, her human self and not her real spiritual self that had made the statements.

During her interrogation, it came out that Stetson and her practitioners had used the same tactics while testifying under oath in the Brush Will case, rationalizing that they were speaking "in the absolute." One of the practitioners boasted that she had been on the stand for two days testifying from the standpoint of the "absolute" and the opposing lawyer never caught her once. Referring obviously though indirectly to this verbal legerdemain, Archibald McLellan wrote in a *Sentinel* editorial that a true Christian Scientist fully understands that to "make the perfection of Christ, of man in the image and likeness of God, a cloak for deception of any kind, whether it be the blackest of sins or the 'white lies' of conventionality, is to commit an enormity; it is what a poet of a century ago aptly termed stealing 'the livery of the court of heaven to serve the devil in.'"[54]

In all these respects, the figure of Augusta E. Stetson looms large in the Christian Science movement, but not as a potential successor to Eddy. She was, rather, a precursor of a tendency among some Christian Scientists to live out an uneasy compromise between the rhetoric of spirituality and the reality of a subtle—and sometimes not so subtle—materialism.

How the World Works

For Eddy, spirituality is at war with the spirit of worldliness, but not with humanity. With advancing years, her concern with the needs of humanity broadened. While her primary emphasis was never on social and political affairs, she became increasingly aware of the growth of power structures in the United States and the vast dimension of world problems, especially the issues of war and peace that reached critical mass with the outbreak of World War I four years after her death.

There was, of course, the friendly, familiar world of Concord at her doorstep. Much as she shied away from the often gaping eyes of Christian Scientists, she relished the role of a public and public-spirited figure in Concord itself. National affairs, too, engaged more of her attention in her last fifteen years or so than in former years. Eddy subscribed to and read a number of magazines, sometimes marking articles about public policy in such periodicals as the *Literary Digest* and sharing passages with members of the household. Nor was she reluctant to express her views publicly. In a message to her church in 1899 she wrote, "I reluctantly foresee great danger threatening our nation,—imperialism, monopoly, and a lax system of religion." When pacifists and isolationists denounced President Theodore Roosevelt's call for naval preparedness in his April 1908 message to Congress, Eddy wrote and asked the Committee on Publication to circulate a statement that, while she believed in arbitration of national disagreements, it is unquestionable that "at this hour the armament of navies is necessary, for the purpose of preventing war and preserving peace among nations." Her tone was less warlike than the president's. But Roosevelt commented in a letter, he wished "that other religious leaders showed as much good sense."[55]

By that time, Eddy's fame had increased to the point that she was frequently asked by leading newspapers for her comments on a variety of domestic and world issues such as peace and war, national politics, divorce, and the death of public figures. She made frequent charitable contributions to such causes as disaster relief for victims of the Galveston flood, the repair of New England churches, the Massachusetts Society for the Prevention of Cruelty to Children, and even a New England hospital.

In one area of world politics Eddy developed surprising expertise. Sarah Pike Conger was the wife of the American minister to China at the time of the Boxer Rebellion. A dedicated Christian Scientist, she relied on her faith during the Boxers' siege of the foreign legation in Peking in 1900. In working through the difficult issues she faced, Conger carried on an extensive correspondence with Eddy, who developed a strong interest in conditions in China. A few years later, a reporter who had been a correspondent there interviewed Eddy, who asked him a question about Chinese affairs. She then proceeded to discuss various aspects of the situation in China in such detail that the reporter wondered to a colleague how so secluded a person could have acquired such extensive knowledge of the history and national habits of the Chinese.[56]

Along with her widening awareness of national and world events and conditions, Eddy developed a strong conviction about the need for the popular press to reach the public with responsible information that would keep readers accurately informed. By 1900, the misrepresentation of Christian Science in the press had convinced her to form the Committee on Publication to correct injustices done her and Christian Science in public forums. Certainly, too, the extreme injustice accorded her by the press, including both the *New York World* and *McClure's Magazine*, sharpened her sense of the need for greater journalistic responsibility and ethics. While journalism as a profession was not of special interest to her, any activity that had so much influence on public thought was a definite concern, especially when it came to the representation of the cause she led.

However sophisticated and worldly the press believed itself to be, she saw it shaped and influenced by operative and often covert mental factors just as much as any other power center in public life. In this respect, the attention accorded Eddy in *McClure's Magazine* and in the *New York World* were illustrations of how unseen influences often shaped the character of major journalistic institutions—and to a significant extent, academic scholarship as well.

On November 2, 1906, the *World's* financial manager, Bradford Merrill, wrote to Joseph Pulitzer—who apparently knew nothing of the matter until this point—that among the major stories the newspaper was pursuing was the "revelation of Eddy's decrepitude." The beat, he said, was the result of a rumor that had been passed along to the paper's city editor, John Spurgeon, from a relative. Spurgeon then followed the tip to Boston and finally got "all the facts" from "Mr. Peabody, a Boston lawyer of the highest standing."[57]

Spurgeon was probably unaware that Frederick Peabody's reputation was exceedingly dubious in Boston legal circles. Peabody was among the least likely persons to share anything like accurate information about Eddy. For nearly two years, he had been providing information—in most instances, disinformation—about Eddy to the staff of *McClure's Magazine* for the series they began running in December 1906. That series was set in motion when Georgine Milmine, an obscure New York journalist who intended to include Eddy in a series of articles on eminent American women, arrived at Pleasant View seeking an interview, but was turned aside by Eddy's staff. Convinced that Eddy had something to hide, she began a series of interviews with disaffected former associates, including William Nixon, Richard Kennedy, and Judge Joseph Clarkson, along with individuals in rural New Hampshire who had known Eddy in the distant past.

Milmine then trekked about New England gathering as much dirt on Eddy as she could, also turning up some useful documentary material in the process. Realizing that she lacked the ability to fashion this material into a coherent biographical narrative, she sold it to *McClure's* in 1904. *McClure's* investigative staff, headed by Ida Tarbell, who had written an influential exposé of the Standard Oil Company, then pursued the leads developed by Milmine.

By this time, Josephine Woodbury was again in the picture. After the loss of her lawsuit against Eddy in 1899, she spent several years in England, living well and continuing her campaign against Christian Science, which was then flourishing in the British Isles. Her hostility toward Eddy had not abated. Indeed, a Christian Scientist who met her in London recalled that after commenting to Woodbury, with no intended reference to Woodbury herself, "your sin always finds you out," she put out her tongue and hissed at her. By 1903 she was at least temporarily back in the United States, evidently relishing any opportunity to get back at Eddy. In early February she wrote twice to Twain from her New York hotel, offered to meet with him and sent him, among other materials, a concocted and misleading description of the "Mother's room" at the Mother Church, an apartment designed for Eddy's occasional use.[58]

William D. McCrackan, New York's Committee on Publication who met with Twain on several occasions, came to the conclusion that Woodbury had more covert ways of influencing Twain. Time and again, Twain told McCrackan, he would be roused from sleep by "an impelling force" to write abusive letters to Eddy. Although he generally tore such letters up (actually he sent two of them to McCrackan, who graciously returned them), he explained that "something forces me to write them." That "something," concluded McCrackan, was nothing but "vulgar hypnotic trickery" engendered by Woodbury. Whatever the merits of McCrackan's view, Woodbury's influence on the developing series at *McClure's* can hardly be doubted. After Milmine had been rebuffed by the staff at Pleasant View, she contacted Woodbury, who predictably put her in touch with Peabody. *McClure's* then hired Peabody to provide new leads for the staff's research. In Gillian Gill's words, "behind the unknown and subtly mythical Georgine Milmine, we find the well-known staff of *McClure's*, and behind the magazine loom the ghostly figures of the strongly implicated Woodbury and the avowedly prejudiced Peabody."[59]

The same chain of influence was at work in the reporting of the *New York World*, which very well may have pursued its own investigation out of rivalry with *McClure's*, a purveyor of a more sober, but, in this instance at least, just as yellow journalism. Woodbury manipulated Peabody; Peabody manipulated the staff of *McClure's* and the *New York World;* its editors manipulated Senator Chandler; Senator Chandler manipulated both George Glover and Foster Eddy, until the Masters' interview with Eddy proved that the picture of her in the *World*'s articles and the charges of her supposed "next friends" had no basis in fact. Yet all the while the editors of both *McClure's* and the *World* viewed themselves as tough-minded professional journalists acting from their own clear and hard-headed motives.

While the influence of the *World*'s articles on Eddy had a strong immediate bearing on the initiation of the Next Friends Suit, the role of the *McClure's* series had a more long-lasting influence in shaping negative views of her in the hostile biographical tradition. To write up the series for publication Tarbell turned to a new subeditor, Willa Cather, just blossoming as America's finest novelist of the Southwest and Midwest. Cather later tried to distance herself from the magazine series and the book that developed from it, probably because she saw it as an exercise in mere journalism. But she was the author of all but one of its fourteen chapters. Her developing skills as a novelist were effectively deployed in the book, which converts the real Eddy into a vivid but essentially fictional character.[60]

Cather's Eddy is a megalomaniac power-seeker intent on dominating those around her, money-grubbing, totally unscrupulous, devoid of originality, and a textbook case of hysteria. By characterizing Eddy as a hysteric, Cather—possibly without even realizing it—drew upon one of the major chauvinist put-downs of women who acted outside of the domestic sphere. In so doing, she put in place a basic interpretive rubric that much of the negative literature about Eddy casually repeated—for example, by the eminent literary critic Harold Bloom, who referred to Eddy as "a monumental hysteric of classical dimensions."[61]

Bloom, among others, thus accepted at face value what turned out to be a wholly unsubstantiated view of Eddy. In her biography of Eddy, written from a feminist perspective, Gillian Gill demonstrates that the picture of Eddy as a hysteric traces back to a single affidavit solicited by reporters for *McClure's* from one Hannah Philbrik, who conceived a strong dislike for Eddy after having attended school with her briefly. Whatever the source of Philbrik's animosity, it illustrates a point about Eddy's effect upon others that was to remain a constant throughout her life. While it is too much to say that she was the sort of person people either loved or hated, it became a prevalent pattern that she either won people's hearts or turned them off completely. Around the same time that she elicited Philbrik's animosity, for example, she won the profound admiration of her minister and tutor, the Reverend Enoch Corser. This pattern was to repeat itself in future decades. It was expressed in the extraordinarily contrasting views of Eddy that took the forms of hostile biographical literature beginning with the Cather and Milmine series for *McClure's*, and a hagiographical tradition that began with Wilbur's *Human Life* series.[62]

From Philbrik's highly biased affidavit, Cather built up a portrait of the young Mary Baker as extremely nervous and hysterical, and, as a child and young woman, subject to violent seizures. Cather then proceeded to draw a trajectory from Mary Baker's presumed early hysterical fits, to symptoms of her illness in North Groton during her thirties, then to her later "obsession" with animal magnetism. With a sure sleuthing instinct, Gill—who also wrote a biography of Agatha Christie—points out that convincing evidence for Eddy's presumed hysterical behavior simply does not exist. The Baker family papers, which came to light only after the Cather biography was published, portray Mary Baker as frequently ill. But they give not the barest hint that she had hysterical fits of any sort or used them to control and disrupt her family. Nevertheless, the view of Eddy as virtually a life-long hysteric has been widely accepted, to a large degree on the authority of Edwin Franden Dakin's highly sensationalized and best-selling biography, *Eddy: The Biography of a Virginal Mind*. Dakin extolled Milmine as "an intrepid, path-breaking researcher" whose biography is "so detailed and annotated that it was nothing short of a monumental piece of work."[63]

In the final analysis, the negative biographical tradition, which includes the journalistic depictions of Eddy in the *World* and the *McClure's* series, were extensions of the portrayal of Eddy that Woodbury had etched in acid in her article for the *Arena*—demonstrating the subtle chain of influences that, then as now, sometimes shapes the covert ways in which the world works.

MONITORING THE WORLD

For Eddy, the influence of Christian Science was at work in the world just as surely as were the unseen influences that shaped human thought via journalism and other areas of life. Christian Science, she believed, will continue to gradually "leaven" the atmosphere of human thought, and will continue to do so until "the leaven of Spirit changes the whole of mortal thought, as yeast changes the chemical properties of meal."[64]

In *Science and Health*, she speaks of this leavening process as particularly applicable to the worlds of "Science, Theology, and Medicine"—the title of a major chapter in the book. The role of the media in the period of the Next Friends Suit convinced Eddy that the influence of Christian Science must become a force in the world of journalism as well. This conviction took concrete form about a year after the conclusion of the suit when, in July 1908, she instructed the board of directors and trustees to begin a newspaper entitled the *Christian Science Monitor.* By late November of the same year the first issue was on the stands.

In her July 1907 interview with Leigh Mitchell Hodges for the *North American,* Eddy had said, "Newspapers should be edited with the same reverence for Truth, God, as is observed in the administration of the most serious affairs of life." At that point, there was little indication that she contemplated founding a newspaper that would fulfill this criterion, but for at least a decade, the idea of a newspaper edited and published by Christian Scientists had been hovering in the background of her thought. The *Christian Science Sentinel,* which she founded in 1898, carried several pages of news in each issue, along with reprints of newspaper editorials. The same year she rejected a plan by several Christian Scientists to buy and operate a Boston newspaper, believing that doing so was premature. That the project was on her mind, however, was clear from a phrase she dropped into a letter to McLellan in 1902: "until I start a widespread press."[65]

The founding of the *Monitor* barely a year after the conclusion of the Next Friends Suit was obviously influenced by the *World*'s example of journalism at its worst. Its character may also have been to some extent shaped by a letter Eddy received in March 1908 from John L. Wright, a Boston newspaperman and a Christian Scientist, who recommended the founding of a "general newspaper" reflecting a constructive rather than a merely sensational view of the news. Upon receiving Wright's letter in March 1908, Eddy drafted a reply, probably never sent, saying that she had had "this newspaper scheme in my thought for quite awhile."[66]

Translating this "newspaper scheme" into a functioning reality was the way Eddy found for Christian Science to leaven world thought, though in a very modest way, by leavening the world of journalism. For Eddy and her followers, the founding of the *Monitor* was in its own way a kind of discovery: the discovery of an appropriate alternative, perhaps the only alternative, to the involvement of so many other churches in social and political affairs. The *Monitor* was an outlet for the expression of social concern by Christian Scientists at a time when the Social Gospel was a hugely important aspect of American church life and an important influence in the shaping of reform programs and socio-economic thought of the Progressive Era.

For advocates of the Social Gospel, the mission of Christianity was redefined so as to include direct involvement in the securing of social justice and greater economic security for the downtrodden victims of industrialization. It was, of course, easy enough for Christian Scientists to hunker down and ignore social problems completely, practicing their faith in order to maintain their health, comfort, status, and success. Eddy and the more earnest of her followers believed, however, that healing was not necessarily confined to individual problems, but could be practiced in relation to the larger problems of the world.

It is really not possible to speak of Eddy as having a set of social or political teachings. But she did make a number of statements that point in the same direction, condemning the worldliness that she saw as the opposite of the spirituality she cherished. In 1901, she cited evidences of this materialism in a message to her followers, "I reluctantly foresee great dangers confronting our nation in the form of materialism, competition, and a lax system of religion."[67]

But Eddy never wanders far from her metaphysical basis. For her, all evidences of conflict and oppression can ultimately be traced to the belief of plural minds separate from the one Mind. Only "by entering into a state of evil thoughts," she wrote, can we "separate one man's interests from those of the entire human family," also stating that the belief in life apart from God "ruptures the life and brotherhood of man at the very outset." Yet she prophesied a time when "the cement of a higher humanity will cement all interests in the one divinity." These words well express Eddy's consistent Christian demands on her followers.[68]

Among the most crucial matters of social and political concern were war and peace. During the early stages of the Russo-Japanese War in 1905, she wrote a statement to the *Boston Globe* including the words, "War is in itself an evil, barbarous, devilish. Victory in error is defeat in Truth." The next June in a message to her church at the time of its annual meeting she requested church members to "pray each day for the amicable settlement of the war between Russia and Japan and pray that God bless that great nation and those islands of the sea with peace and prosperity." Two weeks later she requested that church members cease special prayers for peace and instead trust in "God's disposal of events." Yet her followers believed that their prayers were bearing fruit.[69] Within several weeks, through the mediation of President Roosevelt, a treaty concluding the war was signed in Portsmouth, New Hampshire. To Eddy's followers, the fact that she had called for their prayers to end the war and that the treaty was signed just forty miles from her Pleasant View home showed what prayer could accomplish beyond the healing of individuals.

In future decades, Christian Scientists came to think it natural to pray as individuals about such larger problems as war and natural disasters. That they did so was in itself one consequence of Eddy's founding of the *Monitor.* An excellent newspaper, reflecting the constructive thrust of her teaching, signified that the church was neither ignorant of world problems nor involving itself in them at the level of a social or political movement. Rather, it implied what was suggested in the very term "monitor." In the words of Katherine M. Fanning, editor of the *Monitor* from 1983 to 1988, a monitor "receives and tracks. It is a communicator . . . but I think that most of all, a monitor watches. I think Eddy wanted her newspaper to watch and to report on . . . the causes behind the news."[70]

"SOMETHING IN A NAME"

Once the idea for the *Monitor* came to focus in Eddy's mind, she pushed the project forward with determination. After informing the directors of her intentions, she wrote tersely to the trustees of the Christian Science Publishing Society: "It is my request that you start a daily newspaper at once, and call it the Christian Science Monitor. Let there be no delay. The Cause demands that it be issued now."[71] "Now," it turned out, meant in a hundred days—precious little time in which to accomplish so formidable a task as planning and staffing a major journalistic enterprise. The recently completed publishing house had to be extended, a project that required the demolition of a block of three-story brick apartment buildings. A staff of nearly one hundred had to be recruited and plans put in place for the widespread distribution of the newspaper.

Having given initial instructions for the founding of the newspaper, Eddy followed the implementation of her directive with great interest and some anxiety. There were capable people to carry the work of moving the *Monitor* forward, particularly Archibald McLellan, who became its first editor while still serving as editor of the *Sentinel* and *Journal.* As he observed in a conversation with William Dana Orcutt, who had spoken of Eddy's ability "to plan out and follow through" the manufacture of her books, "she has left us nothing to conceive or originate—simply to carry on and to execute."[72]

To make sure that they did so, Eddy took note that the project they were carrying through was her plan—the *Monitor* as she had conceived of it. On August 12, she had Dickey write to McLellan asking to see a sample mock-up of the newspaper so that "she may have an intelligent idea of what you propose to do. She has been expressing a great deal of anxiety about the outcome of your efforts. . . ." She examined the type-face to be used, requested a better quality paper, and chose the motto for the newspaper: "First the blade, then the ear, then the full grain in the ear." In mid-August she carefully examined a lengthy memo from the trustees of the Publishing Society about the logistical problems they were encountering. Responding through Dickey, she indicated that her original conception had been more modest—that she had not envi-sioned launching so soon "into metropolitan greatness," but that a smaller paper costing much less would have been preferable, at least at the outset. Nevertheless, she did not wish to hamper the trustees, but expressed hope that they would proceed "with wisdom and economy."[73]

When it came to the fundamental character of the newspaper, how-ever, she would make no compromise. Where some of those close to Eddy argued that it should be mainly a Boston paper, she insisted that it be a "real" newspaper, a vehicle for national and international news. Where others argued that it should be an overtly religious newspaper, she confined the direct expression of her teaching to a single daily article on the "Home Forum" page.

Most important, she insisted, was that the title of the newspaper include the term "Christian Science." Irving Tomlinson was present when a group of those involved in the project tried to persuade her that leaving this out would give the paper greater appeal. He recalled that as a last resort McLellan had an interview with Eddy to win her over to their point of view. "The members of the house were on tiptoe, waiting outside of Mrs. Eddy's room while the final decision was being made. The interview was brief. A moment or so, and the editor emerged. Said he, 'Mrs. Eddy is firm, and her answer is God gave me this name and it remains.'"[74]

By taking this position and holding it against the advice of some of those closest to her, Eddy cemented the unbreakable association between the newspaper she founded and the church of which it was a part. In the editorial she wrote for the first issue, "Something in a Name," she said it was the purpose of the newspaper to "spread undivided the Science that operates unspent."[75] The newspaper did not promote Christian Science in any direct way, but it did operate from the assump-tion that the teaching of Christian Science was valid. Christian Science became, therefore, the operative feature in the background of the news-paper, furnishing and guiding its approach to the coverage of daily affairs, shaping the paper's treatment of the good in human life, along with the evils that needed to be confronted and opposed.

The theological basis of the *Monitor*'s approach—why it can be said in Eddy's words to "spread undivided the Science that operates unspent"— was well expressed in a *Monitor* editorial published on August

26, 1954, during an assembly of the World Council of Churches. The editorial was written by Robert Peel, who served as an editorial writer for the *Monitor* for many years before beginning his biographical trilogy on Eddy. Peel saw a deep connection between the theme of the assembly, "Christ, the Hope of the World," and the teachings of Christian Science that undergirds the *Monitor.*

The newspaper, he wrote "was founded on a theology which teaches that the Christ, as the divine manifestation of God, is ever appearing to the humble heart that turns away from materiality to Spirit." This hope is neither "this worldly" nor "other worldly." It is not directed toward "either an earthly utopia or a paradise beyond the grave. It is solidly grounded in the transformation of present human experience by the Christ acting in consciousness to bring to light man's eternal spiritual status as the son of God." Thus the action of the Christ in human life—even, Peel implies, if it is not acknowledged as such—is the basis for "our own large hope in the face of today's monumental problems."[76]

Eddy's editorial for the first issue of the *Monitor* also said that its purpose was "to injure no man, but to bless all mankind." The phrase "to bless all mankind" in its simplicity spoke for itself. But it had a dimension in its effect on Christian Scientists that was caught in an article by Helen Andrews Nixon that appeared soon after the newspaper was first published. William Nixon's excessive emphasis on publishing as the main activity of the church had caused much dissension in the several years before the Mother Church was reorganized. Now, however, his wife wrote in support of a new publication that was both within the church and an expression of its deepest values. The effect of the newspaper, she wrote, "has been to lift one's eyes to an horizon far beyond one's own doorstep. The call to help in the world's thinking is no longer something that can pass unheeded, it is an imperative duty. Things we did not like to look at nor think of, problems we did not feel able to cope with, must now be faced manfully, and correct thinking concerning the world's doings cultivated and maintained."[77]

The more universal scope and mission of the *Monitor* took concrete form in its character as a truly *international* newspaper. The emphasis on the covering of world news, through which the *Monitor* attained much of its distinction, grew in large part through the influence of its first associate editor, Frederick Dixon, a British Christian Scientist with considerable vision and historical background. Eddy approved of editorials that had a broader viewpoint and, through Dixon, made it clear that the *Monitor* should carry world news. By 1910 a European bureau had been established, which in turn set the pattern for a network of bureaus worldwide.[78]

Mary Baker Eddy examining the first issue of the *Christian Science Monitor,*
November 25, 1908. Albert J. Forbes, 1986 drawing.

The first edition of the *Monitor* was published on November 25,
1908, a day Eddy eagerly anticipated. On November 20 she had opened
her Bible to Isaiah 62, verses 7 to 12, which contained the following
words: "Go through, go through the gates; prepare ye the way of the
people; cast up, cast up the highway; lift up a standard for the people."
Beside the passage, Eddy wrote the notation: "6 days." November 25,
when the "standard" of the *Monitor* was lifted up, turned out to be a cold
and foggy day. Irving Tomlinson recalled that Eddy summoned members of her household, then commented that, contrary to the weather
outside, that day is "in Truth the lightest of all days. This is the day
when our daily paper goes forth to lighten mankind."[79]

Speaking of the Monitor as going forth to "lighten mankind" conveys the underlying intent that prompted Eddy to found the newspaper as the last major accomplishment of her life. That the newspaper
marked a strong and sincere, if modest, effort to accomplish this aim
is well attested by honors it has received—including, ironically enough,
a number of Pulitzer Prizes. Next to the healing work of Christian
Scientists, the *Monitor* has been an effective missionary for the movement.
Eddy was particularly pleased with the characterization of the *Monitor*
by William McKenzie as "a most genial persuader of men," saying that

this was "the spirit I have enjoined upon them from the start." The *Monitor* provided proof to those wary of Christian Scientists' approach to human problems that they did not bury their heads in the sand, while, in the words of McLellan, its first editor, it was a paper that went into "the highways and byways of humanity." In the words of Alfred Farlow in a letter to Eddy, "It is wonderful what the Monitor is doing as a missionary. It is opening the way for our literature, including your works. It is a better missionary than the Christian Scientists because it does not talk too much; it does not commit Christian Science unwisely, and does not disgrace us by unwise answers to insincere questions of critics."[80]

The *Monitor* was the way Eddy found to make apparent that her church was in the world, but not of the world. Christian Scientists, Eddy believed, could not on the whole afford to become too immersed in political and social causes. To her, they were engaged in a more consequential and profound reform than was possible in the political arena. She went on record supporting the need for citizens to vote and endorsing the voting franchise for women. And there was nothing to prevent Christian Scientists from making a contribution in the sphere of political affairs and social reform. But Eddy also warned Stetson in 1907 "to avoid being identified pro or con in politics. . . . Keep out of the *reach* of such subjects. Give all your attention to the moral and spiritual status of the race."[81]

In *Science and Health,* she included an extended passage underscoring that the great struggle for human rights, especially the abolition of slavery, foreshadowed the larger struggle for the freedom of humanity from all forms of enslavement to error and evil. "Legally to abolish unpaid servitude in the United States was hard," she wrote, "but the abolition of mental slavery is a more difficult task."[82] Eddy saw the primary work of Christian Scientists as heartfelt participation in the great work of attaining this end.

In the first edition of *Science and Health* she had written, "The time for thinkers has come; and the time for revolutions, ecclesiastic and social, must come." In later years, more active and committed Christian Scientists spoke of their work in the movement as the preeminent reform of a reforming period, one that struck at the roots of social evils while seeking to remove its weeds. Edward Kimball expressed the view of many when he spoke of "this crusade of reform which is now progressing in the name of Christian Science."[83]

The progress of this major reform, Eddy and her followers believed, would eventually leaven and ameliorate the evils that plagued society, since God's government must be demonstrated in all phases of experience.

In the Daily Prayer, she enjoined church members to pray for God's Word to "enrich the affections of all mankind" in the conviction that so doing would eventually ameliorate the sicknesses of society as well as the body.[84] But this larger spiritual transformation, she insisted, was the crucial end for which her followers much work.

In so doing, she maintained, they would help establish a new level of spiritual consciousness at which social and political evils, like other expressions of conflict and error, could no longer occur.

12

Elijah's Mantle

"I HAVE AN EXPERIENCE ALL MY OWN"

IN AUGUST 1909, AS THE STETSON EPISODE WAS NEARING ITS CLIMAX, EDDY
wrote to Alfred Farlow,

> Will you yourself, and get others that are as smart as you are, stir the dry
> bones all over the field, to more words, actions and demonstrations
> in Christian Science. I am weary waiting for the impulse of Christian
> Science to become more active all over our field. Get somebody—and
> more than one—to ring out the first arousal. "Awake thou that sleepest,
> and arise from the dead, and Christ shall give thee light."[1]

Sometime during that same year, Eddy had a visit with her friend
William Dana Orcutt. Applying a phrase she had heard used by her
banker, Josiah E. Fernald, to herself, she told Orcutt that what she was
doing during this period of her life was "consolidating my gains, while
I keep on with the building"—a comment which he called a "wonderful
self-analysis of those final fruitful years."[2]

At that point, despite age, weariness, and intermittently severe
physical difficulties, Eddy was still thinking in terms of the welfare of
the movement as a whole. With her usual determination to wrest something positive from the most difficult experiences, she drew practical
lessons from Stetson's efforts to dominate the New York field. A letter
from Adam Dickey printed in the *Sentinel* for January 15, 1910, stated
her desire that all branch churches "shall follow the growing tendency
to adopt a truly democratic form of church government." He went on to
explain, "She believes that all branch churches that have been controlled by any one teacher, or the students of any one teacher, will find
it greatly to their advantage to change to a broader and more liberal
form of government." By that point she had already written a number

of *Manual* bylaws for the future protection of the church, many of them designed in the first instance to deal with Stetson's excesses.[3]

Eddy's role in the controversy over Stetson was the last occasion in which she was involved in a major way in the affairs of her church. Over the course of the next year, members of the household observed her increasing withdrawal from active concern with church matters. As Eddy put it in a message to be conveyed by Alfred Farlow to his mother, "I have an experience all my own and no one else can enter into it." In June 1910, William Rathvon, who had joined the household late in 1908, noted "the almost total abolition of the features of the ordinary day," and Eddy's "lack of interest in things that formerly meant much."[4]

In her own way, however, she was still striving to fulfill her injunction to Farlow to promote more "actions and demonstrations in Christian Science." At this point, doing so required her to contend with the effects of aging. As she approached ninety, Eddy at times needed assistance in walking and in doing the little things that until a few years before she had managed without help and with no apparent effort. There were also occasional outbursts of extreme temper, suspicion, and accusativeness, generally repented of within a short time.

If Eddy was direct in pointing out the failings of others, she could also be frank about what she had to contend with herself. In a note to Calvin Frye in mid-1908 she wrote, "Beloved, if you knew with what I am beset continually arguments of dementia incompetence old age etc. it would explain why I am so changed."[5] Here the term "argument" is crucial. Eddy believed that she was dealing, not with fixed, inevitable conditions of age and stress, but with mental arguments, generated at least as much by malice against her as by age itself. While she believed that these arguments could and should be opposed, there were times when they temporarily took over. On such occasions, Eddy could lash out without apparent reason against household workers. But these episodes were usually temporary and far from characteristic. In some instances when she had caused an unnecessary furor or treated a member of the household unfairly, once she was herself again she made strong efforts to set things right.

On one occasion in April 1910, for example, Eddy temporarily lost control of herself and raged unreasonably against Laura Sargent for a presumed slight. Sargent, devastated, left the household for several days and took refuge in a nearby hotel. Eddy quickly regained her composure and dictated to Adelaide Still a loving tribute to her household staff called "A Paean of Praise" which she sent to the *Sentinel* for publication. In what Robert Peel has called "her Christian Science treatment for the situation," Eddy wrote that the faces of the Christian Scientists in her home "shine with the reflection of light and love; their footsteps are not weary; . . . Mrs. Eddy is happier because of them; God is glorified in His reflection of peace, love, joy." Still recalled that Eddy missed Sargent so deeply and was so overjoyed when she returned that she clapped her hands, took Sargent's "face in her hands, and kissed her, first on one cheek then another. She could not make too much of her."[6]

While Eddy looked primarily to the Bible for daily light and inspiration, she continued to study and draw help from *Science and Health* and her other writings, just as other Christian Scientists would do. Indeed, she told a student during her last years that she was "just beginning to understand *Science and Health*." Adelaide Still recalled that when she needed support and Laura Sargent read a passage from one of her books, Eddy would sometimes exclaim, "That is wonderful, Laura, where did you find it?" Among the passages that meant much to her was a statement from her book *Unity of Good:* "The scientific man and his Maker are here; and you would be none other than this man, if you would subordinate the fleshly perceptions to the spiritual sense and source of being."[7]

In the copy of *Science and Health* she had at hand during the last months of her life, Eddy carefully underlined a number of passages that she found helpful in fortifying her refusal to submit to age and death as God-ordained necessities. That she was working and praying along the lines of her own teaching is clear from words she confided to Rathvon in January 1909: "I am struggling with the claims of old age and death and if I undertook to handle them as presented, I could never meet them; but I just hold to the allness of God, that there is nothing else, and I want all of you to do just the same." And according to Frye's diary for April 24, 1909, after Eddy called six of her household workers to her room, she said to them: "God is taking me at my word. I have said 'there is no life substance or intelligence in matter.' He is now making me prove it." She had written in *Science and Health*, "Trials are proofs of God's care." Her own trials, she said, "are God's discipline for taking me higher. They are not sickness and discomfort unless I call them so."[8]

"THE GOOD WHICH IS BEING DONE BY THE STRUGGLE"

Eddy saw the struggle she was engaged in as having an effect beyond herself. When a household member observed that her struggle was not only relentless but successful, and that the world had reason to be grateful for it, Eddy commented, "Yes but what comforts me the most is the *good which is being done by the struggle*." When William McKenzie, who had not seen her for several years, visited her in April 1910, he noted that "she appeared as one who had been through conflict, showing evidence thereof, yet remaining victor. Her first question was, 'Did you know me?' My whole heart went out to her in gratitude as I replied, and once more I saw the light from her eyes which made her face shine."[9]

Eddy believed that her efforts to deal with the process of aging were made more difficult by the hostility she incurred. Shortly before her death, she told Calvin Frye that what she was meeting was not a natural result of old age and its limitations, which she had hoped to overcome. Rather, it was "the malice and hate which poured in upon her thought through the next friends suit" and seemed "to undermine her vitality." Again, just one week before her death she dictated this short sentence: "It took a combination of sinners that was fast to harm me."[10]

Who these sinners were she did not say, but there remained a good deal of malice aimed at her from at least several familiar quarters: partisans of the recently vanquished Stetson; William Chandler, who had instituted a virtual death watch near Chestnut Hill so as to be able to contest her will upon her demise; Frederick Peabody, whose attacks on her continued; some of the more vociferous and determined members of the clergy and the medical profession; and, of course, Josephine Curtis Woodbury. In January 1909, Woodbury published in an Italian newspaper a short ditty entitled "Dies Irae!" (Latin for "Days of Wrath," a term borrowed from the standard text of a requiem mass), ending with the verse:

> The Day of Wrath o'ertakes her,
> Bids speak, each tongue-tied minion,
> Sets free her hand-cuffed vassals,
> Strips bare her mock-dominion![11]

The belief that Eddy would soon die was, in fact, very much in the air from the time she moved to Chestnut Hill. The Boston press leaped at every rumor of her illness so as to be able to exploit the news of her death when it occurred. In late July 1908, for example, Calvin Frye wrote in his diary:

> At about 12 o'clock last night an editor of Boston Herald called . . . and asked at what hour Mrs. Eddy died! He said the rumor on the street is that she is dead. She had been having a series of attacks for over a week which kept her in bed and on the lounge almost the entire time and last night she despaired of living until morning: but when this telephone was rec'd it revealed cause of attack and [she] gained much relief.[12]

Eddy's quiet withdrawal during the last months of her life did not mean, however, that she spent her time in some kind of haze. Many of her hours were absorbed in prayer. In September 1910, while Tomlinson was keeping watch in her bedroom, he heard her speaking and realized that she was quietly uttering a prayer. She asked no special blessing for "health, comfort, or prosperity, for herself or her Cause." Rather, she sought "a full realization of the Truth of being for herself and for her followers and for all mankind." She spoke of "God's presence hourly and *momently,*" bringing to Tomlinson's consciousness "the truth that real prayer is the very heart and soul of Christian Science, its founding, its growth and its fruits." As Eddy ceased praying, Tomlinson recalled, he spoke, and her "response indicated that she was awake but in a realm apart from her surrounding." When he said to her that her prayer was heard, meaning heard not by him but by God, "she replied, 'Yes, dear it is,' then within fifteen minutes fell back into a sound sleep."[13]

The same month brought another indication that, while Eddy was definitely thinking her own thoughts, she continued to challenge the world's material sense of things in the broadest spiritual terms. After several members of the household attended a flying exhibition, she dictated to Adam Dickey some reflections on the contrast between spiritual and material flying:

> The elevation desirable worth obtaining or possible to obtain in Science is spiritual ascent, thought soaring above matter—soul overcoming mortal and material sense, holiness discounting sin and destroying the love of sin and the capacity to sin. This elevation is not manifested by kiting the skies or kicking the earth. It is something first felt, second seen, third acted.
>
> This soaring skyward means the going upward of soul and sense, the pure aspiration for holiness, without which no man can see God—know Him and understand good and practice it without danger of the possibility of falling from his safety of Soul and its soaring. Oh when will the age plant its discoveries on spiritual cause and effect on that which is not alone only capable of going up but is ascending physically, mentally, and spiritually. Almost one century of experience has caused me to say How long O Lord, How long![14]

Another evidence of the quiet activity of her inner life is afforded by a fragment she dictated in October 1910 to her maid Adelaide Still, who rarely left her side:

> The deepest hallowed intoned thought is the leader of our lives, and when it is found out people know us in reality and not until then. . . . The wisdom of this hour and the proper labor of this hour is to know of a certainty the quality of the seed which takes root in our thought . . . in short, the moral life's history is, Be good, do good, speak good, and God, infinite good, cares for all that is and seems to be. . . . Who believes what

I have written? He who has the most experience of Good. Who dis-
believes it? He who has the most fear of evil. What is the remedy for this
belief? It is experience, for every moment, hour and day of mortal existence brings each one of us nearer the understanding of the nothingness
of evil in proportion to our understanding of the allness of Good.[15]

These and other indications of Eddy's interior life during her last
year or so indicate that, even in the midst of struggles and setbacks, she
was entering into a new phase in the maturation of her own spirituality. It was quiet, inward, and at points serene. Yet even in the midst of
these periods of apparent detachment, her concern for the future of
Christian Science could suddenly surface, as it did in September 1910
when she dictated a prophetic short piece called "Principle and Practice."
It was both cogent and, in its concluding words, surprising.

Eddy begins by making a distinction between mere human belief
in Christian Science and true spiritual understanding of it. If Christian
Science practice is based on mere belief, it becomes nothing more
than a faith-cure. But the true practice of Christian Science, she wrote,
requires so much more than that. "It is the healer's understanding
of the operation of the divine Principle, and his application thereof,
which heals the sick, just as it is one's understanding of the principle of
mathematics which enables him to demonstrate its rules." Then comes
the stern conclusion: "Christian Science is not a faith cure, and unless
human faith be distinguished from scientific healing, Christian Science
will again be lost from the practice of religion as it was soon after the
period of our great Master's scientific teaching and practice."[16]

About this same time an inquiry from a Christian Scientist roused
her to clarify a vital point in her teaching. A letter that arrived at
Chestnut Hill spoke of how the correspondent had been criticized by a
practitioner for declaring that she was "an immortal idea of the one
divine Mind." The practitioner said that this was incorrect, since she still
lived in the flesh. Eddy's answer, which was published in the October
Journal, reaffirmed the necessity in the practice of Christian Science of
thinking out from the standpoint of spiritual truth, without ignoring the
need for recognizing the human sin and error that needs correction:

> You are scientifically correct in your statement about yourself. You can
> never demonstrate spirituality until you declare yourself to be immortal
> and understand that you are so. Christian Science is absolute; it is neither
> behind the point of perfection nor advancing towards it; it is at this point
> and must be practiced therefrom. By this I do not mean that mortals are
> the children of God,—far from it. In practicing Christian Science you
> must state its Principle correctly, or you forfeit your ability to demon-
> strate it.[17]

The vitality of thought shown in these two statements reprises the pattern of earlier years, in which Eddy would rally with sudden and surprising new energy from periods of weakness and pain. In April 1910, just eight months before her death, William Rathvon recorded in his diary that "all hands" were assembled "in the Pink Room. . . . Then for forty minutes our Leader held forth in most remarkable fashion at her very best. She took high ground and held it; she thrust and parried and had everybody on the run, yet it was all straight Science." In July, he recorded a similar instance when she was "at her best" in "poise, acumen, and graciousness." The entry concluded: "I never saw a better or more wonderful exhibition of clear skill."[18]

Eddy also remained capable of the wry wit that had marked her humor since girlhood. When a student of hers wrote that at the age of eighty-seven she was still an active housekeeper surrounded by children, grandchildren, and great-grandchildren, Eddy instructed her secretary, "Tell her to press on in the strength of her Redeemer." After calling the household together to point out some mistakes, she said she did not wish to be finding fault all the time, then told the story of a poor man who bought a tombstone for his wife on which he wished to have inscribed "Let her rest in peace." But being poor he had to abbreviate it, so that "he put on the initials only so that it read 'Let her rip.' That is about the way I feel." When speaking of what Rathvon called "a delayed demonstration we are making," she sang the words of a song she had heard in the South along the lines of, "Der's a good time comin', brudder, but it's a long time gettin' here."

Everyday events also continued to amuse her. When Tomlinson and Rathvon accompanied her on her first and only ride in an automobile, they found it necessary to perch themselves in an extremely awkward position with their knees practically pushed up to their chins, only to notice Eddy trying to hide her face with her parasol so as to conceal her laughter.[19]

Rathvon also noted in his diary a number of instances in which Eddy shared with him and others the fruits of her long spiritual experience in a natural, unselfconscious way:

- May 8, 1909: A fine day is one in which you can get closest to God. I have had some of my best days in stormy weather.
- June 27: It came to me as a voice out of heaven, "You have all in God and God in all."
- September 3, 1910: When I saw my duty, hell couldn't keep me from doing it.

- September 11: He sets us free on the cross, not on the crown; that known, the cross becomes the crown instantly.
- September 25: There is never a time when there is not something for you to do. Doing that something opens the way for God's blessing.
- Fall of 1910: Keep hold the hand of God.
- November 6: God is giving each of us the experience best adapted to lead us to Him.

OLD GUARD, NEW GUARD

Quietly but purposefully, Eddy was still training promising household members for future service to the church. One day Dickey commented to her on the quality of the members of her household, "Mother, this is the cream of the country." Replied Eddy, "The cream,—I want them to be the butter."[20] Her day-to-day requirements on them, however, were not nearly as stringent as in former years. She did give assignments to the watchers, at least through the early spring of 1910, and asked them to take turns remaining with her through the night while she slept. But once she became less rigorous in her insistence upon a strict observance of the hours of watching, some members of the household took this as a cue that they could relax in a way that in former years would have been unthinkable.

Rathvon took it upon himself to spearhead this change. For him, it involved virtually a pitched battle with Frye for the control of the atmosphere of the home, which he believed had been too long dominated by Frye's excessive influence on Eddy. In May 1910, Rathvon drafted a memo accusing Frye of having pursued "an odious career of aggressive mental suggestion" in the attempt to mentally control Eddy so as to advance his own "personal ends, ambition, and power." Around the same time, Rathvon, his wife, Tomlinson, Dickey, and another household member requested that Frye meet with them and confer on this issue. When he outright refused to do so, they signed a letter to him, again written by Rathvon, stating ominously that "a household divided against itself shall not stand." In his diary, Rathvon defined the point at issue in the following terms: Frye "was different from the rest of us, among other things, in this. We have two aims in our work here: first, to protect our Leader; and second, to protect the Cause. CF has shown his are: first, to protect our Leader; and second to protect our Leader. The Cause never appears to enter his considerations and hence he is always ready to sacrifice its interests."[21]

Calvin Frye during the Chestnut Hill years.
Courtesy of The Mary Baker Eddy Collection.

On the basis of his diary entries, what appears to have entered Rathvon's own considerations had less to do with the welfare of the cause of Christian Science than with his desire to bring greater relaxation and harmony to the atmosphere of the home. When his wife joined the household in September 1909, he noted that "her coming is to be desired mainly as a step in the march we are making, which has for its goal the loosening of the unnecessarily rigorous restraints mainly imposed by C/F's New England viewpoint, which hedge us about right and left." The same month he noted that he had broken more of the traditions of the household than anyone who had preceded him. He rejoiced that he found time to ice skate again, that he along with other members of the household had begun to take walks morning, noon, and night, to ride by car into Brookline for visits to the library, and to motor into Boston on personal errands.[22]

In one sense, Rathvon and other like-minded household members who challenged Frye's role were reflecting a predictable "old-guard, new-guard" mentality. It could also be said that, lacking Frye's long-term experience, including many battles he had fought at Eddy's side for more than a quarter of a century, they were insensitive to needs of hers that he perceived and they did not. From Frye's standpoint, there was no real choice to be made between her welfare and that of the cause, since on the basis of everything he had observed, its welfare depended largely on her welfare and capacity to act as its leader.

By early 1910 Rathvon had come to a very different conclusion. In view of Eddy's frailty and withdrawal from daily involvement in decisions affecting the church, he developed a plan for forming an advisory council to act in her stead in executing the "consent clauses" in the *Manual*—actions that required her verbal or written approval before being implemented by the board. Rathvon discussed the matter with several church officials. He also wrote to Dickey of having presented the plan to Frye, who Rathvon said had endorsed it tentatively, proposing that it be drafted in concise form and presented to Eddy for her consideration. This may have been an adroit ploy by Frye to make sure that the plan would *not* be implemented. The plan was discussed with her on several occasions. But according to Still, when Eddy asked Frye if he thought she should assent to the transfer of power to an advisory council, he replied, "I'd keep it in my own hands, if I were you; it's giving them too much power." Eddy replied, "You are right," and that was the end of the matter.[23]

Eddy may not have known that the whole idea was Rathvon's brainchild to begin with, nor was she probably aware of Rathvon's broader anti-Frye campaign, which involved Dickey and Tomlinson as well. Had she known, her response might well have been similar to the attitude she had expressed several years earlier in a letter to Strang. Speaking of Frye, she wrote: "He dear one is suffering for righteousness while others are at peace in sin." The change in the household that resulted from Rathvon's efforts was, however, very evident to George Kinter. After spending a few weeks at Chestnut Hill in October 1910, Kinter noted in a letter the "increasing release in pressure" on the household. "The folks disport themselves in manners and fashions unknown in days of yore." Eddy was also evidently sensible of the relaxation of the efforts of her household workers, and was troubled by it. Frye records that on August 21, 1910, she watched from her window while Dickey and Rathvon tossed a ball and Dickey tried to walk on his hands. Rathvon's diary records the incident as an attempt to provide Eddy with some diversion by performing these and other stunts in plain sight of her bay window. He referred to it as an "immense success" that brought from her compliments about their "nimbleness and proficiency." But Frye's diary for the next day conveys that her real reaction was the very opposite: the result for her was "a very disturbed night and a fear she could not live!"[24]

Throughout the year 1910, Eddy's demands on the household did indeed lessen. But this was probably due less to Rathvon's efforts than to her gradual retreat into an inwardness that grew more perceptible during her last months. She appears to have felt at that point that she had done all she could do to move the cause forward and that it was now up to her followers, especially the officers of her church, to sustain its progress. On her last carriage ride she was heard saying to herself, "Oh, if the students had only done what I told them, I should have lived and carried the Cause." "If there was any shadow over her last days," wrote Robert Peel in the penultimate paragraph of his biographical trilogy, "it was the recognition that Christian Scientists might have to learn for themselves some of the hard lessons she had hoped to save them from by her teachings and rules."[25]

"SHE HAS 'ENTERED INTO HER REST'"

While Eddy had worked assiduously to plant her church on a firm foundation, she by no means believed that its growth and survival were on automatic pilot. "Christian Science has come to stay!" she affirmed in an undated note dictated to Calvin Frye. But she added that the world said that "Christianity has come to stay when the fact was it was only their false sense of Christianity that stayed nineteen-hundred years and has not yet recovered the genuineness of the Master's teaching and demonstration." If Christian Scientists are satisfied that Christian Science has come to stay, "although they are trying to work out the problem of being contrary to its divine Principle and given rules," they must look into their own hearts and turn upon themselves the magnifying lens of truth that brings to light their errors. Then, she wrote, Christian Scientists must answer the question, "Have you not the gods of popularity and ease to serve, whereas Jesus was the despised and rejected of men and bore the cross resigning all human claims of need or pleasure?"[26]

Eddy was far from sanguine that the cause would survive if her future followers did not answer this question aright and measure up to the exacting demands laid down in her writings. Over the years, at varying times and in varying contexts, she reiterated that these demands must be met or else the very survival of Christian Science as a working church would be put at risk. In *Retrospection and Introspection*, the *Manual*, and other published writings, she gave strong warnings to the movement against adulterating the teaching of Christian Science, sinking "its Principle in personality," and substituting words for works, indicating that in so doing, Christian Science could be lost, at least temporarily, to the ages. Bluntly, she told Mary Armstrong, "Unless there are a few honest workers to save my Church from the money changers, the true pure teachings will be lost through substituting the false teachings for the true teachings from 'Science and Health', and the Science will be lost and go back to the dark ages to be rediscovered." To James A. Neal she wrote in 1899, "God demands a more Christian zealous and persistent effort to resist evil and overcome or our cause will again be covered by the rubbish of centuries."[27]

During the last decade of her life, such warnings grew more urgent, especially in her correspondence and in communications to her household. One household member recorded her as saying in 1903 that the "demonstrating to make matter build up is not Science. The building up of churches, the writing of articles and the speaking in public is the old way of building up a Cause. The way I brought this Cause into sight was through healing; and now these other things would come in and hide it, just as was done in the time of Jesus. Now this Cause must be saved and I pray God to be spared for this work."[28]

Believing that correcting false and misleading statements about Christian Science was crucial to its future, she wrote in 1908 to Alfred Farlow that if the Committee on Publication, to which she entrusted this mission, "neglect their duties, so plainly stated in the By-laws of the Mother Church, they alone must be responsible for it or our Cause at the very hour of its triumph *will go down*." As Dickey records, she declared to her household:

> You must rise to the point where you can destroy the belief in mesmerism, or you will have no Cause. . . . It tried to overcome me for forty years and I withstood it all. Now it has gotten to the point where the students must take up this work and meet animal magnetism. I cannot do it for you. You must do it for yourselves, and unless it is done, the Cause will perish and we will go along another 1900 years with the world sunk into the blackest night.[29]

Unquestionably Eddy meant what she said when she issued such dire warnings. But she could also speak of the future of Christian Science as not being totally dependent on the faithfulness of her students either. Just before the construction of the original Mother Church began, she drew a distinction between the "material superstructure" and the church as a continuing "spiritual idea" which "will stand the storms of ages." When she spoke about the possible loss of Christian Science, she said or implied that it could be eclipsed temporarily, but not permanently. Two months before her death she told Rathvon, "The Cause is not dependent upon man or woman, and God will take care of it."[30]

Eddy was not disposed to making soporific statements and was not inclined to allow her students to relax their efforts. Nevertheless, she did see the cause of Christian Science in the broadest possible terms as in continuity with and completing the tide of scriptural revelation. As she put it in a letter during the Woodbury suit, "Remember that you are talking with the God of Israel and His prophets when you pray— they talked of this hour from that,—you talk of that hour from this." The "God of Israel," she was convinced, would ultimately sustain and renew his cause, which, even if it was temporarily eclipsed, she saw as crucial to the spiritual future of humanity. Her same large estimate of the meaning and magnitude of Christian Science is apparent in a note she dictated for what remained an unfinished response to a question submitted by the *Ladies' Home Journal*. Asked "What is the future of Christian Science?" she replied that the question itself "contains a world of thinking, acting and doing. It is an eternity in itself, Divine Science, I say it with all reverence—the eternity of infinite cycles of time which God metes out in space and time for being."[31]

Something of the depth of Eddy's care and concern for the future of her church is to be found in a statement entitled "Motive," dictated to Dickey in mid-April 1909, in which she prayed: "Oh thou eternal Love, I leave my adopted children—and Thy children—to Thee who art Wisdom, unfailing and unfaltering Wisdom and Love, to guard them in this hour of the attempted reign of malicious animal magnetism,—the reign and rule of all that is selfish, debased, and unjust." She then added: "There is but one way of salvation from sin, disease and death, and this way is to take up thy cross in order to follow Christ; then God, who knows your motive, will reward your act according to that motive and not according to your words."[32]

Although Eddy maintained to the end her sense of the great meaning of Christian Science to humanity, during her last months members of the household got the distinct impression that she now felt the progress of the movement was no longer her responsibility and her fight. When McKenzie visited her in April, he spoke of the many complex problems that had arisen at the church especially in connection with the demands of publishing the *Monitor*, saying how much they wanted her advice and direction. But she had not "elected to give it and so to the best of our ability we had to seek earnestly for the guidance of Mind. Once again I saw her rare smile as with deep earnestness she said to me, 'That is just what I wanted you to do.'"[33]

Mary Baker Eddy getting
into her carriage, 1910.
Courtesy of The Mary
Baker Eddy Collection.

If this was an accurate gauge of her intent, then the relaxation of
some of the most devoted members of her household when she ceased
to make stringent demands on them might have seemed a disturbing
harbinger of what was to come. For many years she insisted that the
board of directors discharge their responsibilities without her prodding
and advice. The first major appointment they made acting largely on
their own was not a promising augur. The month after her last conversation with McKenzie when it came time to replace William B. Johnson
as director, she was presented with the name of John V. Dittemore,
whom she had briefly met but did not remember. Showing no enthusiasm for the appointment, Eddy allowed the directors to make Dittemore
a director entirely on their own responsibility—a decision that turned
out to be disastrous when he helped precipitate a schism in the church
and went on to co-author a hostile biography of Eddy.[34]

Eddy's passing on December 3, 1910, was as quiet and peaceful as her
last months had largely been. Although she caught a severe cold toward
the end of November, she went for her carriage ride on December 1.
Upon her return, she was overcome with weakness. Asking for a tablet,
she penned her last written words: "God is my Life." She spent the next
day on her couch and the following day in bed. Her last words, aside from

a brief response to a helper just before her passing, were set down in the diary of Ella Rathvon sometime on December 3: "I have all in divine Love, that is all I need." When she died at 10:45 P.M., she slipped away so quietly that those who attended her could not be sure when she was gone. Twelve days after her death Calvin Frye recalled in a letter, "There was not more than a half hour's notice of the coming crisis, and scarcely a struggle. She has 'entered into her rest.' "[35]

MISSING MRS. EDDY

As some of those who worked in Eddy's Chestnut Hill household and cared for her deeply recalled, she could be, or appear to be, demanding, ungrateful, nit-picking, and suspicious. They also knew that she showed signs of aging expressed in periods of almost total withdrawal, unprovoked outbursts of anger, and forgetfulness. Nevertheless, at virtually any point during her last two decades, when it came to matters affecting the cause of Christian Science—her own publications, major church policy matters, and moments of crisis—Eddy would almost always snap suddenly into a different mode from the day-to-day vicissitudes of her personal behavior.

At such moments, which continued until her death, she gave renewed evidence that what she asserted in 1888 remained true until the end of her days: "My personality asserted and aimed at by others has been under my feet twenty-two years."[36] Hence the fact that the absence of her direct involvement in church matters, minimal as it had been for some months before her death, was distinctly felt afterward by officials of the church, especially by Dickey. Less than two weeks before Eddy died, Dickey began serving at her request as a member of the board of directors.

Despite their quiet grief when she died, both Dickey and Rathvon, who was to become a member of the board in 1918, at first seemed to take Eddy's passing in stride, making a natural and quick transition from serving her to serving in the church. Calvin Frye took a long trip to Europe and died in 1917 while president of the Mother Church. More vocal in his grief and disorientation was Eddy's groundsman John Salchow. Although he began service at her home nearly twenty years after Frye, his devotion to her ran just as deep. He poignantly recalled his reaction to her death and what he felt at her interment:

It seemed to me as if all the light had gone out of the world. After such long and intimate association with my dear Leader it was hard to find myself suddenly with empty hands, unable to serve her, and a great longing came over me to be with her wherever she was. This longing was so intense that the day of the interment it took definite form. I remember that the casket had been put in the vault at Mt. Auburn Cemetery and just as the door closed I looked at my watch. It was exactly two o'clock, the hour when Mrs. Eddy had usually returned from her daily drive. It seemed then as if everything began to fade out and the material world began to disappear.[37]

Salchow recalled that he had a temporary feeling of being suspended from the earth, until the wife of Archibald McLellan gently laid her hand on his shoulder, saying, "John, she loved you." This gesture awakened Salchow "to a better sense of duty and love for those in the world still dear to me." While he no longer had the opportunity to "continue my personal association with my beloved Leader," he could still serve "her great Cause" through performing humble tasks for the Mother Church. Salchow performed these tasks, as he put it, "with a heart full of love for Mary Baker Eddy and reverent gratitude for all the blessings which Christian Science has brought to me." The tasks were indeed humble: he became a utility man at the Publishing Society.[38]

As directors, Dickey and Rathvon occupied much more exalted offices. Yet along with other church officers, they, too, came to feel Eddy's absence far more acutely than they might have expected when she died. Farlow anticipated something of what they were to feel when he responded to Eddy's request in August 1909 that he help "stir the dry bones all over the field." Farlow wrote to her: "I had already been startled by the apathy, despondency and indolence as well as the want of the real piety of Christian Science. This together with my own experience had convinced me that our people, in their belief, were fast asleep. I do not know what would become of us if it were not for your timely warnings."[39]

After her passing, he and other church officers found out. In numerical terms, the movement appeared to be progressing rapidly. But in another sense, it was reprising a familiar pattern in religious history. As with other movements after the death of their founder, Christian Science became to a significant degree routinized, in the process losing much of the spiritual animus that had accounted for its early growth. The pattern is observable, whether we are speaking of the early Christian church after Jesus, the Islamic movement in the decades after the death of Mohammed, or the Franciscan order after the death of St. Francis.

Eddy appears to have anticipated with great apprehension that the Christian Science church, too, would settle down into a kind of bland predictability when she was no longer on the scene. To her, being a Christian Scientist in any meaningful sense involved not only a strong commitment but, in a sense, a spirit of adventure. "Judge not the future advancement of Christian Science by the steps already taken," she wrote in *Science and Health*, "lest you yourself be condemned for failing to take the first step." Yet a certain cooling and descent into respectability among Christian Scientists in the decades following Eddy's death seemed so obvious even from a distance that in 1929 the noted German author Stefan Zweig concluded an uninformed and highly distorted account of Eddy's life by observing: "Christian Science still lives, but it has grown rigid and formal. What was molten lava when it erupted from the volcanic soul of Mary Baker Eddy, is now cold, and a tranquil fellowship of undistinguished folk has established itself on the lower slopes of the extinct crater."[40]

A journal kept by a thoughtful Christian Scientist, William F. Hillman (1900–1974), usefully amplifies Zweig's point. Hillman became a Christian Scientist in the late 1920s about the time Zweig wrote. Looking back from nearly a quarter of a century's experience in the movement, he later noted the danger of reducing Eddy's teaching to an abstract metaphysical system:

> The awakened Christian sees Christian Science as a means for coming into the full truth of being—the full awareness of God. Christian Science is revolutionary in this regard. It turns man away from system, dogmas, formal creeds, to God. . . . Christian Science describes Mrs. Eddy's experience of God. It is not a theory about God or speculation about Him. In following Jesus she became consciously aware of God. She can help us to have this experience, but it is this experience we are after and not some understanding of a system, metaphysical or otherwise. That is, we can't get into a system called Christian Science and hope to succeed. We must experience God as did Mrs. Eddy and not get enclosed within a system. What she has to say about God and how to experience Him is of vital interest and importance, but only as it takes us to the same experience.[41]

Other passages in Hillman's journals, along with many accounts of healing in the church's periodicals, reveal a dimension of Christian Science that Zweig was probably not in a position to know: the vitality and the intensity of the experiences individual Christian Scientists were still having when they were "up against it"—when they were confronted with major problems such as extreme physical illness, poverty, the need to face grief and personal loss, or the dangerous exigencies of wartime.

In these situations, Christian Scientists often came to grips with biblical texts and Eddy's writings with a new urgency and freshness. In the midst of such spiritual struggles, which they often won and sometimes lost, Christian Scientists took hold of Eddy's teaching in a way that belied what might otherwise appear as their prosaic middle-classness. For Christian Scientists who acted on Eddy's legacy in this way, what erupted as "molten lava" from her "volcanic soul" retained much of its heat. This phenomenon was especially observable in accounts of experiences shared by Christian Scientists in the context of the First and Second World Wars.[42]

Yet in the movement generally, and at the Mother Church specifically, there was a distinct loss of the "volcanic" quality—the vitality and sheer unpredictability—of Eddy's temperament and leadership. Indeed, thirteen years before Zweig's comments were published, church officers who had known Eddy felt this loss acutely and expressed it in language that in an uncanny way anticipated Zweig's own words. In 1916, Dickey and other church officers spoke with one another in a series of informal meetings about what they perceived as a spiritual malaise that was creeping into the movement, despite its strong numerical growth. William D. McCrackan, who participated in the discussions, noted Dickey's claim that the movement was not only dying but was dead. McCrackan further observed:

> The truth is these men were beginning to miss more than they realized the constant activities of Mrs. Eddy while she was visibly watching over them and working for the Cause she had so greatly at heart; they missed her spontaneous enactments which so completely disarmed the foe, her surprises and more than all else the inspiration with which she had guided the movement up from its infancy to its full maturity. They were also beginning to feel the benumbing effect of trying to run a spiritual movement merely with the letter and the law; there was creeping upon them stealthily, but steadily, the fear of an impending rigidity, due to routine and the falling into the inevitable rut.[43]

"Fresh Forms and Strange Fire"

Eddy's "spontaneous enactments," "surprises," and "inspiration" expressed the "volcanic" quality of her life and leadership. They were to some degree observable as components of her temperament well before her work in Christian Science began. The readiness to plunge ahead, to leave behind what had been outgrown, to move in a new direction before it could be fully determined where it would lead— these traits were elements of Eddy's sensibility. They account in large measure for the unpredictable zig-zag quality of the spiritual search that led to her discovery in 1866.

Even as a young woman, Eddy showed an adventurous streak in her willingness to leave New England and join her husband, George Glover, for a new life in the South, although she had been very much a homebound farm girl up to that point. Just so, a combination of intuition, curiosity, and boldness proved strong elements in the steps that led her to Christian Science.

Some indication of these qualities can be found in one of nearly twenty articles she contributed to the Oddfellows magazine, the *Covenant*, when she was in her late twenties. In an article called "The Immortality of the Soul" she suddenly breaks free of the traditional Christian belief in an indefinable spiritual hereafter. Instead of maintaining rigid categories of this life and the next, she views heaven as a larger context of potential experience, wherein all things we now see and value are grasped in their fullness. "We shall there apprehend fully the relations and dependencies incomprehensible to understandings encircled by clay. The boundless ocean of truth will be fathomed and investigated. . . . The obstacles which shackle our present vision and imagination will be gone. . . . Intelligence, refined, etherealized, will converse directly with material objects, if, indeed, matter be existent."[44] Nothing in Eddy's previous development, to the extent that we know about it, prepares us for her almost casual comment, "if, indeed, matter be existent." Yet it did foreshadow the direction her spiritual search was beginning to take.

If there is a pattern to her life, it is the recurrence of new beginnings, and new departures. In the 1850s, she began an intensive investigation of homeopathy, then just as suddenly abandoned it when she came to believe it had no medicinal value but rested on the faith of patients and doctors in its efficacy. Desperately in search of health and confident that Phineas P. Quimby was working along similar lines, she insisted on making an extremely taxing trip to Portland, Maine, in 1862, again with results that strongly propelled her own quest forward. With the broad redirection in her life that began in 1866, everything changed again. Late in that year, she suddenly entered into a new phase of her life by committing herself to exploring the scriptures to discover the basis of her healing the previous February. Again, she dropped most of her teaching work in early 1872 to pursue with single-minded intensity the writing of *Science and Health* until it was completed nearly three years later. After devoting substantial efforts to building up the movement in Lynn, only to see it collapse in 1881, Eddy took another bold initiative by relocating to Boston in 1882 and, in effect, starting over.

In so doing she plunged into a whole new life, one of almost frenetic activity that involved meeting multiple demands that she had never before encountered. As a result, a very different Eddy emerged during the demanding seven years she spent in Boston from 1882 to 1889. Any given day during the mid-1880s might include interviews with students, several hours of teaching, writing multiple letters, and holding conferences on church problems, followed by writing during the evening and sometimes long into the night. The pattern of her life was to change drastically when she abruptly left Boston in May of 1889, over the next several years becoming the "Mrs. Eddy" known to history. But the changes did not stop there. Almost none of the steps she took over the next twenty years were foreseeable, from reorganizing the church in 1892, to writing its *Manual* in 1895, to establishing its basic activities in 1898, to founding the *Monitor* ten years later.

So too, it was the unpredictable quality of her leadership that in large part made it so effective. Gilbert Carpenter, who served as a corresponding secretary in 1905 and 1906, wrote that "she had a quality of forward marching, which sprang from an unusually active mind, and which, when put under the control of divine Love" made her a great spiritual leader.[45] The Eddy who articulated Christian Science and then led the movement with such spiritual determination was in some way akin to, yet different from, the Eddy she had been prior to her discovery. Her life illustrated her own words in the "Prospectus" she wrote for the first issue of the *Journal:* "The mounting sense gathers fresh forms and strange fire from the ashes of dissolving self, and drops the world. . . . Goodness reveals another scene and another self seemingly rolled up in shades, but brought to light by the evolutions of advancing thought."[46]

A QUIET REVOLUTION

In an article written for the *Journal* in 1883 just as she ended her first full year in Boston, she described the process through which "another self" emerges in biblical terms as "the new birth." The "new birth," she says, "is not the work of a moment. It begins with moments, and goes on with years; moments of surrender to God, of childlike trust and joyful adoption of good; moments of self-abnegation, self-consecration, heaven-born hope, and spiritual love." Less a single event such as a conversion experience, the new or spiritual birth is a process through which "man's primitive, sinless, spiritual existence dawns on human thought,— through the travail of mortal mind, hope deferred, the perishing pleasure and accumulating pains of sense,—by which one loses himself as matter, and gains a truer sense of Spirit and spiritual man."[47]

She saw that this spiritual self or "new man" that emerges from the fires of spiritual discipline is, to the degree that it becomes apparent, the true, original, and authentic man whom God already knows as his child. Thus her words, "The scientific man and his Maker are here; and you would be none other than this man, if you would subordinate the fleshly perceptions to the spiritual sense and source of being." Subordinating fleshly perceptions, having the new birth, becoming Christlike,—she believed these to be effects of the study and practice of her teachings. And so doing was the only way to fulfill Paul's injunctions to come "unto a perfect man, unto the measure of the stature of the fulness of Christ" and to "let this mind be in you, which was also in Christ Jesus."[48]

Actually becoming a new or real self—thus being man as God made him—was not a concept easily grasped by those unfamiliar with the term "man" as Eddy employed it. There was a certain amount of confusion over what she meant by this word in an interview she gave to the *New York Herald* for May 1, 1901. When the question came up as to who would succeed her, Eddy was reported as saying, "It will be a man." In a statement for the Associated Press on May 16, she made it clear that she did not mean "any man to-day on earth. . . . What remains to lead on the centuries and reveal my successor, is man in the image and likeness of the Father-Mother God, man the generic term for mankind."[49]

In these words, Eddy prophesies that her successor will not be a human personality but, rather, a new *kind* of man: authentic, spiritual man made in God's image and likeness. What makes the appearing of this new man possible? For Eddy, it is the spiritual revolution that Christian Science was beginning to effect: the "rolling away of the stone" of mortality and death through the new appearing of Christ in our age. "Glory be to God, and peace to the struggling hearts!" she wrote in *Science and Health*. "Christ hath rolled away the stone from the door of human hope and faith, and through the revelation and demonstration of life in God, hath elevated them to possible at-one-ment with the spiritual idea of man and his divine Principle, Love."[50] This, she said, is the great possibility that the advent of Divine Science has opened to humanity by undercutting the foundations of materialism that would limit men and women to the finite selves they seem to be, but in reality are not.

She recognized as well that this possibility must not only be affirmed but to some degree actualized in the lives of her followers. Animated by this conviction, Eddy saw spiritual healing as a great imperative for living Christian experience—but not just for the purpose of making human life more comfortable and convenient. Rather, Christian healing, as she saw it, was a kind of beachhead for establishing the reality of Spirit as an actual presence among men. The only possible answer to the enduring problem of evil must, in her perspective, be a practical one in which this reality becomes felt through acts of healing that cannot rationally be denied.

In this respect, Eddy saw no essential difference between the power of one individual and that of many. A constant theme in her writings is the enormous role that single individuals can play in advancing the consciousness of humanity to the spiritual and breaking the spell of materialism—not, she held, through conventional channels of personal influence and communication, but through the power of Christ that has transformed their own lives. Nothing, she believed, could give human life more purpose and meaning. Thus her words, "Whoever opens the way in Christian Science is a pilgrim and stranger, marking out the path for generations yet unborn."[51]

In her understanding, Jesus' life of self-sacrificial love had made just such a difference, releasing the power of Christ, the divine sonship he incarnated, into human consciousness. And to the extent that individuals follow in his path, take up the cross, and make him truly their Wayshower, they reflect a measure of Christ-power in their own time and circumstances.

For her, there is no way of measuring in advance the capacity of individuals who have awakened to their own permanent spiritual identity to make a decisive difference to the consciousness of humanity. The future of Christian Science she therefore saw as inseparably linked with the commitment and spirituality of her followers. As she put it in Science and Health, "Judge not the future advancement of Christian Science by the steps already taken, lest you yourself be condemned for failing to take the first step."[52]

Eddy thus looked to the *future* of the movement she had founded to make good on the proof of the supremacy of Spirit and her resultant challenge to materialism that defined the meaning of her lifework. "I lay foundations that must not be tampered with," she said late in her life to Laura Sargent. "If the seed I sow bears neither immediate nor abundant fruit it is getting ready for this and the ripening and the harvest is sure to come at the proper time. My plants are not of the hot house kind. They must wait on the evolution of their character, for this is the only soil which brings forth fruitage from my labors."[53]

Eddy saw her own writings in conjunction with the Bible as wholly sufficient sources of spiritual guidance for Christian Scientists in the struggle to "bring forth fruitage" from her labors—if, that is, what she wrote was taken seriously and adhered to. In II Kings, the sign that the spirit of the departed prophet Elijah rests upon his successor Elisha lies in the fact that the mantle of Elijah falls upon him. Taking this biblical metaphor as a "type" for Eddy's life and legacy, "Elijah's mantle" fell—not on any particular individual—but on those of her followers who took what she wrote and taught to heart.[54]

Coda: The Prophetic Voice

In a communication to her followers in 1901, Eddy asked, "Has God entrusted me with a message to mankind?—then I cannot choose but obey." The language that she used clearly indicates her self-identification as a prophet—a term which, as used in a religious and sociological context, is someone who is convinced that he or she communicates the divine will—in the words of Old Testament scholar Bernard W. Anderson, "an intermediary, a spokesperson—one who acts and speaks on behalf of another."[1]

Eddy has sometimes been viewed as an intriguing nineteenth-century woman who acted outside of traditional female roles, pursued new lines of inquiry in religion and medicine, intrepidly engaged in publishing ventures, and founded an important American denomination. But to leave her in the nineteenth century, so to speak, would be to lose sight of the prophetic dimension of her life that defines its larger meaning and gives her whatever significance she may have in the broad stream of Christian thought.

Whether one accepts or rejects Eddy's message, her sense of speaking in the prophetic voice remains a basic fact of her biography and is essential to an understanding of what she wrote. In *Science and Health*, as in most of her writings, Eddy was intentionally addressing not only the religious world of her time, but the decades and centuries that would follow—as indicated by her frequent use of the term "the ages": "When will the ages understand the Ego, and realize only one God, one Mind or intelligence?" And she stated characteristically of Christian Science, "This movement of thought must push on the ages," while telling her students, "As you work, the ages win." "The prophet of to-day," she wrote in *Science and Health*, "beholds in the mental horizon the signs of these times, the reappearance of Christianity which heals the sick and destroys error."[2]

Eddy also anticipated that materialism will deepen and grow more severe as its domination over humanity is challenged. As she put it, "materialistic hypotheses challenge metaphysics to meet in final combat." The final, ultimate nature of this conflict points to the apocalyptic element in her theology—her sense that the alternatives before humanity were stark and becoming more sharply defined.[3]

Certainly her view of the future of humanity was far from roseate. In the first issue of the *Journal* in 1883 she wrote, "The signs of these times portend a long and strong determination of mankind to cleave to the world, the flesh, and evil, causing great obscuration of Spirit." The descent of her best-known adversary, Mark Twain, into the cosmic blackness of his last years would have been no surprise to her. She well understood how what she called a "deadened sense of the invisible God" led inevitably to a despairing view of the human condition.[4]

In no way were Eddy and Mark Twain more alike than in their visceral rejection of the ethos of virtually automatic moral and material progress that was the controlling ideal of their culture. Without discounting the value of scientific and technological progress, they were too aware of the underlying spiritual dilemmas of their time to see the future simply as a continuation of the triumphs of the past, or to buy into specious theological formulas that papered over these dilemmas without addressing them.

As the twentieth century dawned, Twain also anticipated with tragically precise realism the horrors that the world would undergo, including war and bloodshed on a hitherto unimaginable scale. In the fantasies that filled the fables of his later years, he spoke in different ways of the multiplication of human violence and stupidity. In 1900, he wrote that "the time is grave. The future is blacker than has been any future which any person now living has tried to peer into."[5]

Where he and Eddy decisively differed lay in her conviction that there was an option before humanity other than sinking into this blackness: the renewal of the fire of original Christianity that had begun with Jesus and that she believed was being rekindled by Christian Science. Why, then, did so many Christians resist this renewal by rejecting Christian Science?

In responding at various times to this question, Eddy often spoke in the vein of biblical prophets inveighing against the derelictions of the people of Israel. The reason for the rejection of Christian Science by other churches, she maintained, lay in their failure to oppose, or even recognize, the materialism that was corroding Christianity from within. To her, having a God who is really God led inevitably to what she called the great fact of "Life in and of Spirit; this Life being the sole reality of existence," the very essence of her discovery.[6]

This spiritual existence, she held, is real and present now, the only order of being. But in our ignorance of God and our blindness to Spirit, we are entertaining a materialized—therefore a limited and distorted impression—of this one order of reality, thus failing to grasp and live out any more than a fraction of the glory and goodness that is now present to experience. What restricts our vision and limits us so drastically, Eddy believed, are by no means God-imposed limits. Rather, it is the grip of the assumption that God, divine Love, would or even could make his creation out of fragile, finite, and destructible materials—a view that she held to be little short of absurd.

Here, then, lies the basic disjunction between Christian Science and traditional Christianity, Protestant or Roman Catholic. The division is fundamental. The Swiss theologian Karl Barth defined the issue with some surprising ideas of his own along the lines that evil and suffering are elements of *das Nichtige*—of nothingness—and not positive realities of God's creation. Yet when it came to following through on the implications of this insight to the extent that Eddy had done, Barth drew back. Conceding that Eddy's teaching did have several features reminiscent of the New Testament, Barth nevertheless denied that it is genuinely Christian on the basis of this dualistic contention:

> God is the basis of all reality but He is not the only reality. As Creator and Redeemer He loves a reality which is different from Himself, which depends upon Him, but which is not merely a reflection nor the sum of His powers and thoughts, but which has in face of Him an independent and distinctive nature and is the subject of its own history, participating in its own perfection and subjected to its own weakness.[7]

Yet this is the very attitude that Eddy saw as binding Christianity to mortality by blinding Christians to the materialism within their own gates. Many Christians in Eddy's time condemned materialism in the form of Darwinism, positivism, and related cultural influences that threatened to deny much of what they held most dear. Some notable anti-materialists of her time, the great social gospel minister the Reverend Washington Gladden, for example, wrote, "The fundamental truth to which Christian Science has drawn attention is the reality and the supremacy of spiritual forces. The materialists have attacked their reality, and most of us have been sufficiently tinctured with materialism to have little faith in their supremacy. Against this deadly unbelief the Christian Scientist lifts up his battle cry."[8]

But her challenge to materialism had more far-reaching implications, offering a response to forms of materialism that go well beyond the bare-bones version epitomized in Bertrand Russell's classic statement of 1912:

> That man is the product of causes which had no prevision of the ends they were achieving; that his origin, his growth, his hopes and fears, his loves and his beliefs are but the outcome of accidental collocations of atoms; . . . that all the labors of the ages, all the devotion, all the inspiration, all the noonday brightness of human genius, are destined to extinction in the vast death of the solar system, and that the whole of man's achievement must inevitably be buried beneath the debris of a universe in ruins—all these things, if not quite beyond dispute, are nearly certain. Brief and powerless is man's life; on him and all his race the slow, sure doom falls pitiless and dark. Blind to good and evil, reckless of destruction, omnipotent matter rolls on its relentless way.[9]

To what extent is this bleak worldview the result of modern science? Actually, the dense materialism that dominates so much of our time is not on the whole sustained but rather undercut by what has been called the new physics, and especially by quantum theory. An article entitled "Keeping a spiritual perspective on the new physics," written for the *Christian Science Journal* in 1988, points out that in quantum physics "the physicist has been compelled to admit that when physics deals with the basic components of matter—electrons, protons, neutrons, and whatever apparently makes them up—it is no longer dealing with 'objective reality' as such. It is dealing with observer-dependent, observer-created phenomena—with shadows and symbolic descriptions, and not with things." The author cautions that the new physics does not comprise statements of Christian Science and that "physicists generally believe the world we see around us is real enough." But "these admissions of the new physics . . . do indicate the breaking up of material beliefs, a kind of 'mentalization' of mankind's view of matter."[10]

Yet it is also apparent that the very opposite tendency is now becoming prevalent in the life sciences. In the words of Paul Davies, "It is ironical that physics, which has led the way for all other sciences, is now moving towards a more accommodating view of mind, while the life sciences, following the path of last century's physics, are trying to abolish mind altogether." Davies quotes the psychologist Harold Morowitz on this curious reversal whereby biologists "have been moving relentlessly toward the hard-core materialism that characterized nineteenth-century physics. At the same time physicists, faced with compelling experimental evidence, have been moving away from strictly mechanical models of the universe to a view that sees the mind as playing an integral role in all physical events. It is as if the two disciplines were on fast-moving trains, going in opposite directions and not noticing what is happening across the tracks."[11]

This aggressive picture of a universe as the product of a big bang and heading for inevitable extinction also plays a strong role as the background of today's emergent varieties of materialism. If the ultimate destiny of the universe and all that transpires within it is nothing more than a blank, cosmic meaninglessness, then the practical deflation of ethical and religious values in our time becomes harder to resist and more easily understood.

When massive brutality resulting from the political manipulation of primitive ethnic rivalries has become a recurring pathology of contemporary international life; when business ethics sink to the point that we expect maximum selfishness in any area of economic and corporate life that remains unregulated; when gross violence has become so frequent a presence in media and entertainment that one scarcely even notices it; when religious belief concedes point after crucial point to a rigid scientism that views the Resurrection as a patent absurdity; when God is viewed as so lacking in power that he can only suffer with us in pain he cannot prevent; when reductionist views of biblical texts render the Gospels virtually insignificant except in the narrowest ethical terms—then it can only be said that a form of materialism as pervasive as it is subtle has permeated the mental atmosphere of our time.

In the face of these developments which appear to be accelerating rather than diminishing, does religion have a role; or has it compromised itself to the point that it no longer has depth of meaning and value in human experience?

It was Mary Baker Eddy's conviction that this compromised sense of religion had no meaningful role to play in the future spiritual experience of humanity. She maintained that only a new understanding of God as infinite Spirit could make a difference in forestalling the triumph of materialism that she saw as obscuring spiritual light and values. This new understanding for her meant that God's absolute sovereignty and governance of the whole of experience must be taken with a radical new seriousness. For her, this meant turning to new definitions of traditional Christian concepts: "The Ego is revealed as Father, Son, and Holy Ghost, but the full Truth is found only in divine Science, where we see God as Life, Truth, and Love."[12]

One of the first international conferences to address the issues of materialism in public life, under the auspices of the United Nations, was titled "Spiritual and Ethical Dimensions of Social Progress." Out of this seminar, attended by a wide range of representatives from world religions and a variety of professions, emerged a book called *Candles in the Dark: A New Spirit for a Plural World.* Here one contributor, A. W. Phinney, remarked, "Deepening doubt and intellectual distrust of the very existence of the human spirit, like some suffocating stratospheric smog, now drifts across the surface of the globe." He referred, for example, to the "hedonistic consumption, the fascination with self-centered sensuality, and the increasing willingness to market a mindless ennui through the faces of mannequins, models, and rock videos." But he also goes on to "urge the necessity for feeding, not just the literal hunger of man, lessening his poverty, increasing his equality and justice, but feeding his spirit."[13]

This statement raises the largest of questions: whether contemporary religious thought has the wherewithal to feed the spirit and resist the march of materialism in any convincing and substantive way. The tenor of Eddy's writings would indicate that it does not, if it has compromised itself out of all meaningful existence by becoming a kind of poetic embroidery on the edges of human life.

To the extent that this process continued, she saw materialism as potentially obscuring all spiritual values and light, leading to what she termed "the atheism of matter." But she also maintained that Christian Science had put a very different alternative before humanity: taking God's absolute sovereignty and governance of the whole of experience with a new and radical seriousness that, if acted upon, could lead to a truly healing and transforming Christianity. To be sure, healing in Christian Science embraces more than the healing of the body. But physical healing remains a significant part of what Eddy referred to in an 1888 address as "the irrepressible conflict between sense and Soul inaugurated by Science. Mortal thought wars with this sense as one that beateth the air, but Science outmasters it, and ends the warfare." But for this to happen, she maintained, Christian Scientists must engage in the struggle to *make* it happen by giving the world the practical proof of the truth of her discovery.[14]

Thus Eddy's challenge to materialism continues to confront the emerging picture of the human spirit as largely reducible to biological, chemical, and electrical components. To her, there was an ultimate battle to be waged between Christianity understood as science—as a demonstrable understanding of spiritual power at work in human affairs—and a rigid scientism claiming that we must accept finitude as the basic condition of our experience, eking out what meaning we can from a fragile, temporary, and ultimately hopeless existence.

This battle, she believed, would be costly. But it would eventually be won. As she wrote in *Science and Health*, "The night of materiality is far spent. . . . Let discord of every name and nature be heard no more, and let the harmonious and true sense of Life and being take possession of human consciousness."[15]

Chronology

The last two decades of Eddy's life, the period covered by this book, are treated in greater detail than the earlier years in this chronology.

1821	July 16	Birth of Mary Morse Baker in Bow, New Hampshire, the youngest of the six children of Mark and Abigail Baker
1836	January	Baker family moves to farm near Sanbornton Bridge, New Hampshire, twenty-two miles from Bow
1838	July 26	Becomes member of Congregational Church at Sanbornton Bridge
1841	October 17	Brother Albert Baker dies, age 31
1843	December 10	Marries George Washington Glover, building contractor
1844	February 1	Moves with her new husband to Wilmington, North Carolina
	June 27	Glover dies from Yellow Fever. She returns weeks later, pregnant, to Sanbornton Bridge
	September 12	Birth of George Washington Glover II
1849	November 21	Death of her mother, Abigail Ambrose Baker
	December	Death of her fiancé, John Bartlett, in Sacramento, California
1851	May	Son George sent with Mahala & Russell Cheney to North Groton, New Hampshire
1853	June 21	Marries dentist Daniel Patterson; moves with him to Franklin, New Hampshire Probable beginning of her experiments with homeopathic system of medicine
1855	March	Pattersons move to North Groton to be near George, now twelve years old Patterson, disliking George, keeps him from visiting his mother
1856	April	George moves with Cheneys to Minnesota; she receives letter from him in 1861; her health declines sharply, becomes semi-invalid

1860		Pattersons, bankrupt, leave North Groton, moving to Rumney, New Hampshire
1861	June	Travels to Dr. W. T. Veil's Hydropathic Institute at Hill, New Hampshire, in search for health; stays about three months
1862	October 10	First visit to Phineas P. Quimby; remains in Portland, Maine, for rest of the year
	November 7	First letter praising Quimby appears in *Portland Evening Courier*
1863	July	Returns to Portland, which she revisits over next nine months
1865	October 6	Death of Mark Baker at Sanbornton Bridge
1866	January 16	Death of Quimby at Belfast, Maine
	February 1	Severely injured by fall on ice while on way to Temperance Meeting
	February 4	Healing in her home in Swampscott, Massachusetts
1867		Begins work on Genesis Manuscript, completed in 1869
1870		Relocates to Lynn, Massachusetts, her home until she moves to Boston twelve years later
1872	January/ February	Newspaper controversy with Wallace W. Wright; begins writing *Science and Health*
1873	November 4	Secures divorce from Daniel Patterson on grounds of desertion
1875	October 30	First publication of *Science and Health*
1876	July 4	Organization of Christian Science Association, first institution of Christian Science
1877	January 1	Marries Asa Gilbert Eddy
1878		Conspiracy to murder charge brought against Arens and Gilbert Eddy, dismissed January 31, 1879
1879	April 12	Fourteen or fifteen members of the Christian Scientist Association vote to organize the Church of Christ, Scientist; ordained as its pastor on August 16
1881	January 31	Chartering of Massachusetts Metaphysical College
1882	Spring	Calvin Frye chosen by Asa Gilbert Eddy to be her private secretary
	June 3	Death of Asa Gilbert Eddy
	August 14	Frye joins her household where he remains until her death
1884	February 7	Notice in *Journal*: "Mrs. Eddy no longer takes patients"
	May	Teaches a class in Chicago
	August	*Christian Science Journal* becomes monthly publication
1885	March 16	Reply to clerical criticism in Boston's Tremont Temple

	July 30	Engages the Reverend James Henry Wiggin as editorial assistant
1886		Augusta Stetson sent to New York City, where she starts a church
	February	Forming of National Christian Scientist Association
1887	November	George Glover and family arrive in Boston for six-month visit
1888	March	*Unity of Good and Unreality of Evil* published; Abby Corner indicted for manslaughter in deaths of daughter and grandchild, later acquitted June 12; revolt against her leadership by Boston students
	June 14	Addresses National Christian Scientist Association in Chicago
	November 5	Adopts Ebenezer J. Foster as her son
	December 24	Moves to 385 Commonwealth Avenue, Boston
1889	May 22	Abruptly leaves Boston for Barre, Vermont; moves in June to Concord, New Hampshire
	September	Dismantles most of existing organizations of movement through May 1890
1890		Josephine Woodbury gives birth to the "Prince of Peace," claiming that he was immaculately conceived
	September	"Seven Fixed Rules" published in *Journal*, stating that Eddy is not to be consulted on church matters
1891	January 19	Publication of major fiftieth edition of *Science and Health*
	November	Publication of *Retrospection and Introspection*
1892	June 20	Moves to Pleasant View in Concord, New Hampshire, where she is to live for over fifteen years
	Summer	Gathering crisis over William Nixon's effort to substitute publishing house for church
	September 1	Execution of deed of trust creating a four-person board of directors to build and maintain a new church edifice
	September 23	Formal reorganization of the Church of Christ, Scientist, into what would be known as "The Mother Church"; creation of body of "First Members"
1893	March	Begins work with James F. Gilman on illustrations for *Christ and Christmas*, published on December 2
	September 20–22	"Congress of Christian Science" at World's Parliament of Religions in Chicago
	October 1	Ground broken for church edifice in Boston
1894	January	*Christ and Christmas* withdrawn from publication and distribution; republished December 1897

	May 21	Cornerstone of the Mother Church is laid
	December 19	Ordains the Bible and *Science and Health* as the dual and impersonal pastor of her church
	December 30	First service held in Mother Church
1895	January 6	Dedication of new church building
	March 25	Refuses to accept the title of Pastor of the First Church of Christ, Scientist, though later accepts the title Pastor Emeritus
	April 1	First visit to church, followed by first address on May 26 and second address on January 5, 1896
	September	Publication of first edition of *Church Manual*
1896	February	Permanent public Christian Science services begun in London
	August	Sends Foster Eddy to Philadelphia
1897	February 10	Publication of *Miscellaneous Writings:* 1883–1896
	March	Foster Eddy ejected from readership in Christian Science Society in Philadelphia
	March	Suspends all Christian Science teaching for one year
	July 21	Breaks permanently with Foster Eddy, whom she never sees again
1898	January	Founds Board of Lectureship
	January 25	Establishes deed of trust for Publishing Society
	March	First Christian Science church in Germany organized in Hannover
	September	Establishes the *Christian Science Weekly,* renamed *Christian Science Sentinel* in January 1899
	late in the year	Announcement of Board of Education
	November 20–21	Teaches her last class, for two days in Concord
	December 13	Writes bylaw establishing Publication Committee, later renamed Committee on Publication
1899	May	Attack by Josephine Woodbury and Julius Dresser in the *Arena* magazine
	June 4	Communion Message delivered denouncing the "Babylonish woman"
	July 31	Woodbury files lawsuit for libel against her
	October	First of four articles by Mark Twain in the *Cosmopolitan*
1900	May 16	Calls on board of directors to open a Christian Science Reading Room in Boston
	early December	Judge Joseph Clarkson advocates male leadership for church
1901	June 5	Judge in Woodbury suit instructs jury to dismiss charges
	August 1	Frederick Peabody delivers lecture, "A Complete Exposure of Eddyism," in Tremont Temple

	November	Work on major revision of *Science and Health* through December, published in January 1902
1902	January 30	Publication of 226th edition of *Science and Health*, in which chapters take on their final order
	February 13	Copyright obtained for *Footprints Fadeless*, though publication is delayed indefinitely
	June	Limitation of readers' terms to three years
	June 18	Church members resolve to raise $2 million for Mother Church extension
	December	Publication of first of four articles on Christian Science by Mark Twain in *North American Review*
1903	February 19	Adds fifth member to four-member board of directors
	March 29	Begins work on major revision of *Manual*, published September 25
	July 30	Partially in response to Twain attack, requires that Christian Scientists refer to her as "Leader" rather than "Mother"
	November 29	First Church of Christ, Scientist, New York dedicated under Stetson's direction, costing nearly $2 million
1906	June 10	Dedication of extension of the Mother Church
	October 11	Applies for copyright on *The First Church of Christ, Scientist, and Miscellany*, published after her death
	October 28	Publication of first sensational article in *New York World*, followed by over seventy articles through end of summer of 1907
	December	First article in *McClure's* biographical series by Milmine and Cather
1907	February	Decides to appoint trustees to care for her property; publication of Twain's book *Christian Science*
	March 1	Chandler begins Next Friends Suit
	March 6	Appoints three trustees to care for her property
	June	Gives six major press interviews through August; reads *Science and Health* through consecutively for the first time
	August 14	Crucial interview by Masters at Pleasant View
	August 18	Withdrawal of suit with no court finding
1908	January 26	Takes up residence in new home at Chestnut Hill, near Boston
	February 6	Sees Mother Church Extension briefly from carriage
	June	Abolishment of Communion service in the Mother Church

	July 28	Instructs the board of directors to begin a daily newspaper to be titled the *Christian Science Monitor*
	August 8	Gives same instruction to trustees of the Publishing Society
	November 25	First issue of *Monitor* published
	December 9	Augusta Stetson's last visit with Eddy at Chestnut Hill
1909	July	Gathering crisis over Stetson's role in Christian Science comes to a head
	September 25	Stetson stripped of status as teacher and practitioner by board of directors
	November 17	Stetson excommunicated by the board
1910	October	Requires that her picture be removed from present and future church publications
	November	Publication of *Poems*
	late November	Final revision of *Church Manual*
	December 3	After brief illness dies in ninetieth year
	December 8	Funeral service attended by church officials, members of household, George Glover, and Foster Eddy

Notes

Abbreviations and Short Titles Used in Endnotes

Manuscript Collections

Longyear	Longyear Historical Society, Brookline, Massachusetts
Chandler Papers	Papers of William E. Chandler, New Hampshire Historical Society
Twain Papers	The Mark Twain Project, The Bancroft Library, University of California at Berkeley

Unless otherwise indicated, material from letters and reminiscences are reproduced courtesy of The Mary Baker Eddy Collection. Permission to reproduce or otherwise reuse this material may be obtained from The Mary Baker Eddy Collection at 175 Huntington Avenue, Boston, Massachusetts, 02115.

Periodicals

CSJ	*Christian Science Journal*
CSS	*Christian Science Sentinel*

Writings of Mary Baker Eddy

Christian Healing	*Christian Healing, A Sermon Delivered at Boston*
Manual	*Church Manual of The First Church of Christ, Scientist, in Boston, Massachusetts*
Message '00	*Message to The Mother Church: Boston, Massachusetts, June 1900*
Message '01	*Message to The Mother Church: Boston, Massachusetts, June 1901*

Message '02	*Message to The First Church of Christ, Scientist or The Mother Church, Boston, June 15, 1902*
Miscellaneous	*Miscellaneous Writings, 1883–1896*
Miscellany	*First Church of Christ, Scientist, and Miscellany*
People	*The People's Idea of God: Its Effect on Health and Christianity, A Sermon Delivered at Boston*
Pulpit	*Pulpit and Press*
Retrospection	*Retrospection and Introspection*
Rudimental	*Rudimental Divine Science*
S&H	*Science and Health with Key to the Scriptures*
Unity	*Unity of Good*

OTHER FREQUENTLY CITED WORKS

Bates-Dittemore, *Mary Baker Eddy*	Ernest Sutherland Bates and John V. Dittemore, *Mary Baker Eddy: The Truth and the Tradition*
Cather and Milmine, *Life*	Willa Cather and Georgine Milmine, *The Life of Mary Baker G. Eddy & The History of Christian Science*
Dakin, *Mrs. Eddy*	Edwin Franden Dakin, *Mrs. Eddy: The Biography of a Virginal Mind*
Dickey, *Memoirs*	Adam H. Dickey: *Memoirs of Mary Baker Eddy*
Eddy and James F. Gilman, *Painting*	*Painting a Poem: Mary Baker Eddy and James F. Gilman Illustrate Christ and Christmas*
Gill, *Eddy*	Gillian Gill, *Mary Baker Eddy*
Gottschalk, *Emergence*	Stephen Gottschalk, *The Emergence of Christian Science in American Religious Life*
Heart in Protest	*Mary Baker Eddy: A Heart in Protest*
Johnson, *History*	William Lyman Johnson, *The History of the Christian Science Movement*
Meehan, *Late Suit*	Michael Meehan, *Mrs. Eddy and the Late Suit in Equity*
Peel, *Authority*	Robert Peel, *Mary Baker Eddy: The Years of Authority*
Peel, *Discovery*	Robert Peel, *Mary Baker Eddy: The Years of Discovery*
Peel, *Trial*	Robert Peel, *Mary Baker Eddy: The Years of Trial*
Powell, *Portrait*	Lyman P. Powell, *Mary Baker Eddy: A Life-Sized Portrait*
Tomlinson, *Twelve Years*	Irving C. Tomlinson, *Twelve Years with Mary Baker Eddy: Recollections and Experiences (Amplified Edition)*
We Knew	*We Knew Mary Baker Eddy*

INTRODUCTION

1. *CSJ* 7 (May 1889): 89 [the wording of the quotation has been conformed to the text as revised in *Miscellaneous*, 179]; and Sermon, April 5, 1885, A10653.

2. Quoted in "Introduction: The Problem of Evil," in Michael Peterson, ed., *Problem of Evil*, 1; and *Retrospection*, 31.

3. *Miscellaneous*, 24, 366.

4. Stephen M. Barr, *Modern Physics and Ancient Faith*, 1.

5. Richard Tarnas, *Passion of the Western Mind*, 285–86.

6. *S&H*, vii, 65, and 338.

7. Ibid., 259.

8. *Miscellaneous*, 2; and *S&H*, 92.

9. *S&H*, 428.

10. Ibid., 324, 29; *Miscellaneous*, 101; and *S&H*, 65.

11. See Ronald Goetz's seminal 1986 article, "The Suffering God: the Rise of a New Orthodoxy."

12. *CSJ* 15 (June 1897): 240–41.

13. *S&H*, 1902 revision, 608–9.

14. Martin E. Marty, interview, *Heart in Protest*.

PRELUDE: THE WORLD'S LEADEN WEIGHT

1. Peel, *Authority*, 280.

2. *Record*, Perry, N.Y., n.d., quoted in CSS 9 (August 24, 1907): 989.

3. *Message '00*, 10.

4. "Prospectus," CSJ 1 (April 14, 1883): 1 [*Miscellaneous*, 2]; "Christian Science Healing Explained and Defended," *New York Sunday Journal*, n.d., in CSJ 19 (April 1901): 3 [*Miscellany*, 221].

5. *No and Yes*, 34.

6. *Retrospection*, 24–29.

7. Eddy to Mrs. Swarts, September 30, 1884, V00838; and *S&H*, xii.

8. Undated memorandum, A10997.

9. See Chapter 8, "Ayont Hate's Thrall."

10. Richard Norton Smith, review of *Pulitzer: A Life* by Denis Brian, *Columbia Journalism Review* 40 (November–December 2001): 1.

11. "'Choose Ye,'" CSS 24 (July 1906): 659 [*Miscellany*, 4]; Eddy to a student, date unknown, 1897, L02595.

12. "A Letter from Our Leader," CSS 8 (April 28, 1906): 552 [*Miscellany*, 26].

13. "Personal Contagion," CSS 8 (July 7, 1906): 716 [*Miscellany*, 117].

14. Eddy to board of directors, November 8, 1900, V01782.

15. "'I Hold No Enmity,' Says Mrs. Eddy," August 25, 1907, interview by W. T. MacIntyre, *New York American*, quoted in CSS 9 (August 31, 1907): 1004.

16. Lewis Strang statement, CSS 9 (November 3, 1906): 148.

17. Concord Monitor, n.d., CSS 9 (November 3, 1906): 153.

18. Strang to Alfred Farlow, October 31, 1907, L16209.

19. Quoted in Fleta Campbell Springer, *According to the Flesh*, 414.

20. "Dr. Allan McLane Hamilton Tells about His Visit to Mrs. Eddy," *New York Times*, August 25, 1907.

21. Eddy to Albert Metcalf, April 14, 1907, L08840; and Leon Burr Richardson, *William E. Chandler: Republican*, 698.

22. Peel, *Authority*, 281.

23. James P. Wilson to Eddy, January 7, 1907 in Peel, Authority, 278.

24. Eddy to Joseph Armstrong, March 21, 1907, L09466.

25. *Miscellany*, 138.

26. Quoted in Meehan, *Late Suit,* 217.

27. William E. Chandler to Ralph Pulitzer, February 7, 1907, Chandler Papers.

28. Chandler to Joseph Pulitzer, February 27, 1907, Chandler Papers.

29. Eddy to Dr. and Mrs. Ezekiel Morrill, October 6, 1906, quoted in Peel, *Authority,* 260.

30. William Lyman Johnson, *History,* 3: 537; quoted in Meehan, *Late Suit,* 285; and *North American* (Philadelphia): July 14, 1907.

31. Adelaide Still reminiscence; Powell, *Portrait,* 213; Mary E. Eaton reminiscence; and August Mann reminiscence.

32. Lida Fitzpatrick notes, April 5, 1907, *Notes on Mary Baker Eddy's Course in Divinity, Recorded by Lida Fitzpatrick, C.S.D., and Others;* and Eddy, Note to "My beloved Church," April 9, 1907, L08375.

33. Eddy to Irving C. Tomlinson, May 30, 1907, L03867; and "Some Precious Memories of Mary Baker Eddy," *We Knew,* 182.

34. Clara McKee reminiscence; and Hermann Hering reminiscence.

35. Eddy to Farlow, December 22, 1906, L01707; and *New York American,* November 3, 1906.

36. *Cosmopolitan,* August 1907 [reprinted as *What Mrs. Eddy Said to Arthur Brisbane*].

37. *Home Rule,* Abilene, Kansas, in Meehan, *Late Suit,* 289.

38. Adam H. Dickey, Memoirs, 135; and Eddy to Ellen Brown Linscott, September 30, 1885, L12982.

39. Eddy to Calvin Hill, March 24, 1907, L04295; and *New Haven Register,* in *CSS* 9 (August 31, 1907): 1006.

40. "Christian Science," *CSJ* 1 (February 1884): 2 [*Miscellaneous,* 235].

41. Chandler to Ralph Pulitzer, March 28, 1907, Chandler Papers.

42. Quoted in Denis Brian, *Pulitzer: A Life,* 276.

43. Chandler to Dr. Henry Reed Hopkins, March 22, 1907, Chandler Papers; *S&H,* 164, and see also 151, and *Miscellaneous,* 19.

44. *CSS* 3 (September 6, 1900): 10; and The Reverend A. Lincoln Moore, *Christian Science: Its Manifold Attractions,* 44–45, in Gottschalk, *Emergence,* 200.

45. Quoted in Thomas C. Johnsen, "Christian Scientists and the Medical Profession: A Historical Perspective," 73; and Twain, *Christian Science,* 80.

46. Herbert J. S. J. Clancy, *Presidential Election of 1880,* 17–18; and Chandler to Hopkins, July 10, 1907, Chandler Papers.

47. Adelaide Still reminiscence.

48. Bates-Dittemore, *Mary Baker Eddy,* 413.

49. A transcript of the interview with the Masters can be found in Norman Beasley, *Cross and the Crown,* 440–61, and in Meehan, *Late Suit,* 153–66. The stenographer's original report was made available for modification by Eddy, Chandler, the masters, and others who had spoken in court in order to clarify their thoughts, but not apparently to modify anything of substance. See Meehan, *Late Suit,* 167.

50. *Unity,* 37.

51. "Mrs. Eddy Fully Proves Her Competence," *New York American,* n.d. [*CSS* 9, August 24, 1907].

52. "Christian Science Wins," *Boston Journal,* quoted in *CSS* 9 (August 24, 1907): 987–88.

53. Peel, *Authority*, 289; Chandler to Dr. H. R. Stedman, August 18, 1907; and Chandler to Ralph Pulitzer, August 17, 1907, Chandler Papers.

54. "Opening statement by Honorable William E. Chandler," Eddy et als vs. Frye et als, Concord, N. H., August 13, 1907. Quoted portions of Chandler's opening statement were omitted from Michael Meehan's *Late Suit*, but are reproduced in Peel, *Authority*, 284.

55. I Cor. 13:12; and *Miscellaneous*, 87.

56. Chandler, "Opening statement"; and "Conversation," April 1, 1902, A11448.

57. Chandler, "Opening statement"; and *S&H*, viii.

58. Quoted in Meehan, *Late Suit*, 164.

59. *Los Angeles Examiner*, July 17, 1941.

60. See, for example, Claire Warox, *Spontaneous Recovery;* and *S&H*, 580.

61. Quoted in Meehan, *Late Suit*, 203 (emphasis in the original).

62. *S&H*, 103, 583.

63. Ibid., 451.

64. *Miscellany*, 213.

65. *CSJ* 25 (November 1907): 505.

66. See, for example, Larry Dossey, *Be Careful What You Pray For.*

67. "Optic," Quincy, Illinois, quoted in Meehan, *Late Suit*, 314.

68. Chandler to George Glover, May 10, 1912, Chandler Papers.

69. See "The Path Perilous" in Chapter 8, "Ayont Hate's Thrall."

70. Chandler to Frederick Peabody, March 27, 1907 and December 11, 1909, Chandler Papers.

71. "A sympathizer" to Glover, March 3, 1907, Chandler Papers.

72. Adelaide Still reminiscence; and Eddy to Glover, June 16, 1907, L02149.

73. Peel, *Authority*, 295–96.

74. "Christian Science Most Potent Factor in Religious Life, Says Clara Barton," *CSJ* 25 (February 1908): 696.

75. *We Knew*, 182.

76. Michael Meehan reminiscence. See Michael Meehan, *Mrs. Eddy and the Late Suit in Equity.*

77. Frank S. Streeter to Eddy, September 30, 1907, L17994.

78. "Mrs. Eddy's Statements," *CSJ* 18 (July 1909): 250 [*Miscellany*, 143]; and Benjamin O. Flower to Eddy, 7 August 1907, *CSS* 9 (August 31, 1907).

79. Hodges interview, *North American* (Philadelphia): July 14, 1907.

80. Eddy to N. W. Nesmith, May 30, 1907, L13512.

81. *Miscellany*, 136; Chandler to Hopkins, July 23, 1907, Chandler Papers.

82. *S&H*, 34.

83. Quoted in Meehan, *Late Suit*, 319; Quoted in Powell, *Portrait*, 258.

1. "O God, *is it all!*"

1. *S&H*, 26, 33, 47, 34–35.

2. Twain, *Autobiography*, 349.

3. Twain, *Mark Twain Speaks*, ed. Paul Fatout, 222.

4. Twain, *Christian Science*, 3–5.

5. Hamlin Hill, afterword to Twain, *Christian Science*, 5; and Twain, *Fables of Man*, 322–24.

6. Hill, *Mark Twain: God's Fool*, 54; and Twain, *Christian Science*, 102–3, 106.

7. Twain, *Christian Science*, 276, 229.

8. Eddy, "Mrs. Eddy Replies to Mark Twain," *CSS* 5 (January 22, 1903): 323 [*Miscellany*, 302–3].

9. Eddy to Septimus J. Hanna, November 17, 1892, L04930A.

10. Twain, *Christian Science*, 111, 290–92.

11. Quoted in Peel, *Authority*, 201; Frederick W. Peabody to Twain, December 2, 1902, Twain Papers; and quoted in Hill, afterword to Twain, *Christian Science*, 3.

12. Twain, *Christian Science*, 266, 267.

13. Twain, *Mysterious Stranger*, 164–76.

14. Twain, *Christian Science*, 284; and Twain, *Autobiography*, 90.

15. Twain, *Mark Twain's Letters, Volume 4, 1870–1871*, 528.

16. Twain to Samuel E. Moffett, quoted in Stanley Brodwin, "Mark Twain's Theology: the God of a Brevet Presbyterian," in Forrest G. Robinson, ed., *Cambridge Companion to Mark Twain*, 222.

17. Twain to Orion Clemens, quoted in ibid.

18. Twain, *Fables of Man*, 405–6.

19. Twain, *Christian Science*, 284.

20. Jewel Spangler Smaus, *Golden Days*, 42; *Miscellany*, 134; and *Retrospection*, 13.

21. *S&H*, 7.

22. Autobiographical Dictations of June 1906, in *Bible According to Mark Twain*, 330; and *S&H*, 357, 230.

23. *S&H*, 475.

24. Quoted in Brodwin, "Mark Twain's Theology," 241; and "The People's God," *CSJ* 1 (June 2, 1883): 1 [*People*, 3].

25. Twain, *Tom Sawyer*, 68.

26. Twain, *Autobiography*, 68–69.

27. Ibid., 40–41.

28. Albert Bigelow Paine, *Mark Twain*, I, 141; and Twain, *Autobiography*, 190.

29. Clara Clemens, *My Father: Mark Twain*, 173–74; and quoted in Justin Kaplan, *Mr. Clemens and Mark Twain*, 337.

30. Twain, *Autobiography*, 372.

31. Ibid., 372–73.

32. Ibid., 375; quoted in introduction to *Portable Mark Twain*, ed. Bernard DeVoto, 14.

33. Twain, "Letters from the Earth," in *What Is Man?*, 428.

34. Bryce, *American Commonwealth*, 2: 499.

35. Twain, "Letters from the Earth," in *What Is Man?*, 453.

36. William D. McCrackan, "My Interviews with Mark Twain."

37. Abigail Baker Tilton to George S. Baker, July 18, 1837, Baker Papers; and Thomas, *Footsteps*, 26.

38. Quoted in Peel, *Discovery*, 41; and *Retrospection*, 13–14.

39. Lucy Larcom, *New England Girlhood*, 8–9.

40. Perry Miller, *New England Mind*, 3 (see 3–34 for a discussion of "The Augustinian Strain of Piety" discernible in Eddy as well as her Puritan forebears);

Message '01, 15; and Jonathan Edwards, "Personal Narrative," in *Jonathan Edwards Reader,* 285–86.

41. Edwards, *Treatise Concerning Religious Affections,* in *Jonathan Edwards Reader,* 148.

42. *Retrospection,* 31.

43. *Message '01,* 31–33.

44. *Retrospection,* 15.

45. Ibid., 13.

46. Lydia Ann Holmes to Augusta Holmes, August 19, 1838, Baker Papers.

47. Quoted in Peel, *Discovery,* 50.

48. H. A. L. Fisher, *Our New Religion,* 41; and George S. Baker, "Suggestions whilst listening to sermon from the Rev. E. Corser, July 1840," Baker Papers.

49. *Covenant,* April 1846. Eddy had started contributing to this magazine the year before. Although the article quoted here is written anonymously, the editor, who knew Eddy and had written an obituary of her husband, wrote about the anonymous author in terms that makes some Eddy scholars confident that he was referring to her. The article itself is highly descriptive of Eddy's experience.

50. *Miscellany,* 190.

51. Eddy to George S. Baker, November 22, 1849, Baker Papers.

52. Scrapbook 1, SB001.

53. Copybook 1, September 20, 1859, A09001.

54. Twain, *Christian Science,* 102.

55. Copybook 1, August 25, 1843, A09002.

56. *S&H,* 268.

57. David Herbert Donald, *Lincoln,* 225; *S&H,* 156. A useful general discussion of homeopathy and its role in American medicine can be found in Paul Starr, *Social Transformation of American Medicine,* 96–109.

58. *Retrospection,* 30, 33.

59. Tomlinson, *Twelve Years,* 32.

60. This concept is developed in Chapter 1, "Clinamen or Poetic Misprision," of Bloom, *Anxiety of Influence,* 19–48.

61. Quimby, *Phineas Parkhurst Quimby, The Complete Writings,* ed. Ervin Seale, 3: 234–40.

62. Karl Holl, *Der Szientismus,* translation by Mary Gottschalk; and *Miscellaneous,* 234. Interestingly, Eddy's first use of the metaphor "rolling away the stone" occurred in somewhat varying language in her second letter to the *Portland Courier* extolling Quimby (November 1862).

63. Quimby, *Complete Writings,* 3: 291.

64. Ibid., 52.

65. See, for example, *S&H* 127, 272, *Miscellaneous,* 206; *S&H,* 476; and Peel, *Trial,* 153.

66. Quoted in Quimby, *Quimby Manuscripts,* Horatio Dresser, ed., 436.

67. Quimby, *Complete Writings,* 3: 234–240; and see, for example, "Mind is Spiritual Matter," 3: 195–96.

68. *Lynn Transcript,* January 20, 1872; Eddy to Wallace Wright, March 12, 1871, V03416.

69. Warren Felt Evans, *Mental Cure,* 252; and *S&H,* 1st ed., 373–74.

70. "One Cause and Effect," *Miscellaneous,* 24.

71. See, for example, *Miscellaneous,* 365, and *S&H,* 114, 349.

72. *Journals of Bronson Alcott*, ed. Odell Shepard, 467. An extensive discussion of Alcott's relations with Eddy and her students can be found in Peel, *Christian Science*, 47–96.

73. *Miscellaneous*, 38, 69.

74. *No and Yes*, 37; and *S&H*, 466.

75. *Unity*, 9.

76. *Miscellaneous*, 27; and *S&H*, 108.

77. *Miscellaneous*, 196.

78. *S&H*, 561.

79. Ibid., 556; and *Retrospection*, 23.

80. *Lynn Weekly Reporter*, February 3, 1866; Henry Robinson, "Memorandum of an Interview with Mrs. Doctor Eddy, at 'Pleasant View,' Concord."

81. Alfred Farlow, "Historical Facts Concerning Mary Baker Eddy and Christian Science."

82. Eddy to Julius Dresser, February 15, 1866, L07796.

83. These accounts of healing are quoted in Fettweis and Warneck, *Mary Baker Eddy: Christian Healer*, 41–46; and *Retrospection*, 24.

84. *Message '02*, 4.

85. *Miscellaneous*, 169.

86. Eddy develops this interpretation of Genesis in Chapter 15 of *S&H*, 501–57.

87. Ibid., ix.

88. For an analysis of the church fathers' conflict with gnosticism and its results, see Mircea Eliade, *History of Religious Ideas from Gautama Buddha to the Triumph of Christianity*, 396.

89. "The Bible in Its Spiritual Meaning," 37–38, A09000.

90. "To the Christian World," *New York Sun*, December 16, 1898 [*Miscellany*, 105]; and *Unity*, 7.

91. *S&H*, 418.

92. Ibid., 574; and Twain, *Fables of Man*, 131.

93. *Christian Healing*, 11.

94. For the genesis and development of Twain's concept of the dream self, see John S. Tuckey's introduction to *Mark Twain's Which Was the Dream? and Other Symbolic Writings of the Later Years*, 1–29.

95. Twain, *Mysterious Stranger*, 100, 114, 115, 186.

96. McCrackan, "My Interviews with Mark Twain."

97. Quoted in Alfred Bigelow Paine, *Mark Twain*, 3: 1271.

98. See also Clara Clemens's earlier book, *My Husband, Gabrilowitsch*; and quoted in Twain, *Portable Mark Twain*, 786.

99. Twain, *Christian Science*, 286.

100. Eddy, "Mrs. Eddy Replies to Mark Twain," *CSS* 5 (January 22, 1903): 323 [*Miscellany*, 303]; Eddy to Harriet L. Betts, January 7, 1902, L04462; and Eddy to Farlow, December 30, 1902, L01648.

101. McCrackan to Twain, December 11, 1902, Twain Papers. Useful discussions of various aspects of the connection between Twain and Eddy can be found in the chapter "The Metaphysics of Rebellion" in Johnsen, "Christian Science and the Puritan Tradition"; in Chapter 24, "Mark Twain Fails to Come Calling," in Gill, *Eddy*; and in Chapter 6, ". . . remains to be proved . . . ," in Peel, *Authority*.

2. Becoming "Mrs. Eddy"

1. Lee Z. Johnson interview, in *Heart in Protest.*
2. The most useful accounts of the case are to be found in Peel, *Trial,* 50–58, and Gill, *Eddy,* 257–70.
3. Quoted in Peel, *Trial,* 95–96.
4. "To the Public," *S&H,* 3rd ed., xii.
5. Samuel Putnam Bancroft, *Mrs. Eddy as I Knew Her in 1870,* 54.
6. Sermon, n.d., A10762B. For other published examples, see Chapter 6, "Sermons," in *Miscellaneous,* 161–202; "Christian Healing: A Sermon Delivered at Boston"; and "The People's Idea of God: Its Effect on Health and Christianity, A Sermon Delivered at Boston"—all in *Prose Works other than Science and Health with Key to the Scriptures.*
7. *S&H,* xi.
8. "The March Primary Class" *CSJ* 7 (April 1889): 21 [*Miscellaneous,* 282]; C. Lulu Blackman, "The Star in My Crown of Rejoicing—The Class of 1885," *We Knew,* 56–57; and Eddy to Julia Field-King, November 22, 1888, F00063.
9. Eddy, "Massachusetts Metaphysical College," *CSJ* 7 (September 1889): 337; Julia Bartlett reminiscence; and see the discussion of this incident and its ramifications in "Prologue: 'Christian Science in Tremont Temple,' " Gottschalk, *Emergence,* xv–xxix.
10. "Veritas Odium Parit," *CSJ* 3 (April 1885): 1 [*Miscellaneous,* 245–48].
11. Author's interview with Keith McNeil, July 2004; and Eddy to Choate, December 11, 1883, L02519.
12. J. Stillson Judah, *History and Philosophy of the Metaphysical Movements in America,* 177. Also see Gail M. Harley, *Emma Curtis Hopkins: Forgotten Founder of New Thought,* for the most extensive available discussion of Hopkins and her influence.
13. "A Strong Reply," *CSJ* 3 (April 1885): 5 [*Miscellaneous,* 96].
14. *Judah, History,* 1: 202; and Memorandum, 1887, A11365. See also a detailed discussion of the relation of Christian Science and mind-cure in Gottschalk, *Emergence,* Chapter 3, " 'The Tares and the Wheat.' "
15. *Miscellaneous,* xi.
16. Eddy to Ebenezer J. Foster Eddy, June 22, 1888, N00019.
17. Adelaide Still reminiscence. The story was related to her by Calvin Frye.
18. Laura Sargent, quoted in Adelaide Still reminiscence; and newspaper account quoted in Peel, *Trial,* 243. A heavily edited version of Eddy's address is reprinted in *Miscellaneous,* 98–106.
19. William Lyman Johnson, *History,* 1: 151–52; Eddy to Hannah A. Larminie, November 24, 1888, L04491.
20. Eddy to Lizzie L. and John P. Filbert, March 8, 1889, L12782; Eddy to Eldridge J. and Mollie Smith, January 3, 1884, L02060; and Kate Davidson Kimball reminiscence.
21. "To Loyal Christian Scientists," *CSJ* 6 (July 1888): 213 [*Miscellaneous,* 278]; and Eddy to unknown recipient, July 20, 1889, L00007.
22. Eddy to Mary E. Dillingham, May 12, 1889, V03103.
23. Eddy to Carrie Harvey Snider, March 18, 1890, L06054. Eddy did, however, return to Boston for a few weeks later in 1889 to attend to some business.
24. "Notice: Seven Fixed Rules," *CSJ* 8 (September 1890): 249; and Eddy to Helen A. Nixon, August 15, 1890, L04136.

25. "The Way," *CSJ* 7 (December 1889): 434 [*Miscellaneous*, 358].

26. Eddy to Emma C. Shipman, February 6, 1904, L05540; Lex Hixon, quoted in *Heart in Protest*; and *S&H*, 323.

27. Eddy to George W. Glover, October 31, 1887, L02085; Eddy to Clara Shannon, January 16, 1890, L07752.

28. Eddy to Laura E. Sargent, July 8, 1891, L05962; and Eddy to Ira O. Knapp, August 31, 1891, L03403.

29. Eddy to Albert Metcalf, July 29, 1894, L08835.

30. *Miscellaneous*, 136.

31. Jean Leclercq in introduction to *Bernard of Clairvaux*, 57; and *S&H*, 7.

32. Eddy to Carrie Harvey Snider, August 2, 1892, L06073.

33. *S&H*, 1.

34. Pam Robbins and Robley Whitson, *Sign* 59 (July–August, 1980): 16–21, quoted in *Christian Science: A Sourcebook*, 20–21; and *S&H*, 15.

35. *S&H*, 12; and *No and Yes*, 39.

36. *Miscellaneous*, 16.

37. *No and Yes*, 20; and *Miscellaneous*, 174.

38. *S&H*, 465, 361.

39. *S&H*, 202, 115.

40. Phil. 2:5; and *Message '01*, 6–7.

41. Author's interview with Steven Lee Fair, June 2004.

42. Eddy to Eldridge J. Smith, November 4, 1883, L02063.

43. "The November Class, 1898," *Miscellany*, 244; Eddy to Alfred E. and Anna B. White Baker, 1900, F00009; and Eddy to Ellen Brown Linscott, October 15, 1892, L11027.

44. *S&H*, 15.

45. Caroline Foss Gyger reminiscence; *Miscellaneous*, 309; and Eddy to Anna B. White Baker, October 18, 1901, V01901.

46. "Thou Hast Been Faithful over a Few Things," *CSJ* 3 (December 1885): 158 [*Miscellaneous*, 341–42]; and Eddy to Emilie B. Hulin, December 27, 1889, L04566.

47. William Rathvon diary, November 20, 1910; and Calvin Frye diary, December 10, 1893.

48. Eddy to Gilbert C. Carpenter, n.d., L14128; and Henrietta E. Chanfrau reminiscence.

49. *S&H*, 308; Eddy to Edward P. Bates, February 25, 1887, V03058; and Thomas W. Hatten reminiscence.

50. Eddy to Augusta E. Stetson and Carol Norton, February 16, 1896, V01424.

51. Tomlinson, *Twelve Years*, 107; and Eddy to Septimus J. Hanna, August 5, 1897, L14478.

52. Hermann Hering reminiscence; and John Salchow reminiscence.

53. Eddy and James F. Gilman, *Painting*, 115, 151, 166, 149, 156.

54. *Miscellaneous*, 328; *S&H*, 145; and *Unity*, 62.

55. Notes from Mary Baker Eddy, B00017, n.d.

56. Eddy to Marjorie Colles, November 13, year unknown, L08391; and Eddy to Caroline W. Frame, February 24, 1898, L12855.

57. *No and Yes*, 12.

58. *S&H*, xii.

59. Eddy to Susan W. Scott, October 22, 1891, L04052; Eddy to Larminie, October 2, 1890, L04504; and Eddy to Erastus N. Bates, August 28, 1890, L13960.

60. Clara Shannon reminiscence.

61. Eddy to Helen A. Nixon, November 12, 1890, L04137; and Eddy to Joseph S. Eastaman, February 15, 1891, L03475.

62. Mark Twain, *What Is Man?*, 516.

63. Quoted in Peel, *Trial*, 281.

64. Eddy to James Henry Wiggin, April 1890, L02215.

65. *S&H*, 573–74. Quotations from *Science and Health* in this section, "In Her Authentic Voice," have been conformed to the wording of the final edition of the book, rather than the fiftieth edition.

66. Ibid., 25–26.

67. Eddy to Erastus N. Bates, November 2, 1889, L13959.

68. *S&H*, 364.

69. "Notice," *CSJ* 8 (October 1890): 289.

70. *S&H*, 452.

71. *S&H*, 239.

72. Eddy to Julia Field-King, March 13, 1895, L02592B. In 1902 Field-King was removed from the rolls of the Mother Church for teaching doctrines false to Christian Science. See a fuller discussion of this matter in Peel, *Authority*, 114–19.

73. Twain, *Christian Science*, 110. The chapter "The Human Concept" was added shortly thereafter to a later edition of *Retrospection*.

74. *Retrospection*, 94. This quotation and those that follow have been conformed to the wording of the final edition of *Retrospection and Introspection*, rather than the first edition.

75. Ibid., 94–95.

76. Ibid., 94.

3. By What Authority? On Christian Ground

1. Eddy and James F. Gilman, *Painting a Poem*, 172–73.

2. "Mrs. Eddy Replies to Mark Twain," *CSS* 5 (January 22, 1903): 323 [*Miscellany*, 302–3].

3. *Message '01*, 34; and *Message '02*, 4.

4. Controversy over the issue of the "Woman of the Apocalypse" centered largely on the book *The Destiny of The Mother Church* by Bliss Knapp, son of Ira Knapp. Although the book was rejected for publication in the 1940s by the Mother Church board of directors for what it judged to be "questionable conclusions," the Christian Science Publishing Society eventually published *Destiny* in 1991, with the approval of a later church board, in compliance with two multi-million-dollar bequests by Knapp's relatives. For a fuller discussion of Eddy's own view of this issue, see the section "In the *Arena*" in Chapter 8, " 'Ayont Hate's Thrall.' "

5. "A Conversation with the Archivist of The Mother Church: 'Christian healing-Indispensable,' " *CSS* 88 (February 3, 1986): 193; and Eddy, *Speaking for Herself*, 106.

6. Jaroslav Pelikan, *Melody of Theology*, 18; and *S&H*, 547.

7. *S&H*, 126.

8. Ibid., 497.

9. Eddy, Note to "My beloved Church," April 9, 1907, L08375.

10. Memorandum, August 1891, L17954; B00016, 3; B00005, 3; and B00007, 2.

11. Wallace E. Anderson, introduction to "Images of Divine Things" and "Types," vol. 11 of *Works of Jonathan Edwards*, 3.

12. Ibid., 9–10.

13. See the discussion of Swedenborg's possible influence in Peel, *Discovery*, 347–48; and *S&H*, 589, 592.

14. *CSJ* 13 (April 1895): 43; Adam H. Dickey, *Memoirs*, 102–3; and William Dana Orcutt, *Mary Baker Eddy and Her Books*, 61–62. Despite the technical problems that had to be surmounted, an experimental edition of *Science and Health* on Bible paper was run in 1894.

15. *S&H*, 316, 26, 31.

16. *S&H*, 50th ed., 360; and *S&H*, 55.

17. Eddy and James F. Gilman, *Painting*, 63.

18. Ibid., 108, 129, 98.

19. *Christ and Christmas*, 53. This passage and others cited in this section have been conformed to the wording and pictures from the final edition of *Christ and Christmas*.

20. *S&H*, 127; see also *Miscellaneous* 206, 258; and *Unity*, 55.

21. *S&H*, 127; and *Unity*, 52.

22. John 14:16, 17, 26; and *S&H*, 55.

23. *S&H*, 107; 123.

24. Eddy and James F. Gilman, *Painting*, 169, 243.

25. Calvin Frye diary, March 5, 1900; "Queries," *CSJ* 11 (February 1894): 474 [*Miscellaneous*, 33].

26. Eddy to Septimus J. and Camilla Hanna, December 30, 1893, L04995; and Eddy to Augusta E. Stetson, January 22, 1894, H00133.

27. " 'Hear, O Israel,' " *CSJ* 11 (February 1894): 472 [*Miscellaneous*, 308].

28. *S&H*, 556.

29. "Card," *CSJ* 11 (April 1893), 20 [*Miscellaneous*, 321–22]; Eddy to David A. Easton, April 15, 1893, L04688; and Laura Sargent notebook.

30. John Henry Barrows, ed., *World's Parliament of Religions*, 1: 62–64.

31. Quoted in *CSJ* 11 (November 1893): 339.

32. *S&H*, 471.

33. Ibid.

34. Eddy to Edward A. Kimball, September 21, 1893, V03411.

35. Eddy to Barrows, September 27, 1893, L02579. Eddy may well have reconsidered her decision not to have her address published, since it was eventually printed in Barrows's commemorative book.

36. William Lyman Johnson, *History*, 2: 180.

37. Helen Blavatsky and William Q. Judge, "Some of the Errors of Christian Science," 8; and Blavatsky, *Studies in Occultism*, 41–42.

38. *Manual*, 41; and Eddy to Occult Publishing Society, June 22, 1887, L14066.

39. Eddy to Margaret E. Easton, July 2, 1893, L04690.

40. *Miscellaneous*, 22; *Miscellany*, 119; undated memorandum, A10398; *CSJ* 4 (October 1886): 160; and Emma Curtis Hopkins, "First Lesson in Christian Science," 16–17.

41. Richard Hughes Seager, in *World's Parliament of Religions*, discusses this aspect of the influence of the parliament in detail; and Swami Vivekananda, *Letters of Swami Vivekananda, from America*, 118.

42. William P. McCorkle, *Christian Science*, 248; and see, for example, *S&H*, 250, 279, *Unity*, 45, and *Miscellaneous*, 76.

43. Clara Shannon reminiscence; *and Miscellaneous,* 153.

44. Martha H. Bogue, "Notes from Mrs. Eddy's Primary and Normal Classes of 1888 and 1889," quoted in *Miscellaneous Documents,* 70.

45. Clara Shannon reminiscence; and Septimus J. Hanna to Eddy, September 30, 1893, L16544.

46. Eddy to Charles C. Bonney, September 27, 1893, L09475; and memorandum, 24 April 1894, A10388.

47. Memorandum, n.d., A10450.

48. *S&H,* 272.

4. By What Authority? Listening and Leading

1. Eddy to Edward P. Bates, May 3, 1894, L09112.

2. *Retrospection,* 46, *Poems,* 14; written comments on Twain's copy of *Retrospection and Introspection,* Twain Papers.

3. *S&H,* 151; and *We Knew,* 173.

4. Eddy to James Henry Wiggin, July 29, 1888, V01072; *CSJ* 4 (June 1886): 76 [*Miscellaneous,* 255]; *S&H,* 340.

5. Eddy to Ira O. Knapp, June 11, 1892, L03420; Clara Shannon reminiscence; and Eddy to Carol Norton, January 30, 1894, L02356.

6. Eddy to Frank L. Phalen, December 31, 1897, L13284; and "Questions Answered," *CSJ* 6 (October 1888): 342 [*Miscellaneous,* 86].

7. *S&H,* 429; Lida Fitzpatrick notes; and *S&H,* 290.

8. *S&H,* ix.

9. *Message '00,* 9.

10. Peel, *Authority,* 78–79.

11. Eddy to James Henry Wiggin, November 2, 1890, L02226, and November 6, 1890, L02227.

12. Eddy to Edward P. and Caroline S. Bates, March 9, 1895, L08242; and Eddy to Archibald McLellan, June 8, 1902, L07043.

13. Adam H. Dickey, *Memoirs,* 85–87.

14. Eddy to Irving C. Tomlinson, October 28, 1898, L03645; I Cor. 7:10; and Eddy to board of directors, January 10, 1895, L02751.

15. Eddy to Frank S. Streeter, November 7, 1900, V01780.

16. Robert David Thomas, author's interview, May 1987.

17. Eddy to William N. and Frederica L. Miller, May 27, 1902, F00246; Acts 10:34; and "Statement by Helen W. Bingham," in *Miscellaneous Documents,* 146.

18. Gottschalk, *Emergence,* 173; *Manual,* 48. In its final version, this bylaw was named "The Golden Rule."

19. Edward P. Bates reminiscence; and William P. McKenzie reminiscence.

20. Eddy to Anne Dodge, November 13, 1907, L13479, and November 16, 1907, L10530.

21. " 'Hear O Israel,' " *CSJ* 11 (February 1894): 472 [*Miscellaneous,* 308]; "Personal Contagion," *CSS* 8 (July 7, 1906): 716, and *CSJ* 24 (August 1906): 310–11 [*Miscellany,* 116–17]; and McLellan, "Our Leader's Article," *CSS* 8 (July 7, 1906): 716.

22. Memorandum, n.d., A10238.

23. Memorandum, n.d., probably dictated to E. J. Foster Eddy, A10281. For a fuller text of this memorandum, see Peel, *Authority,* 431–32.

24. *Manual,* 40; and *Miscellaneous,* 100.

25. *S&H,* 116, 140; *Miscellaneous,* 282; and *Retrospection,* 67.

26. Quoted in Peel, *Authority,* 79.

27. Quoted in Gill, *Eddy,* 377.

28. Foster Eddy diary, January 2, 1890, Chandler Papers.

29. Foster Eddy to Eddy, May 1, 1894.

30. Eddy to Ira O. Knapp, September 28, 1890, L03380; Eddy to Calvin C. Hill, August 5, 1905, L15550; and Eddy to Foster Eddy, July 9, 1895, L01961.

31. Henrietta E. Chanfrau reminiscence.

32. Foster Eddy to Joshua F. Bailey, June 17, 1892, L12012; and Eddy to Foster Eddy, January 29, 1893, L01811.

33. Eddy to Joseph Armstrong, November 2, 1893, L02695A; and Eddy to Foster Eddy, April 17, 1892, N00238.

34. Eddy to Ira O. and Flavia Stickney Knapp, December 3, year unknown, L03385.

35. Mary E. Armstrong reminiscence.

36. Orcutt, *Mary Baker Eddy and Her Books,* 47.

37. Eddy to board of directors, April 27, 1895, L02664. Foster Eddy's brief stint as First Reader in October 1895 ended with his resignation.

38. Clara Shannon reminiscence.

39. Eddy to Foster Eddy, October 15, 1895, L01975; and January 22, 1896, L01988.

40. Calvin Frye diary, January 5, 1896; and Minnie Weygandt reminiscence. Eddy's last public address to her church was in 1899 at Tremont Temple.

41. Eddy to Foster Eddy, July 21, 1897, L02006.

42. "Strange Tale of Mrs. Eddy's Foster Son," *Boston Evening Record* (March 12, 1907); and John Salchow reminiscence.

43. Eddy to John F. Linscott, April 17, 1896, L11047.

44. *Poems,* 4.

45. Eddy to Augusta E. Stetson, February 20, year unknown, H00134; and Frye diary, March 29, 1896.

46. *Granite Monthly* (October 1896): 199–209. The entire article, in slightly revised form, minus Hanna's introduction, can be found in *Miscellaneous,* 21–30—from which all quoted passages of "One Cause and Effect" in this section are taken.

47. *S&H,* 468.

48. *Miscellaneous,* 27–28.

49. *S&H,* 143.

50. Deut. 4:35; and *No and Yes,* 35.

5. WOMAN GOES FORTH

1. "Editor's Table," *CSJ* 14 (November 1896): 416.

2. Jean A. McDonald, author's interview, June 1987.

3. Martin E. Marty, author's interview, June 1987.

4. See, for example, *Message '01,* 23–24, *Miscellany,* 349, *No and Yes,* 22. See discussion of the relation of Christian Science to philosophic idealism in Gottschalk, *Emergence,* 76–79.

5. *S&H,* 269–70.

6. Ibid., 468, 268.

7. Carol Ochs, *Women and Spirituality*, 27.

8. H. A. L. Fisher, *Our New Religion*, 60.

9. *Retrospection*, 13, 14.

10. Eddy to E. Blanche Ward, June 30, 1896, L05596.

11. Quoted in John White Chadwick, *Theodore Parker*, 215.

12. Mary E. Eaton reminiscence.

13. *S&H*, 691–92, 6.

14. Quoted in Tomlinson, *Twelve Years*, 68.

15. Eddy to John F. Linscott, February 14, 1896, L04127.

16. A quick survey of Eddy's voluminous letter writing, with rough numbers in parentheses, shows that she wrote letters to Septimus B. Hanna, who served as editor of the *Journal* and pastor and first reader of the Mother Church (615); to the prominent lecturer Edward A. Kimball (419); to August E. Stetson, who virtually dominated the movement in New York (393); to the scholarly and faithful William McKenzie (258); to Laura Lathrop of New York, whom Stetson saw as her main rival (111); to John Lathrop, Laura's son, of whom Eddy was fond and who required much nurturing (140); to Pamelia Leonard of New York, who served at her Pleasant View home (119); to Julia Field-King, who prompted Eddy's interest in her possible Davidic descent (154); to Carol Norton, Stetson's promising student whose early death grieved Eddy (153); and to Marjorie Colles, who helped establish Christian Science in England (62). This list does not include her numerous messages to the board of directors or to individual students and churches in the field.

17. Wills, *Certain Trumpets*, 181.

18. Eddy to Laura Lathrop, November 9, 1891, L12950; and Eddy to Septimus J. and Camilla Hanna, October 28, 1895, L05121.

19. "Notes from the Field," *CSJ* 10 (May 1892): 77 [*Miscellaneous*, 152].

20. "The Reason for the Hope," *CSJ* 7 (May 1889): 63.

21. Alfred Farlow to Eddy, May 31, 1901; Twain, "Christian Science," *North American Review* 175 (December 1902): 760; Eddy, "Mrs. Eddy Replies to Mark Twain," *CSS* 5 (January 22, 1903): 323 [*Miscellany*, 302]; and *Manual*, 64–65.

22. Eddy to Sarah G. Baker, March 4, 1890, L12650; and Richard A. Nenneman, *Persistent Pilgrim*, 210.

23. Eddy to Laura Lathrop, January 1890, L04339; and Eddy to Ellen Brown Linscott, March 2, 1890, L11026.

24. Quoted in *We Knew*, 90; and Eddy to Ira O. Knapp, August 13, 1892, V01159.

25. "Obedience," *CSJ* 10 (March 1893): 532 [*Miscellaneous*, 118]; and Eddy and James F. Gilman, *Painting*, 113–14; Eddy to Carrie Harvey Snider, January 21, 1891, L06060.

26. Eddy to Editor, *Boston Herald*, August 4, 1895, L05097B, and August 9, 1895, L05097D.

27. Eddy to board of directors, August 18, 1895, L00117.

28. *Retrospection*, 90.

29. Twain, *Personal Recollections of Joan of Arc*, 429.

30. Quoted in ibid., introduction by Justin Kaplan, xxxvii.

31. *Retrospection*, 5.

32. Gail M. Harley, *Emma Curtis Hopkins*, 34, 32.

33. Eddy to Clara E. Choate, March 15, 1882, L04088.

34. "Veritas Odium Parit," *CSJ* 3 (April 1885): 1 [*Miscellaneous*, 245]; *Retrospection*, 26.

35. Jennie E. Sawyer reminiscence; and Penny Hansen, "Woman's Hour," 156.

36. Margery Fox, "Protest in Piety," 401, 402, 410; and Janice Klein, "Ann Lee and Mary Baker Eddy," 371.

37. Jean A. McDonald, "Mary Baker Eddy and the Nineteenth Century 'Public' Woman," 90, 101, 107, 108.

38. Mary Farrell Bednarowski, *Religious Imagination of American Women*, 156–57.

39. *Miscellaneous*, 207.

40. "Men in our Ranks," *CSS* 12 (February 12, 1910): 470 [*Miscellany*, 355]; and Eddy to board of directors, January 25, 1895, L02755.

41. *Manual*, 99, 100.

42. Julia S. Bartlett reminiscence.

43. Sue Ella Bradshaw, "Truth on the Pacific Coast," *CSJ* 5 (August 1887): 240.

44. Frances Thurber Seal, *Christian Science in Germany*, 11, 20, 78.

45. Josephine Tyter, "The Cause in Richmond, Indiana," *CSJ* 6 (June 1888): 145–46; and "Churches Dedicated," *CSJ* 15 (June 1897): 148–49.

46. Phoebe Haines reminiscence, quoted in Gottschalk, *Emergence*, 246.

47. Eddy, "Man and Woman," A10142B, quoted in *In My True Light and Life*, 623.

48. Margaret M. Elder, *Life of Samuel J. Elder*, 201, 202.

49. Bartlett, in *We Knew*, 47.

50. Eddy to Baxter E. Perry, March 30, 1892, L02573; and Peel, *Authority*, 14–15.

51. Eddy to William G. Nixon, March 13, 1892, L02279.

52. Quoted in Peel, *Authority*, 127.

53. Calvin Frye diary, December 7, 1899.

54. Daisette Stocking McKenzie reminiscence.

55. Memorandum, August 27, 1895, A10105A; and *S&H*, 249, 57.

56. Quoted in *We Knew*, 82; Eddy to Irving C. Tomlinson, December 5, 1900, L03744.

57. *S&H*, 397; and *Miscellaneous*, 206.

58. Eddy, "Man and Woman," A10142B, quoted in *In My True Light and Life*, 620, 621, 622.

6. "THE VISIBLE UNITY OF SPIRIT"

1. *Message '01*, 32.

2. Eddy to William B. Johnson, August 22, 1892, L00021; and Tomlinson, *Twelve Years*, 156.

3. Eddy to Julia S. Bartlett, July 10, 1898, L07742.

4. *S&H*, 18.

5. *Manual*, 41; and *Pulpit*, 22.

6. "National Christian Scientist Association," *CSJ* 6 (June 1888): 154 [*Miscellaneous*, 135].

7. Eddy to the First Church of Christ (Scientist) Boston, November 28, 1889, L00008.

8. "The Boston Church of Christ (Scientist)," *CSJ* 7 (February 1890): 566.

9. Robert Peel made this analogy often in conversations with the author and others.

10. "Communion Service," *CSJ* 5 (August 1887): 264.

11. Quoted in Bliss Knapp, *Destiny*, 53; see Eddy's account of the transactions concerning the property upon which the Mother Church was built in *CSJ* 10 (July 1892), 133–35 [*Miscellaneous*, 139–42].

12. "To Christian Scientists," *CSJ* 8 (November 1890): 335.

13. Helen Andrews Nixon reminiscence.

14. William Lyman Johnson, *History*, 2: 72.

15. "Notes from the Field," *CSJ* 9 (June 1891): 122; and "Organization of Scientist Churches," *CSJ* 7 (April 1889): 13.

16. "Christian Science Publishing House," *CSJ* 9 (May 1891): 55; William Lyman Johnson, *History*, 2: 74.

17. *Manual*, 17; and Eddy to board of directors, May 20, 1904, L00383.

18. *Poems*, 75.

19. *Retrospection*, 1st ed. (1891), 94–95 [*Retrospection*, 76].

20. "Notes from the Field," *CSJ* 9 (July 1891): 168.

21. *CSJ* 9 (March 1892): frontispiece, 514–16; and William Lyman Johnson, *History*, 2: 81, 83.

22. Eddy to an unnamed student, April 30, 1892, L00638; William B. Johnson to Christian Scientists, May 3, 1892, quoted in William Lyman Johnson, *History*, 2: 26; and Eddy to William B. Johnson, May 8, 1892, L00012.

23. "Hints for History," *CSJ* 10 (July 1892): 135 [*Miscellaneous*, 141].

24. Quoted in Knapp, *Destiny*, 84.

25. Eddy to Alfred Lang, August 9, 1892, L07832.

26. "Hints for History," *CSJ* 10 (July 1892): 134 [*Miscellaneous*, 140]; and quoted in *Manual*, 130.

27. Eddy to Lang, August 22, 1892 (estimated), L07833. This trust deed is included in, and thereby is part of, the *Manual*, 128–35.

28. Eddy to Alfred Farlow, October 19, 1892, L01584; "To the Contributors of the Church Building Fund in Boston," *CSJ* 10 (October 1892): 276, 274.

29. Eddy to Edward P. and Caroline S. Bates, January 16, year unknown, L08221; and Eddy to the First Church of Christ, Scientist, Boston, April 17, 1895, L00100.

30. Eddy to Erastus N. Bates, October 1889, L09472.

31. "Love Your Enemies," *CSJ* 8 (April 1890): 2 [*Miscellaneous*, 11–12]; and Eddy to Marjorie Colles, November 2, 1891, L08392.

32. *Manual*, 18.

33. "Hints for History," *CSJ* 10 (July 1892): 133–34 [*Miscellaneous*, 140]; and Eddy to John F. and Ellen Brown Linscott, October 29, 1892, L11056.

34. Eddy to David A. Easton, March 10, 1893, L07876.

35. Eddy to Augusta E. Stetson, December 11, 1894, H00029; and Camilla Hanna reminiscence.

36. "Laying the Corner Stone," *CSJ* 12 (June 1894): 89 [*Poems*, 76].

37. "Nota Bene," *CSJ* 12 (July 1894): 133–34 [*Miscellaneous*, 145]; and "Laying the Corner Stone," *CSJ* 12 (June 1894): 91 [*Miscellaneous*, 145].

38. "A Word to the Wise," *CSJ* 11 (December 1893): 387 [*Miscellaneous*, 320].

39. Gill, *Eddy*, 358.

40. Helen Andrews Nixon reminiscence.

41. "Obedience," *CSJ* 10 (March 1893): 532 [*Miscellaneous,* 117].

42. Eddy to Ira O. Knapp, October 2, 1894, L03447; and Eddy to Ebenezer J. Foster Eddy, April 1894, L01897.

43. Eddy to William B. Johnson, September 17, 1893, L00052; Eddy to board of directors, September 29, 1893, L00053; July 19, 1894, L00065; July 1894, L00066; Eddy to William B. Johnson, October 19, 1894, L03296; Eddy to Stephen A. Chase and Joseph Armstrong, November 23, 1894, L02732; and Eddy to board of directors, December 19, 1894, L02748.

44. Eddy to board of directors, October 1894, V01323.

45. "Hints for History," *CSJ* 10 (July 1892): 134 [*Miscellaneous,* 140–41]. In the revised version in *Miscellaneous,* the original phrase "prayer in brick" has been changed to read "prayer in stone."

46. Ira O. Knapp to Eddy, December 12, 1894.

47. Joseph Armstrong and Margaret Williamson, *Building of the Mother Church,* 25; Edward P. Bates to Eddy, October 6, 1895.

48. Edward P. Bates reminiscence.

49. Ibid.

50. Eddy to board of directors, November 23, 1894, L02734.

51. William Lyman Johnson, *History,* 2: 466–67, 470.

52. Bates reminiscence; Eddy to Flavia Stickney Knapp, April 18, 1895, L03451.

53. *S&H,* 583.

54. Eddy to Harriet L. Betts and Frederick W. Sim, December 3, 1897, L02595; and "Dedication of the Church in Concord," *CSS* 6 (July 23, 1904): 739 [*Miscellany,* 162].

55. Eddy to board of directors, November 1894, L01124; Eddy to Edward P. Bates, Caroline S. Bates, Caroline W. Frame, Emilie B. Hulin, November 25, 1894, V01325.

56. William Lyman Johnson, *History,* 2: 477. Judge Hanna read from an 1894 edition of *S&H,* 340; the final wording appears in *S&H,* 35.

57. *S&H,* 581, 241; *Retrospection,* 94; *Message '02,* 5; and Matt. 3: 17.

58. *S&H,* 35; "Dedicatory Address of Rev. Mary Baker Eddy," *CSS* 1 (April 6, 1899): 4 [*Miscellany,* 188].

59. Eddy to Stetson, December 11, 1894, H00029.

60. *Pulpit,* 2; William Lyman Johnson, *History,* 2: 514.

61. Eddy to Foster Eddy, December 9, year unknown, L03448.

62. *Pulpit,* 2.

63. Ibid., 3, 4.

64. "An Easter Gift," *CSS* 6 (April 16, 1904): 520 [*Miscellany,* 164].

7. "The Preparation of the Heart"

1. Eddy to William P. McKenzie, April 2, 1895, L04851.

2. Clara Shannon reminiscence; and "Mrs. Eddy Replies to Mark Twain," *CSS* 5 (January 22, 1903): 323 [*Miscellany,* 302–3].

3. Clara Shannon reminiscence, "Golden Memories," 52.

4. Ibid.

5. *S&H*, 8, 365–66; and *Miscellaneous,* 107.

6. Norman Pettit, *Heart Prepared,* 1, 2.

7. Eddy to Sue Ella Bradshaw, February 24, 1890, L04643; and "Annual Church Meeting," *CSJ* 14 (November 1896): 368 [*Miscellaneous,* 127].

8. *Miscellaneous,* 115.

9. *S&H*, 146; "Notice," *CSJ* 11 (November 1893): 347 [*Miscellaneous,* 156].

10. *S&H*, 91st ed. (1894), 310 [*S&H*, 4–5].

11. "Church Service," *CSJ* 8 (May 1890): 65; Eddy to Septimus J. and Camilla Hanna, 18 December 1894, L05037.

12. Eddy to board of directors, December 19, 1894, L02748; and *We Knew,* 123.

13. Eddy to Ellen Brown Linscott, June 20, 1895, L04207; and "Church and School," *CSJ* 13 (April 1895): 1 [*Miscellaneous,* 313–14].

14. Septimus J. Hanna reminiscence.

15. "The New Order," *CSJ* 13 (July 1895): 157; and "Notes from the Field," *CSJ* 13 (January 1896): 434.

16. Eddy to Sue Harper Mims, April 24, 1902, L13101; and fragment, n.d., A10903.

17. The first version of this text appeared in *CSJ* 15 (April 1897): 24. The final version can be found in each issue of the *Christian Science Quarterly.*

18. Tomlinson, *Twelve Years,* 184, 185.

19. *Message '01,* 11; and *Manual,* 31.

20. "By-laws," *CSS* 2 (January 4, 1900): 288, and "Church By-laws," *CSS* 2 (January 18, 1900): 320 [*Manual,* 63]; and Eddy to board of directors, May 16, 1900, L00247.

21. "Editor's Note Book," *CSJ* 7 (May 1889): 101; and see Clifford P. Smith, *Historical Sketches,* 180–83.

22. Quoted in William Lyman Johnson, *History,* 1: 89; "Christian Science Dispensaries," *CSJ* 7 (June 1889): i; "Christian Science Dispensaries," *CSJ* 7 (December 1889): iv; and William Lyman Johnson, *History,* 1: 90.

23. "A New Home," *CSJ* 6 (September 1888): 317.

24. "Testimonies from the Field," *CSJ* 27 (October 1909): 427.

25. "The Christian Science Reading-Room," *CSS* 12 (May 7, 1910): 710.

26. "Annual Church Meeting," *CSJ* 18 (July 1900): 206–7.

27. H. A. L. Fisher, *Our New Religion,* 60.

28. *Christian Science versus Pantheism,* 11; and *Miscellaneous,* 187.

29. *No and Yes,* 10; and Rabbi Maurice Lefkovits, "The Attitude of Judaism toward Christian Science," pamphlet, 4.

30. Karl Holl, "Der Szientismus," translation by Mary Gottschalk.

31. *No and Yes,* 33–35.

32. *Pulpit,* 21, 22.

33. "A Cruce Salus," *CSJ* 7 (October 1889): 368 [*Miscellaneous,* 293].

34. *Miscellaneous,* 106–10.

35. *Retrospection,* 67.

36. Harriet L. Betts reminiscence.

37. Eddy to William P. and Daisette McKenzie, January 16, 1896, L13071; and Eddy to Caroline D. Noyes, January 30, 1896, L05459.

38. The original wording of the text appeared in *CSJ* 13 (February 1896): 441–43. The revised text, which is quoted here, is from *Miscellaneous,* 123–25.

39. Eddy to Septimus J. and Camilla Hanna, January 17, 1896, L05130; Eddy to Joseph and Mary Armstrong, February 4, 1896, L02776.

40. Eddy to Thomas W. Hatten, August 29, 1896, L03585; Eddy to Ella Peck Sweet, December 28, 1898, L11255.

41. "Mental Digestion," *CSS* 6 (September 12, 1903): 24 [*Miscellany,* 229]; and Eddy to William B. Johnson, June 28, 1895, L00109.

42. Eddy to Joseph Adams, April 27, 1887, L07892.

43. Hermann S. Hering reminiscence.

44. Eddy to board of directors, November 8, 1902, L00317.

45. Eddy to Septimus J. and Camilla Hanna, May 24, 1896, L05151; "The Church Manual," *CSJ* 13 (October 1895): 268 [*Manual,* 3; *Miscellaneous,* 148]; Eddy to board of directors, February 27, 1903, L00325 (see facsimile of letter in Powell, *Portrait,* 209–10).

46. Tomlinson, *Twelve Years,* 159; and *New York Herald,* May 1, 1901, quoted in "Mrs. Eddy Talks," *CSS* 3 (May 9, 1901): 572 [*Miscellany,* 343–44].

47. *Manual,* 130.

48. In a circulated 1998 document, Lee Z. Johnson, Mother Church archivist (1962–91), explained: "The *Church Manual* actually has three consent clauses more than By-Laws containing them. Two of the thirty-two clause-bearing By-Laws incorporate two clauses apiece, and the Deed of 1903 in the *Manual,* pp. 136–138, supplies the third–for a total of thirty-five clauses all together."

49. Eddy to board of directors, February 27, 1903, L00325.

50. *Manual,* 28th ed. (1903), 88; and *Manual,* 29th ed. (1903), 98 [*Manual,* 105].

51. *Manual,* 29th ed. (1903), 115–25 [*Manual,* 128–38].

52. Quoted in *Proceedings in Equity,* 225; "The Mother Church and the Manual," *CSJ* 40 (April 1922): 5.

53. "Christian Science Board of Education," *CSS* 6 (May 14, 1904): 584 [*Miscellany,* 246–47]; *Manual,* 74.

54. "Take Notice," *CSS* 13 (September 17, 1910): 50 [*Miscellany,* 237]; and "The Church Manual," *CSS* 13 (September 10, 1910): 23–24.

55. "Mrs. Eddy's Opinions," *Baltimore Sun,* May 6, 1901.

56. *Manual,* 40.

57. "Mental Digestion," *CSS* 6 (September 12, 1903): 24 [*Miscellany,* 230]; and *Manual,* 104.

58. *S&H,* 449.

59. Eddy to Ellen Brown Linscott, March 10, 1888, L08753.

60. Eddy to Jessie C. H. Gorham, December 21, 1896, L10548; October 18, 1896, L07980; December 8, 1896, L07989; and October 10, 1896, L07977.

61. "Notice," *CSJ* 14 (March 1897): 575.

62. "Definition of Purpose," *CSJ* 3 (November 1885): 147; "Barmaids and Scientists," *CSJ* 9 (April 1891): 10 (see *Miscellaneous,* 297, for a somewhat toned-down version).

63. *Miscellaneous,* xi–xii.

64. Ibid., xi.

65. *Miscellaneous,* 203–6 [the article first appeared in *CSJ* 10 (August 1892): 177–80]; and *Miscellany,* 265.

66. William Lyman Johnson, *History,* 3: 311; and *Miscellaneous,* 100.

67. *S&H,* xii; *Miscellaneous,* v; and "Letters to Mrs. Eddy," *CSJ* 15 (June 1897): 165.

68. *S&H*, 460.

69. "An Important Event," *CSJ* 16 (December 1898): 588 [*Miscellany,* 244].

70. *We Knew,* 144.

71. Ibid., 149; and Tomlinson, *Twelve Years,* 99.

72. *We Knew,* 142; and *S&H,* 331.

73. *Unity,* 51.

74. *We Knew,* 142; and quoted in Hanna, *Christian Science History,* 11.

75. Eddy to Albert and Mary C. Metcalf, November 25, 1898, L08850; and Daisette Stocking McKenzie reminiscence.

76. *We Knew,* 128, 133.

77. Ibid., 130.

78. Edward Everett Norwood reminiscence.

79. For examples of Eddy's reference to a change of consciousness, see *Unity,* 37, *S&H,* 573, *People's Idea,* 1–2; and quoted in Edward Everett Norwood reminiscence.

80. Eddy to Carol Norton, December 20, 1898, L02402; and Eddy to Julia Field-King, September 19, 1898, F00543.

81. Eddy to Charles A. Q. Norton, January 31, 1900, L10627; "A Notable Meeting," *CSS* 1 (January 5, 1899): 10.

82. *Manual,* 97; Eddy to Albert E. Miller, December 10, 1901, L10048.

83. Deposition of Septimus J. Hanna (June 24, 1919), quoted in *Proceedings in Equity,* 538.

84. "Mrs. Eddy's Letter to the Church," *CSJ* 15 (February 1898): 665 [*Miscellany,* 122].

85. *Poems,* 29; the original version of Eddy's poem appeared in *CSJ* 16 (December 1898): 587.

8. "Ayont Hate's Thrall"

1. *S&H,* 317, 97.

2. "Love," *CSJ* 3 (May 1885): 25 [*Miscellaneous,* 250].

3. Memorandum, April 26, 1890, A10840.

4. Eddy to Ebenezer J. Foster Eddy, September 20, 1894, N00066.

5. Caroline Fraser, *God's Perfect Child,* 118, 148.

6. Eddy to Marjorie Colles, May 15, 1896, F00391.

7. "Looking Back," *CSJ* 4 (May 1886): 34.

8. Antoinette M. Mosher reminiscence.

9. Cather and Milmine, *Life,* 429.

10. Josephine Curtis Woodbury, *War in Heaven,* 40; and "Christian Scientists in Chicago," *CSJ* 6 (July 1888): 209. The article is reproduced in Woodbury, *Christian Science Voices,* 152–55.

11. Quoted in Gill, *Eddy,* 421.

12. Ibid., 426; and Woodbury, *War in Heaven,* 50–52; quoted in Milmine and Cather, *Life,* 421.

13. Eddy to Woodbury, March 24, 1896, L02652; Julia Bartlett testimony, "Investigation into the Character of Josephine Curtis Woodbury Undertaken by William B. Johnson at the Instance of Mary Baker Eddy"; and *S&H,* 8.

14. Gill, *Eddy,* 423; and quoted in Peel, *Authority,* 148.

15. James Henry Wiggin, "Mrs. Woodbury's New Volume, 'Echoes,'" in Woodbury, *Christian Science Voices*, xiii.

16. Woodbury, *Christian Science Voices*, 128, 9.

17. This and subsequent accounts are from "Investigation into the Character of Josephine Curtis Woodbury Undertaken by William B. Johnson at the Instance of Mary Baker Eddy."

18. Randall Steward, ed., *American Notebooks of Nathaniel Hawthorne*, ixxv; and *Message 01*, 20.

19. "*Consistency, Thou Art a Jewel*," *CSJ* 6 (August 1888): 251–52 [*Miscellaneous*, 222–23].

20. See the extensive discussion of Eddy's relation with Kennedy in Peel, *Discovery*.

21. Emma Easton Newman, "The Primary Class of 1889 and Other Memories," in *We Knew*, 94; "A Card," *CSJ* 8 (August 1890): 193.

22. *S&H*, 571, 374; and "Power of Prayer," *CSS* 4 (November 3, 1901): 72 [*Miscellany*, 293].

23. Eddy to the Linscotts, December 11, 1895, L13009.

24. Eddy to Woodbury, October 17, 1886, L02636; and Woodbury to Eddy, January 19, 1886.

25. Peel, *Trial*, 175, 176.

26. "The Scarlet Woman," *CSJ* 6 (November 1888): 409.

27. Eddy to Henry Lester Putnam, April 20, 1889, L11173.

28. Eddy to Woodbury, March 24, 1896, L02652.

29. Eddy to Woodbury, July 6, 1894, L02642; and Eddy to Woodbury, April 8, 1895, L02644.

30. Memorandum, n.d., A10633; Eddy to the First Members of the First Church of Christ, Scientist, March 18, 1896, L00142; and March 24, 1896, L00144.

31. Eddy to the Hannas, December 1895, L14475; and Eddy to the board of directors, April 24, 1896, L02786.

32. Eddy to Oliver C. Sabin, July 19, 1899, N00225; Woodbury to Eddy, n.d. (probably 1891–96), and quoted in Peel, *Trial*, 271.

33. Clara Shannon reminiscence.

34. Bates-Dittemore, *Mary Baker Eddy*, 368.

35. Woodbury, *War in Heaven*, 15; and *Christian Science Voices*, 251–52.

36. "Communion, June 4, 1899," *Miscellany*, 125–26.

37. Reported in the *Boston Post*, October 4, 1899.

38. "The Key to the Scriptures," *CSJ* 4 (July, 1886): 82; *S&H*, 564, 560, 561; and Peel, *Authority*, 162.

39. Edward A. Kimball, quoted in "The Law Suit Decided," *CSS* 3 (June 13, 1901): 653; and Ira O. Knapp, quoted in *Boston Daily Globe* (Morning Ed.), June 6, 1901. See also Peel, *Authority*, 432–33.

40. Memorandum, n.d., A10926; and Eddy, *Footprints Fadeless*, in *Mary Baker Eddy: Speaking for Herself*.

41. Eddy to Samuel J. Elder, Willam A. Morse, Charles W. Bartlett, March 31, 1901, L05362.

42. *Boston Post*, June 5, 1901.

43. Eddy to D. Talbot, December 15, 1900, L05622; Eddy to Ira O. Knapp, November 14, 1899, V01683.

44. Emma Shipman reminiscence.

45. *Manual*, 42.

46. Eddy to William B. Johnson, July 12, 1899, L00226.

47. *Message 01*, 15, 20.

48. The pamphlet was subsequently expanded and revised into Peabody's book *Religio-Medical Masquerade;* Eddy to Henry Robinson, December 15, 1901, L13313; and Eddy to Alfred Farlow, September 1, 1901, V01876.

49. *Retrospection,* 94; and *Footprints Fadeless,* 144.

50. Eddy to Edward A. Kimball, February 29, 1901, L07517; and Eddy to Elder, June 7, 1901, V01851.

51. Eddy to James A. Neal and John Carroll Lathrop, September 2, 1899, L03555; Eddy to Kimball, July 4, 1900, L07496; and Eddy to Alfred E. Baker, October 26, 1900, V01775, quoted in Peel, *Authority,* 169.

52. Eddy to William G. Ewing, January 8, 1900, L08531.

53. Quoted in Peel, *Authority,* 159, 168.

54. *S&H,* 572.

55. *Message '01,* 1; and Frye diary, April 8, 1900.

56. *Poems,* 79.

57. Eddy to William P. McKenzie, December 27, 1899, L13051.

58. Frye to D. E. Fultz, August 29, 1901, L14277; and *S&H,* 586, 33.

59. Eddy to John Henry Keene, August 9, 1902, L02153.

60. "New Commandment" *CSJ* 7 (October 1889); and 339 [*Miscellany,* 292].

61. *S&H,* 24.

62. *Message '02,* 11.

9. A Power, Not a Place

1. Eddy and James F. Gilman, *Painting,* 105.

2. *S&H,* 58; and Eddy to Rachel F. Marshall, August 21, 1903, L05851.

3. Eddy to Edward P. Bates, January 8, 1897, L08187; and Eddy to Edward A. Kimball, January 31, 1901, L07503.

4. Eddy to Daphne S. Knapp, November 24, 1897, L04232; and Eddy to George W. Glover, April 27, 1898, L02127, quoted in *McClure's* 31 (May 1908): 19.

5. *Message 01,* 29; and Eddy to Archibald McLellan, June 8, 1902, L07043.

6. Minnie Bell Weygandt reminiscence; and Eddy to John Austin, October 14, 1894, F00323.

7. Eddy to Calvin A. Frye, January 20, 1908, L17974; and Frye diary, April 19, 1902.

8. Adam H. Dickey, *Memoirs,* 33–34.

9. William R. Rathvon diary, December 23, 1908.

10. Eddy to board of directors, May 16, 1903, L00338; *Manual,* 67–68; and Eddy to board of directors, January 20, 1907, L00524.

11. Eddy to board of directors, May 16, 1903, L00338; and Eddy to William B. Johnson, April 27, 1903, L00336.

12. Eddy to Pamelia J. Leonard, July 24, 1902, L04432; and Ella S. Rathvon to Eddy, January 22, 1909, quoted in "Letters to Our Leader," *CSS* 11 (January 30, 1909): 41.

13. "Significant Questions," *CSS* 5 (April 25, 1903): 540, and (May 2, 1903): 556; see also *CSJ* 21 (May 1903): 65–66 [*Miscellany,* 228–29].

14. Gill, *Mary Baker Eddy*, 395, 396; and John G. Salchow reminiscence.

15. John G. Salchow to "Moike," June 2, 1901, from the private collection of Ralph Byron Copper; and Salchow reminiscence.

16. Henrietta E. Chanfrau reminiscence.

17. Salchow reminiscence.

18. George H. Kinter reminiscence; Hermann S. Hering reminiscence.

19. Mary E. Armstrong reminiscence, Longyear Historical Society.

20. Caroline Foss Gyger reminiscence; and Mary Amstrong reminiscence. It is worth noting that Armstrong disliked Neal, but it seems unlikely that she would have fabricated this incident.

21. John G. Salchow to "Bertha & All," n.d., from the private collection of Ralph Byron Copper.

22. John Lathrop diary, May, November, 1907.

23. Eddy to William B. Johnson, December 19, 1902, L03329; Lauretta Wheelock Blish reminiscence; and *S&H*, 209.

24. *S&H*, 312; and Frye diary, January 5, 1900.

25. Rathvon diary, July 1910; and Carpenter, *Footsteps*, 50, 330–31.

26. Salchow reminiscence; and Clara Shannon reminiscence.

27. Dickey, *Memoirs*, 80–81; and Joseph G. Mann reminiscence.

28. Wilbur, "Glimpses of a Great Personality," *Human Life* 4 (January 1907): 4.

29. *Miscellaneous*, 100.

30. Mann reminiscence.

31. Eddy to board of directors, February 23, 1906, L00469; Armstrong reminiscence; and Eddy to Laura E. Sargent, n.d., L05980.

32. Orcutt, *Mary Baker Eddy*, 68–71. Norton once commented, "Mother Eddy is the most striking and ugliest figure in New England to-day" (Norton, *Letters*, 2: 310).

33. Minnie Bell Weygandt reminiscence; and Salchow reminiscence.

34. *Rudimental*, 2.

35. Adelaide Still reminiscence; and *S&H*, 442; "Take Notice," *CSS* 11 (June 12, 1909), 810.

36. Ella Peck Sweet reminiscence.

37. George H. Kinter reminiscence.

38. Eddy to Calvin C. Hill, April 26, 1905, L18663. Also see quotation from Eddy in section " 'God Has Bidden Me,' " Chapter 4, "By What Authority? Listening and Leading."

39. "Dr. Allan McLane Hamilton Tells about His Visit to Mrs. Eddy," *New York Times*, August 25, 1907; see also *CSS* 10 (September 7, 1907): 7.

40. Eddy to Will S. Farlow, January 1, 1903, L08545; Dickey, *Memoirs*, 45; and Adelaide Still reminiscence.

41. Lida Fitzpatrick notes.

42. Gyger reminiscence; and *We Knew*, 201.

43. Adelaide Still reminiscence.

44. Bonhoeffer, *Life Together*, 94; and Hering reminiscence.

45. Gyger reminiscence.

46. *We Knew*, 113.

47. Carpenter, *Footsteps*, 99–100.

48. Salchow reminiscence.

49. Quoted in Peel, *Authority*, 426.

50. *We Knew*, 197–200.

51. Eddy, "Watching versus Watching Out," *CSS* 8 (September 23, 1905): 56 [*Miscellany*, 232].

52. John B. Willis, "Watching vs. Watching Out," *CSS* 8 (September 16, 1905): 40–41.

53. John Lathrop reminiscence. An earlier version of the story was quoted in *CSS* 1 (March 16, 1899): 12. In a 1923 article entitled "Watching," Lathrop retold the story, including (without attribution) the lessons Eddy had shared with him; see *CSS* 26 (October 13, 1923): 123.

54. Mann reminiscence.

55. *Course in Divinity*, 48, 52, 54.

56. Fitzpatrick notes; *Course in Divinity*, 25; and Rathvon diaries.

57. Adelaide Still reminiscence.

58. Adelaide Still to Gilbert C. Carpenter, Jr., February 26, 1937, from the private collection of Keith H. McNeil.

59. Eddy to Mr. and Mrs. Gilbert C. Carpenter, February 1, 1905, L14144.

60. Frye diary, January 11, 1906.

61. The affair with Strang is discussed in the reminiscences of both Salchow and Weygandt; Eddy to Calvin C. Hill, n.d., L18666.

62. See section "Old guard, new guard" in Chapter 12, "Elijah's Mantle," for a fuller discussion of this issue; and *Message 02*, 4.

63. Mann reminiscence.

64. *Miscellany*, 195.

65. Salchow reminiscence.

66. Weygandt reminiscence.

67. Rathvon diary, January 1910; and February 13, 1910; and Matthew 12:60.

68. Rathvon diary, November 5, 1910.

10. "The Outflowing Life of Christianity"

1. *Miscellaneous*, 199. The original version of the sermon was printed in *CSJ* 2 (June 1884): 4.

2. *Manual*, 47.

3. See section " 'With such a light and such a presence' " in Chapter 1, "O God, *is it all!*"; *S&H*, 143.

4. George H. Kinter reminiscence.

5. Memorandum, n.d., A10261.

6. Twain, *Christian Science*, 284.

7. *S&H*, 138, 31.

8. Ibid., 600.

9. John 15:5, 8.

10. Karl Holl, "Der Szientismus," translated by Mary Gottschalk.

11. See the more detailed discussion of the process of secularization in Gottschalk, *Emergence*, 249–59.

12. *Rudimental*, 2–3; and *S&H*, 270–71.

13. Horton Foote, quoted in *Heart in Protest*.

14. W. Michael Born, "Richard Rust, a minister with a mission," *Cross Currents* 4 (October 16, 2000).

15. See section "In Her Authentic Voice" in Chapter 2, "Becoming 'Mrs. Eddy.'"

16. Anne Dodge, "Lowliness of Heart," *CSJ* 26 (April 1908): 23–25.

17. *S&H*, 149.

18. Ibid., 390, 391, 393, 417.

19. William R. Rathvon diary, June 27, 1909; and *S&H*, 411, 454–55.

20. *S&H*, 366.

21. Ibid., 197.

22. 1 John 4:18; *S&H*, 410, 411; and *Miscellaneous*, 194.

23. Eddy to Janette E. Weller, January 26, 1885, L13426; and S&H, 468, 368.

24. Allison W. Phinney, Jr., "Why Does Christian Science Treatment Heal and How Does It Work?" *CSS* 93 (Sept. 23, 1991): 29–32.

25. *S&H*, 185; *Pantheism*, 10; *S&H*, 456.

26. *Miscellany*, 364; *S&H*, xi.

27. *S&H*, 109.

28. Lee Z. Johnson, author's interview, June 1987; and *Miscellany*, 105–6 ("To the Christian World" was first published in the *New York Sun*, December 16, 1898).

29. Dr. Cushing's affidavit, quoted in Cather and Milmine, *Life*, 84–86; *Lynn Weekly Reporter*, February 3, 1866, quoted in Peel, *Discovery*, 195.

30. *S&H*, 3rd ed. (1881), 1: 152–53 (for details on the correct attribution of this incident, see Peel, *Discovery*, 215, 350 n. 68).

31. This is true, for example, of some—though not all—of the accounts given in the book by von Fettweis and Warneck, *Christian Healer*, since the book appears to establish no reasonable criteria for assessing the historical validity of the many healings it enumerates.

32. Peel, *Trial*, 250.

33. "Healed by Mrs. Eddy," *CSS* 7 (December 24, 1904): 259.

34. Thomas C. Johnsen, "Christian Scientists and the Medical Profession," *Medical Heritage* 2 (January–February 1986): 76; and Alfred Farlow, "Facts about Mrs. Eddy," *CSJ* 20 (July 1902): 216.

35. "Testimonies from the Field," *CSJ* 19 (September 1901): 384–85.

36. Edmund F. Burton, "A Physician's Reasons for Becoming a Christian Scientist," *CSS* 10 (February 1, 1908), first published in the *Milwaukee Wisconsin*, n.d.

37. Ibid.

38. Mary E. Christie, "Wonderfully Sustained by Truth," *CSS* 3 (December 6, 1900): 221–22.

39. Maurine Campbell reminiscence, Longyear Historical Society.

40. *S&H*, 39, x.

41. *S&H*, 226th ed. (1902), 660; and *S&H*, 662–63, 657.

42. *S&H*, 667–69.

43. *S&H*, 224.

44. Rev. Edwin T. Hiscox, quoted in *CSJ* 15 (May 1897): 81; and quoted in *CSS* 4 (January 30, 1902): 348.

45. *S&H*, 475; Haldeman, *Christian Science*, 25–26; Gen. 2:7; and Varley, *Christian Science Examined*, 37.

46. Lambert, *Christian Science Before the Bar of Reason*, 135–36.

47. *S&H*, 148.

48. Ibid., 145–46.

49. *Boston Evening Transcript*, March 24, 1894, quoted in Allen, *William James*, 372.

50. Quoted in "Editor's Table," *CSJ* 16 (April 1898): 68–69.

51. Allen, *William James*, 373; James, *Letters of William James*, 2: 66–67.

52. James, *Will to Believe*, 28; James, *Pluralistic Universe*, 314.

53. James, *Varieties of Religious Experience*, 559; James, *Pluralistic Universe*, 307, 309.

54. James, *Varieties of Religious Experience*, 95–96.

55. Ibid., 121; and see section " 'This crushing out of life, of hope, or love' " in Chapter 1, "O God, *is it all!*"

56. Twain, *Christian Science*, 267.

57. Simon, *Genuine Reality*, 376.

58. *Miscellaneous*, 370.

59. Schoepflin, *Christian Science on Trial*, 114–15.

60. Harriet L. Betts reminiscence; *S&H*, 151; and Eddy to Frank W. Gale, April 4, 1889, L08563.

61. Quoted in "The Harold Frederic Case," *CSJ* 16 (December 1898): 624.

62. "To the Christian World," *CSS* 1 (December 29, 1898): 4–5; and *CSJ* 16 (January 1899): 663–68 [*Miscellany*, 103–8].

63. "The Brush Will Case," *CSJ* 19 (October 1901): 455–67; and Meehan, *Late Suit*, 202–4.

64. "Christian Science Healing Explained and Defended," quoted in *CSJ* 19 (April 1901): 2–7 [*Miscellany*, 219–22].

65. Thomas C. Johnsen, "Christian Scientists and the Medical Profession," *Medical Heritage* 2 (January–February 1986): 76.

66. "An Important Decision," *CSJ* 16 (September 1898): 405–16.

67. "Message of the Pastor Emeritus," *CSS* 1 (June 8, 1899): 2 [*Miscellany*, 128]; and "Christian Science Healing Explained and Defended," quoted in *CSJ* 19 (April 1901): 5 [*Miscellany*, 222].

68. Eddy to Augusta E. Stetson and Carol Norton, March 25, 1894, L02359.

69. "Wherefore?" *CSS* 5 (November 27, 1902): 200 [*Miscellany*, 227]; Eddy to First Church of Christ, Scientist, Columbus, Ohio, March 25, 1905, L05637. For more background on Eddy's letter, see " 'God is the giver,' " *CSS* 7 (April 1, 1905): 488–89 [*Miscellany*, 204–5].

70. *S&H*, 167.

71. Ibid., 443–44.

72. See discussion of this issue in Peel, *Authority*, 238–39, 260, 310–11, 341, 462–63, 507–8.

73. *S&H*, 464.

74. Lydia B. Hall to the board of directors, February 11, 1929.

75. "A Statement by the Directors," *CSJ* 46 (March 1929): 669.

76. *Miscellaneous*, 205–6; and Eddy to William G. Nixon, June 30, 1890, N00034.

77. "Dedication of the Church in Concord," *CSS* 6 (July 23, 1904): 739 [*Miscellany*, 160]; *Manual*, 92.

78. Eddy to Archibald McLellan, June 18, 1903, L03057; and Eddy to Septimus J. and Camilla Hanna, April 6, 1898, L05218.

79. Peel, *Authority*, 98; Eddy to Edward A. Kimball, November 26, 1903, L07602; and Rathvon diary, January 11, 1909.

80. "A Correction," *CSS* 2 (October 19, 1899): 104 [*Miscellany*, 217–18].

81. Eddy to John Carroll Lathrop, March 25, 1905, L04284; Eddy to Frank W. Gale, June 9, 1891, L08565; Mary Eaton reminiscence; Eddy to Joseph S. Eastaman, March 16, 1893, L03485; and "Conversation," April 1, 1902, A11448.

82. James A. Neal reminiscence.

83. *S&H*, 591.

84. Eddy to Neal, January 29, 1897, L03524.

11. "THE KINGDOMS OF THIS WORLD"

1. *Miscellany*, 134.

2. *S&H*, 50; and *Miscellaneous*, 74, 110.

3. Hugh A. Studdert-Kennedy, *Mrs. Eddy*, 422–23.

4. Eddy to John Carroll Lathrop, May 9, 1906, L04290.

5. *Miscellany*, 7–8.

6. Eddy to Solon S. Beman, December 18, 1905, L10494.

7. Eddy to board of directors, July 28, 1907, L00394.

8. *Miscellany*, 8, 43.

9. Quoted in ibid., 66–67, 77, 72, 30.

10. Quoted in Paul Eli Ivey, *Prayers in Stone*, 74, 73.

11. *Miscellany*, 79–80.

12. Gill, *Eddy*, 470.

13. *Miscellany*, 3–6.

14. *Miscellany*, 85; Dr. Alfred Kohn, quoted in Ivey, *Prayers in Stone*, 74; and Studdert-Kennedy, *Mrs. Eddy*, 425.

15. John Salchow reminiscence; and Lathrop to Hermann S. Hering, February 9, 1908, L12397.

16. Salchow reminiscence.

17. Adelaide Still reminiscence.

18. Salchow reminiscence; Eddy to Archibald McLellan, November 1908, L07169; and Eddy to Alfred A. Farlow, September 22, 1907, L01721.

19. Hering reminiscence.

20. *CSS* 5 (November 27, 1902): 206; *CSS* 3 (September 20, 1900): 45; and Sydney E. Ahlstrom, *Religious History of the American People*, 2: 528.

21. Jennie E. Sawyer reminiscence; *S&H*, 6; "Ways that Are Vain," *Miscellany*, 211; *Message 01*, 15; and *Retrospection*, 30.

22. *S&H*, 239; and Blanche Hersey Hogue, "Glorifying God," *CSS* (December 24, 1910), 324.

23. Farlow, "Christian Science in Business Life," *American Business Man* 11 (May 1908): 155–57; and Eddy to Farlow, May 4, 1908, L01764.

24. Quoted in Altman K. Swihart, *Since Mrs. Eddy*, 43–44; and Bates-Dittemore, *Mary Baker Eddy*, 382.

25. Peel, *Trial*, 177.

26. *CSS* 10 (May 12, 1908): 270; and "Mrs. Eddy's Letter to First Church," *CSJ* 21 (January 1904): 585. For the edited version of her message to the church, see *Miscellany*, 193.

27. Swihart, *Since Mrs. Eddy*, 45.

28. "One Mother Church in Christian Science," *CSS* 11 (December 5, 1908): 270.

29. Stetson's recollections of the interview are included in Swihart, *Since Mrs. Eddy*, 62–65.

30. Robert David Thomas, *With Bleeding Footsteps*, 268; and Peel, *Trial*, 297.

31. Henrietta Chanfrau reminiscence.

32. "An Allegory, *CSJ* 2 (April 1885): 1–2; *CSJ* 4 (September 1886): 131–33; and *CSJ* 11 (October 1893): 289–93 [*Miscellaneous*, 323–28].

33. Eddy to Septimus J. and Camilla Hanna, December 13, 1893, L05035; and Eddy to Carol Norton, December 9, 1897, L02391.

34. Eddy to Augusta E. Stetson, October 26, 1897, V01549; March 6, 1899, H00051; and August 4, 1903, L02565.

35. *Evening Journal*, July 1, 1904; Calvin Frye diary, August 2, 1909; and quoted in Swihart, *Since Mrs. Eddy*, 48.

36. Stetson to Eddy, August 5, 1906; Eddy to Stetson, August 9, 1906, L02568; and Peel, *Authority*, 332.

37. Quoted in Swihart, *Since Mrs. Eddy*, 102, 70, 71.

38. Eddy to Stetson, July 11, 1909, H00130; and July 23, 1909, H00131.

39. *Miscellany*, 360.

40. Dakin, *Mrs. Eddy*, 214–15; and Thomas, *With Bleeding Footsteps*, 164.

41. Alison W. Phinney, Jr., "Is Animal Magnetism Old-Fashioned?" *CSJ* 115 (July 1988), 227.

42. Larry Dossey, *Be Careful What you Pray for. . . . You Just Might Get it*, 190–91, 102.

43. Bates-Dittemore, *Mary Baker Eddy*, 438.

44. Quoted in ibid., 437.

45. Virgil O. Strickler diary, 1909. Strickler's diary is by far the richest source available for an understanding of the inner workings of Stetson's circle and the influence she had on its members.

46. "Response by Mrs. Stetson," *Boston Daily Globe*, November 8, 1909; and Eddy to Stetson, October 31, 1905, H00102.

47. "Long Death List in X-Science Circle," *New York Times*, April 25, 1910.

48. *Miscellaneous*, 41; *S&H*, 234, 235; Philippians 2:5; and *S&H*, 467.

49. *Boston Herald*, December 30, 1910; and Billy Sunday, in A. Sheldrick, "What Is a Real Revival?" pamphlet.

50. Swihart, *Since Mrs. Eddy*, 168.

51. Ivey, *Prayers in Stone*, 55, 153, and see 101–3 for a discussion of the Maybeck church in Berkeley, California.

52. Stetson, "The Best Sermon Ever Preached," in *Sermons Which Spiritually Interpret the Scriptures and Other Writings on Christian Science*, 357.

53. *S&H*, 447.

54. Virgil O. Strickler diary; *CSS* 12 (September 18, 1909).

55. *Miscellany*, 129; "War," *CSJ* 26 (May 1908): 65 [*Miscellany*, 286]; and Theodore Roosevelt to Hayne Davis, April 20, 1908, L09772.

56. Michael Meehan reminiscence; and the interview was by William E. Curtis, "Mrs. Eddy a Marvel in Mental Activity," *Chicago Record Herald*, June 18, 1907.

57. Letter from Bradford Merrill to Joseph Pulitzer, November 2, 1906, New York World Papers, Rare Book and Manuscript Library, Columbia University.

58. Lucia C. Coulson, "Report of Miss Coulson's Interview with Mrs. Josephine Curtis Woodbury," June 11, 1930; and Woodbury to Twain, February 3 and 5, 1903, Twain Papers.

59. William D. McCrackan, "My Interviews with Mark Twain"; and Gill, *Eddy*, 566.

60. An extended discussion of Cather's authorship of the biography attributed to Milmine is found in the introduction and afterword by David Stouck to the University of Nebraska Press edition of *The Life of Mary Baker G. Eddy and the History of Christian Science,* which identifies both Milmine and Cather as authors.

61. Harold Bloom, *American Religion,* 133.

62. *McClure's* 28 (January 1907): 236; and Gill, *Eddy,* 39; see Corser's comment in "The original beauty of holiness,'" Chapter 1, "O God, *is it all!*"

63. Dakin, *Mrs. Eddy,* 418.

64. *S∂H,* 118.

65. "An Interview with the Founder of Christian Science," *North American,* August 15, 1907; and Smith, *Historical Sketches,* 131.

66. Eddy to John L. Wright, March 3, 1903, L06998; and quoted in Erwin Canham, *Commitment to Freedom,* 15.

67. *Miscellany,* 129.

68. *Miscellaneous,* 18; and *S∂H,* 571.

69. "How Strife May Be Stilled," *CSS* 7 (December 31, 1904): 8 [*Miscellany,* 278]; "To My Church," *CSJ* 23 (July 1905): 253 [*Miscellany,* 279]; and "Mrs. Eddy's Requests," *CSJ* 23 (August 1905): 323 [*Miscellany,* 280].

70. See the discussion of Eddy's approach to social issues in Gottschalk, *Emergence,* "The Social Question," 259–74; and Katherine Fanning, quoted in *Heart in Protest.*

71. Eddy to board of trustees, August 8, 1908, L07268.

72. William Dana Orcutt, *Mary Baker Eddy and Her Books,* 120.

73. Adam H. Dickey to McLellan, August 12, 1908, L06474; and Dickey to board of trustees, August 14, 1908, L07269.

74. Tomlinson, *Twelve Years,* 125.

75. "Something in a Name," *Christian Science Monitor,* November 25, 1908.

76. *Monitor,* "Reason for Our Hope," August 26, 1954.

77. Helen Andrews Nixon, "An Added Responsibility," *CSS* 11 (December 26, 1908): 324.

78. William McKenzie, "Mrs. Eddy's Instructions re The Monitor."

79. Notation by Laura Sargent in one of Eddy's Bibles, B00007; and Tomlinson, "Monitor's 1st issue," November 25, 1908, A11927.

80. McKenzie, "Mrs. Eddy Instructions re The Monitor"; quoted in Erwin Canham, *Commitment to Freedom,* 74; and Farlow to Eddy, July 30, 1910.

81. *Boston Post,* November 1908; *S∂H,* 63; and quoted in Stetson, *Sermons,* 51. One Christian Scientist who was deeply involved in political life was John Works, a U.S. senator from California (1911–17). Works's papers are in the Bancroft Library, University of California at Berkeley.

82. *S∂H,* 225; the extended passage on this subject includes pages 224–28.

83. *S∂H* (1st ed.), 3; *CSJ,* 17 (May 1899), 103.

84. *Manual,* 41.

12. ELIJAH'S MANTLE

1. Eddy to Alfred Farlow, August 19, 1909, L01775.

2. William Dana Orcutt, *Mary Baker Eddy and Her Books,* 124.

3. Adam H. Dickey, "Democracy in Church Government," *CSS* 10 (January 15, 1910): 390.

4. Eddy to Farlow, March 25, 1908, L01759; and Rathvon diary, June 18, 1910.

5. Calvin Frye diary, July 2, 1908, Peel, *Authority,* 318.

6. Peel, *Authority,* 351–52, discusses the incident in greater detail; "A Paean of Praise," *CSS* 12 (February 12, 1910): 470; and Adelaide Still reminiscence.

7. Edward Norwood reminiscence; Adelaide Still reminiscence; and *Unity,* 46.

8. Rathvon diary, January 9, 1909; *S&H,* 66; and Irving C. Tomlinson notes, April 23, 1909, A11948.

9. Tomlinson notes, June 25, 1910, A11995; and quoted in Clifford Smith, *Historical Sketches,* 100.

10. Memorandum, n.d., L18277; and quoted in Peel, *Authority,* 359.

11. "Dies Irae!," *Florence Herald,* January 14, 1909.

12. Frye diary, July 28, 1908.

13. Tomlinson diary, February 3, 1910.

14. "Soaring," September 1910, A10267.

15. Fragment dictated to Adelaide Still, October 1910, A10355.

16. "Principle and Practice," CSS20 (September 1, 1917): 10; and reprinted in Norman Beasley, *Cross and the Crown,* 573–74.

17. *CSJ* (October 1910): 485, 486.

18. Rathvon diary, April 9, 1910, July 18, 1910.

19. Ellen Bouton and Adam H. Dickey, September 15, 1910, L17334; Tomlinson notes, October 1909, A11972; and Rathvon diary, January 25, 1909, and subsequent references with dates shown.

20. Dickey, *Memoirs,* 77.

21. Unsigned memorandum, May 1910; Johnson, Dickey, Ella and William Rathvon, and Ella Hoag to Frye, May 10, 1910, V04686; and Rathvon diary, November 3, 1909. Rathvon probably wrote both the memo and the letter; given his strong feelings in the matter and his claim to have taken the lead in challenging Frye's presumed influence, it is difficult to believe that anyone else could have written them.

22. Rathvon Diary, September 3, 1909, and October 6, 1909.

23. William R. Rathvon to Adam H. Dickey, June 6, 1910, V03692; and Adelaide Still reminiscence.

24. Eddy to Lewis Strang, n.d. V03522; George Kinter to John Lathrop, quoted in Peel, *Authority,* 357; and Frye diary, August 21, 1910.

25. Adelaide Still reminiscence; and Peel, *Authority,* 366.

26. "False and True," A10131; and *In My True Light and Life,* 652–53.

27. See, for example, *Manual,* 43; *Miscellaneous,* 164; *Retrospection,* 64; *Miscellany,* 197, 117; Mary Armstrong reminiscence; and Eddy to Neal, June 15, 1899, L03552.

28. Lida Fitzpatrick notes.

29. Eddy to Farlow, June 16, 1908, V00418; and Dickey, *Memoirs,* 128.

30. Rathvon diary, October 5, 1910.

31. Eddy to Anna B. White Baker, July 29, 1899, F00160; and "The Future of C. Science," November 24, 1910, A11346A.

32. "Motive," April 16, 1909, A11338.

33. Quoted in Smith, *Historical Sketches,* 100.

34. Adelaide Still reminiscence.

35. Ella Rathvon reminiscence; and Frye to Fred N. Ladd, December 15, 1910, L18276.

36. *Chicago Christian Scientist* II, November 1888.

37. Salchow reminiscence.

38. Ibid.

39. Farlow to Eddy, August 21, 1909.

40. *S&H,* 459; and Stephan Zweig, *Mental Healers,* 246.

41. *Journals of William F. Hillman,* unpublished manuscript, September 1953.

42. See particularly *Christian Science War Time Activities,* concerning experiences of Christian Scientists during World War II. Similar accounts from World War I were not published in book form, due to the fact that many records from this period were destroyed in a flood. There are, however, a number of surviving accounts of the wartime period in testimonies in the Christian Science periodicals.

43. William D. McCrackan, *Adam H. Dickey, C.S.B.,* biographical sketch.

44. *Covenant,* May 1847.

45. Gilbert Carpenter, *Mary Baker Eddy: Her Spiritual Footsteps,* 255.

46. *CSJ* (April 14, 1883): 1 [*Miscellaneous,* 1].

47. *CSJ* (October 6, 1883): 6 [*Miscellaneous,* 17].

48. *Unity,* 46; Ephesians 4:13; and Philippians 2:5.

49. *Miscellany,* 346.

50. *S&H,* 45.

51. Ibid., 51.

52. Ibid., 459.

53. Laura Sargent reminiscence.

54. II Kings 2:9–15.

CODA: THE PROPHETIC VOICE

1. *Message for 1901,* 31; and Anderson, *Understanding the Old Testament,* 248.

2. *Miscellaneous,* 346; *S&H,* 174; *Miscellany,* 188; and *S&H,* 98.

3. *S&H,* 268; see also 95–96.

4. *CSJ* (April 14, 1883): 1 [*Miscellaneous,* 2]; and *S&H,* 55.

5. Twain, "The Missionary in World Politics."

6. *Miscellaneous,* 24.

7. Karl Barth, *Church Dogmatics,* 3: 364–65.

8. Washington Gladden, "The Truths and Untruths of Christian Science," *Independent,* CV (March 19, 1903), 777.

9. Lester E. Denonn and Robert E. Egner, eds., *Basic Writings of Bertrand Russell, 1903–1959,* 67, 72.

10. *CSJ* 106 (July 1988): 20.

11. Davies, *God and the New Physics,* 8.

12. *Unity,* 51.

13. "The Dynamic Now—A Poet's Counsel," in Baudot, ed., *Candles in the Dark,* 237, 249, 243.

14. *S&H,* 580; and *Miscellaneous,* 102.

15. *S&H,* 354.

Bibliography

Ahlstrom, Sydney E. *A Religious History of the American People*. New Haven, Conn.: Yale University Press, 1972.

Albanese, Catherine L., ed. *American Spiritualities: A Reader*. Bloomington: Indiana University Press, 2001.

————. *Nature Religion in America: From the Algonkian Indians to the New Age*. Chicago: University of Chicago Press, 1990.

Alcott, Bronson. *The Journals of Bronson Alcott*. Selected and edited by Odell Shepard. Boston: Little, Brown, 1938.

Allen, Gay Wilson. *William James: A Biography*. New York: Viking Press, 1967.

Anderson, Bernard W. *Understanding the Old Testament*. 4th ed. Englewood, N.J.: Prentice-Hall, 1986.

Armstrong, Joseph, and Margaret Williamson. *Building of The Mother Church: The First Church of Christ, Scientist in Boston, Massachusetts*. Boston: Christian Science Publishing Society, 1980.

Bancroft, Samuel P. *Mrs. Eddy as I Knew Her in 1870*. Boston: G. H. Ellis Press, 1923.

Barr, Stephen M. *Modern Physics and Ancient Faith*. Notre Dame, Ind.: University of Notre Dame Press, 2003.

Barrows, John H. *The World's Parliament of Religions*. Chicago: Parliament Publishing, 1893.

Barth, Karl. *Church Dogmatics*. Edited by G. W. Bromiley and T. F. Torrance. Translated by G. W. Bromiley. Edinburgh: T. & T. Clark, 1975.

Bates, Ernest Sutherland, and John V. Dittemore. *Mary Baker Eddy: The Truth and the Tradition*. New York: Knopf, 1932.

Baudot, Barbara Sundberg, ed. *Candles in the Dark: A New Spirit for a Plural World*. Seattle: University of Washington Press, 2002.

Beasley, Norman. *The Cross and the Crown: The History of Christian Science*. New York: Duell, Sloan and Pearce, 1952.

Bednarowski, Mary Farrell. *New Religions and the Theological Imagination in America*. Bloomington: Indiana University Press, 1989.

————. "Outside the Mainstream: Women's Religion and Women Religious Leaders in Nineteenth-Century America." *Journal of the American Academy of Religion* 48 (1980): 207–31.

————. *The Religious Imagination of American Women*. Bloomington: Indiana University Press, 1999.

Blavatsky, Helena. *Studies in Occultism*. 1891. Reprint, Pasadena, Calif.: Theosophical University Press, 1967.

Blavatsky, Helena, and William Q. Judge. *Some of the Errors of Christian Science*. Point Loma, Calif.: Aryan Theosophical Press, 1907.

Bloom, Harold. *The American Religion: The Emergence of the Post-Christian Nation*. New York: Simon & Schuster, 1992.

―――. *The Anxiety of Influence: A Theory of Poetry*. New York: Oxford University Press, 1973.

Bonhoeffer, Dietrich. *Life Together*. Translated and with an introduction by John W. Doberstein. San Francisco: Harper SanFrancisco, 1993.

Born, Michael. "Richard Rust." *Cross Currents: New England Conference of the United Methodist Church* 4 (Oct. 16, 2000).

Braden, Charles S. *Christian Science Today: Power, Policy, Practice*. Dallas: Southern Methodist University Press, 1958.

Braude, Ann. *Radical Spirits: Spiritualism and Women's Rights in Nineteenth-Century America*. Boston: Beacon Press, 1989.

Brian, Denis. *Pulitzer: A Life*. New York: John Wiley & Sons, 2001.

Brisbane, Arthur. *What Mrs. Eddy Said to Arthur Brisbane*. New York: M. E. Paige, 1930.

Brodwin, Stanley. "Mark Twain's Theology: The God of a Brevet Presbyterian." In *The Cambridge Companion to Mark Twain*, edited by Forrest G. Robinson. Cambridge: Cambridge University Press, 1995.

Bryce, James. *The American Commonwealth*. New York: Macmillan, 1896.

Buswell, A. T. "Human Leadership and Heavenly Liberty in Christian Science Culture." *Mental Science Magazine* 3 (July 1887): 217.

Canham, Erwin D. *Commitment to Freedom: The Story of The Christian Science Monitor*. Boston: Houghton Mifflin, 1958.

Carpenter, Gilbert C., C.S.B., and Gilbert C. Carpenter, Jr., C.S.B. *Mary Baker Eddy: Her Spiritual Footsteps*. Rumford, R.I.: private printing, 1934.

Cather, Willa, and Georgine Milmine. *The Life of Mary Baker G. Eddy and the History of Christian Science*. London: Hodder and Stoughton, 1909. Reprinted with an introduction and afterword by David Stouck. Lincoln: University of Nebraska Press, 1993.

A Century of Christian Science Healing. Boston: Christian Science Publishing Society, 1966.

Chadwick, John White. *Theodore Parker: Preacher and Reformer*. New York: Houghton Mifflin, 1900.

Christian Science: A Sourcebook of Contemporary Materials. Boston: Christian Science Publishing Society, 1990.

Clancy, Herbert John. *The Presidential Election of 1880*. Chicago: Loyola University Press, 1958.

Clemens, Clara. *Awake to a Perfect Day: My Experience with Christian Science*. New York: Citadel Press, 1956.

―――. *My Father, Mark Twain*. New York: Harper, 1931.

―――. *My Husband, Gabrilowitsch*. New York: Harper, 1938.

Dakin, Edwin Franden. *Mrs. Eddy: The Biography of a Virginal Mind*. New York: Charles Scribner's Sons, 1929, 1930. Reprint, New York: Scribner, 1970.

Davies, Paul. *God and the New Physics*. New York: Simon & Schuster, 1983.

Dickey, Adam H. *Memoirs of Mary Baker Eddy*. Brookline, Mass.: Lillian S. Dickey, 1927.

Donald, David Herbert. *Lincoln*. New York: Simon & Schuster, 1995.

Dossey, Larry. *Be Careful What You Pray for . . . You Just Might Get It: What We Can Do about the Unintentional Effects of Our Thoughts, Prayers, and Wishes*. San Francisco: Harper, 1997.

Dresser, Annetta G. *The Philosophy of P. P. Quimby*. Boston: G. H. Ellis, 1895.

Eddy, Mary Baker. *Christian Healing: A Sermon Delivered at Boston*. 1886. In *Prose Works Other Than Science and Health With Key to the Scriptures*. Boston: The First Church of Christ, Scientist, 1925.

———. *Christian Science versus Pantheism*. 1898. In *Prose Works Other Than Science and Health With Key to the Scriptures*. Boston: The First Church of Christ, Scientist, 1925.

———. *Church Manual of The First Church of Christ, Scientist, in Boston, Massachusetts*. 1895. Boston: The First Church of Christ, Scientist, 1910.

———. *The First Church of Christ, Scientist and Miscellany*. In *Prose Works Other Than Science and Health With Key to the Scriptures*. Boston: The First Church of Christ, Scientist, 1913.

———. *Message to the First Church of Christ, Scientist or the Mother Church, Boston, June 15, 1902*. In *Prose Works Other Than Science and Health With Key to the Scriptures*. Boston: The First Church of Christ, Scientist, 1925.

———. *Message to the Mother Church: Boston, Massachusetts, June 1900*. In *Prose Works Other Than Science and Health With Key to the Scriptures*. Boston: The First Church of Christ, Scientist, 1925.

———. *Message to the Mother Church: Boston, Massachusetts, June 1901*. In *Prose Works Other Than Science and Health With Key to the Scriptures*. Boston: The First Church of Christ, Scientist, 1925.

———. *Miscellaneous Writings*. 1897. In *Prose Works Other Than Science and Health With Key to the Scriptures*. Boston: The First Church of Christ, Scientist, 1925.

———. *No and Yes*. 1892 (first edition 1887). In *Prose Works Other Than Science and Health With Key to the Scriptures*. Boston: The First Church of Christ, Scientist, 1925.

———. "One Cause and Effect." *Granite Monthly* (November 1896): 199–209. Reprinted in *Prose Works Other Than Science and Health With Key to the Scriptures*. Boston: The First Church of Christ, Scientist, 1925.

———. *The People's Idea of God: Its Effect on Health and Christianity—A Sermon Delivered at Boston*. 1883. In *Prose Works Other Than Science and Health With Key to the Scriptures*. Boston: The First Church of Christ, Scientist, 1925.

———. *Pulpit and Press*. 1895. In *Prose Works Other Than Science and Health With Key to the Scriptures*. Boston: The First Church of Christ, Scientist, 1925.

———. *Retrospection and Introspection*. 1899 (first edition 1891). In *Prose Works Other Than Science and Health With Key to the Scriptures*. Boston: The First Church of Christ, Scientist, 1925.

———. *Rudimental Divine Science*. 1891 (first edition 1887). In *Prose Works Other Than Science and Health With Key to the Scriptures*. Boston: The First Church of Christ, Scientist, 1925.

———. *Science and Health with Key to the Scriptures*. 1875. Boston: The First Church of Christ, Scientist, 1911.

———. *Speaking for Herself, Autobiographical Reflections: Retrospection and Introspection, Footprints Fadeless*. Boston: The Writings of Mary Baker Eddy, 2002.

———. *Unity of Good*. 1892 (first edition 1888). In *Prose Works Other Than Science and Health With Key to the Scriptures*. Boston: The First Church of Christ, Scientist, 1925.

Eddy, Mary Baker, and James F. Gilman. *Christ and Christmas*. Boston: The First Church of Christ, Scientist, 1894.

———. *Painting a Poem; Mary Baker Eddy and James F. Gilman Illustrate* Christ and Christmas. Twentieth Century Biographers Series. Boston: Christian Science Publishing Society, 1998.

Edwards, Jonathan. *Notes on Scripture*. Edited by Stephen J. Stein. New Haven, Conn.: Yale University Press, 1998.

———. "Personal Narrative." In *A Jonathan Edwards Reader*, edited by John E. Smith, Harry S. Stout, and Kenneth P. Minkema. New Haven, Conn.: Yale University Press, 2003.

———. *Religious Affections*. Edited by John E. Smith. New Haven, Conn.: Yale University Press, 1959.

———. *Typological Writings*. Edited by Wallace E. Anderson, Mason I. Lowance, and David H. Watters. New Haven, Conn.: Yale University Press, 1993.

Elder, Margaret Munro. *The Life of Samuel J. Elder*. New Haven, Conn.: Yale University Press, 1925.

Eliade, Mircea. *A History of Religious Ideas from Gautama Buddha to the Triumph of Christianity*. Translated from the French by Willard R. Trask. Chicago: University of Chicago Press, 1985.

Essays and Bible Lessons Ascribed to Mary Baker Eddy with Repaid Pages; Footprints Fadeless by Mary Baker Eddy with the Science of Man or Questions and Answers in Moral Science; Early Papers; Visions; Mind-Healing: Historical Sketch. Compiled by Richard Oakes. Capetown: Rustica Press, 1959.

Evans, Gillian R., trans. *Bernard of Clairvaux: Selected Works*. With preface by Ewert Cousins and introduction by Jean Leclercq. New York: Paulist Press, 1987.

Evans, W. F. *The Mental-Cure, Illustrating the Influence of the Mind on the Body, Both in Health and Disease, and the Psychological Method of Treatment*. Boston: Carter, 1869.

Farlow, Alfred. "Christian Science in Business Life." *American Business Man* 11 (May 1908): 155–57.

Fatout, Paul, ed. *Mark Twain Speaks for Himself*. West Lafayette, Ind.: Purdue University Press, 1978.

Fettweis, Yvonne Caché von, and Robert Townsend Warneck. *Mary Baker Eddy: Christian Healer*. Boston: Christian Science Publishing Society, 1998.

Fisher, H. A. L. *Our New Religion: An Examination of Christian Science*. New York: Jonathan Cape and Harrison Smith, 1930.

Fox, Margery. "Protest in Piety: Christian Science Revisited." *International Journal of Women's Studies* 1, no. 4 (July–August 1978): 401–16.

Fraser, Caroline. *God's Perfect Child: Living and Dying in the Christian Science Church*. New York: Metropolitan Books, 1999.

Fuller, Robert C. *Mesmerism and the American Cure of Souls*. Philadelphia: University of Pennsylvania Press, 1982.

Gardner, Martin. *The Healing Revelations of Mary Baker Eddy: The Rise and Fall of Christian Science*. Buffalo, N.Y.: Prometheus Books, 1993.

Gill, Gillian. *Mary Baker Eddy*. Reading, Mass.: Perseus Books, 1998.

Gilman, James Franklin. *Recollections of Mary Baker Eddy, Discoverer and Founder of Christian Science*. Rumford, R.I.: Privately printed, 1934. Reprint, Freehold, N.J.: Rare Book Company, 1970.

Gladden, Washington. "The Truths and Untruths of Christian Science." *The Independent* CV (March 19, 1903).

Goetz, Ronald. "The Suffering God: The Rise of a New Orthodoxy." *Christian Century* (April 16, 1986): 385.

Gottschalk, Stephen. "Christian Science and Harmonialism." In *Encyclopedia of the American Religious Experience: Studies of Traditions and Movements*, vol. 2. Edited by Charles H. Lippy and Peter W. Williams. New York: Charles Scribner's Sons, 1988.

———. *The Emergence of Christian Science in American Religious Life*. Berkeley: University of California Press, 1973.

Haldeman, Isaac M. *Christian Science in the Light of Holy Scripture*. New York: Revell, 1909.

Hanna, Septimus J. *Christian Science History*. Boston: Christian Science Publishing Society, 1899.

Hanson, Penny. "Women's Hour: Feminist Implications of Mary Baker Eddy's Christian Science Movement, 1885–1910." Ph.D. dissertation, University of California at Irvine, 1981.

Harley, Gail M. *Emma Curtis Hopkins: Forgotten Founder of New Thought*. Syracuse: Syracuse University Press, 2002.

Healing Spiritually: Renewing Your Life through the Power of God's Law. Boston: Christian Science Publishing Society, 1996.

Hearst, William R. *Faith* (pamphlet). San Simeon, Calif.: Privately printed, 1941.

Hick, John. *Evil and the God of Love*. New York: Harper and Row, 1966.

Hill, Hamlin. *Mark Twain: God's Fool*. New York: Harper & Row, 1973.

Hillman, William F. "The Journals of William F. Hillman, 1946–1974." Unpublished manuscript.

History of Woman Suffrage. 1881. Edited by Elizabeth Cady Stanton, Susan B. Anthony, Matilda Joslyn Gage, and Ida Husted Harper. New York: Arno Press, 1969.

Holifield, E. Brooks. *Theology in America: Christian Thought from the Age of the Puritans to the Civil War*. New Haven, Conn.: Yale University Press, 2003.

Holl, Karl. "Der Szientismus." Originally published in *Zeitschrift für die gesamte Strafrechtswissenschaft* 1916, slightly revised for inclusion in Holl's collected essays in *Gesammelte Aufsätze zur Kirchengeschichte*. Tübingen: J.C.B. Muhr, 1921–28: 3.

Hopkins, Emma Curtis. *First Lessons in Christian Science*. Chicago: Purdy, 1888.

———. *Sixth Lesson in Christian Science: From the Private Lessons*. Chicago: Purdy, 1887.

Howard, Stephen. "Exploring Mary Baker Eddy's Revisions to Science and Health with Key to the Scriptures." *Longyear Museum: A Report to Members and Friends* (Summer 2003).

In My True Light and Life: Mary Baker Eddy Collections. Boston: The Writings of Mary Baker Eddy and The Mary Baker Eddy Library for the Betterment of Humanity, 2002.

Ivey, Paul Eli. *Prayers in Stone: Christian Science Architecture in the United States, 1894–1930*. Urbana: University of Illinois Press, 1999.

James, Henry. *The Bostonians*. London: Macmillan, 1886.

James, William. *The Letters of William James*. Edited by Henry James. 2 vols. Boston: Atlantic Monthly Press, 1920.

———. *A Pluralistic Universe: Hibbert Lectures to Manchester College on the Present Situation in Philosophy*. New York: Longmans, Green, 1909.

————. *The Varieties of Religious Experience: A Study in Human Nature*. 1902. Reprint, New York: Penguin Books, 1982.

————. *The Will to Believe, and Other Essays in Popular Philosophy*. 1897. Reprint, Cambridge, Mass.: Harvard University Press, 1979.

Jewell, F. S. "The Claims of 'Christian Science' as so Styled and Its Peculiar Philosophy" (pamphlet). Milwaukee: Young Churchman, 1897.

Johnsen, Thomas C. "Christian Science and the Puritan Tradition." Ph.D. dissertation, Johns Hopkins University, 1983.

————. "Christian Scientists and the Medical Profession: A Historical Perspective." *Medical Heritage* 2 (January–February 1986): 70.

————. "Historical Consensus and Christian Science: The Career of a Manuscript Controversy." *New England Quarterly* 53 (March 1980): 3–22.

Johnson, William Lyman. *The History of The Christian Science Movement, I and II*. Brookline, Mass.: The Zion Research Foundation, 1926.

————. "The History of the Christian Science Movement: The Thousand Pages." Brookline, Mass.: unpublished manuscript, n.d.

Judah, J. Stillson. *The History and Philosophy of the Metaphysical Movements in America*. Philadelphia: Westminster Press, 1967.

Kaplan, Fred. *The Singular Mark Twain: A Biography*. New York: Doubleday, 2003.

Kaplan, Justin. *Mr. Clemens and Mark Twain: A Biography*. New York: Simon & Schuster, 1966.

Kaufman, Martin. *Homeopathy in America: The Rise and Fall of a Medical Heresy*. Baltimore: Johns Hopkins University Press, 1971.

Kazin, Alfred. *God and The American Writer*. New York: Alfred A. Knopf, 1997.

Kenyon, F. E. "Mary Baker Eddy, Founder of Christian Science. The Sublime Hysteric." *History of Medicine* (London) 6 (1975): 29–46.

King, Karen L. *What Is Gnosticism?* Cambridge, Mass.: Harvard University Press, Belknap Press, 2003.

Klein, Janice. "Ann Lee and Mary Baker Eddy: The Parenting of New Religions." *The Journal of Psychohistory* 6 (Winter 1970): 362–75.

Knapp, Bliss. *The Destiny of the Mother Church*. Boston: Christian Science Publishing Society, 1991.

Lambert, Louis A. *Christian Science before the Bar of Reason*. New York: Christian Press Association Publishing Company, 1908.

Larcom, Lucy. *A New England Girlhood, Outlined from Memory*. Boston, New York: Houghton Mifflin Company, 1889.

Lefkovits, Maurice. "The Attitude of Judaism toward Christian Science" (pamphlet). Cincinnati, 1912.

Lewis, C. S. *Mere Christianity*. New York: Macmillan, 1952.

Marsden, George M. *Jonathan Edwards: A Life*. New Haven, Conn.: Yale University Press, 2003.

Marty, Martin E. *Modern American Religion*. Vol. 1: *The Irony of It All, 1893–1919*. Chicago: University of Chicago Press, 1997.

Mary Baker Eddy: A Heart in Protest (documentary). Videocassette. Boston: First Church of Christ, Scientist, 1988.

McCorkle, William P. *Christian Science, or, The False Christ of 1866*. Richmond: The Presbyterian Committee of Publication, 1899.

McDonald, Jean A. "Mary Baker Eddy and the Nineteenth Century 'Public' Woman: A Feminist Reappraisal." *Journal of Feminist Studies* 2 (1986): 105–11.

Meehan, Michael. *Mrs. Eddy and the Late Suit in Equity*. Concord, N.H.: Michael Meehan, 1908.

Meyer, Donald. *The Positive Thinkers: Religion as Pop Psychology, from Mary Baker Eddy to Oral Roberts.* New York: Pantheon Books, 1980.

Miller, Perry. *The New England Mind: The Seventeenth Century.* Cambridge, Mass.: Harvard University Press, 1954.

Miscellaneous Documents Relating to Christian Science and Its Discoverer and Founder, Mary Baker Eddy, Author of the Textbook Science and Health with Key to the Scriptures. Rumford, R.I.: Privately printed, 1935. Reprint, Freehold, N.J.: Rare Book Company, n.d.

Moore, A. Lincoln. *Christian Science: Its Manifold Attractions.* New York: T. E. Schulte, 1906.

Neider, Charles, ed. *The Autobiography of Mark Twain.* New York: Harper, 1959.

Nenneman, Richard A. *Persistent Pilgrim: The Life of Mary Baker Eddy.* Etna, N.H.: Nebbadoon Press, 1997.

Notes on Mary Baker Eddy's Course in Divinity, Recorded by Lida Fitzpatrick, C.S.D., and Others; Watches, Prayers, Arguments Given to Students by Mary Baker Eddy; Items from Gilbert Carpenter's Collectanea Not Already Included in the Above; Instructions in Metaphysics from Mary Baker Eddy, Recorded by Dr. Alfred E. Baker, M.D., C.S.D., Together with Some Notes on Metaphysical Work. Freehold, N.J.: Rare Book Company, n.d.

Ochs, Carol. *Women and Spirituality.* Totowa, N.J.: Rowman & Allanheld, 1993.

Orcutt, William Dana. *Mary Baker Eddy and Her Books.* Boston: Christian Science Publishing Society, 1950.

Paget, Stephen. *The Faith and Works of Christian Science.* London: Macmillan, 1909.

Paine, Albert Bigelow. *Mark Twain, a Biography: The Personal and Literary Life of Samuel Langhorne Clemens.* New York: Harper & Brothers, 1912.

Parker, Gail Thain. "Mary Baker Eddy: New Thought Parodied." In *Mind Cure in New England: From the Civil War to World War I.* Hanover, N.H.: University Press of New England, 1973.

Peabody, Frederick. *The Religio-Medical Masquerade: A Complete Exposure of Christian Science.* New York: Fleming H. Revell Co., 1910.

Peel, Robert. *Christian Science: Its Encounter with American Culture.* New York: Holt, Rinehart and Winston, 1958.

———. "A Church Designed to Last." *Christian Science Journal* (June–September 1982).

———. *Health and Medicine in the Christian Science Tradition: Principle, Practice, and Challenge.* New York: Crossroad, 1988.

———. *Mary Baker Eddy: The Years of Authority.* New York: Holt, Rinehart and Winston, 1977. Reprint, Boston: Christian Science Publishing Society, 1982.

———. *Mary Baker Eddy: The Years of Discovery.* New York: Holt, Rinehart and Winston, 1966. Reprint, Boston: Christian Science Publishing Society, 1972.

———. *Mary Baker Eddy: The Years of Trial.* New York: Holt, Rinehart and Winston, 1971. Reprint, Boston: Christian Science Publishing Society, 1973.

———. *Spiritual Healing in a Scientific Age.* San Francisco: Harper & Row, 1987.

Pelikan, Jaroslav. *The Melody of Theology: A Philosophical Dictionary.* Cambridge, Mass.: Harvard University Press, 1988.

Permanency of The Mother Church and Its Manual. Revised ed. Boston: The Christian Science Publishing Society, 1954.

Peterson, Michael L., ed. *The Problem of Evil: Selected Readings.* Notre Dame, Ind.: University of Notre Dame Press, 1992.

Pettit, Norman. *The Heart Prepared: Grace and Conversion in Puritan Spiritual Life.* 2nd ed. Middletown, Conn.: Wesleyan University Press, 1989.

Pioneers in Christian Science. Brookline, Mass.: Longyear Historical Society, 1993.

Powell, Lyman P. *Mary Baker Eddy: A Life Size Portrait*. New York: Macmillan, 1930.

Proceedings in Equity 1919–1921 Concerning Deed of Trust of January 25, 1898 consti-tuting the Christmas Science Society. Boston: Christian Science Publishing Society, 1923.

Putnam, Ruth Ann. *The Cambridge Companion to William James*. New York: Cambridge University Press, 1997.

Quimby, Phineas P. *The Complete Writings*. Edited by Ervin Seale. Marina del Rey, Calif.: DeVorss, 1988.

———. *The Quimby Manuscripts: Showing the Discovery of Spiritual Healing and the Origin of Christian Science*. Edited by Horatio W. Dresser. New York: Thomas Y. Crowell, 1921.

Richardson, Leon Burr. *William E. Chandler, Republican*. New York: Dodd, Mead and Co., 1940.

Robins, Pam, and Robley Whitson. "Mary Baker Eddy's Christian Science." *Sign* 59 (July–August 1980): 16–21. Reprinted in *Christian Science: A Sourcebook of Contemporary Materials*. Boston: Christian Science Publishing Society, 1990.

Russell, Bertrand. *The Basic Writings of Bertrand Russell, 1903–1959*. Edited by Lester E. Denonn and Robert E. Egner. New York: Simon & Schuster, 1961.

Schoepflin, Rennie B. *Christian Science on Trial: Religious Healing in America*. Baltimore: Johns Hopkins University Press, 2003.

Seager, Richard Hughes. *The World's Parliament of Religions: The East/West Encounter, Chicago, 1893*. Bloomington: Indiana University Press, 1995.

Seal, Frances Thurber. *Christian Science in Germany*. Privately published, 1931.

Silberger, Julius Jr. *Mary Baker Eddy: An Interpretive Biography of the Founder of Christian Science*. Boston: Little, Brown, 1980.

Simon, Linda. *Genuine Reality: A Life of William James*. New York: Harcourt Brace, 1998.

Smaus, Jewel Spangler. *Mary Baker Eddy: The Golden Days*. Boston: Christian Science Publishing Society, 1966.

Smith, Clifford P. *Historical Sketches: From the Life of Mary Baker Eddy and the History of Christian Science*. Boston: Christian Science Publishing Society, 1992.

Smith, Louise A. *Mary Baker Eddy: Discoverer and Founder of Christian Science*. Boston: Christian Science Publishing Society, 1991.

Smith, Richard Norton. Review of *Pulitzer: A Life* by Denis Brian. *Columbia Journalism Review* 40 (November–December 2001): 1.

Snowden, James H. *The Truth about Christian Science: The Founder and the Faith*. Philadelphia: Westminster Press, 1920.

Springer, Fleta Campbell. *According to the Flesh*. New York: Coward-McCann, 1930.

Starr, Paul. *The Social Transformation of American Medicine*. New York: Basic Books, 1982.

Steiger, Henry W. *Christian Science and Philosophy*. New York: Philosophical Library, 1948.

Stein, Stephen J. "Retrospection and Introspection: The Gospel According to Mary Baker Eddy." *Harvard Theological Review* 75 (1982): 97–116.

Stetson, Augusta. *Reminiscences, Sermons, and Correspondence, Proving Adherence to the Principle of Christian Science as Taught by Mary Baker Eddy*. New York: G. P. Putnam's Sons, 1917.

———. *Sermons Which Spiritually Interpret the Scriptures and Other Writings on Christian Science*. New York: G. P. Putnam's Sons, 1924.

Stewart, Randall, ed. *The American Notebooks of Nathaniel Hawthorne.* New Haven, Conn.: Yale University Press, 1932.

Story of Christian Science Wartime Activities, 1939–1946. Boston: Christian Science Publishing Society, 1947.

Studdert-Kennedy, Hugh A. *Christian Science and Organized Religion.* San Francisco: Farallon Press, 1930.

———. *Mrs. Eddy: Her Life, Her Work and Her Place in History.* San Francisco: Farallon Press, 1947.

Swihart, Altman K. *Since Mrs. Eddy.* New York: Henry Holt and Company, 1931.

Tarnas, Richard. *The Passion of the Western Mind: Understanding the Ideas That Have Shaped Our World View.* New York: Harmony Books, 1991.

Thomas, Robert David. *"With Bleeding Footsteps": Mary Baker Eddy's Path to Religious Leadership.* New York: Knopf, 1994.

Tomlinson, Irving C. *Twelve Years with Mary Baker Eddy: Recollections and Experiences.* Boston: Christian Science Publishing Society, 1945. Amplified Edition, 1996.

Tuckey, John S., ed. *Mark Twain's Fables of Man.* Berkeley: University of California Press, 1972.

Twain, Mark. *The Adventures of Huckleberry Finn.* 1885. Edited by Shelley Fisher Fishkin, with an introduction by Toni Morrison. Reprint, New York: Oxford University Press, 1996.

———. *The Adventures of Tom Sawyer.* 1876. Reprint, New York: Oxford University Press, 1993.

———. *The Bible According to Mark Twain: Writings on Heaven, Eden, and the Flood.* Edited by Howard G. Baetzhold and Joseph B. McCullough. Athens: University of Georgia Press, 1995.

———. *Christian Science.* 1907. Reprint, New York: Oxford University Press, 1996.

———. *Mark Twain's Fables of Man.* Edited by John S. Tuck et al. Berkeley: University of California Press, 1972.

———. *Mark Twain's Letters.* Vol. 4: *1870–1871.* Edited by Victor Fischer and Michael B. Frank. Berkeley: University of California Press, 1995.

———. "The Missionary and World Politics." Letter addressed "To the Editor of the Times," enclosed in a letter dated July 9 (?), 1900, to C. F. Moberly Bell. Microfilm Edition of Mark Twain's Manuscript Letters, Mark Twain Papers, Vol. 9. Prepared by Anh Quynh Bui, Victor Fischer, Michael B. Frank, Lin Salamo, and Harriet Elinor Smith. The Mark Twain Papers of the Bancroft Library. Berkeley: University of California Press, 2001.

———. *No. 44, The Mysterious Stranger: Being an Ancient Tale Found in a Jug and Freely Translated from the Jug.* Foreword and notes by John S. Tuckey. Berkeley: University of California Press, 1969.

———. *Personal Recollections of Joan of Arc.* 1896. Reprinted with foreword by Shelley Fisher Fishkin. New York: Oxford University Press, 1996.

———. *The Portable Mark Twain.* Edited by Bernard A. De Voto. New York: Viking Press, 1946.

———. *What Is Man? and Other Essays.* New York: Harper & Brothers, 1917.

———. *What Is Man? And Other Philosophical Writings.* Edited by Paul Baender. Berkeley: University of California Press, 1973.

———. *Which Was the Dream? and Other Symbolic Writings of the Later Years.* Edited by John S. Tuckey. Berkeley: University of California Press, 1967.

Varley, Henry. *Christian Science Examined*. New York: Revell, 1898.

Vivekananda. *Letters of Swami Vivekananda*. Calcutta: Advaita Ashrama, 1964.

We Knew Mary Baker Eddy. Boston: Christian Science Publishing Society, 1979.

Warox, Claire. *Spontaneous Recovery: Unexpected Health after Chronic or Incurable Illness—The Medical Phenomenon*. Boston: Addison-Wesley, 1994.

Weddle, David L. "The Christian Science Textbook: An Analysis of the Religious Authority of Science and Health by Mary Baker Eddy." *Harvard Theological Review* 84 (1991): 273–97.

Wilbur, Sibyl. "Glimpses of a Great Personality: The Four Meetings with *Mrs. Eddy Face to Face; My Impression of Her as She Is Today; Her Home, and How She Lives and Works*." *Human Life* (January 1907): 3–4.

———. *The Life of Mary Baker Eddy*. New York: Concord Publishing Company, 1908.

Wills, Garry. *Certain Trumpets: The Call of Leaders*. New York: Simon & Schuster, 1994.

Wilson, Bryan R. *Sects and Society: A Sociological Study of the Elim Tabernacle, Christian Science, and Christadelphians*. Berkeley: University of California Press, 1961.

Woodbury, Josephine Curtis. *Christian Science Voices*. Boston: Usher, 1897.

———. *Echoes*. New York and London: G. P. Putnam's Sons, 1897.

———. "Quimbyism, or the Paternity of Christian Science." *Arena* (May 1899). Reprinted in pamphlet form by Garden City Press, Letchworth, England, 1909.

———. "War in Heaven: Sixteen Years in Christian Science Mind-Healing." Pamphlet by Press of Samuel Usher, Boston, 1897.

———. "The Wonder in Heaven." Unpublished manuscript, 1894.

Zweig, Stefan. *Mental Healers: Franz Anton Mesmer, Mary Baker Eddy, Sigmund Freud*. Translated by Eden and Cedar Paul. New York: Viking Press, 1932.

Index

Page numbers in italics refer to illustrations.

Chamberlin, Robert N., 19, 27, 31

Chandler, William, *17;* accusations of
delusions, 34–38; and malice for
Eddy, 396; and Next Friends Suit,
9, 10, 17–18, 19–20, 25, 26,
27–28, 31–34, 383; and Peabody,
258; post-trial, 38–41; on projected
malice, 373

Chanfrau, Henrietta, 294, 369–70

charity, 380

Chase, Stephen A., *216*

Chestnut Hill home, *362;* household
workers, 288, 290, 293, 300,
316; life at, 114; move to,
361–64, 396

Chicago, Ill., 98, 115, 231, 378

Chicago Inter-Ocean, 141

Chicago Tribune, 138

children, 64–65. *See also* Glover,
George (son)

China, 221, 380

Choate, Clara, 95, 278, 366

Christ and Christmas (Eddy), 113,
128–34, *132,* 153

Christian Science: branch churches,
195, 217; community of, 195–97,
206–7; defense of, 93–94;
denominational congress, 136–38,
139, 158; dissension in, 90–91, 96,
97, 98, 154, 175–76, 207, 211, 242
(*see also* Stetson, Augusta;
Woodbury, Josephine Curtis);
early failures, 11–12; early
followers, 89–91, *229;* after Eddy's
death, 403–5, 409–10; Eddy's
definition of, 67, 76; Eddy's
founding of, 96, 279, 280; Eddy's
role in, 175; and First
Commandment, 164–65; foes, 25;
governance of church, 199,
242–43, 393; growth in, 6, 203,
355; history, 120; household
workers, 303, 313; influence of,
384; inner psychology of, 247; and
Manual of the Mother Church,
238–45; membership, 14, 164;
men in, 184–85, 189–93; and
mesmerism, 273; and mind-curers,
96; missionary function, 231,
232–33, 390; and Next Friends Suit,

40; and "one cause," 164–67;
one-heart emphasis, 210;
paganization of, 365–66; and
Pleasant View, 103; purpose of,
321–22, 329; reactions to, 26–27;
rejection of, 416; schism of 1888,
115; and science, 137–38; spirit of
adventure in, 408–9, 410; spiritual
malaise in, 410; teaching, 119–20;
Twain on, 45–46, 47–48, 50,
86–87, 322, 342; visibility of, 195;
welfare of movement, 393–94;
women in church leadership, 168,
181–84

*Christian Science, with Notes Containing
Corrections to Date* (Twain), 45,
47–48

Christian Science Association, 100,
177, 211, 262

*Christian Science in the Light of Holy
Scripture* (Haldeman), 338

Christian Science Journal (formerly
known as *Journal of Christian
Science*): accounts of healing, 33;
during Boston crisis, 100;
dissension in, 207; on dissolution
of Boston church, 197; Dodge's
article, 325; on Eddy's mission, 99;
on Eddy's role in the church, 47;
on foolish virgin parable, 110;
founding of, 97; on Hotel Boylston
reading room, 231; on
immortality, 398; on importance of
Christian Science, 10; on legal
issues, 346; on mental malpractice,
36; on mesmerism, 374; on
Miscellaneous Writings 1883–1896,
246; on Mother Church, 200,
201–2; on "the new birth," 412;
and Nixon, 211; and one-heart
emphasis, 210; on pastors, 227; on
quantum physics, 418; "Seven
Fixed Rules," 100; on suffering, 6;
after Tremont Temple appearance,
94; and Woodbury libel suit, 275;
Woodbury's articles, 261

Christian Science Monitor, 40, 228–29,
385, 387–91, *390,* 405, 426

Christian Science: No and Yes (Eddy),
97, 114, 235

STEPHEN GOTTSCHALK was an independent scholar, an authority on Christian Science, and a former member of the Church's Committee on Publication. His works include *The Emergence of Christian Science in American Religious Life* and numerous articles.

MAY 1 1 2006   T-05

WITHDRAWN
from
NEWTON PUBLIC LIBRARY

DRAWN
11
IC LIBRARY

NEWTON PUBLIC LIBRARY
NEWTON, KANSAS 67114